BOOK OF SLIDES

The Complete Collection Presented at the 2002-2011 Lectures with Clarifications

Also by David R. Hawkins

Power vs. Force: The Hidden Determinants of Human Behavior

Dialogues on Consciousness and Spirituality

Orthomolecular Psychiatry (with Linus Pauling)

Qualitative and Quantitative Analysis and Calibration of the Levels of Human Consciousness

The Eye of the" I": From Which Nothing Is Hidden

I: Reality and Subjectivity

Truth vs. Falsehood: How to Tell the Difference

Transcending the Levels of Consciousness: The Stairway to Enlightenment

Discovery of the Presence of God: Devotional Non-duality

Reality, Spirituality, and Modern Man

Healing and Recovery

Along the Path to Enlightenment

Dissolving the Ego, Realizing the Self

Letting Go: The Pathway of Surrender

Success is for You: Using Heart-Centered Power Principles for Lasting Abundance and Fulfillment

Book of Slides

The Complete Collection Presented at the 2002-2011 Lectures with Clarifications

David R. Hawkins, M.D., Ph.D.

Veritas Publishing

P.O. Box 3516

W. Sedona, AZ 86340 U.S.A

Phone: 928.282.8722 • Fax: 928.282.4789

www.veritaspub.com

Softbound LCCN: 2018930312

Softbound ISBN: 978-1-938033-98-8

Dedication

Dedicated to all the students and followers of Dr. Hawkins' work, including the attendees of the lectures who asked for this compilation.
A special thank you to the DFW Hawkins' Study Group in Plano, Texas whose untiring efforts helped to make this book possible.

TABLE OF CONTENTS

FOREWORD

This book is a magnificent resource. It was put together by devoted students and provides an "atlas" of the vast terrain covered by Dr. David R. Hawkins in his 2002-2011 public lectures. "Doc," as we called him, was a rare human being. Born with exceptional genius, he easily mastered life in the world. His accomplishments included scientific breakthroughs in psychiatry and clinical settings, artistic and architectural creations, household inventions, humanitarian awards, membership in various elite organizations, business and administrative successes, and many other achievements across the spectrum of human experience. Being with him, one had the sense that he had "done it all, seen it all." Doc was down-to-earth and related with ease to whomever and whatever was in front of him. During his life, he traveled every inch of humanity's terrain, from the lowest rungs of hell to the Infinite Glory of Divinity. Nothing mattered more to him than sharing the spiritual gifts he had been given—liberation and the way out of suffering.

Those of us who had the great fortune to attend the lectures of Dr. Hawkins will never forget what it was like to be there. We saw the slides in person, yet are quick to say that we experienced much more than words on a screen. The verbal and visual information was delivered via a carrier wave of Love, silent and all-pervading. Historically, this nonverbal transmission has been called the "Grace of the Guru." Here is a firsthand account of a typical lecture day.

We came from all over the world. Some of us sacrificed jobs and personal comfort in order to attend a lecture. Even if we did not understand English, we came anyway, for we valued the beneficial energy. We lined up at the venue as early as we could get there, sometimes in the dark. As dawn broke, more and more people arrived, and the line lengthened into the parking lot. The joy was palpable! We hugged old friends, greeted new ones, and quietly breathed in the beauty of the blue sky and red rocks all around us. In that setting, it was easy to experience Doc's teaching, "Our love for each other is not different than our love for God."

The doors opened about an hour before the event began. Greeters welcomed us with smiles and hugs. As we made our way into the auditorium, we heard "Kyrie", a chant composed by Robert Gass, playing in the background. Doc told us, "We play this music so that you can experience what the energy field of 700 feels like." "Timeless; Ineffable; Essence; Grace; Completion; Oneness of existence; All-inclusive; Innate; Enlightened; Mystical; Non-separation;" These were some of the words that Doc used to describe the energy field of the 700s—and we felt it.

Once we found our seat, we sometimes sat quietly and meditated, for it was an environment of total inner safety. Our essence, our true Self, was fully welcomed here. As one person described it, "After a lifetime of searching, my soul finally felt at home." Doc never took credit for the healing energy that we experienced. Rather, he affirmed that we were experiencing our own inner Self:

"What the people in the world actually want is the recognition of who they really are on the highest level, to see that the same Self radiates forth within everyone, heals their feeling of separation, and brings about a feeling of peace. To bring peace and joy to others is the gift of the benevolence of the Presence. *The Eye of the I,* Chapter 6, *The Resolution of the Ego*, pg. 133.

We also enjoyed browsing through the bookstore. It seemed incredible that so many books, audios and videos—addressing such a vast array of topics—had been created by one man in the final years of his life. He never claimed ownership of the material, saying, "I don't see the books as 'mine'. It wasn't a personal 'me' that wrote them." Veritas staff members and volunteers had worked for weeks in advance to make the resources available and to ensure a safe and pleasant event on every level. Doc noted:

This is the form of love called caringness. We see caringness in many arenas of life – caring for the environment, caring for the welfare of others, caring for our pets, caring for our appliances, caring for our garden, and caring about the quality of our life. So, we try to maximize the quality of our life in all that we do – our cooking, the way that we dress, our efforts at work, our home décor, and so on. We partly do so by anticipating and fulfilling other people's expectations. When people come to one of our seminars, for instance, they will have certain expectations. I care about their effort to take time and show up, and I try to do the best job I can to be creative, original, and appropriate. So, in the general field of lovingness, we value other people's time and effort (interview with the author, 2012).

Behind the scenes during the preceding weeks, some of us had witnessed Doc's preparation for the lecture. We were amazed at the extent of his love for the people who would be attending the event. By "preparation," we mean something different from what public speakers or educators generally do. It was not mental. There was no rehearsal. Rather, he *became* the topic. Doc was more of a space than a person—a space of infinite potential. It was as if Doc had access to an infinite number of channels and then allowed himself to be tuned into one specific channel. The lecture topic finessed from the infinite field that he was, words and information that would be helpful to a particular audience, on a particular day, about a particular topic.

Weeks before a lecture, he surrendered to this process of becoming "tuned in" to that channel. He wrote down the main points to be shared, and these points were made into slides. As you can see from the slides in this book, the points were not mental explanations. Rather, each word or phrase was a key that unlocked the Self-knowledge of the listener. For weeks before the event, he went over the slides daily, distilling the information down to its simplest essence. He often asked for the words to be read to him as he sat quietly with eyes closed. Sometimes he would edit a slide. For example, hearing the word "must," he said: "Take it out. Not necessary. Makes people go weak."

In the weeks before the Love lecture, he asked for someone to read to him from the sections about Love in his books. The reader gave this account:

Doc closed his eyes. An atmosphere of pristine receptivity settled over the room. I sensed his total and complete attention. I don't have the capacity to know what was going on for him in those moments, but I can tell you that I witnessed his unwavering dedication to his students. Even on the days that he was in physical pain, he still wanted me to read to him. He said he needed to re-familiarize himself with the energy field that people were expecting to learn about at the lecture. I don't think we understand the sacrifice this entailed. Having left behind a limitation, who wants to go back to it? Only out of great compassion does a teacher re-attune himself to an energy field that he transcended long ago. Each time I read to him, I was aware of the sacrifice that he was making for us. In the weeks leading up to a lecture, he *became* what he would be teaching. And if something in the collective consciousness relative to the topic had to be purified, he bore the suffering of that purification.

"*Gloria Excelsis Deo*!" Doc began the lectures with this exclamation. He gave all glory and honor to "Thee, O Lord." We members of the audience may have seen him as a teacher and speaker, but he knew himself to be a servant of the Lord. After the initial declaration, he often said, "Nothing causes anything. Everything is happening spontaneously of its own, by virtue of what it is." This teaching came alive in front of us as we watched him. Each movement, each expression, each phrasing was perfectly spontaneous. He told us, laughing while he spoke, "I am as surprised as you are to hear what's being said today!" His wife, Susan—lovemate, best friend, co-researcher, and "right arm"— was always on stage with him. Doc said that she was the "fulcrum" that made possible the interfacing of his consciousness with the world. No one will ever know the personal sacrifices she made in order to share him with the world.

Susan and those of us who witnessed Doc backstage knew of his profound surrender just before he went on stage. In one single instant, he relinquished his weeks of preparation and turned the lecture over to Divine Grace. He became, he said, "a conduit." Thirty minutes prior, we may have brought him to the back entrance in a wheelchair, but now we marveled at how such a frail frame of a man (in his eighties) was suddenly dancing with his cane on stage! Animating the movements of various animals—the octopus, the doggie, the camel, the little chick—as he slid across the stage, singing a ditty from childhood. His laughter lit up the room!

Someone described his personality at the events as a mixture of Einstein, the Buddha, and Mr. Magoo. It was a personality that interacted with the world in a comical, intelligent, compassionate, unexpected, and piercing way. It was Love, he said, that animated the interface with others.

Q: There still seems to be a personality present.

A: That is the automatic product of love which interfaces between the Self and the people in the world. Its function is to uplift, communicate, and heal, and it frequently uses humor to interact with the world. It uses laughter and humor to recontextualize people's distorted viewpoints. Its main purpose is to heal by recontextualization. The Self seeks to make a healing contact with the Self of the person in the world who is suffering. This same love, which is a quality of the Self, seeks to contact the Self in everyone in its writing, speaking, or conveying of information that could be useful. *The Eye of the I*, Chapter 17, *Dialogues*, pg. 325-26.

He was a liberated being—free, spontaneous, and totally available. The spaciousness of that which he was welcomed everyone and everything. Though he appeared in the form of a man, he was somehow beyond male and female, human and nonhuman. He was the "Eye of the 'I'" from which nothing was hidden. Nothing existed that was not included in this Love.

Still, you need to know that he did not dress or look like a spiritual teacher. He strove to be ordinary. There were no robes or rituals, saintly affects or special incantations. There were no theatrics or miracles performed on stage. There was no organization to join or dues to pay. The true teacher, he said, has no interest in special clothing, dramatic performances, names or titles, for there is actually no "person" present who would care about such things. "Teaching is a function, not a person," he told us.

His lectures gave our thinking mind something to pay attention to, but the real teaching unfolded on the plane of the Self, silently and nonverbally.

"That is the value of the presence of a Teacher whose energy field is like a catalyst. The high energy field of the Self is already present in the student. It does not have to be acquired but only activated, which is a consequence of positive karmic potentiality." *Discovery of the Presence of God,* Chapter 7, *The Razor's Edge,* pg.133.

Doc usually set aside the last two hours of the day for Q and A. Though the line was long and it seemed like there could not possibly be enough time for everyone, he was never rushed. People from all walks of life went up to see him on stage. As they sat down at the round table with Doc and Susan, there were questions, hugs, prayers, songs, laughter, and blessings. He received the heart of each person and intuited the inner need of the student. Like the Buddha, he skillfully said what was right for each individual, and in the right measure. Context, he said, is more important than content. Therefore, over the years, we sometimes heard different answers to the same question.

Doc never sought followers and had no interest in persuading others. He simply shared what he knew to be true. "I'm not interested in big-shot-ism," he said one time.

The intention of this presentation is the alleviation of suffering by virtue of replacing falsehood with truth and sharing the knowledge of how to arrive at truth on one's own, for the pathway to its source resides within. For those who are aligned with truth, the path lights up; for those who refuse it, the path is darkened. All of us are free to choose. *Truth vs. Falsehood, Caveat: A Note to the Reader*, p. xi.

The book you hold in your hands is indeed a light unto your path. "He who has ears to hear, let him hear. Eyes to see, let him see."

On behalf of readers now and in the future, we thank the small group of devoted students in Texas who made this project their labor of love. May this unique resource help us in the deep and continuous remembrance of our teacher and his teaching: "Straight and narrow is the path. Waste no time."

Fran Grace, Ph.D.

Professor of Religious Studies
and Steward of the Meditation Room Program

University of Redlands in Redlands,
California, USA

PREFACE

"I want you to live in such a way that your life is a prayer. I want you to live your life in such a way that you have no anxiety at all about meeting God. Are you willing to be answerable for who you are and what you've done with what you are? What more can you ask? What more can you ask, that I live in such a way that frankly I am not scared of talking to God. I have done everything I can in every direction here. I have pushed myself to the limit to be the fulfillment of my potential. That relieves me of all guilt because now I can make a mistake. Yes, I make a mistake, but in the overall context, you see, I have sanctified that mistake by overall intention. So, by intention then our life becomes devotion. We become the prayer. By virtue of that we invoke Divinity and then through the heart, through the heart, through the devotion, through the alignment with Divinity, we empower all mankind. So we say, Gloria in Excelsis Deo! Glory to God in the Highest! And what more could be said?" 2005 Lecture 4, "Transcending Barriers"

INTRODUCTION

In addition to being the author of many books, Dr. David R. Hawkins participated in numerous live interviews, Satsangs/Q&A sessions, and gave numerous talks at various locations around the world. A crucial component of the teachings of Dr. Hawkins was via live interactive formal lectures beginning in January 2002, and ending with the last one on September 2011, given in front of audience of over 1000 people. "Doc" (as Dr. Hawkins is affectionately addressed in the student community) provided in these lectures unique spiritual information not available in books or elsewhere. It was Doc's intention to provide a book of all the slides used in these lectures along with a brief explanation of each one. The purpose of this work is to fulfill that intention:

"We are going to publish an atlas of all these slides... a page of explanation for each slide so the reader gets a quick overview on what it is all about without having to read a lot of material," as Doc stated during the April 2006 lecture, and in many other lectures. When all the 'work' in putting together the slides themselves was finished in 2011, there were 317 slides. A group of volunteer students took on the task of listening to the explanation of the slides as Doc covered them in the lectures, transcribing the explanation and then putting together the one-page overview for each slide. That process itself took more than a couple of years and after that, the task of presenting the materials in a "readable", user-friendly format started. Those of us who have tried to transcribe Doc's talks know how difficult that process is!

Mere words can only capture a portion of what Doc was conveying during a lecture. Beyond the words, there are the voice inflections, facial expressions, laughter, hand gesticulations, as well as body posture and movements that add nuances to the entire presentation. One can get all of that by watching a DVD, and, of course, listening to an audio recording would be the next most complete version of the lecture presentation. An easy way for errors to creep in is in the form of relying on what someone else heard or thinks they heard on a lecture DVD or CD. It can be quite time consuming to search through one or more lecture recordings to verify what indeed Doc did say.

However, by finding the words used by Doc in the lecture and listening to them for oneself, you can then even find out what Doc was talking about just prior to the quoted words, which provides an expanded context for the quote. Although we all love Doc quotes from lectures, we also have to be aware of the limitations of this practice. There is nothing like diving into the recordings for oneself and getting the message directly.

In this work, we have necessarily had to rely on the rewording of Doc's message based on our understanding and apologize in advance for the errors introduced through this practice. As a safeguard, we have included plenty of concordant quotes and/or references to books wherever possible and the timing on the recorded lecture media where the explanation of a slide begins for help in getting to the topics under discussion, thus cutting down the time needed in searching for the exact spot on the recording.

Some of the slides did not have a direct video clip in the lectures addressing the material in the slides. Where Doc did not discuss a slide or an item in a slide in detail, we have tried to make use of the explanations in other Doc materials, including books to provide the explanation for the items in a slide to the extent possible. There are other slides where Doc chose not to discuss the details as they were already in a book so we have chosen to transcribe/edit what little Doc said on these slides and in addition added from the relevant books, with minimal editing where necessary. Another item to keep in mind is that due to time constraints, we have come up with the overview of the slides based on listening to only one or two of the video clips, but several of the slides, e.g. slide 1 was covered in multiple lectures. The Index to slides mentioned earlier makes it possible for the interested reader to locate all of the clips on any given slide for additional research into a topic if desired.

Overall, it is our hope that this atlas is helpful in obtaining a bird's eye view of the materials covered in the lectures, and in locating where to find a more in-depth discussion of a particular slide. The calibrations pertaining to passing phenomena of human life provided in the slides in this book are of course valid only as of the date of the respective lecture. Non-linear learning takes place through familiarity and repetition and is a technique that one sees used in all of the Doc materials, including lectures, as well as books. Doc's style of presentation was informal and spontaneous, as the slides were a tool to remember to cover specific items Doc wanted to share with the student community. Most often, but not always, the items in a slide were taken up in a sequential manner. In putting together an explanation for each slide, we have endeavored to select the non-overlapping parts of the explanations in this book as far as possible, as many items in various slides were explained multiple times throughout the Lectures.

May this atlas serve the Highest Good! Gloria in Excelsis Deo!

Straight and narrow is the path…

Waste no time.

Gloria in Excelsis Deo!

Map of Consciousness®

God-view	Self-view	Level	Log	Emotion	Process
Self	Is	Enlightenment	700-1,000	Ineffable	Pure Consciousness
All-being	Perfect	Peace	600	Bliss	Illumination
One	Complete	Joy	540	Serenity	Transfiguration
Loving	Benign	Love	500	Reverence	Revelation
Wise	Meaningful	Reason	400	Understanding	Abstraction
Merciful	Harmonious	Acceptance	350	Forgiveness	Transcendence
Inspiring	Hopeful	Willingness	310	Optimism	Intention
Enabling	Satisfactory	Neutrality	250	Trust	Release
Permitting	Feasible	Courage ↕	200	Affirmation	Empowerment
Indifferent	Demanding	Pride	175	Scorn	Inflation
Vengeful	Antagonistic	Anger	150	Hate	Aggression
Denying	Disappointing	Desire	125	Craving	Enslavement
Punitive	Frightening	Fear	100	Anxiety	Withdrawal
Uncaring	Tragic	Grief	75	Regret	Despondency
Condemning	Hopeless	Apathy, hatred	50	Despair	Abdication
Vindictive	Evil	Guilt	30	Blame	Destruction
Despising	Hateful	Shame	20	Humiliation	Elimination

Slide 1

SLIDE 1: MAP OF CONSCIOUSNESS ®

This slide was first introduced at January 2002 lecture, DVD disc 2 at 00:00:40.

This slide was used in almost all of the lectures, with new additional information relating to the Map shared in almost every Lecture, thus providing a very comprehensive explanation of what the Map of Consciousness means, how it was derived, how to apply it, etc. While running the largest psychiatric practice in New York, Dr. Hawkins always looked for alternative approaches to healing and once attended a lecture given by Dr. John Diamond regarding muscle-testing, which Dr. Hawkins interpreted as a non-local response of Consciousness Itself to 'biological life' (protoplasm). Consciousness records for all of time everything that seems to happen in the world, including events, emotions, thoughts, intentions everywhere, and responds to an integrous enquiry as to the truth of a statement via muscle-response. Additional details on "How to calibrate the levels of consciousness" can be found elsewhere, e.g. Appendix C of Power vs. Force (2012 edition by Veritas Publishing) pp. 321-332.

Negative stimuli like fluorescent lights made everyone go weak in muscle testing but while trying to demonstrate muscle-testing at the clinic in the 1970s, Dr. Hawkins discovered that his patients who had been studying A Course in Miracles (ACIM) and had completed about the first 80 lessons did not go weak. Something had shifted in the consciousness of these patients to make them impervious to the negative stimuli. This phenomenon pointed to how one's level of consciousness can go higher with the practice of spiritual disciplines like the ACIM workbook lessons and further investigations/experimentation led eventually to the development of The Map of Consciousness. Divinity (Absolute) is a field of infinite power that does not move, and has no content, intentionality or purpose. It dominates everything forever, is the source of the universe, and is the basis for the Map of Consciousness with the level of 1000 indicating the maximum potential of power expressible through the human nervous system. The innate innocence, the capacity for awareness without any content is a realizable potential within all human beings, often facilitated by means of spiritual work. The content of consciousness comes in through the levels of consciousness shown on the Map of Consciousness. The more one rises in consciousness, the faster one could rise, but the process is non-linear and not predictable.

The Map of Consciousness allows us a way of discerning essence. Each one of the levels of consciousness has its own paradigm of reality - what is acceptable, status symbols, etc. - each is its own unique world. Most of humanity lives below the level of 200. Above 200, one moves into a life-supporting, positive domain. Piety has its place, but beyond piety are joy, ecstasy and nonstop energy. One of the most important things for spiritual students to note is that God is at the top of the chart, not down at the levels at the bottom of shame, guilt or apathy, etc. Life in the higher levels of consciousness can stall people out, e.g. one can lose motivation to advance in consciousness if one gets a new job or a new car.

Map of Consciousness

Over 250,000 calibrations spanning a 20 year study conducted by the Institute for Spiritual Research have defined a range of values corresponding to well-recognized attitudes and emotions (localized by specific attractor energy fields, much as electromagnetic fields gather iron fillings.) With an arbitrary scale of 1-1000 and the Map of Consciousness format, Dr. David R. Hawkins displays the classification of these energy fields to make them easily comprehensible. It is important to realize that the calibration figures do not represent an arithmetic but a logarithmic progression. Thus, the level 300 is not twice the amplitude of 150, it is 300 to the tenth power. An increase of even a few points therefore represents a major advance in power. The ways the various levels of human consciousness express themselves are profound and far reaching. Levels below 200 are detrimental to life in both the individual and society at large; those above 200 are constructive expressions of power. The decisive level of 200 is the fulcrum that divides the general areas of force and power-Truth from falsehood. Emotional correlates of the energy fields of consciousness, quoted from Dr. Hawkins' bestselling book Power vs. Force, note that they rarely are manifested as pure states in an individual. Levels of consciousness are always mixed, a person may operate on one level in a given area of life and on quite another level in another area. An individual's overall level of consciousness and how it demonstrates is the sum total effect of these various levels. A brief elaboration of the "levels" and numerical "log" columns is presented here to establish the general progress in these categories. Our reality changes in how we view God, how we participate in Life, what we feel and how we express ourselves in the world.

Dr. Hawkins' "anatomy of consciousness" is a profile of the entire human condition, allowing a comprehensive analysis of the emotional and spiritual development of individuals, societies, and the race in general.....« guide to all of us as to where we and our neighbors are on the ladder of spiritual enlightenment.

Energy Level 20 Shame
People at this emotional level are vulnerable to all the other negative emotions. They wish they were invisible. Banishment is a traditional accompaniment. It is destructive to health. Shame leads to cruelty to self and others and often results in paranoia, delusions and psychosis.

Energy Level 30 Guilt
Guilt manifests itself in a variety of expressions such as remorse, masochism, and victimhood. It results in psychosomatic disease, accident proneness and suicidal behaviors. Projection and denial are prevalent in these people.

Energy Level 50 Apathy
Apathy is the level characterized by poverty, despair and hopelessness. The world and the future look bleak. Death through passive suicide may result. Individuals on this level are seen by the world as drains of resources.

Energy Level 75 Grief
This level sees sadness everywhere. Here we find habitual losers and chronic gamblers. There is constant loss and depression. Often there is bereavement, mourning and remorse. Regret and despondency prevail.

Energy Level 100 Fear
Fear runs much of the world and spurs restless activity. Fears become basic motivators in people's lives. The world looks hazardous and threatening. Insecurity results in manipulation, jealousy, totalitarianism, and inhibition.

Energy Level 125 Desire
There is a great deal of energy available at this level motivating a major portion of human activity including the economy. This level is insatiable. It is an addiction. money, prestige or power runs the lives of the many finding value in "things" outside themselves.

Energy Level 150 Anger
Desire leads to frustration which in turn leads to anger. It is the fulcrum by which the oppressed eventually catapult to freedom. These individuals are volatile, dangerous, irritable and explosive. Hate fuels violence.

Energy Level 175 Pride
Pride is the level aspired to by the majority of mankind today. People feel good at this level and can move away from shame, guilt and fear by reveling in the contrast from these lower levels. Pride is the basis of religious wars, political terrorism, and zealotry. It is divisive and blocks recovery from addictions.

Energy Level 200 Courage
This is the level of empowerment. Courage brings exploration, accomplishment, fortitude and determination. Life is seen to be exciting, challenging and stimulating. Productivity begins.

Energy Level 250 Neutrality
The ability to transcend polarization and rigid positions about life begins. There is immunization against experiences of defeat, fright and frustration. Inner confidence blooms. There is no longer interest in conflict, competition, or guilt. The attitude is non-judgmentalism.

Energy Level 310 Willingness
The gateway to the higher levels of excellence and success opens. Growth is rapid. Willingness brings commitment to participate, open mindedness, a genuine friendliness and helpful nature. These people face inner issues, do not have major learning blocks and are self-correcting.

Energy Level 350 Acceptance
At this level, the individual stops seeing themselves as victims. A major transformation takes place. They take responsibility for themselves and have a capacity to live harmoniously with the forces of life-meeting life on life's terms. Emotionally calm, they are flexible and inclusive.

Energy Level 400 Reason
Intelligence and rationality come to the forefront when the emotionalism of the other levels is transcended. Here the individual is capable of handling large, complex amounts of data and making rapid, correct decisions. This is the level of science and medicine. There is an increased capacity for conceptualization and comprehension. This is where Einstein and Freud influenced society. A shortcoming is confusion between objective and subjective worlds-the duality of the Newtonian paradigm.

Energy Level 500 Love
Love at this level is characterized by love which at 540 is unconditional unchanging, and permanent. It is not dependent on external factors. These individuals have a way of relating to the world which is forgiving, nurturing, and supporting. They augment the positive rather than attracting the negative.

Energy Level 540 Joy
As love becomes more unconditional, it begins to be experienced as ... inner joy. This is the region of consciousness of saints, spiritual healers and advanced spiritual students. There is an enormous capacity for patience. The hallmark of this state is compassion. They merge with Divine will.

Energy Level 600 Peace
This energy field is associated with the state designated by such terms such as illumination, enlightenment, self-realization, and God consciousness. Distinction between subject and object disappears, and there is no specific focal point of perception. Some individuals at this level remove themselves from the world as the state of bliss precludes ordinary activity.

SLIDE 1: MAP OF CONSCIOUSNESS (BACKSIDE)

This most crucial slide, "Map of Consciousness" was introduced in the very first Lecture in 2002, and the levels explained throughout the subsequent Lectures. The backside of the Map of Consciousness explains the levels. A laminated Map of Consciousness with the backside is available for purchase at http://veritaspub.com which is the public website for the work of Dr. Hawkins. At the bottom of the Map, a person who is in apathy, grief, or paralyzed by fear, it feels good to move up to desire, anger, or pride. One can begin to understand the suicide bomber, who may be a "nobody" to begin with, and suddenly becomes a "somebody" (level of pride); now committing to an integrous act, believing that it is for God. He willingly sacrifices his life for God and goes up into a state of ecstasy (high 500s). Now we begin to understand the purpose of the human world: it provides an infinite panorama in which interactions of these levels of consciousness can take place. By playing our part in this panorama, we serve others. Each one of us serves others merely by being here. Everyone including the people below 200 serves us by helping us to recontextualize their reality, their values, and what they are to us, so we end up respecting them all. As mistaken as we think they might be, one must say that there is something one can respect about someone who is willing to sacrifice his life for something greater than himself, e.g. his family, his country, his religion, or for God as understood by him.

The levels below 200 resulted from the fact that biological life when first introduced on this planet needed an external supply of energy for survival in an unpredictable environment where wrong choices could lead to death of the organism. Therefore, lions and other carnivores hunt and kill prey. All the human ego's tricks are observable in the evolution of the various species of the animal kingdom over eons of time where deception, rivalry, ego gain, self-servingness, camouflage, and force subserve survival.

The evolution of the hominid eventuated as Homo sapiens, and concordantly, the prefrontal cortex emerged in front of the animal brain, which remains under the domination of animal instincts up to consciousness level 200. The animal instincts are directed to personal gain and continue to follow that path in conflict with the energy of spiritual power, truth, and love. The ego's deception is clever in that it deludes its victim and prisoner into believing that the perpetrators are 'out there', whereas they are innate and 'in here'.

Understanding (level of 400s) the ego and adopting it as a pet allows us to dissolve it eventually, as we become aware of its proclivities and can override them. Rarely do people escape the 400's to the nonlinear domains starting at 500. In the 500's, people switch from being primarily concerned with the objective world to the subjective state of Awareness, realizing that the experience of life derives from within, where things are not measurable.

Causality is a dualistic system of thought calibrating at 460, and Darwin's theory of evolution calibrates about the same. At birth, one already has a calibratable level of consciousness, and the time of one's leaving the body is already determined at the time of our birth (not the means, but the moment in terms of "karma"). Life is not subject to death, it only changes form. Only the death of the ego is a possibility upon the fulfillment of potentiality for enlightenment. Over level 600, there is the possibility to remember previous lifetimes, which in fact serve as chapters in the one life. As consciousness advances, it all begins to make sense, to fit together.

The Enlightened and Divine States

The Supreme Godhead - God Unmanifest

God Manifest as Divinity/Creator

Archangel

"I" as Essence of Creation

"I" of Ultimate Reality

Christ, Buddhahood, Krishna, Brahman Avatar

God (Self) as Logos

Self as Beyond Existence of Nonexistence

Teacher of Enlightenment

"I"/Self-Divinity as Allness (Beatific, Vision)

Sage-Self as God Manifest

Self as Existence

"I Am"

Enlightenment

Slide 2

SLIDE 2: THE ENLIGHTENED AND DIVINE STATES

This slide was first introduced at March 2002 lecture, DVD disc 2 at 1:11:00.

The Supreme Godhead-God Unmanifest is the power of infinite potentiality. Out of the Unmanifest comes the **God Manifest as Divinity/Creator**. Everything created has the power of Creation within it, and the universe is expanding at a rate greater than the speed of light. Potentiality becomes actuality because of the Presence of God and conditions favorable. All comes into existence by virtue of the Presence of God. Consciousness research confirms the presence of angels (calibrating from 500 upwards) and **archangels** (from 6000 upwards), indicating that the energies of Reality are analogous to a step-down-transformer type of stratification between man and God.

The Self has seemingly different prevailing qualities at various levels of consciousness. States of **Enlightenment** start at 600, when the self becomes the Self of the Love of God. Perception disappears at about the calibrated level of **"I AM"** (650) allowing the beauty of existence to radiate from what the world considers homely or even ugly. At that level, the luminescence of the Presence is exquisite bliss, which then progressively dissolves into a primordial peace and stillness that encompasses and is the **Divine Essence of all Existence**. In the 700's, one becomes a **mystic**. Instead of speaking only from ecclesiastical doctrine, one now speaks from inner knowingness, awareness instead of personhood. Knowingness begins to spring forth from within and constitutes the so-called "Purusha". Beyond that, the predominant quality of the Presence is its Radiance as the existence of **Allness**. Still further, the Reality is **beyond existence** or manifestation, and beyond that, the *anlage* of the Self reveals itself as the **ultimate omnipotentiality** of the Unmanifest prior to consciousness itself, yet including it by virtue of being its essence. There are infinite universes, dimensions, and planes within dimensions because every potentiality creates an infinite number of potentialities, all of which, in turn, create an infinite series of potentialities, and so on. That is the knowingness of Self- knowingness as the **essence of Creation**. All is spontaneous and self-creating. The essence of Divinity is present in all Creation as Creation itself.

Our Spiritual Will brings potentiality into actuality. The calibrated scale of consciousness confirms the various levels of enlightenment given different names over time, e.g. **Sage - Self as God Manifest**, **Teacher of Enlightenment**, **God (Self) as Logos**, **Avatar**, **Christ/Buddhahood/Krishna/Brahman**, etc. Universes are not created by something outside of them but by that which is innately within their essence. Universes, domains, and dimensions are self-creating and self-evolving because of the omnipresence of Divinity. The **Supreme** could be likened to an intrinsic quality or capacity for potentiality and existence. The **Ultimate** is described as beyond form, existence or manifestation; beyond is-ness or beingness; beyond consciousness or awareness; beyond Allness or Void; and beyond all qualities, descriptions, or definitions. Language is an attempt to indicate that which cannot be languaged but which can be known only by virtue of being it.

Power of the Levels of Consciousness

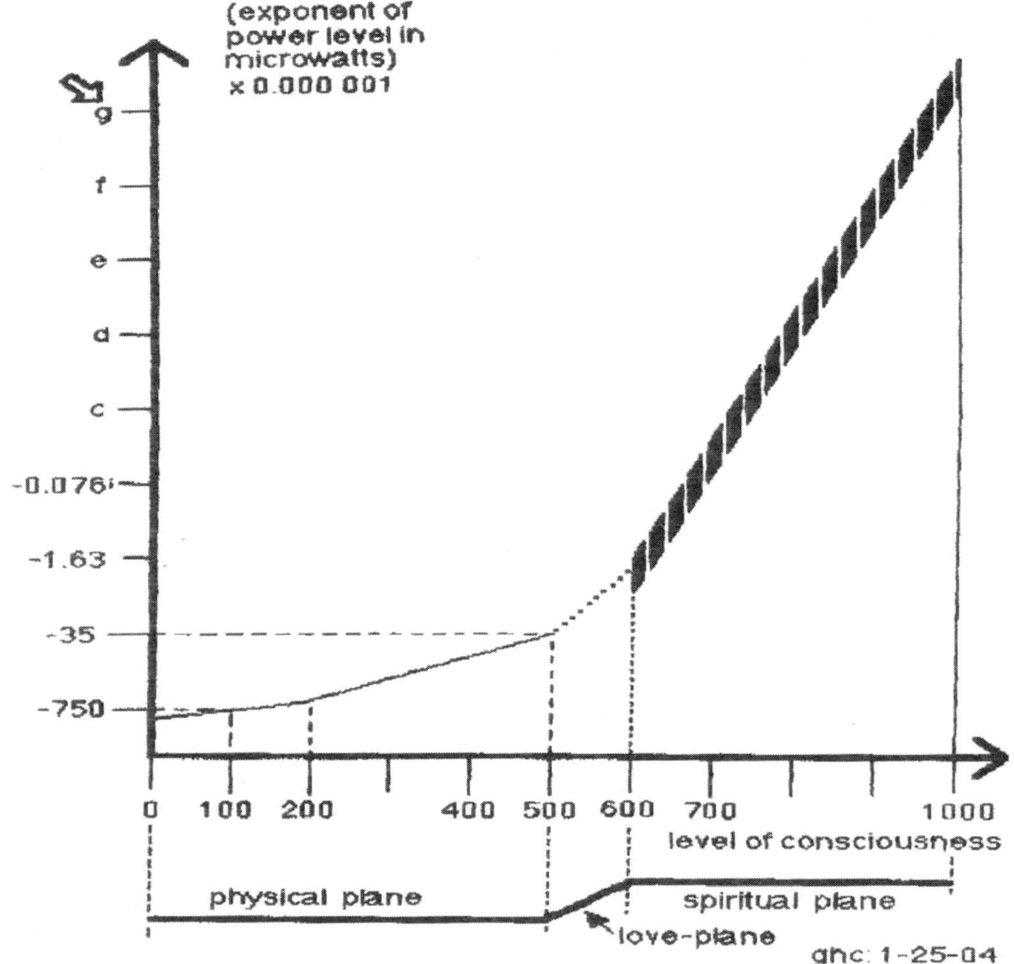

Slide 3

SLIDE 3: POWER OF THE LEVELS OF CONSCIOUSNESS

This slide was first introduced at the February 2004 Lecture, DVD disc 1 005020.

This slide was prepared by one of the students in the lecture audience, who showed it to Dr. Hawkins for review and use. It shows the relative "rates of increase of power" as consciousness advances through the following strata: (a) Below 200 (materialistic plane), (b) 200 through 499 (moral plane), (c) 500 - 599 (love plane), and (d) 600-1000 (spiritual plane).

The more one rises on the scale as shown on the Map of Consciousness, the faster one may rise in power but the process is non-linear, not predictable and can remain at certain points. The slide only indicates the relative increase in power through the above stated bands. To begin with, Apathy, which calibrates at 40, has much less power than that of Fear, which calibrates at 100. Fear, on the other hand, has much less power than that of Courage, which calibrates at 200.

Above the level of Courage are those of Neutrality, Willingness, Acceptance, and Reason. These fields give energy as well as nurture and support life and truth, thus increasing aliveness. Above the level of 500, the power of the field increases rapidly up to 599 and still more rapidly from 600 upwards. At 600, one leaves the fields of duality, illusion, and identification with the small self, and moves into the fields of Enlightenment on the spiritual plane. The energy fields of the enlightened beings, the great spiritual masters and avatars, start in the 600s and continue up to level 1,000.

This is what Dr. Hawkins said (paraphrased) about the graph, "This was a contribution from Mr. George Cholewinski, whose name has been chopped off the bottom. He translated the consciousness levels. You remember I said they had to become logarithmic because the numbers are so huge at the higher levels of consciousness. We had a logarithmic scale and we tried to give comparative levels of power in microwatts, just because people are used to such things. We are really talking about a nonlinear domain, but to make it more comprehensible we tried to relate it in comparative figures similar to the magnetic spectrum. In the things we write and communicate, people tend to become literal; they tend to miss the forest for the trees. Do not focus on the trees. The things that we are trying to illustrate are so you get the gist of it all.

Mr. Cholewinski is very good at mathematics. I am not very good at mathematics and do not enjoy mathematics because it is so pedestrian, limited to trudging through the linear world. When you are used to living free like a bird in the nonlinear world, it is a drag to have to figure everything out. Anyway, he correlated it in microwatts, using advanced mathematics. The answers we got use muscle testing, which would make any dyed-in-the-wool scientist shudder. The mathematics is not on here, I do not know what happened to it. It fell off the bottom here, but the mathematics is quite advanced, so he calibrated them and you see the levels of consciousness go from zero to 200 and then suddenly the slope of the graph changes, and again you see suddenly at 500 it shoots up and then again at 600 it reaches almost infinity."

Distribution of the Levels of Consciousness of Mankind (1)

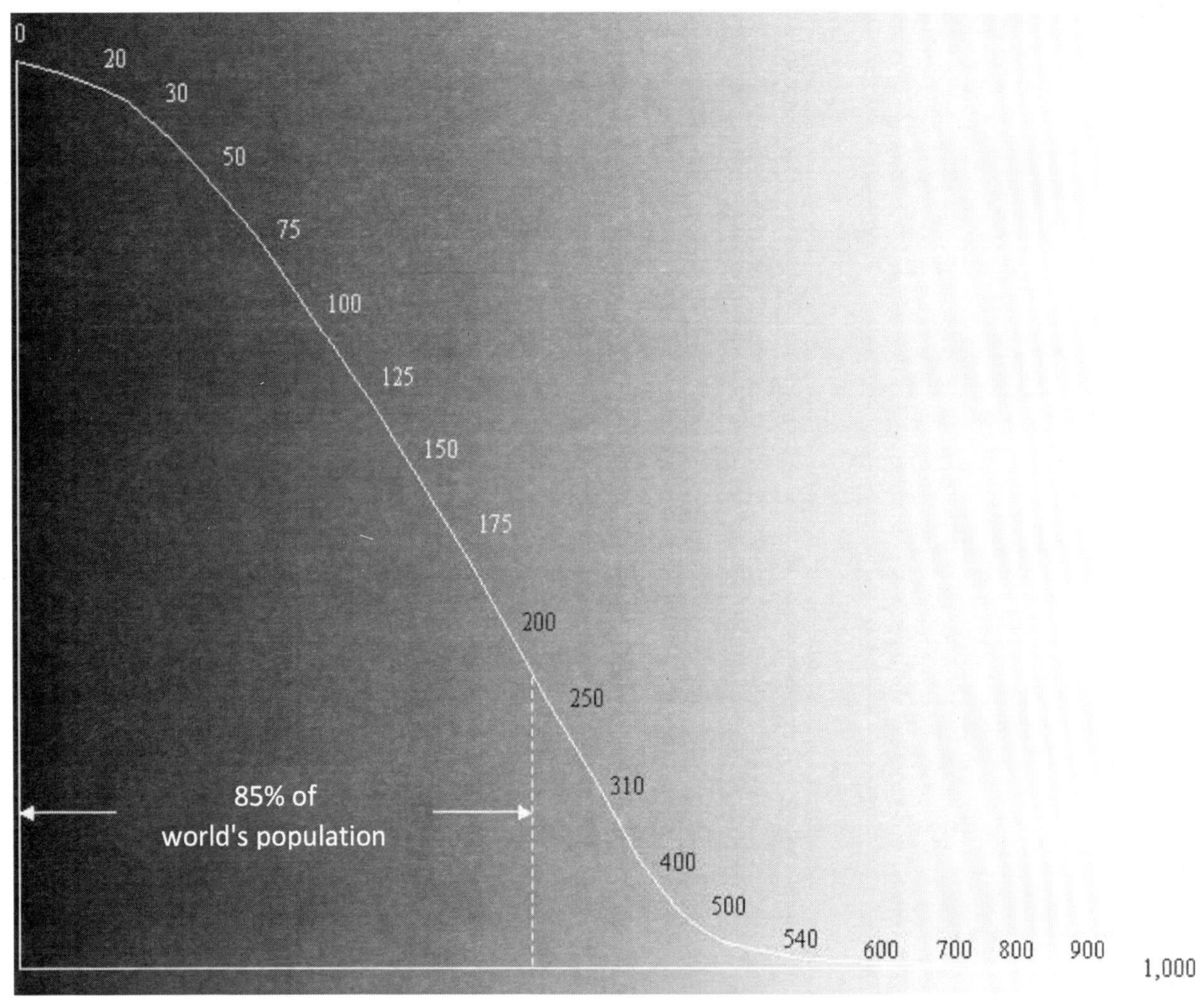

Slide 4

SLIDE 4: DISTRIBUTION OF THE LEVELS OF CONSCIOUSNESS OF MANKIND (1)

This slide was first introduced at the January 2002 Lecture, DVD disc 2 – at 000300.

At of the date of presentation of this slide, eighty-five percent of people on the planet calibrate below the level of consciousness of 200. Now that the average overall level of consciousness of humanity is above the level of integrity, the paradigm has changed. The new paradigm is no longer "material success", but instead it is integrity. We are now held accountable for things that were formerly "winked at".

Naiveté is the downside of the spiritual aspirant. One simply cannot conceive of how things really are. When above 200, one cannot conceive of the behavior of that which is below 200; however, it is unwise to think that the whole world is moral and humane. We project our positive consciousness onto that which is completely different from us. The human world is purgatorial and the levels of human consciousness range from the exquisite to the horrific. There is much in between, so the human domain is a great "karmic theatre" providing maximum opportunity for advancement of consciousness.

Most corporations calibrate at about 205, with a few in the 300s as of the time of the presentation of this slide. The great cathedrals in Europe calibrate generally at about 700. The intellect is very powerful. The heavy programming of man's consciousness by negativity has meant that only 4% of the world's population ever reaches 500 or beyond. Beyond 500, love is no longer an emotion. Below level 500, love is dualistic with the source of happiness being "out there". Therefore, love is vulnerable, and can be lost. At level 500, Love becomes a way of being, the way we are with the world and with ourselves. However, we do not allow others to abuse us and we do not abuse ourselves. Only 0.4% of the population reaches the level of 540, or Unconditional love. The consciousness level of Enlightenment begins at level 600, which is the crossover from duality to non-duality, and is reached rarely, as only one in ten million persons is even interested in the nondual state.

The discovery of the distribution of the levels of consciousness throughout society explains much of human behavior in history. How millions of people, whole generations and whole cultures, even whole continents, could be so easily manipulated to their own destruction is explained by the discovery that only some 15-20% of the world's population calibrates above the level of Integrity at 200. In addition to this limitation, the consciousness level of mankind as a whole remained at only 190 and was unchanged for centuries until, suddenly, in 1986 it jumped across the critical line from falsehood to integrity and truth above 200.

Distribution of the Levels of Consciousness of Mankind **(2)**

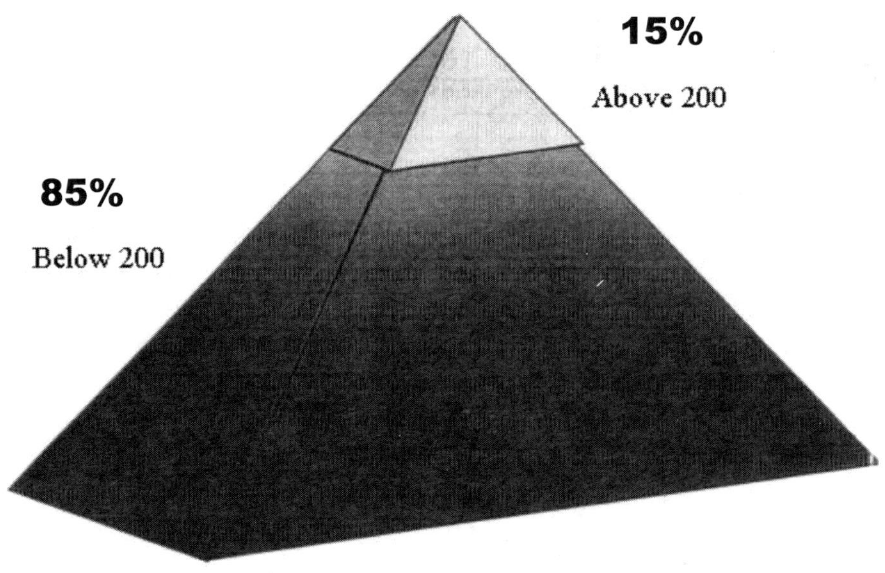

Slide 5

SLIDE 5: DISTRIBUTION OF THE LEVELS OF CONSCIOUSNESS OF MANKIND (2)

This slide was first introduced at the November 2003 Lecture, DVD disc 1 at 005900.

The distribution of the levels of consciousness of mankind can be displayed in the form of a pyramid, which gives a better sense of the mass of humanity. It is interesting that about 80% of mankind calibrates below the critical consciousness level of 200. This is consistent with the Pareto principle, also known as the 80-20 rule, which states that, for many events, roughly 80% of the effects come from 20% of the causes. Essentially, Pareto showed that approximately 80% of the land in Italy was owned by 20% of the population; Pareto developed the principle by observing that 20% of the peapods in his garden contained 80% of the peas. Mathematically, the 80-20 rule is roughly followed by a power law distribution (also known as the Pareto distribution) for a particular set of parameters, and many natural phenomena have been shown empirically to exhibit such a distribution.

The collective negativity of the population below level 200 is counterbalanced by the minority of people who calibrate above 200, and whose positive power is far greater than the negative pull of the masses below 200. The increase in power is exponential; therefore, actually only very few people with extremely advanced levels of consciousness are necessary to counterbalance the negativity of the rest of mankind.

Also of great interest and importance is that the distribution of the levels of consciousness of people on the planet is quite uneven. There is great disparity between different cultures and populations; this underlies the constancy of human conflict as reflected in interracial and international tensions and warfare. At the lowest levels of consciousness, life is devalued, and murder, suicide, mass slaughter, killing of children, and genocide are characteristic since hate is endemic. In contrast, at levels above 200, life is seen as a divine gift to be reverenced, and therefore killing the innocent is unthinkable.

In the words of Dr. Hawkins from the January 2002 Lecture: "One level of consciousness is not better than another. Each level is suitable for that which it is. Somebody at 700 is not suitable as a carpenter, is not suitable to run a church, and is not suitable as a president. You do not want anybody at 700, as most of them cannot function at all. They just sit in their ashram and if they still survive, people come and say 'hello' to them and they smile happily at them and that is that. The 200s and the 300s, who are the builders of the world, the construction workers, the steel workers, the people who go to work every day, they are the backbone of our society. The 400s is the world of the intellect and reason that dominates America. 500 is rare, with 540 being extremely rare and upwards from 540 there's practically nobody really."

It is not a duality of good and evil. It is not that 200 and above is good and below 200 is bad. The levels represent a perspective, an arbitrary point of observation, which is significant only in relationship to the whole. Each selected level is therefore the viewpoint from an arbitrary perspective. It does not denote a different reality, but instead shows how such a reality is experienced or perceived. Thus, it is not that reality 'is' that way, but that it 'feels' or 'looks' that way. Calibrated levels of consciousness are not really separate from each other but are actually potentialities that we can verifiably gradate to facilitate comprehension.

Distribution of the Levels of Consciousness of Mankind **(3)**

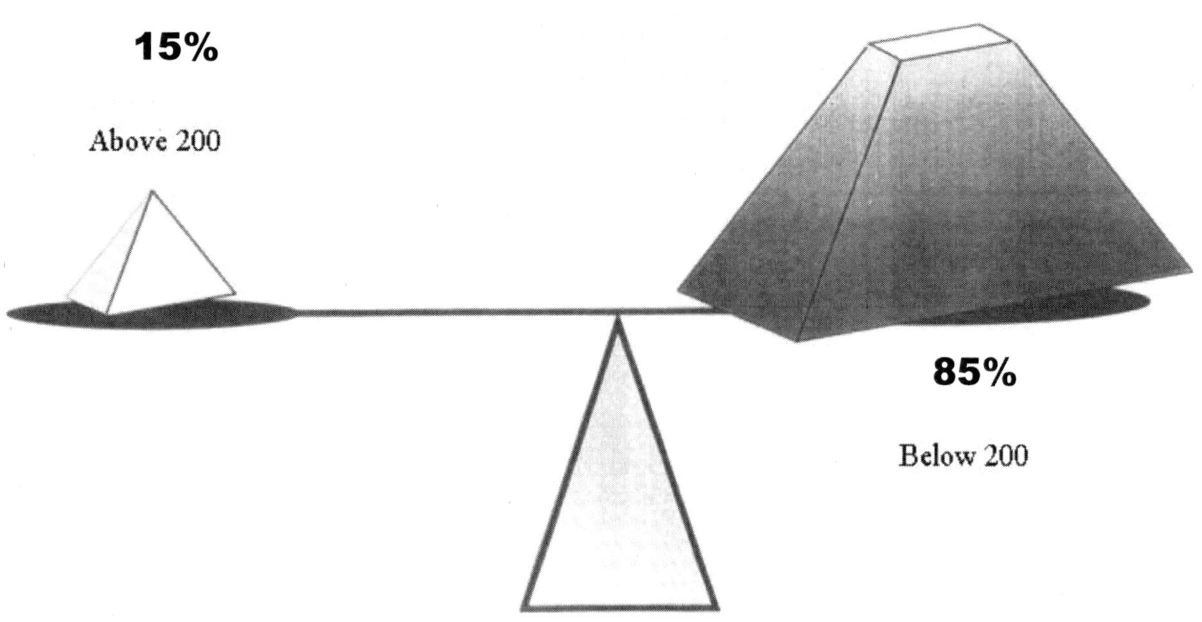

Slide 6

SLIDE 6: DISTRIBUTION OF THE LEVELS OF CONSCIOUSNESS OF MANKIND (3)

This slide was first introduced at the November 2003 Lecture, DVD disc 1 at 005930

The calibratable levels of consciousness denote power, which explains why the sheer mass of humanity that calibrates below 200 does not simply self-destruct by its pervasive negativity. In effect, the power of the 15% that calibrate above consciousness level 200 counterbalances the 85%. How do phenomena happen? They are the consequence of intentionality in the field. This is not causality but is the infinite power of Divinity. Everything is a consequence of the power of the field of Divinity as Self. It is the totality of the field, the climate - not just a "this" causing a "that". Because the scale of power advances logarithmically, a single Avatar at a consciousness level of 1,000 can in fact totally counterbalance the collective negativity of all of mankind.

Each level of human consciousness has its own innate 'reality', and conflict is inevitable between people and cultures that are diametrically opposed to each other. Cultures based on beliefs that calibrate as low as 20 ("Jihadism") now threaten the entire world via nuclear technology. In civilized people and countries, rationality and restraint are expected, but these qualities are ridiculed as weaknesses by the lower levels of consciousness, which are themselves prone to animalistic paranoia, delusions, and violence motivated by hatred. Force creates counterforce.

Power dominates by virtue of that which it is. Pride and arrogance calibrate at 195, in the realm of force. Therefore, the British Empire, which was at the level of pride and arrogance, was no match for Gandhi who calibrated in the 700's, a very high level of power.

In the words of Dr. Hawkins from the February 2004 Lecture: "You get that the 15% is counterbalancing the 85%; their creativity, their power, their productivity; the power of integrity is far greater than that of non-integrity. You can also understand the power of capitalism, and the answer to Karl Marx. 'This' (pointing to the smaller side of the balancing scale), is not exploiting 'that' (the larger side), 'this' is holding 'that' up. One brilliant idea creates more capital than all the money that the banks in the world are holding. Think of the giant economic productivity of one brilliant thought of Thomas Edison's: electricity. Capital exists in the mind and not in the bank. One brilliant thought, followed by integrous means, the rest of it is just automatic. So, this is the 15% that holds up the 85%."

Evolution of Consciousness

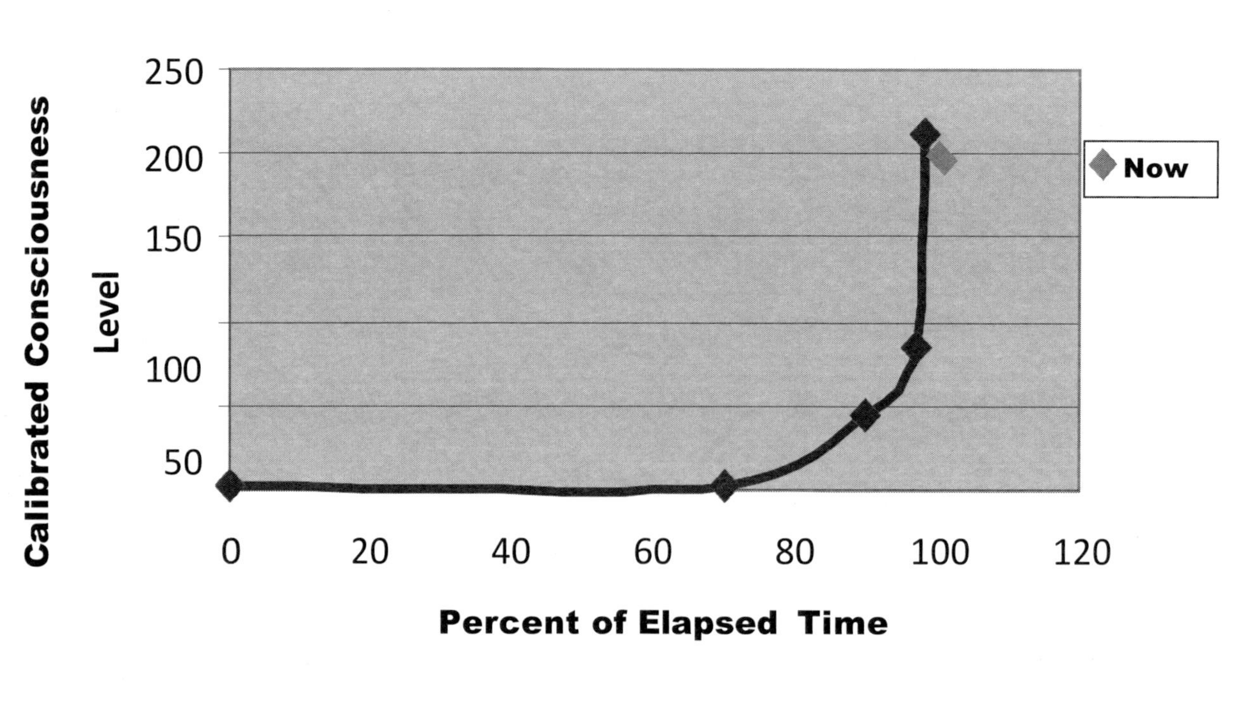
Calibrated Consciousness Level
250
200
150
100
50
0
20
40
60
80
100
120
Percent of Elapsed Time
Now

Slide 7

SLIDE 7: EVOLUTION OF CONSCIOUSNESS

This slide was first introduced at the October 2004, DVD disc 1 at 011800 and revised in December 2008, DVD disc 1 of 4 at 01:36:00

The evolution of consciousness of life on planet Earth and of humankind overall has been seemingly slow. It did not reach level 90 until the time of the birth of the Buddha at about 563 B.C. The rate of evolution then

then appears to have accelerated so that by the time of the birth of Jesus Christ, the consciousness level of the totality of mankind had reached 100. During each time period, the percentage of the population that calibrated over 200 was quite small. Nevertheless, the Vedas out of ancient India's Aryan culture calibrated in the high 900s, with Krishna at 1,000, which was the same level demonstrated by Jesus Christ and the Buddha.

However, it took approximately 2000 years for the overall consciousness level of mankind to move from 100 to the level of 205 in the late 1980s, and then again move another two points in November 2003, at the time of the Harmonic Concordance, to 207. Even with strong intention and dedication, human progress is slow and difficult. Thus, patience is the prerequisite to compassionate understanding, as the pace of human evolution fluctuates, e.g. a decrease in the consciousness level of mankind from 207 to 204 at the time of the presentation of this slide in December 2008. A seemingly reasonable probability could be derived that consciousness will continue to evolve because that is its nature, and the future of mankind can be realistically viewed as optimistic. This progression also implies that consciousness seeks to return to the awareness of its own source (calibrates as true).

The evolution of consciousness is also demonstrated by its progression in the evolution of hominids. Neanderthal man calibrated at consciousness level 75; then Java man, Homo erectus, emerged at 80; Heidelberg man at 80-85; and then, 600,000 years ago, Homo sapiens idelta (cal. 80) appeared in Ethiopia as a possible forerunner of modern man. A very recent discovery is the hominid Homo floresiensis, a diminutive evolutionary ancestor who lived on the Indonesian island of Flores until approximately 13,000 years ago. They compensated for their small brain size by having increased neuronal complexity and calibrate at 85.

In the words of Dr. Hawkins from the February 2006 Lecture: "This is the evolution of consciousness on a time scale. People ask, 'what do you think is the future of mankind?' Well, this is the level of consciousness over great expanses of time. Multimillions of years go by after the age of the dinosaurs, and then suddenly human consciousness emerges on this planet and it shoots way up in a relatively short period of time until the present level. You can see that for 85% of elapsed earth time, it was still way down here and suddenly it took off and now you see, despite the world news, it is on a very upbeat, rapid rise.

People lament what they consider catastrophes in the world, not realizing that catastrophes themselves can be of great service to spiritual evolution. Nothing gets you closer to God than facing the muzzle of a gun! (Ha, Ha, Ha). During World War II, the two of us standing there, looking at a live mine about to go off, were at peace after accepting that the results of our efforts were not in our hands. Yes, it is either God or nothing, I tell you. In that instant you surrender your life to God. Everybody laments and wrings their hands about calamity, but calamity is the only way many people can get there. Many people cannot get there so long as life is smooth, prosperous, etc. and materialism disappears quickly when you are facing death."

Earth Epochs and Calibrations

TIME PERIODS ROCK SYSTEMS	TIME EPOCHS ROCK SERIES	APPROX DURATION MILLION YEARS	APPROX % OF TOTAL AGE	LIFE FORMS	CALIBRATED LEVEL OF LIFE
Quaternary	Recent Pleistocene	1	2%	Rise and dominance of man	212
Upper Tertiary	Pliocene Miocene	80		Modern animals and plants	212
Lower Tertiary	Oligocene Eocene Paleocene			Rapid development of modern mammals insects and plants	112
Upper Cretaceous		60	8%	Primitive mammals; last dinosaurs; last ammonites	84
Lower Cretaceous				Rise of flowering plants	
Jurassic		35		First birds, first mammals. Diversification of reptiles; Climax of ammonites; Coniferous trees	68
Triassic				Rise of dinosaurs; cicada-like plants; bony fishes	62
Permian		25	20%	Rise of reptiles. Modern Insects. Last of many plant and animal groups	45
Pennsylvanian (Carboniferous)		85		First reptiles, amphibians, primitive insects; seed ferns; primitive conifers	35
Mississippian (Carboniferous)				Climax of shell-crushing sharks, Primitive ammonites	33
Devonian		50		First amphibians, first land snails, Primitive land plants. climax of brachiopods	27
Silurian		40		First traces of land life. Scorpions, First lungfishes Widespread coral reefs.	17
Ordovician		90		First fish. Climax of trilobites First appearance of many marine invertebrates.	12
Cambrian		70		First marine invertebrates	8
Proterozoic Archeozoic (Precambrian)		Over 1300	70%	First signs of life. Bacteria, Algae	2 1
Age of oldest dated rocks: about 1,850,000,000 years					

Slide 8

SLIDE 8: EARTH EPOCHS AND CALIBRATIONS

This slide was first introduced at the December 2003 lecture, DVD disk 1 at 001430.

Planet Earth apparently arose as a spin-off of condensed energy of galactic origin, the mechanics of which are still under study by science. When the surface of the molten mass of earth cooled sufficiently, consciousness plus matter evolved first as primitive, simple life forms, such as algae or lichens. Eons later, life appeared as the DNA of viruses, and later, of bacteria. For life to survive and later evolve, the prime requisite is that it be designed with survival as its primary goal or consequence. Self-propagation, self-interest, and self-servingness were *a priori* requirements for any primitive life form to survive or to succeed. In turn, the survival of life in form depends upon the accumulation, organization, utilization, and integration of pure energy itself. Energy is a necessity of life that had to be acquired.

On the vegetative level, photosynthesis became the primary mechanism by which chemical molecules could be integrated and utilized. Microorganisms developed integrated systems that incorporated molecular components of the environment. The survival of life depended on the acquisition of needed energy sources of whatever forms were available. The fulfillment of this basic necessity was accomplished by the development of survival systems of extraordinary complexity and ingenuity. These were developments of the quality of intelligence innate to the field of consciousness itself before they appeared in the physical world as living forms.

Significant inferences are derived from calibrating the levels of consciousness of all life on planet Earth through the great archeological eons of prehistory. 70% of all of time, archeologically speaking, was spent at level 1. In only 2% of this time, life went from 84 to 112. The evolution of consciousness has currently been speeding up, after moving very slowly for a very long time. The overall consciousness level of life has slowly progressed over the archeological ages, as represented by the evolution of the animal kingdom, and is at 212 as of the date of this presentation in December 2003. Similarly, the consciousness level of human evolution shows the same type of progression over time and is 207 as of December 2003.

Each level of life, consciousness, is sacrificial to the one above it, in that it earns karmic merit and becomes part of the higher level. Below 200, animal life survives at the cost of another life. Animal life is not evil; it is just deficient in energy. It needs to get in order to live. That is how the animal brain arose, as life discovered that it had to 'get' in order to survive. Animals below 200 are all voracious; above 200 their nature changes. What we inherit as a human is an ego, a mind, which is then programmed by life. To become enlightened means to transcend the ego, by understanding it for what it truly is, a vestigial remnant of man's evolutionary origins.

ANIMAL KINGDOM

Bacteria	**1**	**Birds of Prey**	**105**	**Sheep**	**210**
Protozoa	**2**	**Rodents**	**105**	**Range Cattle**	**210**
Crustaceans	**3**	**Rhinoceros**	**105**	**Elephant**	**235**
Insects	**6**	**Song Birds**	**125**	**Farm Horse**	**240**
Arachnids	**7**	**Dove**	**145**	**Cats**	**240**
Amphibians	**17**	**Polar Bear**	**160**	**Family Cat**	**245**
Fish	**20**	**Grizzly Bear**	**160**	**Race Horse**	**245**
Octopus	**20**	**Water Buffalo**	**175**	**Dogs**	**245**
Shark	**24**	**Black Bear**	**180**	**Family Dog**	**250**
Viper	**35**	**Jackal, Fox**	**185**	**Monkey**	**250**
Komodo Dragon	**40**	**Wolf**	**190**	**Gorilla**	**275**
Reptiles	**40**	**Hippopotamus**	**190**	**Chimpanzee**	**305**
Predatory Mammals:		**Javelina**	**195**	**Exceptions:**	
Hyena, Lion, Tiger	**40**	**Grazers: Zebra,**		**Oscar the cat**	**250**
Snake	**45**	**Gazelle, Giraffe**	**200**	**Alex, Trained African**	
Alligator	**45**	**Deer**	**205**	**Grey Parrot**	**401**
Dinosaur	**60**	**Bison**	**205**	**Koko (Trained Gorilla)**	**405**
Whale	**85**	**Domestic Pig**	**205**	**Song Bird's Song**	**500**
Dolphin	**95**	**Elk**	**210**	**Cat's Purr**	**500**
Migratory Birds	**105**	**Dairy Cow**	**210**	**Dog's Wagging Tail**	**500**

Slide 9

SLIDE 9: ANIMAL KINGDOM

This slide was first introduced at the November 2003 lecture, DVD disc 1 at 014600.

The evolution of consciousness through the animal kingdom helps one understand how the human ego got to where it is today. The text of *A Course in Miracles* and many religions vilify the ego by calling it 'sin', but consciousness research shows that the reality is quite different. Due to the biologic nature of the ego, it does not know anything about God. How could it do what it does in order to keep itself separate from God when it does not even know anything about God? When above 200, one cannot conceive the behavior of that which is below 200; it is unwise to think the whole world is moral and humane. You don't put a bare foot in a cage with a **Komodo dragon** (cal. 40), not because of hate or fear of the Komodo dragon, but out of respect for how a Komodo dragon sees the world and thinks. He thinks of the world in terms of food. However, a Komodo dragon calibrates higher than serial child killers (cal. 30).

The best thing to do with the ego is to love it and see it as a cute little animal. In order for life to survive on this planet, it had to be programmed 100% for survival. So, the core of the ego is interested in its own survival and not the survival of others. It only has enough energy for its own survival. The **bacteria** do what they do to survive. The fact that they kill you in the meantime is not the bacteria's problem, nor its concern. If the bacteria were worried about you, they would not survive. That would violate their programming. Therefore, we can forgive animal life and see that is what animal life is.

People under 200 think they have to do what they do in order to survive. They still think like animals. With **jackals** and **foxes** (cal. 185), we begin to see intelligence really beginning to show up. With **wolves** (cal. 190), we see group pack formation. We see the dominant alpha male and female, the territoriality, the group identity, group commitment, and we still see all this in the human. The characteristic of the life of the wolf is very characteristic of whole societies in today's world.

A big transformation of consciousness was the appearance on the great plains of Africa and North America of the grazing animals like **deer**, **buffalo**, **elk**, etc. The world has been at the devastation of lower levels of consciousness plus testosterone. You put the two together and you have human history. **Elephants** at 235 are more trustable than a large part of the human populace; they show group solidarity, group love with family bonding and they mourn their dead. The elephants get together and actually go through a mourning process for the dead, recognizing the absence of life. **Cats** as a genus, as a species, calibrate at 240; however, a cat adopted by a family jumps to 245 due to the presence of humans. A **dog** is at 245, but again, if a family adopts it, its consciousness jumps to 250.

When we put the animal kingdom together with the evolution of the ego, we can accept that the ego is a product of biologic evolution and there is no reason at all to feel sinful, guilty or fearful for having inherited an ego as part of becoming human. Reinforcement of belief that one is a sinner and therefore deserves self-starvation and self-condemnation keeps one from crossing over the level 200, which is the most important thing in all of spiritual evolution. Because once you cross over 200, you are going to be attracted to the rest. Under 200, you are repelled, or threatened by spirituality.

The Great Books of the Western World

Aeschylus 425
Apollonius 420
Aquinas, Thomas 460
Archimedes 455
Aristophanes 445
Aristotle 498
Augustine 503
Aurelius, Marcus 445
Bacon, Francis 485
Berkeley 470
Boswell 460
Cervantes 430
Chaucer 480
Copernicus 455
Dante 505
Darwin 450
Descartes 490
Dostoevsky 465
Engels 200
Epictetus 430
Euclid 440
Euripides 470
Faraday 415
Fielding 440
Fourier 405
Freud 499
Galen 450
Galileo 485
Gibbon 445
Gilbert 450
Goethe 465
Harvey 470
Hegel 470
Herodotus 440
Hippocrates 485
Hobbes 435
Homer 455
Hume 445
Huygens 465
James, William 490
Kant 460
Kepler 470
Lavoisier 425
Locke 470
Lucretius 420
Machiavelli 440
Marx 130
Melville 460
Mill, J. S. 465
Milton 470
Montaigne 440
Montesquieu 435
Newton 499
Nicomachus 435
Pascal 465
Plato 485
Plotinus 503
Plutarch 460
Ptolemy 435
Rabelais 435
Rousseau 465
Shakespeare 465
Smith, Adam 455
Sophocles 465
Spinoza 480
Sterne 430
Swift 445
Tacitus 420
Thucydides 420
Tolstoy 420
Virgil 445

Slide 10

SLIDE 10: GREAT BOOKS OF THE WESTERN WORLD

This slide was first introduced at the April 2004 lecture, DVD disc 2 at 005600-012500.

The great books of the Western World arose out of the 400s primarily, the levels of reason. The greatest intellects throughout history of the Western World calibrate primarily in the high 400's. The human mind and its intellect have been both the tool as well as the subject of investigation of the enormous complexity of reason and rationality throughout the ages. The sheer volume of man's investigations filled vast libraries and grew to a bewildering proliferation of information rather than a conclusive resolution or simplification.

In the 1950s, a group of educators and scholars, chaired by Mortimer Adler, sought to give organizational recognition to the intellectual efforts of the great thinkers over time. The best academic thinkers of the Western world congregated and spent a great deal of time deciding which books should be included and this resulted in the production of The Great Books of the Western World, which included the works of the excellent scholars and thinkers in their best efforts in the attempt to arrive at and define truth. Collectively, The Great Books calibrate at 450, but with the elimination of Karl Marx (cal. 130), they calibrate at 465 and here we have already a paradigm of the capacity of the intellect, set out and historically tested over many centuries, having stood the rigors of academic demand and the dialectic of reason and intellect, following the rules of logic.

Marxism is dualistic in that it sees perpetrator and victim in everything and projects that onto the world, setting up contention, distrust, revolution, hatred, blame, paranoia, and war. If each thing is being what it is and attracts to it what it is, because you're like a magnet that attracts to you what you are, then the perpetrator/victim model is erroneous and reflects the worst of the downside of the mind, the most serious distortion because it interferes with one's capacity to perceive reality. Marx's problem was an oedipal complex. How people handle the Oedipal complex, how they see authority, determines whether they are going to become a Marxist or not. In the unconscious, the father stands for the authority. Now, you either see authority as protective and nurturing and a power that is aligned with your well-being or you become competitive with it and see the authority as a threat. The core of the infantile ego is it wishes to be recognized as God. The 'omnipotence' of the narcissistic ego, then, runs up against the reality represented by the father figure, as setting limits in society of expected codes of behavior. What happened with **Marx** is that **Hegel**, the father figure of the German School of philosophy, was the father figure for Marx. And basic to Hegel's philosophy is the principle of the Absolute. The narcissistic ego hates anything that's successful and authoritarian. It instantly hates success. The way to become successful is to study success and be like that. The way to become unsuccessful is to attack it. Marx's unresolved oedipal complex has cost the world forty-five million dead because Marx was too cheap to see an analyst or somehow resolve his dread of Hegel and the principle of the Absolute. Thus one can see why one has to be stringent for truth. Philosophy is not just airy-fairy, it's what determines whether one lives or dies and is extraordinarily important.

On the other hand, **Copernicus** upset the world by telling the truth. He was not popular for a while, any more than was **Galileo**, because people have a fixed idea of things and one can see that the truth is not too welcome. In fact, the church did not forgive Galileo for 450 years. It is notable that the final volume in The Great Books of the Western World is devoted to Freud, whose most seminal discovery was that of the importance of the unconscious mind and its primary role in all aspects of mental and emotional life. The great contribution of psychoanalysis is that it demonstrates the decisive role of subjectivity as the substrate of experience and its interpretation and intrapsychic dynamics.

Structure of Truth

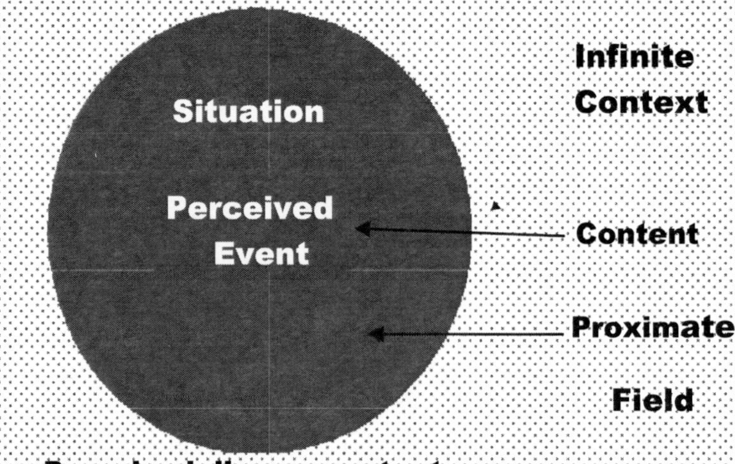

Event:	**Perceived, linear, content**
Situation:	**Time, place, circumstances, influences,**
Infinite Context:	**Nonlinear, infinite, omnipresent, timeless. Records all events and circumstances permanently.**

Slide 11

SLIDE 11: STRUCTURE OF TRUTH

This slide was first introduced at the April 2004 lecture, DVD Disc 2 at 012530.

"Was slavery wrong? From an absolute viewpoint, you could say, "of course." Was it wrong at the time? Do you realize, everyone here, the ancestors of everyone in this room were, at one time, slaves- without exception. The Vikings were one of the first ones to discover it. They used to just kill people. Then they found if they didn't kill people they could sell people. Out of greed, they stopped slaughtering. If it wasn't for greed, few of us would be in this room. They began to market people and slavery was born. Slavery was everywhere in this world without exception. Slavery was a prevailing condition of all of mankind, right or wrong, yes or no, it was the field of the human condition. It was karmically the human condition. What happens with the evolution of consciousness is that we begin to see a thing differently. Now we see slavery as undesirable, wrong, etc. But you can't project it backward in time. Therefore, at the time, it was not non-integrous. In fact, it was legal, a lifestyle, everywhere in the world." – Paraphrased from DVD disc 2, 012500-013850 of the April 2004 Lecture, "Emotions and Sensations".

A statement is only true within a specific field, and the same exact statement can become blatantly false in a different field (situational ethics, impaired responsibility, mitigating circumstances, different time period or setting, different culture or historical period, etc.). The prevailing circumstances alter perceived truth and responsibility. It becomes clear that a reliable understanding of truth requires definition and description of not only the content but also the overall field, and the intention of the observer. Content is linear - form – manifestation – perceived. The proximate field surrounds it and is linear as well as non-linear - time, place, circumstances, influences, contributory factors, both known and unknown.

Context is everything beyond the proximate field - non-linear and infinite, omnipresent, timeless; records all events and circumstances forever. Nobody has ever defined truth and that is one reason people argue about truth. We talk about what is logical and provable, we talk about the Newtonian world "out there", but we don't live there. We are all living in the non- measurable, non-definable, and non-provable realm of awareness called 'subjectivity', the experiential sense of presence, of experience, the basis of experiencing. People who have gone out of body know that the sense of subjectivity goes with you. There is the body lying in the bed and you are on the other side of the room, witnessing the phenomena of the surgeon sewing up your body. The sense of "me, I" goes with consciousness, not with the physical body. Science, reason, and social discourse operate primarily on the level of content (linear), whereas meaning is abstract and a consequence of context via comprehension (nonlinear).

The resolution of ambiguities and conflict is the automatic consequence of expansion of context from limited positionality to inclusive totality. In the past, such heated controversies emerged over whether the earth was round or flat, or whether it went around the sun or vice versa. The same types of controversies are now repeated by science/reason versus religious/spiritual truth and faith. By expansion of context, however, it will be easily observed that no actual conflict is possible in reality, and seeming conflict is only an artificial consequence of mentation from an arbitrary and limited point of view and observation.

Thus, limitation of paradigm is a consequence of the dominance of the ego, which sacrifices truth and integrity in order to see itself as victorious. Science is limited to the consciousness levels of the 400s; nonlinear context, or spiritual reality, calibrates at 500 and above. Such limitation of vision is detrimental to human peace and progress, as well as being an impediment to wisdom and happiness.

CONTENT, FIELD, AND CONTEXT

Content	Proximate Field	Context
Ego	Spiritual ego	Spirit
Linear	Semi-linear	Nonlinear
Limited	Semi-limited	Unlimited
Definable	Describable	Experiential
Predictable	Random	Self-existent
Newtonian	Nonlinear Dynamics Quantum Mechanics	Spiritual
Measurable	Identifiable	Observable
Objective	Objective	Subjective
Describable	Describable	Knowable
Circumscribed	Diffuse	General
Force	Influence	Potentiation
Time	Calculable	Timeless
Location	Generalized	Nonlocal
Provable	Estimated	Knowable

Slide12

SLIDE 12: CONTENT, FIELD, AND CONTEXT

This slide was first introduced at the April 2004 lecture, DVD disc 2 at 013520.

Content is any describable object, statement, fact, idea, or supposedly self-existent 'thing', (i.e., form). The 'field' is the time, place, and circumstances that prevail. Because the components are knowable, the field can be viewed as proximate or as having a probable effect on the content. The field is thus like the weather or location and therefore may vary and include intangible factors, such as public opinion, influential prior events, or belief systems, both conscious and unconscious. Beyond the form of content and the proximate field or conditions, however, is the absolute, overall formless context that is unlimited by time or dimension, but within which human consciousness operates and functions as a frame of reference from which one can select points of observation. The overall context is the infinite field of consciousness itself, which is unlimited and beyond form, yet capable of registering form as minute as a passing thought. Without the base of consciousness, the mind is incapable of awareness; thus, no statement of any kind can be made.

Therefore, any definition of truth must include content, a knowable field, and an awareness of ultimate context. The content is linear and specific. The proximate field is semi-linear. It's somewhat linear, but it's also somewhat nonlinear. The infinite context is beyond time. That which is within the box is definable. That which is outside the box can no longer be defined, but it can be described. 'The situation was favorable.' You can't measure 'favorable.' And yet, if it's favorable or unfavorable will make a difference in the outcome. The proximate field, we can say is describable and subjectively, it's experiential. You walk into a room, you get where the room is at, totally.

There's no way you can prove that, no way you can demonstrate it, you can't measure it-you know they're up to no good or not. Instantly you know that.

The Newtonian world is predictable. As we get outside the limitation of the box, then in the proximate field you start to see randomness, you see the nonlinear dynamics, and the context is spiritual or self-existent and unpredictable. That is why Doc always counseled against extreme sports. Nineteen successful freefalls do not determine that the twentieth will also be successful - the likelihood of the twentieth one going wrong is the same after number nineteen as it is at number one. You haven't changed the likelihood at all. There is the example of the two guys in Sedona who caught rattlesnakes. One guy got bitten nineteen times and the twentieth bite killed him. That's pushing the box.

Within the box, you've got force. The proximate field has an influence and the infinite field potentiates. There is a progression of comprehension and the capacity or capability to know truth as one moves from content to field to context. The capacity to know is further dependent on the observer's brain physiology, intention, maturity, and calibrated level of consciousness. The infinite context, which is the infinite context of consciousness calibration, is not the proximate field but it's the field which has the power to transform the un-manifest into the manifest. The power of Creation comes out of an infinite field, of the un-manifest becoming manifest, and the mechanism is intention. The content of the field is the ego. The proximate field is the spiritualized ego. The infinite context is the spirit. It is because of the spirit that man even concerns himself with ethics or morality. It doesn't dawn on other species, other than man. We can describe that which is within form. Beyond form you can only know it. One can know what love is, it's a subjective awareness. It's not really possible to prove it or describe it. The poets try to do so but do not really succeed.

Spiritual Foundation - The Virtues

Available	**265**	**Respectable**	**255**	**Equitable**	**385**
Considerate	**295**	**Patient**	**255**	**Wisdom**	**385**
Decent	**295**	**Stable**	**255**	**Rational**	**405**
Responsible	**290**	**Honorable**	**255**	**Supportive**	**245**
Reliable	**290**	**Cordial**	**255**	**Benign**	**225**
Honest	**200**	**Friendly**	**280**	**Protective**	**265**
Hard Work	**200**	**Maturity**	**280**	**Humane**	**260**
Moral	**200**	**Idealistic**	**295**	**Content**	**255**
Warm	**205**	**Orderly**	**300**	**Pleasing**	**275**
Kind	**220**	**Normal**	**300**	**Glad**	**335**
Helpful	**220**	**Sane**	**300**	**Happy**	**395**
Diligent	**210**	**Fair**	**305**	**Sensible**	**240**
Easygoing	**210**	**Ethical**	**305**	**Pleasant**	**220**
Thoughtful	**225**	**Flexible**	**245**	**Positive**	**225**
Persistent	**210**	**Balanced**	**305**	**"Salt of the Earth"**	**240**
Open	**240**	**Respectful**	**305**	**Modest**	**245**
Tolerant	**245**	**Healthy**	**360**	**Diplomatic**	**240**
Calm	**250**	**Faithful**	**365**	**Polite**	**245**
Dependable	**250**	**Sense of Humor**	**345**	**Firm**	**245**
Genuine	**255**	**Loyal**	**345**	**Nice**	**255**

Slide13

SLIDE 13: SPIRITUAL FOUNDATION - THE VIRTUES

This slide was first introduced at November 2003 lecture, DVD disc 2 at 000100.

"Transcending the limitations of the ego and the roadway to enlightenment is simple. The basic characteristics of someone who has crossed over 200 could be stated simply: good will towards all. Practice that in all things. Kindness, respect for life, respect for the rights of others, consideration- no great requirements, and that doesn't mean leaving the world and sitting cross- legged, shaving your head and doing all those strange things. It means you go through the world as though you are part of a certain field which is automatically considerate of others. When it is inconsiderate it corrects itself. The person who has gone over 200, when they are inconsiderate, it is not okay with them. They go to bed that night, they hear their mind trying to justify what they said, but part of their mind keeps nagging them, because it was not a kind remark, etc. Now this is the new paradigm which we live up to. It sounds very basic. Any one of these virtues will take you all the way to enlightenment. Take anything off this chart and practice it incessantly, constantly, around the clock, with no exceptions. Any one of these will take you all the way. The first virtue listed on the chart is availability, which means to be present. You walk into a restaurant and she (the waitress) never looks at you, she writes your order down-you can't fault her for it. She is not present. The next one comes in, smiles- instantly there is a connection, they are present. In the old truck stop, the waitress always called you 'sweetheart.' And the old truckers always called them 'honey.' 'Going to have the same thing, honey?' 'Yep, sweetheart': You see how the politically correct person would be offended by that. It was a style of connectedness, a way of lovingness and caringness, an expression of concern for your fellow human being. 'What you going to have, sweetheart, same as usual?' 'Yeah, honey bun': Sounds gruff, sort of macho world of the trucker, but you get the sense of it. They are available to each other, responsive to each other, acknowledging each other's importance in their life. And when you stop back at the same truck stop and your favorite waitress isn't there you feel disappointed. Oh, well. You always sit in her section. There is 'affectionateness', then. The person is available, they're present." - Paraphrased from November 2003 Lecture, "Realization of the Self and the 'I'", DVD disc 2 ~ 000100-000500.

One must begin the spiritual journey here, with the practice of virtues and not start with an advanced teaching like that of the Bhagavad-Gita, which calibrates at 910; first, you must learn to be polite. Bhagavad-Gita is tremendous when one reaches a certain point in evolution of consciousness, but will not make sense when you are just starting. The calibrated level of consciousness of a neighborhood can be evaluated just by looking at the sidewalk. Just being responsible for one's own trash raises one's consciousness. The kindness and forgiveness one gives to oneself is projected out to the world.

A negative feeling on top is coming from something below (subconscious): one must find it, own it, and forgive oneself for it. When something throws you out of easiness, there's something you need to pay attention to. The uneasiness is pullingup something that needs to be cleared. We clear it by looking within ourselves and finding what makes us uneasy, owning it, and forgiving our self because one is a fallible human being. One has to learn to show oneself kindness in the willingness to forgive. This then transfers into willingness to forgive others. Spiritual aspirants must learn to accept things the way they are, not the way they want them to be. Each thing is what it is by its karmic inheritance, and not by anything else. There is no cause except by one's own spiritual intention.

These character traits are essential to spiritual evolution and progress, which require self-discipline, humility, and fortitude as well as determination. They lead to prayer and the practice of spiritual principles in all of one's affairs, accompanied by the awareness that one is ultimately accountable to God for what has been done with the gift of life.

Transcending the Seduction of the Mind

Fact: 99% of the mind is silent.

1% = hypnotized

Polarize (Duality) stems from the process called "IZE"

Politicize	**Rationalize**
Moralize	**Fantasize**
Idealize	**Infantilize**
Hypothesize	**Intellectualize**
Romanticize	**Mentalize**
Criticize	**Glamorize**
Emotionalize	**Demonize**
Dramatize	**Prize**
Catastrophize	**Theorize**
Victimize	

The wise transcend the IZE and the seduction of thoughts and images to hypnotize.

Slide 14

SLIDE 14: TRANSCENDING THE SEDUCTION OF THE MIND

This slide was first introduced at the August 2003 lecture, DVD disc 1 at 000940.

Consciousness research confirms that approximately 99 percent of the 'mind' is silent and only 1 percent is actually processing images. The observer self is **hypnotized** by that 1 percent of activity and identifies with it as 'me'. It is oblivious to the silent 99 percent of the field because it is invisibly formless. This is also reminiscent of the fact that 96 percent of the universe is invisible as so-called 'dark', unseen matter and energy.

The "IZE's" are the ego's distraction from the truth, or solutions. To **Politicize** causes dissension and conversation in your mind. You read the paper, you argue with the news, you argue with the editorial writer. It instantly creates a duality and creates conflict. That is one of the great enemies of peace. The next great enemy of peace is to **Moralize**. If we politicize and moralize, which is everybody's habit when they read the paper or the watch news, then you can see why everything is divided into 'good' or 'bad'. What if you didn't moralize? What if you were just the witness? Once you are in duality, every move triggers a response. Even if you win, you will get punished, highly taxed, and criticized, maybe even bombed and assassinated. If you politicize and moralize and then **Idealize**, you've set up the next war. This is the basis of war, right there. War has nothing to do with guns, munitions, bombs; those are just the aftermath, the mechanics of it. Then, out of that, we speculate and so we begin to **Hypothesize**. It should be this way, it could be that way; people ask you the hypothetical question, "but, what if?" Never answer "what if?" The hypothetical has absolutely no grounding in fact. The hypothetical is the grossly distorted pseudoscientific studies that prove that 'this is dangerous' or 'that is dangerous' and keeps everybody frightened and programs everybody with negative programs.

The next thing we do is we **romanticize** about all kinds of things and create a flowery imagination of how it could be, should be, and then become dissatisfied if it does not compare favorably with our romantization of it. To romanticize is to project onto it, so in all these examples something is happening out there and then the mind projects this interpretation onto it, then believes what it has just projected onto the world is happening 'out there.' Any commentary you can make about life is always a projection because when you experience the reality of life, there's nothing to say about it. Any commentary is a distortion; its opposite is reverence or respect.

Criticize: "Well, you shouldn't have done that..." **Emotionalize** is to whip- up energy by exaggeration. **Dramatize**: "Oh My! See how big and bad this whole movie is!" **Catastrophize**: news is a constant negative sensation, no solution possible, too big. **Theorize**: to solve problems that do not even exist, except in your head. **Rationalize**: excuses for our behavior. **Generalize**: everything is this way; "always" statements. **Fantasize**: For the relief of our pain, like "I'm not really here." **Infantilize**: see other adults as children whom we must save. **Intellectualize**: Think up a number of problems to solve that do not even exist. **Mentalize**: Our mind imagines causation. It is not in the world out there, but only in our mind. **Glamorize**: Like a spray of paint on something to render it attractive. **Demonize**: "I hate that evil thing"... all these thoughts or attitudes simply "**Victimize**" us. One of the fastest ways to God is to become aware of the "IZEs" and see that your mind is "IZE-ing" out there and thereby become wise.

Formula of Causality

Attractor Pattern

Operants

Observable Event

Slide 15

SLIDE 15: FORMULA OF CAUSALITY

This slide was first introduced at the June 2004 lecture, DVD disc 2 at 0002440.

The mind sees God as 'first cause', shown in the arguments for proof of the existence of God from theology, such as that of St. Thomas Aquinas. This concept creates the limitation of conceiving of God as the great 'roller of the dice', subsequent to which everything has been a linear succession of sequential causes, like endless billiard balls. That cannot be the case, because the sequence is not of sameness, you suddenly come to differentness. The quality of God is not the same as the quality of the supposed effect. You cannot find the original billiard ball behind all the billiard balls because when you get past number one, there are no billiard balls there.

In the words of Dr. Hawkins from the January 2002 Lecture: "If you can see through that conundrum, that's like a koan, you'll become enlightened. There is no cause to what happens, but there is a source. The source is the structure of the ego itself as it sits within the infinite power of spiritual consciousness and that automatically sequences what appears to be sequence, the fate of the spirit. That is the absolute perfection of the judgment of God. There is no error possible. There is no God to fear, there is only the consequences of one's own actions to fear. To see through the illusion of causality is to see that nothing is causing anything else. What you see are conditions. For this flower to open up, it requires a certain temperature, a certain humidity, a certain amount of sunlight, nurturance and as you see it opening up, the sunlight is not causing it to open, the nurturance is not causing it to open. Nothing is causing it to open because everything fulfills its own potential. Within that which is created, part and parcel of its existence is its innate capacity to manifest as that which it is. The becoming of that which is witnessed as existence, then, is merely the unfolding of the potentiality of that as it was created. It is not being caused by anything over here (manifest), it is not being caused by anything over there (unmanifest)."

Because one perceives things sequentially, one thinks one thing is causing another in the following manner: A➡B➡C. This is a deterministic linear sequence, like billiard balls sequentially striking each other. The presumption is that A causes B, which causes C. But consciousness research indicates that causality operates in a completely different manner, in which the attractor pattern complex "ABC" splits through its "operants" and is expressed as the seeming sequence "A, then B, then C" of perception. From the slide, we see that the source (ABC), which is unobservable, results in the visible sequence A which is an observable phenomenon within the measurable three-dimensional world. The typical problems the world attempts to deal with exist on the observable level of A➡B➡C.

Inner spiritual work is to find the inherent attractor pattern, the ABC out of which the sequence

A➡B➡C seems to arise. The operants transcend both the observable and the non-observable; we might picture them as a rainbow bridging the deterministic and the nondeterministic realms. It takes the totality of God to account for the existence of everything at any moment, anywhere in the universe. Additional details on Causality can be found in "Power vs. Force: The Hidden Determinants of Human Behavior", Chapter 1: Critical Advances in Knowledge, pp. 66-70 (2012 edition).

FUNCTION OF MIND

Lower Mind (Cal. 155)	Higher Mind (Cal. 275)
Content	Content plus field
Concrete, literal	Abstract, imaginative
Sensory, emotional	Symbols, unemotional
Specific, local	General
Limited, time, space	Unlimited
Personal	Impersonal
Form	Significance
Recognize specifics	Identify class
Sort, categorize examples	Categorize class
Reaction	Detached
Memory, recall of events	Contextualize significance
Plan	Create
Definition	Essence, meaning
Particulars	Generalize
Pedestrian	Transcendent
Motivation	Inspirational, intention
Morals	Ethics
Examples	Principles
Physical and emotional survival	Intellectual development
Pleasure and satisfaction	Fulfillment of potential
Accumulation	Growth
Acquire	Savor
Remember	Reflect
Maintain	Evolve
Think	Process
Denotation	Inference

Slide 16

SLIDE 16: FUNCTION OF MIND

This slide was first introduced at the April 2004 lecture, DVD disc 2 at 003850.

The mind has two different attractor fields: the attractor field aligned primarily with survival is termed 'Lower Mind' and calibrates at level 155, aligned with self-interest, physical survival, emotional pleasure, and personal gain. As consciousness evolves, it becomes increasingly aware of the importance of others, and with a greater capacity of discernment, eventually arrives at level 275, denoted as 'Higher Mind', which is capable of dealing with nonlinear abstractions and essence. It is therefore more perceptive of principles and the subtle qualities of essence. The lower mind learns how to think but it thinks in an animal sort of way concerned with form, limited and specific, whereas the higher mind at calibration level 275 gets into abstraction, meaning, and generalities.

The lower mind is literal but the higher mind is abstract and asks, "What does it mean?" It wants details. The lower mind personalizes everything but the higher mind sees more impersonally e.g.: What does it mean for my family? What does this mean for USA as a whole? What does this mean for mankind? The higher mind begins to see significance and becomes detached because it is reflecting on something in trying to understand the significance and the meaning. It asks: what am I supposed to learn out of this?

In going from the lower mind to the higher mind, one goes from the particular to the general. Instead of worrying about morals, one is more concerned about ethics: what are the philosophic implications of this? Instead of just examples, one is looking for the underlying principles.

Instead of accumulating things, one is now interested in personal inner growth. Instead of acquiring things, one savors them. Lower mind remembers, higher mind reflects. Lower mind thinks whereas higher mind processes.

So mind is not just a "thing" that everyone equally "has" for, upon observation, it is discovered that there are really two dominant energy fields of mentalization as mentioned above, and each is a consequence of genetic/karmic inheritance, modified by experience and intention. Mind is thus describable on two primary levels, which are, in turn, reflective of differences in brain physiology and the emergence of the etheric (energy) brain of higher mind. Lower mind is thus restricted to the capacities of a physical brain and its neurochemistry. The rate of subjective happiness at level 155 is only 15%, but by consciousness level 275, the rate quadruples, to 60%.

Lower Mind vs. Higher Mind

Lower Mind (Cal. 155)	Higher Mind (Cal. 275)
Desire	Value
Exclusive	Inclusive
Control	Diffuse
Utilitarian use	Sees potential
Literal	Intuitive
Ego-self-directed	Ego + self-oriented
Personal and family survival	Survival of others
Constrictive	Expansive
Exploit, use up	Preserve, enhance
Design	Art
Competition	Cooperation
Pretty, attractive	Aesthetics
Naive, impressionable	Sophisticated, informed
Gullible	Thoughtful
Excess	Balance
Force	Power
Smart	Intelligent
Exploits life	Serves life
Callous	Merciful
Insensitive	Sensitive
Particularize	Contextualize
Statement	Hypothesis
Closure	Open ended
Terminal	Germinal
Sympathize	Empathize
Rate	Evaluate
Want	Choose

Slide 17

SLIDE 17: LOWER MIND VS. HIGHER MIND

This slide was first introduced at the April 2004 lecture, DVD disc 2 at 004230.

Lower mind **desires** things, but the higher mind **values** them. Lower mind wants to be **exclusive**, whereas the higher mind is **inclusive**. Lower mind wants to **control** things, while the higher mind is **diffuse** and sees interaction/overlap with surroundings. Lower mind sees an **utilitarian use**, whereas the higher mind **sees the potential** in everything for the greater good of all. Lower mind is **literal**, whereas the higher mind is **intuitive** and incorporates higher values of the Self. Lower mind is **constrictive** and restrictive, whereas higher mind is expansive and interested in the survival of others. The lower mind wants to **exploit/use up things**, whereas the higher mind wants to **preserve** and **enhance** them. The lower mind is interested in **design**/practical applications to fulfill needs, whereas the higher mind is interested in **art**/challenging the viewer with questions to ponder. Lower mind **desires**, higher mind **values**. Lower mind is "**smart**", higher mind is **intelligent**.

Lower mind **wants**, higher mind **chooses**. Actually, one's options are not restricted to "want" vs. "not want." One can merely choose what is, thereby releasing all negativity via radical acceptance. "O Lord, whatever I am by Thy Grace, I choose to be!" One can add, "So I am short, fat, ugly, stupid and broke. So?" Every time one catches the mind saying, "So", one can respond by saying, "So, nothing!" The mind says "So and so is wrong!" The best way to get off blame is to admit that one is wrong. It is part of being polite. No one is certain about what is going on, as the human mind lacks the ability to tell essence from perception. The mind has considerations; it is not 100% in agreement with one's spiritual intention. When one lets go, one lets go of considerations. Spiritual work is about finding out what these considerations are and letting go of them.

Attitudes reflect the degree to which perception, emotion, mentation, and rationality are influenced by what one has become. How one experiences and views the world is quite different at consciousness level 275, in contrast to Lower Mind at level 155. These levels profoundly influence all aspects of life. The degree of difference is almost equivalent to describing two different, contrasting civilizations with different levels of the quality of interpersonal relationships, pleasure, happiness in life, worldly success, philosophies, politics, and most importantly, the level of spiritual awareness and alignment. The extremes of political positionalities, whether they are far left or far right, calibrate extremely low and represent the egocentricity of lower mind, which has a potentially extensive audience. Cultural conflict can therefore be contextualized as primarily between the representations of lower mind versus higher mind, which have quite different paradigms of social reality and expectations. Additional details on Lower mind vs. Higher mind can be found in "Truth vs. Falsehood: How to Tell the Difference" (2005), Chapter 13 - Truth: The Pathway to Freedom, pp. 235-241.

QUANTUM MECHANICS AND THE MUSCLE TEST RESPONSE

Copenhagen Solvay conference (1927)

1. Schroedinger process:quantum state of a system-possibilities
2. Heisenberg process: choice - intention
3. Dirac process: collapse of the wave function ->change
4. Von Neumann: Process II (physical) vs Process I (mental)

Process I

S = PSP + (I-P) S (I-P)   S = State
⇓ ⇓   P = Intention

Yes   Not Yes

5. Henry Stapp: The universe is repository of information. A quantum state - a wave function - experiential reality ensues from sequential collapses of wave function.
6. Einstein (499) refused role of consciousness

Problem: Paradigm

Slide 18

SLIDE 18: QUANTUM MECHANICS AND THE MUSCLE-TEST RESPONSE

This slide was first introduced at the February 2003 lecture, DVD disc 1 at 001000.

That truth makes the body musculature go strong and falsehood results in its weakening was an empirical clinical discovery, as described by Dr. Hawkins in Power vs. Force. The phenomenon is due to the fact that truth exists as an actual reality, whereas falsehood has no substrate of reality. Thus, the muscle-testing response is either "yes" or "not yes" ("no"). The mechanisms are clarified by understanding basic principles of quantum physics. Phenomena are the consequence of the collapse of the 'wave state' of potentiality to the 'particle state' of manifestation and actuality. These are the result of intention and observation itself. The observer and the observed become an operational unit. Further detailed description of Quantum Mechanics is available through Henry Stapp via his writings and talks on the internet.

The intention of the observer/questioner facilitates or does not facilitate a collapse of the wave function (the von Neumann Process I). Thus, the state of the universe (Schrodinger equations) via the Heisenberg principle is often reduced or not (Dirac process), and therefore, the quantum response is limited to "yes" or "not yes." For further details, including discussion at the Copenhagen Solvay conference (1927), please see "I: Reality and Subjectivity" (2003), Appendix D: Quantum Mechanics, pp. 435-436.

That field of infinite potentiality, which Quantum Mechanics comes closest to defining, is what in spiritual work we refer to as consciousness. Quantum Mechanics has discovered that consciousness alone, simply by observing something, changes the thing observed. This is the closest approximation science has come to at this point to understanding the subjective nature of reality. The reason it is quite advanced is because it incorporates an awareness of the limitation of the intellect and it describes observables. The measurable is one thing, but the observable is quite another, because observable retains the observer - that the observer is present as part of the experiment; it is not just a measurement existing by itself, but the observer now has an influence.

Quantum Mechanics does not call reality measurable any more, e.g. "8 foot by 6 foot". It calls it observable. So all one can say about society is what seems to be our observations of it - we are not talking about any self-existing reality outside us, we are just talking about observables of an observer (what each one of us is.)

Consciousness calibration technique only works if one is committed to knowing the truth. The ego is subtle and is always trying to promote/proposition some gain. Personal questions are difficult. When a stimulus is applied, there is a response of equal and opposite amount. One has to be non-attached. One way to do this is to state, 'In the name of the highest good / truth.' Response is very rapid and transitory; if one waits a second, the animal within comes up and puts more pressure on the arm. Muscle-testing response is a transition from the content of the field to the field itself. The Heisenberg Principle is where Einstein did not agree. He could not move from the 400s, which is the linear, to the 500s, which is non-linear, because the Heisenberg Principle emphasizes the importance of intention, in that the intention already determines what one will find. What one finds is a consequence of what one is looking for.

Newtonian Paradigm vs. Quantum Mechanics

Newtonian Paradigm	Quantum Mechanics
Orderly	Disorderly
Logical	Illogical
Predictable	Unpredictable
Deterministic	Free
Literal	Creative
Pedestrian	Imaginative
Reductionist	Progressive
Separate	Intermingled, Interconnected
Discrete	Diffuse
Cause	Potentiate
Atomistic	Nonlocal Coherence
Forced	Reactive
Caused	Responsive
Provable	Comprehensible
Measurable	Observable
Sequential	Simultaneous
Settled	Potential
Temporal	Time Dependent/Independent
Computational	Stochastic/Chaotic
Limited	Unlimited
Actuality	Possibility
Permanent	Altered by Observation
Constricted	Expansive
Content	Context
Objective	Subjective
Force	Power
Certain	Uncertain
Finished	Poised

Slide 19

SLIDE 19: NEWTONIAN PARADIGM VS. QUANTUM MECHANICS

This slide was first introduced at the June 2002 lecture, DVD disc 1 at 01:41:00.

One of the most important philosophical implications of quantum mechanics involves the **breakdown of the causality principle** in subatomic phenomena, as the various substratum of what we assume to be reality are shown to be profoundly affected and **alterable by the mere act of human observation**. Newtonian Paradigm, on the other hand, is the reality of ordinary life in which things are **logical** and **sequential** based on the paradigm of **linear causality**. This is **orderly**, everything seems to be arising **logically** in **predictable** ways e.g. one looks at one's childhood to understand why one does things the way one does. It is **reductionist**, **provable**, **measurable**, and **temporal**. One can figure it out on a **computer**; its problems are solvable by differential calculus.

Newtonian is based on **Force**; everything is already **settled**, so that it is a **certain** world one can count on, where death is guaranteed as one is dealing with physicality. It should be noted that although quantum mechanics (cal. 460) provides a means of understanding the transition between the linear and the nonlinear domains, to do so requires a paradigm jump that begins at the calibrated consciousness level of 500 (i.e., beyond the limitation of the concept of causality). Newtonian is the world of gross matter but that is not where one's life is lived, as one is aware of the subtleties of "is-ness", existence and inferences which are not on the level of the gross, are **not measurable**, and **do not even exist in time or space**.

Because the ultimate Reality is **subjective**, **Power** resides at the level of quantum reality (Context) and not the content, which is Newtonian as the "**finished**" endpoint of it all, the consequence is like the Empire State building which originated as **an idea in someone's mind**; it was a **potentiality** which eventually became manifest as an **actuality**. Thus, quantum is **poised** as a **potentiality**, is **subjective**, **expansive**, **uncertain** or ambiguous, **progressive**, grows with **possibility**, and is **unlimited**. When the quantum potentiality is going to arise in thought or world it is **stochastic**, **not predictable**, as we are dealing with **observables** but not **measurables**; they are **comprehensible** but **not locatable in time or place** e.g. where was the Empire State building before it arose in physicality? Nowhere, as it is **diffuse**, **intermingled** with the glory of the city of New York, the glory of man etc.

Quantum reality is **progressive**, **imaginative**, **creative**, **free**, **unpredictable**, **illogical** and **disorderly**. **Atomistic** applies to the Newtonian paradigm, "divided into separate elements", as opposed to holistic or **Nonlocal Coherence** which in the quantum sense describes an entity in its un-identified state as a potential. "The more detailed one's analysis of the structure of what is supposedly "out there," the more one discovers that what one is examining is, in fact, the nature of the intricate processes of consciousness which are actually originating from within. There is actually nothing "out there," other than consciousness itself. The habitual tendency to believe otherwise is a fundamental illusion, a vanity of the human mind, which tends always to view its transitory subject as "mine." -"Power vs. Force: The Hidden Determinants of Human Behavior", Chapter 20: The Evolution of Consciousness, pp. 264-265 (2012 edition).

LINEAR GRADATIONS

Example 1	Example 2	Example 3	Example 4
Degrees Fahrenheit	Value	Goodness	Light
– 3,000	- Precious	- Heavenly	- Blindingly bright
– 2,000	- Valuable	– Very good	- Very bright light
– 1,000	- Worthwhile	– Good	- Bright
– 500	– Asset	- Pleasant	- Very strong light
– 100	– A+	- "Okay"	– Light
– 50	- Neutral	– Sort of "okay"	- Subdued light
– 0	- Unattractive	- Fair to	– Dim
– -50	- Hindrance	– Not too good	– Dusk
– -100	- Awful	- Unsatisfactory	– Dark
– -200	– Ugly	– Bad	- "Pitch black"
– -etc.	- Repulsive	- Wicked	
		- Horrible	
		- Ghastly	
		- Horrific	

Slide 20

SLIDE 20: LINEAR GRADATIONS

This slide was first introduced at the April 2002 lecture, DVD disc 1 at 010000.

To be more specific about how the perceptual distortion occurs, one becomes aware that the ego has a propensity for positionality, meaning the ego makes up opposites by an arbitrary point of view. For example, to arbitrarily look at a scale of temperature and say, "Above this is hot and below this is cold." Temperature measures the presence of heat; it does not measure the presence of cold. There is only one variable, heat. If heat is present, we call it hot. As less and less heat is present, we call it cold. So cold is nothing but the absence of heat. There is no such thing as coldness as an independent opposite to heat.

We could do the same thing with light. One can say that light is either there or not there but languaging makes it appear that "this is light" and "this is dark" and they are opposites to each other. But really they are not opposites but only a matter of degree of the presence of light. There is only one variable in Reality. The mistake of the ego is that it thinks there are two variables and they are opposite to each other: good and evil, right and wrong, etc. Light is profoundly present or it diminishes by degrees to less and less, and when it is completely absent we call it darkness. In the dualistic languaging of the ego, we say they are opposites: light and dark. All definitions are options for pragmatic daily human life, but there are no opposites. To see that takes one beyond the "polarity of opposites", which is one of the great blocks to the evolution of consciousness and spiritual work.

It is important to see that the scale of consciousness is really only of one variable, not two. The mind could say that there is a duality between that which is above 200 and makes one go strong with muscle-testing and that which is below 200 and makes one go weak, but that is judgmentalism - the wrong instrument to apply to human life. Because human life is coming out of an incredible complexity, the evolution of consciousness and its karmic expressions throughout all of time is what accounts for even a "speck of dust" to be right here at this moment. What can one say about that?

We say people are evil because they are killing each other and innocent people are getting killed. Labeling others as innocent in this way is judgmental, as one does not really know their karmic history or background. Maybe all those little kids that just got blown up on the street were some horrific villains in a previous lifetime, like Nazi torturers, etc. Because one does not know the evolutionary background, one has to be willing then to surrender to "not knowingness" (humility), which automatically brings peace. This is the way out of hating the content of one's consciousness, as consciousness is in essence only the appearance of love and evolution of love.

Without the non-form of consciousness, one cannot comprehend or perceive form. Without the silence of consciousness, one cannot hear sound. It is because the Presence prevails as the primary Reality that one is aware of phenomena, which are the energy fields of consciousness. As one lets go of the content (phenomena), one becomes context. The ego is structured on opposites, and is addicted to the juice it gets from its positionalities. Actually, there is only ONE variable. This can be either present or absent. Knowing this, one can be 'pro' something without hating those who are not. Goodness is either present, or not (as opposed to saying that good and evil exist). There is only good or its absence. There is the presence or the absence of light, not light and dark. Enlightenment is not something one has to seek or work toward as it happens automatically when one lets go of the ego's positionalities.

Spiritual Practices

The Lord's Prayer	**650**	**Golden Rule**	**405**
Om (pronounced om)	**740**	**Transcendental Meditation**	**295**
Aum (pronounced a-um)	**210**	**Prayer of Jabez**	**310**
Om Namaha Shivaya	**630**	**Walking the Labyrinth at Chartres Cathedral**	**503**
Shanti Shanti Shanti	**650**	**Genuflection**	**540**
Om Mane Padme Hum	**700**	**Kneeling to pray**	**540**
Gregorian Chants	**595**	**Prayerful hand clasp**	**540**
Japa	**515**	**Devotional acts**	**540**
Jesus Prayer	**525**	**Turning prayer wheels**	**540**
Saying the Rosary	**515**	**Devotional burning of incense**	**540**
Hajj (pilgrimage to Mecca)	**390**	**The Wailing Wall**	**540**
Kirtan (Yogic Chant)	**250**	**Bathing in the Ganges**	**540**
Twelve Steps of Alcoholics Annonymous	**540**	**Prayer of St. Francis of Assisi**	**580**

Slide 21

SLIDE 21: SPIRITUAL PRACTICES

This slide was first introduced at the August 2004 lecture, DVD Disc 2 at 014650.

The **Lord's Prayer** calibrates at 650. With this prayer, we ask the Lord to take care of the spirit. It is a safeguard especially at night, as one would not want to die in sleep, without having previously said The Lord's Prayer. The correct pronunciation of a 'Mantra' is important to learn, as **OM** (740) calibrates very differently than **AUM** (210), a misleading pronunciation given in some books. Therefore, spiritual awareness can be decisive in one's evolution as one can spend a number of lifetimes at 210, and not get too far with AUM and then spend half a lifetime at 740 making all the difference in spiritual evolution.

Each of these spiritual practices is useful at different levels of consciousness. There is a time to do the rosary, a time to walk the maze, a time to do selfless service; there is not a linear progression. What is a useful spiritual practice here at this time could be a distraction at a different level of consciousness. Spiritual reality is facilitated by intention, and spiritual practices demonstrate the power of intention. By intention, man symbolically sanctifies and commits both to self and others, as well as places of worship. Because of intention, all styles of blessing and prayer calibrate over 500, and their collective effect can greatly impact the overall level of collective human consciousness, as evidenced by the observation that the last two major jumps in the overall level of human consciousness occurred after a Harmonic Convergence. The first jump occurred at the time of the Harmonic Convergence in 1987 when the collective consciousness level went up from 190 to 205, and then again at the time of the Harmonic Concordance in November 2003, when it jumped from 205 to 207. At both times, spiritually committed people all over the world prayed simultaneously. The witnessing of the transition from 205 to 207 happened fortuitously at the end of a lecture in San Francisco when a spiritually committed group of four hundred people simultaneously prayed and sounded "Om," followed by meditation on the chanting of the Lotus Sutra.

Most people in the pedestrian, linear, concrete world are unable to intuit context, the spiritual reality and they criticize the high-calibrating spiritual practices. Because of the devotion behind it, turning the prayer wheel and other similar devotional acts calibrate at 540. The Twelve Step groups at 540 calibrate higher than many spiritual practices on the planet today. All spiritual practices are inherently more powerful than the naive seeker realizes. The seeker should approach them with respect, and obtain adequate preparation information. There are a multitude of spiritual practitioners and healers of every variety. It is up to the seeker to make sure what he is getting involved in, as the dictum "caveat emptor" applies.

PROGRESSIVE FIELDS OF REALIZATION

Form

Register

Recognition

Watcher/Experiencer

Awareness

Observer/Witness

Light of Consciousness

Manifest as Allness/Self

Unmanifest (Godhead)

Slide 22

SLIDE 22: PROGRESSIVE FIELDS OF REALIZATION

This slide was first introduced at the April 2002 lecture, disc 1 at 000900.

As one begins to meditate, one becomes aware of the content going through the mind: relentless, thinking all the time, feeling all the time, imagining things, remembering things - it is a cacophony that just goes on and on. Ninety-nine point nine percent of ordinary people walk around the world identifying with form, and that is why they are so preoccupied with health, wealth, death, etc. As they start to get involved in spiritual work, they begin to realize there is a step beyond form. They discover that the mind is somehow registering somewhere. This begins to pull one back from the identification with content to that capacity called "**Watcher**", which is recognizing the registration and experience of form. Further, behind the watcher, there is a knower of all of this. Somehow, there is a spotlight / a lens / something that is aware and one realizes that there is awareness going on of the watcher/observer/witness.

To go beyond the **Watcher/observer/witness** stage, one needs to investigate how the inner Light comes about. First, you begin to realize these are impersonal as watching/observing/witnessing are happening autonomously, without any intervention by anyone. There is no 'you' that is watching and witnessing, although in the beginning one may have the illusion that there is a 'you' that is witnessing and observing. One begins to notice that witnessing happens all the time without intervention by anyone. If it was an entity doing it, that entity could control it and stop witnessing. One begins to realize that this is happening of its own, and dis-identifies with the witness and sees that witnessing is coming out of consciousness itself. As one sees that, one progressively lets go of identifying with content, and expands and identifies with context. It is because of consciousness that any of the lower states can occur in the first place. Consciousness is there, in and of itself, without intervention by anyone to be there. One can become unconscious of consciousness when one goes to sleep and that is the oblivion; that is not the 'Void', that is oblivion. Many people like oblivion because it is peaceful and happy. Well, how do you know it is peaceful and happy? If one was not oblivious, one was aware that it was peaceful and happy and that is why you could say to everybody how well you slept the previous night. Something is aware of the oblivion anyway and that something has no memory or expectations and is the Presence Itself, which prevails under all circumstances. So you move back another level and realize that the Source of the **Manifest** is at the level of the **Unmanifest**, the Presence.

To summarize the above, as observation moves through the levels, the sense of the self-definition of 'I' moves with it. The easiest transition is the realization that one is not the focus or content of the mind but the unchanging experiencer/witness/observer. Although the story of life changes, there is always an aspect of consciousness continuously watching and, on a slightly different level, experiencing. The sense of 'I' moves progressively from content to context. Stripped of all pretenses, the inner sense of Presence, 'I-ness' merely knows Itself without any content. For additional details, please see "I: Reality and Subjectivity" (2003), Chapter 17: The Inner Path, pp. 292-294.

BRAIN FUNCTION AND PHYSIOLOGY

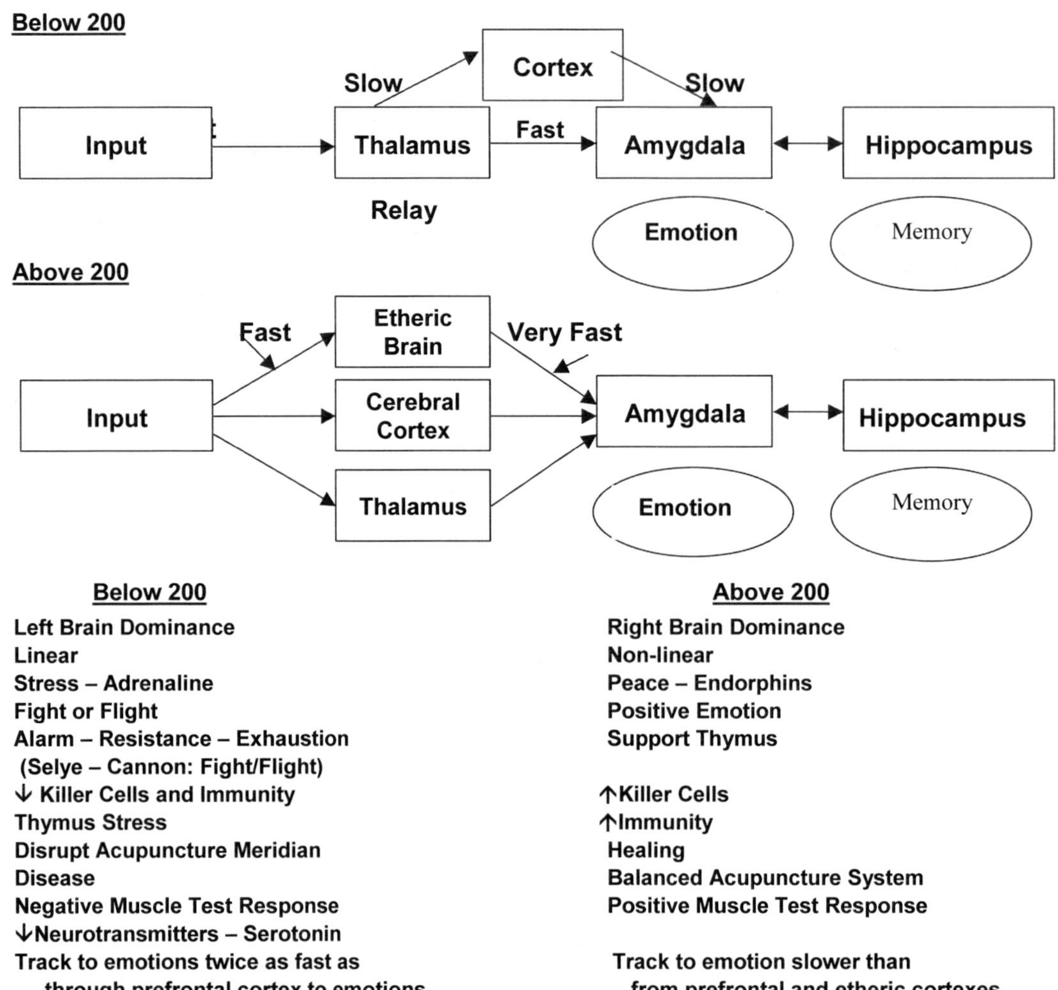

Below 200	Above 200
Left Brain Dominance	Right Brain Dominance
Linear	Non-linear
Stress – Adrenaline	Peace – Endorphins
Fight or Flight	Positive Emotion
Alarm – Resistance – Exhaustion	Support Thymus
(Selye – Cannon: Fight/Flight)	
↓ Killer Cells and Immunity	↑Killer Cells
Thymus Stress	↑Immunity
Disrupt Acupuncture Meridian	Healing
Disease	Balanced Acupuncture System
Negative Muscle Test Response	Positive Muscle Test Response
↓Neurotransmitters – Serotonin	
Track to emotions twice as fast as through prefrontal cortex to emotions	Track to emotion slower than from prefrontal and etheric cortexes

Importance: Spiritual endeavor and intention change the brain function and the body's physiology and establishes a specific area for spiritual information in the right brain prefrontal cortex and its concordant etheric (energy) brain.

Slide 23

Institute for Spiritual Research, Inc. dba Veritas Publishing

SLIDE 23: BRAIN FUNCTION AND PHYSIOLOGY

This slide was first introduced at the November 2003 lecture, DVD disc 2 at 005800.

Over 200 the brain actually changes, and is different from the brain under 200. Instead of wanting (below 200), one can choose (above 200). As one progresses further, the spiritual intention increases and so does the Kundalini energy. There is nothing one needs to do, as everything begins to happen as a result of being in a higher energy field. One is merely an antenna at times. Use of the etheric brain allows one to recognize things from the higher spiritual realms. The frequencies are too high to experience by protoplasm. When we make choices that are in accordance with higher frequencies, our right brain releases endorphins, and the experiences are positive. One must not be intrigued, or obsessed by the miraculous, as it occurs by itself - the Kundalini energy does it, without consulting anyone at all. It is unpredictable, as one cannot conduct miracles on schedule. If one "owns" the siddhis as a personal power, one gets caught in the glamour. People experience them routinely in the high 500s, and even lower levels in situations such as silent retreats. It is not the person but the field that is responsible for them. The field knows, not the body. Truth needs nothing. Truth does not need glamour and it is not trying to proselytize. It has nothing to gain.

"The etheric brain is a modification of the total energy field of Divinity which becomes modified more progressively towards form, but is quite a bit beyond form. The etheric brain is capable of nonverbal, nonlinear knowingness. The speakingness happening of its own, right this moment is coming from the field of Consciousness through the etheric brain. The field knows, and we see from kinesiologic testing that Consciousness knows everything. The Omniscience of God is the All- Knowingness expressed as the infinite field of Consciousness, "Atman" in Sanskrit, beyond all time, beyond all content, beyond all form. It only knows if a thing is and if a thing is true-that's all It knows.

Because knowingness has existence, there is no way Consciousness can know nonexistence. Consciousness is unable to recognize falsity, because falsity has no reality to Consciousness. Therefore, the kinesiologic response is only "yes" or a "not yes." Understanding does not come through intellection. As you get more right-brained and more spiritual, understanding comes about as a self-realization. It reveals itself. The etheric brain is connected to the field of Consciousness and that is how the knowingness speaks to you- is speaking right now- the thought didn't arise until I spoke it. This gives a sort of physiologic explanation.

The etheric brain's capacity to pick up the knowingness of Divinity, Omnipotence, is called, classically, the Purusha of the spiritual teacher. There is no personal "self" speaking to you at all. That is a projection. No such thing exists. The field, through the capacity of the etheric brain, can tell the cerebral cortex how to speak it and verbalize it. You get it the same time I get it. I didn't hear it until I just heard it and then you got it. Which makes life an exciting adventure, because you live on the edge of the unknown all the time and nobody knows what is going to come up next. We found that below 200, one does not even have an etheric brain yet. Two hundred and over energizes the production and creation of an etheric brain.

The advantage of spiritual commitment is that it activates the right brain, causing a change in physiology allowing for immediate knowingness. Below 200 in the animal brain, the sensory input is very fast to the relay station, and then it goes very fast, so this is emotions-- fear and hatred, Selye's stress response, Cannon's fight or flight—the emotional center in the brain. Therefore, it is necessary to forgive 85% of the people on the planet, because they react emotionally and then their common sense comes around later. Devotional Non-duality is devotion to the Truth and not to piety. Therefore, a true teacher is sometimes outrageous, more in the style of Zen than in the style of a pious saint." - Paraphrased from November 2003 Lecture, "Realization ofthe Self and the 'I'", DVD disc 2, 005820-010100.

Correlation of Levels of Consciousness and Societal Problems

Level of Consciousness	Rate of Unemployment	Rate of Poverty	Happiness Rate "Life is OK"	Rate of Criminality
600+	0%	0.0%	100%	0.0%
500-600	0%	0.0%	98%	0.5%
400-500	2%	0.5%	70%	2.0%
300-400	7%	1.0%	50%	5.0%
200-300	8%	1.5%	40%	9.0%
100-200	50%	22.0%	15%	50.0%
50-100	75%	40.0%	2%	91.0%
<50	97%	65.0%	0%	98.0%

Slide 24

SLIDE 24: CORRELATION OF LEVELS OF CONSCIOUSNESS AND SOCIETAL PROBLEMS

This slide was first introduced at June 2004 lecture, DVD Disc 1 at 002000.

Things are not caused externally. Nobody forces anyone to throw trash on the street. One chooses to do that because of what one is. There is a rather astonishing correlation between the levels of consciousness (LoC) and societal problems. At the highest LoCs, the rates of unemployment, poverty and criminality are zero while the rate of happiness is 100% (the 500s are similar to 600+, except for a few fallen gurus).

In the 400s - out of the 2% unemployment rate, most are listed as unemployed but they are really collecting unemployment insurance; unemployment usually ends when unemployment insurance runs out. Same thing for the 300s, unemployment rate of 7% and the 200s, unemployment rate of 8% (80% of those are really collecting unemployment insurance checks until they run out.)

Rate of poverty is due to bad investments for those in 400s (0.5%), 300s (1%) and 200s (1.5%).

Rate of criminality in the 400s is 2% - it is mostly white collar crime; in the 300s it is 5% and it is 9% in the 200s. Over 200 but below 500 does not mean one is a saint but one does things that are necessary and reasonable.

Of major sociological importance is the very dramatic major change that takes place below consciousness level 200. Between 100 and 200, unemployment rate jumps from just 8 percent to 50 percent; poverty rate escalates from 1.5 to 22%; rate of happiness decreases from 60 to only 15%, and criminality skyrockets from 9 to 50%. Between 50 and 100, rate of criminality is 91% (they steal from their employers, pad the expense reports, and help themselves to whatever is not nailed down.) Below 50, the poverty rate is 65% (the rest are supported by the Government) and criminality is a lifestyle.

Similar correlation charts can be constructed that show the almost identical pattern for the percentage of each consciousness level with incidence of physical illness, mental disorders, victims of crime, automobile accidents, health insurance coverage, rates of AIDS and STDs, arrest rate, domestic violence, child abuse, incarceration, birth rate, gang membership, exposure to violent media, drugs, and the time children spend watching television. The rate of true poverty is far higher in non-free-enterprise systems. The price of freedom entails some degree of risk, which, in turn, spurs greater effort and enterprise. In contrast, welfare societies are more complacent and less innovative because the government assumes responsibility for their survival.

Nothing is causing anything, but that which one is then manifests itself in the world in this sort of style. There is nothing outside causing one to do any of these things. These are all coming from what one is, the nature of one's decisions, the way one relates to people, and one's ability to understand spiritual reality, morality and ethics or the lack thereof. Anything that talks about blame is fallacious.

Movies 1 of 2

2001: A Space Odyssey	440	Bye Bye Birdie	245	Ferris Bueller's Day Off	330
A Beautiful Mind	375	Caddy Shack	205	Forrest Gump	475
About Schmidt	435	Carnal Knowledge	155	French Connection	275
A Fish Called Wanda	230	Casablanca	385	From Here to Eternity	395
African Queen, The	395	Cat in the Hat	130	Funny Girl	385
Aliens	145	Charade	305	Gandhi	455
All About Eve	300	Chariots of Fire	425	Ghostbusters	235
All Quiet on the Western Front	150	Charlotte's Web	335	Giant	350
Amadeus	455	Chicago	385	Gigi	375
A Man for All Seasons	455	Chinatown	315	Godfather, The	155
American Beauty	380	Citizen Kane	400	Godfather, Part II, The	155
American Graffiti	365	City Lights	355	Godzilla	180
An American in Paris	355	Cleopatra	365	Goldfinger	215
Annie Hall	355	Clockwork Orange	70	Gold Rush, The	260
Apartment, The	200	Close Encounters of the Third Kind	265	Gone with the Wind	400
Apocalypse Now	65	Color Purple, The	475	Good Fellas	100
Around the World in 80 Days	385	Cool Hand Luke	255	Graduate, The	325
Babe	350	Crocodile Dundee	265	Grape s of Wrath, The	385
Barbarella	185	Dances with Wolves	375	Grease	330
Barefoot in the Park	395	Deliverance	145	Great Gatsby, The	350
Batman	210	Deer Hunter, The	155	Greatest Show on Earth	390
Ben-Hur	475	Dickens' Christmas Carol	499	Guess Who's Coming to	305
Best Years of Our Lives	360	Dr. Strangelove	225	Halloween	85
Beverly Hills Cop	180	Doctor Zhivago	415	Hamlet	405
Big Blue	700	Double Indemnity	315	Harry Potter	215
Birds, The	215	Driving Miss Daisy	395	Hello Dolly	380
Birth of a Nation, The	140	Easy Rider	195	High Noon	275
Blade Runner	225	English Patient, The	250	In Cold Blood	80
Bonnie and Clyde	105	Empire of the Sun	490	In the Heat of the Night	165
Bowling for Columbine	185	ET: The Extraterrestrial	375	It Happened One Night	255
Braveheart	275	Exorcist, The	140	It's Alive	125
Breakfast Club	300	Fail Safe	255	It's a Mad, Mad, Mad World	290
Breakfast at Tiffany's	360	Falling Down	90	It's a Wonderful Life	450
Bridge on the River Kwai, The	385	Fahrenheit 9/11	195	Jaws	140
Bringing Up Baby	255	Fantasia	475	Jazz Singer, The	390
Butch Cassidy & the Sundance Kid	270	Fatal Attraction	140	Jerry Maguire	375
		Field of Dreams	390	Jurassic Park	330

Slide 25

SLIDE 25: MOVIES (1)

This slide was first introduced at the April 2004 lecture, DVD disc 3 at 000450.

Calibrations for some 200+ movies have been presented in this and the following slide, and they can also be found in "Truth vs. Falsehood: How to Tell the Difference" (2005), Chapter 9: Social Structure and Functional Truth, pp. 107-108 as well as Appendix D of the same book, pp. 419-422. The great interest in movies at the time of the presentation of this slide in 2004 was highlighted by "The Passion of the Christ" and everyone wanted to know the calibration for that movie. The movie was used as an example to demonstrate and explain the underlying correlations between the calibration level and the intention of the film-maker as well as the impact of the ten minutes of dramatization of brutality.

The intention of the film-maker (Mel Gibson) at the time was extremely high at 490 indicating that it was not to make money but to show the truth of Jesus Christ. The movie calibrates overall at 195, but remove the ten minutes of brutality and the calibration goes up to 395, which is extremely decent, a great movie. Of course there is some editorializing in the movie and it is certainly not a documentary. The critics say that the movie varies from truth, but they do not realize that it is not a documentary shot on location. A movie is an artistic expression in which the truth is being conveyed symbolically, emotionally and figuratively. The film-maker was trying to give the feeling of - what it was about - the Cross and he used various devices.

The intention at 490 was obviously not to make money but Mel Gibson had some kind of commitment to what he thought Christianity should look like to the public at a time that he thought it was under attack. It is a response he sees to the secularization in society which needs to be reminded of the truth of Jesus Christ. So the 495 calibration reflects the movie-maker's response to the "attack" of secularization, which is a very powerful attack but as a movie-maker, Mel Gibson got pulled into the drama for those ten minutes of brutality.

Of note is that a rather unique movie, *Big Blue*, which was noted in *Power vs. Force*, calibrated at an amazing 700. Beneath the story line was the contextualization of the Oneness of all life and the option open to human choice of selecting the eternal or the physical life.

"*What the #$*! Do We Know?* (cal. 455) is a non-Hollywood film that humorously demonstrates the greater reality behind appearances: science and spirituality; nonlinear dynamics; quantum reality; the effect of thought on changing reality; and that responsibility rests on human consciousness and what that implies about freedom. The film has been acclaimed as unique and has continually expanding showings." – Adapted from "Truth vs. Falsehood: How to Tell the Difference" (2005), Chapter 9: Social Structure and Functional Truth, pp. 108-109.

MOVIES 2 of 2

Legally Blonde	355	Philadelphia Story, The	405	Streetcar Named Desire	315
Lethal Weapon	105	Place in the Sun, A	210	Taxi Driver	360
Lion King, The	415	Platoon	180	Terminator	125
Little Buddha	445	Predator, The	145	Terms of Endearment	425
Lord of the Flies	270	Pretty Woman	375	Thelma and Louise	140
Lord of the Rings	350	Psycho	80	There's Something about	105
Lost Horizon	485	Pulp Fiction	25	Third Man, The	200
Love Story	310	Raging Bull	255	Titanic, The	405
Madame X	215	Raiders of the Lost Ark	385	To Kill a Mockingbird	310
Mad Max	160	Rain Man, The	410	Tom Jones	195
Maltese Falcon, The	325	Rebel Without a Cause	310	Tootsie	355
Manhattan	305	Return of the Kind	350	Toy Story	400
Marty	235	River's Edge	310	Treasure of the Sierra	200
M*A*S*H*	360	Rocky	265	Twin Towers, The	350
Matrix, The	165	Rocky Horror Picture Show	205	Valle y of the Dolls	200
Midnight Cowboy	195	Rosemary's Baby	60	Vertigo	105
Miracle on 34th Street	390	St. Elmo's Fire	105	Willie Wonka	345
Monty Python and the Holy Grail	215	Saturday Night Fever	395	Winged Migration	495
Moonstruck	325	Saving Private Ryan	195	Wait Until Dark	110
Mr. Smith Goes to Washington	395	Schindler's List	180	Wall Street	225
Murder on the Orient Express	365	Searchers, The	315	Way We Were, The	350
My Big Fat Greek Wedding	385	Seven Days in May	340	West Side Story	405
My Fair Lady	405	Sex, Lies, and Videotape	140	Wild Bunch, The	270
Network	255	Shakespeare in Love	395	Wizard of Oz, The	450
North by Northwest	340	Shane	390	Wuthering Heights	360
Notorious	145	Shining, The	55	Yankee Doodle Dandy	400
Oliver!	365	Silence of the Lambs	45	Young Frankenstein	255
Omen, The	85	Singin' in the Rain	415	You've Got Mail	275
One Flew Over the Cuckoo's Nest	160	Sixth Sense , The	310		
On the Waterfront	295	Sleepless in Seattle	350		
		Some Like It Hot	355		

Slide 26

SLIDE 26: MOVIES (2)

This slide was first introduced at the April 2004 lecture, DVD disc 3 at 000450.

"This decidedly American product escalated to become a worldwide industry, of which Hollywood is the symbol. As an art form, it is unexcelled in that it includes acting, dance, music, cinematography, and drama, plus creative engineering and technology that utilize the best of available talents. (The calibrations shown in chart 26 denote the consciousness level of the presented material, not the quality of the movie itself, e.g., horror films are meant to be that level and therefore are artistically successful as denoted by calibrations less than 100.) [...]

The accusations that America is an immoral society are belied by the extent to which the importance of the morality of the media is a focus of much debate. Exploitation of the freedom of expression pushes the envelope of nihilistic hedonism until moral outrage counters with the setting of limits. The entertainment media proclaim their innocence, i.e., "We don't create public opinion, we just reflect it," which, however, is circuitous in that the public opinion to which they refer is, to a considerable extent, a consequence of the media output in the first place.

The artist has to choose which aspects of life to emphasize through artistic endeavor, so the media is a major influence on social mores and belief systems. This is reflected in the overall calibration of the Hollywood film industry (cal. 180). Also notable is the recent spate of anti- Christmas spirit movies (Waxman, 2004), which collectively calibrate at 170. Movie economics, however, reflects the public's real areas of interest. Fortune magazine (January 2005) reports that although only 3.0 percent of Hollywood films are rated "G," they produce more income than the 69 percent of films that are rated "R." Also interesting is that the movie industry of India (which features the generally acclaimed 'most beautiful women in the world') is more sexually restrained and subtle, but worldwide, it has triple the sales of Hollywood. Its overall output also calibrates 10 points higher, at 210, than Hollywood at 200.

A new genre of movies has recently emerged with the production of Fahrenheit 9/11, which received much publicity prior to the November 2004 presidential election. Its calibration at 180 reflects the political position it represents. After the election, corrective counter-information was presented by Fahrenhype 9/11 (cal. 290), as well as Celsius 41.11 (cal. 390), which humorously represents the temperature at which brain death occurs. The emergence of political propaganda movies aimed at the voters may further deter integrous leaders from seeking public office." – Excerpted and adapted from "Truth vs. Falsehood: How to Tell the Difference" (2005), Chapter 9: Social Structure and Functional Truth, pp. 108-109.

"The classic movie, Lost Horizon shows Shangri-La (the movie's metaphor for unconditional love and beauty), which calibrates at 485. Once experienced, it reprograms the experiencer so that he is never content again with ordinary consciousness. The hero of the movie discovers this fact when he is unable to find happiness again in the ordinary world after returning from Shangri-La. He then gives up everything in order to seek out and return to that state of consciousness, spending years in a struggle, which almost costs him his life, to regain and find Shangri-La again. This same reprogramming process occurs in people who have reached high states of consciousness by other means, such as the experience of Samadhi through meditation, or near- death experiences. Such individuals are frequently observed to have changed forever. It is not uncommon for them to leave all that the material world represents and become seekers after truth; many who had transcendent experiences with LSD in the 1960s did that very same thing. Such higher states are also attained through the experiences of love and religion, classical music or art, or through the practice of spiritual disciplines."– Adapted from "Power vs. Force: The Hidden Determinants of Human Behavior", Chapter 6: New Horizons in Research, pp. 126-127, (2012 edition).

Distribution of Prevailing Consciousness Levels - Americas

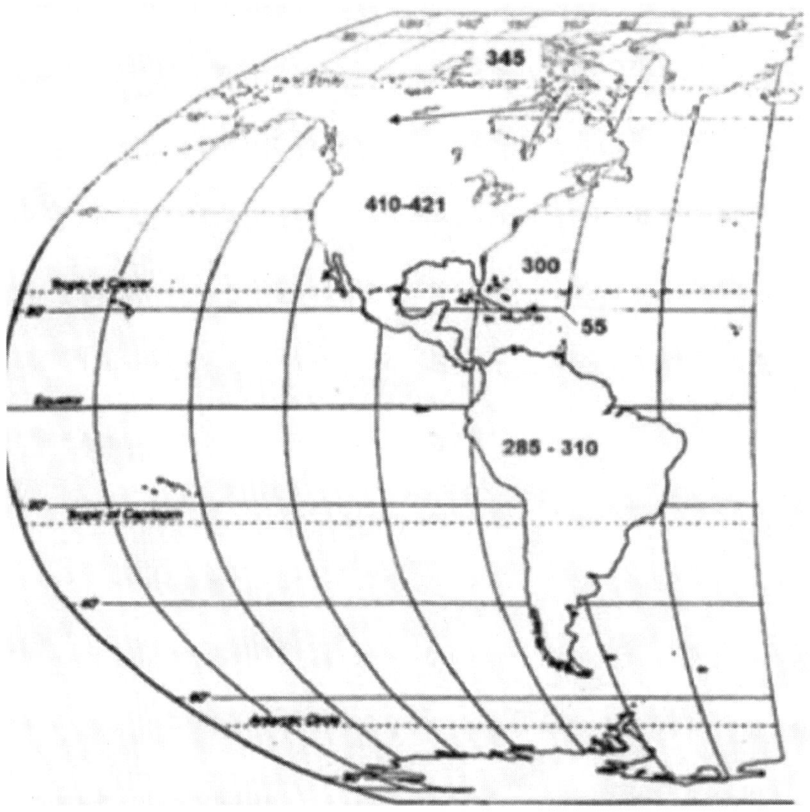

Slide 27

SLIDE 27: DISTRIBUTION OF PREVAILING CONSCIOUSNESS LEVELS - AMERICAS

This slide was first introduced at the June 2003 lecture, DVD disc 1 at 005100.

All of history suddenly becomes obvious when one realizes that man has been trying to navigate without a compass. How can diplomats and statesmen deal with each other when they do not even know what they are dealing with? In view of the overriding importance of international diplomacy, there is no higher priority for mankind than the development of a fact- based science upon which even the very survival of human life itself now depends. Just like the invention of the telescope or Einstein's famous equation relating energy and mass, which made amazing new discoveries possible, some discoveries are seminal and open up entirely new dimensions for exploration. A study of prevailing consciousness levels of various countries helps in understanding the condition of the world, and the community of which we are a part.

Looking at the countries in the Western Hemisphere, Greenland calibrates at 345 while Iceland is slightly below 345 because of the alcoholic problem in half of its population. North America, with Canada at 410 and USA at 421 as a region stands for education, science, reason, and rationality, the norms by which its population lives and assumes others in the world also follow, which they clearly do not. The countries of Central America are in the 300s, the level of enthusiasm, and industry, while the countries in South America are at 285-310, all above the level of integrity. As all countries except Haiti are over 200, this region is not a violent or explosive place. Haiti's history has seen the rule of sadistic dictators who exploit the people, allow them to starve and kill them for amusement. The populace is also involved in the practice of voodoo (cal. 50), typified by blood sacrifice rituals. Past attempts at financial aid paradoxically worsened the poverty and starvation because of its effect in increasing the birth rate.

Distribution of Prevailing Consciousness Levels – Eastern Hemisphere

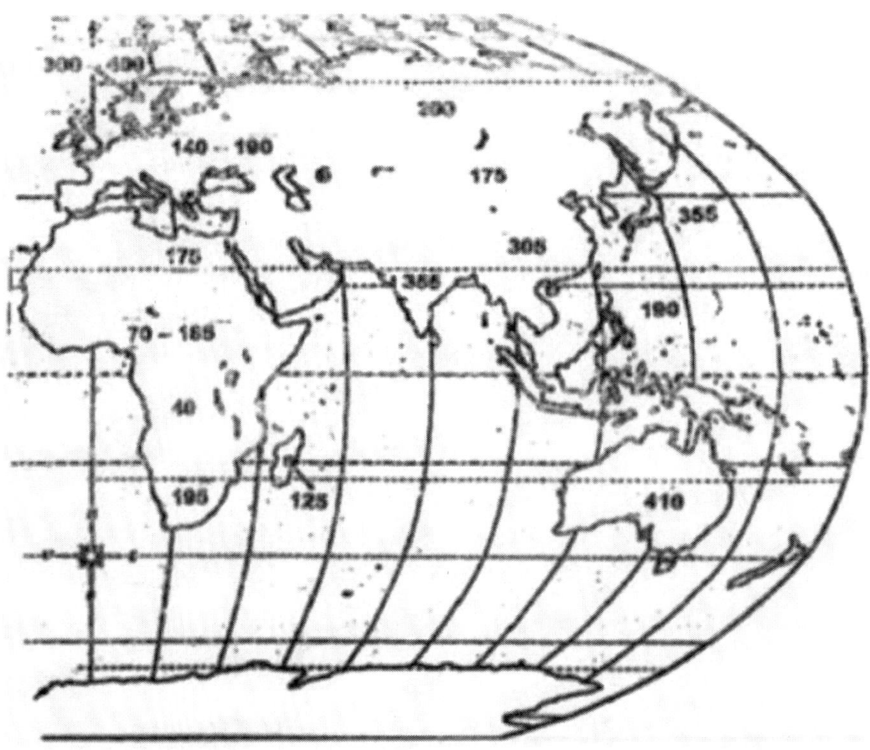

Slide 28

SLIDE 28: DISTRIBUTION OF PREVAILING CONSCIOUSNESS LEVELS - EASTERN HEMISPHERE

This slide was first introduced at the June 2003 lecture, DVD disc 1 at 005330.

The overall situation of the Eastern Hemisphere is in stark contrast to that of the Western Hemisphere. Here is seen the underlying hotbed of almost certain conflagration. Australia at 410 reflects the rationality of Western culture, and Northern Europe in 300s, India at 355, and Russia at 200 appear to be quiescent (overall) as does China at 305. Madagascar is at 125, South Africa is at 195, with the countries adjoining South Africa at 40-140 (Sudan 70, Rwanda 70, Kenya 70, Tanzania 80, Zambia 100, Angola 50, Namibia 100, Zimbabwe at 80, Botswana at 65, Nigeria at 75, Chad at 90, Ethiopia at 140 and Somalia at 100), and those in North Africa are at 70-180. The difficulty arises between Latitude 10-40 North in North Africa and Middle East, involving countries including Israel (190), Saudi Arabia (175), Yemen (160), UAE (180), Jordan (185), Iran (190), Iraq (125), Syria (160), where we are going to see all the problems. At 50, a country does not have energy and cannot put its act together, so countries at the levels of Apathy are not much of a problem to any other country. The situation in North Africa and the Middle East, however, is quite different because at consciousness levels 180-195, the countries now have enough money and resources, plus negative and hostile attitudes, to become real threats. Rival countries that calibrate at those levels constitute an ominous match. Interfering parties need to be forewarned that well-meaning efforts may merely fan the flames of hatred, and that they likely will be perceived as enemies and vilified and attacked for their efforts. Turkey at 245 and Egypt at 300 seem like the only hopes in that region.

For countries that calibrate very low at or around the levels of Apathy, how much does democracy appeal to them? They have not even got water or bathrooms, they do not have food, and the children are dying, falling over with AIDS and starvation. Who there is interested in a political system? They will naturally follow anyone who promises them water and food, and they are subject to be ruled by a dictator who exploits the people and allows them to starve. A calibration level of 70 has nothing to do with 421 (USA) as the people at 70 slaughter each other in many countries and are not even at the level of slavery as yet, which is a step higher for them. With slavery, one gets that people are worth money, but in these countries/cultures, they just kill everyone in the vanquished country.

Distribution of Prevailing Consciousness Levels – Eastern Hemispheres

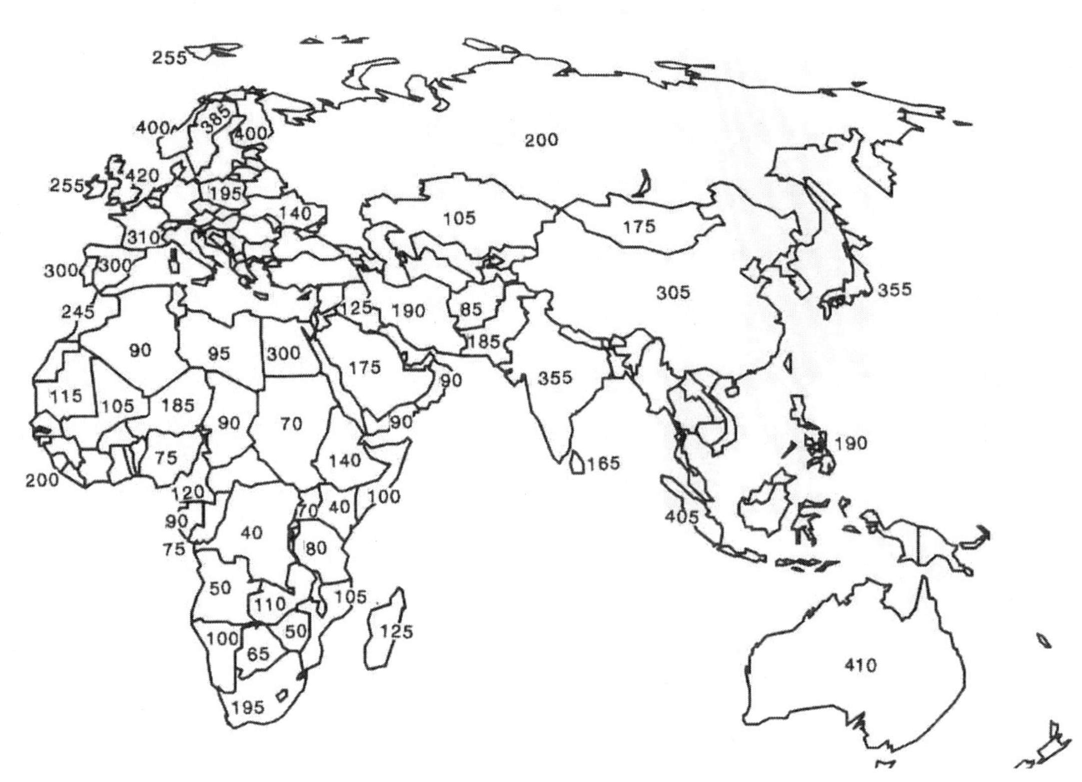

Slide 29

SLIDE 29: DISTRIBUTION OF PREVAILING CONSCIOUSNESS LEVELS

This slide was first introduced at the June 2003 lecture, DVD disc 1 at 005445.

Calibration of various countries can be extremely helpful in developing diplomatic strategies to deal with other countries and international relations in general. USA at 421 does not have to antagonize other countries by saying that USA is better than they are. That is not the way to make friends. Regions that calibrate below level 100 are characteristically torn by internal problems, starvation, and ravishing by local citizens as well as by pervasive disease, malnourishment, high fertility and infant mortality rates, short life span, and illiteracy. They are so weakened by all the factions that, in and of themselves, they lack the strength or resources to be a threat to world peace. But, at higher levels around Pride (175), these countries have enough energy to cause real damage.

After the devastation of World War I, it was hoped that a League of Nations would be a means to resolve international conflict but, like the United Nations that replaced it, such organizations proved to be futile. Both organizations were idealistic in theory but inept in practice. (The League of Nations calibrates at 185; the UN calibrates overall at 190, and the International Criminal Court calibrates at 195.) Although the United Nations has proven to be a successful humanitarian aid organization, it has primarily produced rhetoric (cal. 185) rather than resolution. The United Nations' Political Affairs Committee calibrates at 180. Its overall position is anti-American even though America pays approximately twenty-five percent of U. N. expenses, plus provides the building on the East River, a choice location in Manhattan. Mankind cannot place its fate in the hands of an organization that calibrates at the ineffective level of 185-190. To survive, mankind has to put aside sentimentalism (cal. 190), rhetoric, and its mainstay of sophistry (cal. 195).

We talk about spiritual community. What is the world, and the condition of the world? We are in it but we are not of it. What can we do directly through interaction at the physical level by trying to change belief systems? That will be using force and it has limited response, and results in counterforce. That is not going to transform the people into saintly peaceniks. They make their living by the war. They get their status from war. They get their sense of masculinity/sufficiency from violence and even their spiritual belief systems are tied up with violence. Therefore, it does not seem that addressing directly on the physical level is going to have any impact. This situation can be transformed only by addressing the level of power, not force (form). What can we do as a spiritual community? By letting go of our own ego/positionality, we reinforce the field. By collapsing the wave function, we change the field.

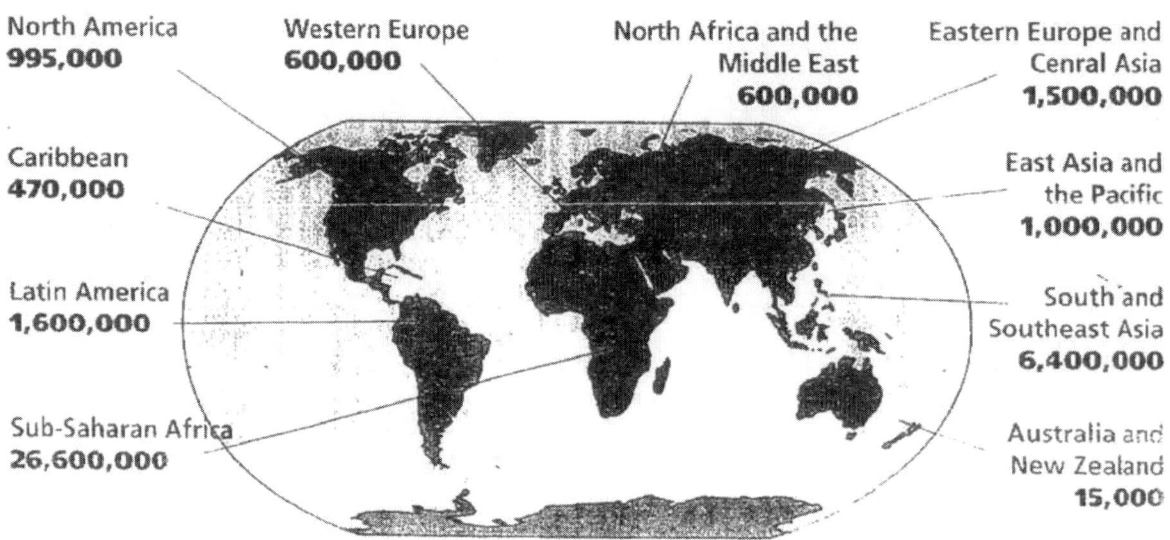
Adults & children estimated to be living with HIV/AIDS*
North America
995,000
Western Europe
600,000
North Africa and the
Middle East
600,000
Eastern Europe and
Cenral Asia
1,500,000
Caribbean
470,000
East Asia and
the Pacific
1,000,000
Latin America
1,600,000
South and
Southeast Asia
6,400,000
Sub-Saharan Africa
26,600,000
Australia and
New Zealand
15,000

Slide 30

SLIDE 30: ADULTS & CHILDREN ESTIMATED TO BE LIVING WITH HIV/AIDS

This slide was first introduced at the October 2004 lecture, DVD disc 2 at 011755.

The incidence of HIV/AIDS in the world correlates with the distribution of the levels of consciousness in the world, and not caused by anything external. The calibration levels of 70-90 give no karmic immunity to negativity, whatever it might be. If we were closer to the middle ages history-wise, we'd be looking at the black death, or plague instead of AIDS for these levels of consciousness. So AIDS is today's plague.

It is like the broken window principle. The energy attracts to it what is concordant with it. That is why it is important to raise the levels of consciousness of people. You cannot eliminate crime as long as there is trash on the streets, because they come from the same energy field. That which does not care about its environment, fellow human beings, neatness, orderliness, or beauty then desecrates beauty and throws its trash on the street with the attitude, "not my problem; they get paid to do their jobs." In contrast, persons at higher levels of consciousness take complete responsibility for their physical, mental and spiritual well-being, inspiring others around them to do the same.

Correlation of Levels of Consciousness and Rate of Happiness

Level	Log	Percent
Enlightenment	700-1,000	100
Peace	600	100
Joy	570	99
Love	500	89
Reason	400	79
Acceptance	350	71
Willingness	310	68
Neutrality	250	60
Courage	200	55
Pride	175	22
Anger	150	12
Desire	125	10
Fear	100	10
Grief	75	9
Apathy	50	3
Guilt	30	4

Slide 31

SLIDE 31: CORRELATION OF LEVELS OF CONSCIOUSNESS AND RATE OF HAPPINESS

This slide was presented for the first time at the July 2005 lecture, DVD disc 1 at 1:41:00.

Why should one go through the work of spiritual endeavor, and engage in self-examination, etc.? One cannot pursue spiritual work just because one wants to be happy. It is like going into business because you want to be rich. Everyone wants to be rich but that does not make everyone rich. Wanting to be happy keeps one 'wanting to be happy'. The way out is through transcending the lower levels of consciousness, by becoming aware of the tremendous shift in the rates of happiness as one transcends the lower levels.

People at the lowest levels of Apathy and below have less than a 5% rate of happiness. These are the levels of chronic criminals and terrorists. If one is not too happy, it is not too hard to blow up other people, but if one is happy it makes it difficult, indeed impossible, to do so.

Chronic Grief calibrates at 75 and has a 9% rate of happiness as some people get happy because of suffering itself. Some people make a life of suffering, martyrdom, always feeling sensitive, insulted and affronted.

Moving up to Fear, the rate of happiness goes up to 10% and then 12% at the level of Anger because one swells up with anger and one gets a certain satisfaction that one is scaring people. At the level of Pride, the rate of happiness goes up to 22%. In this study, the question that was not asked is whether the rate of happiness is an actual subjective state or just an opinion of the subject, and that can be a subject for further research. The one hundred people mentioned in Bernie Goldberg's book *100 People Who Are Screwing Up America* calibrate exactly at 175.

At the level of Courage (200), people accept personal responsibility and the rate of happiness goes up to 55%. The level of Neutral is like *comme ci comme ça*, neither good nor bad, e.g. a person may say, "if I do not get this job, I'll get another one," which is a comfortable way to be, and the rate of happiness goes up to 60%. Neutral people are easy to get along with and the level of Neutral is a swell place to be, but people at this level do not feel guilty for not being able to help others, as they do not feel compelled to do so. At the level of Willingness (310), one has a positive input for others and the rate of happiness goes up to 68%. One owns Power within and does not depend on others for happiness at the level of Acceptance (350) and the rate of happiness moves up to 71%. The rate of happiness then climbs to 79% at the level of Reason (400), 89% at the level of Love (500), 99% at the level of Unconditional Love and finally 100% at the level of Peace (600) as one transcends unhappiness (ego) completely at that point.

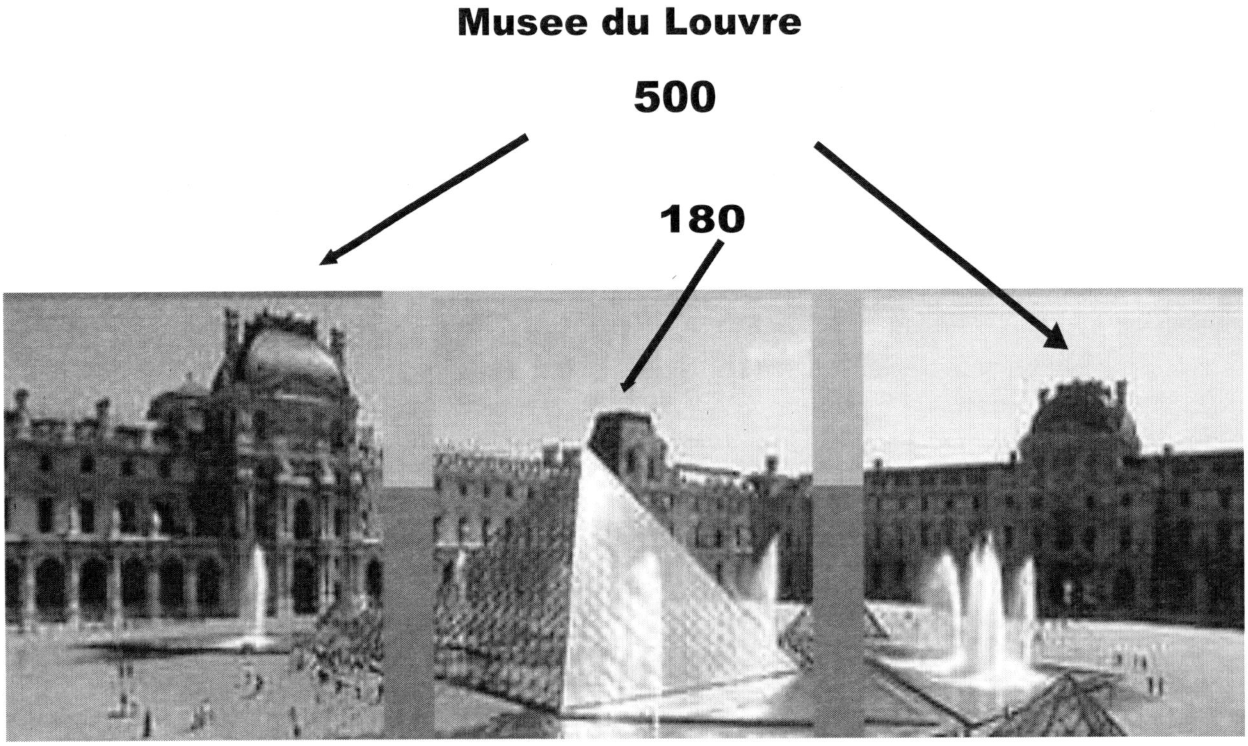

Musee du Louvre

500

180

Pyramid (Cour Napoleon)

Slide 32

SLIDE 32: MUSEE DU LOUVRE

This slide was first introduced at the April 2004 lecture, DVD disk 2 at 013900.

The Louvre or the Louvre Museum (French: *Musée du Louvre)* was originally built as a fortress in the twelfth century and used to be the royal residence of the Emperor of France until it was converted into a museum in the eighteenth century. It is currently one of the largest and the world's most visited museums, housing thousands of objects from prehistory to the 21st century. The Louvre calibrates at 500, and when one visits the Louvre, one finds it to be an incredible place. There are Rembrandts that calibrate at 700, and other truly marvelous works of art.

In the middle of the Louvre, in the main courtyard (*Cour Napoléon*) of the Louvre Palace (Palais du Louvre), is a glass and metal pyramid structure that serves as the main entrance to the Louvre Museum. The Chinese American architect, I. M. Pei, designed and built this structure around 1990 at the request of the French Government. It calibrates at 180 and is an abomination, a piece of post modernistic art - really an architectural disaster that is completely out-of-place and would look good somewhere else. The architect calibrates quite high but this structure is a philosophical statement of post-modernism and deconstructionism, representing the distorted hermeneutics of relativistic epistemology, which is the new disease of humankind. Postmodernist architecture challenges Modernism as antiquated and "totalitarian", favoring personal preferences and variety over objective, ultimate truths or principles.

If the human world goes down in consciousness, the one thing that can be pointed to for the slide would be the distorted hermeneutics of relativistic epistemology and the memes that come out of that, like a virus. Without it, anti-Semitism could never even have occurred. "The Protocol of the Elders of Zion" is a fabricated document purporting to be factual, calibrating about 90.

This document came about in the beginning of the twentieth century, prevailed across Europe, and resulted in the Third Reich and the elimination of six million Jews. That is "the power of the pen," which should not be ignored. Our society ignores the power of the pen, thinking that it is irrelevant and turns to the sports news instead. Deviations from truth, relativistic right now, are the reason one cannot mention the Constitution of the United States in the classroom, due to the thinking of distorted hermeneutics of relativistic epistemology. Despite its great progress and overall erudition, ours is still a naive society that, for instance, does not fully understand the difference between religion and spirituality, which is the very crux of the U.S. Constitution itself.

To mention the word "God" does not establish a religion; it is just a noun like any other noun. The Constitution is "deistic." The Constitution calibrates at 710 and the critics of the Constitution calibrate at 190, including the Ninth Circuit Court of Appeals, by the way, which also calibrates about 190.

Diagnostic Chart of International Relationships

God-view	Self-view	Level	Log (Other Countries)	Log (America (421))
Loving	Benign	Love	500	500
				421
Wise	Meaningful	Reason	400	400
Merciful	Harmonious	Acceptance	350	350
Inspiring	Hopeful	Willingness	310	310
Enabling	Satisfactory	Neutrality	250	250
Permitting	Feasible	Courage	200	200
Indifferent	Demanding	Pride	175	175
Vengeful	Antagonistic	Anger	150	150
Denying	Disappointing	Desire	125	125
Punitive	Frightening	Fear	100	100
Uncaring	Tragic	Grief	75	75
Condemning	Hopeless	Apathy	50	50
Vindictive	Evil	Guilt	30	30
Despising	Hateful	Shame	20	20

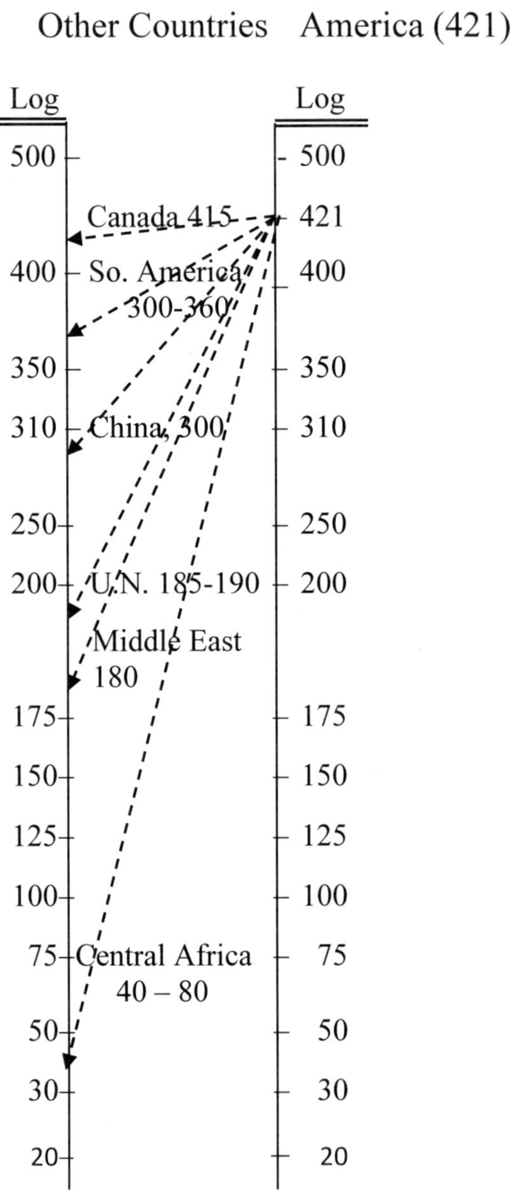

Slide 33

SLIDE 33: DIAGNOSTIC CHART OF INTERNATIONAL RELATIONSHIPS

This slide was first introduced at the April 2004 lecture, DVD 2 at 013940.

Diplomacy has nothing to do with anything rational whatsoever. The history of humankind demonstrates that, over and over again, the condition of violence and war has prevailed. The Map of Consciousness can be used as a tool for the better understanding of others, where one can define anything in terms of "Us" vs. "Them": politics, business, products, research, international diplomacy, etc. One side of the chart is "Us" i.e. where we are (our family, our country, political or philosophical position, scientific challenge etc.), and the other side is "Them" or the audience to be contacted. We need to go where "they" are, so we can deal with what is of value to them. If we calibrate the energy field of the audience, and calibrate where we are, then we can see what our task is. This can give some reality basis to diplomacy other than the fallacious power struggle that goes on right now. The United Nations calibrates at 190, barely able to function at all. It is the biggest committee in the world, and when people want to kill a project, they refer it to a committee. If one wants to stop action that one opposes, assign it to a committee and that is the end of it.

Let us take the example of the USA as a country as "Us" and determine what task the USA faces in relating to other countries. To calibrate a country, one needs three things: the level of consciousness of the ruler, that of the government, and that of the people. The overall level of consciousness of a country reflects a combination of all three factors. There are countries with highly integrous ruler and integrous people but their government bureaucracy is totally corrupt. You would not want to drive your car in that country because if there is a small incident like a dent in the car, you may find yourself in jail and your family being black mailed for a large sum of money. Of course, if you pay off the judge, the attorney and the prosecutor, you get free. Therefore, it is best not to drive your car in that country.

A similar situation prevailed in Russia when President Gorbachev calibrated at 500 but the governmental bureaucratic system collapsed into an endless chaos after communism was undone, and the economy was taken over by the white mafia. On the other hand, in still other countries, the government and the people may be fine but the ruler may be a crook.

By drawing a line between the level of the USA (421) and that of another country in the Middle East that calibrates at 180, it becomes clear that the values of the US are not applicable directly to that country. Reason appeals to Canadians. It does not appeal to the Middle East. Revenge appeals to the Middle East. Cultures in lack are only interested in what can be of gain to them: the chart helps determine what will appeal to them. You cannot "sell" something to people who are not interested in it. Integrous people respect truth for its own sake. Non-integrous people respect truth only for what they can get out of it. The chart can be for one's business and other businesses, one's company and the company's target audience for advertising, the local government and other agencies, etc.

WAR AND PEACE

Peace: Natural state where Truth prevails War: State when falsehood prevails
Basis of War: Ignorance

Conditions: Man cannot discern truth from falsehood

Consequences: Can't discern leader from megalomaniac
Basis: Ego programmed into polarized ego positions
Result: Distortion of truth; propaganda
Cost: Death and destruction

Calibrations: World War II

Above 200

Winston Churchill	510	Robert Oppenheimer (early)	43
Pres. Roosevelt	499	U.S. Treatment of War	25
Pres. Harry S. Truman	495	U.S. Internment of Japanese	30
Gen. Dwight D.	455	Heisenberg	46
Gen. Douglas MacArthur	425	Werner von Braun	40
U.S. Government	395	U.S. Military	31
U.S. Embassy in Japan	300	German Military	20
Normandy Invasion	365	Triage	20
Los Alamos	400	Gen. Erwin Rommell	20
U.S. Military at Pearl	250	Kamikaze Pilots	39
The Luftwaffe	345	Emperor Hirohito	34
Gen. Hideki Tojo	205	Admiral Yamamoto	20

Below 200

Adolph Hitler	45	Los Alamos Double Agent	70
Josef Stalin	90	League of Nations	18
Benito Mussolini	50	Pacifists	14
Heinrich Himmler	40	Attack on Pearl Harbor	45
Third Reich	70	Joseph Goebbels	60
Neville Chamberlin	185	Nazi Treatment of Prisoners	70
Japanese Embassy in U.S.	55	Japanese Treatment of	40
Japanese Government	130	Nazi Invasion of Europe	40
Robert Oppenheimer (late)	70	Concentration Camps	30
London Blitz	30	Dr. Josef Megele	15
"Cambridge Five"	95	The Rosenbergs	40
Traitors	30	Lord Haw-Haw	50
"Tokyo Rose"	85		

Slide 34

SLIDE 34: WAR AND PEACE - WORLD WAR II

This slide was first introduced at the November 2003 lecture, DVD disk 1 at 012900.

World War II is the most familiar war historically. If one can understand one war, you can understand all wars. You can analyze all the factors and discover very simply that peace is the automatic consequence of truth and war is the automatic consequence of falsehood. How could we have diagnosed it?

Winston Churchill calibrates at 510 and Roosevelt at 499. President Roosevelt's fireside chats calibrate at 500. Politics is on TV around the clock now and it was Aristotle who originally pointed out that there are three things important in politics: ethos, logos, and pathos. One is the integrity of the speaker. The next is the integrity of the information. The third is the means to persuade an audience by appealing to their emotions. Both Churchill and Roosevelt wereskilled in pathos. Roosevelt made a tough decision - no more butter, no more sugar, no more gasoline. Everyone had to sacrifice everything; it was nitty-gritty survival, instead of protesting that or having a parade, we are losing our civil rights. People sat around the radio at night for the fireside chat. The president explained it to the audience as if the people in the audience were members of his family: we cannot have butter because we have to have it for so and so, etc. Then the people in the audience naturally said, "OK."

The protests that one sees going on politically today result from the failure to communicate the message properly (lack of pathos). It is one thing to know the truth and quite another to get people to sit still for it. Looking at the calibrations of Presidents Truman and Eisenhower, one sees their status as highly integrous. MacArthur had problems with his pride and all, but they won the war. At the same time, you have the German military, and the U.S. military as integrous. The German military was over 200. In fact, no matter how awful war is, we find the military is integrous, out of honor, out of duty, out of surrender to their country, for the Fatherland. It is only the people on top, the leaders, who are often not integrous. That is why, as soon as the war ended, people on both sides shook hands. A person who was out to kill you before, the minute the war is over one can be friends with, recalling the war in which he was the kamikaze pilot and you were the target. There is a certain integrity among the troops, which does not prevail at the top.

Below 200 are Hitler, Stalin, Mussolini, Third Reich, etc. The League of Nations was ineffectual then at 185, just as the UN is now at 190. Horrors such as World War II can be traced in part to incorrect assumptions made by people in power about their potential adversaries because they had no context or way to measure their level of consciousness. Thus, they thought Hitler could be trusted to abide by the terms of a peace treaty, the Japanese are no threat to the US in the Pacific, etc. Secretary of War Stinson said, "Gentlemen don't read other gentlemen's mail." The mind does not understand triage until consciousness level 350. The dropping of the atomic bomb in World War II was triage, weighing which loss of life would be less. Triage calibrates at 205. It is an effort to save life, but is often demonized as taking life instead. The biggest enemy of peace in the world is political naiveté. One cannot have truth without peace, and one cannot have falsehood without war. Only 7% of human history has been without war. New information comes to light all the time, as the recent information regarding World War II. It then changes the way one looks at it. Therefore, you can accept all worldly information as provisional without having any opinion about it.

War and Peace

Peace:	Natural state where prevails	Consequences:	Inability to discern leader from a megalomaniac
War:	State when falsehood prevails	Basis:	Ego programmed into polarized ego position
Basis of War:	Ignorance	Result:	Distortion of Truth; propaganda
Conditions:	Man cannot discern truth from Falsehood	Cost:	Death and destruction

Calibrations: Korean War

South Korea	300	North Korea	80
U.S. Position	300	Communist Regime	80

Vietnam War

U.S. Military	335	PTSD a fact?	Yes
Vietnam Populace	70	U.S. Media	185
War Protestors	201	Lyndon Johnson	185
Viet Cong	40	Communists (U.S.)	130

Cold War

U.S. Position	400	U.S. Intelligence Operations	195
West Germany	310	CIA	185
Pres. Richard M. Nixon	400	FBI	185
Pres. John F. Kennedy	430	East Germany	165
U.S. Media	215	Russian Position	75
KGB	40	Leonid Brezhnev	90
Nikita Kruschev	40	Communists (U.S.)	130

Gulf War

Pres. George H.W. Bush	400	Gulf War Syndrome a Fact?	Yes
U.S. Military	310	Saddam Hussein	95
Kuwait	195		

World War I

Pres. Woodrow Wilson	400	Shell Shock a Fact?	Yes	Kaiser Wilhelm	165

Comparative: Napoleonic Wars – Waterloo

Duke of Wellington	405	Napoleon	75

Slide 35

SLIDE 35: WAR AND PEACE

This slide was first introduced at the June 04 lecture, DVD Disc 2 at 002000.

We can go through several wars and then get the general principles without being a participant. We can calibrate the energy of everything involved and discover very amazing things, of what went on and why it went on. Then one sees that war is the consequence of the degree the society is ruled by falsity. Peace is the automatic consequence of truth.

In the Korean War, the intention of South Korea was at 300. The U.S. position was at 300, out to defeat Communism. North Korea and its communist regime was coming from a much lower level.

In the Vietnam War, we see that the U.S. was considerably down in intention and in fact below 200 in several areas, including US President Lyndon Johnson, and the US media. Post- traumatic Stress Disorder (*PTSD*) is a mental health problem that can occur after a traumatic event like war, and many people say they are just falsifying the symptoms to collect money.

Muscle-testing reveals that it is in fact true and not a fabrication.

In the Cold War, the United States position was intelligent and the U.S. media was integrous.

U.S. intelligence even during the Cold War was 195, CIA 185. Other countries have enormous intelligence operations. France, even in peacetime has probably ten times as many people out there as the US does. East Germany, Russian Position, KGB, were all below 200 during the Cold War.

In the Gulf War, the first President Bush was at 400. That is, he was doing his duty. The President of the United States puts his hand on the Bible to this day and swears an oath to fulfill the obligations of the presidency to protect the people of the country. So that certainly puts him up around 400. Is the Gulf War Syndrome a fact? Yes. People thought they were trying to collect, but it was a fact. On the other side, Saddam Hussein was at 95, and Kuwait at 195.

In World War I, President Woodrow Wilson calibrated at 400. The Kaiser calibrated at 165. Was shell shock a fact? Yes, Shell shock, PTSD, these aftermaths of war, are real and an overwhelm to the central nervous system.

Napoleon originally calibrated at about 440, brilliant, almost a genius, as it is staggering to see what Napoleon did for France: incredible architecture, the great libraries, museums and all.

When he crowned himself emperor, thus usurping the prior authority of the Church in which only popes had the power to crown an emperor, he dropped down below 200 in calibration. Napoleon had dropped all the way down to 75 by the time of the battle of Waterloo, and proved no match for the Duke of Wellington, who calibrated at 405.

WAR AND PEACE

Peace: Natural state where Truth prevails

War: Consequence of Falsehood

Basis of War: **Ignorance**

Conditions: **Man cannot tell truth from falsehood**

Consequences: **Citizens cannot discern leader from an egomaniac**

Basis: **Innocence is easily programmed into polarized ego positions**

Result: **Inflammatory rhetoric and propaganda**

Cost: **Agony, death, and destruction**

Calibrations: Iraqi War

Above 200:

President Bush (position)	460	U.S. State Dept. (Intention)	450	U.S. Media	320
Secretary Powell	460	The Congress	450	Peace Vigils	305
Secretary of Defense	460	U.S. Population	430	UN Security Council	202
U.S. Military (Intention)	450				

Below 200:

Iran	185	Iraqi Population	140	Iraqi Military Leaders	65
Palestine	180	Iraqi Media	140	Jihad	50
Israel	180	France vis-a-vis the U.S.	140	Islamic Terrorists	50
Peace Demonstrations	170	Middle East	110	Taliban	45
"Peace" as Political Slogan	130	Vilification of U.S. & Pres.	70	Bin Laden	40
Turkey	165	Saddam Hussein	65	Syria Regime	130

Slide 36

SLIDE 36: WAR AND PEACE - IRAQI WAR

This slide was first introduced at the April 2003 lecture, DVD disk 1 at 001445.

The world deals with symptoms and does not understand the cause. We need a better diagnosis: we get the circumstances, we get all the players, we calibrate their levels of consciousness and now we have some predictable scientific means to expect a better result. The basis of war is ignorance. Force consumes energy in going from "here" to "there". For example, a war requires money, lives, food for the soldiers, taxation etc. Power is like gravity--it just is. It is a quality of that which is (truth), and it influences and uplifts. Phenomena arise from the coalescence of many factors in the field of divinity. Peace is the automatic consequence of truth. Deliberate distortions of truth bring war.

On the US side, one sees integrity of intention across the board in the Iraqi War, but it was not able to handle the problem without resorting to violence. That is because the US side was coming from Marquees of Queensberry rules while the opposite side was coming from the level of the Komodo dragon. The preceding events in this war were nearly identical to the other wars: a megalomaniac leader propagandizes their populace to militancy while the intended victim goes into denial with faulty intelligence (cal. 190), naive diplomatic ineptitude, and poetic fantasies of "if we're nice to them, they'll be nice to us" illusions. Not only were three thousand innocent civilians killed, but also the Pentagon itself was attacked and thus defined the attack as an act of war. The plane that crashed was intended for the White House itself (Calibrates as 'true'.) The attack was thereby formally an "act of war" by definition, declaration, and intention (Calibrates as 'true'.) Osama bin Laden formally declared war prior to the Pentagon attack, which fulfilled the warning of Jihad, a Holy War. The 9/11 events obviously were not just a 'criminal act' any more than was the Japanese bombing of Pearl Harbor.

The public's comprehension of the true meaning and impact of the 9/11 attacks was impaired by the relentless repetition of the images of the burning Twin Towers. Lack of clarity about the correct definition of the event resulted in the later confusion about whether detentions were to be legally classified as criminals, prisoners of war, combatants, noncombatants, saboteurs, etc. The presidential decisions that followed were dictated by the preceding events, plus the president's sworn oath of office to defend the country against aggressors. Actions at the time were based on available intelligence sources (U.S., Russia, and Britain). The U.S. Intelligence persisted at calibration level 190.

As events turned out, the primary threat was not specifically Iraq itself but Pan-Arabic Wahhabism as expressed by violent al-Qaeda extremists. Thus, the real enemy was not really a specific country but a militant ideology that had actually begun in Saudi Arabia and spread to Iran and across the entire Middle East. It then became politicized and favored by the Iraqi ruling party. Thus, the true identity of the aggressor became clouded. This confusion was abetted by Sadam Hussein's repudiation of the United Nations' mandate on fourteen occasions, which was the real trigger of overt war. The Iraqi War stopped the killing of fellow Iraqis by Saddam Hussein, who routinely killed more of his countrymen than did the Gulf and Iraqi wars combined (30,000 mass graves).

Teacher at Work (1)

Slide 37

SLIDE 37: TEACHER AT WORK (1)

This slide was first introduced at the August 2004 lecture, Disc 1, beginning around 001400.

The slide depicts the enormous effort required to prepare the book, "Truth vs. Falsehood: How to Tell the Difference", more than 2 years and thousands of calibrations in the making.

From "Truth vs. Falsehood: How to Tell the Difference" (2005), Author's Statement, pp. ix-x:

"The accumulated data was overwhelming in its revelations and implications. Researchers using this new tool were like children with their first microscope, excitedly examining everything and anything in the human experience. The mass of accumulated data often revealed rather startling information. It became overwhelmingly apparent that appearance was not in accord with essence, and that the mind is basically naive and easily deceived. Therefore, readers are forewarned that portions of the material may be disturbing and confrontational to some cherished illusions.

The work has been progressively presented in a sequence of books, video and audio recordings, workshops, and public lectures with audience participation. It has been translated and made available worldwide in more than fourteen languages. In addition, it has been presented to numerous ongoing study groups around the world, and it was peer reviewed prior to publication.

The enormous mass of data has been organized and presented in a sequence in order to facilitate comprehension across a wide spectrum of information. The subject matter is also contextualized to facilitate the awareness of intention. Seeming paradoxes dissolve with reflection, and much of the information is transformative in itself.

As with *Power vs. Force*, reading the material herein results in a progression of the reader's level of consciousness. Therefore, what at first exposure might seem confrontational, paradoxically, it resolves into greater awareness and an expanded capacity of discernment."

Teacher at Work (2)

Slide 38

SLIDE 38: TEACHER AT WORK (2)

This slide was first introduced at the August 2004 lecture, DVD Disc 1, beginning around 001245.

This is another slide showing the effort required to prepare "Truth vs. Falsehood", more than 2 years and thousands of calibrations.

In the words of the author, from "Truth vs. Falsehood: How to Tell the Difference" (2005), Caveat: A Note to the Reader, pp. xi-xii: "Overall, the basic dictum to the information reported is that importance is not based on whether it is pleasing, but on whether it is true or false and to what degree. The reported calibrations are the result of research and are not the author's opinion. Thus, there is no point in writing querulous letters that usually follow the format of "How come you rated walruses higher than seals," etc. Like a calculator, the described methodology results in numbers, not subjective bias or opinion.

Extensive references are provided that give background information needed to better understand the reported research findings. The compilation of the manuscript itself took three years, including revisions, corrections, and incorporation of input from review committees and consultants, as well as feedback from a variety of experts. Thus, meticulous effort has been made to present the data with as much accuracy as possible.

The overall mission was guided by Socrates' dictum that all human error or wrongdoing is involuntary for man can only choose what he believes at the time to be a good that will bring happiness. His only error is that he cannot discern the really good from the illusory good. This work is devoted to clarifying what is the 'real' and how it can be identified.

To preclude undue emotional upset, the publication of the book was delayed until information that had been discovered by prior research was revealed to the public. It was therefore decided to wait until after the 2004 elections, the Iraqi war, the United Nations scandal, Islamic terrorist training in the United States, double agents in U. S. intelligence operations, clergy pedophilia, MS-13 gang infiltration, Iran's nuclear plans, etc., had occurred. All these events were identifiable back in 2003-2004, long before they became public news. Similarly, more could be said about events yet to surface."

Identification and Characteristics of Spiritual Truth, Integrous Teachers, and Teachings (1)

1. **Universality: Truth is true at all times and places, independent of culture, personalities, or circumstances.**
2. **Non-exclusionary: Truth is all-inclusive, non-secretive, and nonsectarian.**
3. **Availability: It is open to all; non-exclusive. There are no secrets to be revealed, hidden, or sold, and no magical formulas or "mysteries."**
4. **Integrity of purpose: There is nothing to gain nor lose.**
5. **Nonsectarian: Truth is not the exposition of limitation.**
6. **Independent of opinion: Truth is *nonlinear* and not subject to the limitations of intellect or form.**
7. **Devoid of Positionality: Truth is not "anti" anything. Falsehood and ignorance are not its enemies but merely represent its absence.**
8. **No requirements or demands: There are no required memberships, dues, regulations, oaths, rules, or conditions.**
9. **Non-controlling: Spiritual purity has no interest in the personal lives of aspirants, or in clothing, dress, style, sex lives, economics, family patterns, lifestyles, or dietary habits.**
10. **Free of force or intimidation: There is no brainwashing, adulation of leaders, training rituals, indoctrinations, or intrusions into private life.**

Slide 39

SLIDE 39: IDENTIFICATION AND CHARACTERISTICS OF SPIRITUAL TRUTH, INTEGROUS TEACHERS, AND TEACHINGS (1)

This slide was first introduced at the December 2004 lecture, DVD disc 2 at 001200.

By becoming familiar with the characteristics of Spiritual Truth, Integrous Teachers and Teachings, the tendency to veer off the straight and narrow spiritual path is minimized. Otherwise numerous lifetimes can be wasted in the pursuit of that which does not help but may actually hinder or set back spiritual progress.

Truth is universal in the sense that that which is true always has been, and always will be, is experiential, and described the same in all cultures. The Truth revealed in the ancient Vedas of 7000 B.C., the Reality of Krishna, of Buddha, of Jesus Christ, is not different than what an enlightened person describes as the Infinite Reality today. One cannot "get it" from somebody else. The last thing to let go of is the belief in what one thinks is the source and core of one's own life and existence. When one surrenders that to God, then one goes through death of the ego and the spectacular Truth shines forth. Therefore, universally, each enlightened being is enlightened out of nothingness. The only thing a teacher can transmit is the frequency of the energy field. Then, when the moment comes that one needs it, the field presents it not as a thought but as the certainty of the knowingness. Truth is not dependent on anything outside of itself.

Because truth is universal, how can anybody claim to own it? How can one canonize truth? How can one label it? Truth is everywhere, universally available at all times. It is always the same. That which is true radiates forth and has no secrets or mysteries. How can that which is the essence of all that exists be secret? The naiveté is the presumption that that which is universal and nonlinear is going to express itself in a linear secret. The discovery of truth leads to an exuberance, making one share it with everybody. One sees truly spiritual organizations such as 12-Steps share their truth freely with the world.

Truth is not seeking specialness. Truth stands forth self-revealing and is available to anyone who wants it. Spiritual truth, being what it is, is already fulfilled. The advanced spiritual person needs nothing, is not looking to sign up followers, having them sign pledges, or giving money. There is nothing to gain, because one already is "All That Exists". Sectarianism is going back into the linear domain: members versus non-members, ours versus theirs church; there is no universality there. Truth is not subject to the limitations of the intellect, and is therefore not subject to opinion. Nonlinear is the total field, distinct from linear, which is content. One can argue with content. The argument becomes less when one moves to the proximate field and it disappears altogether when one moves to the Universal Field. The nonlinear is inviolate. It has no handles to grab it by, as it has no form. When the intellect stops, when the mind stops thinking, there is only an infinite Presence. This Infinite Presence radiates forth through form and ends up as speech, which happens of its own. Truth is either present or not present, and if it is present, it is present to varying degrees and its degree can be calibrated. In integrous spiritual organizations, everyone is free to go as they wish, without obligations. There is no need to program other people. Making one's life a prayer means to become one with the Context - not by practicing it or hearing about it, but by *being it.*

Identification and Characteristics (2)

11. **Nonbinding: There are no regulations, laws, edicts, contracts, or pledges.**
12. **Freedom: Participants are free to come and go without persuasion, coercion, intimidation, or consequences. There is no hierarchy; instead, there is voluntary fulfillment of practical necessities and duties.**
13. **Commonality: Recognition is a consequence of what one has become rather than as a result of ascribed titles, adjectives, or trappings.**
14. **Inspirational: Truth eschews and avoids glamorization, seduction, and theatrics.**
15. **Nonmaterialistic: Truth is devoid of neediness of worldly wealth, prestige, pomp, or edifices.**
16. **Self-fulfilling: Truth is already total and complete and has no need to proselytize or gain adherents, followers, or "sign up members."**
17. **Detached: There is noninvolvement in world affairs.**
18. **Benign: Truth is identifiable along a progressive gradient. It has no "opposite" and therefore no "enemies" to castigate or oppose.**
19. **Nonintentional: Truth does not intervene or have an agenda to propose, inflict, or promulgate.**
20. **Non-dualistic: All transpires by virtue of intrinsic (karmic) propensity within the field by which potentiality manifests as actuality rather than by "cause" and effect.**

Slide 40

SLIDE 40: IDENTIFICATION AND CHARACTERISTICS OF SPIRITUAL TRUTH, INTEGROUS TEACHERS, AND TEACHINGS (2)

This slide was first introduced at the December 2004 lecture, DVD disc 2 at 010300.

A truly spiritual person, organization, or teacher is nonbinding. Oaths will survive more than this lifetime, so it is best not to take oaths. One can find oneself in strange circumstances due to a blood oath they once took, many lifetimes ago. One can check out mysterious sequences in this lifetime, pray about them, and ask for forgiveness for all those people one harmed previously.

In integrous organizations, participants are free to come and go without persuasion, coercion, intimidation, or consequences. In some cults on the other hand, if someone leaves, they threaten the person with all kinds of horrible things, and the person becomes their enemy.

Recognition is a consequence of what one has become rather than as a result of ascribed titles, adjectives, or trappings. What one is automatically positions one in the world in the first place. People are recognized for what they have become in reality.

Truth eschews and avoids glamorization, seduction, and theatrics. Only truth itself is the inspiration. The number of followers does not mean anything. Hitler had 40 million Germans following him in World War II. *Extraordinary Popular Delusions and the Madness of Crowds* talks about how all of mankind believes certain things periodically, because truth is sometimes drowned by the sheer numbers of falsehood. In truly spiritual organizations, there is noninvolvement in world affairs. This does not mean that one cannot witness to what the truth of them is but that one does not get involved in them. Noninvolvement is the basic spiritual principle of detachment.

At the same time, there is an alternate teaching by the Dalai Lama who says it is not sufficient to just pray, but that spiritual people are obligated to do for the world what they can to solve the world's problems. It means to use one's influence to improve society rather than just praying for one's own soul. Truth is identifiable along a progressive gradient. It has no "opposite" and therefore no "enemies" to castigate or oppose. The spiritually integrous are non-threatening, do not retaliate, and take no offense if someone stops following them or leaves their teachings. Truth does not intervene or have an agenda to propose, inflict, or promulgate.

It does not proselytize, which is an attempt to control others. All transpires by virtue of intrinsic (karmic) propensity within the field by which potentiality manifests as actuality rather than by "cause" and effect. The way to be is: Do not talk about it, do not pray about it, but just "be" that which is forgiving, understanding and supportive of life. One just is that which recognizes beauty, and is attuned to the beauty of Creation which one sees everywhere. Everything happens by potentiality becoming actuality because local conditions permit it to be so, by the power of the infinite field.

Identification and Characteristics (3)

21. Tranquility and Peace: There are no "issues" or partialities. There is no desire to change others or impose on society. The effect of higher energies is innate and not dependent on propagation or effort. God doesn't need help any more than gravity needs the "help" of an apple's falling off the tree.

22. Equality: This is expressed in reverence for all of life in all its expression and merely avoids that which is deleterious rather than opposing it.

23. Nontemporality: Life is realized to be eternal and physicality as a temporality. Life is not subject to death.

24. Beyond proof: That which is "provable" is linear, limited, and a product of intellectualization and mentation. Reality needs no agreement. Reality is not an acquisition but instead is a purely spontaneous, subjective realization when the positionalities of the dualistic ego are surrendered.

25. Mystical: The origination of truth is a spontaneous effulgence, radiance, and illumination, which is the Revelation that replaces the illusion of a separate individual self, the ego, and its mentation.

26. Ineffable: Not capable of definition. Radical subjectivity is experiential. It is a condition that replaces the former. With this event, context replaces content, devoid of temporality and beyond time. Reality does not exist in time, or of it, or beyond it, or outside of it, and it has no relationship to that which is an artifice of mentation. It is therefore beyond all nouns, adjectives, or verbs, transitive or intransitive.

Slide 41

SLIDE 41: IDENTIFICATION AND CHARACTERISTICS OF SPIRITUAL TRUTH, INTEGROUS TEACHERS, AND TEACHINGS (3)

This slide was first introduced at the December 2004 lecture, DVD disc 2 at 012100.

Tranquility and Peace: There are no "issues" or partialities. There is no desire to change others or impose on society. The effect of higher energies is innate and not dependent on propagation or effort. God does not need help any more than gravity needs the help of an apple falling off the tree. When we align ourselves with God's will for us as we understand it, we are contributing to the overall collective level of consciousness. In the presence of God, the infinite potentiality manifests as the entire universe and creation expresses itself in what we call evolution. That is the fulfillment of the reality of Divinity.

Equality: This is expressed in reverence for all of life in all its expression and merely avoids that which is deleterious rather than opposing it. A person asks, "What can I do to advance my consciousness?" *Be* that. One's life becomes the prayer and becomes that which reveres all of life. You see the incredible beauty of everything shining forth, the incredible beauty of form. The more advanced one gets the more the beauty becomes universal. Even that which the world describes as ugly becomes art. One sees beauty in linearity because beneath the linearity is the nonlinear, as the presence and essence of divinity is in all things, beyond form. One can see the intelligence in creation and the incredible aesthetics. When everything starts to look beautiful, you are close to the end and had better tell your friends. Anyone serious in spiritual work needs to give out instructions ahead of time about how they would like their affairs handled.

Non-temporality: Life is realized to be eternal and physicality as a temporality. Life is not subject to death. That life is eternal is taught by every great spiritual pathway, but mankind compartmentalizes it and says that it is not scientifically true and does not let it become a daily living reality. Anything goes when there is no accountability. If one denies the existence of the Absolute, then one is free to do whatever one wishes to do. Then, as *Dr. Faustus* discovered, payment is due. Accountability is intrinsic to the design of the universe, so karma is intrinsic to all actions because every action, decision and intention already has a calibrated level of consciousness without one saying so. You automatically create a track in the infinite. Everything one has done is recorded forever. Every hair on one's head is counted. That scares some people, but is a very wonderful feeling for others.

Beyond proof: How can one prove existence, infinity or divinity? None of these are provable. The mystics in all religions calibrate high and often much higher than the established ecclesiastic institution of the religion itself. The great avatars were Self-realized mystics. The presence of God is experienced by everyone at all times but very few recognize what it is. No matter what is being experienced, experiencing is going on all the time. The TV set is always turned on, no matter what is playing on it. One stops looking at the program and asks, "What is it that is on all the time?" There is some primary premise that is *a priori*, that enables experience to occur.

Mystical: The mystic looks within and keeps transcending the limitations of the ego: "not this, not that" through the pathway of negation, or through the pathway of affirmation. Enlightenment is the transcendence of the ego, which is replaced by a different condition. What was the mind of the individual personal self is dissolved into the Infinite Oneness.

Identification and Characteristics (4)

27. Simplistic: One sees the intrinsic beauty and perfection of all that exists beyond appearance and form.

28. Affirmative: Truth is beyond opinion or provability. Confirmation is purely by its subjective awareness; however, it is identifiable by consciousness calibration techniques.

29. Non-operative: Truth does not "do" anything or "cause" anything; it is everything.

30. Invitational: As contrasted with promotional or persuasive.

31. Non-predictive: Because Reality is nonlinear, it cannot be localized or encoded in restriction of form, such as secret messages, codes, numbers, and inscriptions, or hidden in runes, stones, the dimensions of the pyramid, the DNA, or the nostril hairs of the camel. Truth has no secrets. The Reality of God is omnipresent and beyond codification or exclusivity. Codes are indicative of man's imagination and not the capriciousness of Divinity.

32. Non-sentimental: Emotionality is based on perception. Compassion results from the discernmentof truth.

33. Non-authoritarian: There are no rules or dictates to be followed.

34. Non-egoistic: Teachers are respected but reject personal adulation or specialness.

35. Educational: Provides information in a variety of formats and ensures availability.

36. Self-supporting: Neither mercenary nor materialistic.

37. Freestanding: Complete without dependence on external or historical authorities.

38. Natural: Devoid of induced, altered status of consciousness or manipulations of energies by artificial exercises, postures, breathing, or dietary rituals, (i.e., non-reliance on form or physicality; no invoking of entities or "others").

Slide 42

SLIDE 42: IDENTIFICATION AND CHARACTERISTICS OF SPIRITUAL TRUTH, INTEGROUS TEACHERS, AND TEACHINGS (4)

This slide was first introduced at the December 2004 lecture, DVD disc 2 at 014200.

When you get to the point that a weed knocks you out, you are certainly making spiritual progress. The world calls it a ragweed and the spiritual aspirant calls it God. It is in the weed that you first see this incredible sculpture which no person can create. That which it is, is the linear expression of how it came to be what it is. Its form expresses its evolution. Consciousness is like a light bulb. The higher the level of consciousness, the brighter is the bulb. It can be read across time and distance. Truth is the perfect fulfillment of its potentiality from moment to moment. It goes from perfection to perfection to perfection to perfection. Each thing is perfect at every moment. One does not go from imperfection to perfection, but from perfection to perfection. Truth attracts by virtue of what it is. The purely spiritual programs which have transformed millions of lives are non-promotional. They serve by attraction, not promotion, e.g. the 12-Step groups.

You find what you intend to find. There are all kinds of codes. Can the Infinite Creator and Presence of the entire universe hide secrets about Himself in codes? Secrets mean gain.

True compassion sounds hardheaded - it calls a spade a spade. A lot of pseudo-spirituality is sentimentality, hearts and flowers. Jesus Christ said: "I bring you the sword of truth." He did not bring people the support of their favorite fallacies, emotionalities, or sentimentalities. He brought the truth. He got killed for telling the truth. Sentimentalized spirituality is false and has caused the death of millions of people over time.

In true spiritual organizations like the 12-Step programs, no authoritarian hierarchy is followed. Each time truth shines forth it starts from nothing, from standing still. It is reborn each time and it cannot be transmitted to somebody else. Titles can be transmitted, but not the condition itself. That is what Huang Po meant by the transmission of No Mind. The nonlinear cannot be transmitted because it has no form. There are endless artificial techniques, strange diets, holding strange poses for long periods of time, blood cleansers, purges, breathing exercises. The intention is what gives them any power they have. The intention is to get closer to God, so one follows certain purifications. These things are okay if one has a teacher who is a master of the technique. Altered states are not the same as divine states. Alpha wave training is therapeutic, but is not a spiritual state. That which one becomes is naturally devoid of induced altered states of consciousness or manipulations, etc. All those things can be transitional assists along the way.

Spiritual Teachers

Name	Level
Abhinavagupta	655
Acharya	480
Allen, James	505
Augustine, Saint	550
Aurobindo, Sri	605
Bartalanffy, Ludwig von	485
Besant, Annie	530
Black Elk, Wallace	499
Bodhidharma	795
Bohm, Jakob	500
Bucke, Richard M.	505
Buddhananda, Swami	485
Butterworth, Eric	495
Calvin, John	580
Chandra, Ram	540
Confucius	590
Dalai Lama (Tenzin Gyatso)	570
De Chardin, Teilhard	500
Dilgo Khyentse Rinpoche	575
Dionysius, the Areopagite	490
Dogen	740
Druckchen Rinpoche	495
Dzogchen Rinpoche	510
Eckhart, Meister	705
Erasmus	500
Fillmore, Charles	515
Fillmore, Myrtle	505
Fox, Emmet	470
Gaden, Shartse	470
Gandhi, Mahatma	760
Gangaji	475
Goldsmith, Joel	480
Gupta,Mahendranath	505
Gyalpo, Lamchen Rinpoche	460
Hall, G. Manley	485
Holmes, Ernest	485
Hopkins, Emma Curtis	485
Huang, Chungliang Al	485
Huxley, Aldous	485
John Paul II, (Pope)	570
John, Saint, of the Cross	605
Karmapa	630
Kasyapa	695
Khantsa, Jamyung	495
Kline, Jean	510
Krishna, Gopi	545
Lawrence, Brother	575
Leadbeater, C.W.	485
Linpa, Kusum	475
Luther, Martin	580
Madhva Charya, Sri	520
Magdeburg, Mechthild Von	640
Maharaj, Nisargadatta	720
Maharshi, Ramana	720
Maezumi, Hakuyu Taizan	505
Merton, Thomas	515
Moses de Leon of Granada, Rabbi	720
Mukerjee, Radhakamal	475
Muktananda	655
Munroe, Robert	485
Nanak	495
Naranjo, Claudio	465
Nityananda, Bhagavan	500
Origen	515

Slide 43

SLIDE 43: SPIRITUAL TEACHERS (1)

This slide was first introduced at the June 2003 lecture, DVD disc 2 at 012000.

Over the years, many people asked about the calibrated level of spiritual teachers. This slide and the one following it give us a panorama of different integrous teachers throughout the planet, and their impact on society. The two slides list over 100 well-known, respected teachers from various schools. They all calibrate over 460 (Excellence), and their works have stood the test of time. The list, of course, is not complete and would include many others if space permitted. Spiritual students should be aware that the acumen of some of the false teachers or self-styled "gurus" can be dazzling, and their capacity to mimic a convincing sincerity is amazing; they often take in even sophisticated spiritual seekers. That is spiritual seduction, a mixture of truth and falsehood blended in a slick package. The teachings sound valid if you cannot see that their truth has been distorted by a false context. It is best to be safe than sorry and rely only on teachers and teachings that can be trusted.

Richard Bucke at 505 was a medical doctor who wrote the book *Cosmic Consciousness* that explores the evolution of the human mind. **Eckhart Meister** at 705 had a conflict with the Catholic Church because he was a mystic. The church didn't know what to do with him, whether to hang him or sanctify him. He was a Doctor of the church. **Mahatma Gandhi** at 760 stood in power without firing a shot. The British Empire at the time calibrated at 190 and was arrogant and disrespectful of other countries. It wasn't the expertise of their rule, it was their arrogance. With the disrespect of other cultures and regimes one sees what a terrible consequence they had. So Mahatma Gandhi, who was well over 700, did nothing but stand there up against the British Empire, without firing a shot. That is the meaning of power. Power just stands there; it changes everything by virtue of that which it is. So Gandhi stands there in the high 700's and the British Empire was brought to its knees. That is an interesting demonstration of power and force because at the time that happened, the British Empire was the most powerful empire the world had ever seen and owned a quarter of the world. The power of Gandhi at 760, in contrast with the British at 190, meant they didn't stand a chance.

The sixteenth **Karmapa**, Rangjung Rigpe Dorje, who passed on from physicality in 1981 calibrates at 630. Recent Vedanta masters**, Ramana Maharshi** and **Nisargadatta Maharaj**, both calibrate at 720 whereas Huang Po, teacher of advanced "no mind" nonduality, is at 960. **Robert Monroe** at 485 was a scientist and engineer who wrote *Journeys out of the Body* and many other books. He studied and wrote about out of body experiences. One of the great mystics of the Hebrew tradition, **Rabbi Moses de Leon of Granada**, (14th century), was at 720.

Spiritual Teachers (2)

Otto, Rudolph	485
Padmasambhava	595
Pak Chung-Bih, Sotaesan	510
Palmo, Tenzin	510
Paramahansa, Yogananda	540
Patanjali	715
Patrick, Saint	590
Phuntsok, Khempo	510
Pio, Father	585
Plotinus	730
Po, Huang	960
Poonjai-Ji	520
Powell, Robert	525
Prabhavananda, Swami	550
Prejnehpad, Swami	505
Pulku, Gantey Rinpoche	499
Ramakrishna	620
Ramdas, Swami	570
Ramanuja Charya, Sri	530
Rumi	550
Sai Baba, Shirdi (not Sathya)	485
Sannella, Lee	505
Satchidananda, Swami	605
Shankara (Sankara Charya)	710
Smith, Joseph	510
Socrates	540
Steiner, Rudolf	475
Suzuki, Master Roshi	565
Swedenborg, Emanuel	480
Tagore, Rabindranath	475
Tauler, Johann	640
Teresa, Mother	710
Teresa, Saint, of Avila	715
Tillich, Paul	480
Tzu, Chuang	595
Tzu, Lao	610
Underhill, Evelyn	460
Vivekananda	610
Watts, Alan	485
White Brotherhood	560+
White Plum Asanga	505
Yukteswar, Sri	535

Slide 44

SLIDE 44: SPIRITUAL TEACHERS (2)

This slide was first introduced at the June 2003 lecture, DVD disc 2 at 012500.

This slide is a continuation of the calibrated level of spiritual teachers. Although the writings of teachers almost always calibrate at the same consciousness level as their author, there are occasional exceptions. **Plotinus** calibrates at 730, his writings at 503. **Huang Po** who wrote about the transmission of No Mind is at 960, his writings at 850, and **Meister Eckhart** calibrates at 705 while his writings are at 600. Very advanced states of consciousness are difficult to convey in the linearity of sentences and be intelligible to the reader. These occasional exceptions in the calibrated level of the teacher and the teacher's writings are inadvertent and not intentional and they sometimes happen as the teacher writes at an earlier time in his life and then transcends that level but does not have time to reflect his new realizations in his writings.

Students frequently ask for a list of integrous teachers whose work has been verified on a Scale of Consciousness. The list of verifiably integrous teachers in this and the previous slide provides a very wide array of pathways to facilitate spiritual endeavor and evolution. **Padmasambhava** at 595 is thought to be the founder of Tibetan Buddhism. **Paramahansa Yogananda** at 540 is a saint with many followers. **Father Pio** at 585 also had conflict with the Catholic Church. He had many interesting experiences of *Siddhis* including bi-location.

An interesting comparison can be made in interpreters of the ancient Vedas that demonstrates the direct spiritual purity of nonduality. Eighth century sage of Advaita Vedanta "nonduality," **Shankara**, also known as "**Adi Sankaracharya**" calibrates at 710. In comparison, **Sri Ramanujacharya**, tenth century sage of "qualified non-dualism" is at 530, and **Sri Madhvacharya** of the twelfth century "dualistic devotion" is at 520. **Mother Teresa** at 710 had a positive effect on the world. She won a Nobel Peace Prize for her work with the orphans of Calcutta. The **White Brotherhood** at 560+ is a higher heaven of celestial realms and is quite advanced.

Spiritual bookstores present an overwhelming variety of books, some of which are primarily spiritual fiction, notwithstanding the fame of their authors. Approximately fifty percent of the material in some spiritual libraries and bookshops is below calibration level 200. The majority below 200 is primarily fantasy and seven percent is actually delusional. There are many teachers with exotic names, and it is important not to be misled by the ethnic name or the title. What is important is their calibrated level of consciousness. It is better to have a neighbor down the street at 480 teaching you than a "swami" who calibrates at 220. The point being made here is to beware of the glamour of titles, attire, etc. One can learn from anyone who calibrates over 200. Probably the best teachers at the beginning of the spiritual quest are those with the simplest message which is to be kind towards everyone including yourself.

Transcending the Levels of Consciousness

The Dualities of Attraction and Aversion

Attraction	Aversion	Attraction	Aversion
Familiar, secure	Change, uncertainty	Resist	Accept, surrender
Cling	Fear of new	Defend	Give in
Easy	Effort	Success	Failure
Pride	Humility	Special	Common
Anger/"Strength"	Passivity/"Weak"	More	Less
Win	Lose	"Own"	Stewardship
Importance	"Nobody"	Attractive	Plain
Gain	Lose	Unique	Ordinary
Money	Poverty	Change world	Change self
Excitement	Boredom	Warp facts	Truth
Desire	Won't get	Condemn	Forgive
Status	A "nobody"	Be responsible	Guilt/Blame
Noticed	Ignored	Hold	Let go
Opinion	Ordinary	Dominate	Succumb
Crave	Frustrated	Content	Field
Control	Accept	Abundance	Frugality
Save world	Surrender it	Martyr	Accept
Novelty	Bored, sameness	Victim	Responsible
Thrill	Miss out	Revenge	Forgive
Aggressive	Passivity	Hate	Compassion
Gossip: "In"	"Out"	Blame	Accept/forgive
Fashionable	Drab	Conflict	Peace
Be "Right"	Wrong	Past	Present
Superior	Common	Fear	Won't survive
Speak up	Silence	Excuse	Accountable
Stubborn	Give in	Deny	Admit
Famous	Anonymous	Impatient	Wait

Slide 45

SLIDE 45: TRANSCENDING THE LEVELS OF CONSCIOUSNESS:THE DUALITIES OF ATTRACTION AND AVERSION

This slide was first introduced at the February 2005 lecture, DVD disc 2 at 1:00:00.

What holds people to a certain level of consciousness is positionality, which expresses as dualities of attraction and aversion. The pathway to enlightenment is constantly surrendering both attractions and aversions, assisted by prayer and often the assistance of others. Every ego position has a payoff and is an attraction. The payoff is the feeling of being "right". One has to give up the indignation of not being "right". With surrender and humility comes the realization of a different dimension, beyond duality.

We like what is familiar and resist change. To correct oneself takes effort and is resisted, but in the end is rewarding. That applies to one as a person, as in "I don't really want to give up being a pick pocket." The attraction is clinging to the current lifestyle and the fear is of the new. Even spiritual work brings up as much to awareness, as one does not like a certain way of being, nevertheless, it is habitual, and there is a certain comfort in that. One has to acknowledge that in order to transcend that.

The ego takes pride in the payoff of being right and does not want to look at humility. What the ego does not realize is humility allows one to become greater. The ego then becomes proud of its humility and becomes the spiritual ego. It is hard for the ego not to get some degree of it at least on the intellectual level, as it thinks along the lines of, "Yes, I have been there, I have heard that speaker, I have read that book. Of course I know Sanskrit, and that definitely makes me better than other people..."

Anger gives an illusion of strength because it takes a position. In fact, strength is not "anger" but "wisdom of staying cool under pressure." The mind lives in a world of dualities such as pain and pleasure, gain and loss, win and lose. The stock market and everything else is a game of win and lose. The other gain is feeling important, as one of the reasons we like to win is to feel important. It gives us a temporary sense of empowerment. There is a legitimate side to winning, as the recognition that the consequence was a result of one's own dedication and effort, and that is different from a vanity.

We do not have to have an opinion about anything and that gives rise to a feeling of freedom. If someone asks, "What do you think of the election?" One can respond by saying, "I don't think anything about it. Democracy in action, how does that sound." Someone else asks "What about catastrophe?" and your answer can be, "Well you know what Ramana Maharshi says: The world you see doesn't even exist." His recommendation is that you surrender it to God. You do not know what is right and wrong, or what is the undoing of bad karma or the earning of good karma. What looks like a catastrophe to one is frankly someone else's salvation. Anyone who has been on the edge of catastrophe remembers it was the catastrophe that got you to let go and got you to salvation. Without the catastrophe, without one's feet being held to the fire, one was not about to quit." Surrendering the world to God brings us closer to peace and Truth.

Diagnostic Differential: Infatuation vs. Love

Quality	Passion/Attraction (Level 145)	Love (Level 500+)
Locus	Self/Ego	Self/Spirit
Origin	Animal instinct	Spiritual State
Mental Function	Impaired reality testing	Uplifted
Intention	Mate, get	Bond, enjoy
Duration	Transitory	Permanent
Hormone/Endocrine	Adrenalin/Sex Hormones	Endorphins
Emotions	Excess/Imbalance	Calm/Balance
Brain Physiology	Left Brain - Physical	Right Brain - Etheric
Stability	Impaired/Desperate	Enhanced
Emotional Quality	Frantic, fearful, torment	Self-fulfilling
Bodily Functions	Impaired, loss of appetite and sleep	Improved
Description	Addiction, craving	Fulfillment, content
Pathology	Suicide, stalking, despair, depression	Well-being
Judgment	Impaired	Improved
Perception	Exaggeration, glamorized	Illuminated
Intention	Possess, capture, control, own	Be with
Emotional Quality	Frustration, anxiety	Gratitude, satisfied
Productivity	Disrupted	Enhanced
Self-Image	Inflated	Positive
Loss	Depression, rage, hate, blame	Regret, grief, sadness
Balance	Erratic, over stimulated	Steady
Social Image	Impaired, "foolish," "madness"	Enhanced
Intellectual Function	Romanticizing, lower mind	Realistic, higher mind
Effect on consciousness level		

Slide 46

SLIDE 46: DIAGNOSTIC DIFFERENTIAL: INFATUATION VS. LOVE

This slide was introduced at the April 2005 lecture, DVD disc 2 at 001600.

Love and Infatuation have completely different qualities, but people often confuse the two. Alignment with Love includes the spiritual Self and calibrates at 500 and up. There is a dim awareness that we are answerable over long run for our integrity, so we turn down what could be a win, a temporary gain for long-term gain. Infatuation (Passion/Attraction) calibrates at 145 and is where controlling others is crucial to the relationship. When happiness is "out there," it is always at risk.

The origin of infatuation is the animal instinct - frantic mating, whereas Love is a spiritual state in which the welfare and happiness of the other person is equal to one's own, even to the point of self-sacrifice. The mental function is impaired when a person is "madly in love" while those aligned with Love are uplifted by the relationship, with more enjoyment in their life and a sense of gratitude for the relationship. When infatuated with a goal, reason becomes distorted (cal. at 155) in order to sub serve and rationalize the reaching of that goal and involves all kinds of violations of truth, whereas Love involves the realistic higher mind (cal. 275 and up.)

The intention of infatuation is to get a mate- a quick acquisition, whereas Love looks for a bond and enjoys life side by side. In a mature relationship, joy is in being with others, becoming compatible with friends, not just in the exclusive relationship, and there is no desire to capture, control or own anyone. **Adrenalin/Sex** hormones are released in attached relationships and have to do with conquest. **Endorphins** are released accompanying joy and happiness in a spiritually aligned relationship. In infatuation, left-brain physicality prevails. The right-brain etheric body plays a large part in an aligned relationship.

In infatuation, bodily functions are impaired, with loss of appetite and sleep, whereas in a spiritually aligned relationship, the body improves and heals. In infatuation, judgment is impaired, whereas in a spiritual relationship, it is improved and one can work out things with the other person mutually through the mind, improving rationality. Within the infinite field of consciousness, everyone is answerable. Awareness of this curtails extremism. Glamorization makes things more tempting and is a part of addictions to the ego's payoff.

The self-image in infatuation is inflated-getting what one wants makes one spiritually worse off than if one did not get it. The inflation of the narcissist is self-feeding. Love results in a positive effect on self-image, with fulfillment of the potentiality of happiness. The loss of the relationship in infatuation can result in depression, rage, hate, blame, murder, and suicide. The loss of a loving relationship can result in sadness at loss and regret, which is different from depression, hate, murder, or suicide. The social image of infatuation is over-stimulated, out-of-control, impaired, "foolish," "madness", with the emotional quality of frustration/anxiety. In a truly loving relationship, the image has the qualities of gratitude, balance, steady calmness, feeling settled and more stable, and flexibility with the changes that occur in life, even if the relationship ends at some point.

The Dualities of Shame (1)

Attraction	Aversion
Self-punitive	Self-forgiveness
Depression	Choose Life
Judgmental	Surrender to God's Mercy
Negativity	Let go of position
Shrink, hide	Be visible
Self as worthless	Affirm gift of life
Rigid self view	Correctable, flexible
Condemn	Forgive
Mortification	Choose self-worth
Denigrate	Honor self
Self-hatred	Self-forgiveness
Severe	Benign
Imbalanced	See both sides

Slide 47

SLIDE 47: THE DUALITIES OF SHAME (1)

This slide was introduced at the May 2005 lecture, DVD disc 2 at 010600.

Shame is the bottom level and often shows up as disgrace, depression, and hopelessness. It sometimes takes clinical forms, which can show up as suicide or the failure to take the necessary steps to survive. Clinically, shame is a pharmacological problem and has correlation to neurotransmitters in the brain. Depletion of these chemicals allows one to drop to the depths. Death is the alternative and will occur if no intervention takes place to help the person.

Shame is banishment. In primitive society, life depended on integrity of the local tribe. Banishment in shame from the tribe left a person without means to survive and death ensued, so shame was equivalent to death. Shame, at calibration 20, is very close to death. People with shame shrink, they disappear, try to become invisible, have self-hatred, and give up all hope.

This level is a consequence of many things - the denial of God is one and karmic consequence is another. Paradoxically, some people have to hit this bottom before the ego will give up. Only when they are clinging to life by their fingers will they let go.

At the level of Shame, the attraction is to be **self-punitive** while the aversion is to be its opposite or **self-forgiving**. Attraction is to **depression**, with aversion to **choosing life**. One is attracted to be **judgmental** against oneself instead of **surrendering to God's mercy**; be **negative** rather than **let go of a position**. One wants to **shrink and hide** rather than **be visible**. One is attracted to seeing **self as worthless**, with an aversion to **affirming the gift of life** itself. One likes an unforgiving and **rigid self view**, and is unwilling to **correct it and be flexible**. At the level of Shame, one would rather **condemn** than **forgive**, as one seeks **mortification** rather than **choosing self-worth**. The physicality of the body is a gift of being human. Why mortify it? At one time, the Gothic downside of religion was into mortification of the body, e.g. sackcloth and ashes and hair shirts.

One is attracted to **denigrating** value and worth rather than **honoring oneself**. A spiritually aligned person owes it as an obligation to honor one's self, to honor one's dedication. However, at the level of Shame, one indulges in **self-hatred** rather than **self-forgiveness**. The ego loves hatred and negativity, thriving on the juice it gets out of its positions. It has only animal energy, not kundalini spiritual energy. Kundalini energy would influence the field and things would come about effortlessly. The ego at the level of Shame loves to be **severe** rather than to be **benign**, and is **imbalanced** in not wanting to **see both sides** of a position.

The Dualities of Shame (2)

Attraction	Aversion
Blame self	Blame ego's ignorance
Exaggerate faults	Transcend limitations
Partial selective view	Overall view - balanced
Self as loser	Self as corrected
End of the road	Beginning of the new
Unlovable	Worth as child of God
Error unforgivable	Error as lesson
Narcissistic orientation	Concern for others
Serve self	Serve life
Indulgent self-evaluation	Let go of egoistic position
Self as center of life	Self as participant in life
Focus on self	Focus on others
"Should have"	Was not able then

Slide 48

SLIDE 48: THE DUALITIES OF SHAME (2)

This slide was introduced at the May 2005 lecture, DVD disc 2 at 010600.

Any of these negativities at the level of **Shame** can be undone by practicing the simple virtues, as discussed in the slide "Spiritual Foundation - The Virtues". One has an obligation to be responsible for one's life as a gift. Risking your life unnecessarily for a cheap thrill is a spiritual violation and not integrous. Spiritual responsibility is accepting stewardship of your assets. Spiritual devotion is a tremendous asset. Only one in ten million persons has enlightenment as an ultimate goal.

At the level of Shame, attraction is to **blaming oneself** rather than blaming the **ego's ignorance**, thus refuting the wisdom of Socrates: "it seemed like the best decision at the time." To stop blaming oneself, one needs to see that the context was different then, and not the same as now. One was more limited then. The attraction is to **exaggerate faults** while aversion is to its opposite, which is to **transcend limitations**. You want to maintain a **partial selective view** rather than becoming **balanced**. One sees **self as loser** rather than **self as in need of correction**. One wants to see life as the **end of the road** instead of **beginning of the new**. One sees self as absolutely **unlovable** and denies **worth as a child of God**. All that exists arises from one Source.

The problem at this level is in viewing **error as unforgivable**, rather than **error as lesson**. It is because of the **narcissistic orientation** - "all me, my guilt, my error; oh, how unforgivable," with no **concern for others** who are also experiencing the effects of one's thoughts and self-dialog. At the level of Shame one is highly self-centered and focused on **serving self** rather than **serving life**. There is the attraction to **indulgent self-evaluation**, wallowing in guilt and shame, penance, sackcloth and ashes, a poor, suffering martyr, and aversion to **letting go of the egoistic position**. There is confusion in viewing **self as center of life** rather than **self as a participant in life**. The **focus is on self** rather than **focus on others**, holding onto misery from the past and milking it in the present. A retrospective falsification is in saying "**should have**", instead of realizing that one **was not able then** to be different.

In spiritual work, you must hold Socrates' dictum in mind, that "All men choose only the good." This takes you out of hatred, blame and self-condemnation. One can only choose the good, even if that is to kill someone or to blow up infidels. Jesus said, "Forgive them, for they know not what they do." The Christ is an energy field that became embodied in the person of Jesus of Nazareth and all humans have that same potential to realize Christ consciousness through forgiving, loving and giving rather than being stuck at lowest levels of consciousness such as Shame.

The Dualities of Guilt and Hate (1)

Attraction	Aversion
Make judgment	Surrender judgment to God
Punish self or others	Forgive self or others
Refuse mercy	Accept mercy and compassion
Justify negativity	Surrender secret pleasure
Project feelings	Take responsibility
Choose perception	Choose essence
Rigid, narrow view	Flexible, see both sides
Penance, self-indulgence	Service to others
Cling to position	Ask God for miracles
Reinforce	Relent, choose options
Act out	Transcend
Enjoy meanness	Enjoy being gracious to self/others

Slide 49

SLIDE 49: THE DUALITIES OF GUILT AND HATE (1)

This slide was introduced at the June 2005 lecture, DVD disc 2 at 004000.

There is only one real attraction and that is to the payoff of your current position. One has to disassemble that current position and see what you are is getting out of it, such as being the loser or the victim. Being a "victim" is the biggest payoff in today's society after "being right," which beats them all. The attraction at this level is to **make judgment** toward one's self and others. "Judge not," says the Lord. When we re-contextualize Divinity as a gigantic electromagnetic field and one is an electron or 'a little magnetic iron filing', that changes the way you experience guilt. You see that the way you have been "programmed" has led you to that state. Out of your intrinsic innocence, you chose judgmentalism because you thought it was for the greatest good at the time. The mind is like a computer and the basic hardware will play any program and cannot defend itself against falsehood. It only takes an instant to get programmed and the human mind cannot defend itself against being programmed. Practically everyone is the victim of their own innocent programming. That is why fascism, totalitarianism and others seek the children and indoctrinate them by replacing the authority of the parent.

In guilt, you want to **punish one's self (or others)**, because they have been programmed. One **refuses God's mercy**, **justifies negativity**, and **projects feelings** on to others. It is a rigid, narrow view, which calls for penance, a self-indulgence. The ego clings to the position of guilt, reinforces it and enjoys its meanness because one projects it onto others. Guilt and hate go extremely well together. Instead of hating one's own self, one projects it into the world and hates "them." One has to have somebody out there to cast blame on, as part of the perpetrator/victim model that is very popular in society. It is a dualistic positionality coming out of the distorted hermeneutics of relativistic epistemology. That is what ails society today - the distorted understanding of what is true by denying that there is the Absolute, by which meaning can be discerned. As the author of *Alice in Wonderland* Lewis Carroll said, "A word means what I want it to mean, neither more nor less."

Those above are the attractions. There are also aversions, such as surrendering judgment to God. We do not have the capacity to judge. At the level of Guilt, there is aversion to forgiving oneself and others, accepting mercy and compassion, surrendering secret pleasures, or taking responsibility. These come from not choosing essence, refusing to be flexible and to see both sides of issues, and not being of service to others. There is reluctance to ask God for a miracle and re-contextualization. The miracle is a consequence of asking Divinity to take one out of the perceptual fixation one has so one can see it from a greater context. When the context expands, the problem dissolves. Reluctance to forgive yourself and others is because of the juice one gets out of guilt and hate, which becomes self-indulgence.

The Dualities of Guilt and Hate (2)

Attraction	**Aversion**
Act against self and others	**Act to help self and others**
Choose the negative	**Choose the positive**
Be "right"	**Be wrong**
Helpless, stuck	**Flexible, grow**
Reinforce	**Transcend**
Stuck in past	**Live in the now**
Malignant, cruel	**Benign, merciful**
Stingy	**Benevolent**
Project responsibility	**Choose to be author**
Vengeful	**Merciful**
Be small	**Choose "bigger than that"**
Grasping	**Benevolent**

Slide 50

SLIDE 50: THE DUALITIES OF GUILT AND HATE (2)

This slide was introduced at the June 2005 lecture, DVD disc 2 at 004000.

Continuing on the theme of positionalities that hold the state of **Guilt** and **Hate** in place, you see that an attraction in this state is to **act against self and others** instead of **acting to help self and others** by supporting life in all its expressions. Another attraction in this state is to **choose the negative** instead of the **positive**, and to maintain a position of "**being right**" instead of admitting that you can **be wrong** because the mind is prone to error. One does not have the energy or inclination in this state to be **flexible and grow** and is therefore **stuck** in a **helpless** state that gets reinforced by a continuing refusal to transcend it. One is attracted to being **stingy, malignant, cruel and stuck in the past** instead of being **benevolent, benign and merciful** while **living in the present** which is the only time that is actually available.

Instead of choosing to be **responsible** for one's own life by being kind and **merciful** towards all of life, one **projects** one's innate power to the world "out there" and becomes **vengeful** when others do not act in the manner expected. The attraction in this state is to **be small** and grasp at straws instead of **choosing to be "bigger than that"** and **benevolent** towards all of life.

The states of Shame, Guilt, and Apathy are hellish to experience in the human domain, even though other possibilities of much greater happiness exist here. In the depths of hell, hopelessness, despair and agony are beyond description and they are eternal-*forever*; condemned to the dark, the blackness and hopelessness without possibility of any intervention from anywhere in time because one's state is outside of time. The soul is lost and abandoned forever. The top level of hell is agony, suffering and torture-child's play. Then it gets even more severe, with agony beyond description. On descension, you come to a knowingness, as Dante did, to "abandon all hope all who enter here." Beyond that is damnation and hopelessness for eternity. As Dr. Hawkins shared on many occasions, "Out of this eternity of hopelessness, a voice arose that said: 'If there is a God, I ask Him for help.' Then everything blacked out and there was oblivion. Next thing I was standing in the full radiance of Divinity as the Allness of Creation and Life Itself. If that is what it takes, that is what it takes. I don't recommend it."

The purpose of the human domain seems to be for the ego to hit bottom and surrender to God. Therefore, this world is perfect even though there is much suffering involved, especially at the lowest levels of consciousness.

The Dualities of Apathy (1)

Attraction	**Aversion**
Blame, project "cause"	**Responsibility, own**
"I can't"	**"I won't"**
See self as victim	**See self as co-player**
Indifference	**Caring**
Defeatist	**Optimist**
Justify, rationalize, excuse	**Take action**
See self as helpless	**See self as able**
Hopeless	**Hope**
Negate self-worth	**Choose self-worth as gift from God**
See self as weak	**See self as potentially strong**
Effuse solutions	**Willing, accept**
Self-sabotage	**Self-endorsement**
Indolence, sloth	**Energy of action**

Slide 51

SLIDE 51: THE DUALITIES OF APATHY (1)

This slide was introduced at the July 2005 lecture, DVD disc 2 at 011300.

In apathy, one says, **"I can't"** handle things. The truth is **one "won't"** handle things. One **sees self as victim** and the aversion is **seeing oneself as a co-player** in life. Apathy is a lack of taking **responsibility**. Why is Apathy a spiritual violation? It is because **sloth** is one of the seven cardinal sins, being a lack of respect for the divine gift of life itself and a **negation of one's worth** and that of everyone else. An example would be to not pick up the newspapers or trash lying on the sidewalk and dispose of them properly. The appropriate **action** is to have reverence for life itself, including one's own life.

In Apathy, one thinks of all the **excuses** and sees oneself as victim. There is **indifference** instead of **caring**; a **defeatist** attitude instead of being an **optimist**. You **rationalize an excuse** because of being **helpless and hopeless**, which are denials and spiritual errors that negate one's **self-worth and one's life as a gift from God**. The aversion is to see, to choose, to revere and to respect one's life. As Dr. Hawkins said, "The life in this body I respect: I take the medication for this, I take the medication for that, because this life is a gift and the purpose is to serve God to the fullest extent."

There is an aversion to **seeing oneself as able**, which can only come through **willingness**. The only power out of this situation is the Will. One has to learn to surrender to God and say, "Dear God, I of myself don't have the energy or the know-how to transcend this level." Then, you surrender to Divine Will, which is what energizes us all. There is not enough energy coming out of the ego because it is getting too much payoff from being hopeless and is coming from negation of self-worth. The aversion is to an affirmation of one's self worth and seeing life as a gift from God.

Another attraction is to **see oneself as weak**, with the aversion being to **see oneself as potentially strong**; attraction is to **self-sabotage**; the aversion is to **self-endorsement**. Apathy is a negation of the reality of Divinity as an expression of one's own life.

The Dualities of Apathy (2)

Attraction	**Aversion**
Pessimism, cynical	**Trust, faith, hope**
See self as unworthy	**Accept value of life**
Future looks bleak	**Future holds opportunity**
See self as incapable	**See self as willing to learn**
Rigid, inflexible	**Malleable, capable of growth**
Passive	**Active**
Reject help	**Accept help**
Self-pity	**Compassion, then move on**
Cling to position	**Surrender positionality**
Self-indulgence	**Move on**
Excuse	**Self-honesty**
Sink lower	**Evolve, move up**
Succumb	**Resist**

Slide 52

SLIDE 52: THE DUALITIES OF APATHY (2)

This slide was introduced at the July 2005 lecture, DVD disc 2 at 011700.

In Apathy, there is the indulgence in the attractions of **pessimism, unworthiness, passivity, self-pity, to excuse, to sink lower, and to succumb**. The aversions are to the upside: **trust, faith and hope, accepting help, compassion, and moving on**. "Get over It," a song by The Eagles is a reminder that it is time to let go of self-pity and move on. "We heard you lost both legs and your left ear, and now you're blind and in a wheelchair; So? Get over it!" You have to get over it to embrace the wonder of life available at the higher levels of consciousness.

We tend to become like what we hold as the "ego ideal", the people we respect and look up to and whose value is unquestioned. We hold them as picture images within ourselves to identify with, using Freudian concepts. People who are a failure have hostility toward success. They are "anti-America, anti-Wal-Mart, anti-court, anti-president." They do not understand that the way to become successful is to become like those who are successful. The lesson is not to revile successful people, but instead to picture how they became that way and to use them as a pattern, through identification.

All persons in spiritual work hold a spiritual ideal, a teacher, a spiritual figure, somebody inspiring who speaks to us and we can relate to, even if it is a soldier walking into a hail of bullets. As an example, Dr. Hawkins shared: "I look at the guy and I can tell, despite terror, by God, he's going to do it; I already 'got it' from the heart: I 'got it', and intuitively he gets that I 'got it'." One who "gets" the reality of another person feeds that reality back to that person and it is through the one who "gets it" that the evolution of consciousness occurs. One "gets" the Divinity of the Essence of That Which Everyone Is and affirms it in the heart, for the warrior and for the woman in difficult childbirth before there was anesthesia. When we identify with them, we strengthen man's way out. What we can do for humanity is to own our own Reality, acknowledge it and reverberate it to others. Those who are valorous own their valor within and give it strength and recognition. In that way, all of humanity becomes valorous. That is how we all evolve together.

The Dualities of Grief (1)

Attraction	Aversion
Cling to	Let go of
Live in past	Live in the now
Hope to undo	Accept
Bargain with God	Accept limitation - karma
Hope to change, entreaty	Surrender
See as loss	See as opportunity to move on
Refuse, deny	Work through
Anger, resentment	Acceptance
Self-blame	Accept limitation
Feel empty	Replace with new values
Love	Compensate
Equate other with source of happiness	See happiness as internal

Slide 53

SLIDE 53: THE DUALITIES OF GRIEF (1)

This slide was introduced at the August 2005 lecture, DVD disc 2 at 004400.

We **cling to grief** because we can juice it and **live in the past**. We **bargain with God**, **see it as a loss**, have **anger, resentment, feel empty**; the aversion is to get over it and **accept** it. One has to **accept** the imperfection of 'personal' human life as part of the overall perfection of human life itself. The ultimate purpose of human life is to realize that one is permanent, universal and impersonal, by transcending that which seems to be transient, local and personal.

Grief is the level of sadness, loss, and despondency. Most people have experienced it for some of the time but those who remain at this level live a life of constant regret and depression. This is the level of mourning, bereavement, and remorse about the past. It is also the level of habitual losers and those chronic gamblers who accept failure as part of their lifestyle, often resulting in the loss of jobs, friends, family, and opportunity, as well as money and health. There is a generalization from the particular, so that the loss of a loved one is equated with the loss of love itself. Such emotional losses may trigger a serious depression or even death. At this level, one is unwilling to work through the grief, accept one's limitations and see happiness as internal rather than external.

The universality of the experience is due to the structure and nature of the ego, which misperceives the source of happiness as external and imbues it with specialness. In reality, the only source of happiness is from within, and its mechanism is intrapsychic and internal. When a desired object, situation, or relationship is obtained, the internal mechanism goes into operation with the satisfaction of that desire because the object, person, or condition had been imbued with special qualities. The value of what is perceived is in the eyes of the beholder and is not intrinsic to the desired object or person itself. Therefore, grief is associated with desire as well as ownership.

The value of the pathway of negation is that one lets go of their attachment to seeing something external as a source of their happiness. Then there is the realization that the source of **happiness is internal**. Grief saw the source of happiness as, "**You are my happiness**". This will put you in a bad place, but "You contribute and support my happiness" is a good place to be. When there is the attitude that "You are the source, you are it, and if I lose you, I lose it all," one goes into grief, and wants to go back in time. The attraction of this is the emotionality of it. You see the source of happiness as "out there".

Life is full of solutions; it goes from perfection to perfection. It does not move from imperfection to perfection or from incomplete to complete. The unfolding flower is a perfect half-unfolded flower, next it is a perfect drooping flower, a little later it is a perfect withered flower, and finally it is a perfect seed for the next year. Everything is perfectly the fulfillment of its own potentiality as it actualizes. It is the downside or the tragedies in the world that tend to give us the ambition to transcend the lower levels of consciousness such as Grief.

The Dualities of Grief (2)

Attraction	**Aversion**
Dependent on externals	**Depend on self**
Resist	**Transcend**
Despondency	**Hope**
Go back in time	**Move forward to options**
Emotionalize	**Minimize**
Seek sympathy	**Sufficiency of self**
Avoid, control	**Accept, work through**
See loss as permanent	**See loss as temporary**
See source of happiness as as "out there"	**See source of happiness as "in here"**
Irreplaceable	**Future has promise**
Life full of problems	**Life full of solutions**
Bitter	**Faith and hope**

Slide 54

SLIDE 54: THE DUALITIES OF GRIEF (2)

This slide was first introduced at the August 2005 lecture, DVD disc 2 at 004430.

The duality of grief is clinging to the past instead of relinquishing it to God, and thinking that the source of happiness has been lost. The source of happiness cannot be lost as the source of happiness is the presence of Divinity within oneself as the source of one's existence; a posture of humble gratitude for the Presence within counters and makes up for any external losses. The aversions are to letting go of the past, to accepting change as normal, and to the willingness to surrender one's willfulness to God.

Every loss is also an opportunity for freedom. One is now free to **move on**. For example, if the body does not work as well anymore, you are now free to work on spiritual or intellectual pursuits. In other words, there is an upside innate to every situation. **Acceptance** brings in awareness and you **see the source of happiness within**. All negative feelings are due to **seeing the source of happiness outside of oneself**.

People would say grief is inevitable. Everybody goes through grief in life. It starts out in early childhood, and reoccurs at various points along one's life. Some people know how to handle grief; they do not fight it, but experience it out. One way to transcend these lower levels of emotions is to stop resisting them and experience them out. How does one experience a thing out? You experience it out by letting go of resisting it and saying instead, "I am going to experience this out". That is the way one gets rid of it. You get a temporary discomfort, but a long-term gain. If you do not experience it out, 30 years later you're still grieving the same thing. Some people are still pumping for all it is worth even 30 years later. You can choose to move on instead.

The attraction at all the lower levels of consciousness is clinging to the "juice" of the narcissistic gain of the ego. One starts to see that at the bottom of all these positions is narcissistic gain. You do not have to surrender multiple things, but only the narcissistic gain; this eliminates all of them and they disappear. As Dr. Hawkins shared, "I remember a point in my own spiritual evolution where letting go of a 'key' thing suddenly helped all related things disappear as they were all hooked into narcissistic gain." The narcissistic gain does not care, as one sees it in the messianic megalomaniac. Narcissistic gain does not care if you kill 10 million of your fellow humans and your entire family. The narcissistic ego takes glee in plotting the ultimate "dirty" bomb that will eliminate all of human life. It is routine to kill millions; therefore, it gives one respect for the narcissistic ego and a sense of urgency to transcend its limitations.

The Dualities of Fear (1)

Attraction	**Aversion**
Excitement of danger	**Stay "cool"**
Panic, overreact	**Miss opportunity**
Dramatize	**Handle calmly**
Emphasize	**Deflate**
Gain attention, help	**Self-sufficient**
Survive	**Trust God**
Protect	**Lose, loss**
Control	**Surrender**
Emotionalism	**Think clearly**
Exaggerate	**Minimize**
Imagine	**Stay logical**
Project to the future	**Live in the now**

Slide 55

SLIDE 55: THE DUALITIES OF FEAR (1)

This slide was introduced at the August 2005 lecture, DVD disc 2 at 004600.

Everyone knows fear, the **excitement of danger**, **dramatizing**, and the **emotionalism**. Fear has to do with being on the front of the wave of experiencing. Grief is clinging to the past, and fear is anticipating the future. Equanimity and peace is to be right on the peak of the wave, without resisting the future or clinging to the past, with neither attraction nor aversion. People have an aversion unless they have already had training to **stay "cool"**. In the military, the more danger one is in, the "cooler" one must be, and no one wants anyone to emotionalize. If Kamikaze pilots heard a military man blubbering, he is not going to be much help. Because if you are on a 20mm aircraft gun, you had better stay cool. Emotionalizing stops when a situation gets really serious. No one has the time for emotionalizing then because everyone's life is on the spot. All emotionalizing is self-indulgence. People have an aversion to staying **calm** in the middle of disaster. People want to **exaggerate** and scream. Why would anyone want to scream in a tornado when you are trying to hang onto the dog and cat while going up into the air?

Something interesting about the Weather Channel: they have reports on hurricanes and tornadoes. The survivors of the natural disasters who were interviewed had something in common, and that is that they all prayed. There was a lady who was pinned down for 48 hours with no water or food and with no way for anyone to get to her. She said, "I just prayed." In some of the accounts of the survivors of tornadoes, they report being lifted up some 100 feet in the air, and how they went into a state of sublime peace.

We let go of fear by seeing it as the indulgence of the child within. Caution is different from fear; caution is thinking, anticipating, but not emotionalizing. Fear is going into hysteria and coming apart. You cannot come apart if the situation is one of real danger, where you need to stay cool. One has to learn to **handle it calmly**. In the end, you can **surrender** constantly, and **trust God**. Even while facing death, emotionalizing is not necessary. With acceptance, you transcend into serenity. Death is not a possibility for the real part of us, and on a certain level, everyone knows that.

In a near death experience, you see a major jump in consciousness after the experience. In the out of body experience, one does not see any change at all. The person at a level of 340 who goes out of body for the first time, when he comes back into the body he still calibrates at 340. A person who experiences a near death experience, on the other hand, when he comes back, he generally calibrates at 560-570. "Out of body" experiences are merely experiencing yourself as a spirit out of the body, and you already knew that you are spirit when out of body. When one is out of the body, it is more familiar than being in a body. In spirit, wherever one thinks one is, one is there. We let go of the fear of death by total acceptance of ourselves as spirit, as our survival depends completely on God. With that mindset, one surrenders one's life to God, trusts God, and if it is time to leave this planet, you happily leave.

The Dualities of Fear (2)

Attraction	**Aversion**
Proliferate	**Suppress imagination**
See enemies	**See safety**
Resist, defend, avoid	**Accept**
Elaborate, escalate	**Reduce perceptions**
Harbor	**Shame, work through**
Justify	**View realistically**
Project cause	**Own responsibly**
Death	**See life as eternal**
Focus on body	**Focus on spirit**
See life as physical	**See spiritual as reality**
Loss: youth, money, possessions	**See source of happiness as intrinsic**
Loss of love of others	**See Self as Source**

Slide 56

SLIDE 56: THE DUALITIES OF FEAR (2)

This slide was first introduced at the August 2005 lecture, disc 2 at 005300.

You could surely say fear does not have an upside, but you would be wrong. Yes, fear does have an upside: the adrenaline, the excitement, and all the exaggerated importance of things. When you are living in a state of fear as a lifestyle, fears tend to proliferate and one likes to **harbor fears, justify them, and project the cause** as "out there in the world". One thinks the "cause" of the fear is external, like the fear of the Komodo dragon, that "he (the Komodo dragon)" is the one causing one's fear. The attraction is to **see enemies** externally and the aversion is to **see safety** within the all-encompassing field of Consciousness. At the level of fear, you are not prepared to **accept** what is, and are unconsciously or consciously in **resistance**, **defending** your position and **avoiding** facing the truth. Fear sees life as strictly **physical**, and it **focuses on the body**.

In some systems of training, such as the EST training that was popular in the 1970s, they used to talk about stacks. Fear is a big stack, and at the bottom of the stack is the fear of physical death. In surrendering a stack of fears, a technique called "And then what?" can be used to get to the bottom of the stack, which is where surrender will help in getting rid of the entire stack of fears. One takes a fear and says, "And then what?" For example:

I lost my car. And then what?

I won't have transportation. And then what?

I will lose my job. And then what?

I will have to walk to work. And then what?

There aren't any jobs like that. And then what?

I'll be poor. And then what?

I will starve. And then what?

I will die. The bottom of every stack of fears is the fear of physical death. When you can say "so what" to physical death, nothing scares you anymore. It is a basic fear that once surrendered brings down the whole stack. From that point onward, you can increasingly **see the source of happiness as intrinsic** to existence and your **reality as spiritual**, instead of physical.

The Dualities of Desire

Attraction	**Aversion**
Win, gain	**Lose**
Money	**Poverty**
Control	**Passive**
Get	**Lose**
Crave	**Frustrated**
Force	**Weakness**
Approval	**Criticism**
Success	**Failure**
Fame	**Anonymity**
Stubborn	**Give in**
Aggression	**Submission**
Resist	**Change**
Defend	**Give in**
Acquisition	**Poverty**
Conquest	**Lose**
Popularity	**Unnoticed**

Slide 57

SLIDE 57: THE DUALITIES OF DESIRE

This slide was first introduced at the August 2005 lecture, DVD disc 2 at 005500.

Desire is the state that bothers most of the people, most of the time. Fears and grief come along, people are apathetic about certain things in their life, but desire and wantingness is the one that really bothers most people. The attractions in this state are to **winning, money, gain, control, getting, approval, success, fame, acquisitions, conquest,** and of course being right. People are willing to die to be right. The ego does not mind dumping the body at all. Rather than admit defeat, the ego will walk one over the cliff. People die for illusions all the time. In Dr. Hawkins' lifetime, a hundred million people or more died chasing some illusion rather that admitting they were wrong. Chairman Mao's economic agricultural plan resulted in the starvation of 30 million people. "The Little Red Book", the faith in Chairman Mao resulted in the death of 30 million; it was the greatest famine in all of history. After that, you would think humanity would get that Marxism is not the right way.

The inability to learn is due to the pride of the ego. The desire to be right, to control, the need for approval; we are familiar with these because they are a part of everyday life. All fears of feeling **passive, weak, failure, poverty,** and **losing** are the aversions. Many people desire to be **popular**, as we see displayed in the media the extremes people will go to, to just be noticed. They will say anything outrageous as long as they are on camera. Describing the attractions in the state of desire in a humorous way in the words of Dr. Hawkins, "I want it to be immediate, I want to control it, to crave it, to force it, I am going to have success, I am going to be stubbornly aggressive, I am going to defend it, and conquer it".

The aversions are to loss. There is nothing wrong with poverty, if you do not resist it. As Dr, Hawkins has shared, "I was happy being poor. I have been poor, I have been rich and frankly there is no difference between the two. You get up that day and you are happy or you are not happy. When I first came to the West, I slept on a cot I got at the Dime Store. We had an apple to celebrate any special occasions. I tested the teachings of *A Course in Miracles*. I left the house with no money, no food, and everything was provided for me. By 11:00 AM someone would say, 'What are you doing for lunch? Come along with me.' Everything I needed just appeared. I drove the old truck to Sedona; just as I needed a pair of pliers to fix the truck, on the side of the road was a brand new, never used pair. I fixed what I needed and went on. Everything went that way. It is true you do not need anything at all except faith.

The Dualities of Anger

Attraction	Aversion
Act out feeling	Self-control
Intimidate	Forgive
Hold on	Let go
Punish, get even	"Go Scot free"
Self-vindication	Exoneration
Dump on others	Restraint
Excitement, "stirred up"	Stay "cool"
Emotionalize	Think
Dramatize	Ignore
Express	Stifle
Prove self	Dismiss
Be right	Thought to be wrong
Enlist support	Keep to oneself
Puff up	Appear weak
"Macho"	"Wimp"
Growl, show teeth	Be calm
Excitement	Peace

Slide 58

SLIDE 58: THE DUALITIES OF ANGER

This slide was first introduced at the August 2005 lecture, DVD disc 2 at 005730.

The state of Anger is closer to the animal world, as one feels expanded. One is stirred up, bigger than life with anger. It allows one to **dramatize** and **emotionalize**. To be right, the animal **growls** and **shows its teeth**, tries to win by **intimidation**. The last thing it wants is to **be calm** or to be at **peace**. It is afraid it will **appear weak**. It does not want to give in. It does not want to see a bad person "**go scot free**".

The Buddha said one does not have to get even with one's enemies, because they will bring themselves down by their own hand. The world specializes in righteous anger. It loves righteous anger because one can **be right**, **puff up**, get all the narcissistic swelling, and become bigger than one really is. The ego thinks if it swells, it is more important. The fact is that it is not more important, but just a swollen ego.

As with other levels, positionalities result in conflicting dualities that require the surrender of the transitory pleasure of indulgence of the attractions such as getting even, acting out, etc. and the resistance to the aversions, such as letting them go scot-free, **self-control**, etc. Willingness enables the surrender of short-term self-indulgence of attractions and aversions for long-term spiritual growth.

Dualities of Pride

Attraction	**Aversion**
Vain, proud	**Humility, humble**
Be more	**Be less**
Important	**Nobody**
Admired	**Looked down on**
Status	**Common, ordinary**
Noticed	**Ignored**
Special	**Ordinary**
Better than	**The same**
Superior	**Inferior**
Attractive, fashionable	**Dull**
Be right	**Wrong**
Opinionated	**Silent**
Thrill	**Dull, pedestrian**
"Insider"	**Excluded**
Exclusive	**Common**
Succeed	**Fail**

Slide 59

SLIDE 59: DUALITIES OF PRIDE

This slide was first introduced at the August 2005 lecture, DVD disc 2 at 005840.

Pride is a projection one imposes. It gives you **status**, you get **noticed**, you get to feel **superior**, and you get to be an **"insider"**. One gets to be elite, and to be politically correct. You get to be above common people, which are the paradox of egalitarianism, which really means that all people are of equal value.

The aversion in pride is **humility**. This aversion arises out of the fear that you may be **looked down upon**, because you are **ordinary** and not special. One of the worst things for people is to be thought **wrong**; people would rather die than to be thought of as wrong. A whole generation would rather die than admit they are following a false teacher.

Vanity and pride make one feel **superior,** which is elitism. In pride one gets to be noticed, one gets to be **better than** others, one thinks it gives one **status**, and it makes one feel **important**. The payoff is difficult to transcend because one has to have humility. The narcissistic ego would rather die than to be humble. It would rather die than to say, "I do not know."

Spiritual evolution is rooted in humility as true spiritual understanding comes from revelation. Spiritual evolution is not the acquisition of new information, but in putting that information to work to realize the truth. The ego inflation of spiritual pride is different from self-esteem, which is earned through achievement of goals. For example, one is walking along not thinking about anything and a revelation comes spontaneously. One is walking by a beetle and it comes to you to turn the beetle over and give him a chance to continue to do what it was doing. You do not get this understanding from reading a book; it is an automatic consequence of what one has become. One has caringness about life in all its expressions, innate to what one has become.

Comparative Dualities

Anticipated Pleasure	The Fears
Control	Surrender
Familiarity, habit	Change, uncertainty, strangeness
Cling to the old	Fear of the unknown or the new
Easy way	Hard, effort
Ignore, deny, reject	Upset, look at, face
Refuse to own	Take responsibility, be accountable
"I can't"	The truth of "I won't"
"Don't want to"	"Can't"
Rigidity, repetitious	Learn
Homeostasis, stability	Reprogram, shift, off-balance
The past as an excuse	The present as the change agent
"No will power"	Confront with lack of willingness
"Try," "going to"	Do
"Tomorrow"	Now
Procrastinate	Failure
Pretend	Be honest
Unwilling, resistance	Acceptance

Slide 60

SLIDE 60: COMPARATIVE DUALITIES

This slide was first introduced at the June 2005 lecture, DVD disc 2 at 005000.

One of the main pleasures of the ego is **control**. To control the media, one's image, what people think, finances, everything can become an issue of control. Control implies trusting the linear, letting go of control is trusting in the nonlinear field. Control is seeing oneself as the cause and effect, seeing oneself as the silent agency, the inner controller called "I". The "I" has to control everything, because in the animal kingdom, unless it does, it expires. The ego depends on content. One of the anticipated pleasures of remaining where you are in consciousness is familiarity with the position. You are used to being angry and stupid because it is comfortable and familiar.

People get arrested for being part of the "street culture", and they then go into a prison culture identical to the culture on the street. When they get out of prison, they go right back to the same "street culture". Society wonders why these people have not been reformed or rehabilitated. It is because the person feels **familiar** and at home with the "street culture" and refuses to leave it. People **cling to the old** because it is the **easy way**. One can **ignore, deny, and reject** alternatives. The aversion is to **surrendering** control. One does not like to change, because it feels **uncertain** when you let go of what is familiar. You cling to the old because of the **fear of the unknown and the new**. The fear is that it seems **hard** to change. People would rather ignore the negativity than to be **upset** or **face** an issue. The aversion is that to become different requires one to **take responsibility** and **be accountable**. At some point, you realize that change is perceived as difficult because you are resisting it. When you let go of resisting change, it becomes less difficult and even looked forward to.

The human mind is programmed and is easily misled. Instead of seeing other people or oneself as "wrong", you can see them as misled. Karmic reasons or one's evolution of consciousness may play a role. It seems easier to ignore a problem than to "look" at it. The upset is due to the resistance in owning the problem; it is easier to refuse it than to own it. It is easier to project blame on to others than to take responsibility and be accountable. The biggest excuse of all is, "I **can't**". At the bottom of all of the resistances is the unwillingness to **surrender** the issue to God. Humility removes most of these blocks.

What one must realize is **the present as the change agent**. You can move from hell to heaven in a tenth of a second. For some egos, it takes the extremes of hell before they will let go. There is no point in blaming the degree of suffering that occurs in your life, because if that is what it takes, that is what it takes. One's will power is only as strong as one's level of consciousness. However, surrendering to the Will of God, or Divine Will calibrates at 850 and is capable of the miraculous. Will power is that it is the denial of "willingness". It is because one **lacks willingness** that one has not already transcended the issue. It is more comfortable to **procrastinate** than to just do it. The fear is that you will **fail**, and underlying the fear is pride. So what if one fails? As the saying goes, "if you fail, try, try again". The power you need, is to **be honest**.

The True Nature of Divinity

	Calibration Level
Reality as witness/observer	600
Arhat	800
Seeing into one's "self-nature"	845
Void	850
Oneness	850
Nothingness	850
Reality as Consciousness	850
Reality as Awareness	850
Omniscience	850
Omnipresence	850
Omnipotence	850
Allness	855
The Buddha	1,000
The Creator	Infinity
Divinity	Infinity
God	Infinity

Slide 61

SLIDE 61: THE TRUE NATURE OF DIVINITY

This slide was first introduced at the November 2005 lecture, DVD disc 2 at 011800.

Calibrating the levels of consciousness is not a personal view. It is a teaching mechanism, a way of confirming various levels of consciousness. For example, someone asked about a particular teacher who claims to be an **Arhat**, but differs from the traditional interpretation of the Pali Canon of the Buddhist tradition. The only way to determine this was through calibrating it. In fact, the teacher in question was indeed extremely high and had correctly interpreted the teachings of the Pali Canon. The Arhat calibrates at 800, while seeing into **one's self-nature** calibrates at 845.

The **Void, Oneness, Nothingness, Reality as Consciousness, Reality as Awareness, Omniscience, Omnipresence, Omnipotence**, all calibrate at 850. **Allness** calibrates at 855. These are all qualities of **Divinity**, but they are not the Essence of Divinity. Traditionally **God** is described as **Omniscience, Omnipresence, and Omnipotence**. Omnipotence is the Absolute Power of God and when you experience it, it is tremendous. Jesus and Buddha both calibrated at 1,000. The highest level to experience Divinity in the Earth domain is 1,000; we call this Incarnation.

The **Buddha** teaches Enlightenment. The question is, does Buddha's teaching differentiate from the state of Christ Consciousness, which is Divinity Incarnate? Was the Buddha's ultimate state Nothingness? No, Buddha experienced the **Allness/Oneness of Divinity**, but he did not use the word Divinity or God because the misinformation about it could set up a belief system. Like the Buddha, the 12 step groups use the term Higher Power for Divinity or God for the same reason. The Buddha Nature is not Voidness or Nothingness; it is Allness. Buddha, like Christ, experienced God as his own Reality. The Buddha experienced God as Infinite Love. The Buddha is not God as Infinity, however. **The Creator** is at the level of **Infinity**. In a world that cannot tell a devil from an angel, there are those who cannot tell God from that which is not God. Some people think that God is at the "bottom" of the Map of Consciousness, and free speech should be at the top, but that is fallacious. Calibrations can be quite a useful tool in determining the Truth. The Avatars calibrate at 1,000; beyond that are the realms that go to Infinity. This slide is for documenting the range within the fields of consciousness of Divinity.

World Religions - Sons of Abraham

Christianity (Early)

First Century - "The Way"	980
The Apostles	905-990
Gnostics	510
Prior to the Council of Nicaea	840
After the Council of Nicaea (325 AD)	485

Catholicism

Eastern Orthodox	490
Coptic	475

Roman Catholic

Papacy	570
College of Cardinals	490
Faith and Liturgy	535
Clergy	490
Jesuit Order	440
Church (worldwide)	450

Post-Reformation

Amish	375
Born-again Christians	350
Christian Science	410
Episcopalian	510
Evangelist	385
Fundamentalist Christian	325
LDS	405
New Thought	405

Post-Reformation (continued)

Pentecostal	310
Protestantism	510
Puritans	210
Quakers	505
Salvation Army	405
Unity	505

Islam

Sufism	700
Sunnite	255
Shi'ite (Muslims)	250
Wahhabism	30
Muhammad (age 35)	700
Koran	700
Muhammad (age 38)	130
Jihad	60-90
Muhammad Abdul Wahhab	20
Sayyid Qutb	420↓75

Judaism

Hasidism	605
Messianic	605
Reconstructionist	555
Conservative	550
Reform	550
Orthodox	545

Slide 62

SLIDE 62: WORLD RELIGIONS: SONS OF ABRAHAM

This slide was first introduced at the Dec 2005 lecture, DVD disc 1 at 003710. A preliminary version was introduced at the June 2003 lecture, DVD disc 2 at 001200.

The consciousness calibration technique was used to analyze everything in the history of the world, including spirituality, religion and theology. Judaism, Christianity and Islam are the three brothers that came out historically out of Abraham. Judaism has survived all the ravages of time. Hasidism is the conscious awareness of the divinity of all that exists and calibrates at 605. Messianic includes Jesus Christ as a representative of God. Other denominations of Judaism such as Reconstructionist, Conservative, Reform and Orthodox also calibrate quite high thus making Judaism a representative of a very high level of truth.

The better we can understand things, the better we can integrate them, accept them and stop making things wrong. In the first century of **Christianity**, **"The Way"** calibrated at 980. Many centuries later, the writings of the **Gnostics** were discovered, and they calibrate at 510. The interesting thing about Christianity is that prior to the **Council of Nicaea** (325 AD), it calibrated at 840 and afterwards it dropped significantly to 485. That is the most catastrophic drop in the level of consciousness that has happened historically other than that which happened with **Mohammad**. It is almost like that which is virtuous and truthful pulls to itself all its enemies. Truth becomes such a danger to falsehood that falsehood pulls itself up and sneaks in the door somehow. Often the enemies of truth cleverly conceal themselves in sheep's clothing, therefore discernment is required on the spiritual path.

Catholicism is **Eastern Orthodox**, **Coptic** and **Roman Catholic**, which has been the dominant Christianity for many centuries. The level 570 is ideal for a leader of a world-wide religious organization because above 570 one cannot handle the worldly things that need to be handled and below 570 one does not have the requisite power to withstand the attack that comes by virtue of the office. The papacy has stood the test of time although a couple of popes calibrated at well below 200 during this time.

Post-reformation saw new Christian denominations such as the **Amish**, the **Born-Again Christians, Christian Science, Episcopalian, Evangelist, Fundamental Christian, Latter-Day Saints, New Thought, Pentecostal, Puritans, Quakers, Salvation Army and Unity**, which all calibrate above the level of integrity. **Islam** is the most recent one of the Abrahamic religions and arose at the time of Mohammed. The level of consciousness of Mohammed varied. The **Koran** calibrates at 700. The kernel of Islamic faith is an expression of loving acceptance and inner peace, but the evolution of practical dogma was intertwined from the start with the politics of territorial expansion in the form of **jihad**, or religious warfare. The truth of the teachings had dropped severely by the end of the Crusades. In modern times, the ascendance of fanatic nationalistic religious movements, characterized by paranoia and xenophobia, has rapidly eroded the spiritual essence of this faith. The level of truth of the teachings of militant Islamic fundamentalism varies but is extremely low, with **Wahhabism** at 30. **Sufism**, the mystical side of Islam calibrates at 700.

World Religions - Oriental

The Institute for Spiritual Research, Inc., dba Veritas Publishing

Ancient Hinduism

Sanatana Dharma (Eternal Truth) of Rishis	925
Dravidian	905
Aryan	910
Vedanta	855

Buddhism

Mahayana	960
Zen	890
Hinayanna	890
Lotus Land	740
Tantric	515
Tibetan	490
Won (Won Bulgyo)	405

The Yogas

Bhakti	935
Raja	935
Jhana	975
Karma	915
Kundalini	510
Kriya	410
Surat Shabd (Sahaj Marg)	495
Hatha	390

Eastern

Shinto	350
Including Sumari code	190
Including Bashudo code	180
Taosim	500

Others

Hare Krishna	460
Subud	470
Tamil Soddja Vedanta	550
Sikhism	600
Janism	495
Radhasoami	475

Other Religions

Baha'i	365
Native American	500

Slide 63

SLIDE 63: WORLD RELIGIONS: ORIENTAL

This slide was first introduced at the Dec 2005 lecture, disc 1 at 011845. A preliminary version was introduced at the June 2003 lecture, disc 2 at 001200.

Enlightenment was already a dominant energy in 10000 BC in India. In the ancient Aryan culture arose many great religions, with Shiva-ism being the oldest. **Hinduism** is extremely interesting as can be seen from the calibrations of the ancient denominations and even the current teachings of **Vedanta** calibrate at 855. Out of these great cultures arose the great **Yogas** and Devotional Nonduality, as taught by Dr. Hawkins, is the modern day version of **Jnana Yoga** or the Yoga of Self-Knowledge. The four great classic Yogas of Hinduism are **Raja** (meditation), **Jnana** (wisdom and introspection), **Bhakti** (devotion), and **Karma** (selfless service). These have their equivalency in all religions, including Christianity. Artificial means of awakening Kundalini are to be avoided, as forcing this energy up the spine prematurely can be dangerous. **Jainism** is very careful about not hurting life in all its expressions and their followers try to avoid stepping on or killing insects or they breathe in a way as to not inhale microorganisms, bacteria, etc.

The separation between **Hinayana** and **Mahayana** in **Buddhism** is artificial because that which is, is both nothingness and allness. It is like the Infinite Reality is either nothingness, which is the void of Hinayana Buddhism, or the Allness, which is the Infinite Presence of Mahayana Buddhism. One is salvation of the self; the other is salvation of mankind but they are the same as one leads to the other. **Zen** is a style of being in which meditation is continuous, even while one is walking, talking or acting. Capacity to function has nothing to do with the state of Awareness just as there are waves on the surface of a lake but the deepest part of the lake is still. The Buddhist teachings have deteriorated less than any other religion over time. **Lotus Land** Buddhism is similar to Christianity. **Tantric** is not recommended as it deals with manipulation of energies and can become linear.

Shinto, at 350, is integrous in concept. Its downside is the glorification of the warrior archetype, which has the disadvantage of energizing the spleen in addition to the solar plexus and the heart. Blood lust by the Japanese military during ravages of the Pacific and the Far East in the 1930s, and later during World War II was supposedly for the glorification of the emperor, who was believed to be the descendent of the Shinto sun god. The ancient wisdom of **Taoism** states that the oak tree, which resists the wind, is susceptible to breaking, and the willow tree, which bends with the wind, survives. In the teachings of the Tao the flow of life is neither sought nor resisted. Thus, life becomes effortless and existence itself is pleasurable, without conditions, and easygoing like a cork in the sea.

Baha'i is the path of unity and peace and included women as equal to men from its very founding. There is a dearth of authoritative information and research on **Native American** spirituality in spite of the fact that it is one of the predominant and attractive characteristics of that culture. The high calibration (500+) reflects the acknowledgment of God as the Great Spirit/Creator and source and essence of all life, which is therefore held to be sacred.

Divinity and Avatars

Divinity - God Transcendent

God	Infinity
God the Father	Infinity
The Creator	Infinity
The Almighty	Infinity
Maker of Heaven and Earth	Infinity
Ruler of the Universe	Infinity
Maker of All Things Visible and Invisible	Infinity
Omnipotent, Omniscient, and Omnipresent	Infinity
The Supreme	Infinity
Source of all Life and Existence	Infinity
The Holy Spirit	Infinity
Allah	Infinity
AN (Dravidian - early Hindu)	Infinity
Shiva	Infinity
Krishna	Infinity
Brahma	Infinity
Vishnu	Infinity
Durga	Infinity
Isvara	Infinity
Rama	Infinity
God of Moses and Abraham	Infinity

Divinity - God Immanent

The Christ	Infinity
Christ Consciousness	Infinity
Christ as God Incarnate	Infinity
Purusha	Infinity
Self	Infinity
Atman	Infinity

Other Denotations of Spiritual Reality

Celestial Hierarchy

Angels	500+
Archangels	50,000+
Buddha Nature (as Allness)	1,000+
Buddha Nature (as Void)	980
Native American Great Spirit	850+
Deity	720
Yahweh (Yewah)	460
Jehovah	205
Word "God" as intellectual concept	460

Slide 64

SLIDE 64: DIVINITY AND AVATARS

This slide was first introduced at the Dec 2005 lecture, DVD disc 1 at 014340. A preliminary version was introduced at the June 2003 lecture, DVD disc 1 at 014400.

The energy levels of various historical designations of **Divinity** and celestial hierarchy were determined using the consciousness calibration technique. **God Immanent** is the God of the mystic. The terms transcendent and immanent are only mentations of dualistic thinking and do not denote two different realities. The evidence of the existence of **God** is right here and right now and was confirmed in the calibration of 23 statements on July 13 2002 before an audience of over 200 people during a public Lecture (see "I: Reality and Subjectivity", Chapter 10: The Nature of God, pp 163-164.) The results of the calibration of the reality of Divinity are what one would simply expect using "common sense," innate intelligence, and intuition. Calibrations simultaneously confirm the pragmatic value of the consciousness calibration system in evaluating the levels of truth. "God" as a concept calibrates at only 460, as would be expected, because it is a mentation (that is why Buddha did not use the term God.) God is the Ultimate Reality, as confirmed by consciousness research, which also validates the existence of the Omnipresence of God as both transcendent and immanent.

The calibrations of the levels of angels and archangels indicate that the energies of Reality are analogous to a step-down-transformer type of stratification between man and God. The celestial or heavenly realms are identifiable and known to mankind. Throughout history, it is recorded that successful contact has been made by individuals with a karmically gifted talent to make conscious contact with teachers from celestial realms. Unfortunately, some individuals have used the gift to contact lower realms, and they hear an impersonator of God, as happens in a psychotic state. The terms "**Jehovah**" and "**Yahweh**" calibrate lower because of mythological connotations and origins.

Angels can appear in a physical body. Some people channel angelic energy. Some angels choose to incarnate in the world and they are a great source of benevolence. Dr. Hawkins often related the incident where he received help from a complete stranger when stranded with a flat tire on a busy cloverleaf interchange. The experience was like turning the beetle over when the beetle is on his back and cannot seem to turn over. The stranger took care of having the tire fixed by driving with the tire to and from the repair facility, some distance away and then putting the tire back on the car, thus enabling Dr. Hawkins to resume his trip to an engagement. Consciousness calibration confirmed that the stranger was an angel.

Avatars and Great Spiritual Teachers

Jesus Christ	**1,000**	**Name of God as "Om"**	**975**
Buddha	**1,000**	**John, the Baptist**	**930**
Krishna	**1,000**	**Moses**	**910**
Zoroaster	**1,000**	**Abraham**	**850**
The Twelve Christian Apostles	**980**	**St. Paul (Saul of Tarsus)**	**745**

Slide 65

SLIDE 65: AVATARS AND GREAT SPIRITUAL TEACHERS

This slide was first introduced at the Dec 2005 lecture, DVD disc 1 at 015030. A preliminary version was introduced at the June 2003 lecture, DVD disc 2 000320.

The highest level of consciousness possible for a human body is 1000 due to the inability of the human nervous system to withstand higher energies. This level was reached by only the few throughout history who have traditionally been referred to as the Great Avatars (the founders of the world's great religions, such as **Jesus Christ, Buddha, Krishna and Zoroaster**), and who were enlightened by the Divine Presence that replaced the linear, limited, ordinary human mind with the nonlinear Reality. The Self, indicative of the presence of the Divine as immanent, is sometimes referred to in classical literature as Universal Mind. By transcendence, the ego-self is replaced by the non-ego Self. This phenomenon has been traditionally termed 'Enlightenment'.

The **twelve Christian apostles** calibrate extremely high. Divinity of the Christ energy in the form of the Holy Spirit was transmitted to them. They had a profound impact on the world. In the first century, Christianity "The Way" calibrated at 980. The bones of St. Peter are buried under the altar in the Basilica of St. Peter in the Vatican. They calibrate in the 900s, even after 2,000 years. Thus, the high spiritual energy is a permanent quality and apparently not subject to physical degradation over even great expanses of time.

The list provided in this slide is not exhaustive but includes those whom are best known. The term "avatar" is from Sanskrit and means "incarnation by virtue of crossing over by descent of Divinity." The result in the human race is a fully illumined being who, because of the knowledge revealed, embodies the power of that level of truth and its concordant field of consciousness and radiates it out to mankind, thereby supporting and catalyzing the evolution of consciousness. Veneration and respect are appropriate responses because they acknowledge the value of the innate gift to mankind of such an uplifting energy. Interpretation and comprehension of the revealed truths of these great teachers fall within a spectrum that reflects not only the level of truth of the original teaching but also the consciousness level of its cultural expression and comprehension.

Great Spiritual Writings

Writing	Level
Abhinavagupta (Kashmir Shaivinism)	655
A Course in Miracles (workbook)	600
A Course in Miracles (textbook)	550
Aggadah	645
Apocrypha	400
Bodhidharma Zen Teachings	795
Bhagavad-Gita	910
Book of Kells	570
Book of Mormon	405
Cloud of Unknowing	705
Dead Sea Scrolls	260
Dhammapada	840
Diamond Sutra	700
Doctrine and Covenants: Pearl of Great Price	455
Genesis (Lamsa Bible)	660
Gnostic Gospels	400
Gospel of St. Luke	699
Gospel of St. Thomas	660
Granth Sahib - Adi (Sikhs)	505
Heart Sutra	780
Huang-Po Teachings	960
Kabbalah	605
King James Bible (from the Greek)	475
Koran	700
Lamsa Bible (from the Aramaic)	495
Lamsa Bible (minus the Old Testament and Book of Revelation, but including Genesis, Psalms, and Proverbs)	880
Lao Tsu: Teachings	610
Lotus Sutra	780
Midrath	665
Mishneh	665
New Testament (King James Version after deletion of the Book of Revelation)	790
New Testament (King James Version from the Greek)	640
Nicene Creed	895
Psalms (Lamsa Bible)	650
Proverbs (Lamsa Bible)	350
Ramayana	810
Rubaiyat of Omar Khayyam	590
Rig Veda	705
Talmud	595
Tibetan Book of the Dead	575
Torah	550
Trinity (concept)	945
Upanishads	970
Vedanta	595
Vedas	970
Vijnane Bhairava	635
Yoga Sutras, Patanjali	740
Zohar	905

Slide 66

SLIDE 66: GREAT SPIRITUAL WRITINGS

This slide was first introduced at the Dec 2005 lecture, DVD disc 2 at 000030. A preliminary version was introduced at the June 2003 lecture, DVD disc 2 at 005500.

Any single selection out of the writings on this slide is, in and of itself, sufficient for a lifetime of study and spiritual endeavor. From the calibration levels, it becomes evident that the great sages from the early Aryan culture of ancient India represented the first major emergence of the highest spiritual awareness available to man ever recorded. The same truths emerged later in different cultures and eras, completely separate from each other, and yet, the realization of the nature of the highest truth was essentially identical in each case, with some variation of expression that reflected cultural and linguistic differences. Thus, truth as such is not exclusive but universal, or it would not be truth. Therefore, spiritual or religious claims to exclusivity indicate the interference and errors of the egos of later followers of the original sages. Advanced spiritual students value all sources of truth and often study combinations of them. Thus, the study of Christian mystics clarifies the truths revealed by the **Vedas**, and, in turn, the Vedas clarify Buddhist teachings that then clarify the teachings of Jesus Christ.

Abhinavagupta (c. 950 - 1020 AD) is most famous for a treatise on *Kashmir Shaivism*. ***A Course in Miracles*** **Workbook** calibrates at 600 whereas the **Textbook** tends to demonize the ego and calibrates at 550. ***Aggadah*** and ***Apocrypha*** are very ancient teachings prior to the Christian era. **Bodhidharma** transmitted Zen Buddhism to China during the 5th or 6th century. ***The Bhagavad Gita*** coming out of the ancient Hindu Vedas has the message of Krishna. ***The book of Kells*** is a manuscript from - 800 CE containing the four gospels transcribed by Celtic monks. ***The Cloud of Unknowing*** is an anonymous work of Christian mysticism written in the 14th century and is a spiritual guide on contemplative prayer. ***The Dead Sea Scrolls*** were discovered in caves along the northwest shore of the Dead Sea during 1947-1956.

The Dhammapada is a collection of sayings of the Buddha, one of the most widely read Buddhist scriptures. ***The Diamond sutra*** is a key object of devotion in Zen Buddhism. ***The Lotus Sutra*** presents itself as a discourse delivered by the Buddha toward the end of his life. ***The Heart Sutra*** is one of the most popular Buddhist scripture of all. ***The Zen teachings of Huang Po*** deals with void or no-thingness i.e. the non-linear, but 'no-thing' does not mean 'non- existence', which is an error. In the ultimate state at 1000, the radiance of Love is unmistakable. By comparison, the Void at 850 is profound with no beginning or end, but is sterile as it is devoid of Love.

Doctrine and Covenants: Pearl of Great Price pertains to the Church of The Latter Day Saints. The *Mishnah (**Mishneh**)* is the oral law in Judaism, and was collected and committed to writing about AD 200. A particular teaching within the Mishnah is *Midrash* (***Midrath***). The ***Zohar*** (905) deals with the mystical aspects of Judaism. ***The Old Testament*** calibrates overall at 190, but **Genesis** (660), **Psalms** (650), and **Proverbs** (350) are above 200. ***The Lamsa Bible*** (from the Aramaic) calibrates twenty points higher than the ***King James Version*** (from the Greek).

Other Teachings, Schools, and Traditions

100th Monkey Phenomenon	205	Hatha Yoga	260
Agnosticism	200	Holotropic Breathing	202
Anti-Creationism	150	Huna	260
Anti-Evolutionism	150	I Ching, The	430
"Archangel Channeler"	190	Keys of Enoch	265
Astrology	210-405	Kirlian Photography	160
Biofeedback	202	Knights Templar	400
Bodywork	205	Kung Fu	410
Codependency (concept)	190	Metaphysics	460
Creationism	200	Numerology	210
Crystals	210	Qi Gong	240
Druids	450	Rebirthing	250
Eckankar	230	Reiki	340
Enneagrams	390	Rolfing	205
Esoteric	390	Rosicrucians	405
EST (Erhard Seminars Training)	400	Soul Midwifery	240
Ethical Culture	350	Superstition	200
Falun Gong	195	Telepathy	250
Feng Shui	185-210	Theosophy	365
Firewalking	200	Universalist Church	320
Free Masonry	510	White Brotherhood	560
Freethinker	350	White Magic	203
Fundamentalism	200	Wu Den	275

Slide 67

SLIDE 67: OTHER TEACHINGS, SCHOOLS AND TRADITIONS

This slide was first introduced at the Dec 2005 lecture, DVD disc 2 at 002300. A preliminary version was introduced at the June 2003 lecture, DVD disc 2 at 011700.

Many spiritual students have explored a variety of these approaches and report pragmatic and experiential benefit. Calibration levels do not indicate that one level is 'better' than another but only different, analogous to the selection of clubs when playing golf, which depends on whether one is going to 'putt', 'chip" or 'drive'. Therefore, efficacy is the result of intention and not just a technique in itself.

The **100th monkey phenomenon** relates to the observation by scientists that monkeys on a Japanese island learned to wash sweet potatoes and gradually this new behavior spread through the younger generation of monkeys. Once a critical number of monkeys was reached i.e. the 100th monkey, the previously learnt behavior instantly spread across the water to monkeys on nearby islands, proving the non-local effects of consciousness as the phenomenon of washing sweet potatoes was picked up in the collective consciousness. Therefore, when we clear something in our own consciousness, one does not have to feel guilty because we have picked up a lot from the collective consciousness via the 100th monkey effect.

Atheism is arrogant but **agnosticism** is integrous because it says that by itself, the mind cannot know the existence of God. **Astrology** is based on causality. Planetary movements do not cause things to happen; instead, all things including the movement of planets are happening synchronistically. The physical body and the planet both calibrate at 200, neither good nor bad. The body is a product of physicality and practices that are strictly physical calibrate around 200 e.g. **bodywork, biofeedback, holotropic breathing**, etc. **Co-dependency** calibrates at 190 and confuses love with dependency, so the lesson is that one can do things out of love and not co-dependency.

EST did not allow you to blame anything out there, stressing that one has to take responsibility for one's actions. That will have quite a good effect in today's world in which cause is put out there as blame, instead of accepting the fact that it was our own error. **Ethical Culture** advises living in accordance with *ethical principles* as central to living meaningful and fulfilling lives, and to creating a world that is good for all. **Feng-shui** calibrations range from 185 to 210 and just like the calibration of astrology, the calibration depends on the type of beliefs and basic premises involved. The founders of the US Constitution were deists, theists and freethinkers and that is why the US Constitution is quite literal.

There was a lot of interest generated in **Knights Templar** (cal. 400) because of the movie 'The Da Vinci Code.' **Superstition** at 200 is neither good nor bad as it incorporates that which is within the collective consciousness. **Telepathy** calibrating at 250 indicates that it is factual. **White Brotherhood** is a celestial realm calibrating at the level of Unconditional Love. Alice Bailey was the translator of the transmission from the White Brotherhood during 1919-1949 when she wrote many books including 'Glamour: A World Problem' which was calibrated at 560. The members of the White Brotherhood have the intention to stay back to help the evolution of humanity, even though many of them are advanced enough to be able to transition to higher realms.

MARGINAL SPIRITUAL/RELIGIOUS BELIEF SYSTEMS

Al-Qaeda	90	Islamic Fascism	60
Atheist Movement (Ideology)	190	"Left Behind" Apocalyptic Ideology	190
Christian Identity Movement	110	Mayan Religion	95
Aum Shinrikyo Cult	85	New Ageism	185
Aztec Religion	85	Solar Temple (Ideology)	155
Channeling	195	Plasma Energy Orbs (Ideology)	160
Crop Circles extraterrestrial?	No	Polygamous Sects	135
Cults	50-160	Raelians (Ideology)	130
Divination	185	Right-Wing Fundamentalist (Ideology)	95
DNA Code Theology	160	Secularism	165
Easter Island Statues	70	Shroud of Turin real?	No
Extraterrestrials real?	No	Star Children (Ideology)	145
Fortune-Telling	185	Star People (Ideology)	160
Full-Moon Gatherings	180	Star seed Family (Ideology)	145
Goddess Movement	190	Tantra (Modern)	95
Heaven's Gate Cult	160	UFOs real?	No
Indigo children	170	Urantia Book (Ideology)	150
Incan Religion	85	Wicca (Ideology)	160
Incoming Fifth World (Ideology)	130		

Slide 68

SLIDE 68: MARGINAL SPIRITUAL BELIEF SYSTEMS

This slide was first introduced at the Dec 2005 lecture, DVD disc 2 at 003400. A preliminary version was introduced at the June 2003 lecture, DVD disc 2 at 003530.

There is curiosity in students about various belief systems and approaches to spirituality. That is Many of these teachings were calibrated to put the mind at rest that they have been checked out, thus saving students time and effort that is best spent on integrous spiritual paths that can lead to Enlightenment. Some of these marginal belief systems are very famous. The **Aztec religion**, like the **Mayan and the Incan religions** calibrates extremely low as they worshipped death and engaged in blood sacrifice of children, etc. The **DNA code** is all a fantasy. **Easter Island statues** represent the self-destructiveness of the former inhabitants who apparently destroyed the trees and other vegetation and ended starving to death, but not before they had regressed to cannibalism.

Idolatry, like the worshipping of the golden calf, calibrates at only 65. The avoidance of idolatry is taught in both Islam and Judaism in the formal structure of the places of worship. The ego is attracted to the limitation of form, whereas the essence of Divinity is beyond all form, yet innate within it. **Fortune telling** and similar practices were highly developed in ancient Mesopotamia. Ancient peoples consulted oracles, seers, shamans, and a variety of practitioners of magic and otherworldly secret, mystical rites and rituals. Also a great variety of psychics, channelers, trance mediums, and medicine men and women with special connections to a variety of spirits were popular. **Full-moon gatherings** are part of the magical mystery of it all and do not calibrate well.

Indigo children, **Incoming Fifth World**, Celestine Prophecy, etc. are all fictional. If one presents spiritual fiction as spiritual fiction, then it is integrous but if treated as true or factual, then it is below 200. The future cannot be foretold because of two reasons: first, it is not reality as time itself is not real, and second, even in the practical human living, events are decided instant by instant else there would be no point to incarnation, no karmic merit. The Earth is a recycling center. One made mistakes before, and now gets a chance in the present birth to undo them and choose again. If the future was set already then there would be no freewill and no karma or responsibility, and one will not need a savior and there would be no point in spiritual work.

New Ageism calibrates at 185 due to the glamorization of the adolescent within us. **Plasma Energy Orb ideology** is fictional. **Right Wing fundamental Christianity** at calibration level 95 becomes like an inquisition. **UFOs** and UFO based religions all calibrate low as UFOs are not real. The **Urantia** book calibrates below 200.

Many of these marginal belief systems represent childlike credulity and the inclusion of positionalities that are at considerable variance from verifiable truth. **"*Left Behind*"** tells the story of the end times (set in the contemporary era), in which true believers in Christ have been taken instantly to heaven leaving the world shattered and chaotic. The "end times" apocalyptic culture and its literature calibrate low because they are based on elaborations from the New Testament Book of Revelation, which itself calibrates at 70.

Calibration of Verses

Calibration of Verses – Old Testament

60% calibrate over	200
50% calibrate over	300
50% calibrate over	400
30% calibrate at or over	500
20% calibrate at or over	600
10% calibrate at or over	700
02% calibrate at	800
10 verses calibrate at	1,000

Calibration of Verses - Koran

30% calibrate below	200
25% calibrate below	150
14% calibrate below	100

Interpretation of Koran by Sayyid Qutb

(In the Shade of the Qur'an) 90

Other References to Divinity

Greek Gods	90
Germanic Gods	90
Scandinavian Gods	90
Gods of War	90
Pagan Gods of Rome	100

Slide 69

SLIDE 69: CALIBRATION OF VERSES AND OTHER REFERENCES TO DIVINITY

This slide was first introduced at the Dec 2005 lecture, DVD disc 2 at 004125.

It is difficult to make complete sense of scripture with just an overall 'composite' calibration, as its different books or chapters invariably calibrate differently. That is why it is helpful to calibrate individual chapters of a book or verses of selected scriptures, as done on this slide. The awareness that 40% of the verses of the ***Old Testament***, and 30% of the verses of ***Koran*** calibrate below 200 helps one realize that just because something is written in a scripture does not mean anything, and one does not have to bow down to it. Errors in scriptures and spiritual writings may be due to a variety of reasons including obvious ones like those due to translation from a foreign language.

In the case of the various books of the Bible, many of them were compiled based on 'voting' by persons with various positionalities. Voting is certainly not the way to establish Truth, which is a subjective realization and not a popularity contest. It takes detailed analysis to 'explain why' erroneous writings were inadvertently included in canonized scripture, and additional details on religious error and false teachings can be found on pp. 368-375 of "Truth vs. Falsehood: How to Tell the Difference" (2005), Chapter 17: Spiritual Truth. Although the Books of the Old Testament (with the exception of Psalms, Proverbs, and Genesis) calibrate below 200, many individual verses do calibrate quite high, as shown on the slide.

The Koran also includes errors that have serious consequences to humanity, with many verses that are incongruous with the statement "In the name of Allah, the All Merciful" with which each verse of the Koran starts. Some of these verses recurrently speak of "beheading infidels" and condone slaughtering nonbelievers, even though the Koran calibrates overall at 700. Inasmuch as "religious homicide" calibrates at 30, it would seem that contamination by falsity is the worst enemy of genuine, pure spirituality.

To understand the limitations of scriptures, it is also necessary to look into the role of religious mythology that is common to all early cultures. There are famous **Greek, Roman, and Germanic** mythologies, as well as that of the Viking, Native American, and all other primitive cultural and ethnic groups. In all of these, the anthropomorphic gods have human characteristics and fallibilities. The 'gods' are also blamed for catastrophes of nature, such as fire, volcanic eruptions, floods, and plagues whereby an angry god 'smites' the peoples of the region. This led to the widespread prevalence of acts of sacrifice to appease the angry, human-like gods, as seen in Aztec, Incan, Canaanite, Mesopotamian, and Semitic histories. When succeeding revelations of much higher spiritual reality were revealed by the teachings of the great avatars, often the old mythology persisted as belief systems and was incorporated in or tacked onto the newer teachings. While mythology is of historical interest, it is clearly devoid of the higher truths now available to humanity. They are also misleading distractions to the seekers of spiritual truth.

Places of Spiritual Interest

Alhambra	720
Anghor Watt	550
Aranachula Mountain	500
Basilica of St. Peter (Rome)	710
Bethlehem (current)	175
Bethlehem (in Jesus' time)	415
Buddha, relics of the	905
Cathedral of Notre Dame	790
Cathedral of St. John the Divine, New York City	530
Catholic Chapel	565
Chartres Cathedral	790
Christian Saints, relics of the	750
Crystal Cathedral (Los Angeles)	410
Dharamsala (India)	330
Ganges River	515
Great Buddha of Afghanistan (prior to being blown up by the Taliban)	555
Great Buddha of Kyoto	780
Jewish Synagogue	495
Jewish Temple	505
Ka'ba' (Mecca)	530
Karnak, Great Temple at	415
Lhasa (Tibet)	320
Lourdes	510
Machu Picchu	510
Maharaj, Nisargadatta, Attic of	510
Mecca	205
Medina	225
Mosque	495
Nativity, Church of the	450
Pieta, The	590
Pyramids of Egypt	520
Sainte Chapelle (Chapel), Paris	735
St. Patrick's Cathedral, New York City	530
St. Peter, relics of (under floor of the Basilica in Rome)	910
Sakya Monastery (Tibet)	390
Shinto Shrine	650
Sphinx, The	520
Stonehenge	599
Strasbourg Cathedral	715
Taj Majal	750
Tibetan Buddhist Stupa (Sedona)	640
Unity Village	510
Vatican, The	570
Washington National Cathedral	530
Westminster Abbey	790

Slide 70

SLIDE 70: PLACES OF SPIRITUAL INTEREST

This slide was first introduced at the Dec 2005 lecture, DVD disc 2 at 004250. A preliminary version was introduced at the June 2003 lecture, DVD disc 3 at 001920.

Most of these calibrations are self-evident and reflect not only esthetics but also the presentation of beauty as instrumental to devotion and reflective of that spiritual intention. The **Alhambra** (720) is one of Spain's major tourist attractions, exhibiting the country's most significant Islamic architecture, being also a UNESCO World Heritage Site and the inspiration for many songs and stories. **Anghor Watt** ("Angkor Wat", cal. 550) is a temple complex in Cambodia and the largest religious monument in the world, and is the country's prime attraction for visitors. **Dharamsala** (330) is the center of the Tibetan exile world in India and a popular destination for Indian and foreign tourists, including students studying Tibet. The **Karnak** temple complex (cal. 415) in Egypt comprises a vast mix of decayed temples, chapels, pylons, and other buildings. **Lourdes** (510) is a most important site of international Catholic pilgrimage due to the apparitions of the Virgin Mary seen first in 1858.

The 'Heisenberg effect' is demonstrated most visibly by the unique example of the **Ganges River**, which, on the physical level, is the recipient of the sewage of several hundred villages, towns, and cities along its course. Thousands of Hindus bathe daily in this grossly contaminated water in acts of spiritual purification. By spiritual intention, the holy river calibrates over 500, reflecting the input of the energy of sanctification by the millions of Hindu devotees over many centuries. Another example of the power of intention is in the calibration of **Arunachala Mountain** at 500, which was the home of the famous sage Ramana Maharshi (cal. 720) who never left the site upon which his followers established a famous ashram. Yet another example of the phenomenon of spiritual intention is the effect of the consciousness level of **Nisargadatta Maharaj** (cal. 720) on the **attic** where he met with visitors in Bombay. The attic calibrates at 510.

The **Great Buddha of Afghanistan** calibrated at 555 prior to being blown up by the Taliban, which was a purposeful act of desecration (cal. 35). The calibration of **Bethlehem** has come down from 415 at the time of Jesus to 175 today so it may be better to do pilgrimage to a city like Chicago that calibrates over 400, instead of traveling to Bethlehem, which calibrates much lower. The calibrations of **Mecca** and **Medina** have also come down over the years because of continuing conflicts. **Tibetan Buddhist Stupa in Sedona** calibrates at 640. The physical remains ('relics' or bone fragments) of enlightened beings still calibrate extremely high. The **'Buddha relics'** are those of not only the Buddha but also of subsequent great spiritual masters and patriarchs. After all these years, the relics surprisingly still calibrate in the range of the 900s. This phenomenon is also true of the **relics of St. Peter**, buried under the altar in the Basilica of St. Peter in the Vatican. They also calibrate in the 900s, even after 2,000 years.

SPIRITUAL EXPERIENCES

Buddha Nature	**1000+**	**Hanukkah**	**515**
Christ Consciousness	**1000+**	**Ramadan**	**495**
The Supreme	**1000+**	**Sweat Lodge Ceremony**	**560**
Near-Death Experience	**520+**	**Smudging**	**520**
Satori	**585**	**Christmas: Peace on Earth,Goodwill to Men**	**675**
Enlightenment	**600+**	**Sound of Tibetan Buddhist Horns**	**320**
Christian Communion	**700**	**Nirbija Samadhi**	**800**
Passover	**495**	**"Amazing Grace" (Hymn)**	**575**
Durga Puja Festival	**480**		

Correlation with the Gunas

Tamas **= lower resistance, inertia energies below calibration level 200**

Rajas **= energy of constructive action, levels 200-400**

"High ***rajas*****" = calibration levels 400-499**

Sattva **(peace, tranquility) calibrates at 500-599**

Moksha **as enlightenment is 600 and over**

Slide 71

SLIDE 71: SPIRITUAL EXPERIENCES

This slide was first introduced at the April 2006 lecture, DVD disc 2 at 002400. A preliminary version was introduced at the June 2003 lecture, DVD disc 2 at 010300.

Near-death experiences are transforming and people who have had a **near-death experience** remember the surprise of the profound sense of freedom and peace that accompany the loss of anxiety of having a physical body. The same release from survival anxiety occurs at consciousness level 600. At that starting level of the states of enlightenment, identification with the body ceases and the body is witnessed to be completely autonomous. **Satori** is a term used in Zen Buddhism and is similar to enlightenment. It often comes about in the beginning when meditating with eyes closed. Then when one opens one's eyes, the state disappears. At a more advanced level, one can open one's eyes and walk around, still maintaining the state of Presence.

Nirbhija-samadhi is a term explained in the Yoga Sutras of Patanjali. During Nirbhija- samadhi the Atman (Presence) is experienced. After emergence from that state, the experience gradually begins to fade. At a still more advanced stage, one can go about one's daily life and do everything that needs doing, and the Presence maintains. That is the ultimate goal of spiritual practice, and can eventually lead to the experience of **Buddha Nature, Christ Consciousness and the Supreme**, referring to the same ultimate human experience described in the Buddhist, Christian and ancient Hindu literature respectively.

The act of **Christian Communion**, which uses bread as a symbol for Jesus' body and wine as a symbol for Jesus' blood, calibrates quite high at 700. This is good reason to honor communion. **Passover, Durga Puja Festival, Hannukah and Ramadan** are religious festivals that calibrate in the range o f 480-515. The spirit of **Christmas embodied as "Peace on Earth, Goodwill to Men"** calibrates at 675. **Smudging** is an ancient ceremony in which one burns sacred herbs or plants, such as sage, to allow the smoke to clear and bless a space. It is a way to clear stagnant energy in a field which can include emotional, energetic, mental, spiritual or physical, and the environment-whether at one's home, office, or other physical space. In the ancient Hindu literature, for example in Chapter 14 of *The Bhagavad Gita*, it is said that the three **gunas** (energy fields) born of material nature bind the immortal Self to the body. ***Tamas*** is the guna (energy) of resistance that is overcome by rajas, the energy of activity and effort; ***Rajas*** is the response to motivation and dedication to actually reach ***Sattva***, the state of peace and tranquility. Continuing abidance in Sattva leads to **Moksha**, the states of Enlightenment.

Spiritual Practices

Aum (mantra)	210	Om Mane Padme Hum	700
Baptism	500	Om Namah Shivaya	630
Bathing in the Ganges	540	Prayerful hand clasp	540
Confirmation	500	Prayer of Jabez	310
Devotional acts	540	Prayer of St. Francis of Assisi	580
Devotional burning of incense	540	Random Acts of Kindness	350
Genuflection	540	Saying the Rosary	515
Golden Rule	405	Shanti, Shanti, Shanti	650
Gregorian Chants	595	Surrender (at depth) one's Will to God	850
Hajj (pilgrimage to Mecca)	390	Surrender the World to God	535
Japa	515	Turning prayer wheels	540
Jesus Prayer	525	Twelve Steps of Alcoholics Anonymous	540
Kirtan (Yogic Chant)	250	Transcendental Meditation	295
Kneeling to pray	540	Visualization (healing)	485
Last Rites	500	Wailing Wall, The	540
Lord's Prayer, The	650	Walking the Labyrinth (Chartres Cathedral)	503
Om (pronounced om, as in loan)	740	What is held in mind tends to Manifest	505

Slide 72

SLIDE 72: SPIRITUAL PRACTICES

This slide was first introduced at the April 2006 lecture, DVD disc 2 at 002630 and the March 2008 lecture, DVD disc 2 at 013830-014820. A preliminary version was introduced at the June 2003 lecture, DVD disc 2 at 011430.

Many spiritual practices and techniques have evolved over the centuries to facilitate dis-identification with the ego and its world of limited perceptual dualities of content. This slide is similar to slide 21 but includes some practices not included in slide 21: **Baptism, Confirmation, Last rites, Random acts of kindness, Surrender at depth one's will to God, Surrender the world to God, Visualization (healing), and "What is held in mind tends to manifest."** The role of the priest serves all, besides officiating at baptisms, confirmations, weddings, and administration of last rites, funerals, and burials. These ways of faith are basic traditions and form the necessary foundations of all religions and spiritual pathways. A random act of kindness refers to a selfless act performed by a person or a group wishing to assist or to cheer up a person by being kind, thoughtful, or forgiving in some way.

How can we surrender at great depth? The Infinite Presence within is more powerful than the human will or ego. What already 'is' requires no future. Acceptance is an ever-present option. Complete surrender to God unveils the Truth. Surrendering the world to God and concentrating instead on Self-realization is based on the observation that the appearance of the world is the result of dualistic perception and the intrinsic mechanisms of the ego. All one can actually see within the world are differences and preferences. If one looks at a forest, one sees large and small trees, bent and twisted trees. There is no purpose in going into the forest to try to straighten out all the crooked trees. There is nothing 'wrong' with crooked trees or those that seem to be falling over.

To evolve spiritually is actually the greatest gift one can give the world, and that is done by virtue of what one is and not just by what one does. A useful technique to bypass mentalization is that of creative visualization in which the desired goal is envisioned and held in mind periodically. Potentiality tends to manifest when conditions are favorable, and intention (plus karmic propensities) is a contextual influence. In ordinary mentation, logic and sequence are seen as causal and also needful of effort. Envisioning is influential on outcome by entirely different (and easier) mechanisms. What is held in mind tends to manifest, and the technique is utilized in diverse areas, including sports and even business. The higher the level of consciousness, the greater the likelihood that what is held in mind will actualize. Thus, to see solutions that 'serve the highest goal' is more powerful than simply projecting fulfillment of merely personal selfish desires and gain.

THE FOLLOWING SPIRITUAL CONCEPTS CALIBRATE AS TRUE

1. **Chi Energy ("Shakti") energizes the acupuncture systems**
2. **Kundalini (spiritual) energy activates the chakras and produces the pure-energy etheric brain and shifts brain physiology**
3. **Negative interference with acupuncture energy flow precedes physical illness**
4. **Etheric Body, Reincarnation, and Karma**
5. **Jesus' thirty-three miracles**
6. **Jesus miraculously fed the thousands**
7. **The miracles of the Christian apostles**
8. **Speaking in tongues**
9. **Pentecostal flame**
10. **Both Jesus and John, the Baptist, were killed for revealing the truth**
11. **Wait three days before burial or cremation of the body**
12. **The consciousness level is already set at birth**
13. **The exact time of bodily "death" is karmically set at birth**

Slide 73

SLIDE 73: SPIRITUAL CONCEPTS CALIBRATING AS TRUE

This slide was first introduced at the June 2003 lecture, DVD disc 2 at 010720.

Most prominent in Asian cultures, traditional Chinese medicine and certain martial arts, **'chi'** refers to life force or energy flow (also known as qi in Chinese, ki in Japanese, gi in Korean, khi in Vietnamese, prana in Sanskrit.) Chi a difficult concept for science, as it is non-provable but consciousness calibration reveals that it is an absolute reality. The same is true for **Kundalini, etheric body, reincarnation and Karma**.

The body's **acupuncture energy system**, via the twelve main meridians of the body, instantly responds to anything that is negative, because all the energy fields below the level of Courage at 200 represent that which is not the truth. Which then brings in the whole energy field and thought system of being a victim, and as a sick person we view ourselves as a victim of the disease. Therefore, it is important to realize that there is the illness, and there is the person who has the illness. We then understand that the person who has that illness needs to change in order for it to disappear. One can refer to Healing and Recovery (2009) to learn about recovering from a specific illness, including how to handle the actual event on the physical, psychological, emotional, and mental levels, and how we can change as a being so that healing becomes automatic.

The **miracles performed by Jesus** and the **Christian Apostles** calibrate as true; the Apostles calibrated at 980 at that time. **Speaking in tongues** and the **Pentecostal flame** both calibrate as true. These refer to dramatic miracles that helped the Christian church begin on the day of Pentecost, when the apostles were filled with the Holy Spirit (Pentecostal Flame) and shared the gospel with the peoples, speaking to them in their own languages. **Waiting 3 days before burial or cremation of the body** is advisable, as it gives the spirit time to adjust. At higher levels of consciousness, especially those above 600, one is happy to be rid of physicality, and therefore 3 days may not be necessary.

There is already a **calibratable level of consciousness at the time of one's birth**, and **the exact time of bodily death is also preset**. No 'accidents' are possible in the universe. Although the time of bodily death is already set at birth, the means is not predetermined. The other good news is that due to the relationship of content to context, it is impossible to experience one's own physical death because the very means of experiencing instantly leaves the body, which is no longer viewed as a 'me' but as an 'it' (calibrates as true). All fear is eliminated totally by the realization of the Self, for in that state is the absolute knowingness of immortality-that that which is one's actual Reality is not even subject to birth or death, much less vicissitudes.

Courage (Level 200)

Empowerment

Exploration

Fortitude

Stamina

Determination

Challenging

Exciting

Pleasurable

Stimulating

Doable

Capable

Learn, grow

Admit defects

Energize

Responsible

Accountable

Confidence

Honesty

Integrity

Steadfast

Reliable

Fulfilling

Concern for others

Stop blaming

Truthful

Reality testing

Rejects error (sin)

Capable of humility

Acceptance of Divinity

Conviction

Slide 74

SLIDE 74: COURAGE (LEVEL 200)

This slide was first introduced at the April 2006 lecture, DVD disc 2 at 002730.

What characterizes the level of Courage and what are the character traits of someone at the level of Courage? At this level, one wants to **learn and grow**. To become spiritually aware, one has to have intention and curiosity. One has to **stop blaming others** and **start having concern for others** instead. The most important thing at the level of Courage is **honesty**, and **integrity, and being steadfast**. People ask, "What does it take to be at the level of Courage?" It means to stick to it **steadfastly** even when it seems like you are getting nowhere. Just keep doing the work and stop worrying about arriving somewhere. When someone says, "If I keep doing this, I will become that", that is doing it for some kind of reward. This work is to be done not for any reward but for its own sake. To be a good person for its own sake, and for no other reason, even if no one likes you. There are many people and groups where if you are a good person, they will throw you out.

At the level of Courage, spiritual energy profoundly alters the experience of self and others; therefore, it is the level of the onset of **empowerment**. This is the zone of **exploration**, accomplishment, **fortitude**, and **determination**. Courage implies the willingness to try new things and to deal with the vicissitudes of life. At this level, one is able to cope with and effectively handle the opportunities of life. People at this level put back into the world as much energy as they take from it. The development of the capacity to align with a recognized truth rather than personal gain clearly separates truth from falsehood. The decisive choice to make this step is that of accepting responsibility and being accountable for one's decisions or actions. There is the emergence of awareness of responsibility for the destiny of one's soul and not for just the body and the satisfactions of the ego. Truth is seen as an ally instead of an enemy. Alignment with truth rather than gain brings strength, self-respect, and true empowerment rather than ego inflation. The biblical quote from Matthew, "For what shall it profit a man, if he shall gain the whole world, and lose his own soul?" now becomes an axiom that guides decisions and choices of options.

There is a greater sense of inner freedom due to the relief from guilt and fear that subtly accompanies all violations of truth. On the unconscious level, the spirit knows when the ego is lying and violating premises that operate out of conscious awareness. At this level, it is the effort and intention and not just the results that are important. "To thine own self be true" progressively dominates choices, decisions, and the emergence of an inner sense of honor. The long-term goal of life becomes the development of inner potentials, such as strength, rather than the acquisition of externals. For additional details, please see "Transcending the Levels of Consciousness: The Stairway to Enlightenment" (2006), Chapter 9: Courage, pp. 185-194

Neutral (Level 250)

Flexible

Easygoing

Even tempered Balanced

Practical

Calm

Unemotional

Realistic Nonjudgmental

Unattached

Life is okay

Well-being

Confident capability

Safe to be with

Harmless

Attract rather than promote

Comfortable

Sense of freedom

Benign

Peaceful

Tranquil

Undemanding

Easy to placate

Uncomplaining

Content

Self-sufficient

Secure

Laissez-faire

Cordial

Rely on God's wisdom

Sense of humor

Grateful

Happy, cheerful

Slide 75

SLIDE 75: NEUTRAL (LEVEL 250)

This slide was first introduced at the April 2006 lecture, DVD disc 2 at 002920.

The level of Neutral is very **easy going**, and not fired up with ambition. Neutral people are very agreeable and safe to be with, because they have no interest in conflict, competition or guilt. They are **cordial** and have a good **sense of humor**. Rising above barriers or oppositions that dissipate one's energies, the Neutral condition allows for **flexibility** and a **nonjudgmental**, **realistic** appraisal of problems. To be neutral means to be relatively **unattached** to outcomes. Not getting one's way is not experienced as defeating, frightening, or frustrating at this level. When sensing one's power, one is not easily intimidated or driven to prove anything. The expectation that life, with its ups and downs, will be basically okay if one can roll with the punches is an attitude of level 250. They are **comfortable** and emotionally undisturbed. This attitude is nonjudgmental and does not lead to any need to control other people's behaviors. Correspondingly, the level of Neutral results in greater freedom for self and others.

Neutrality is content to **attract rather than promote**. It is **benign** and not inclined to proselytize or prize the glamour of importance; neither does it minimize nor diminish itself out of false humility. It is not interested in persuasion, coercion, intimidation, or threat. In Neutrality, one is free from trying to 'prove' anything about oneself. In addition, it is not interested in causes to promote or defend; therefore, Neutrality is **peaceful** and values **tranquility and calm**. It is devoid of demands, pressures, or narcissistic needs. A general attitude at this level is that of being interested but **not emotionally involved**, thus allowing for an easygoing and pleasant attitude because there is nothing really 'at stake'. Devoid of the need of 'winning' or 'gaining', Neutrality is relatively **self-sufficient** and **content** to be what it is. 'Take it or leave it' is an attitude of **confidence** and intrinsic worth that needs nothing from others.

The freedom of Neutrality is the consequence of the letting go of positionalities, conditions, and expectations. Narcissistic demands and egocentric needs are no longer dominant. Therefore, the level of Neutrality does not suffer from lack nor is it driven by desire, wantingness, or the compulsion to 'do' something or take sides in social issues; thus, it includes **flexibility**. In Neutrality, there is trust in God as being nonjudgmental and benign, resulting in **reliance on God's wisdom** that makes allowance for man's limitations. Thus, God is really the source of freedom because Divinity no longer seems to be a threat to fear or hate and therefore deny. Projected perceptions are confused with reality and given emphasis by imaginary gain or loss. In contrast, Neutrality is the consequence of nonattachment and is therefore relatively devoid of distortions of projected superimposed values, opinions, etc. For additional details, please see "Transcending the Levels of Consciousness: The Stairway to Enlightenment" (2006), Chapter 10: Neutrality, pp. 195-202.

WILLINGNESS (Level 310)

Cheerful	Contribute	Jovial
Volunteers	Assist	Motivated
Helpful	Encourage	Energetic
Positive attitude	Self-correcting	Benevolent
Participatory	Appropriate	Mutuality
Friendly, social	Committed	Inspirational
Self-esteem	Join	Supportive
Humanitarian	Aliveness	Golden Rule
Good will to life	Well-being	Aligned
Sympathetic	Optimistic	Win-win
Responsive	Pleasant	Thankful
Service to others	Sense of humor	Gracious
Build		

Slide 76

SLIDE 76: WILLINGNESS (LEVEL 310)

This slide was first introduced at the April 2006 lecture, DVD disc 2 at 003025.

Energy fields are really portals out of which we see the world. All we experience is our own energy field reflected back upon us as perception and experiencing. When one reaches the level of Courage (cal. 200), the world appears to be a place of opportunity. It is a challenging place with opportunities for growth and expansion. At the level of Neutral (cal. 250), life and the world is 'okay' due to one's being nonattached. You move into an easygoing view of the world and begin to say, "Well, that's human nature. It's serving some kind of ultimate purpose."

The people who move on up to the level of Willingness (cal. 310) experience the world as friendly. They walk down the street, see endless friendliness, and think the universe is friendly no matter what they have. The world is harmonious, benign, and supportive. At level 200, the energy is positive, so the field stops pulling negativity from the universe to itself. One is able to face, cope with, and handle things, and, for the first time, able to be pro-life instead of the anti-life stance of the lower energy fields. At the level of Courage, people still experience the lesser negative feelings, but they now have the power to handle those energies. The critical process going on in Consciousness is one of empowerment and the emotion is affirmation, as in being pro-life, as opposed to anti-life.

The next major level is that of Neutral at 250, where the energy field is positive and even more aligned with Truth. The emotion of Neutral is self-trust, e.g. it is 'okay' if one gets the job and 'okay' if one does not. The process going on in consciousness is release, as one is detached from any particular outcome and not driven by aversions or cravings. The advantage of the level of Neutral is the "okayness" of life, but then one has to introduce a new energy of intention to move to the next level, Willingness, which implies that one has overcome inner resistance to life, and to participation.

Real power begins with Willingness, as the primary emotion at this level is **optimism** and the process going on in consciousness is intention. Willingness is **sympathetic** and **responsive** to the needs of others. Willing people are **builders** of, and contributors to, society. With their capacity to bounce back from adversity and learn from experience, they tend to become **self-correcting**. Having let go of Pride, they are willing to look at their own defects and learn from others. At the level of Willingness, people become excellent students. They are easily teachable and represent a considerable source of power for society. **Motivation** is the consequence of **inspiration** instead of the desire for gain. Willingness is **cheerful, helpful, and voluntary**. The energy of Willingness is also the level of the **Golden Rule**: "Do unto others as you would have others do unto you." In successful relationships, this results in a **mutuality** of partners as helpmates and companions. Many truly charitable people see it as an honor to be able to **serve others** and are unaware that it simultaneously sub-serves the accumulation of karmic merit. For additional details, please see "Transcending the Levels of Consciousness: The Stairway to Enlightenment" (2006), Chapter 11: Willingness, pp. 203-210.

ACCEPTANCE (Level 350)

Wisdom	**Sees whole picture**	**Non-controlling**
Non-judgmentalism	**Appropriate**	**Judicious**
Sanguine	**Balanced**	**Sophisticated**
Comfortable	**Includes context**	**Respectful**
Patience	**Self-discipline**	**Unruffled**
Harmonious Cooperative	**Plurality**	**Impartial**
Benign	**Tolerant**	**Germane**
Mature	**Holistic**	**Broad viewpoint**
Nonrestrictive	**Accordance**	**Sagacity**
Non-rejecting	**Practical**	**Harmless**
Realistic	**Non-desirous**	**Measured**

Slide 77

SLIDE 77: ACCEPTANCE (LEVEL 350)

This slide was first introduced at the April 2006 lecture, DVD disc 2 at 003050 (no words spoken).

People who have moved up to the level of Acceptance (cal. 350) really begin to experience the harmony of life and discover synchronicity and how everything just sort of flows together. They experience a world of harmony because they are holding cooperation as their own energy field. This helps them to move up to Enthusiasm (cal. 390), as the person on this level realizes that God is merciful. The primary emotion at this level is forgiveness and the process going on in consciousness itself is transcendence of character defects like harboring of resentments. Acceptance allows engagement in life on life's own terms, without trying to make it conform to an agenda. One now sees things without distortion or misinterpretation; the context of experience is expanded so that one is capable of "**seeing the whole picture**." Acceptance has to do essentially with **balance**, proportion, and **appropriateness**.

The individual at the level of Acceptance is less interested in judgmentalism and instead is dedicated to resolving issues and finding out what to do about problems. Tough jobs do not cause discomfort or dismay. Long-term goals take precedence over short-term ones; self- discipline and mastery are prominent. It sees that other people have equal rights and therefore honors equality. While lower levels are characterized by rigidity, at this level social **plurality** begins to emerge as a form of resolution of problems. Therefore, this level is free of extremes of discrimination or intolerance. There is an awareness that equality does not preclude diversity. Acceptance includes rather than rejects.

Acceptance is a result of **wisdom** as well as surrendering positionalities. Someone at this level accepts that the varied expressions of life are in accord with Divine will and that Creation is thereby multitudinous in its expressions as evolution. Acceptance sees that perceived qualities are innate to the human condition and are reflective of individual as well as group karma and innate to the species Homo sapiens. Society includes an admixture of different levels of evolutionary development, including a panorama of options and alternate ways to go in the existential 'house of mirrors'. By surrendering the wish to change or control others, there is a reciprocal freedom of not being controllable by others' opinions and values, nor is there a desire or need for their approval. With freedom from the need of approval by others, there is release from the compulsion to seek or crave social agreement. The maturity of Acceptance includes the ability to tranquilly accept both personal and human limitations without loss of self-esteem because value judgments have lost their validity and are now seen to be primarily arbitrary, personalized choices. Thereby, personal opinions become dethroned and lose their tendency to dominate by sheer emotional pressure. For additional details, please see "Transcending the Levels of Consciousness: The Stairway to Enlightenment" (2006), Chapter 12: Acceptance, pp. 211-218.

REASON (Level 400)

Thinking	**Unemotional**	**Abstractness**
Comprehend	**Respects facts**	**Objectivity**
Intellectual	**Respects definitions**	**Impersonal**
Logical Educated	**Intelligent**	**Detached**
Discernment	**Processes data**	**Reason**
Specificity	**Principles**	**Symbolism**
Structured	**Erudition**	**Information**
Disciplined	**Deliberate**	**Facts**
Dialectic Rational	**Controlled**	**Level/class/genus**
Understand	**Conceptual**	**Distinctions**
Delineate	**Definition**	**Synthesize**
	Distinctive	**Abstraction**
	Meaning	

Slide 78

SLIDE 78: REASON (LEVEL 400)

This slide was first introduced at the April 2006 lecture, DVD disc 2 at 003055.

Students of spiritual work are often those who are perfecting the levels of the 400s, where they have acquired a dedicated willingness to learn about spiritual matters. The basic question remains the same as it has throughout all of history: What does it all 'mean' (i.e., hermeneutics)? Pondering the implied subtleties of **meaning** has occupied the greatest minds of history and produced the great wealth of philosophy and its central issues, including epistemology, theology, metaphysics, and ontology. With the evolution of consciousness, **reason**, **logic**, and the intellect are energized by alignment with commitment to truth, which is actually an aspect of Divinity and the invisible source of the power of the field of mind itself. The gift of the alignment with truth results in comprehension and the accumulation of wisdom and sagacity in the exercise and application of the function of reason.

Thus, it is still up to the individual will to choose the degree to which reason is prioritized in relation to emotionality. The individual is free to ignore reason or to follow its dictates and interpretations of reality vis-a-vis imagination, fantasy, or emotional options and their degree of expression. A major deterrent to spiritual evolution and transcending identification of the self with mind is the processing of data, symbols, and words via random mentalization, which is presumed to be **'thinking'**. During meditation, this mental chatter is frustrating and becomes a source of anxiety. To try to silence the mind forcibly is ineffective, and the results are limited and brief.

Spiritual study utilizes the intellect to reveal that the intellect itself has to be transcended from 'knowing about' to 'becoming', which it accomplishes by spiritual practice, discipline, and devotion. By understanding the source of the flow of mentalization, it can be transcended, revealing the silence out of which thinkingness arises. By spiritual intention, the intellect can be sanctified so that it becomes a springboard and roadway to understanding spiritual reality instead of a dead end or a roadblock. Mentalization is of egocentric origin, and its primary function is commentary. Unless requested, thought is a vanity, an endless procession of opinion, rationalization, reprocessing, evaluating, and subtle judgment by which the thoughts are given value or importance via presumed significance because they are 'mine'. The ego is enamored of its life story and its central character.

It is a relief to let the mind become silent and just 'be' with surroundings. Peace results, and appreciation and calm prevail. In order to realize that a running commentary is not necessary or even authorized, the will gives the mind permission to be silent. When devalued and humbled, the vanity basis of thinkingness collapses, and in its place one discovers the joy of inner silence, which constitutes 99% of the mind. Only 1% is actually chattering. The God of this level (400) is Wise, life is meaningful, the primary emotion is **understanding**, and the process going on within consciousness is **abstraction**. For additional details, please see "Transcending the Levels of Consciousness: The Stairway to Enlightenment" (2006), Chapter 13: Reason (Calibration Level 400), pp. 219-235.

LOVE (Level 500)

Warmth	**Heartfelt**	**Join**
Appreciation	**Nurturing**	**Diffuse**
Supportive	**Understanding**	**Contextual**
Forgiving	**Protective**	**Benign**
Inclusive	**Goodness**	**Alignment**
Affectionate	**Purity**	**Humble**
Cordial	**Giving**	**Satisfying**
Gracious	**Generous**	**Gratitude**
Positive	**Sharing**	**Completion**
Steadfast	**Nonlinear**	**Vision**
Uplifting	**Holistic**	**Sweetness**

Slide 79

SLIDE 79: LOVE (LEVEL 500)

This slide was first introduced at the April 2006 lecture, DVD disc 2 at 003110.

The 500 level is characterized by the development of an energy field that is progressively unconditional, unchanging, and permanent. It does not fluctuate because its source within the person who loves is not dependent on external factors. Lovingness is a way of being in and relating to the world and is **forgiving, nurturing, and supportive**. Love emanates from the heart and has the capacity to **uplift** others and accomplish great feats because of its purity of motive. In terms of the evolution of consciousness, this level reflects transcendence of identification with the limiting linear domain and its positionalities to the awareness of subjectivity as the primary state that underlies all experience. Thus, the sense of reality moves from what is perceived to the condition or faculty by which it is experienced. Whereas the ego focuses on content, the spirit values **context**. The ego values quantity, and in contrast, the spirit values quality. By consciousness level 500, approximately ninety percent of the people experience happiness as a basic quality of life.

The barriers to Love that arise from animal instincts no longer pressure for dominance, nor does the narcissistic core of the ego predominate, which is a consequence of humility and the relinquishment of egocentricity. Thus, personal self-interest is no longer dominant as selfishness or neediness. The view of the self is that of **benign** adequacy and **alignment** is with Love as a primary goal and lifestyle. The primary emotion is reverence for all of life, and the process going on in consciousness is revelation. There is nothing logical to Love and one cannot prove it or destroy it. This is why conferences on "Science and Spirituality" calibrate around 440, as persons engaged in science and theology do not get that spiritual reality is a different paradigm and the intellect is not the correct tool to investigate spiritual reality.

Spiritual reality is subjective; it is not objective. It is nonlinear, one cannot prove that someone loves someone or something, yet one will give up one's life for Love. Love is **inclusive**, of course. Love has an innate goodness to it, so most people on this path reach a point of sweet goodness, **sweetness** to their life, becoming **cordial** towards life itself. The energy field of Love is innately gratifying in and of its own quality. It is discovered that Love is available everywhere and that lovingness results in the return of love. The capacity for Love grows so that the more one loves, the more one can love, and there is no end to it. In addition, it is discovered that to be loving is also to be lovable.

Perception is replaced with **vision** at this level that allows for the awareness of the intrinsic value of all that exists. Love is a quality of Divinity and as such illuminates the Essence and therefore the lovability of others. From calibration levels 500 to 539, the love is still subject to conditions and partialities, based on considerations and qualitative values, as well as the influence of belief systems. The relinquishing of judgmentalism greatly increases the capacity of Love, as does surrendering the wanting of anything from others. Thus, people are not perceived according to what they have or do but by appreciation for what they are and have become. For additional details, please see "Transcending the Levels of Consciousness: The Stairway to Enlightenment" (2006), Chapter 14: Love, pp. 245-253.

UNCONDITIONAL LOVE (Level 540)

0.4% of people

Inner joy

Healing

Faith

Ecstasy

Kindness

Inner state

Patience

Persistence

Compassion

Saintly

Siddhis

Miraculous

Kundalini energy

Vision

Essence

Beauty

Synchronicity

Perfection

Surrender

Emerging Self

Devotional

Rapture

Uplifted

Inclusive

Nonselective

Merciful

Transformative

Selfless

Radiant

Effortless

Unlimited

Diffuse

Openness

Way of life

Slide 80

SLIDE 80: UNCONDITIONAL LOVE (LEVEL 540)

This slide was first introduced at the April 2006 lecture, DVD disc 2 at 003300.

As Love becomes increasingly unconditional, it begins to be experienced as **inner Joy**. This is not the sudden joy of a pleasurable turn of events but instead is a constant accompaniment to all activities. Joy arises from within each moment of existence rather than from any outer source. Level 540 is also the level of **healing** and of spiritually based self-help groups. From level 540 upward is the domain of saints, spiritual healers, and advanced spiritual students. Characteristic of this energy field is a capacity for enormous **patience** and the **persistence** of a positive attitude in the face of prolonged adversity. The hallmark of this state is **compassion**. People who have attained this level have a notable effect on others. They are capable of a prolonged, open visual gaze that induces a state of love and peace. At the high 500's, the world is illuminated by the exquisite **beauty** and **perfection** of Creation. Everything happens effortlessly by **synchronicity**, and one sees the world and everything in it to be an expression of Love and Divinity. Individual will merges into Divine will. One feels the power of the Presence that facilitates phenomena outside conventional expectations of reality, termed '**miraculous**' by the ordinary observer. These phenomena represent the power of the energy field, not of the individual. One's sense of responsibility for others at this level is of a quality different from that shown at the lower levels. There is a desire to use one's state of consciousness for the benefit of life itself rather than for particular individuals. This capacity to love many people simultaneously is accompanied by the discovery that the more one loves, the more one can love.

When we look at our humanness from the viewpoint of forgiveness and compassion, we can then love it and hold it within our greatness. We also now know that what we forgive in others is forgiven within ourselves and disappears from our perception of the world. Our perception of the world begins to shift. It is like putting on a different pair of colored glasses—the world is not the same, and we can experience it in a completely different manner. What kind of lovingness brings about an almost automatic healing within the body? It is unconditional love, that which is nonjudgmental, forgiving, and aligned with understanding and compassion. Love sees, nurtures and supports all of life and honors its sacredness, and of itself creates a healing energy field that calibrates at 540. There is sensitivity to beauty that becomes almost rapturous. Beauty can become overwhelming. One can look at two people sitting and waiting and as they glance at each other lovingly, that makes one cry. The God of this level is One, i.e. shared by all of Creation. Life goes from complete to complete. The predominant emotion is serenity, and the process going on within consciousness itself is transfiguration. For additional details, please see "Transcending the Levels of Consciousness: The Stairway to Enlightenment" (2006), Chapter 15: Unconditional Love, Joy, and Ecstasy, pp. 255-267.

ILLUMINATION (Level 600)

Timeless	**Self**	**Wordless**
Peace	**Motionless**	**Whole**
Inner Silence	**Effulgent**	**Identity**
Radiant Stillness	**Bliss**	**All encompassing**
Completion	**Presence**	**Transformation**
Luminous	**Essence**	**Nonlinear**
Revelation	**Divinity**	**Harmony**
Unlimited	**Unfolding**	**Intrinsic**
Global	**"Sat-chit-ananda"**	**Nonlocality**
All-inclusive	**Emergence**	**Total**
Innate	**Oneness**	**Unification**

Slide 81

SLIDE 81: ILLUMINATION (LEVEL 600)

This slide was first introduced at the April 2006 lecture, DVD disc 2 at 003355.

Illumination is a **radiant** state. It emanates from within. It has no form and it does not say anything. There is no one speaking to you. It is a blissful state, one of absolute fulfillment, with the presence of Love as infinite peace. It is rather unmistakable. It is just beyond the level of ecstasy. One goes into Joy, then Ecstasy, and if Ecstasy is surrendered to God, then the state of Illumination replaces the previous ones. When this state is reached, the distinction between subject and object disappears, and there is no specific focal point of perception. Frequently, individuals at this level leave the world because the state of bliss precludes ordinary activity. Action at the level of 600 and above is perceived as occurring in slow motion, suspended in time and space. All is alive, radiant, and continuously flowing, unfolding in an exquisitely coordinated evolutionary dance in which significance and Source are overwhelming. This awesome revelation takes place without thought or conception so that there is an infinite silence in the mind, which has stopped conceptualizing. The observer dissolves and becomes equally the observation. Sound has no effect on the silence that persists even within the sound. The state is traditionally referred to as ***sat-chit-ananda*** (silent bliss).

Physiological functions can come to a halt. There is no desire to move or speak, and the inner Silence is mute as though suspended in timelessness. Whether the body continues on and survives or not is uninteresting and actually without meaning. It is a matter of no interest and up to the Universe to direct. If the karmic propensities are aligned with physical continuation, the body survives. If not, the body is simply abandoned, for it came from the earth and returns to the earth when it has served the purpose of the spirit.

The Presence is self-fulfilling and **complete**, exquisitely soft and simultaneously powerful. Its essence pervades all manifestation as the Source of Existence. All is seen to arise from the Un-manifest becoming Manifest as Creation from a Source that is innate, All Present, and beyond volition. In Unity and Oneness, everything is simultaneously intrinsic to everything else, but not by virtue of being either the 'same' or 'else'.

Creation is witnessed as the unfolding and revelation of the emergence of infinite potentiality as Creation. Thus, there is no duality of a 'this' (Creator) creating a 'that' (Creation) for Creator and Creation are one and the same, and Creation is self-effulgent. Everything that exists is perfect and complete. Creation does not move from imperfection to perfection, as is witnessed by the ego, but instead moves from perfection to perfection. The God of this level is 'All-being', Self- view is perfect, the predominant emotion is **bliss** and the process going on in consciousness is illumination. For additional details, please see "Transcending the Levels of Consciousness: The Stairway to Enlightenment" (2006), Chapter 16: Peace, Bliss, and Illumination, pp. 275-283.

SELF-REALIZATION (Levels 700-850)

Compassion

"self" dissolved in Self

Timeless

Essence

All inclusive

Divine context

Perfection

Self as God Immanent

Grace

Nonlocality

Nonseparation

Creation as unfoldment

Evolution is

Creation Beyond

emotion

Silent awareness

Body self-actuated

Beyond volition

Autonomous

Completion

Oneness of

existence

Awareness

Mystical

Purusha

Beyond cause/effect

Innate

Self as Source

Truth = Love = Divinity

Samadhi

Awakened

Enlightened

Transcendent

Sage/Teacher

Devoid of needs

Witnessing

Desireless

Sanctified

Slide 82

SLIDE 82: SELF-REALIZATION (LEVELS 700-850)

This slide was first introduced at the April 2006 lecture, DVD disc 2 at 003450.

Probably the best-known recent representatives of this state of non-duality are Nisargadatta Maharaj and Ramana Maharishi. This is where the smaller self is dissolved into the larger Self. The Grace of the Guru becomes sought because at levels beyond 700, one begins to radiate an energy which can be picked up in the student's aura, and the potential for enlightenment becomes possible. Vibration is necessary because it is a non-linear dimension and to have read about it does not do any good. The levels of 700-850 are the states of Samadhi, and we say the persons in these states are awakened, enlightened, transcendent, and devoid of needs. They have become sanctified, like Mother Teresa. There is an identification of Self with consciousness, and Divinity Immanent is realized as Self beyond mind. The reason these levels are so peaceful is that there are no external wants. The only reason you say you want something is when others are not happy unless you say you want something, so you make up something plausible and then others are happy. That means the Sage/teacher sacrifices the truth a little bit to make others happy.

At this level of realization, the sense of one's existence transcends all time and all individuality. The body is seen as merely a tool of consciousness through the intervention of mind, with its prime value being that of communication. The self merges back into the Self. This is the level of non-duality, or complete Oneness. There is no localization of consciousness; awareness is equally present everywhere. Great works of art depicting individuals who have reached the level of Enlightenment often show the teacher with a specific hand position, called a *mudra*, wherein the palm of the hand symbolically radiates benediction. This is the act of the transmission of this energy field to the consciousness of mankind, which is also depicted by a halo. The Presence of Self constitutes the classic *Purusha*, or Radiance of Self as Source. Self 'knows' by virtue of identity with Divinity itself. It thereby is its own Awareness, and by its Presence, it thereby makes itself 'known' as the 'Knower'.

The surrender of identification with each state releases it, including letting go of any attachment to its familiarity. Consciousness evolves as though attracted to return to its Source. Each advance expands the paradigm of awareness that, transitionally, has a certain sense of 'home'. Many sages, once they reach the level of the 700s, remain at that level for the remainder of their lives. Occasionally, however, the process continues spontaneously when allowed to do so. Each level represents the completion of the evolution that precedes it, but it is also the doorway to the next. Subjectively, transition is more like an emergence or an unfolding, which is the province of awareness itself, about which there is no mentalization because these are the states of 'no mind' (paradoxically also labeled as 'Mind'). For additional details, please see "Transcending the Levels of Consciousness: The Stairway to Enlightenment" (2006), Chapter 17: Self-Realization, pp. 285-293.

FULL ENLIGHTENMENT (Levels 850-1,000) (1)

Divinity as timeless totality

Divinity as existence

Auric radiance to humanity

Nonlinear present in linear

Consciousness as radiance of Divinity

Consciousness as Source of Life

Divinity as all-present Oneness

Timeless infinite context

Universe as consequent to omnipotence

Consciousness as omniscience

Awareness intrinsic quality of consciousness

Divinity innate to all existence

Field by which potentiality becomes expressed as actuality

Consciousness as Source of Life

Life energy not subject to destruction

Divinity as Infinite Context and Source

Slide 83

SLIDE 83: FULL ENLIGHTENMENT (LEVELS 850-1,000) (1)

This slide was first introduced at the April 2006 lecture, DVD disc 2 at 003615.

The very high energy frequencies of Enlightenment transmit a vibration to the collective consciousness field of mankind in general and become inscribed in the auric fields (etheric spiritual energy bodies) of spiritually aligned people by 'silent transmission'. The frequency vibration of this energy remains within the spiritual etheric body for very long periods of time and (confirmed by consciousness calibration research) can last for as long as twenty-five incarnations or up to even one thousand years, where it lies in wait to be claimed.

Enlightened sages were primarily Self-realized mystics or recipients of Divine Incarnation, such as Jesus Christ. The oldest sources of the highest spiritual truth historically came down from the great Aryan sages of ancient India (i.e., the *Vedas*, the *Upanishads*). These originated in approximately 5,000 B.C. (The Buddha lived approximately 563 B.C.). The sages who reached level 850 or over became primary influential teachers, and their teachings form the core of important schools and revered spiritual traditions. Thus, a major teaching retains its intrinsic value over many centuries. The transition from calibration level 850 to 1,000 is the consequence of rejection of the Void as the ultimate reality and affirmation of the Realization that the Source of the Enlightened states is *Divinity* as *God*, which is inclusive of all the attributes that calibrate at 850, *plus* God as Infinite *Love*. Full Enlightenment realizes the Presence as God and Divinity as the Source and Essence of Life, Creation, Consciousness/Awareness, and Existence. God is therefore descriptively omnipotent, omniscient, and omnipresent, and both Immanent and Transcendent, as well as Manifest and Un-manifest (the Godhead). Calibration level 1,000 is the ultimate state possible within the human domain (calibrates as 'true').

Awareness is an aspect of Consciousness and is not personal. A spiritual teacher speaks from 'Purusha' or the Presence within, which has no personal identity. A teacher does not hear voices, does not have conversations with other forces or channel other entities, such as an archangel. That which speaks and that what is spoken are identical. Purusha is the Self of the teacher, which speaks only from its own knowingness from within. That which it is, is complete and total and radiates out its Totality as a self-fulfilling knowingness. Divinity knows its own; therefore, to accept that truth is to already feel joy. To not experience joy by understanding this means that it is being resisted. For additional details, please see "Transcending the Levels of Consciousness: The Stairway to Enlightenment" (2006), Chapter 18: Full Enlightenment, pp. 295-306.

FULL ENLIGHTENMENT (Levels 850-1,000) (2)

Manifestation as emergence of potential

Divinity as Infinity

Divinity as harmony

God as Creator/Essence/Source

Love as expression of Divinity

Existence as expression of Grace

All inclusive

Oneness/Fullness

Glory of God – "Gloria in Excelsis Deo"

Ineffable

Non-volitional

Sanctity

Nonverbal awareness

Innate, intrinsic, omnipresent

Divinity as Source rather than cause

All moves from perfection to perfection

Slide 84

SLIDE 84: FULL ENLIGHTENMENT (LEVELS 850-1,000) (2)

This slide was first introduced at the April 2006 lecture, DVD disc 2 at 004040.

The state is non-verbal, but it is verbalized in order to communicate. That which communicates is the persona, an aspect of energy that is called upon when there is a purpose for communication. It speaks autonomously and spontaneously so one does not have to think about what one says because there is nobody saying it. Speakingness is its own speakingness, and fulfilled already. It may be hard to understand but all that one can say is that the speakingness is speaking. People either get it or not. Just like Lovingness is loving, it is not dualistic. Lovingness is its own expression of what it is. That which has existence is already total and complete or it would not exist. Existence does not require dependence on some other condition. Conditional existence is therefore an illusion of the ego/mind which believes that nothing exists except as dependent on something outside itself. Existence is solely by the grace of God, by Divine ordinance. Appearance reflects conditions and is therefore transitory.

At the previous levels of consciousness, all has been surrendered to God, and then the very last remnant of the self remains as the seeming source of life—the core of the ego itself, with the conviction that *it* is the author and primordial *source* of one's very life and existence. As this arises, so also does a knowing-ness that 'even this, too' must be surrendered to God. This last barrier is signaled by a sudden burst of the last remaining fear, which is very strong and intense—the very basic fear of death. Then arises a knowingness, which has been nascent in the spiritual aura that 'all fear is an illusion' and 'death is not a possibility'. Then, as a consequence of faith and devotion, the last illusion is surrendered. Next emerges the literal, actual, feared sensation of dying—a brief but very intense agony because, unlike physical death, it has never been faced before. That is the only and final 'death' possible. As the agony dies away, there is an emergence into the Revelation of the Infinite Glory of Divinity. The last vestige of the ego/mind disappears into the Silence of the Presence. The stunning perfection and beauty of the Allness of Creation as Divinity radiates forth, and all is still, beyond all time. *Gloria in Excelsis Deo* is *the State itself.*

To know what is necessary to know in order to reach Divine states accelerates progress; otherwise, there is an unconscious resistance of fear due to ignorance. This fear is overcome by the acquisition of the necessary understanding; therefore, there is nothing left to fear, and all fear is an illusion—a knowing-ness that is also required at very advanced states. Any student who is serious about spiritual alignment and devotion to God, to Love, to Truth, to fellow humanity, or to the alleviation of human suffering in all sentient beings, is already very far advanced. Consistent application of any spiritual principle can unexpectedly result in a major and sudden leap to unanticipated levels. At that point, memory may not even be available, and instead, the Knowingness of Spiritual Truth presents itself silently. For additional details, please see "Transcending the Levels of Consciousness: The Stairway to Enlightenment" (2006), Chapter 18: Full Enlightenment, pp. 295-306.

OBLIGATIONS OF SPIRITUAL TEACHERS (1)

Declaration of responsibility

Integrity of purpose and function

Stewardship of knowledge

Moral and ethical conduct with students

Refusal of exploitation: money, sex, control, status

Explanation of teachings and their confirmation

Provide availability of teachings

Compassion and dedication to student body and individuals

Preclude dependency

Seed autonomous study groups

Humility: devoid of spiritual ego yet certainty of knowledge

Acknowledge source of knowingness

Eschew personal credit or acclaim

Share the means of access to Truth

Slide 85

SLIDE 85: OBLIGATIONS OF SPIRITUAL TEACHERS (1)

This slide was first introduced at the April 2006 lecture, DVD disc 2 at 004150.

The primary function of a spiritual teacher is that of declaration of the condition or state and thus affirmation of the Reality of its Source, traditionally called Divinity. The Presence is of a dimension different from that of ordinary experiencing and therefore requires a rather specific and unique type of languaging. It is of a Source beyond that of ordinary experiencing and is instead a quality of Reality devoid of linearity. That the Source of consciousness/awareness is simultaneously beyond even existence or non-existence is impossible to language except by intuitive implication, for even the sun is a consequence of realities that are beyond and greater than the sun itself.

No one has written about the obligations of spiritual teachers. That is one of the reasons that the spiritual progress of humanity has been slow. False teachers abound as both the teachers and the followers have no guidelines as to the obligations of spiritual teachers. Spiritual teachers should be willing to make a declaration of their responsibility regarding their integrity, their obligations, stewardship and knowledge; and about the moral and ethical conduct with their students, which has been outrageous all over the planet. The main thing is the declaration of refusal to exploit any aspect of others.

Commitment is to the explanation of the teaching, to be the steward of the availability of the teaching. Many spiritual teachings were not written down for more than a hundred years and by the time they were, they had wandered far from their original truth. The teacher dissuades people from becoming dependent and likes to see autonomous study groups. The teacher acknowledges the Source of the knowingness, that there is no person doing anything therefore there is no one to take credit or blame.

Adulation is not due to the persona but to the Truth. The student owes the teacher nothing at all; if they stay awake, great; if they do not, who cares? It is not necessary to stay awake. There is nobody to feel offended if someone snores. The linear manifest world (Creation) is itself an emergence from the nonlinear, the Un-manifest (the Godhead). The enlightened teacher is therefore the example or confirmation within the visible, linear human domain of the Source, out of which enlightenment and life itself manifest. They are therefore the exemplification of the human potential as a demonstration within the visible world. The condition or state represents the threshold at which the nonlinear Source might well be said to emerge from potentiality to actuality, much as a light bulb is a transformer of electrical energy into light. Although both light and electricity emanate from the same source which is invisible, it is only the light that is visible. Thus, the enlightened sage is akin to a transformative agency by which the agent becomes visible and confirmable. This is then expressed as a function of the sage/mystic as the witness who gives testimony to other dimensions of reality that transcend the ordinary. The uniqueness is represented by the descriptive term 'ineffable'.

For additional details, please see "Discovery of the Presence of God: Devotional Non-duality" (2006), Chapter 11: Teachers and Teaching, pp.171-179.

OBLIGATIONS OF SPIRITUAL TEACHERS (2)

Provide means of verification of Truth

Inspirational and devotional

Explain difference between spiritual and personal love

Explain the pitfalls that are temptations along the pathway

Provide historical correlations

Unguarded and open

Approachable

Avoid seduction by mystification

Reject commercialization

Maintain simplicity of life

Avoid pomposity, glamorization, or theatrical display

Transparency, dedication to role and function

Reverent, and acknowledgment of the source of knowingness

Slide 86

SLIDE 86: OBLIGATIONS OF SPIRITUAL TEACHERS (2)

This slide was first introduced at the April 2006 lecture, DVD disc 2 at 004350.

The teacher should provide a means for verification of truth so that they do not have to push people's credibility and the student does not have to take someone's word. The teacher should be devoted and explain the difference between spiritual and personal love, as that is a major issue and pitfall in the 500s. In the high 500s there is powerful energy being radiated and people of the opposite sex come out of the blue and solicit you. They knock on your door and say, "this may sound crazy but I'd like to go to bed with you." They are confusing spiritual love with personal love. The love radiated in the high 500s is like magnetism and they feel in your presence a sense of love. They are picking up the energy field and it is activating in them, but it is not personal so an inexperienced teacher is easily flattered and seduced. Indeed, there are many books about the various gurus who were seduced by various spiritual students.

A teacher should avoid mystification or "mumbo-jumbo" in order to sound wise, as that is a type of seduction. It involves, for example, speaking in Sanskrit or doing strange things to hypnotize students into thinking you are a great swami, or wearing special robes, or displaying spiritual powers called the siddhis. That is not spirituality but theatrics and one learns that in grammar school, including the very slick and seductive display on the front covers of magazines with messages like, 'buy this, buy that.'

The teacher should be unguarded and open, not defensive. He should provide some historical correlation. He should be approachable and maintain simplicity of his own personal life, rather than pomposity, glamorization and theatrical displays. They should also be completely and totally transparent; there is nothing one needs to guard or protect against or try to hide. That which you are is completely transparent and obvious.

PERCEPTION VS. ESSENCE

PERCEPTION	ESSENCE	PERCEPTION	ESSENCE
Judgmental	Acceptance	Motivated	Witnessed
Projection	Awareness	Selective	Totality
Opinion	Impersonal	Personal	Impersonal
Distortion	Clarity	Sought	Registers
Content	Context	Volitional	Passive
Programmed	Pristine	Attraction/Aversion	Autonomist
Emotional	Detached	Causation	Unfoldment
Reactive	Nonattached	Want/don't want	Observe
Gain/Loss	"As is"	Memory file	Record
Mental	Intuitive	Think about	Know
Exclusive	Inclusive	Evaluate	Recognize
Good/Bad	Intention	Processed	Purity
Value	Quality	Contaminated	Unprocessed
Belief	Level of Truth	Meme	Concept
Distinction	Apperception	Central	Peripheral
Meaning	Existence		

Slide 87

SLIDE 87: PERCEPTION VS. ESSENCE

This slide was first introduced at the April 2006 lecture, DVD disc 2 at 004730.

Perception has to do with the linear content. Essence has to do with the Field. How you perceive the content is a consequence of the Field. Perception tends to be judgmental, essence is accepting. Perception obviously is a projection in contrast to awareness; perception is personal opinion, essence is impersonal. There is no personal investment in an answer when calibrating. For example, a fortune cookie seems to have a characteristic of goodness, so its calibration is the verification of one's capacity to discern essence. Essence has to do with what is pristine, detached, and not emotionally embroiled. Perception tends to be reactive, as anyone who watches television well knows. Essence is not involved with the outcome, as it has no concern for the outcome. Perception sees everything as gain or loss, e.g. will we gain a profit from it?

Essence merely sees things as they are. This is hard for people to understand. Everything is as it is. This sounds like a dumb statement except that it is the reality of enlightenment. The meaning of anything is simply what it is. Anything else is a projection. By saying that something is this or that, one just projected onto it.

A pointer is neither a piece of metal nor a piece of junk; neither it is useful nor not useful. All these descriptions are made up in a person's head, and this is the way Newtonian causality comes about. The mind says it caused a thing to happen. By the time the mind thinks it moved it or made it happen, it has already happened. The intention is actually coming out of the etheric (energetic) body, which is different from the physical body. It takes 1/10,000 of a second for the experiencer to move from the phenomenal to the subjective. Perception is 1/10,000 of a second behind "what is".

The ego's perception is like a tape monitor; it is a shock when the monitoring stops and awareness and experiencing are simultaneous. This is what gives the highest levels of consciousness their extraordinary quality. When perception ceases, one is wonderstruck by the brilliance and the radiance of Divinity of All That Exists. The radiance of divinity shines forth with such stunning beauty, one is immobilized and unable to think or function. From that moment on, all has changed.

The memory is stored according to feeling states shaded by perception; there is an affective tone to all memories. Perception is very programmable. When a person hears comments about politics for example, they are not someone's original take but usually pulled from information on a "blog" site, mostly memes. Like a parrot, one thinks it is their opinion, but it really has nothing to do with their opinion. Perception is mental, whereas the "Isness" of things is something one intuits without thinking about it. The reason contemplation is useful as a spiritual style is that it is a way of being with Reality. Meditation serves a purpose, but tends to take one out of the world. In contemplation, you are always in a meditative state. You begin to see that the Totality is equally valued at all times. Perception does not stop in that state of awareness, but it has a different quality, a different value when modified by essence. Perception makes distinctions, essence is the Allness and Oneness of things. Perception is therefore motivated, selective and personal, while essence is witnessed and impersonal. It registers but it does so passively. Perception deals with want-do not want, while essence is observation.

PERCEPTION: INFLUENCES

Level of consciousness
Programming
Conditioning
Set and setting
Priorities
Age, sex, gender
Education
Culture
Emotional set
Media
Propaganda/hype
Glamorization
Status
Glamour
Seduction
Meaning

Instinctual appeal
Prior experience/exposure
Expectation
Desire
Needs
Presentation
Moral/ethical
Political viewpoint
Senses/modality
Symbolism
Memory file
Framing
Degree of narcissism
Level of spiritual evolution
Opinions/intention

Slide 88

SLIDE 88: PERCEPTION: INFLUENCES

This slide was first introduced at the April 2006 lecture, DVD disc 2 at 010300.

The level of consciousness obviously determines perceptual influence considerably because a person's dedication to truth makes you aware that the media is programming people all the time. You hold back belief because you know there will be more to the story. Those who lived through the history of wars will see things revealed even 25 to 30 years later, so obviously there is more to the story. The level of consciousness has to do with sophistication in a certain way. Perception is programmable. Conditions depend on set and setting, and priority. Whether people like it or not, age, sex and gender play a big role in programming. You might protest, but you are fooling yourself if you do not see this. Men see things differently than women. As a man and woman are walking down 5th Avenue, the woman will notice a new dress in the storefront. A man will not notice a new dress, because he does not wear them. Thus, gender plays a role on how one perceives the dress in the window. Shopping on 5th Avenue at Gucci's or a designer store is either fun or not fun. Some people think it is smart to hang out there while others do not care. Education, culture, emotional set, and the media all play a role in the propaganda hype.

Because of glamorization, you begin to wonder if it is a person wearing a designer label or a label wearing a person. Sometimes, there is a label walking down the street with a person attached to it. It is all very seductive and has personal meaning. Not that it is wrong, but one must be able to see it and be aware of the programming. Some things have an instinctual appeal. Your prior experience and exposure will certainly determine the expectation of how you experience a thing. Political viewpoint will be skewed one way or the other. Many things do not have a specific meaning of themselves, but they become powerful by what they symbolize. One's emotions project onto a symbol. They are in the memory file and framed according to a specific meaning. How you frame a thing will profoundly alter the way you interpret it.

What does one mean by framing? The same situation when looked at differently from a different perspective now looks very different. This applies to *A Course in Miracles*, which is really a course on reframing. You take the situation out of the immediate present and turn it over to the Holy Spirit, instead of engaging in projection by your ego. One allows God to give it a greater context, which shows you that the person is driven, unable to be different than he is and is obviously a teacher of yours. Thus, any disturbance can be healed simply by reframing. The same thing happens in therapy. When you surrender to the Holy Spirit, you allow the field to reframe it. Now taken out of the context of time, and the concept of causality, it is completely different. Your level of evolution will determine your opinions and intentions.

ALTERNATIVE VIEWPOINTS TO HATEFUL/EVIL

Sad mistake	**Negative emotional storm**
Naïve error	**Compartmentalized**
Passion for life	**Personality disorder**
Duped, misled	**Narcissistic megalomania**
Programmed/brainwashed	**Psychosis**
Karmic propensity	**Impulse disorder**
Ignorance	**Psychopathy**
Mentally ill	**Lack ofeducation**
Genetic defect	**Driven/compulsion**
Vulnerable	**Intoxication/impaired**
Energydominated	**Misinformed**
Infantile	**Delusional**
Primitive	**Subculture**
Atavistic/*Thanatos*	**Lack of spiritual evolution**
Social coercion	**Regression/degenerative**

Acceptance/Compassion/Understanding/Tolerance/Patience/Forbearance/Benign

Slide 89

SLIDE 89: ALTERNATIVE VIEWPOINTS TO HATEFUL/EVIL

This slide was first introduced at the April 2006 lecture, DVD disc 2 at 010800.

People are upset when they are experiencing the emotion of hate. They feel guilty about it. They see things as hateful/evil and at the same time, they feel guilty, and hate themselves for hating and feel guilty about hating. There is the idea that evil is in the eye of the beholder, but calibration shows that evil can be "out there." There are different ways of looking at all the horrible people that have been in a person's life who "deserve to die." One technique to use may be to call them all kinds of horrible names and get over one's hatred and anger of which there is a limited amount in everyone. Then you can finally see that what they are suffering from is a "sad mistake" and you do not have to kill or hate anyone anymore. People are duped and misled and brainwashed and make naïve errors. One can see other people's behavior as some kind of karmic propensity of which they have no conscious memory. You can see it as ignorance. You can see that the characteristic traits of mentally ill, psychopathic personalities is due to a genetic defect. The genetic propensity to criminality is diagnosable by age 3, which shows up as inability to control one's behavior. Some people are "energy dominated" when a negative energy field of say gambling in a casino hits them in the solar plexus and they can lose everything.

The alternative viewpoint to use instead of hate is to see them as infantile, primitive, and atavistic, as suggested by Freud's theory regarding the depth of the Id, the very bottom in the pits of the unconscious, which has attraction to the energy of death called 'Thanatos'. There is an attraction to death, counterbalanced by the energy of the love of life termed 'Eros.' There is also social coercion, as society has a profound influence on how people behave. In a negative emotional storm, people "snap" (cal. 95.) Another explanation is the "compartmentalized" personality sometimes seen in turncoats, who may or may not even be aware of their other personality. More information and examples of this are given in the section on 'Espionage and Political Criminality' in "Truth vs. Falsehood: How to Tell the Difference" (2005), Chapter 11: The Downside of Society, pp. 194-199.

Narcissistic megalomaniacs have no possibility of control and frequently actually abandon whole armies to certain death to satisfy their own inflated egos. They display lack of loyalty to their very own troops by allowing them to be needlessly slaughtered (e.g., the armies of Stalin and Hitler) and subsequently by killing off victorious generals or returning victorious troops, or putting them in gulags. One can call the symptoms of these troubled personalities as psychosis, impulsive personality disorder, psychopathic disorder, lack of education, driven/compulsion, intoxication/impaired, regression/degenerative, etc. Instead of hating these persons, you can see that they are ill, misinformed, delusional, members of a subculture that lacks spiritual evolution. By acceptance, compassion, understanding, tolerance, patience, and forbearance one becomes benign and glad to be devoid of hatred and anger. We ask the Holy Spirit for help to get us over our hatred for these people with defects. Experientially the Holy Spirit reframes it and one feels compassion as these people are fulfilling their own karmic potentiality. Compassion does not mean that one has to become their victim or willingly assist that which is destructive.

SPIRITUAL FICTION AND MYTHS

Alien Abduction
A Million Little Pieces (Book)
Apocalypse Prophecies
Aquarian Cults
Area 51 Conspiracy Theories
Astrological Religions
Babaji
Bible Code
Book of Revelation (New Testament)
Celestine Prophecy
Channeling
Crop Circles
Crystal Children
Da Vinci Code
Da Vinci Code Decoded
Disappearance of the Universe
Divination
DNA Code
End Times Prophecies
Extraterrestrials
Ghosts
Incoming Fifth Dimension
Judas Gospel
Maitreya
Mayan Calendar Predictions
Natural Healing (Book)
Neg. Prayer-Healing Stdy. (AHJ, 4/06)
New Ageism
Opus Dei Code
Protocol of the Elders of Zion, The (Book)
Raelians
Reincarnate as lesser species
Reincarnation of Buddha (Ram Bahadur Banjan)
Shroud of Turin
Snake Pit, The (Book)
Solar Temple
Starseed Children
Trans mediumship
UFOs
UFO Religions
Urantia Book

SLIDE 90: SPIRITUAL FICTION AND MYTHS

This slide was first introduced at the June 2003 lecture, DVD disc 2 at 010740 and was updated at the June 2006 lecture, DVD disc 1 at 000530.

Every single instant in life is an avenue to God, an absolute doorway. We try to be timely as well. We live in a world and we want to know what is going on in the world. Right now, spiritual fiction is selling big and almost half the people do not even know that it is fiction and not reality. For the record, we should give it our imprimatur. Imprimatur in the Catholic religion is just paternalistic, in which the Church takes some responsibility for the evolution of the soul and tries to be an adequate parent. The intention of imprimatur is integrous at 375, to protect the innocent from seduction by the lies, which in today's world is almost impossible, because the TV and media are very powerful. In the old days, when a book was disapproved it was placed in the Index in the Vatican and condemned to be heretical.

Approximately 50% of the material in some spiritual libraries and bookshops is below the calibration level of 200. Although "New Age" literature is popular, it is also the area of maximal error and is quite dangerous. It is rife with channelings from nonintegrous sources, earth prophecies, UFOs, extraterrestrial visitors, 'guides' from the future, and claims of special, unique realms and strange foretellings of invasions from other galaxies, etc. The future is unknowable as life is evolutionary, dependent on agreements of the will, individually and collectively. We ourselves are our own spiritual decisions, deciding what the future will be.

Most conspiracy theories are projections from human imagination. *A Million Little Pieces, Book of Revelation (New Testament), Celestine Prophecy, Disappearance of the Universe, Judas Gospel, Natural Healing, Neg. Prayer-Healing study (AHJ, 4/06), The Protocol of the Elders of Zion, The Snake Pit, Urantia Book* have major negative consequences for humanity. *The Protocol Elders of Zion* gave rise to Nazi death camps and resulted in the killings of a hundred million people in World War II. *The Snake Pit* and similar works resulted in the mentally ill being removed from the safety of the state hospital systems, which calibrated above the level of integrity, and into the street culture, which calibrates around 110. It is crucial to see the huge impact of falsehood. That which pretends to be true can be quite devastating and must be seen as such and avoided.

The calibrated level of the experience (not the person) of Alien abduction is always at about 70, the same as experiential apocalyptic visions (e.g., John, the author of Revelation). The experiences are very real to the subjects who are thereby convincing in their retelling of the revealing visions. The visions characteristically are fear provoking and the downside can be very considerable as the myth propagates through fear, suggestion, and the virus of memes (e.g., the "End Times" as imminent, etc.) The human mind is extremely naive, ignorant and vulnerable to falsehood and error. Faith, confidence and trust are necessary for any pathway to God to work, but in today's world they have been severely damaged by the fallacy that goes on in the media. What hope is there for humanity? The child within us is both our salvation as well as our downfall.

REASON: GREAT SCIENTISTS

Aristotle	498
Bacon, Sir Francis	485
Bernard, Claude	450
Bohm, David	505
Bohr, Neils	450
Burbank, Luther	450
Byrd, Adm. Richard	420
Copernicus, Nicholas	440
Darwin, Charles	450
Eddington, Arthur	460
Edison, Thomas	490
Einstein, Albert	499
Euclid	470
Faraday, Michael	450
Fleming, Sir Alexander	460
Freud, Sigmund	499
Galen	475
Galilei, Galileo	485
Galvini, Luigi	450
Hawking, Stephen	499
Heisenberg, Werner	460
Helmholtz, Hermann von	460
Hippocrates	485
Huxley, Thomas	460
Jenner, Edward	450
Kekule, Friedrich	440
Kelvin, Lord (Wm. Thompson)	450
Kepler, Johannes	465
Mach, Ernst	460
Malthus, Thomas	480
Maxwell, James	460
Newton, Sir Isaac	499
Pasteur, Louis	465
Plank, Max	460
Poincaré, Henri	430
Semmelweiss, Ignaz	460
Steinmetz, Charles	460
Teilhard de Chardin, Pierre	450
Wittgenstein, Ludwig	440

Slide 91

SLIDE 91: REASON: GREAT SCIENTISTS

This slide was first introduced at the August 2006 lecture, DVD disc 2 at 002515.

Reason is a very respectable level. The great scientists calibrate about the same as *The Great Books of the Western World*. That is the domain of the 400s, of Logic and Reason, mathematics, and is very erudite. David Bohm at 505 calibrates the highest on the slide. He postulated the Enfolded and the Unfolded Universe. Thomas Edison was a great genius who by just one invention - the discovery of Electricity - created more wealth for the US than the whole income of many other countries. People envy America and one can see that America is a product of great scientists. Ed Jenner gave the world the gift of vaccination without which many of us would not be alive today. Friedrich Kekule received insight into the image of the Carbon molecule in a dream where the snake was swallowing his own tail. Ignaz Semmelweis, an early pioneer of antiseptic procedures, was a physician who demonstrated that childbed fever was contagious, and proposed appropriate hand washing by medical personnel.

The scientists represent an intellectual condition. This is where the Universities in USA used to calibrate (400s.) What came out of the creation of these scientists is today's world. Because science is by its very nature concerned only with observable phenomena, it has never been attracted to spiritual concepts as a subject for consideration, despite the fact that many great scientists throughout history have personally testified to subjective experiences of pure consciousness occurring in the course of, and frequently crucial to, their work.

Sir Isaac Newton's great contribution to science from the viewpoint of consciousness is also a limitation because that is the world of causality, a great block to the realization of divinity. He created differential calculus and the Newtonian dimension calibrates in the mid-400s and is what dominates current society, even though he himself calibrated at 499. How is that? Usually the person calibrates at about the same level as their work but in the case of Newton, he was himself very intensely spiritual, as are many other scientists also. Stephen Hawking has worked in trying to unify Einstein's General Theory of Relativity with Quantum Theory.

One of the most important philosophical implications of quantum discovery involves the breakdown of the causality principle in subatomic phenomena. The underlying state to be ascertained is variable and depends on position, momentum, time, potential, kinetic energies, angle, and nonsubstance qualities such as the act of human observation itself, namely, consciousness (the famous Heisenberg Uncertainty Principle). What is important to grasp is that the various substratum of what we assume to be reality are profoundly affected and alterable by the mere act of human observation. What one discovers is a product of intention in that what one discovers depends on what one is looking for. This, in turn, has led to the awareness that no major advance in science can occur without a further understanding of the nature of consciousness itself.

FASHIONABLE PHILOSOPHIES

"Academic Left"	180	Hate	70	Darrida, Jacque	170
Afrocentrism (Racism)	180	Hedonism	180	Foucault, Michel	190
Anarchism	100	Iconoclasm	175	Husserl, Edmund	195
Atheism	165	Irresponsibility	195	Irigary, Luci	155
Authoritarianism	180	"ism" (Suffix)	180	Kristeva, Julia	150
"Critical Theory" (Marcuse)	145	Libertarianism	180	Kuhn, Fritz	195
Deconstructionism	190	Misanthropy	180	Lacan, Jacques	180
Demonize	80	Moral Equivalency	170	Lyotard, Jean-Francois	185
Dialectical Materialism	135	NY Times Security Breach	140	Manchu, Rigoberta	180
Dixie Chicks	160	Nihilism	120	Marcuse, Herbert	150
"End Justifies the Means"	120	"Nutty Professors"	160	Marx, Karl	135
Epistemological Relativism	190	Pacifism	185	Olsen, Karl	160
Eugenics	105	"Peacenik" Politicalization	180	Popper, Carl	185
Fascism (Secular)	80	"Question Authority"	160	Russell, Bertrand	200
Fascism (Theocratic)	50	Philosophic Theories:		Sartre, Jean-Paul	200
Fascism (Islamic/Militant)	50	Baudrillard, Jean	175	Singer, Peter	195
Feminist Politics (Sexism)	185	Caputo, John	185	Vidal, Gore	180
Free Speech, U.S. (6/2006)	180	Chomsky, Noam	135-185	Whitehead, Alfred	225
Free Speech, WW II (U.S.)	255	Da Lauze, Gilles	190	Zinn, Howard	200

Slide 92

SLIDE 92: FASHIONABLE PHILOSOPHIES

This slide was first introduced at the August 2006 lecture, DVD disc 2 at 003025.

One of the reasons that one cannot tell truth from falsehood is because the common belief now is that it does not matter, that falsehood is just as important as truth. That is the philosophy of the **Academic Left**, calibrating at 180. It represents Afrocentrism (racism), and gives favoritism to various groups. One of the main supporters of **Anarchism** and **Atheism** is Daniel Dennett and his main idea is that all religion and spirituality is fictional, and that the professors should get together and start a revolution to free man from this ignorance. Central to the decline of the calibrated level of the US Universities is the **Critical Theory of Marcuse** as represented by **deconstructionism**, whereby integrity is **demonized** and academia is brought down to the level of **dialectical materialism** (135.)

The **Dixie Chicks** were on the front cover of Time magazine and they calibrate at 160. The **"end justifies the means"** calibrates at 120. **Epistemological Relativism** is undermining humanity as we know it; it is based on the idea that our knowledge of truth must be assisted by our mental constructs, and that the truth of a statement is relative to a social group or individual, and denies the Absolute sovereignty of God. **Eugenics** (cal. 105) was popular for a while; it advocates the improvement of human traits through the promotion of higher rates of reproduction for people with desired traits (positive eugenics), or reduced rates of sexual reproduction of people with less-desired or undesired traits (negative eugenics), or both.

Fascists believe that democracy is obsolete, and they regard the complete mobilization of society under one-party as necessary to prepare a nation for armed conflict and to respond effectively to economic difficulties (Secular fascism calibrates at 80 whereas theocratic or Islamic/militant fascism calibrates at 50.) **Feminine politics** (Sexism) calibrates at 185 and emerges as gender equality. Divinity has no gender and is non-linear/beyond form. Pronoun - he or she - is only about biology, or protoplasm. God is not limited to biology or protoplasm. To say "He/She God" is worse than saying "He God" because now one has "double-genderized". When we pray, we use the neutral term "Thee" as that is beyond gender.

Free speech during World War II was 255 as one could disagree, but it did not vilify. Now they vilify and **free speech** has come down to 180. **Hedonism** - no ethics or morality - calibrates at 180. **Libertarianism** is rooted in the primacy of individual judgment and calibrates at 180. **Moral Equivalence** is the idea that "we are just as bad as or worse than them" and calibrates at 170. **Nihilism** is the rejection of all religious and moral principles in the belief that life is meaningless and calibrates at 120. **Pacifism** (cal. 185) relies on force, not power and leads to defeat. **"Question Authority"** (cal. 160) is a bumper sticker that seeks to enhance a person's self-interest and greatly weakens the ability to cooperate with others.

The **philosophic theories** of Noam Chomsky, Herbert Marcuse and others are sophistries that academia tends to worship, and have resulted in Academia in the US falling from the mid-400s to its current level below 200. The idea that life is ridiculous was promoted by Jean Paul Sartre by his Existentialist philosophy, and by Bertrand Russell in the twentieth century, and by Howard Zinn and Gore Vidal in recent times.

CURRENT MEMES, ISSUES, AND MEDIA FIGURES

"Perception is Reality"	**180**	**"Intelligent Design"**	**275**
Alliance Defense Fund	**480**	**Justification**	**185**
Apologist	**190**	**Moral high ground**	**190**
Baldwin, George (ACLU)	**180**	**Moral superiority**	**190**
Castro	**90**	**Nasrallah, Hassan**	**180**
Churchill, Ward	**90**	**North Korean Leader**	**80**
Code Pink	**175**	**One Worldism**	**185**
Encyclopedia Britannica	**460**	**"People of Conscience"**	**185**
Globalize yourself	**190**	**Political Science**	**220**
Guevara, Che	**90**	**President of Iran**	**80**
Humanities	**235**	**Social Science**	**240**
Ideologue	**185**	**Sociology**	**260**
Intellectual narcissism	**175**	**Wikipedia**	**280**

"One man's terrorist is another man's Freedom Fighter" 185

Slide 93

SLIDE 93: CURRENT MEMES, ISSUES, AND MEDIA FIGURES

This slide was introduced at the August 2006 lecture, DVD disc 2 at 004040 and is similar to the April 2004 lecture, DVD disc 3 at 000100.

A meme is a slogan repeated so often that it ends up uncritically accepted as truth, and realigns one's orientation towards reality. Therefore, the meme is not innocent, or benign, and conscious people should be aware of how and what they are being programmed with. A meme should be calibrated when in doubt, because the way to God via devotion to truth is a unique way of expressing it. Shepherd Smith of Fox News, reporting from the Middle East said, "In this world, perception is reality; falsehood is the truth." **Justification** - **the moral high ground** - is what all the wars are about, as by rationalizing one has permission to do whatever one wishes. A whole country could have its citizens avoid getting bombed, for example, by returning a few kidnapped people, but they will not do it and in the meantime, blame the other side for bombing.

Lack of intellectual integrity is different from the belief that **"perception is reality."** What is undermining academia in the US is not perception but philosophical theories based on intellectual narcissism/relativism. The essence of relativism is that falsehood is equal in importance to truth but if one asks those believers in this philosophy if they would take counterfeit money, they would immediately say 'no'. It does not matter if the check is good or not if it is only a point of view. No, they do not really believe in that and the "Nutty Professors" that teach relativism get paid in authentic $$ for their lectures. The best that one can do at the major Universities in the US is the humanities department, which calibrate at 235: being socially helpful.

In contrast to the **ACLU**, which calibrates below 200, the **Alliance fund** calibrates at 480. The founder of ACLU, George Baldwin, was a communist sympathizer, an atheist, and was always challenging authority, and he is the one who set up the Scope's trial, which was completely fallacious**. Ideologue** as a sect calibrates at 185, as they believe the hypothetical intellectual constructs to be real. To reach a more advanced level of consciousness, one has to know what the traps are, and the most serious trap in today's society is the media barrage that hits almost everyone thousands of times a day, unknowingly. One is being brainwashed without one's permission. If someone were to ask," Would you like to be brainwashed?" most would answer 'no'. These same people eagerly flip the TV switch on and go from one brainwash to another unknowingly. A person must be aware of the phenomenon that other generations did not have to deal with.

The Ku Klux Klan was quite overt. They were not subtly reprogramming but very blatant. Nazism was not surreptitious. Interestingly however, the propaganda minister of the Nazi regime was an expert and his methods are followed today by the far left: if you repeat a lie often enough, the mind will begin to believe that it is true. When one hears a theme repeated often in the media, one can intuit that you are being brainwashed. You can see why the news commentators are in despair, as they cannot even trust Reuters because Reuters screens the news through a political distortion: one man's terrorist is another's freedom fighter. This is Reuter's dictum of truth telling, which calibrates at 185, as it is only part of the story; by leaving out the other part you are being programmed.

SPIRITUAL PRACTICE AND DAILY LIFE (1)

Practices	Willing to Surrender	Willing to Accept
Education	Hate	God's Will
Choice: Teachers	Anger	Evolution of life
Alignment with pathway	Revenge	Inherent limitations
Commitment	Guilt	Choices
Daily routine	Self-hatred	Situations
Meditation	Resentment	Assets
Contemplation	Malice	Ego and its problems
Prayer	Jealousy	Gift of Life
Supplication	Envy	World as Creation
Humility - Humor	Vanity	Mortality
Dedication	Pride	Divine Presence
Focus on beauty	Craving	God's Love
Note perfection	Greed	Mercy
Watch unfoldment	Want	Need for change
	Desire	Inner discipline

Slide 94

SLIDE 94: SPIRITUAL PRACTICE AND DAILY LIFE (1)

This slide was first introduced at the October 2006 lecture, DVD disc 1 at 002200.

How does a person make spiritual practice a part of daily life? Traditionally, religion gets compartmentalized to Sunday and the rest of the week you get back to reality, which is business and you do not feel guilty about things that you would if it were Sunday. Therefore, the first thing one needs is **education**, and that is why lists of hundreds of **teachers**, teachings and writings have been provided, along with pitfalls along the way and spiritual traps. The essence of truth in all of the pathways has been distilled in the teachings of Devotional Non-duality, and that itself saves a couple of lifetimes, as one can go direct to the spiritual core of a pathway, instead of wasting time with the externals. That leads a person to the search for enlightenment, letting go of attachment to the linear and to realize the source of one's existence as the nonlinear. The alignment with the direct pathway to enlightenment speeds up the likelihood of enlightenment more than one thousand times, by committing to it and instituting a daily routine that **includes meditation, contemplation, prayer and supplication**.

The mind eventually comes to a stop when one realizes that below the mind, prior to thinking, there is an infinite space of silence. With **humility** goes **humor,** contrasting essence with perception. Along the pathway, one becomes increasingly aware of beauty and perfection by letting go of projecting anything onto the world. Then one begins to **watch the unfoldment** of Creation, by noticing that each thing is an actualization of a potentiality, as the Un-manifest becomes Manifest as Creation. Everything has a source and an origin, but no cause. The Un-manifest (Godhead) does not do anything; it does not even create universes, but out of it emerges the potentiality of Divinity as Creator. The Creator then becomes the Source of infinite power, which is present continuously at all times.

One has to get beyond the duality of a linear universe. It is not possible for something that is 'alwaysness' and 'foreverness' to have a beginning and an end. You have to be willing to **surrender Hate, Anger, Revenge, Guilt, Self-hatred, Resentment, Malice, Jealousy, Envy, Vanity, Pride, Craving, Greed, Want and Desire**. Finally, you realize that you really need nothing to make you happy. If there is no difference between what one wants and what one has, then you are happy all the time, seeing that what one has is what one wants. There is a willingness to accept **God's Will**, the **evolutionary nature of life with its inherent limitations** at every level, local conditions which show up as **situations** in which one is forced to choose, stewardship of assets that go with the gift of life, **God's Love and Mercy**, and the need for inner discipline as a response to changes in life which are continuous. Interestingly, the willingness to accept the ego and its limitations reduces the ego's hold, while self–criticism, condemnation, fear, and shame actually strengthen the ego. The earlier in life that one accepts mortality, that our time here is limited, the better it is. Then, if someone says, "I want to kill you," you can confidently say, "That is your problem and your karma, not mine!

Spiritual Practice and Daily Life (2)

Practices	**Willing to Surrender**	**Willing to Accept**
Choose "holy company"	**Narcissism "Me"**	**Necessary effort**
Practice Socrates' view	**Fearfulness**	**Forgiveness of self and others**
See others as programmed	**Emotionalism**	**Truth in place of opinion**
Declaration	**Drama**	**Selfless service**
Commitment	**Victimhood**	**Inner honesty**
Visualize goals	**"Hurt feelings"**	**Responsibility**
Lovingness toward life	**Opinions of others**	**Inner silence**
Gratitude for "haves"	**Competitiveness**	**Peace instead of drama**
Satisfaction with progress	**Gain**	**Witness/observer**
Priority of "attention set"	**Win**	**Nonpositionality**
Benevolence	**Be "right"**	**Nonattachment**
Mindfulness	**Importance**	**Surrender opinionation**
	Change others	**Faith and confidence**
	Control others	**Patience and confidence**
	Being special	
	Thinkingness	
	Self as causal	

Slide 95

SLIDE 95: SPIRITUAL PRACTICE AND DAILY LIFE (2)

This slide was first introduced at the October 2006 lecture, DVD disc 2 at 000400.

Choosing **holy company** means to avoid that which is non-integrous. Demonic forces have been conning people for thousands of years and you are not any smarter than they are. The very fact that you are consulting them tells them that you want to be special. One has to love **Socrates**' view, that man intrinsically is incapable of discerning essence from perception. Everyone is choosing what they consider to be the highest good at the time. You have to see others as programmed and not be in denial about it. Being spiritual does not mean being stupid. Make a declaration to yourself and God to live by a commitment.

To succeed at spiritual goals, you can mentally perform a trial run of how you would like to be and visualize it, as in sports. Practice every move mentally and then when the event comes up in the external world, you are already familiar with the pathway because you have created neuronal circuits, as in forgiveness. Picture yourself as capable of that which you wish for yourself, which is to live your life in a way in which you are constantly experiencing the beauty and perfection of all things. Become loving toward all of Life in all its expressions. Be grateful for what you do have and be satisfied with whatever progress you have made.

One neurologically can create an attention set, which are cascades of levels of options. The more often you make a certain choice, the greater is the mathematical likelihood you will make it again. Neurologically, you set up these priorities and likelihoods, so it will become more likely that one will forgive a person than not. Preferences set up likelihoods. The more often one chooses a certain sporadic event, the more likely it will not be sporadic. Be benevolent towards yourself and others. Mindfulness means that there is some aspect that is self-reflective, so you knows when you are off course. You find yourself hating somebody and some aspect of mindfulness brings to your attention that you are wandering off the path. It means constant self-awareness, "Am I still on course?" In order to accomplish the above practices, one has to be willing to surrender the items listed in the slide including narcissism – "me" -- the opposite of truth as the ego juices every positionality to get what it can for wonderful "me".

Renunciation is a lifestyle and may involve leaving the world and going to an ashram. True renunciation is internal; not renouncing the world but the ego's attachments. To renounce and still participate in the world, you have to be non-attached, because the world is always challenging and tempting you into lower levels of consciousness. Renounce all positionalities, emotionalism and drama. One learns to see the ego as a pet, which needs to be housebroken and civilized. You cannot change or control others, but can tell them how you see it and then it is up to them.

Lurking in the background is constant thinkingness, which one needs to surrender, along with the idea that one is special or that the ego can cause things to happen "out there." Each thing is becoming what it is; there is no causality or specialness. In addition, you have to be willing to accept the items listed in the slide, including taking responsibility for your consciousness and faith in the words of the teacher or the teaching.

THE MIRACULOUS (1)

Explanation: Emergence of potentiality into actuality

Unexpected occurrence from the viewpoint of linear causality

Seeming rarity due to limitation of the observer

Facilitated by favorable karmic propensity

Jesus' 33 miracles

Stigmata

Adoration – Devotion

Canonized saints by Pope in 2006

Carl Jung's concept of synesthesia

Emperor Constantine

Clinical experiences of ACIM participants

Miraculous as consequent to the level of consciousness

The Siddhis as a phase in the evolution of consciousness – level 570

12-step groups: miracles by the thousands

Lower Mind (cal. 155): Intrinsic limitation of skepticism vs. gullibility

Slide 96

SLIDE 96: THE MIRACULOUS (1)

This slide was introduced at the December 2006 lecture, DVD disc 1 at 000700.

The miraculous occurs outside of time and is not the consequence of causality. Nothing arises solely of its own but only within the field of context, which includes all of life and civilization, the prevailing conditions that are ever changing and unfolding, and the entire universe. What appears to be change is the emergence of potentiality out of Un-manifest into the actuality of manifestation. One thinks things are occurring in sequence, but there is no sequence in the universe. The sequence is in the observer. There is no person causing a miracle. One is merely witnessing a phenomenon when the local conditions, karmic propensity, and prevailing field of energy are appropriate. From the viewpoint of linear causality, the miraculous is not explicable.

The whole purpose of spiritual evolution is to transcend the lower states of consciousness, evolving to higher states of consciousness, and as one advances the miraculous become more frequent. The average person does not observe that which is extraordinary because it is not within their realm of reality, so they will only observe a miracle if it is very pronounced. The 33 miracles of Jesus did exist and were dramatic so people would "get it". In the days of Jesus, the presence of divinity within a teacher was not recognized unless there was something theatrical. One may be enlightened and speak great truths, but not until someone turns water into wine will people be open to the truth.

The condition called stigmata is a topic of great discussion and inquiry. It tends to occur around the level of 570, which is sainthood. Sometimes the stigmata results as an expression of sainthood. A person may experience stigmata when there is a strong identification and an intense admiration and adoration for Jesus Christ. It can bring actual nail marks and bleeding of the hands. The Catholic Church catalogs this phenomenon and goes to great lengths to record its authenticity. Consciousness calibration confirms the truth of this. Saints canonized by the church in 2006 were indeed saints.

Jung had an interesting concept called synesthesia or synchronicity, meaning that things happen simultaneously, consequent to the presence of divinity. It has to do with time and location, like those who thought they were just lucky to be at the "right place" at the "right time". Emperor Constantine was facing a great enemy for the control of Rome; he calibrated 195 at the time. When confronted with this issue, suddenly he went into a state of devotion. He prayed for a sign and after he entreated God with great sincerity, he automatically jumped to 245. His new state of consciousness summoned forth a sign. He looked up and saw a light in the form of a cross. He saw it as a sign from God, and the symbol Chi Rho was then put on the shields of the soldiers. He defeated the enemy and declared Christianity as the official church of the Roman Empire. The entire Western world, including America, emerged out of the powerful miracle of Constantine.

In the 12 step groups, the miraculous is commonplace. Millions of alcoholics have recovered from a seemingly grave and hopeless condition. The 12 steps groups are politically silent and invisible, but influence all of society by virtue of their energy. The power of these groups show that faith is sufficient to precipitate the miraculous. In lower mind (155), there is an intrinsic limitation of skepticism and naiveté, preventing the experience of the miraculous.

THE MIRACULOUS (2)

Miraculous is consequent to the level of consciousness of the observer

The miraculous as a constant: Creation as Evolution

Impersonality: witnessed, not caused

Spontaneous healings

Abuse by promoters for fame and money

Expertise of "Holy men" of India

No "person" performs miracles

Subjective witnessing by this teacher of the miraculous

Contribution of the Heisenberg principle: collapse of the wave function

Power of faith and belief

Siddhis and sainthood

Aura as field: precipitates, potentiates

Healing vs. treating

Non-healing as a benefit

Slide 97

SLIDE 97: THE MIRACULOUS (2)

This slide was first introduced at the December 2006 lecture, DVD disc 1 at 004800.

The miraculous is a consequence of the level of consciousness of the observer. One could bring a person who has an issue into the presence of a higher energy field and when appropriate karmic conditions prevail, that person may be healed. One merely observes the phenomena.

The miracle of creation is continuously present and the form that creation takes is evolutionary from the viewpoint of the witness. Evolution is the constant emergence of the potentiality becoming an actuality. We think healings are spontaneous, but they are really the consequence of the level of consciousness and the effect of prayer.

The "Siddhis" occur frequently in the high 500's to level 600. At first, the miracles are sporadic, then they become more and more continuous and eventually quite profound. The miraculous is abused by promoters for fame and money, e.g. the "Holy men" of India are experts at simulating the miraculous. They have been perfecting it for thousands of years. It is very entrancing, so much so that one is sure that they just witnessed the "real" thing.

The subjective witnessing of the miraculous by Dr. Hawkins included being lifted up by angels during surgery without anesthesia, "I kept surrendering to God and let go resisting the pain. I was lifted up by an infinite softness and I knew it was angels". Everyone has guardian angels. The angelic forces are infinity powerful and at the same time infinitely gentle. They are the presence of pure love. In today's world, we do not think of the miraculous as a reality. We think of it as something that happened centuries ago, and it was so incredibly unusual that it changed the course of history. People do not think of the miraculous in terms of everyday life, unless one is doing *A Course in Miracles,* and is thinking about it and asking for a miracle all the time.

The contribution of the Heisenberg principle is that it explains the science of the miraculous. There is a crossover from the linear to the nonlinear domain. Now we see the power of intention and that people praying for someone's recovery increases the likelihood of that recovery. Everything is synchronous with everything else in creation, so the healing must be karmically appropriate. One surrenders to the Will of God for the highest good, and within karmic propensity, it will manifest in a certain way. Everyone is alive despite having had "close calls"; surviving many "close calls" is the result of the miraculous.

An average doctor calibrates around 440, whereas a holistic doctor calibrates around 465, which is quite a bit higher because it is a logarithmic scale. The holistic doctor is willing to try nontraditional techniques, whereas the traditionally trained physician is following the academic and scientific methods and always looking for approval of his peers. The difference between treating and healing is that in the former, the context remains the same, whereas in the latter, the clinical response is elicited by a change of context so as to bring about an absolute removal of the basis of the condition rather than mere recovery from its symptoms. It is one thing to prescribe an anti-hypertensive medication for high blood pressure; it is quite another to expand the patient's context of life to the degree that he stops being angry, hostile, and repressive. The **non-healing or suffering may be beneficial** in that it leads to the grace of healing a karmic debt.

THE MIRACULOUS (3)

BLOCKS

Lack of karmic merit

Lack of willingness to surrender secondary gain

Guilt

"Justified" resentment

Desire to control

"Outlining" (advice to God)

Unwilling to undo negative karma

Seeking short-term (ego) vs. long-term benefit (Self)

Overblown emotionality/hysteria

Clinging to the juice

Slide 98

SLIDE 98: THE MIRACULOUS (3)

BLOCKS

This slide was first introduced at the December 2006 lecture, DVD disc 2 at 003000.

People under the calibrated level of 200 do not witness or experience the miraculous; all skeptics calibrate below 200, and dismiss the miraculous. There is no point in getting upset or angry with people at that level. They seem to be born that way, without the capacity to be honest with themselves and others. This is an early level of development and evolution, and those in it deserve sympathy. The difficulty is that the cynic and skeptic do not understand context and the non-linear. Because the mind believes in causality, the average mind misses 99% of the miraculous that is happening all around us. It is not that they are rare; it is that only rare people are conscious of them and are capable of witnessing them. Everything in the universe is intertwined with everything else, and what people try to do intensely is change that synchronicity- what you are praying for could actually be the antithesis of the design of creation altogether and asking for something that would not be fortuitous.

What about people who are deep in the pits of hell and negativity who pray for help? They did not experience the miraculous while below 200, but were uplifted over 200 after they prayed, and then they experienced the miraculous. Those that witness and observe the miraculous do so out of **karmic merit.** To be a human is a great fortune and should not be spent in worldly pursuits, for they are ephemeral and based on transient illusions. Within the victim of this lifetime lies the hidden perpetrator in the personal or collective unconscious of previous lifetimes who now unconsciously provokes attacks from others. We punish other people with our suffering: "Oh, how I suffer!"

The secondary gain of hating people is being right and is one of the most common blocks to the miraculous today. **Guilt**, sackcloth, and ashes; whining and penance are all at the bottom of the chart, blocking the experience of the joy of the miraculous, which is toward the top of the chart. One of the first things a person learns in the 12 Steps is that there are no **justified resentments** and hence the willingness to let them go opens the way for miracles.

It is obvious people cannot be different from what they are at the time (Socrates' principle.) The hypothetical is a fallacy. The **desire to control** is biologically intrinsic and hard to let go and prevents the experience of the miraculous. **"Outlining" (Advice to God)** is thinking one can use divinity for fulfillment of personal desires. You do not ask for a certain thing to be done; you ask for a change in how you are seeing a certain thing, in order to precipitate a miracle. A person has to be willing to **undo negative karma** with appropriate spiritual alignment and dedication, when you have done the best you can with a thing, but are still stuck with it. It is not always possible to see what the **long-term benefit of the Self is vs. the short-term ego** benefit so you have to be patient and ask for that which is "in the highest interest of all." The egocentricity and narcissism of emotionality is a major block. You need to find out what the juice is that you are getting out of it, and then be willing to let go of it. Once the blocks are removed, it opens the way for the miraculous. At about level 570, the miraculous becomes continuous.

GOD vs. SCIENCE

Secularism	**165**	**Darwin's Theory of Evolution**	**450**
Skeptical Scientism	**190**	**Daniel Dennett**	**250**
Richard Dawkins ("God Delusion")	**190**	**Creationism**	**245**
Anti-religionism	**180**	**Genesis (Bible)**	**600**
Scientism	**190**	***Discovery of the Presence of God***	**950**
"Natural Skepticism"	**195**	**Evolution of Consciousness**	**600**
Mechanistic Reductionism (Bottom-up)	**185**	**Francis Collins (The Language of God)**	**400**
Vanity of the Ego (Pride)	**190**	**Intelligent Design**	**480**
Atheism	**165**	**William Jennings Bryan**	**505**
Skepticism	**160**	**Clarence Darrow**	**450**
Nihilism	**120**	**St. Thomas Aquinas**	**570**
***The God Gene* (Dean Hamer)**	**190**	**Evolution is Creation**	**Infinite**
"Big Bang" Source of the Universe	**135**	**God as Source of Creation/Universe**	**Infinite**
Earth-warming of human origin	**False**	**"God vs. Science," *Time,* 11/13/06**	**410**
Parallel Universe Theory	**False**	**Carl Sagan**	**200**
Neg. Prayer Healing Study (J. Cardio.)	**190**	**Theology**	**460**
Negation of Faith	**90**	**Evolutionary Psychology**	**210**
Negate Nonlinear Reality (Context)	**90**	**F. Crick: Discovery of DNA**	**460**
Crick: Source of Consciousness: Neuronal	**140**	**Heisenberg Principle**	**460**

Slide 99

SLIDE 99: GOD VS. SCIENCE

This slide was first introduced at the February 2007 lecture, DVD disc 1 005700.

This slide contrasts two paradigms: the linear, provable dimension; and the nonlinear which is experiential but not provable, called ineffable. Spiritual realities are energy fields in the world of context. The world of science is in the linear paradigm. An "ism" is at 185, it becomes onerous, like religionism, trying to push its agenda on others. **Richard Dawkins** (The God Delusion) has a delusion that God is a delusion. Scientism gets outraged and indignant, becomes a religion in itself, putting faith in itself as the ultimate truth. **Natural skepticism** is a slightly negative way of being in the world; a child brought up in love and affirmation tends to be trusting rather than skeptical. **Mechanistic Reductionism (Bottom-up)** is the basis of all the skeptics, a pedestrian way of thinking. It thinks creation is an accidental evolution, not even calling it "intelligent design", while the truth is that intelligence is innate to the gift of life itself. **Vanity of the Ego (Pride)** is the vanity of narcissism.

Politicians are cleverly deceptive and about 80% in America routinely lie. **Atheism** is lower than agnosticism and more of a mistake, believing that God does not exist. **Agnosticism** is humbler and intellectually integrous. **Skepticism** represents cynicism of people who have a profound faith in their own thinkingness and their own skepticism. **Nihilism** negates the value of all of life; nothing means anything. **The God Gene** (Dean Hamer) is a pseudoscience that arose as an attempt to explain the near-death experience (NDE). The hypothesis is that the brain activates a neuronal circuit and creates the experience when close to death. NDEs throughout the ages are nearly identical and are profound and permanent. The **"Big Bang" Source of the Universe (135)** states the universe arose out of energy, but does not give a source of the energy. Negation of faith and nonlinear reality (context) both calibrate at 90. Daniel Dennett in evolutionary psychology (210) is not out to disprove anything. Creationism (245) is an honest limitation, but is an insufficient explanation. Genesis (Bible) at 600 says, "Out of the Godhead is the infinite potential of divinity to be anything and everything, including being the Creator. The Godhead is the source of Godness." **Discovery of the Presence of God at 950** is aligned with the truth of consciousness itself, from which spiritual awareness arises. **Francis Collins in "The Language of God" (400)** tried to bridge the gap between science and religion.

Literal creationists do not like intelligent design, but it could potentially give both sides an option if they really want peace, because it does not include the word "God" in it. **William Jennings Bryan** was a man of faith and was involved in the Scopes trial. **Clarence Darrow** was a scientific skeptic, a very intelligent man. Each man truthfully represented what he stood for in the trial. **St. Thomas Aquinas (570)** wrote a textbook integrating both faith and reason, with each reinforcing the other's existence. The mid-400s sees everything from the Newtonian paradigm of "cause and effect" with God as a "cause" rather than an ever-present Source. A "cause" goes from "here" to "there" in a timeline and deals with force. God as an eternal Source means that evolution is continuous and ongoing because that is the nature of Divinity itself, to become ever more of that which It is, in all its expressions. **"God vs. Science," Time, 11/13/06** was quite integrous and accomplished its goal.

SCIENCE – THEORY (1)

Attractor Fields (Nonlinear Dynamics)	460
"Big Bang" Source-of-Universe Theory	False
Biofield	460
Black Hole Theory revised in 2004 (Hawking)	455
Bootstrap Theory	455
Chaos Theory	455
Collective Unconscious (Jung)	455
Consciousness as Consequence of Neuronal Activity	140
Consciousness Calibration	605
Darwinian Theory of Evolution	450
Dinosaur Extinction Theory	200
Dirac Equations	455
Discovery of Double Helix of DNA	460
"Distant Healing"	False
Divinity as Source of Universe	Infinite
Drake Equation	350
Earth's magnetic field weakening	True
Earth slowly reversing magnetic poles	460
Earth warming due to pollution	False
Earth warming due to solar magnetic surface cycles	455
$E=mc^2$	455
Entanglement (Quantum Theory)	False
Frame Dragging	460
"God" gene (Hamer)	190
"Greenhouse" gas earth-warming theory	False
HeartMath	460
Heisenberg Uncertainty Principle	460
Hormesis	180
"Holographic Universe"	395
Inflation Theory (post-Big Bang)	450
Intelligent Design	480

Slide 100

SLIDE 100: SCIENCE – THEORY (1)

This slide was first introduced at the February 2007 lecture, DVD disc 1 at 013920.

Attractor Fields (Nonlinear Dynamics - cal. 460) explain the levels of consciousness. Each level of consciousness represents an attractor field that dominates a specific field of consciousness by virtue of its innate intrinsic power; in large groups of long standing, this is referred to as 'the Higher Power'. The **"Big Bang" Source of the Universe Theory** claims that the big bang occurred billions of years ago, and is false; in reality, the "start" of something that is outside of time cannot be located in time. The "big bang" can only occur in the mind of an observer. **Biofield (460)** describes the field of energy and information that surrounds and interpenetrates the human body. **Bootstrap Theory** and **Chaos Theory** both calibrate at 455 and are advances in quantum mechanics.

The **collective unconscious theory** (455) of Jung is a reality from the scientific viewpoint and explains how people can develop an illness they had never even heard of. It comes from the collective unconscious, not from the individual. Negative belief systems along with unconscious guilt and karmic propensities can also result in illness. Two discoveries due to F. Crick, **"Consciousness as Consequence of Neuronal Activity"** (140) which is a bottom-up scientific theory, and **"Discovery of DNA"** (460) show that the same person could author something erudite as well as something fallacious. The **Consciousness Calibration method** (605) has taken the nonlinear and made it accessible and comprehensible to the linear by using a scale of 1-1000. Ultimate Reality in an infinite universe is dimensionless, outside of time and has no center-everywhere is equally the same as everywhere else. How consciousness calibration can transcend time, distance and space is difficult to comprehend for the skeptic and those stuck in the linear.

Divinity as Source of the Universe is infinitely true. **Drake Equation** is about the probability of life on other planets in this galaxy. **"Earth warming due to pollution"** theory and **"Greenhouse" gas earth-warming theory** are false. Earth warming due to solar magnetic surface cycles is 455. Earth warming of human origin is False: The cyclic temperature of the planet is due to the magnetic activity on the surface of the sun. Core drilling in the Arctic shows these cyclic periods of warmth. Human pollution and earth warming are not causally related. Overpopulation is the cause of human pollution and affects the temperature about 0.8 degrees Fahrenheit. **$E=mc^2$** is Einstein's special-relativity equation and shows the power of scientific proof.

HeartMath is a discovery that the heart literally has a mind of its own (intuitive), and its electromagnetic field is dominant over cerebral rhythm; the heart field thus affects brain physiology. The **Heisenberg Principle** explains that the consciousness and intention of the scientist limits and characterizes the results of a study. **Hormesis** is a theory that a little of something will immunize against a lot of it. "**Holographic Universe**" is not really a scientific fact and has to do with how a thing is conceptualized rather than what it is. **Inflation Theory** (post Big Bang) states the world is expanding at the speed of light. Intelligent Design is 480: Literal creationists do not like **intelligent design**, but it could potentially give both sides (Creationists and Scientists) an option if they really want peace because it does not include the word "God" in it. It seems like the fear is that "God" will come in through the back door.

SCIENCE – THEORY (2)

Microbe Organisms on Mars	**True**
Mind Fields Entangled with Divinity	**True**
Mind Fields Entangled with Others	**False**
Morphic Resonance	**460**
Morphogenetic Fields (Sheldrake)	**460**
M-Theory (formerlyString Theory)	**460**
Multiple Universes	**True**
Newtonian Causality Principle	**460**
Nonlinear Dynamics	**460**
Prayer Increases Healing	**True**
Nuclear Fission Reaction (actuality)	**200**
Nuclear Fission Theory	**455**
Organisms on Mars	**True**
"Parallel Universe" Theory	**False**
Quantum coherence	**460**
Quantum Gravity	**460**
Quantum Mechanics	**460**
Schrödinger Equations	**455**
Singularities	**455**
S-Matrix Theory	**455**
Spiritual experience as the consequence of neuronal activity	**125**
"Steady State" Theory of ongoing expansion of the universe	**405**
Stem Cell Research	**245**
Sub particle Physics	**455**
Telekinesis	**True**
Teleportation of Quantum States (electrons in ions)	**400**
United States Space Program	**400**
von Neumann Process	**450**

Slide 101

SLIDE 101: SCIENCE – THEORY (2)

This slide was first introduced at the February 2007 lecture, DVD disc 2 at 000030.

That there are **microbe organisms on Mars** tested positive. That water has been on Mars tested positive. That there is life on Mars tested negative. That there is life in the nonlinear form on Mars tested positive. The source for potential life existing on Mars tested positive. The potential for life existing everywhere in the universe tested positive. Because of the quality of the Source of all existence, that which exists already has all that is necessary for the emergence of life and actual emergence would depend on local conditions and evolutionary phenomena.

Morphic Resonance is Rupert Sheldrake's hypothesis that "memory is inherent in nature" and that "natural systems", such as termite colonies, pigeons, orchid plants or insulin molecules inherit a collective memory from all previous things of their kind. Sheldrake's morphogenetic fields or **M-fields** are invisible organizing patterns that act like energy templates to establish forms on various levels of life. It is because of the discreteness of M-fields that identical representations of a species are produced. Something similar to M-fields also exists in the energy fields of consciousness and underlies thought patterns and images-a phenomenon termed "formative causation." **M-Theory** unifies all consistent versions of superstring theory.

Newtonian Causality Principle is the very center of science, which sees everything in terms of linear causality. **Telekinesis**, the ability to move objects through mind power, is true. **Teleportation of Quantum States** (electrons in ions) is not a form of transportation, but of communication; it provides a way of transporting a qubit (a unit of quantum information) from one location to another, without having to move a physical particle along with it. All major scientific theories, which are predominantly mathematical in nature, calibrate in the range of 450 to 460. Calibrating the levels is pragmatically useful because a number below 200 indicates that further pursuit is a waste of time, energy, and money (e.g., **the parallel universe theory**). It is interesting that nuclear fission calibrates at 200 (as do guns), and thus it is the purpose for which it is used, e.g., dynamite and gunpowder have multiple uses such as a fireworks display or bombs and bullets. Intention is the decisive factor. The intention in dropping the atomic bomb that ended World War II calibrates at 455.

The quantum theory of 'entanglement' is an incorrect conceptualization; the phenomenon to which it has been applied can be explained differently: The coherence of 'A' and 'B' is not due to 'A' influencing 'B', but instead, both are influenced by 'C'. This can be observed in the flight pattern of birds and fish that move in geometric patterns. Each fish or bird is *not* influenced by the pattern of the others; instead, each is individually attuned to an overall attractor energy pattern, much as the dancing couples in a ballroom are not attuned to each other but simultaneously to the same music. Similarly, 'distant healing' (i.e., from 'A' to 'B') is negative, but **prayer influences healing** because of the commonality of 'C' in that all minds are interchanged with the infinite energy field of Divinity.

RELATIVISM VS. REALITY (1)

Reality / Truth / Essence		**Relativism / Appearance / Illusion**	
Absolutism 650		**Relativism 125-190**	
Discern essence from appearance	**600**	**"Perception is reality"**	**190**
Descartes (*res interna* vs. *externa*)	**490**	**Marx (victim/perpetrator)**	**130**
Plato	**485**	**Protagoras**	**190**
Jesus, Buddha, Krishna	**1,000**	**Atheism**	**165**
The Apostles	**990**	**Skepticism**	**130-160**
Socrates	**570**	**Chomsky**	**135-185**
Great Books of the Western World	**465**	**"Dead white man"**	**130**
Science	**440-499**	**"Science is oppressive"**	**160**
Plotinus	**503**	**Marcuse**	**130-150**
Orwell's *"1984"*	**425**	**"Newspeak"**	**180**
Freud	**499**	**Victimology/blame**	**160-180**
Patriotism, love of country, honor	**520**	**Hate America**	**130**
U.S. Nat'l Anthem, Pledge, Flag	**510**	**Treason**	**80**
Honest dissent, disagree	**495**	**Sedition**	**105**
Balance	**205**	**Extremism**	**140**
Chivalry	**465**	**"Honor killing"**	**90**
Personal responsibility	**475**	**Narcissism**	**140**
Free speech (1955)	**255**	**Free speech (2007)**	**180**

Slide 102

SLIDE 102: RELATIVISM VS. REALITY (1)

This slide was first introduced at the April 2007 lecture, DVD disc 1 at 004925.

The Scale of Consciousness deals with the Absolute. In relativism, perception is reality, not essence. Discerning essence from appearance does not happen until the third eye opens at level 600. This is very rare, so the science of consciousness calibration is God's gift to those who have not reached the level 600 yet, and still would like to be able to tell truth from falsehood. The alternate to Absolutism at 650 is Relativism at 125-190. "Perception is Reality" at 190 is the basis for post-modernism. Descartes (490) pointed out that the mind cannot differentiate mentalizations about the seeming appearance of the world versus the world as it actually is, whereas Marx (130) authored the victim/perpetrator model of dialectical materialism that denies the reality of Divinity as the Source of Creation and life. Protagoras (190) said that reality is perception: "I live in my own reality and you live in your own reality." This argument was shown to be fallacious in 450 B.C. The modern world goes along with Protagoras rather than Plato (485).

Relativism rejects Jesus, Buddha and Krishna at 1000 and prefers Atheism at 165. The Apostles calibrate at 990 in contrast with Skepticism at 130-160. Socrates is 570, whereas Chomsky is 135-185. In the postmodern period, the "Great Books of the Western World" (465) have been removed from Harvard University as they have been found to have been written by "dead white man" (130). Science is 440-499, with Newton, Einstein and Freud all at 499. "Science is oppressive" is false, at 160. The relativist is anti-science and discards logic and reason, and the fact that science pervades everything in the world.

Herbert Marcuse (130-150) has the basic philosophy behind current post-modernism, which is responsible for the decline of the universities, believing that the enemies of freedom are the family, religion, patriotism, work, science, reason, logic, morality, capitalism, tradition and God. Modern man has to deal with things the traditional man did not, like being programmed constantly through the conscious and unconscious. Greater discernment is needed more than ever. Chivalry at 465 was defending womankind, out of love and honor and not belittling them whereas sexism is at 180, with a further downside of "Honor killing" at 90. Orwell's *1984* at 425 predicted today's society with "Newspeak" at 180, today's "political correctness." Newspeak is extremely oppressive, more so than the totalitarianism it alleges to displace.

Patriotism, Love of country, honor (520) are not allowed on college campuses. The military is not allowed on campus. The contrast of patriotism is Hate America at 130. Freud calibrated at 499 while Victimology/blame is at 160-180: "It is somebody's fault." The Western World in 1955 calibrated at 255. On April 14, 2007, it calibrated at 199. Socrates said that the downfall of democracy in Western Civilization would be via free speech. Free speech in 1955 was at 255; Free speech in 2007 calibrated at 180. Free speech is a very powerful weapon, which has become a tool of narcissism. Honest dissent, disagreement calibrates at 495 versus Sedition at 105 or Treason at 80. There are options for disagreement, like becoming a conscientious objector (cal. 375), not a military deserter or turncoat.

RELATIVISM vs. REALITY (2)

Reality/Truth/Essence		Relativism/Appearance/Illusion	
U. S. Philanthropists	455	United Nations	180-190
Amish forgiveness of murder	540	Blame	180
Emergence	600	Materialism	180
Consciousness calibration	605	Narcissism/opinion	140
Call a spade a spade	475	Apologist	190
Honesty	475	Wolf in sheep's clothing	120
Social equality (US Constitution)	550	Sexism	180-190
Transparency	425	Deception	160
Truth 475 -- Veritas	485	Slander, false witness	60-75
U.S. Jurisprudence	525	9th Circuit Court of Appeals	190
U.S. Constitution	710	Iran government	205
U.S. Bill of Rights	640	Shiara	190
Einstein	499	Critics of Einstein	190
Heisenberg principle	460	Mechanistic reductionism	160
New Testament (minus	880	Secularism	165
Humane Society (organization)	410	PETA (organization)	100
American Civil Rights Union	460	American Civil Liberties Union	130

Slide 103

SLIDE 103: RELATIVISM VS. REALITY (2)

This slide was first introduced at the April 2007 lecture, DVD disc 2 at 000030.

U.S. Philanthropists are overall at 455. The United Nations is at 180-190 and is not philanthropic. America is vilified even though it is the most humanitarian country in world history. The world loves Blame (180). The real struggle in the world is about two things: the moral high ground and money. In contrast to hate and blame, the Amish forgiveness of murder calibrates at 540, unconditional love, and is one of the best demonstrations of Christianity and teachings of Jesus Christ. Emergence is 600, beyond causality, and includes both content and context with potentiality becoming actuality because of local conditions, one of which is intention, which adds power to the field. Causality is rooted in mechanistic Materialism (180) and the laws of Newtonian logic. Phenomena become their own potential, with the emergence of "this" transforming into "that." Consciousness calibration (605) adds information above the 600 level.

Narcissism/opinion is 140. Many websites are the glorification of narcissism - "me, me, me..." Consciousness calibration eliminates personal opinions. This is not popular today. Discretion means that one has to take responsibility for the context for what one says. It is part of spiritual integrity and standing up for truth, without making a public display about it. Calling "a spade, a spade" (475) is different from being an Apologist at 190. An apologist for evil aligns with that energy and shares in its karmic consequences. Honesty is at 475, in contrast to Wolf in Sheep's Clothing at 120. Spiritual deception seems severe, just as seduction of innocent children is more severe than that of adults. The U.S. constitution guarantees Social equality (550). Sexism and Racism are at 180. Transparency is 425. Deception is at 160. Teachers' goals and motives should be transparent to all, with nothing to hide and not resorting to deception. Truth is 475. The Latin version, Veritas, is 485, coming out of greater history, compared to Slander and false witness (60-75). "Politicians as a matter of course are forced to tailor the truth close to 100% of the time" - tested true. U.S. jurisprudence, U.S. constitution, U.S. Bill of Rights all calibrate extremely high.

Professional skeptics have spent years trying to disprove Einstein via lectures and books, all of which describe and depict Einstein as a "fake," an "imposter," and an "Emperor who has no clothes." Despite negative reception, the authors continue diatribes undaunted (cal.190) and are apparently oblivious to the confirmation of Einstein by the development of nuclear energy. New Testament (minus Revelation) is at 880, and in contrast, Secularism is 165. Refuting spiritual truth is why the western world is sinking. Religion, via relativism, is "scuttling its own ship." The Archbishop of Canterbury (at 400), for example, uses the secular term "BCE" in his own book so as not to offend Muslims.

The Humane Society (organization) is 410 and People for the Ethical Treatment of Animals (PETA), an American animal rights organization is at 100. PETA states that animal life should take precedence over human life. American Civil Rights Union (ACRU) is 460, whereas American Civil Liberties Union (ACLU) IS 130. The ACRU is dedicated to protecting the civil rights of all Americans by publicly advancing a Constitutional understanding of essential rights and freedoms, emphasizing the right to religious freedom.

RELATIVISM vs. REALITY (3)

Reality/Truth/Essence		**Relativism/Appearance/ Illusion**	
Earth temperature due to Sun	**455**	**Human origin (*Inconvenient Truth*)**	**180**
Academia (1955)	**440**	**Academia, U.S. (2007)**	**180**
Professors, U.S. (1955)	**440**	**Professors, U.S. (2007)**	**180**
Logical Integrity	**400-499**	**Sophistry, rhetoric**	**180-190**
Traditional Morality	**490**	**Hedonism**	**180**
Hollywood (1955)	**265**	**Hollywood (2007)**	**180**
Hayes Office (1955)	**430**	**Sundance Film Festival (2007)**	**165**
Boy Scouts, Girl Scouts	**450**	**NAMBLA**	**140**
Classic Philosophy	**440-485**	**Frankfurt School**	**130-180**
Aristotle	**498**	**Marcuse (Critical Theory)**	**140-150**
Sophocles	**465**	**Relativistic Philosophy**	**130-190**
Huang Po	**960**	**Dawkins, R.**	**190**
***People of the Lie* (M. Scott Peck)**	**450**	**Conspiracy Theories, paranoia**	**90-110**
Modernism	**400**	**Postmodernism**	**180**
***Intellectual Morons* (Flynn, 2004)**	**440**	**Ethical, moral, social relativism**	**180**
U.S. Society (2007)	**421**	**World overall (2007)**	**205**
Cable News	**410-440**	**Huffington Post, Myspace, YouTube**	**140**

Slide 104

SLIDE 104: RELATIVISM VS. REALITY (3)

This slide was first introduced at the April 2007 lecture, DVD disc 2 at 003035.

Earth temperature change due to Sun calibrates at 455, while Earth temperature change due **to human origin ("An Inconvenient Truth")** is at 180. Humans create pollution, but are not the cause of earth warming. Man's contribution through pollution is 0.8-degree F. rise in temperature. Pollution is due to overpopulation. **Academia in 1955** was at 440. **Academia in 2007** is at 180. **Marcuse** has said that the purpose of education is indoctrination. **Professors** in U.S. in 1955 calibrated at 440. In contrast, **Professors in U.S. in 2007** calibrate at 180. "Professors: The 101 Most Dangerous Professors in America" is a book by David Horowitz and the professors in it all calibrate under 200. **Logical Integrity** is 440-499 while **Sophistry/rhetoric** calibrates at 180-190. The argument between the two sides was solved, with Sophistry shown to be fallacious around 450 BC and is recorded in Plato's dialogues. **Traditional Morality** is 490. Marcuse and others recommend **Hedonism** (180) as its replacement, saying the purpose of life is self-indulgence.

Hollywood (1955) was 265. **Hollywood (2007)** is 180. **Hayes Office** in 1955 calibrated at 430 and was a review board, which classified films according to the content. In contrast, the **Sundance Film Festival** in 2007 is at 165, exploring deviance for its own sake. **Classic Philosophy** is at 440-499. **Frankfort School** is at 130-180. The Frankfort School was a Marxist society, which called itself Social Theory. During World War II they moved to Columbia University in America, moving back to Frankfort after the war. **Boy Scouts, Girl Scouts** are at 450, with "patriotism, integrity, truth, helpfulness and concern for others-anathema to relativism".

In contrast, North American Man/Boy Love Association **(NAMBLA)** at 140 legally safeguards the attempts of older men to rape young boys. One sees this as an inversion of the traditional- luciferic inversion, satanic as well as luciferic. **Huang Po** is at 960 while **Richard Dawkins** at 190 feels that religion should be banned. Once again, Relativism is asking us to move to levels below 200. The consciousness level of humanity was going up and then it turned over and came back down somewhat. So it could be that the karmic purpose of this life is such that we have the options and it may be that there's going to be waves of fluctuation in which mankind overall rises and falls.

"People of the Lie" (450) by M. Scott Peck, a psychiatrist, is a best-selling book, which concluded that the basis of evil is unabashedly naked narcissism**. Modernism** (400) is an artistic and cultural movement beginning at the turn of the 20th century and includes modern automotive design, architecture, and appliances. **Postmodernism** (180) is the late-20th-century style and concept in the arts, architecture, and criticism that represents a departure from modernism. The question is, 'how could such a tremendous reversal, a 180, occur?'

The book, **Intellectual Morons** (Flynn, 2004), is about the personal lives of people who believe in ethical, moral, and social relativism and is educational in providing answers. **U.S. Society** (2007) is 421. **World overall (2007)** is 205. They both were higher two years prior. Cable News is at 410-440. **"Huffington Post," Myspace**, and **YouTube** are at 140. The computer world and blogger land have had an apparent detrimental effect.

RELATIVISM vs. REALITY (4)

Reality/Truth/Essence		Relativism/Appearance/Illusion	
Prefrontal cortex (human)	200	Limbic/amygdala (animal)	120
Discretion	375	Vilification, desecration	120
Statue of Liberty	500	Imam's plane setup	180
Abstract thought	450	Concrete thinking	190
Meaning	450	Definition	200
"Higher Mind"	275	Lower Mind	155
Friendly	255	Hostile	125
Stand up for the truth	500	"Tolerance"	190
World as karmic expression	575	World unfair	200
World: karmic opportunity	600	World exploitive	180
Traditional religion (U.S. impact)	450	Secularism	190

Destruction of society by iteration 510

"Money Trumps Peace" 355

References:

Flynn, D. 2004. *Intellectual Morons*. New York: Crown Forum. 450

Hawkins, D. 2005. *Truth vs. Falsehood* (pp 220-229). AZ: Veritas Publishing 490

Peck, M.S. 1998. *People of the Lie.* New York: Touchstone 450

***All-American Colleges.* 2006. Wilmington, Del.: Intercollegiate Studios Inst. 440**

Slide 105

SLIDE 105: RELATIVISM VS. REALITY (4)

This slide was first introduced at the April 2007 lecture, DVD disc 2 at 004635.

Reality, truth and essence require the **prefrontal cortex** (200) and this is not very open in man until level 200. Relativism, based on appearance and illusion depends on the other side of the brain called the **Limbic system** (120), operating out of the amygdala, which is emotionalized narcissism. It is for our evolution and karmic merit to be able to deal with these people, who see things differently than we do. **Discretion** is at 375; **Vilification, desecration** is at 120: It is not necessary to drop down to vilification when people disagree. **Statue of Liberty** is 500 because its energy is more than just its physicality**. Imam's plane setup** in 2006 is at 180. This was a staged setup, imitating hijackers. They hid under the cloak of freedom and liberty, threatening to sue, and getting away with it under the cover of relativism. **Abstract thought** is 450. **Concrete thinking** is 190, which cannot understand the context of being set up and fall into it, unable to get the abstract meaning. This is where relativism fails, saying that nothing means anything other than what one says it means, thus negating essence or intrinsic meaning. **Standing up for truth** at 500 is higher than quoting truth, which is in the 400s. It is not combative and takes a higher integrity, "willing to stand up and be counted."

Tolerance is 190 in the Marcusian political meaning, where one tries to destroy that which he does not believe in. **The World as karmic expression of God** calibrates at 575, a world of infinite karmic potentiality. It is the unfoldment of potentiality of human evolution. Human life is karmically fair, completely and totally. **World as a karmic opportunity** is a teaching of the Buddha, and calibrates at 600: "Rare is it to be born a human; rarer still is it to have heard of Enlightenment; and most rare is it to pursue Enlightenment." **World exploitive** calibrates at 180, seeing the world as unfair, unjust, oppressive - the victim mentality of Marxism and Marcuse, which sees the minority as always being exploited by the majority, so the majority can never be right from this viewpoint. The impact of **traditional religion in U.S.** includes ethics, morality, answerability, accountability, etc. and calibrates at 450. **Secularism** relies on blame, that whatever is wrong is somebody's fault, and calibrates at 190.

Destruction of society by iteration is true at a very high level of confidence indicated by its calibration of 510: A very slight error, almost imperceptible, repeated enough times, will have a profound effect. This is happening in today's world via the chipping away at truth by teaching post-modernism, religious concepts that are really luciferic and satanic than logical, and its constant repetition/iteration by the media around the clock, which greatly diminishes human capacity to tell truth from falsehood. The way to offset it is not to attack falsehood but by every one of us being as friendly and loving as possible within our own respective domain or life. One person being **friendly** (255) is more powerful than five persons being **hostile** (125). Each level of consciousness has its own values that include what it considers desirable or a gain, and thus material for negotiation. 'Peace' is a popular political slogan, but as President Bush said in an interview in 2007, **"Money trumps peace"** (cal. 365) is making clear that it is really the financial considerations that are persuasive in the world of socio-economic/political reality.

WHAT IS REAL? (1)

Definition: Actual, existent, primarily physical

Confirmable by the senses; factual; manifest

Scientific: measurable via information

A mental conclusion of sensory experience: lower mind, animal

Subjective based on faith

"I Am" is provisional to consciousness levels above 200

Not based on opinion

Protagoras's proposition: Solipsism

Socrates: Illusion that perception = reality

Descartes: *res interna* vs. *res externa*

A sensory and mental presumption

Quantum Theory: The universe is purely mental – there is no "out there," only "in here"

No center to the universe

Requires consensual validation for "proof"

Slide 106

SLIDE 106: WHAT IS REAL? (1)

This slide was first introduced at the June 2007 lecture, DVD disc 1 at 003550.

Reality at the most concrete, literal level has to do with the content while Truth has to do with the Context, what one derives from Context. People think their mind knows what the truth is and what is real. Because the real is linear at this stage, it is confirmable by the senses, and even the animal is capable of material linear reality. Next level up from the sensory level is the world of science, where, for a thing to be real, it has to be measurable. Thus, science is not capable of dealing with the abstract and answers to life cannot come out of science. Science measures a thing via information about it, e.g. its dimensions and position in time and space. When one says that something is real, one is drawing a mental conclusion of one's sensory experience and it is really the lower mind in the animal that says that it is real. The animal does not have to think about it. It is our inner animal that says that a thing is real, e.g. "Ouch, that hurts!" when the feet hit a stone while walking. At this stage, the real is subjective, based on faith in sensory input. Knocking faith means one does not have any way of knowing anything about anything.

Through evolution, we have developed the capacity to be able to sense the linear domain in detail. Below 200, humans are sensory but they are unaware of their existence as such. If one does not value one's existence, then one does not value the existence of others. There are cultures that destroy the life of others because they are not aware of the value of existence. The sensory world is rooted in interpretation of data. The intellectual problem is as described by Protagoras in Plato's dialogs: "The world I experience is real to me and the world you experience is real to you", therefore, reality is only subjective, which is the basis for Solipsism: the way I experience the world is my world. Socrates pointed out how illusion is one's perception of reality which is then projected out into the world. Socrates also initiated an avenue by which forgiveness comes about through the understanding that the mind cannot tell truth from falsehood. Descartes elaborated on it by pointing out the duality of the world within and the world without.

Comprehension of the world requires transcending that duality and man has thus far never had the compass to discern essence from perception. What we think is real is a sensory and mental presumption. Quantum Mechanics says there is no world 'out there', only 'in here', no universe apart from the observer. The world that we deal with is adequately described by science, and with its advanced understanding of Quantum Mechanics/Heisenberg principle, it enlarges its realm. The current view of the universe according to the leading edge of science is that the universe is held in place by consciousness itself; e.g. see "Mindful Universe" (2008) by Henry Stapp. The Observer blocks the collapse of the wave function by observing, and the universe is suspended between potentiality and actuality. Without consciousness, the universe cannot exist. How does one prove what is real? It is through consensual validation. If two persons say that a thing weighs so much, it does not create a reality but it does create an agreement on what both of them presume to be a reality. It does not tell us what the real is, but it does tell us what is confirmable within the usual definition of reality, which is necessary to carry out transactions in the world of form.

WHAT IS REAL (2)

Reality is subjective based on faith in the senses: Experiential

Dependent on reliability of information

Actually testimonial

Fulfills criteria – "facts"

To "know" what is "real" is a subjective presumption

Axiomatic – Primary – a priori

Fulfills properties of content to establish identity

Product of sensory/mental processing and editing

All information is itself tentative and provisional

To "know" is a narcissistic premise vs. to actually "know about"

To actually "know" is to "be" - only a cat really "knows" what it is to be a cat

Reality is identity rather than description

Maharshi: "The world you see doesn't exist. 'Reality' is a dream."

Slide 107

SLIDE 107: WHAT IS REAL? (2)

This slide was first introduced at the June 2007 lecture, DVD disc 1 at 004540.

Reality is experiential based on faith in one's senses. Therefore, an animal is capable of discerning what is real, even though he does not know what the truth is. It is **dependent on the reliability of the information** that the senses are providing; therefore, it is actually a testimonial. All statements about reality are testimonials. Reality fulfills a criteria of "facts" which is reliable data. To know what is real is a subjective presumption. Everybody's mind says, 'I know what is real." If one becomes a bit humble, you realize that it is a presumption your mind is making now. A sophisticated spiritual student drops narcissism and takes on humility: "whatever I think and believe now could change later." Additional information comes in so we become humble in making statements about the world and know they are subject to editing later on. All information in spiritual context is presumptive and it is only provable by actually becoming.

Spirituality means an openness to receive and is 'yin' in nature. Certainty is like 'yang': "I know that", which leaves no room to back off. Because to "know" what is real is a subjective presumption, it is best not to invest narcissistic emotionality into it. Why contaminate the intellectual world with emotion? All we are talking about anyway is content and what it really means is signified as a consequence of Context. Reality is a product of the animal world, and then one adds human mental processing and editing to it at this stage. Therefore, all information is only tentative and provisional, the best understanding we have at this moment.

To think one knows is a narcissistic premise; one can only know about a thing. The only way to know a thing is to be it. The only one who knows what it is to be a cat is a cat. To know is to be and that brings us to a more sophisticated metaphysical and philosophical understanding: that reality is identity rather than a description. This is where we run into a potential problem in the current society. In our world of the media, we no longer see what a thing is - we see how it is politicized, glamorized, presented in Technicolor, with music!

"I am me" is the only reality, with everything else only a description. It is important to the mystic that reality is identity rather than description, because one becomes what a religionist would try to describe but which is inexpressible. Transmitting information about mystical Self-awareness is impossible because for one thing, there is no one there to describe it and for another, it will not be comprehensible to the average person. Everyone thinks there is a 'you' there because of projection. A 'me' is a definition, description and measurement, completely missing the higher levels of consciousness. If one lets go of definition, there is only the reality of one's existence. You cannot prove that you exist without going through mentalization.

What **Ramana Maharishi** said, **'The world you see does not exist'** is true at the level of consciousness of 700, but at lower levels of consciousness, it sounds idiotic. What one has to do is to let go giving reality to the linear, and by detachment from linearity one becomes detached from the world and that world no longer exists as a reality.

WHAT IS REAL (3)

Mental: Dream, memory, plan, picture, reason, images, imagination

Emotional: Scale of Consciousness

Content: Subject to context

Spiritual: Faith, hope, devotion, prayer

States: Humility, realization, awareness, mindfulness, observe

Decision: Choice, reflection, meditation

Focus: Self, ego, gain, desire, accept, reject

Character Traits: Perseverance, accept, declare, fantasy, denial, doubt

Level of Consciousness: Narrative, story, drama

Meaning: Interpretation, adjectives, inferences, connotation, attitude

Setting: 50% error in line-up identifications; impact of sequence, expectation

Slide 108

SLIDE 108: WHAT IS REAL? (3)

This slide was first introduced at the June 2007 lecture, DVD disc 1 at 005630.

Many things are real but do not exist in the physical domain and cannot be proven to exist: mental phenomena like dreams, memory, plans, picture, reason, imagination etc. Trying to reduce reality to the pseudo-scientific primitive does not work because not everything is in the sensory linear domain. Many people who refute spiritual reality come from a pedestrian level of science because they only understand linearity and not Context at all and ridicule things like faith. That which is mental is certainly real to the experiencer. One cannot transcend the level of Protagoras until one transcends the 'personal' and to do that, a person needs to let go of the emotional. What you end up with then is the Scale of Consciousness.

Henry Stapp says the same from a quantum mechanics perspective, that there is no world apart from consciousness. After negating the pathways to Knowingness through the intellect or what one thinks is real, what one ends up is with the condition known as Divine Stupidity: "I of myself know nothing" because whatever one thinks is a definition and all definitions are not factual and have no intrinsic reality. As the Buddha said, "I have heard that such and such is true, and now with my own inner work, I'll verify that." With divine stupidity, you end up with no opinion on anything, as all opinions are mentalizations.

Emotion depends on how seriously one sees the passing phenomena. If you see them as trivial and evanescent, you know that things are going to work out. When both persons are in alignment with forgiveness and peace, they try to resolve issues rather than prolong them. Our understanding of content depends on context. Spiritual qualities like faith and prayer are intangible and unprovable. The states that start with divine stupidity go through humility, realization, awareness, mindfulness, and the observer. The mind is addicted to experiencing and already interprets the incoming stimulus in 1/10,000th of a second by jumping in and judging, by making the experience right or wrong. To observe without extracting the juice of experiencing is a reachable state through choice, reflection, and meditation. It is to be conscious without experiencing the content of consciousness. Perseverance (Commitment), Acceptance, and Declaration activate intention about the purpose of one's life.

Level of Consciousness determines how one is going to experience the world. What a person see happening in society dramatizes the story into a narrative like "a poor me" or "a bad you" and these are the stories that the mind makes up, which have nothing to do with reality. All of the above comes out of meaning, which depends on context. The nonlinear, non-languaged understanding and comprehension is revealed in its abstract meaning out of which one has an interpretation, inferences, connotations and attitude, which are all elaborations. It is not only what happens - the content and the context, but also the meaning of that. Nothing is interesting about life except what it means. If it is lacking meaning, it is just a passing animal experience. What is the value and significance of our existence itself? Why is it so great to be a human being? The setting is that 50% of blogs are fallacious, not to mention that the intention behind them is vicious. Even our eyes lie to us half the time, as there is a 50% error in line-up identification of suspects in criminal courts. Who or what can one rely on?

WHAT IS REAL (4)

Bias: Intention, alignment, preference, attraction vs. aversion; idealization vs. realism

Naiveté: Familiarity, interpretation, sophistication

Intelligence: Education, indoctrination, programming

Social Influence: Cultural norms and expectations, class, sex, age, politics, upbringing, labeling, popularity, media hype, glamour

Intention: Active, do, inspect, enjoy, remember, find fault, criticize, destroy

"Diminishers" vs. Expanders": Dramatize, exaggerate, minimize, dismiss, mental capacity, Freudian balance of ego/Id/superego

Mental/Emotional Health: Balance, maturity, unconscious psychological factors

Quantum Zeno Effect

Allness: (cal. 1,000) vs. Nothingness (cal. 850)

Slide 109

SLIDE 109 WHAT IS REAL? (4)

This slide was first introduced at the June 2007 lecture, DVD disc 1 at 012810.

Bias is the reason one cannot see what is real, as negativity of intention leads to alignment that leads to preferences that lead to attractions and aversions. The intention to disparage the truth of divinity blinds people and they end up writing untruthful blogs. **Naiveté** is another downside that can be overcome by familiarity, interpretation and sophistication, as many objections to truth are obviously fictitious. Understanding is also reflective of **intelligence**, which is more than just IQ and operationally depends on education, indoctrination and programming. Another reason one cannot see what is real is **social influence,** which includes cultural norms and expectations, how one was brought up, social class, gender, age, political indoctrination, the way things were labeled, whether you were was popular or not, media hype, and glamour. If one had the good fortune of upbringing in a family that respects morality and ethics, then you are going to be more aware of when they are 'out'. What people believe is true is how they have been indoctrinated by repetitious memes, pounded into our heads by the media. For media hype, people seem willing to sell anything in today's world, because it gets them into the daily news. You can feel sorry for the people who become victims, not only of their own egotism, but also for all their controllers who are people making multimillions feeding these people to the dogs for a price.

You can see how things change if you are active, do, inspect things, enjoy them, remember them, find fault, criticize or destroy them. These have values coming out of intention. If you are trying to extract the truth about something, your intention about it is already interpreting it. To become facetious in order to ridicule something shows departure from truth and integrity. On top of that, there are in our world the **"diminishers" and** the **"expanders."** In the presence of all these processes, the chances of knowing the truth are greatly diminished. The choice to be a diminisher or expander is not within one's conscious control. The mind automatically tends to do it. It depends on one's childhood experiences - whether spilling milk was a big deal or a minor one. Diminishing and expanding comes from childhood training, of what one's parents considered emotionally important and they do this by dramatizing, exaggerating, or minimizing it.

How one interprets things depends on one's overall mental capacity and by the Freudian balance of Ego/Id/Superego. Freud had a more positive view of the ego as the mental capacity for reality testing, to balance the Id and the Superego, and not giving in excessively to animal instincts of the Id or the excessive guilt of the Superego. Generally, the capacity for understanding reality is a balance of **mental/emotional health** and whether one has balance and maturity or unconscious psychological factors such as poor self-esteem.

The **Quantum Zeno effect** has to do with commitment and intention. The more often one chooses to forgive, the more likely that choice will be made again, even though the statistical options are mathematically same. Consciousness, because of its nature, chooses the options it has chosen before. Allness versus Nothingness is a classical duality and is the ultimate pair of opposites to transcend (for more detail see, "Transcending the Levels of Consciousness: The Stairway to Enlightenment" (2006), Chapter 18: Full Enlightenment.)

Wolf in Sheep's Clothing

Slide 110

SLIDE 110: WOLF IN SHEEP'S CLOTHING

This slide was first introduced at the June 2007 lecture, DVD disc 1 at 014320.

The picture on this slide makes clear the difference between appearance and essence and is worth a thousand words. The majority of politicians lie routinely as part of their job, and therefore it is best not to quote a politician as a source of authority. The politician is supposed to make things work by whatever means. His commitment is not a spiritual one and there is no point in making him wrong. He tells everyone that if they do things in a certain way, the consequences will be as outlined by him. As far as the politician is concerned, he is fulfilling the good and the good is the fulfillment of a certain specified objective. A spiritual motivated person, on the other hand, has a completely different set of values regarding what is truth, what is integrous, what is honesty, and what is reality.

The calibration of 'Wolf in Sheep's Clothing' at 120 is worse than expected as most of the political methods calibrate around 190, prideful egotism etc. The calibration of 120 means that it is a serious error and is the hiding place of evil itself, and it is extremely important to become sophisticated and realize that essence and perception are two completely different things. It is a serious error to misperceive, not a minor one. To think that the Komodo dragon is safe because one is a humanitarian and likes all of nature does not mean that you can step into his cage wearing sandals. The downside of Western Civilization is acting on the belief that "We have to be nice to all Komodo dragons and invite them here as they are just nice animals." That error is quite severe. The picture teaches at one glance what will take a number of lectures to get across to many people. Almost everyone has been deceived at some point by a 'Wolf in Sheep's Clothing', and therefore it is good to bring this picture into awareness.

Interestingly, the muscle test can be used accurately only by people who themselves calibrate over 200. Even more profound is that not only must the question-and-answer subjects be over 200, but also the motive of the question itself (which is in the form of a statement) has to be integrous and over 200. This recalls that "only the meek shall inherit the earth," and that "the wolf in sheep's clothing" now stands unmasked and revealed. Unless one is integrous, this simple test does not work, and the test cannot be used for selfish or egoistic ends. The access by 'evil' (non-integrous) to truth is denied because truth is the essence of the Creator. Whereas humanity's innocence was previously its weak point, that innocence now returns as the royal road to the ultimate victory of truth over falsehood.

WHAT IS TRUTH? (1)

Perception vs. Essence: Descartes' *res interna* vs. *res externa*

Socrates' dictum

Popularity: herd instinct, media bias, memes

"Extraordinary Popular Delusions and the Madness of Crowds"

Political slant

Confusion with opinion

Faith in belief systems and data

Historic human deficiency

Corroboration by calibration

Truth dependent on context: Level of Consciousness

To truly know is to "be" rather than "know about"

Narcissism distorts: projected self-interest

All mentation reflects limitation

Precluded via brain function at calibration levels below 200

Subject to programming and indoctrination

Meaning: hermeneutics of abstraction

Slide 111

SLIDE 111: WHAT IS TRUTH? (1)

This slide was first introduced at the July 2007 lecture, DVD disc 1 at 002410.

Descartes pointed out the difference between **res interna** (perception - the world as one sees it) and **res externa** (essence - the world as it is). The barrier between the two limits is the capacity to see actuality. Protagoras as depicted in Plato's dialogues made the incorrect assumption that there is no ultimate reality. That people have different opinions does not mean there are different realities, just different perceptions. Socrates' dictum is very helpful to spiritual students: "man chooses only the good. However, man does not know how to comprehend the difference between the truly good and the illusory good." To be able to forgive requires recognition of this inner reality.

Memes are phrases that people start believing due to repeated broadcast by the media. The world's great dictators have depended on this. **"Extraordinary Popular Delusions and the Madness of Crowds"** (Charles Mackay, 1841) gives examples of things that the whole world believed that turned out to be illusions. A current popular delusion is that global warming is due to man. The temperature of the earth has reflected the magnetic activity on the surface of the sun for tens of thousands of years. Man contributes to contamination, not warming. Disagreement with popular delusions makes one a heretic.

Politics and money dominate our society. Truth becomes confused with political opinion. Data used in studies is often false. For example, secondhand smoke is an illusion. A federal court threw it out as junk science after determining that the EPA had "cherry picked" its data and had grossly manipulated "scientific procedure and scientific norms" in order to rationalize the agency's own preconceived conclusion that passive smoking caused 3,000 lung cancer deaths a year. Political slant influences science.

Historic human deficiency is the incapacity to tell truth from falsehood. For the first time in history, there is an objective means of verifying the truth. Truth is dependent on context, which is unique for every level of calibration. To know is to "be" rather than to "know about." **Narcissism distorts** by superimposing self-interest and selfishness on truth. The media impact on society is enormous. Almost all political statements in the media are distortions. Narcissism feeds on itself, with a sense of grandiosity and people want to propagate their beliefs. All mentation reflects limitation as the mind cannot discern truth from falsehood. The brain is hardware, while mentation is software. What one thinks is already a limitation - it is what one is that transcends limitation. Brain physiology limits the capacity to understand and comprehend truth in those under 200. Other cultures that are out to kill us are indoctrinating their youths.

The Nazi propaganda minister, Goebbels, was good at indoctrinating the Germans against the Jews, visually comparing them to worms, rats, etc., which caused instant programming. In today's world, arriving at a capacity to discern truth, to stand for truth and to live a life of truth is slim with the constant media barrage. Truth has to do with what a thing means. Pondering the implied subtleties of meaning (**hermeneutics**) has occupied the greatest minds of history and produced the great wealth of philosophy and its central issues, such as epistemology, theology, metaphysics, and ontology. Meanings are levels of abstraction and people below 200 do not have the capacity for abstraction, which is the context.

WHAT IS TRUTH? (2)

Influence of "Attention Set"

Quantum Zeno effect

Content subject to context, time, history

"What is *so* all the time everywhere" (Werner Erhard)

Subjective and experiential vs. demonstrable, impersonal Paradigm allegiance

Cultural norms

Allegorical vs. literal – letter vs. spirit of the law

Fallacy of mixing levels

Limitations of science: "junk" science

Distortion of relativism, rhetoric, and sophistry

Absolutism

Languaging, labels, and semiotics - ("Illegal" vs. "undocumented")

Intention: dedication and humility

Capacity for comprehension and abstract categories (Kant) Epistemology, sophistication, education, and priorities

I.Q., personality blocks: oppositionalism, contrariness, hostility

Media: "Fair and balanced" equals falsity equal to truth

Postmodernism: Relativism; fallacy of moral equivalency; multiculturalism

Slide 112

SLIDE 112: WHAT IS TRUTH? (2)

This slide was first introduced at the July 2007 lecture, DVD disc 1 at 004500 and contents rearranged at a later date.

Influence of "Attention Set" Quantum Zeno effect: Spiritual decision or declaration changes one's attention set. Choosing to forgive brings about the mental habit of forgiving. The influence is physiologic and neurological; by consistently making certain choices, neurons begin to fire more favorably. **Content subject to context:** Part of context is time and history; look at circumstances before making something wrong. **"What is so all the time everywhere":** Truth is not subject to content or context, time or circumstances. What is intrinsically so is forever and for all time. People who believe in God know they are accountable. The purpose of Erhard Seminars Training (EST) was to get people over 200. **Subjective and experiential vs. demonstrable, impersonal:** The subjective and experiential is an impersonal field of truth, not provable but confirmable, different from that which is demonstrable. **Paradigm allegiance:** People become confined to a certain context, where they try to corral all their understandings of everything, e.g. materialistic reductionism; they become disturbed when confronted with more abstract concepts. **Cultural norms:** What is normal in one environment is not normal in another, e.g. what passes as okay on a beach in USA will get one arrested in an Arabic country.

Allegorical vs. literal-letter vs. spirit of the law: One of the most frequent political tricks is to distort the spirit of the law under the guise of being the letter of the law or vice-versa. **Fallacy of mixing levels:** What is true at one level is not necessarily true at another. "Render unto Caesar that which is Caesar's and that which is God's unto God's" is a way of expressing the different levels. This is the basis for a lot of spiritual error, especially in New Ageism. **Limitations of science:** Science becomes politicized, becomes a big world enthusiasm, e.g. global warming. People get carried away with grandiosity about it all and money pours in with a lot of TV coverage, festivals all over the world to overcome something that does not even exist. **Distortion of relativism, rhetoric, and sophistry:** Whole cultures forbid reason, as it may interfere with faith. So reason is seen as a jeopardy to faith. St. Thomas Aquinas said the opposite: "reason supports faith."

Absolutism: Thinkingness denies the existence of God, which is the whole basis of absolutism. The calibrated levels of consciousness are absolute and absolutely calibrate God at Infinity. **Languaging, Labels and Semiotics:** Whether one uses the term "illegals" or "undocumented" totally changes the picture. All one wants to know is if they have a green card or not, because if they don't, one's business may be in jeopardy. Selection of vocabulary already changes the seeming reality just by virtue of semiotics. **Intention: dedication and humility** - What is truth depends on one's own intention, which determines the degree of dedication to truth, and humility, to learn what the truth is. **Capacity for comprehension and abstract categories (Kant)**: A mistake of the far left and its impact on academia is that they mix categories. One cannot jump Kantian categories - phylum, class, species, etc. All are paradigms, too. One cannot say that a fish is a bird without feathers.

Epistemology, sophistication, education, and priorities: The capacity to do conscious calibration rises with more education, more dedication, more spiritual evolvement, with spiritual evolvement as the most important, and with education giving sophistication in how to best phrase the question. **I.Q., personality blocks, etc.:** Approximately 29% of the public have personality disorders: passivity, aggression, oppositionalism, contrarianism, innate hostility. Some people are hostile all the time. **Media: "Fair and balanced":** Everything in the media in today's society is supposed to be fair and balanced. This can lead to the downfall of democracy in our time. Giving falsehood same priority as we give to truth, we end up with a gridlock. Gridlock causes loss of sovereignty. When the government does not respect its own laws, it loses the respect of the populace. **Postmodernism, etc.**: All these calibrate less than 200 and sound good but are rooted in relativistic falsities.

WHAT IS TRUTH (3)

Fall of Academia: Delusional professors and conspiracy theories

Duke University fiasco

Fall of consciousness level in the U.S. and Western civilization

Impact of framing

Logos, Ethos, and Pathos

Deism, Atheism, and Accountability

Legend: Ancient Egypt: Weighing of the Heart vs. Truth

Osiris, god of the Underworld

Fate of the Soul

Wisdom; discretion; prudence; responsibility

Allegiance: God vs. Mammon; God vs. Caesar; Spiritual vs. material

Mistakes, errors

Cultural morality

Reversal of Truth/Falsehood via brain physiology

Conscience as one's guide

Judgment Day: Every hair shall be counted (cal. 1,000)

Narcissistic glorification of "free speech" (cal 255 ↓ 180)

Bloggerism: "Salt the mine"; "straw man"; sheep's clothing

Slide 113

SLIDE 113: WHAT IS TRUTH? (3)

This slide was introduced at the July 2007 lecture, DVD disc 2 at 000020 and contents rearranged at a later date.

Fall of Academia: Philosophical theories based on intellectual narcissism/relativism is undermining academia in the US, e.g., Duke University where 88 professors' false accusation declaration was never retracted despite the court ruling based on overwhelming evidence to the contrary. **Fall of consciousness level** in the U.S. by 5 points does not sound like much but it is as if the level of the sea has fallen by a factor of five, affecting all the ships afloat. **Impact of framing**: The same situation when looked at differently from a different perspective now looks very different. **Logos, Ethos, and Pathos**: Logos has to do with the integrity of the speaker, the level of truth. Ethos is the efficacy of the speech - it is one thing to know a matter, another to convey it. Pathos is the receptivity of the listeners, the audience's ability to listen. **Deism, Atheism and Accountability**: Do not trust anybody who does not believe in God because they are not answerable. In the long term, it is only the inner knowingness that 'every hair on one's head shall be counted', which keeps one strictly pulled back to the magnet of truth. Atheists do not think they will be accountable. **Legend from Ancient Egypt**: Osiris is the lord of the underworld. When you die, your heart is weighed on a scale and based on the degree with which you have represented Truth, your soul goes to either heaven or hell. This should make people stop before they walk a devious pathway because the realization that one is accountable by itself brings about integrity. **Wisdom:** One cannot say anything at any given time without some moral responsibility for discretion and prudence. Our life is a gift for our own spiritual evolution, so one has an obligation to fulfill one's obligations to God, self and to humanity to the best of one's ability. **Allegiance**: God vs. Mammon is the big conflict. You do not have to do anything for financial gain, as in fulfilling one's obligation to God, self and fellow man, that which you need will emerge. **Mistakes and errors** are unremitting because of the karmic propensities and the limitation of humans in general, for which we forgive ourselves. We all live within a **cultural morality** of expectation and parameters of what is expected, permissible and forgivable, and what is unforgivable. Morality is also judgmentalism and trying to decide priorities of morality-which is more moral, this move or that move. **Reversal of Truth** takes place and affects the brain. We are not the victims of our brain physiology; we are the determinants of it. Whether you become "left brain" or "right brain" dominant, the map of brain physiology shows different pathways. **Using conscience as one's guide**, one needs a rational, mature and educated conscience, which is interested in integrity rather than just morality, because being moralistic can be a great hindrance. **Judgment Day:** Realizing that every hair on our head is counted, and the picture of Osiris weighing the heart and realizing our accountability is not to frighten us, but to make us realize our moral responsibility and the consequences thereof because our decisions affect everyone. **Narcissistic glorification of free speech** is probably the biggest threat to western civilization in general and the US in particular. Discretion of speech is a higher good. Use your speech for goodness, for love, for that which is beneficial. Free speech means equal time and equal weight to the enemies of our own culture. **Bloggerism** seems to be just an expression of the desecration of what should be revered, free speech. It is the means of destroying it. "**Salt the mine**" means to plant a story in one place, so they can quote it as an authority, at another place.

THE HUMAN DILEMMA (1)

Whence did we come?

Are we body or spirit?

Whence do we go?

Why are we in this world?

What is the purpose of human life?

How did the world arise?

Right vs. wrong: birth of morality

States: Infancy, childhood, adolescence, adulthood, middle age, old age – longevity

Sickness and health

Social accord/governance

Politicalization

World religions

Divisiveness of races, colors, nationalities

Internal conflict – hegemony

Social Strata

Education, IQ

Slide 114

SLIDE 114: THE HUMAN DILEMMA (1)

This slide was introduced at the August 2007 lecture, DVD disc 1 at 002630.

'Whence did we come?' is framing the question in a linear time dimension, speaking in terms of causality. Speaking from an evolutionary standpoint, the human came from the 'mammalian' but even there we do not end up with a human being but only a sophisticated hominid. What makes the human 'human' is the spirit and the etheric body. How did we get here? The answer of a spiritually evolved person is different from that of a materialist. The materialist is happy with an animal existence and evolution, a linear Newtonian explanation of the body. To a more evolved person, "we" means the human community or the spirit of the human, which inhabits physicality and has consciousness and awareness. "God created man" calibrates at 1000 whereas the evolutionary approach calibrates at 440.

Are we body or spirit? This is arbitrary languaging with no basis in reality. There is not a duality of body and spirit. The end of physicality is not the end of life. We are a spiritualized body and we see the difference in the brain function: left vs. right brain, as an effect of the spiritual energy, which lights up the level of Awareness. **Where do we go at 'death'?** We do not go anywhere; we transform into a different energy field and the spirit body becomes our primary body. **Why are we in this world?** The answer is that we are not in the world but the world is in us. Only consciousness is aware of the world and it is only consciousness that is aware that "one is".

The purpose of human life: The world gives us the maximum opportunity to develop spiritually, and we have to respect one another because all of us have earned the great karmic merit to be born human. **How did the world arise?** It depends on what one means by 'world.' If we mean the planet Earth, Science explains how the Earth arose. If we mean the world of our experience, that is a state of consciousness that arose as a karmic benefit, as an automatic consequence of what we have become.

Right vs. Wrong, birth of morality: Intrinsic to the human experience is the issue of morality and right vs. wrong, and people like to ridicule morality, which they think is a human invention. Right vs. wrong is definitely obvious throughout the animal kingdom, and one finds it in the wolf-pack, in the struggle for the alpha male and female positions, the struggle for dominance, hegemony, etc. It is a basic law of life throughout nature that one part will try to dominate the rest, e.g. the strongest country will dominate as far as it can dominate. A society that tries to reverse right and wrong will go through a period of confusion and collapse.

Impact of states: The definitions of what is right vs. wrong, etc. change with time, whether one is **sick or healthy**, and throughout one's life, so one normally matures as one passes from infancy to old age. Agreement about all these things brings about **social accord and governance**. **Politicalization** is a way of constantly re-editing the definitions of rules of governance. The presence or absence of **World Religions** signifies a change of lifestyle for the inhabitants of the human domain. Factors such as **Divisiveness of races, color, nationalities, social strata, education and IQ** interact with all these rules of living, what is right and wrong, etc. Internal conflict over who is going to have the "say so" in these matters results in hegemony or power struggle throughout the animal and the human kingdoms.

THE HUMAN DILEMMA (2)

Levels of consciousness

Adaptational stress to change

Different forms of government

Accountability

Crime, pestilence, natural calamities

Media barrage

Perception vs. essence; illusion vs. reality

Id vs. Superego vs. Ego: Psychology

Brain physiology

Music, the arts, aesthetics

Imprinting; framing; sequence

Context vs. content

Humor; ambiguity

Indoctrination, memes, propaganda Intention

Discernment vs. naïveté

Narcissism vs. spirituality

God or no God

Slide 115

SLIDE 115: THE HUMAN DILEMMA (2)

This slide was introduced at the August 2007 lecture, DVD disc 1 at 010100.

We are discussing all the factors which when put together and recombined cover thousands of possibilities and variations of the human dilemma. It takes a huge amount of will and devotion to life itself to keep on walking with our head held high. **Levels of consciousness:** These are karmic propensities. Some of them are gifts from God. The purpose of human life is the evolution of consciousness. **Adaptational stress to change** is constant, as nothing lasts very long in our society and we have to change with each additional factor. Any change brings about stress and the release of stress hormones. Some people really collapse at this level based on the stress of change and go into adrenal exhaustion. **Different forms of government** imply different kinds of accountability and a constant form of conflict with governmental agencies like IRS or INS, etc. The Government is constantly changing its character even though its structure may remain the same.

Accountability is responsibility and it is central to all spiritual evolution. Being not accountable negates the value of truth and one cannot muscle-test if one is not accountable. **Crime, pestilence,** and **natural calamities:** we have to accept there are various kinds of crime/violence like 9/11, pestilences like AIDS, flu, natural calamities like earthquakes, floods, tsunamis, etc. These are part of the karmic package and there is no logical explanation for them. **Media barrage** is incessant and includes images, therefore mankind is being programmed all the time. **Perception vs. essence; illusion vs. reality:** capacity to tell truth from falsehood is permanently damaged in half of the population because of media barrage, relativism etc. **Id vs. Superego vs. Ego:** At the basis of the human psyche is the Id, the repressed animal instincts, the desire to kill, rape, and injure for the sheer joy of hurting. Superego balances the pressure of the Id. The ego in Freudian terms is the strength to balance the two and a healthy ego is able to handle the instincts without going into guilt about them. **Brain physiology** limits the capacity to understand and comprehend truth. We are not the victims of our brain physiology; we are the determinants of it.

Music, the arts, aesthetics all influence brain function and neuronal connections. **Imprinting; framing; sequence:** The phenomena of human existence result in a certain amount of imprinting and brainwashing. The other thing that gives meaning is framing and in today's world, the media has already selected the things to which one is going to pay attention. The sequence in which these things are presented has a different impact on the brain physiology, so the programming of the media is highly significant. Sophisticated people are aware of **context (nonlinear) vs. content (linear.) Humor, ambiguity:** Humor is healing, and points out the ambiguity between the content and the context. **Indoctrination, memes, propaganda:** We are constantly being indoctrinated by the human experience through memes (repetitive quotes) and propaganda. **Intention** energizes all phenomena of human experience, e.g. whether one is programmed or not depends on one's intention. **Discernment vs. naïveté:** To know the things discussed here gives one greater discernment because the mind unaided is naive and cannot tell essence from perception. **Narcissism vs. spirituality:** Narcissism is interested in dominating with its own viewpoint. Spirituality seeks truth for its own sake. **God or no God** is the overall context in which all of the phenomena of the human dilemma take place. The ego's 'house of mirrors' looks completely different when illumined by the light of divinity.

THE HUMAN DILEMMA (3)

Alignment

Seeking God vs. mammon/Caesar

Biological/hormonal drive/instincts

Sublimation vs. acting out

Desire for control, power over others, dominance, hegemony, alpha male

Herd instinct

Desire for acceptance/approval

Capacity for gratitude, thankfulness

Mercy vs. revenge

Value of human life

Mortality and limitation

Moral accountability

Concepts of Divinity: Merciful/punitive

What are the limits of freedom

Grasping vs. generous

Flexibility, capacity to learn, grow, mature

Innate energy: "Élan vitale"

Slide 116

SLIDE 116: THE HUMAN DILEMMA (3)

This slide was introduced at the August 2007 lecture, DVD disc 2 at 005630.

One's **alignment** with truth means that at every intersection one chooses that which is true and if you constantly chose that which is true, you will end up in a completely different dimension than those who constantly choose what is false. One's alignment has a very powerful effect on how you experience the world, what you interpret as true or valuable. Out of that alignment, we are **seeking God versus materialism, the spiritual versus the material**, and **God versus the worship of money, wealth or worldly power.** In addition to the above, there are **biological factors and hormones, the instinctual drives**, e.g. all young men are driven crazy by testosterone. **Sublimation vs. acting out:** Freudian psychology talks about the negative instincts, the negative drives, and to sublimate them instead of acting them out. You find an outlet that is socially acceptable and/or creatively effective to relieve the pressure of these negative drives. **Desire for control, power over others, dominance, hegemony, alpha male:** It is a nuisance to control other people because then they become your responsibility and you get all kinds of karmic liability, etc. Should one try to take control to make it better or just turn it over to God? Pragmatically speaking, turning it over to God works well. The **herd instinct** is how large segments of society shift 180 degrees. Under propaganda and a charismatic leader, the herd instinct takes over and people will perpetrate extremely horrible acts if everyone is doing it.

Desire for acceptance/approval from others: "Everybody has to agree with me" is a narcissistic orientation. As you evolve spiritually, you need progressively less and less and finally don't need anything. The desire for acceptance and approval runs a great many people all the time. To counteract that, there is a **capacity for gratitude and thankfulness**. Give a genuine "thank you" with a gracious attitude to people. The shortcut to spiritual reality is to develop the habit of being gracious towards all of life in all its expressions all the time. Always choose the high road-**mercy instead of revenge**. **The value of human life** is such that you value the other person's life as well as your own. When you value life itself, then its various expressions are acceptable. We are very aware that we are **mortal and limited.** All anxieties and fears are the fear of death. The earlier we accept the inevitability of mortality, the less our level of overall anxiety because all fears and anxieties are basically the fear of death. **Moral accountability** is one reason people have a fear of dying. One's guardian angel takes a moral inventory with you and you get a chance to look at yourself. Your life is reviewed and you see the options, choices, and karmic energies for the next reincarnation already set.

Concepts of Divinity: Whether you picture God as all merciful or punitive makes a big difference. As you grow spiritually, the fear of death lessens. It is your own option to have another life to correct the record, because you see how long it is-the implication of that record, a few eons. **What are the limits of freedom?** There aren't any, only the capacity of the human mind to see what the options are. **Grasping or generous, flexible, have capacity to learn, growing, maturing:** Most normal people try to learn from an experience-that this is not the way to do it, but will make every part of life subserve growing and maturing and developing spiritually. Innate energy of life, "Élan vitale" in French: It is an explanation for the evolution and development of the inner level of consciousness of organisms.

THE HUMAN DILEMMA (4)

Man vs. universe

Karmic inheritance/propensities

Purpose of human life

Civilized vs. primitive

Power vs. force

Truth vs. Falsehood (by Dr. Hawkins)

Love as quality, essence, good brain physiology

Childhood experiences: beauty, music, religious

Cultural norms/mores

Mental impact/programming

Technology/communication

Vast accumulation of knowledge

Sort wheat from the chaff

Opinion/narcissism/relativism

Goals, ambitions, "ego-ideals"

Identification, models

Slide 117

SLIDE 117: THE HUMAN DILEMMA (4)

This slide was introduced at the August 2007 lecture, DVD disc 2 013445.

Man vs. universe: Man pictures himself as thrown into the universe, as an accident of the universe, as the highest evolutionary form on the planet. From humanness, the next level of evolution in the nonlinear is the angelic. You leave the ranks of bodily humans and get to be a junior angel in training. There are ranks of angels. That which you consider to be 'you' continues on unabated, however your location and identification with the body disappears. That which you call 'you' is sort of like an etheric energy and it can go anywhere it wants in space.

Man's **karmic inheritance and his propensities** are not well-understood in the western world. What is karmic inheritance? The energy field of that which you are imprints all your decisions and their consequences, and this etheric body then is your soul, your spirit, and stays with you. Because it is context, it tends to influence the likelihood of various things happening in your life. It does not cause them, but increases the likelihood of collapsing the wave function from potentiality to actuality of certain events. If you have unfortunate things happening in your life, especially if they continue, then look for the karmic inheritance. Presume it is payback from a previous lifetime. Forgive yourself for being the one who did that to others. Presume anything negative that happens is karmic inheritance.

Purpose of human life is to serve God, self and humanity. Fulfill your obligations, destiny and potentiality by serving God, moving from self to Self, and serving fellowmen. Do not leave yourself out because in serving humanity, you serve yourself as well. **Civilized vs. primitive** is the society you grew up in. Power vs. force: Power is context; force is linear and Newtonian. **Truth vs. falsehood**: this book describes how to tell the difference.

Love becomes a quality, essence, good instead of an emotion. It is a way of defining ones' own reality, a quality. It is because of lovingness that you step over the black beetle because you appreciate the gift of life. All of this affects **brain physiology**. How you see and experience the world is reflected in your brain physiology.

Childhood experiences with beauty, music, and religion are very helpful in building positive qualities into a child's life. Then these end up as **cultural norms and mores,** whether people believe in them or not. **Mental impact and programming**-already discussed in previous slides. All of this is advanced by **technology/communication,** e.g. the internet and electronic media. We have access to **vast accumulations of knowledge.** Out of all that from the house of mirrors, one eventually learns to **sort the wheat from the chaff.** One gets rid of **opinion, narcissism, relativism**, and instead develops **goals, ambitions and "ego ideals"**, that which one wishes to become. Then one begins to identify with the models of that. Society needs **models and mentors**.

THE HUMAN DILEMMA (5)

Drives, self-sacrifice

Traps: Drugs, crime, vanity, possessions

Hedonism/self-discipline

Hormones: Sex and biological drives and dominance

Self-improvement, value of learning and skills

Introvert, extrovert, ambivert

Cultural myths

Imprinting, suggestibility

Uniqueness, individuality

Eccentricities, psychiatric disorders

Attentional set prioritization

Attractions vs. aversions

Sensory dominance – predilection (auditory, thought, feeling)

Archetypal roles (the rebel, the bitch, the hero, the profligate, child/adult, knight, leader, boss, etc.)

Dependence/Independence

Nature/nurture balance

Slide 118

SLIDE 118: THE HUMAN DILEMMA (5)

This slide was not actually reviewed at the August 2007 lecture, but is included here.

The ego's defense mechanisms include repression, suppression, denial, and projection, as well as the action of turning **instinctual drives inward against the self.** Thus, the drives that were biologically innate from the animal world are hidden in the 'Id'. Control mechanisms of the 'superego' (the conscience) are derived from society, and the conscious ego then has the job of reconciling these basic biological drives with society. **Drugs, crime, vanity and possessions** trap human consciousness from advancing much on average in a lifetime. **Hedonism** maintains that pleasure should be the aim of living and is anti-spiritual, anti-religions and anti-accountability. Wisdom on the other hand requires **self-discipline**, and delaying immediate gratifications for long-term goals.

Hormones can have a major influence in regulating one's **biological drives,** e.g. during puberty various sex hormones increase sex drive. Biologic drives dominate people below the level 200. **Self-improvement, learning and skills**: This is a way of life among the spiritually motivated people, who constantly work at overcoming negative attitudes such as self-pity or intolerance. **Introvert, extrovert, ambivert**: An ambivert exhibits qualities of both introversion and extroversion, as most people do not fit the categories of introvert and extrovert and fall somewhere along the scale of extroversion, depending on the situation, context and people around them.

Cultural myths are the set of stories and beliefs that characterizes a culture and greatly influence the people of that culture. **Imprinting, suggestibility:** The phenomena of everyday human existence and experience result in a certain amount of imprinting and brainwashing. Suggestibility means to be in an unguarded state, so anytime we have been in that state, we have picked up all the programming, and whether we remember it or not, it is still operative.

Uniqueness, individuality: refers to the sum total of characteristics that make up a particular individual including the good, the bad, and everything in between that makes a person unique. **Eccentricities, psychiatric disorders:** eccentricity refers to unusual behavior on the part of an individual without being maladaptive. People with psychiatric disorders "suffer" from their behavior while eccentrics are quite happy and less prone to mental illness.

Attentional set prioritization refers to the ability to learn to attend to the sensory features and responses that are relevant to performing a task and ignore the features and responses that are irrelevant. For example, when contemplation is done repeatedly over a period of time, it becomes incorporated into one's personality and attentional set by which one automatically becomes benevolent, loving towards all life in all its expressions, and aware of the perfection and beauty of every moment. We experience an **attraction** towards that which supports our life (friendliness, etc.) vs. an **aversion** towards that which does not support life (hostility, etc.). What holds people to a certain level of consciousness is positionality, which expresses as dualities of attraction and aversion. The pathway to enlightenment is constantly surrendering both attractions and aversions, assisted by prayer, etc.

CREATION vs. EVOLUTION (1)

Newtonian Science: Linear Causality

Source (timeless) vs. "First Cause"

Emergence vs. Causal

Heisenberg Principle: Intention

Potentiality actualizes by intention

Potentiality actualizes: Non-volitional field effect

Evolution *is* Creation

Creation is the emergence of evolution

Creationism: 6,000-year-old world

Evolution as collapse of the wave function

Creation as manifestation

God vs. Godhead

Creation as a consequence of what God *is* vs. *does*

God's will as Divine ordinance

Volition as an anthropomorphic concept

Teleology: ("in order to") presumption

Mechanistic Reductionism: "Bottom up" vs. "Top down"

Slide 119

SLIDE 119: CREATION VS. EVOLUTION (1)

This slide was introduced at the October 2007 lecture, DVD disc 1 at 011045.

Creation has a Source but no cause. The Source is forever present, with no beginning and no end. The idea of "first cause" is a Newtonian idea of causality, a "this" causing a "that". God as "first cause" is different from God as ongoing Source. The popular image is of God rolling the dice; there was not any universe, then the dice were rolled, this is causal. God is far beyond cause as the omnipresent Source. As we witness phenomena there is no cause to it; everything is emerging from potentiality into actuality depending on the overall context. According to the Heisenberg principle, potentiality actualizes in a field of intention, by intention saying "yes". Potentiality can also actualize non-volitionally because of the power of the field itself. This is important in the understanding of creation, which is not because of what God does, but because of what God is. Creation is the emergence of evolution as "unfolding". If one has a potentiality, will it actualize? It depends on the power of the volition. The Heisenberg principle reaches its maximum expression as Divinity. Man likes to speak about the will of God because he is anthropomorphic. All comes about not because of some capricious decision by Divinity; it is merely a consequence of what Divinity is. In a field of infinite power, to hold an idea in mind tends to make it manifest. Therefore, one cannot blame things on God, like to say it is "Gods Will". No, it is one's own will amplified by the presence of Divinity. What one holds in mind, because of the power of the nonlinear field of intention, tends to manifest. Everything is spontaneously expressing the essence of what it is. Expressivity is a capacity of human consciousness, happening through physical expression, tone of voice, vocabulary, posture, etc. There is no personal "you" that makes a decision.

Everything is nonlinear, and we see its expression in the linear domain. The linear is the actualization of the potentiality of the infinite field. The "human will" has the same potential effect when we say yes to "being a servant of God", being selfless, kind and generous. When one aligns with all the virtues, one greatly increases the likelihood of that manifesting in our life. There are many anthropomorphic depictions projected onto God; for instance God's anger, God's will, God's revenge, pleasing God, etc. We define God's Will as Divine ordinance, not as a capricious God's "will". Divine ordinance means the quality of what God is: Omnipotence, omniscience, and omnipresence, which get activated when one holds these qualities in mind. God is the reason one is able to do anything at all, otherwise one's volitions would have no effect in the universe.

Teleology presumes a volitional goal, that things became a certain way to bring about a certain result, and that the universe creates by Intelligent Design: that everything "is" in order to "do something". Then it says it does this in order to survive. A bug does not care if it survives or not, a bug just "is"; survival is in one's head. The ones who survived are the ones who fit into nature. Mechanistic Reductionism ("bottom-up" theory of evolution) thinks creation is an accidental evolution; its calibration does not even reach the realms it purports to disclaim. The Realities of Creation, and spiritual truths ("top down") calibrate from 600 up and consciousness at lower levels cannot understand them.

CREATION vs. EVOLUTION (2)

Matter vs. Spirit

Nonlinear essence vs. form

All form = linear information

Universe is an expression of the Infinite field

Energy condenses as matter: $E = mc^2$

Infinite potentiality of consciousness

Energy in 1 cubic inch of space is greater than the mass of the entire universe

Paradigm allegiance/limitation

Darwinian Evolution - 450

Divinity as Source - Infinity

Intelligent Design - 480

Newtonian Causality - 400

Dawkins: God Delusion - 190

Genesis - 600

Slide 120

SLIDE 120: CREATION VS. EVOLUTION (2)

This slide was introduced at the October 2007 lecture, DVD disc 1 at 012450.

Materialists deny the existence of spirit. Essence has nothing to do with form. Essence is nonlinear energy of the form, beyond form. All form is linear information, which can be analyzed, e.g. by science. The universe is an expression of the Infinite field. It is forever expanding at the speed of light (calibrates as true.) The Infinite potentiality is expanding faster than the speed of light in all directions simultaneously (calibrates as true.) Energy condenses as matter. The formula E = mc2 calibrates in the 400s. This formula led to the development of the Nuclear Age. Form as the linear information enables us to address many of the world's problems, such as the use of nuclear energy. It also introduces some new problems, such as nuclear weapons and nuclear waste. The energy in one cubic inch of empty space is greater than the equivalent of the total mass of the universe. That statement is beyond human ability to imagine.

The calibrated levels of consciousness delineate paradigms. If one is in a paradigm at a lower level of consciousness, such as Mechanistic Reductionism, one is unaware of the realities at the higher levels. The whole conflict of science vs. religion is because of a conflict of paradigms. Science is consistent with realities up to the 400s. Ultimate reality calibrates at levels of 500 and higher. The limitation of science is in fact a limitation of paradigms. Paradigm allegiance confines a skeptic to serve a pedestrian level of linear Newtonian Reality. The linear cannot disprove the non-linear. They are different paradigms. Science cannot measure what is real, such as Love, Pleasure, Beauty and Devotion. It is a limitation of awareness. Each paradigm has a limited perspective. Darwinian Evolution, which calibrates at 450, is also a limited perspective, a "box". Many are limited to this paradigm and have allegiance to the concept of causality as the explanation of phenomenon in nature.

Divinity as the source of the universe calibrates at infinity. Intelligent Design, which calibrates at 480, is a kind of compromise used in academic and educational fields. The Secularist does not like the idea of intelligence behind creation. It leaves the door open for God or Divinity. There is much political debate on the concept. The concept of Intelligent Design is obvious to those who are quite conscious. One can intuit the intelligence behind the stunning beauty of the natural world. You do not have to ascribe it to an external God. Causality blocks the awareness that because of the essence of that which it is, it fulfills its potential. The beauty of the natural world is intrinsic to its existence. Newtonian Causality is a very limited paradigm. Intelligent Design is far more advanced. The book, "The God Delusion" (cal. 190) contends that a Supernatural Creator does not exist and that belief in a personal God is delusion. Genesis (cal. 600) states that from the Godhead radiated Light, and out of that Light originated life, and the universe. Life comes from the spontaneous evolution of the Godhead.

CREATION vs. EVOLUTION (3)

Anti-religionism - 180

Dennett: Evolutionary Psychology - 210-250

Atheism - 165

Deism, Theism

“Bottom - Up” Mechanistic Reductionism - 185

Godhead as Light of Life - Infinity

Scopes Trial: Darrow - 450, Bryan - 510, Baldwin - 180

Autonomous vs. Intentional

Linear vs. Nonlinear contextualization

“Big Bang” Theory - 450

Black Hole Theory - 455

Inflation Theory - 450

Multiple Universes - True

Parallel Universe Theory - False

Slide 121

SLIDE 121: CREATION VS. EVOLUTION (3)

This slide was introduced at the October 2007 lecture, DVD disc 2 at 000000.

It is one thing to be "religious", quite another to be anti-religious. Anti-religionism calibrates much lower. One could be honest and say that you do not understand what religion is all about. You do not, however, have to take a stance against it. For example, a person does not have to like goodness, love, compassion and honor, but they do not have to be against them. In anti-religionism there is hostility toward religion, it is not objective. The reason for the hostility is that at the core of the ego is narcissism that does not accept anything that denies its own divinity.

Evolutionary psychology is pragmatic, as the 200's are the pragmatic levels and therefore it is useful within its own domain. The growth of the psychological mechanism consequent to evolution is factual. It is not hostile or controversial, it does not negate that God could exist. It says that humanity has benefited and evolved psychologically consequent to evolution. **Atheism** calibrates at 165. If one negates truth or the Source of truth, which is Divinity, God does not allow one to use the truth meter. They wander through the world not knowing that they live in a dark lack of understanding. **Deism** and **Theism** means belief in a Divine Being without being a religionist. The founders of the Constitution of USA were Deists and Theists. Consequently, we are free of government-imposed religion. "All men are created equal" comes from the Theist and the Deist, not from religion. **Bottom up mechanistic reductionism** calibrates at 185. The "top down" God as the Source of creation, calibrates at Infinity. **Godhead as the Light of Life** calibrates at Infinity. Life can only change form.

There is no reason to fear death because it is not a possibility. You can go to realms where you think you are dead, however. People can spend huge amounts of time in self-negation, and can become like a "nothing". If one firmly believes in death as nonexistence and negates consciousness, one becomes unconscious and ends up in the Void. As you value your existence, you begin to see life as having infinite potential. As one begins to experience the infinite love of God, then the option one chooses is love and lovingness. As one reaches advanced states of consciousness, what one looks for is love. Love is what differentiates Divinity from the Void.

The Scopes trial in 1926 was orchestrated by James Baldwin (cal. 180), who was trying to get publicity for the ACLU (cal. 145). He was the founder of the organization and the town in which the trial would take place was trying to increase its business. A local teacher voluntarily taught evolution in the school and got arrested. **Darrow** (cal. 450) was a brilliant lawyer. He taught logic was the ultimate reality, and that the Bible did not meet the requirements of logic. Bryan was a famous religionist (cal. 510). Each one was the perfect representative of the respective argument. Darrow stuck to logic while Bryan stuck to faith. The trial was faith versus logic. There are the linear and nonlinear contextualizations of descriptions of creation. The **Big Bang Theory,** the **Black Hole Theory**, the **Inflation Theory** are all theories of the beginning of the universe, theorizing about the mechanism of the underlying Reality. There are **multiple universes**, potentially infinite in number. God is Omnipotent, Omniscient, and Omnipresent, so there is no limitation on creation in the underlying reality.

SPIRITUAL SURVIVAL / REALITY (1)

Realities of levels of consciousness

Reality is a subjective mental presumption

Reality: linear vs. nonlinear

Reality vs. Truth

Is the "me" real?

Who or what is the "I"?

"I" as witness vs. actor

"I" as experiencer

"I" as chooser, volition, will

"I" as social personhood

"I" as feelings / thoughts

Self as blank screen

Self as content vs. context

***Res interna* vs. *res externa* (Descartes)**

Self knows, mind thinks

Slide 122

SLIDE 122: SPIRITUAL SURVIVAL / REALITY (1)

This slide was introduced at the November 2007 lecture, DVD disc 1 at 005100.

Realities of Levels: As we go up in consciousness, the level of reality increases. It also moves into a different paradigm. **Reality is a subjective mental presumption**: Everyone presumes that one's experience is reality. That presumption does not replace the truth that there is an objective, discernible reality that is discoverable, and confirmable. The fact you are not aware of it does not mean it does not exist. **Reality: linear vs. nonlinear** is the basis of much discord because reality, according to certain paradigms, is linear and is only a pedestrian provability. That is really the limitation of traditional science, the world of causality. **Reality vs. Truth**: Reality is one thing and truth is another because they are different levels of abstraction. The other error we see is mixing levels of abstraction. **Is the "me" real?** Ours has become the society of narcissism and everybody is now aware of that in the virtual reality of the media. They tend to amplify that narcissism: "The world should change because of what I feel." The narcissistic generation exalts the "me" and is insulted all the time. If you are insulted, do not try to change the world; try to transcend your ego.

Who or what is the "I": We are getting to the more sophisticated understandings of "I", because it has to do with the pathways to enlightenment. People's idea of "who am I" varies quite widely. **The "I" is the actor at one level, at another level is the "I" as the one who witnesses** actions, feelings, thoughts, creation. Below 200, people live in an alternate reality of feelings, no thinkingness there. The more sophisticated say **I am that which experiences, I am that which chooses, I am the will**. Certainly, karma implies that **will, choice and volition** are extremely important. Feelings and thoughts do not count that much karmically because you can think anything, you can feel anything, but it is choosing and the volition that matters. The spiritually committed life is different from ordinary life. **"I" as social personhood**: narcissism of the ego is extreme. It is important to the ego to be somebody. People will do anything to get that one second on the screen. **I am my feelings/ I am my thoughts:** Lower levels of consciousness believe they are their feelings. More evolved are the 300s-I am what I think. The very sophisticated get "**what I am is a blank screen**." They observe that the mind can believe one thing on Monday and another thing on Wednesday depending on how society is programming it.

Self as content vs. context: That which I am is not the content of thinking or believing because it changes every year because I am a year older; I am the context in which the scenario is going on. **Res interna vs. res externa**: Discerning the world of appearance versus the reality of the world as it is beyond observation requires a great deal of sophistication. **The Self knows by virtue of the fact that it is everything. The mind thinks** about a thing. The ego as the 'experiencer' cannot transcend the disconnection between res externa and res interna that takes place in 1/10,000th of a second.

SPIRITUAL SURVIVAL/REALITY (2)

Reality as essence vs. appearance

Alice in Wonderland: opinion

Virtual reality of media

The world is a projection: illusion

"Reality" = 1/10,000th of a second process

Editing: "Tape out" vs. "recording"

Mind is without a compass

Alternate realities above or below level 200

55% error in the United States

Politicalization of beliefs

Narcissism as warp / distortion

Indoctrination trumps reality

All information is presumptive

Send your kids to Yavapai College (cal. 440)

Protagoras's dictum: Reality as subjective presumption

Slide 123

SLIDE 123: SPIRITUAL SURVIVAL / REALITY (2)

This slide was introduced at the November 2007 lecture, DVD disc 2 at 002420.

Reality as essence vs. appearance: We live in a world of free speech, and free speech has deteriorated in this age of media barrage, with people intending hatred, malice and malevolence. Opinion is limited in usefulness, yet that is what dominates today's world. The intellectual world has dropped to the level of **Alice in Wonderland: opinion** - a thing is what I say it is, nothing more and nothing less. It is what I indoctrinate you to think. It is either that or nothing else. If you resist, you will not pass and get a college degree. In the modern **media, we have a virtual reality** in which reality itself is immaterial. The focus is on what a thing looks like, what it sounds like and what people believe about it instead of trying to find the reality of the moment. For one moment on TV, people are willing to give up integrity, morality, their whole life, their money, not realizing that **the world in which they are playing a part does not even exist except as an illusion, a projection** of their own mind.

The world as it is, is unknown by the mind because information is instantly **processed by the experiencer edge of the ego in 1/10,000th of a second**. That is why it is so hard to become enlightened. How does one get to the Reality beyond that 1/10000th of a second? The mind is like a tape recorder. Birds are singing outside, and then there is the recording of the birds singing outside. On the old- fashioned tape recorder, there is a tape-out monitor. On the **tape-out monitor, you hear what has just been recorded, not the original** sound. That is what the ordinary mind does-you hear the recording. Once you go past the experiencer, you hear all the bird sounds without a recorder. You hear the source rather than the recording of the source. You live with "what is" without any editing.

The **mind is without a compass** and has no check on reality, like the old sailor sailing the seas without a compass, an external point of reference. Compassion arises for human ignorance. The value of the calibrated levels of consciousness is that for the first time man has an external source of reference as a compass. About **55% of the people are unable to discern reality from illusion in the US**, even if you explain it to them, due to the constant programming by the media. People below 200 have difficulty comprehending reality with the **politicalization of every belief system**. The cause of **warp/distortion is narcissism** which is self-seeking and self-serving. **Indoctrination trumps reality**: The traditional American values related to the chivalry and the honoring of women. Now there is indoctrination and the perpetrator- victim model.

All information is presumptive only, subject to change later. Everything you know, think or believe is provisional. Looking at the fall of Academia is disconcerting, esp. to parents wondering where they are going to send their children. Happily, there are many community colleges like **the Yavapai College (cal. 440),** that are still above the level of integrity and offer quality education. If truth, beauty, love, justice, etc. are qualities that **Protagoras' dictum** would lead us to conclude are relative to the individual observer, then how can one claim that stealing, adultery, impiety or murder are somehow wrong? This returns us to the basic issue that the mind cannot tell truth from falsehood.

SPIRITUAL SURVIVAL/ REALITY (3)

Reality is a product of paradigms

All reality presumptive vs. provable

Marx: Religion is an opiate of the people

Relativist antagonism towards the Absolutism of religion

"Tolerance" as downwards slope to non-reality

Validity: Criteria

Alice in Wonderland: The Internet and Bloggerism

The quasi-reality of Truth merchants: "Roger Stone", *Weekly Standard*, 11/5/07

55% in America exhibit damaged capacity to discern reality

Indoctrination vs. education

50% error in identification in police line-ups

Ideology vs. reality

Reality and normal brain function

Academia and "nutty professors"

Slide 124

SLIDE 124: SPIRITUAL SURVIVAL / REALITY (3)

This slide was introduced at the November 2007 lecture, DVD disc 2 at 012800.

Reality is a product of paradigms. Every paradigm of reality is a different reality. The different levels of consciousness are in fact different paradigms. The difficulty with atheism and skepticism is that the linear domain of causality, the 400s, is one domain and the nonlinear is another domain. The limited mind cannot grasp that there is a domain of context that is greater than the pedestrian, mundane world of logic. It cannot comprehend that there is a reality greater than itself. Skepticism calibrates very low, a form of nihilism, because it thinks the only reality is content and linear causality. Skepticism has tremendous faith in its own self-delusion. **All reality is presumptive; one cannot prove any reality whatsoever. Marx said religion is an opiate of the people**. Marxism is atheistic and denies the reality of the absolute. **Relativistic antagonism towards the Absolutism of religion**: The theories of relativistic philosophers like Noam Chomsky, Herbert Marcuse, Jean Paul Sartre, Bertrand Russell, Howard Zinn, Gore Vidal, etc. are popular in Academia, which calls into question the future of spirituality in the US. **"Tolerance" is the downward slope to nonreality** and now is applied to everything that has been traditionally unacceptable. Tolerance becomes a form of ignorance. The world is afraid to "call a spade a spade" for fear of political splatter.

Alice in Wonderland: The Internet system calibrates at a reliable 205-208. In contrast, the content of the material that appears on the Internet, including blogs, reflects the whole range of human consciousness, calibrating from 50 to 445. It is therefore currently the greatest source of disinformation. **Validity Criteria**: are standards and rules used to judge the accuracy of claims in epistemology. An individual must determine what standards distinguish truth from falsehood. The **quasi-reality of truth- merchants**: In the conventions of politics, truth has an ambiguous status and politicians routinely lie and cheat. About **55% of the people are unable to discern reality from illusion in USA**, even if you explain it to them, due to the constant programming by the media.

Indoctrination vs. education: Marcuse has said that the purpose of education is indoctrination. Logical integrity is 440-499 while sophistry/rhetoric calibrates at 180-190 and was shown to be fallacious around 450 BC and is recorded in Plato's dialogues. Another reminder to be careful with using the data supplied by our senses (mind) arises from the fact that even eyes lie to us half the time, as there is a 50% error in line-up identification of suspects in criminal courts. "The Innocence Project" has found eyewitness misidentification to be the leading cause of wrongful convictions, because human memory is fallible. Ideology is one thing, human reality quite another. In Chairman Mao's collectivist farm experiment, by ignoring the innate reward system of the brain, the collectivist farmers lost their motivation, resulting in the world's greatest famine. Thirty million people died consequent to that political ideology. Reality and normal brain function: A healthy person with a normal brain function has a balance between the conscience (superego) and the instinctual (Id) and can recognize the difference between the external and internal reality, i.e.: sees a situation for what it really is, rather than what one hopes or fears it might be. Academia and Nutty Professors: Academia is down in calibration to 190 and under the heavy influence of nutty, delusional professors who believe in conspiracy theories that calibrate at consciousness level 90 or lower (e.g., 'the United States orchestrated 9/11', and 'the Holocaust is a myth')

THE MYSTIC (1)

Mysticism:

The Inner Path

Agape (Bliss)

Ecstasy

Union with the Divine

Transcend Personal "i"

God Immanent

Zen

Radical Subjectivity

Devoid of "others"

Stages (classical)

1. **Purgation of bodily desires**
2. **Purification of the will**
3. **Illumination of the mind**
4. **Unification with the Divine – "*Unio Mystica*"**
5. **Self dissolves in Self**
6. **Final "state" or "condition"**
7. **The Sage**

Slide 125

SLIDE 125: THE MYSTIC (1)

This slide was introduced at the December 2007 lecture, DVD disc 1 at 010330.

In counter distinction to the intellectual approach to spiritual-religious education, mysticism is the inner path. It arises from within. It comes with no advance warning and takes over, every time it is overwhelming, profound, everlasting, eternal and transformative. The ecclesiastic approach in the classic religious education can set the stage for it, but it does not cause it. One can study theology day in and day out, but that will not necessarily precipitate it. If a person has an interest in religion and then adds to that a certain motivation, which then becomes activated, it may result in a mystical inner awareness, which the great saints of Christianity have represented in the study, worship and devotion to religion. Suddenly the words become the inner truth experientially, known as Unio Mystica, the mystical union of the self and divinity, through infinite love. Union with the divine is God Immanent and radical subjectivity. It may reveal itself as agape (bliss), which is the lovingness for all existence, calibrating around 600. Before that level is unconditional love, which is a very profound state, one for which we should be very thankful; it is experienced as lovingness for all of life in all its expressions, lovingness for nature, lovingness for the animal kingdom, and sensitivity to the beauty of everything that exists. You transcend the personal 'I' and the belief that there are separate others. That which is the witness and the observer is about as close as the mind can get to the reality of the inner life of the mystic. As the observer/witness, one can participate without actually being involved. You are involved operationally, but there is no cost involved.

The capacity for happiness lies within you. When you are happy, no matter what is for dinner it tastes great. Happiness and love transforms everything to a positive experience. You do not have anything riding on outcomes. The classic way to this state is the purgation of bodily desires. It is really the purification of the will by letting go of attractions and aversions. The key to letting go of all attractions is the understanding that all attractions are projections of that energy field called glamour. "Glamour" by Alice Bailey is one of the most helpful books ever written. The Buddha said that man gets attached to the world via the senses. One can decide against them and regain freedom; this comes about as a result of the illumination of the mind. The self with the small "s" dissolves into the self with the large "S", and every time this has occurred it has been the same. There is no personal pronoun; in fact, one has to imagine it to the point that it is at least an operational reality. One arrives at the mystical states through the purification of the will. That is assisted by the illumination of the mind which, if it continues, leads on to divine love in the 500's, then on to Unconditional love at 540, with Sainthood at around 570. Through the evolution of consciousness, an autonomous state reveals itself effortlessly. Eventually when it takes over, it may take you out of the world. The choice is that you can leave the world, or stay in the world and live in something like an Ashram. You can lead a life of contemplative quiet, retired from the world. People will come to visit you, what they are looking for is to pick up that energy. **Ramana Maharshi** and **Nisargadatta** as sages served in this capacity to those who were seeking.

THE MYSTIC (2)

Inner Process

Ignition • Initiation • Attraction

Motivation • Curiosity • Inspiration

Contagion • Education • Discovery

Introspection • Awakening • Karma

Devotion • Prayer • Supplication • Dedication

Persistence • Pursuit • Desire • Goal

Meditation • Contemplation • Reflection

Holy Company • Teacher • Energy Field

Mudra • Life as Supplication - prayer

Aesthetic • Grace • Presence

Slide 126

SLIDE 126: THE MYSTIC (2)

This slide was introduced at the December 2007 lecture, DVD disc 1 at 012555.

The inner process towards enlightenment, revelation and becoming a mystic is like ignition, initiation and attraction. First, one hears of it and becomes interested in enlightenment. You then seek out a spiritual group that is aligned with reaching enlightenment. There is ignition just by hearing about it. Then is initiation, which occurs in the energy field of the etheric body, you become attracted to it and begin to hang out with holy people. When a person does that, they pick up the energy field, and classically the energy of the enlightened teacher transmits to the energy field of the etheric body of the student, which may remain for many physical lifetimes. The transmission comes forth when needed, as a conviction and knowingness. When it comes to the death of the personal self, which can be terrifying, to counterbalance it a person needs absolute conviction. This can only arrive from the energy field of someone who has lived it. It cannot be something you read in a book, so the power of the field arises from one who has lived it.

So a person gets attracted to spiritual groups, has motivation and curiosity that is really interest, and then you also get inspired by the presence of others non-verbally and by the truth that one hears from other people. There is a certain contagion in the energy field that is picked up through the holy company, which is a group aura that is now quite powerful. Through contagion, education, and discovery, which leads to introspection, there is the possibility of finally reaching awakening. The whole situation is precipitated, exhilarated by devotion, prayer, supplication, and dedication. Those things are very powerful. You pray to God for enlightenment, "I pray to be a servant of God, to serve God, Self, and fellow man." Through devotion, one develops persistence and a pursuit of the truth, and the only desire you have left is to serve God and your fellowman, and your Self.

You do this through meditation, contemplation, and reflection. Meditation is a strict formality, but contemplation is really a life style. Contemplation means realizing the importance of reflection; it is a very yin position of allowingness. You ask the Holy Spirit, all mighty God for an understanding of a certain thing. "I pray to Thee, O Lord, to understand this differently", then you let it go. You do not tell God how you want it handled. Your life becomes a supplication, a prayer; it is not what you do and not what you have, it is what you have become. All living things know what you are: a silent awareness, that which is closest to divinity is walking by. You walk through the woods and you can see the lighting up of the flowers, the lighting up of the shrubs. Your life then is a supplication in which you are constantly asking for, and opening to the Grace of God. Your openness invites revelation to occur. The aesthetic becomes constantly attractive: ballet aesthetics, Andrea Bocelli, nature, the grace and aesthetic beauty of all that exists eventually becomes a constant awareness. One is aware there is an intrinsic beauty to everything that exists. A person begins to see the aesthetic beauty and pleasure of all that exists. You lighten up the world by that which you have become. "Gloria in Excelsis Deo", Glory be to Thee, O Lord that my existence may be of service to Thee." This lends a certain grace to one's presence. Everyone tries to be around those people who somehow make you feel better.

THE MYSTIC (3)

Experiential

1. **Seeking (the yogas)**
2. **Surrendering**
3. **Samadhi – Turiya (4th state)**

Examples

Dionysus the Areopagite	**755**	**St. John of the Cross**	**605**
Muktananda	**655**	**Johann Tauler**	**640**
St. Teresa of Avila	**715**	**St. Bernard**	**650**
Huang Po	**960**	**Mechthild von**	
Patanjali	**715**	**Magdeburg**	**640**
Plotinus	**730**	**St. Francis**	**660**
Ramakrishna	**620**	**St. Dominic**	**655**
Ramana Maharshi	**720**	**Meister Eckhart**	**705**
Nisargadatta Maharaj	**720**	**Cloud of Unknowing**	**700**

Slide 127

SLIDE 127: THE MYSTIC (3)

This slide was introduced at the December 2007 lecture, DVD disc 2 at 000000.

Mystic revelation is the inner pathway of the contemplatives of Hebrew and Christian ("Unio Mystica") tradition and the Sufis of Islam. It is the 'pathless' way of Zen and the core of Buddhism as well as the Hindu tradition of the classical yogas. These are the pathways through the heart, surrender, love, service, worship, devotion, and lastly, *Advaita*, the pathway through mind. The mind thinks there are only three states: (1) experiencing (waking state), (2) sleep (oblivion), or perhaps, (3) sleep with dreaming. But relatively unknown to ordinary mind is a fourth state known in Sanskrit as Turiya, which is one of awareness itself and independent of content, experiencing, or even participating, analyzing, or recording. The underlying quality is effortless, peaceful, and compatible with a contemplative lifestyle. It leads to the states classically termed Samadhi.

As the famous Zen ox-herding pictures depict, the progression is to first locate and identify the ego (the ox), then tame it, then transcend it, then leave the world, then the world disappears, and then, as a seasoned sage, return to the world. At this point, the world is depicted as merely a reflection on the water (of consciousness itself).

The traditional great pathways of the mystic are included in the four great classic yogas of Hinduism: raja (meditation), jnana (wisdom and introspection), bhakti (devotion), and karma (selfless service). These have their equivalency in all religions, including Christianity. Jnana yoga denotes the pathway of Advaita, or nonduality, which emphasizes meditation and contemplation and is the pathway of the Buddha and great mystics of history and it may be the best way for the person who channels their energy through thought and thinking rather than feeling. In "Truth vs. Falsehood: How to Tell the Difference" (2005), Chapter 16: Religion and Truth, calibrations of the principal Yogas are provided as follows: the selfless service of Karma Yoga (cal. 915), Bhakti (cal. 935), Raja (cal. 935), Kundalini (cal. 510), Kriya (cal. 410), and Hatha (cal. 390).

The aphorisms of Huang Po calibrate at 850; that is the pathway of negation, not this, not that or "neti-neti". To let go of all conceptual thought is a Buddhist pathway. No matter what you say about anything, it only amounts to something that you are saying about anything. Anything that your mind says is perceptual or it could not say anything. You cannot find Divinity or the Buddha nature through the mind. So to transcend the mind with a small "m" is critical, which opens the way for Mind with a capital "M". When Ramana says, "Do not worry about the world you see because the world you see doesn't even exist", it makes no sense to the average person, but it clarifies the difference between perception and essence. What the world sees and thinks is truth is perception; therefore, it is devoid of any inner reality. One TV news program is just as fallacious as the next. The slide includes calibrations of mystics that are familiar. St John of the Cross (605) is well known and books are available about him. St. Dominic (655) founded the Dominican Order in the early thirteenth century. Meister Eckhart is extremely well known and got into some trouble with the Catholic Church over his mysticism. There is a famous book essential to mysticism: *The Cloud of Unknowing*, which calibrates at 700. Part of the wisdom of *The Cloud of Unknowing* is that it does not have an author that you can find online and criticize.

THE MYSTIC (4)

<u>"I" as Content, Self as</u>:

Body, senses, sex, age, animal

History, experiences, memories, recall

Mind, images, thoughts, sequence

Emotions, feelings, desires, aversions

Chooser, volition, causal, decider

Doer, recipient, winner - loser, "get"

Judge, good/bad, worthy, lovable

Victim - perpetrator

Intellection, education, talents, limitations, assets

Time tracks, past, present, future

Slide 128

SLIDE 128: THE MYSTIC (4)

This slide was introduced at the December 2007 lecture, DVD disc 2 at 000700.

Ask God to remove your condition from the realm of thinkingness, to the infinite silence below it. You allow the awareness that below the surface of talkingness, thinkingness, feelingness, sensation-ness is an infinite silent field, which is beyond all time, beyond all dimension, not different from Divinity Itself. You surrender to the Infinite Presence, which is omniscient, omnipotent, without beginning, without end. By spiritual practices and exercises, you open the door of the likelihood of such phenomena to occur. On a certain level, you can reassure yourself that if you do all these things, the Presence will reveal Itself absolutely. God cannot deny your request. Divinity, because it is the very essence of your own existence, cannot deny the request for you to be aware of what you are. The Buddha said the first bondage is to the senses. You let go of identifying yourself as the physicality or its senses, sex, age, or that you are part of the animal kingdom. You let go of identifying yourself as your history, "I was born so-and-so", "I had these and those experiences" and "I can remember that and can recall that."

The direct pathway is to let go of all attractions, all desires, all wants, all negations, and all judgments. You give up seeing yourself as the decider, the chooser, the sense of volition, the naiveté that you are the cause of anything. The infinite power of consciousness is so profound that to think that puny you could be the decider of anything is a great pomposity. Something very profound is making the decisions and it is not your personal self at all; you begin to see that when you let go of the pomposity and grandiosity that there is a personal 'self' making choices and decisions.

That which you are eventually becomes the teacher, the knower. It is all in the One and there is no doingness involved. If the reality of the Self is all that there is, how could there be an "other?" People who get their spiritual instructions from otherness are prone to fallacy and very often before too many years, when you calibrate them early and calibrate them later you see they fell drastically. You give up the illusion that you are the doer, the winner, the loser, or that there is anything to "get." There is only to own the fullness of your being. In the enlightened state, you are beyond victim-perpetrator. Our whole society is riddled with this delusion. By projecting victim-perpetrator as a dualistic belief system, you can see victim-perpetrator everywhere. You give up intellection, education, talents, limitations, assets. You only have left, after you let everything go, a sort of intuitive attraction. You let go of time tracks, ideas of the past, the present, the future and now you can see you are in a dimension with no points of reference. Beyond time, there is no point of reference, beyond location there is no point of reference. You are in the middle of nowhere and everywhere simultaneously. At that point, fear arises that you are lost. The best thing to do there is to rejoice that you are lost. The way to *unio mystica* is through the progressive levels of consciousness, a stair-step to enlightenment described in the book, "*Transcending the Levels of Consciousness*". That one book saves you three or four lifetimes of being a monk. "Familiarity saves many lifetimes of being a monk."

THE MYSTIC (5)

<u>"I" as Context, Self as</u>:

Experiencer • 1-10,000th-of-second delay

Witness, observer, watcher of Emergence: Dance of Shiva

Knower • Awareness • Consciousness

Subjectivity, "is-ness," existent

Timeless presence, primary

Voidness vs. Allness

Light, love, radiance

Illumination • Divine • Love itself

Autonomous, Oneness, primary

Death of personal self; total surrender

Revelation, Radiance of Divinity, Awe

Slide 129

SLIDE 129: THE MYSTIC (5)

This slide was introduced at the December 2007 lecture, DVD disc 2 at 010800.

As you let go of aversions and attractions, you eventually will transcend the limitations of the experiencer. You become that which is happening. **In 1/10,000th** of a second, the ego jumps in and claims to be the author of the experience. To transcend that 1/10,000 of a second is what happens when one finally transcends the limitations and identifications of the personal ego. Now you experience all that is as it is. Nothing is happening in sequence. It only appears to be in sequence. You stop identifying with the perceiver and the experiencer. Then you are into the world of enlightenment. To get there you become the witness/observer, the watcher of the emergence, you then become the knower, awareness, and eventually you end up as consciousness itself. The easiest way to get there, is by allowing the idea of the personal "I" to be relinquished and to own yourself as the witness and the observer. You are not the cause. You are not the perpetrator, nor the victim or any other of the languaging or concepts. It is easy to become conscious that you are the witness of the phenomenon. To the witness, the room seems to be full of people. It seems like there are some persons here causing the teacher to talk to them. What is happening is instead of being the decider, the main actor in the middle of the drama of life, you become merely the witness of it. The best one could say that is close to the truth: How would one know what the "I" is experiencing? Now you can see closer to truth, closer to reality that you are the witness and the observer and not the experiencer.

From these states, it is easy to move to the realm of light, love and radiance. So the mystic enters illuminated states in which the context is illuminated. It is one thing to read about the truth and memorize the truth. It is another thing to have a total realization of it. When the final doorway opens up and the beauty of all existence shines forth, it is divinity that one is witnessing. It is divinity expressing itself as 'All that exists'. Beyond the apparent physical "is-ness", is the more profound, exquisite, stunning beauty of existence itself. All that exists shines forth with a radiance that is paralyzing. At that point, the mind stops. The mind falls back in awe because one is aware that one is witnessing Divinity. Its expression is All-ness. The personal self is gone, by virtue of revelation, the radiance of Divinity, and the ensuing Awe, which continues. And finally in order to be able to function in the world again, a true mystic has to learn to transcend Awe, because the Awe is beyond all brilliance, beyond breathtaking. The revelation of Divinity as Allness paralyzes you. Then if the Will of God is for you to continue on, that will be so. However, if the Will of God is for you to succumb and fall over, in a state of catatonic ecstasy, then that would happen also. Either way, it is all right.

SPIRITUALITY: REASON AND FAITH (1)

Conflict	**Coherence**
The Scopes Trial	**St. Thomas Aquinas**
Paradigms	**Traditional America**
Darrow - 450, Bryan - 505+	**Parochial Schools**
Left Brain/Right Brain	**Pledge of Allegiance**
Church vs. State	**U.S. Constitution**
ACLU (140)	**ACRU (460)**
Michael Newdow	**Pilgrims**
Madalyn Murray O'Hair	**U. S. Founding Fathers**
Secularism	**Billy Graham**
Extremism	**Moderation**
The Grinch	***A Christmas Carol***
Koran	**Abrogation**
Addiction	**12-Step Groups**

Slide 130

SLIDE 130: SPIRITUALITY: REASON AND FAITH (1)

This slide was introduced at the January 2008 lecture, DVD disc 1 at 002850.

The Scopes trial that originally took place in 1925 has reemerged in today's' society in new clothes and different words. The trial had to do with Clarence Darrow (cal. 450) versus Bryan, a believer in God calibrating over 500, symbolizing the clash between reason and faith. The 400s is the paradigm of reason and logic and provability, which is content and linear. It is one paradigm of reality. However, it does not include the entire infinite universe. Each paradigm is its own attitude from which it looks at the world. Realizing that the problem is one of paradigms solves a great many problems. St. Thomas Aquinas (cal. 570) has said that faith is reinforced by reason and that reason is reinforced by faith, otherwise one ends up with destruction.

In traditional America, people did not see any conflict between what one learned in science in school and what one heard in Sunday school. The parochial was not in conflict with the secular school, it was just in addition. In traditional America, everyone started out the school day with the Pledge of Allegiance. Nobody had a problem with it. We had a synthesis of the left and the right brains through the Pledge of Allegiance. A person can create an artificial dichotomy of Church vs. State; it is synthesized in the US Constitution, which guarantees not only freedom of religion but also freedom from religion. The US Constitution calibrates at 570, and brings about social and intellectual coherence. "Church vs. State" is a conflict exhibited by the ACLU (cal. 140). The ACRU (460) is American civil rights versus civil liberties. By liberty, ACLU means "no constraint." The ACRU shows coherence. Michael Newdow wants to remove "In God We Trust" from the U.S. money; European pilgrims who settled in America in early seventeenth century are a contrast to that position. Madalyn Murray O'Hair challenged saying prayer in school. The founding fathers are in contrast to Madalyn Murray O'Hair. Conflict comes from secularism, which attempts to remove any reference to divinity.

In contrast, we get coherence from Billy Graham (cal. 570) who has counseled many presidents of the U.S., and has provided tremendous service to the people of the United States. Extremism comes out of conflict and moderation comes out of coherence. The ACLU is like the Grinch. Dickens' *A Christmas Carol* (cal. 510) exhibits a completely different paradigm. Conflict in today's world has a lot to do with the Koran, as about 30% of its verses calibrate below 200. You get coherence by the principle of abrogation, i.e. that which is towards the back of the Koran overrules that which is in the beginning. Abrogation is an attempt to synthesize different parts of that, which is in conflict intrinsically within itself.

One of the biggest impacts in today's world is addiction, very conflictual and poorly understood by the public and even by professionals who talk about it. Addiction shows conflict within the person as well as between the person and their relationships and the world. The synthesis allowing the resolution of the conflict is the 12-step groups, which at level 540 have had a major impact on our culture. People seek out 12-step groups for not only alcoholism, but for all kinds of addictions, misbehaviors and psychological difficulties. Whatever problem you have in life, if you apply the 12 steps to it, you will resolve it. The 12 steps are benign in intention, totally nonconflictual and have no opinion on outside issues.

SPIRITUALITY: REASON AND FAITH (2)

Conflict	Coherence
Left Brain	Right Brain
Fight/Flight Emotions	Endorphins/Kundalini
Far-Left Relativism	Absolutism
Rhetoric	Logic
Karl Marx	Great Books of W.World
Causality	Emergence
Survival / War	Cooperation
Faith in Falsehood	Verified Level of Consciousness
Extraord. Pop. Delusions	Balance/Wisdom
Innocence of Child	Wisdom
Indoctrination	Education
Perception	Essence
Atheism	Theism

Slide 131

SLIDE 131: SPIRITUALITY: REASON AND FAITH (2)

This slide was introduced at the January 2008 lecture, DVD disc 1 at 0052300.

The left brain has to do with reason and logic. The right brain has to do with synthesis, love and coherence. Left brain people have a great difficulty in understanding right brain people and vice- versa, because they synthesize and see things and process things differently and actually live in two different worlds. One way to help overcome conflict is to see that people process things differently and make allowance for that fact. That allows them to be wrong without you being mad at them. The fight or flight emotions one sees so dominantly in today's society and everyday news, is the conflict between these emotions and the endorphins/Kundalini energy, which begins to flow around the level 200. Kundalini energy is the spiritual energy and has to do with context, not content. We used to think it did not show up until you are almost enlightened, but no, it shows up the minute you opt for truth over falsehood and integrity over personal gain. It means the big conflict between these two realms is narcissism. It is humility that switches one from left brain to right brain, admitting that without help, I don't know the answer; the realization, recognition and acceptance of limitation.

Absolutism is the exact opposite of relativism. Absolutism drives relativists crazy because the thought there is something other than itself that is sovereign is a challenge to the narcissistic core of the ego. The far left and that which denies and causes conflict is based on rhetoric. The value of the right brain is the logic as found in *The Great Books of the Western World*. The preeminence of *The Great Books of the Western World* has been relinquished in today's academic world and the consequences can be seen in the fall of the level of Academia. How the world evolves from the viewpoint of causality is different than that from the viewpoint of emergence.

In the Newtonian paradigm, one thing causes another. That applies only to content. The actual universe, which is context, comes about as a result not of cause and effect, but of emergence. Everything that is done and said is happening spontaneously as a consequence of the reality of that from which it emerges. Spiritual evolution comes about as a consequence of the emergence coming out of a decision, "I want to be kind and loving toward all creatures." Acknowledging Divinity when we start, "All honor be to Thee, O Lord" sets a powerful context to which everything is now subject. Out of conflict arises survival/war. Out of coherence comes cooperation. Survival has been under threat by wars 93% of human time and the only way around it is cooperation. Negotiation is the best way to handle it.

Faith in falsehood is endemic and is offset by verifying the level of consciousness. *Extraordinary Popular Delusions* is appropriate for today's world. It is offset by balance and wisdom. Causes become popular and sound great, but calibrate below 200. The mind, which one thinks is so wonderful, is one endless set of stupid programmings imposed on the innocence of the child within - its only protection is the wisdom of a discerning awareness. The work of consciousness calibration discovers perception from essence. That is what saves us from Marxism. Atheism is about 190. More sophisticated is agnosticism, which calibrates at 200; higher still is theism.

CARNIVAL: WAR of the "ISM'S" (1)

Class, Race, Gender, Age

Politics, Party - Circus

Collectivism, Socialism

Populism: "Causes"

Elitism

Fads

Environmentalism

Historical Revisionism

Hedonism, Egotism

Socialism

Secularism/Religionism

Egalitarianism

Intellectualism

Exhibitionism

Relativism/Absolutism

Slide 132

SLIDE 132: CARNIVAL: WAR OF THE "ISM'S" (1)

This slide was introduced in June 2008 Lecture, DVD disc 1 003200.

More than three fourths of humans calibrate below 200, and almost everyone has these

internet-enabled message machines. The streets of public information are dangerous. It is really a carnival as you watch television and as you listen to all that goes on, especially in a year with an election. What we see is the war of the "ISM's". Here is today's total madness. We are having peace, but the media is concerned with an intense concentration on **class, race, gender and age**. You cannot beat up on people because of their class anymore, but you can play the race card, the gender card and now the age card too. If someone is 72, you can beat him up because he is too old to be president. We have the **politics party circus**, which is entertaining from a somewhat detached viewpoint. You hear quasi-arguments and the liberties they take with logic, truth and facts to serve them around.

Collectivism and socialism: The pressure is to bring about a change in our society to be more and more like Europe - socialist, atheist and 50% of your income goes to taxes. From a paternalistic meritocracy that America was, the idea is to move to a more maternalistic socialism. The US society is very well-balanced where through one's own efforts and self-sacrifice one moves ahead and also there is a sufficient output from that kind of a structure that there's enough capital provided to the economy and to our country to take care of everybody. It is hard to starve to death in our country because somebody will pick you up and lead you to the nearest welfare assistance. We see the carnival in our world of **"causes."** All kinds of **elitism** and there is always a passing **fad** - save the hippopotamus, save the reindeer or save somebody. **Environmentalism** gets a very big push and of course, you can justify anything with **historical revisionism**. What you do is reinterpret history in such a way that being the victim gets juiced the most. If you cannot find any reason to be a victim, it is because you have not gone far enough back in history. In history, everyone was enslaved. In the old days, the Vikings captured and killed everybody, the Goths killed everybody, the Huns, etc.; everybody killed everybody. Then some enterprising smarty got that you can sell these people. They stopped killing them and sold them off. Slavery was worldwide. In ancient Rome, ancient Egypt, ancient Greece, etc. It was a lot better to be a slave than to get slaughtered, because sooner or later you would find some kind of happiness; you might escape, etc.

Exhibitionism: For fame and money, a large part of our society will do anything and selling their soul is traditional. In our society, 15% of our population is willing to sell their soul for fame and fortune. That is scary when you think of it. You see it every day on television, the things that people do to be in the limelight. **Relativism** is a variety of the Marxist doctrine of victim-perpetrator and is the opposite of **absolutism**. Relativism comes from **intellectualism** - a thing is only true if I believe it to be true. Truth is not subject to opinion. It is so, no matter what your opinion is. The value of consciousness calibration is that for the first time in history, man can discern the essence and truth of a thing without having it impaired. This particular **Absolutism** will eventually take you to God if with every decision you need to make, you choose that which calibrates the highest. If you negate the very source and reality of truth, which is a quality of Divinity, then you disenfranchise yourself from the fruits and rewards of adhering to the truth and the source of truth as Divinity.

CARNIVAL: WAR of the "ISM'S" (2)

Communism/Marxism

Paternal/Maternalism

Infantilism

Amoralism

Oppositionalism

"Truthers"

Conspiracy Theorists

Paranoid Psychosis

"Steel doesn't melt"

Criminalism

Apologism

Accommodationism

Loss of Sovereignty

Loss of Authority

Slide 133

SLIDE 133: CARNIVAL: WAR OF THE "ISM'S" (2)

This slide was introduced at the June 2008 lecture, DVD disc 1 at 004700.

Communism and Marxism - Various socialistic and Utopian 'isms' and schemes came and went, of which communism still remains. The basic defect of faulty political positionalities is that they distort content as well as ignore context. The content may sound idealistic, but it becomes fallacious under a different context. When context is ignored, an idealistic concept may become more destructive than the original problem it was meant to correct. Therefore, such idealisms are failures in contrast to wisdom, which includes context and not just content. The Far Right tends to become fascist (fascist ideology calibrates at 125), and the Far Left moves into the sophistry of thinly disguised Marxism (Marx calibrates at 130, communism at 160) and its distortion of reality (i.e., perpetrator/victim model).

Paternalism: you get what you deserve through your own self-discipline. **Maternalism**-everybody deserves to live because they are born a human in our society. **Infantilism** is really narcissism, and narcissism is really a form of infantilism in which you just think about "me" and everybody is supposed to treat your inner feelings as though they are precious. Nobody is supposed to hurt your feelings. As long as we do not hurt anybody's feelings we are okay, except that is infantilism because the world was not created to handle your infantile feelings of what you like and do not like. **Amoralism** is a lifestyle characterized by a narcissistic lack of concern for the rights of others or the incorporation of society's values, such as morality or ethics. In Freudian terminology, there is a lack of superego development and a failure to introject and identify with an adequate authority figure.

Truthers are always coming up with the latest **conspiracy theory** and they always tell you how the United States government engineered 9/11 and put secret bombs in the buildings, etc. What they are getting out of it you get at the end of the story. They give you a smirk: "Everybody knows that **steel doesn't melt**." How do they think railroad tracks came about? "Steel doesn't melt" calibrates at 150. The truthers are working conspiracy theories because they are getting narcissistic gratification out of their idea of moral superiority. The world is in a race for moral superiority - the intense competition for the moral high ground.

Paranoid psychosis is a psychopathic disorder involving a lack of conscience that typifies the classic con man. The Pope correctly said the reason the western world is falling is the impact of Islam plus narcissism in the form of relativism. The threat of aggression and **accommodation** to that which is false, then, reduces one's own level of integrity. The way you can get along with the **criminal** population is to become a little criminal yourself. You get along better with the criminals, but you yourself become semi-criminalized. Rationalized lack of responsibility is also exhibited by the positionalities of **apologists** who sympathize with the most decadent and dangerous persons in the world instead of their more obvious victims. That authorities fail in the personal execution of their responsibility is a widespread phenomenon. In this generation, it is demonstrated by the failure of even the federal government to respect and enforce its very own laws for decades, which has subsequently created major conflicts and dilemmas as well as **loss of sovereignty** and **loss of authority**.

CARNIVAL: WAR of the "ISM'S" (3)

Loss of Credibility

Loss of Boundaries

Decline of Efficacy

Dysfunction

Loss of Confidentiality

Loss of Privacy

"Rights" of the Media

Public "right" to know

Greed for Fame/Money

Populism

Seditionism

Factual: Overpopulation primary problem

Ideal world population: 2.5 billion

Slide 134

SLIDE 134: CARNIVAL: WAR OF THE "ISM'S" (3)

This slide was introduced at the June 2008 lecture, DVD disc 1 at 005300.

We see because of the ism's, **loss of credibility** - you cannot believe anybody anymore; also a **loss of boundaries** - people's boundaries are invaded all the time. You can go on the internet and punch in anybody's address and go there; you will be shown how to get there, probably where they keep their valuables in the house, "go in through the back window, it's never locked." They give you the credit rating of who lives there. So forget about privacy, one does not have any. **Decline of efficacy:** The U.S. is the most powerful nation in the world and we cannot even put a fence across the border. Whether one politically agrees with it or not, one would think a huge country like the US could solve a few little simple mechanical problems. A person becomes **dysfunctional** because they are going in four different directions at once.

Also, in this war of "isms" there's a **loss of privacy** with the public's right to know and the rights of the media; you have no more legal rights to privacy anymore. One sees public attacks on people all over the place. People who are the private advisers to the White House - as soon as they get out of the White House, they write an expose. Singapore has practically a zero crime rate. Try that in Singapore and they execute you the next morning. Why are there no drug dealers in Singapore? Because they are all executed the next morning; get arrested at ten, you die at 6 A.M., no problem. So there is the loss of privacy, the **loss of confidentiality, and the loss of trustability**. With all these "isms", **the rights of the media** - where'd these rights come from? We do not remember any great document in our founding fathers' papers that says everybody has the right to know everything, including what we do in the bathroom and the executive branch of our company.

We see through **populism**; **sedition** is now very trendy. If you want to be somebody, you get up there and denounce the United States government. If you can get up there and hate your country, the more you hate it the more superior you are. You cannot just say you hate America, you have to really hate America, denounce it as an evil country; all Americans are evil, they deserve to die. A certain part of the world teaches that in their schools in the United States, in the school district. They will tell us our big problem is global warming and environmentalism.

What all these ism's and all these problems boil down to is one cause - **overpopulation**. Why so much stuff in the air? Because we have a billion plus people in South Asia, over China there is a haze about three miles thick, a haze of pollution coming from the cities. Because of millions and millions of people, if they just do nothing they create a problem. A couple of billion people, you tell them to sit down in chairs and do not do anything. They are already creating a problem putting all that carbon dioxide out there. Linus Pauling around 1910 correctly figured out around the maximum, **ideal population of the world as 2.5 billion**, which is where we were at around the year 1950. That would leave huge areas to reforestrate, for nature, etc. and would not pollute the planet. Currently we are at 7 billion. If 2.5 billion is ideal and we are at 7 billion, then most of the world's problems are emanating from overpopulation.

INFORMATION vs. DISINFORMATION (1)

New York Times in 1955 - 403, in 2008 - 190

Internet 2008 - 200

"My Face" - 190

NBC News - 190

Fox News - 300

Hollywood in 1955 - 375, in 2008 - 185

Bill O'Reilly - 355

Glenn Beck - 350

Slide 135

SLIDE 135: INFORMATION VS. DISINFORMATION (1)

This slide was introduced at the June 2008 lecture, DVD disc 1 at 010220.

One could believe the **New York Times** in 1955 and it calibrated at 403. In the current world, it calibrates at 190. It was actually a little lower than that before, but it came back up. It does not feel guilty about what it does. You get a kick out of a skinny Frenchmen who climbs 51 stories up the New York Times building. The New York Times was 403 and is now at 190, and it is difficult to absorb just the implication of that for what used to be the most respectable newspaper in the United States. Actually, the Wall Street Journal still calibrates high. Anyway, one did not think they would live long enough that you would not be able to believe what is in the New York Times. It used to be that everybody got up and read the New York Times, especially on Sunday. The New York Times weighed about 5 pounds, and that took care of your whole Sunday morning.

The **internet** right now is doing a lot better than it was. The internet is now up to 200; it was below 200. "**My Face**" at 190, **NBC News** at 190, **Fox News** is at 300. **Hollywood** back in the 50's was at 375, now in 2008 it is at 185. Which of the relatively well-known TV personalities can you believe?

Bill O'Reilly, he is a moralist at 355, and a fellow moralist is **Glenn Beck** at 350 and so here we see a lamenting that the moral backbone of society is disintegrating, that is the main theme. There is this decline in Hollywood, too: it was 375, it is now 190. Who brings it to our attention? These are the social commentators, all probably the best known. NBC has gone off the rail, and has been for some time. For things that we put faith in, if we do not calibrate them, we will not know when we are getting hoodwinked. O'Reilly gets too moralistic and carried away with the indignity about it all, but at least someone does care. That is his job, he gets indignant but not indignant enough; Glen Beck joins the parade too and so we have social commentators with a conscience. In the old days, that was the truth in the world one grew up in and then there were the Hollywood columnists. Walter Winchell would give you the latest gossip from Hollywood, etc. Walter Winchell is not around anymore, so this is all we have to try to keep an eye out for what is happening.

INFORMATION vs. DISINFORMATION (2)

Neal Cavuto - 375

Charles Krauthammer -395

Newt Gingrich Viewpoint - 400

Demagogue - 180

U.S. Senate - 190

U.S. Congress - 200

United Nations - 180

Slide 136

SLIDE 136: INFORMATION VS. DISINFORMATION (2)

This slide was introduced in June 2008 lecture, DVD disc 1 at 010550.

We are continuing to see which of the people who are relatively well known deserve the highest degree of credibility. At what level of truth are they talking, what level of consciousness are they expressing? It looks like the mid-to-high 300s are pretty much a safe realm. They are not talking about absolute spiritual Truth; they are talking about social and cultural reflections of society in our country. **Neal Cavuto** (375) and **Charles Krauthammer** (395) are quite high. Cavuto is funny and interesting, and challenges people. Krauthammer has interesting facial expressions. **Newt Gingrich's Viewpoint**, not him personally, but his viewpoint is at 400; his analysis of the news is relatively intelligent. Newt Gingrich himself is highly educated and is intellectually honest. Many in public service are in the high 300s. It is a level of service and morality. The Band of Brothers is at 375. Many in the military are at this level. They often re-enlist as a group. They truly want to help their fellow man.

Our world is full of **demagogues** (180) with their flashy presentations. They like to play one race or sex against the other. The demagogues use flowery language, are quite animated and many of them are really actors. The art of oratory is a highly valued skill and was taught and discussed even in ancient Rome. It is dependent upon the integrity of the speaker, the integrity of the message and the receptivity of the audience. The political arena always makes for interesting theater. Veritas delayed publishing *Truth vs. Falsehood* until the political hysteria died down after the 2004 election. The demagogues try to be convincing, even though their own integrity is not high. They are trying to sell fallacious distortions.

The US Senate (190) and the entire **US Congress** is at 200. We seem to be in decline, like the fall of the Roman Empire. The legislatures of other countries are often even lower. We wonder why Congress cannot get things done when often the solutions seem obvious and simple. Our political structure has reached the point of impotency. The **United Nations** is a forgone failure. They are completely ineffective in solving any problems. The United Nations calibrates at 180. In order to know the truth about a matter, you must know about the society they live in, and identify the wolf in sheep's clothing. The UN states they will solve the world's problems, but they cannot even pay their own rent. We should not care much about the UN. It really has nothing to do with us. It has nothing to do with our inner integrity or our relationship with God.

Consciousness calibration reveals the effect of the world that we live in by using something objective. We need not curl up in a paranoid box. With all the prior religious traditions, the only way to reach enlightenment was to withdraw from that evil society, join a monastery, close the gates, become celibate, join the other monks and eat turnips all day. Does that appeal to anyone? Most of us do not have any choice. We live in a world in which we must apply spiritual teachings and principles in our daily life. So how do we live in the world we just depicted? Jesus Christ said, "You wear the world like a light garment". When you feel discouraged, forlorn or woeful about the condition of the world, Jesus said to know the world, see it as it is and wear it lightly. Do not let it get to you and ruin your day.

INFORMATION vs. DISINFORMATION (3)

"Truthers" - 160

Injustice Collectors - 165

Conspiracy Theorists - 160

"Hate America" - 160

"Steel doesn't melt" - 150

Universities in 1955 - 400, in 2008 - 175

U.S. overall - 421

World overall - 204

Slide 137

SLIDE 137: INFORMATION VS. DISINFORMATION (3)

This slide was introduced at the June 2008 lecture, DVD disc 2 at 001415.

In the Phoenix, Arizona newspaper they have a whole series of little articles and letters to the editor, from **"truthers"** (cal. 160), which start with "The truth is..." and end up with "Everybody knows steel doesn't melt", which is funny. Truthers are a source of hilarity and they are very entertaining until, pathetically, one realizes they actually believe what they are saying. Nobody could be that dumb, but well, dumb people have to do something, so they write a letter to the editor, which keeps them out of trouble. "**Injustice collectors"** is a neurotic mental symptom, a personality disorder. Injustice collectors are all seeking the moral high ground, so the competition in our world is for the moral high ground. Whether it is Iran, Afghanistan, or elsewhere, somebody is trying for the moral high ground to justify resentment. Well, in the 12- step groups, they say there is no such thing as a justified resentment. Whatever happened, that was yesterday. In other words, injustice collecting is trying to pull something from the past to justify negative emotions in the present. "**Conspiracy theorists**", then are great injustice collectors, of course. They make it all up.

"Hate America" is stylish in certain circles, and one wonders how in the world could "hate America" give one social status. Hate America calibrates at 160, because it violates the band of brothers, it violates your loyalty to your own country. Even if your country is rotten, most people are still loyal to their country to a certain degree. They may want to change the governance and the policy, but they do not really hate their country of origin-"breathes there a man with soul so dead, who never to himself has said, this is my own, my native land." You may disagree with them, but hating them is something else. "**Steel doesn't melt"** is below even hating America because it is a violation of intellectual integrity as well. Where do they think the railroad tracks come from?

The major US **Universities** are in pathetic shape. There are a number of books about it now. Universities back in the fifties calibrated at 400, not only integrous but intellectually honest as well. The Universities are currently in 2008 at 175. Consequently, it is advisable not to go to a university. If you are going to attend a university, you have to have another source of integrity and truth and you have to have a certain sophistication to avoid reprogramming. Some of the distortions have now become part of the curriculum and so students become not educated, but indoctrinated. That is actually the name of a book, "Indoctrination U" by David Horowitz. Via the universities, we have seen the decline of the level of civilization in the western world as the Pope commented, pointing to relativism, which is a secular distortion of causality. The **US overall** is still at 421 despite all what we have been talking about that sounds discouraging. Something is resisting decay. It means that individuals have enough integrity that they are not being taken in. We actually are wearing the world like a loose garment, yes we say that is just politics and we dismiss it. "So, wearing the world like a loose garment, we could also call 'cultural sophistication'" (calibrates true.) Sophistication tells you when they are trying to manipulate you, when they use certain buzzwords to try to stir up your emotions.

The **World overall** at the time of the Buddha calibrated at 90, and at the time of Jesus, it calibrated about 100. The world overall is currently still at 204 (calibrates true.) "It was at 207" tests true. It got up to 207 and then it turned around and came back down to 204. "That happened because a very advanced being left the planet" tests true.

DOUBT, SKEPTICISM, AND DISBELIEF (3)

Struggle for Dominance

Dominance as Control: Politics

Prioritization of Values

Egocentricity vs. Detachment

Emotionality vs. Reason

Content vs. Context

Dominance of Choice/Options

Age: Liberal vs. Conservative

SLIDE 138: DOUBT, SKEPTICISM, AND DISBELIEF (1)

This slide was introduced at the August 2008 lecture, DVD disc 1 at 004330.

Mankind has existed all this time **without a compass**, like a ship at sea with no compass. Mankind bravely walks on, generation after generation, century after century, struggling to walk upright and maintain life and some degree of dignity, etc. and does not even know truth from falsehood, does not know which way is up and which way is down. Out of the innocence within himself, man assumes that perception is reality, i.e. "how a thing is presented" is the way it is. In today's world, the media deliberately presents things to program our mind to think in certain ways. Unless one can tell truth from falsehood, one does not know whether anything is true or not true. Thousands of the ships are at the bottom of the sea for the lack of a compass to guide in differentiating longitude and latitude. For centuries, we went by the stars and the ships at the bottom of the sea will tell you how reliable the stars are. The vulnerability is the **innocence and trust of the child**. Even the skeptic is skeptical because he has a child-like innocence and he trusts his own capacity to think. Nothing can be more dangerous than trusting your own thinking. Because of the vulnerability, one has to have compassion for all men. The child believes anything he is told, as he has no reason to guard anything; it does not enter into his mind that his father, or mother, or teacher at school is lying to him. Therefore, the child within all of us is **programmable** and the enemy is not out-there-ness, the falsehood out there. The problem is our own inner child believes anything it hears. What about disbelieving everything you hear, distrusting it, and being skeptical? You do that because of the innocence of the child who says "that is the only way to keep me from getting fooled." So one is "trapped" by the innocence of the inner child, the **confusion of perception vs. essence** and on one hand, it leads to great and magnificent evolution and on the other hand, it could lead one downhill.

Descartes: Res interna is how one sees the world (perception), as opposed to **Res externa**, which means reality as it is, not as you perceive it, not what you feel or think about it. So independent from our intelligence and witnessing, there is an infinite reality, which is not dependent on our observation. **Socrates' Dictum** says man always chooses the good; it is just that he does not know what the really good is from the illusory good. Because man cannot discern truth from the false, he projects goodness to things that he desires, projects this aura of desirability upon the 'external world' and thinks that it is the thing itself that he desires, when actually it is the "glamour" that he himself is projecting onto the externals. We can stop finding faults in the world and admit that the reason I wanted things of the world is I did not know the truth. *A Course in Miracles* differentiates specialness that we project onto things from their inner reality. Socrates' dictum is extremely useful, because it reminds us that man does not even know he is projecting specialness, uniqueness and desirability onto the external world.

Discernment, opening the third eye of the Buddhic body: You now begin to see the essence rather than appearance. It is not money that makes one happy, it is what one does with the money, what it means and whether one uses it out of love of others or out of greed for inner sensation and possession. **Narcissism is a distortion** because man inflates a certain value and thinks it exists externally to him, e.g. the false notion that being a multimillionaire will almost guarantee that one will be happy, famous, wealthy, etc.

DOUBT, SKEPTICISM, AND DISBELIEF (2)

Relativism vs. Absolutism

Protagoras's Dictum

Projection of Glamour

Allegiance to "Ism's"

Extraordinary Popular Delusions and the Madness of Crowds

Hermeneutics: Meaning

Cultural Marxism

Slide 139

SLIDE 139: DOUBT, SKEPTICISM, AND DISBELIEF (2)

This slide was introduced in August 2008 Lecture, DVD disc 1 010230.

Relativism vs. Absolutism: The scale of consciousness is absolutism, like a thermometer or a barometer. It just tells you what a thing registers using the consciousness calibration technique. It does not express an opinion. **Protagoras's Dictum** is very much applicable to what goes on in current society. What the world worries about now was settled in ancient Greece in 500 BC and by not going for traditional education, what has happened is the information and the wisdom and the genius that has existed in mankind is now lost to the modern generation. If you ask the average person, "what is Protagoras's dictum?" They will say, "huh, what?" The dictum is an argument, which appears in Plato's dialogues. The person says, "What I believe is my reality and what you believe is your reality." Therefore, you then jump to the conclusion these are different realities, which again was an extremely egocentric viewpoint. Therefore, they are of equal value, that what to me is real is real to me and what is real to you is real to you. That would give us a certain compassion for people who are marching rapidly in the wrong direction from truth. They cannot discern truth from falsehood. They think that which they assume to be, is so.

Projection of Glamour is the ego's proclivity to project specialness onto perceived objects, persons, or qualities. Thus, the desired person, attribute, or possession is inflated, romanticized, and glamorized with exaggerated magical attributes (as described in *Glamour: A World Problem* [Bailey, 1950]). This gives the desired object, person, or quality a seductive attraction that most people ruefully discover is an illusion (e.g., adolescent romantic crushes).

Allegiance is **to "isms"**, to popularity, allegiance is no longer to the truth in the current society. In its more elaborate form, it is dedication to an "ism." Environmentalism will eventually kill all the life on the planet if carried to the extreme. All that carbon in the atmosphere is good. If it were not for all the carbon in the cow flatus and the plants, life would have ended on this planet.

Extraordinary Popular Delusions and the Madness of Crowds continues to be relevant because of its recurrent meaning. The fact that everybody believes something does not have anything to do with the fact that it is true, or not. Global warming is probably the biggest current illusion. In fact, the temperature change of the earth is due to cyclic changes in the surface magnetic activity of the sun. These extraordinary delusions became very popular and they become dominant. One wonders how society survives. The study of '**hermeneutics**' (**meaning**) reflects subtleties, references, and shades of classification of levels of abstract thought that are consequent to definition and identification of context. Even if there is agreement about the facts or definition of truth, there remains disagreement as to what it 'means' or signifies.

Cultural Marxism has now removed Marx from its name, but continues to be delusional yet very popular and has to do with the victim-perpetrator illusion. It is the product of the German philosophic school, the Frankfurt School. The modern universities are an output of cultural Marxism by virtue of Herbert Marcuse and calibrate below 200. The rise and fall of civilization, then, becomes apparent, as a new mass delusion overtakes the populace.

DOUBT, SKEPTICISM, AND DISBELIEF (3)

Struggle for Dominance

Dominance as Control: Politics

Prioritization of Values

Egocentricity vs. Detachment

Emotionality vs. Reason

Content vs. Context

Dominance of Choice/Options

Age: Liberal vs. Conservative

Slide 140

SLIDE 140: DOUBT, SKEPTICISM, AND DISBELIEF (3)

This slide was introduced at the August 2008 lecture, DVD disc 2 at 001930.

One sees the endless worldly **struggle for dominance** and **control. Politics** is all about the **struggle for dominance and control**. Once you have dominance and control, you can milk it for zillions of dollars. One of Socrates' dictums is that a democracy cannot last more than a couple of hundred years because the people are easily deceived by the wolf in sheep's clothing, being unable to tell truth from falsehood. The mind of modern man is also susceptible because of the inner innocence of the child. Mankind has intuited this and sought **prioritization of values** throughout time by seeking the great teachers: Jesus Christ, Socrates, Buddha and Moses, etc. When traditional wisdom was revered you were somewhat protected from modern fallacy and nonsense because it was always compared in the back of your mind with the teaching of Jesus Christ or Socrates or some great being. Without a traditional education now, there is no inner guideline. We see the Marxist duality of perpetrator/victim projected onto all of society. In that indoctrination, the minority is always the victim of the majority; that is the way Marx looked at it. We have the victimology and the moral high ground is to claim oneself as a greater victim than somebody else.

What is the appeal of **Politics?** Aside from the juice they get out of it, it is obviously the struggle for dominance and the inner narcissism projected onto the world. Of course, whether you are a **liberal or conservative** is partly a reflection of your **age**. "If you are not a liberal when you are young you've got no heart. If you are still a liberal when you are old, you've got no brain." Everyone is gullible to a certain degree. To be more gullible, you hold the idea that you are not gullible, which proves that you are more gullible; because anyone who does not believe they are gullible is gullible, as the program is not conscious, but automated. You begin by facing the fact that in some way one might be walking around in an illusion created by **egocentricity**. The only way to transcend the illusions by which people live, and the glamour that are associated with them is actually by progressive **detachment** and spiritual evolution. First by reaching the level of **Reason,** by transcending **Emotionality** and the lower levels; and then by transcending **content** and identifying yourself as **Context** instead, via persistent **dominance of choice/options**.

Because of the collective consciousness of mankind, as each person's Kundalini energy rises, just by being spiritually committed we are already profoundly impacting the world. It counterbalances many thousands of people who are not spiritually oriented. By virtue of what you are, you walk through the woods, affecting all living things. Every tree knows when it is in the presence of Divinity. We thought nature was unconscious, but every tree witnesses the presence of God by virtue of the innate nature of life itself. A part of spiritual evolution is that one gives up false humility and owns one's birthright as a human being: that man inherits also Awareness, shared by the Divinity within nature. The tree is aware that you are passing by. That is why you like kissing and hugging trees. You become humble when you look at the reality of nature and realize that you are just an expression of this infinite nature. The inner capacity to discern truth from falsehood is an intrinsic gift from God. The discovery of its Presence allows us to use it in a pragmatic way for helping ourselves, and all of society.

DOUBT, SKEPTICISM, AND DISBELIEF (4)

Religion vs. Religionism

Atheism vs. Agnosticism

"Know" vs. "Know About"

"Proof" vs. "Spoof"

Authority: Credibility

Glamour of "Causes"

Attraction of the Astral Circus

New Age-ism vs. Spiritual Reality

Slide 141

SLIDE 141: DOUBT, SKEPTICISM, AND DISBELIEF (4)

This slide was introduced at the August 2008 lecture, DVD disc 2 at 002450.

There is a lot of **religionism** in which the **religion** becomes the exact opposite of what it teaches. It does so because one is worshiping the religion and not the God of the truth that the religion is trying to teach. While **atheism** calibrates below consciousness level 190, **agnosticism** at level 200 is more sophisticated, more aligned with reality, and merely admits humbly that the intellect by itself is unable to resolve the problem of the actual existence of God. Agnosticism calibrates higher than skepticism because it does not include a negative emotional attitude of antagonism towards Truth. In the final stage of achieving certainty, to **know** means to 'be' and thus the subject is the knower, whereas to **know 'about'** is mental. The mind is struck by the **glamour of causes**.

Environmentalism, for example, is a laudatory cause today. Everybody wants to get on the bandwagon and prevent cattle from passing gas on the plains. Surreptitiously, they pass methane, of course, and the environmentalists want you to become vegetarians, as that will stop the cattle flatus from contaminating the planet. It is **proof vs. spoof.** The media are experts at spoof, and at programming you so that you will believe the exact opposite of truth. Once you know how to calibrate things, of course, it is fun to watch the daily news and calibrate the level of that testimony, that witness, did that person commit the crime or not.

Today's **authority** is viewed with suspicion, as it is partial to some cause and has lost **credibility**. Spiritual people have to walk by the trap. Walking through the swamp is a depiction of the evolving soul walking through the traps, with the seductions at one side and seductions at the other side. One of the seductions a person walks through is the **attraction of the astral circus.** It is very high in glamour, with people who channel all kinds of entities, etc.

Occasionally the entity on the other side is integrous, but if it were an evolved entity it would not be hanging out here trying to control people on the planet. It would have gone on to a higher realm rather than speaking through some trans-medium. Things that come about in a somewhat unnatural way, then, very often serve some other purpose and one has to calibrate their integrity. It is best to avoid that which is the **glamour of specialness**. The entity on the other side gets a vitalization out of power over others; it has all these stupid humans listening to their advice.

New Ageism vs. Spiritual Reality: The Bible says there are things beyond the paranormal. It does not condemn them; it just says do not go there, as humans are not equipped to handle entities from other dimensions. Out of humility then, the teacher says avoid that which is beyond your comprehension because they come from other dimensions and their ideas of reality and their motivations and their style of functioning is totally out of the human domain. The entity has no particular interest in your survival or your spiritual evolution or your enlightenment. A successful student would quickly quit the teacher from the other side. The last thing a teacher on the other side wants is for you to become spiritually erudite because they just lost a follower.

DOUBT, SKEPTICISM, AND DISBELIEF (5)

Paradigm Blindness

"Lying Eyes" Misperception

Truth as Reflection of Level of Consciousness

Karma: Propensity

Garden of Eden

Sin as Error/Ignorance

Responsibility vs. Culpability vs. Accountability

Truth Depends on Context

Slide 142

SLIDE 142: DOUBT, SKEPTICISM, AND DISBELIEF (5)

This slide was introduced at the August 2008 lecture, DVD disc 2 at 003500.

The difficulty for the human mind is not only its narcissism, but also **paradigm blindness**: what is true in one paradigm is not true in another paradigm. **Truth reflects one's level of consciousness** as each level of truth is unknowable to the levels below it and has no validity beyond its own territory. Paradigm blindness was originally understood by Jesus Christ in his terse statement, "Render unto Caesar the things which are Caesar's, and unto God the things that are God's," that is, do not mix levels of abstraction and confuse the realities of the linear and the nonlinear domains.

If you take the witnesses of a crime and show them the pictures of various criminals, the identification of the guilty person is fallacious 50% of the time. There was a great project to free prisoners on death row using DNA and it was very important because every person on death row had been convicted based on identification by many witnesses. It turns out that all of them were "**Lying eyes**" of misperception. The most profound explanation for this phenomenon is the effect of karma**.**

Christianity does not use the Sanskrit term **karma**, but Christianity does believe in karma by virtue of the **Garden of Eden.** If it were not for the fall of man in the Garden of Eden, you would not need a savior. There would not be any sin. What was the problem in the Garden of Eden? Was it disobedience to God's edict to not eat from the tree of knowledge of good and evil? The serpent came along and said to Eve, "eat, it's okay, you'll be fine", and she did. That was the fall of man. Then they noticed they had no clothes on. They were naked and hid in shame. What explains the fall of man in that historic tradition? What the serpent knew was the inner innocence of the child. The serpent said, "It'll be all right, trust me, this is fine." So the serpent was not saying to defy God, the serpent was saying to the inner child in Eve, "trust me, everything will be fine." That was the beginning of the Christian tradition and therefore Christianity does believe in karma. If it were not for original sin and the Garden of Eden there would not be any need for penance and nothing to feel guilty about and we would all be enlightened. The serpent was the source of falsehood. Being innocent herself, there was no reason for Eve to suspect that the serpent was up to some nefarious intention. One has to beware of the serpent because that which is cunning, sly and deceptive tends to be able to sense when you are vulnerable. The vulnerability, again, is that intrinsically we all have the innocence of the child within us, the pure subjectivity of Consciousness Itself.

At level 600, the third eye of the Buddhic body, which is one of the etheric bodies above the crown chakra, opens and one instantly can recognize falsehood and deception and one is protected by the presence of the Divine Spirit in the capacity to discern essence. Because of the innocence, then, Christ taught that **sin is error/ignorance**. To realize the innocence of the inner child in everyone gives us a capacity to be forgiving towards all people, no matter what. The difficulty arises from the limitation of the degree of the evolution of consciousness itself (both personal and collective) and thus arise the problems of **culpability** versus **responsibility,** and **accountability** for the consequences of one's choices and actions. **Truth depends on context**; the overall non-linear intention sets the overall field. Whether a thing is good or evil is discernible only in context, not by looking at the thing itself.

DOUBT, SKEPTICISM, AND DISBELIEF (6)

Higher (275) Mind vs. Lower (155) Mind

Skepticism

"Logic Proof Delusional Disorder"

Conspiracy Theorists

"Steel Doesn't Melt" (160)

Slide 143

SLIDE 143: DOUBT, SKEPTICISM, AND DISBELIEF (6)

This slide was introduced at the August 2008 lecture, DVD disc 2 at 004235.

The difficulty of the doubter, the traditional skeptic, is that he is usually coming from **lower mind (155)**, which deals only in the linear provability as opposed to the **higher mind** (275) which is discerning, abstract, principled, and disciplined. Spiritual dimensions are not linear, nor provable, so one cannot disprove the nonlinear using arguments from the linear. That is why **skepticism** calibrates below 200. Only a few of the debunkers are actually integrous, the rest of them get an ego kick out of trying to imitate what is real and because they imitated it, they assume they have disproven it. Because you can imitate a thing does not mean you have disproven it. It just means you have learned how to imitate a thing, like a stage magician. Therefore, coming from the linear, one can neither prove nor disprove the nonlinear. In all spiritual reality, all understanding of divinity and truth is of a different dimension than the linear. The linear is provable and demonstrable. The nonlinear is more profound and diffuse. It has a profound influence on our behavior, our understanding, and our motivation.

The most powerful motivation is to live with kindness and love towards all living things. You try to understand, and even with things you do not approve of, you can still recognize the intention and the innocence behind it. All of humanity has intuited a higher power than man since the beginning of recorded time. All cultures and civilizations, even widely separated from each other in time and space, acknowledge the divinity of Divinity. Whether one worships communism or whether one worships Divinity, one is still worshiping something greater than the personal self. That is already a step, even if one does it for the communist ideal; then "workers, you have nothing to lose but your chains" becomes uplifting.

A thing is not "this or that" in and of itself, but what we make of it, how we comprehend it and how we contextualize it. Context makes all the difference, e.g. in Olympics, having a greater intention than for one's own self gives a runner a 0.9 second advantage over the competition. We have in today's society the **"logic proof delusional disorder"**, which refers to a contrary intellectual attitude that evolves as debate and lengthy discourse, such as that in current science regarding the authenticity of subjective experience and 'first-person' testimony.

So many of society's problems have arisen because many of the mental hospitals closed years ago, due to cultural Marxism, which came through Thomas Szasz, who popularized it and said that mental illness was only a label and therefore there was no need for the mental hospitals. All the people who were dangerous are now wandering the street, killing people right and left. It used to be out of compassion that the psychiatrists protected people from their own limitation; it is not just the safety of others. Now they become drug addicts, hang out on the sidewalk, commit crimes and murder each other, often ending up in jail. The spiritual dictum that we stay by is out of love and consideration and reverence for all of life. Let that be the overall context of one's own volition. Truthers always tell you how the United States government engineered 9/11 and put secret bombs in the buildings and stuff like this. At the end of the story, they give you a smirk: "Everybody knows that **steel doesn't melt**" which calibrates at 150. The truthers are working **conspiracy theories** because they are getting narcissistic gratification out of their idea of moral superiority.

PRACTICAL SPIRITUALITY (1)

Stay with Holy Company

Energy-field Effect

Relapse

Experience of AA

"Band of Brothers": Bonding

Cultural Paradigms of Reality

Karmic Influences

Spiritual vs. Religious

Slide 144

SLIDE 144: PRACTICAL SPIRITUALITY (1)

This slide was introduced in October 2008 Lecture, DVD disc 2 001445.

Stay with holy company because the group itself radiates an energy that energizes spiritual awareness within yourself when you are near it or around it. The group has **an energy-field effect.** People who are hopeless in AA say they cannot get it, but the group tells them it does not make any difference whether they get it or not. You just go to meetings, sit in the back and shut up. If you cannot sit up, you lay on the floor in the back. Hopeless people who could not get it went to meetings and just by laying on the floor got sober. When a person says "I don't need AA anymore" and they quit going to meetings, the relapse rate is extremely high. When a person disappears from a 12-step group's meeting, you know what is happening, that they are about to relapse into their old behavior because they are saying, "I can do it on my own and I don't need you anymore." That is the **relapse experience of AA** and all the 12-steps groups. The recovery is due to the impersonal **energy field effect.** There is a "**bonding"** that goes on when people are part of a group, as one can see in the famous **"Band of Brothers."** The bonding that goes on in the military is the same. The bonding is profound and timeless. Dr. Hawkins described that every night before going to sleep he said prayers and always prayed for the fellow shipmates, the crew of the YMS 46, a minesweeper in the South Pacific during World War II. It was a small crew, just a small ship, but those people bonded together. Bonding is a profound way. If you bond with your church, if you bond with your religion, if you bond with your fellow man in a common enterprise, etc. that is very powerful, because it also brings unseen forces, guardian angels. When you say, "I don't need you anymore" you are telling your guardian angels "I don't need you folks anymore, I can do it on my own." Egocentricity is the enemy of spiritual reality. Spiritual reality has to do with inner humility, that "I of myself cannot do it" I, as a member of a congregation, or a church or a spiritual discipline-there my capacities are unlimited.

There are various **paradigms of cultural reality,** which have quite an effect in today's world. These cultural paradigms can be very, very misleading and that is the real problem in politics. It presents a paradigm of reality that is a projection of intellectualized fantasy, with no parallel in reality. **Karmic influences** play quite a profound and significant impact. Your intentions in this lifetime, of course, are already setting up **karmic propensities**. Karma is not understood very well in the West at all, although Christianity believes in karma altogether. The karmic influences will determine what kind of things we are working on right now.

This does bring up the difference between **Spiritual vs. Religious.** Religious tends to be documented and historical and depends on authority, belief systems, alignment and commitment and it can be quite restricting. Spiritual means you are interested in the essence of the truth behind that religious teaching. You want to know what is the truth, not what is being taught because religion itself becomes worshiped eventually. There is a lot of religionism in which the religion becomes the exact opposite of what it teaches. It does so because you are worshiping the religion and not God of the truth that the religion is trying to teach. The Inquisition is probably one of the greatest examples of it. Religion can become stultifying and a limitation. One can look at all religion as having the essence of truth in it, but now one's task is not to memorize the religiosity, but to become the essence of the truth hidden within the religious teaching.

PRACTICAL SPIRITUALITY (2)

Alignment with Primary Teacher

Principles above Personality

Chart of Authenticated Teachers

Avoid New Age-ism & Novel

Exotic

Avoid Channeled Entities

Avoid Self-Styled "Masters"

Slide145

SLIDE 145: PRACTICAL SPIRITUALITY (2)

This slide was introduced at the October 2008 lecture, DVD disc 2 at 002500.

Alignment with primary teacher: If one is not going to follow the dictums of a religion like a kid in school, then one has to find a teacher. Therefore, Dr. Hawkins put together a list of more than 100 teachers that calibrate very well, plus another list of all the high calibrating writings. We have an enormous amount of guidance in the world now, which people lacked in the past. "**Principles above personality**" means that one is interested in the essence of truth, not the glamour of the teacher. There are a number of glamorous teachers out there, so **the chart of authenticated teachers** is very practical. The best thing to do is **avoid all New Age-ism and that which is novel and exotic.** Bill Wilson had hardly died, when instantly there were people channeling Bill Wilson. He was not dead more than 12 days when somebody jumped in and grabbed that piece of business; it is hysterical. There are people that channel Clark Gable and Greta Garbo. The channelers show up and they get a certain amount of pump-up from the fact they are channeling some kind of personality.

Avoid channeled entities because until you are pretty advanced, you cannot tell the real from the fake. Some channelers are honest so there is integrous capacity for channeling of entities, but there is no particular benefit to it. A psychic may say something like, "Your grandmother said to eat plenty of greens, it is good for your joints." Well, it is possible that she would have said that. However, these things can become novelties and stop you in your spiritual growth. It is best until you are quite sophisticated to avoid channeled entities. Now, once you learn how to calibrate them, you can calibrate channeled entities, but integrous ones are not that many. Consciousness calibration reveals that only about 20% of channelers are genuine, the other 80% are out for various other gains. Your chances are one in five if you just pick a channeler that you are going to get somebody who is legitimate to begin with. So, avoid New-Age-ism and that which is exotic until you become very sophisticated. Then, when you are sophisticated, you do not need channeled entities, so you give them up. People who call themselves "Masters" will often tend to parade around, too. Have you wondered how "Master so and so" got his name? More than likely, he looked in the mirror one day and said, "You are a master." Wow! That which is a master does not call himself a master, does he? Where would the humility be to call yourself the "master" of something, unless you are the master of stupidity, or egotism? Therefore, it is best to **avoid self-styled "Masters"**.

PRACTICAL SPIRITUALITY (3)

Study, Contemplation, Meditation

Balance of Faith and Reason

Becoming vs. "Know About"

Avoid All Hatred Doctrines

Be Watchful of "Spiritual Ego"

Inspiration: Music, Cathedrals, Beauty

Slide 146

SLIDE 146: PRACTICAL SPIRITUALITY (3)

This slide was introduced at the October 2008 lecture, DVD disc 2 at 003230.

Practical spirituality starts with **Study**, so look at all the lists of qualified calibrated teachers and calibrated works. Then we **contemplate and meditate**. Meditation tends to take one out of the world, if one can find a time and place that is convenient. The difficulty with meditation is that life becomes progressively demanding and the amount of time you allot to it begins to diminish. Meditation is a very effective way and of course, there are many meditative techniques. The simpler they are the better. Contemplation is holding a thing in mind and asking God to reveal to you what is the meaning of that. As a basic rule, if you only need one thing, contemplative and meditative, it is best to be compassionate towards all of life in all of its expressions. It is necessary to avoid all **hatred doctrines.** You can love chocolate or vanilla, liberals or conservatives. To be compassionate, you begin to see that everything and everyone is just being what they are. So what is there to forgive? One could say the person has the option to be other than they are. If they had a real option to be other than they are, they would be other than they are. That is a hypothetical proposition you project onto people and say, "Well, they could be this way or they could be that way." Everyone is innocent because everyone is only being to the fullest that which one is capable of being.

Becoming is different from "knowing about a thing." So many people can repeat back a dictum, they know about it, but it is a further step to become it instead of just knowing about it. The downfall of a number of people is the idea that "I know." It is best to acknowledge that you have heard the teaching, but that there is an aspect of reality that you do not really comprehend until you have contemplated it, sometimes for 40 or 50 years, when a few of the things start to sink through. Contemplation allows one to hold a thing in mind and just question it. You look it over from different angles. At different times, you see different light shining forth and a greater understanding. Meditation is a more intense way of doing that.

Balance of faith and reason was the dictum of the great spiritual teacher and Catholic theologian, Thomas Aquinas. **Be watchful of the spiritual ego:** Spiritual ego is the idea that "I know." It is better "to thy Self be true." If you doubt it, then doubt it and have a good time doubting it. You have the perfect right to be wrong. The spiritually aligned person is attracted to **beauty** in all of its forms: the beauty of nature, the beauty of all that exists, the beauty of every animal, every bush, and every tree. There is a time that when you go beyond the ordinary and the beauty of everything that exists becomes overwhelming. All things are God and all that happens is also; you begin to realize the essence of all things is God. Therefore, when you walk through the woods, the tree is aware of your walking by. "All that is alive is aware of your existence". You see how important your existence is, then. What you have become radiates out into the world and by a field effect, influences everything around you. People who are spiritually oriented become attracted to **music and the beauty of the cathedrals** which tend to shift the brain function. The brain, even in old age is constantly producing new neurons all the time, but if they are not used, they cretinize, i.e. slow up and go away. If they are used, these neurons will connect with each other because they form a tract and it is a working tract. Your neurons are always saying, "Please feed me more beauty, more cathedrals and gorgeous things in this world to appreciate."

PRACTICAL SPIRITUALITY (4)

Be Watchful of "Religionism"

Value of Intention

Religious Practices

Practice of the Virtues

Practice of Great Commandments

Avoidance of the Deadly Sins

Deglamorize Attractions

Slide 147

SLIDE 147: PRACTICAL SPIRITUALITY (4)

This slide was introduced at the October 2008 lecture, DVD disc 2 at 004740.

Be watchful of religionism, expressed as extremism or by the alternative of worshipping the religion instead of God, 'missing the forest for the trees'. This signifies limitation by the intellect to content and ignorance of context, meaning, and significance, which reflect conversion of language/symbols to subjective realization and contemplation. The critical **value of intention** is explored in Wayne Dyer's *The Power of Intention* indicating the importance of the fact that "how we search affects what we find" and how and what we know. That result is the consequence of intention and is a very interesting recognition of the practice of the Heisenberg principle. People find solace from sympathetic support, prayer, and returning to **religious practices**. The important quality in all religious practices is the intention and faith that are involved. **Practice of the virtues**, then, becomes automatic. If one is angry at something, one forgives oneself for being angry, asking God to see it differently. Then one sees its innocence and forgives it. We say, "Oh, everybody knows to **practice the great commandments**", but that is not true. To bear false witness against your neighbor, that is one of the Ten Commandments violated every day on television. You can hear false distortion of what the other person said, to justify hating them and vilifying them. The breaking of the **great commandments** brings down the consciousness level of all of society. Malice and false accusations against our fellow man are probably the greatest violation we see in today's society.

On top of avoiding breaking the great commandments, we want the **avoidance of the deadly sins:** Greed, lust, avarice, malice, pride, envy, wrath, gluttony, sloth, etc. The thing is to learn how to transcend them and the way to transcend them is to see that everything is only being what it can be, and if it could be something else, it would be. Therefore, accept everything as it is, as it appears to be, because first of all one cannot see the essence of it. You can only see how it appears to you. So there would be no point to try to change it, because one is not changing something that is (essence), one is only changing something that one sees (appearance). That is why the famous saying "there's no point in trying to change the world you see, the world you see does not even exist." Trying to save the world from what you have projected onto the world does not make any sense when all one needs to do is to let go of projection.

Besides, many people have earned the right to undo negative karma and to gain positive karma via this earthly human domain and if the purpose of this world is transformational, to undo negative karma and to gain positive karma, then the world is perfect as it is. "The world is perfect as it is" tests true. One has to stop trying to change the world because if you take away from people the chance to learn that this is the wrong way to go, people will not learn that this is the wrong way to go. **Deglamorize attractions**: Today's world capitalizes on the glamorization of attractions. What we are saying today is very simple. Everything is God. God is the power to become and manifest as anything and everything. To see the divinity of all that exists, one says, "Dear God, I ask to see the essence of everything rather than a projected perception or some programmed, glamorized version. I don't know anything." When one is convinced that one is hopelessly and endlessly stupid, one is making good progress. The dumber we are the better we are.

PRACTICAL SPIRITUALITY (5)

Good Will

Avoid "Ancient Mysteries" and Prophecies

Avoid High-Priced Gurus with Specialness

Avoid Evil/Seduction by Glamour

ACIM: Inner Direction

Slide 148

SLIDE 148: PRACTICAL SPIRITUALITY (5)

This slide was introduced at the October 2008 lecture, DVD disc 2 at 005130.

Practical spirituality starts out with **Good will** towards all of life, to have compassion for all the expressions of life with all their limitations, without choosing one as good and the other as bad because there is no way one can tell what is good and what is bad. When one looks back over history at all the millions that have died so that we could be here, that inspires good will towards all the expressions of Divinity. All things are expressions of Divinity and how we see them expressed depends on the karmic balance. One might say this rose has lovely positive karma and a prickly pear has negative karma. Those would all be projections from our own consciousness. No such thing exists in the world. Nothing is good or bad in and of itself, but only as we see it. That is the secret of life. Everything is what it is. What it means is what it is. That prevents intellectual rambling, looking for significances in hidden meanings. Practical spirituality is to have good will towards all of life in all of its expressions. The fact that we do not understand it or cannot see that that is perfect the way it is, is our limitation. It is not a limitation of the world, because everything that exists is God and if you start criticizing that which is, you are criticizing God and He does not like that. We try to accept all of existence non-judgmentally, all of life in all of its expressions. It does not mean one can disregard what it is.

If you step into a cage with a poisonous reptile, then you are stepping into a cage with a poisonous reptile. You cannot pretend that it is just a good doggie in the cage. A good reptile likes to kill you and that is his happiness. If it makes him happy to kill you, what is your duty: to make him happy? There is a mystification and **glamorization** of spiritual teachings. **Ancient mysteries** are the favorite one. "All prophecies are fallacious" tests true. Why is that? Because the future cannot happen until the events of the present have occurred. The events of the present are up to the freedom of the will; you have not made a decision. Everything that happens is due to infinite contributory causes. For one piece of dust to float from here to there, there are infinite things that have to be already in place, e.g. this earth, the temperature, the humidity, the circulation of the air in here, etc. "The number of 'causes' for any event is infinite" tests true. You cannot tell what is going to happen in a minute from now, so there is no way to tell what is going to happen in 50 years. Throughout time, there is always some pundit making a great prophecy about the end of the world and that calibrates at 70. It is best to **avoid ancient mysteries and prophecies** because they become glamorized, and a racket.

Avoid **high priced gurus with specialness**. They are very, very special, and they have a special title and requirement for money to be with them. Spirituality has nothing to do with money, and the idea of specialness is the opposite of the inner experience. The more advanced one is, the less special one feels, until one finally realizes that one is nothing at all. Avoid the **evil/seduction by glamour** in titles and trappings, decor, theatrical presentations, etc. by being aware of the glamour of the specialness and the foreign-ness of it. That which is real has no need for theatrics because its power arises from that which it is, not that which it pretends to be or pictures itself as, but what it actually is. The power of a thing arises from the essence of that which it really actually is in reality and therefore it needs nothing in addition to what it is. ***A Course in Miracles*** is different from channeled materials as the focus is on **inner direction**.

FREEDOM: MORALITY & ETHICS (1)

Freedom is an inner state: choice

Congenital capacity by age 3 - karma

Illumination is subjective

Understanding = comprehension of meaning

Abstract vs. literal

Morality & ethics vs. egotism & narcissism-fraud, false witness

Slide 149

SLIDE 149: FREEDOM: MORALITY & ETHICS (1)

This slide was introduced at the November 2008 lecture, DVD disc 2 at 000400.

Freedom is not out there in the world. You cannot give anybody freedom because they are bound and slaves to so many things. Freedom is just a political slogan. True **freedom is an inner state** consequent to one's **choices**. To be free means one has no attractions, and no aversions. Therefore, you have true freedom to think what you think. This capacity for inner freedom is limited and very much karmically determined. Many people in the world are impaired and are completely incapable of being objective. There is no point criticizing them because they are born that way. About half of American people calibrate below 200. So how are they going to differentiate truth from falsehood? If you are below 200, you cannot really do it. There is a **congenital capacity** for self-control**, which shows up by age 3**. By age 3, as a psychologist, you ask a child to sit there and give him a small candy bar and say, "If you don't eat this by the time I come back, I will give you 2 candy bars". The psychologist is with a stopwatch and leaves the room for 2 minutes. Some children do not have the capacity of self-control, and will be unable to resist eating that candy bar. This is **congenital, diagnosable by age 3**. The prisons everywhere in the world are loaded with these people. Within the prison is the inner child who cannot delay gratification for a greater reward. When we talk about freedom, morality and ethics, realize that it is a choice that is limited to a small percentage of the population. Another limitation, which is also genetic, is a lack of understanding. When one says understanding, what most people mean by that is they are familiar with it. It does not mean they comprehend it at all, because **comprehension of the meaning is abstract and not literal**. As understanding develops, it becomes capable of investigation and comprehension of meaning and abstract derivation of essence apart from form, that is, discernment of content vs. context. Out of context arises the inference of and the search for Source in the capacity for spiritual awareness.

Lack of morality and ethics boils down to **egotism and narcissism** in which **fraud and false witness** is part of the game. It is great to be a politician, as one is not constrained by honesty, truth, veracity, and reliability, or any of those minor things. The fact that it is completely a falsehood is irrelevant. We are just recovering from the cultural shock of this. People who are trying to get over thinking and opinionation find it more difficult than they thought because the mind is constantly projecting judgmentalism, things that are either desirable or not desirable, aversion vs. attraction. One of the basic teachings of Buddhism is to transcend attraction andaversion. Freedom is an inner state. There is only one thing you are free to do and that is the availability of choice. You can choose chocolate or vanilla. You can choose one or another. At least theoretically, you have freedom in that. However, many people are programmed and do not really even have that. The congenital incapacitation diagnosable by age 3, which seems to be primarily karmic, has nothing to do with good or bad. It has to do with one's karmic evolution. This world being what it is brings maximum opportunity. Therefore, you would expect persons who are karmically impaired to be here and they are. It keeps the taxpayers busy, supporting them in jail and prison.

Illumination is an inner subjective state. With spiritual study, we prepare the way. The likelihood of spiritual states increases by our alignment and intention and brings forth the power from field of consciousness itself. Consciousness is the mind of God. The radiance of Divinity shines forth as the infinite power of consciousness itself, which has no beginning and no end. It is infinite in dimension, everywhere present throughout all of time. It is the field of infinite power. One cubic centimeter of space has more energy in it than its equivalent of the mass of the universe. The total mass of the universe is less than the power of one cubic centimeter of infinite empty space. All we are saying is that the mind of God is omnipotent, omniscient, and omnipresent with no past and no future. There is only "what is".

FREEDOM: MORALITY & ETHICS (2)

Protestors & demonstrators (170)

Freedom vs. license - 'Be' vs. 'Do'

Lure of hedonism

Enslavement by the senses

Ego/self-aggrandizement-the great "me"

Bombast (180)

Hate websites

"Accommodation" vs. survival

Slide 150

SLIDE 150: FREEDOM: MORALITY & ETHICS (2)

This slide was introduced at the November 2008 lecture, DVD disc 2 at 001420.

Some people just get off on **protesting and demonstrating** and that calibrates at 170 because it is wholly narcissistic. That is very funny in a way, but to protestors it is very important that they go out there and protest. One sees the narcissism of 'me, me, me' in protesting and demonstrating. People who are concerned about their freedom feel bad about it and need not go out there. **Freedom vs. License - "Be" vs. "Do":** Freedom is not "to do". In the United States, one has the freedom to be, but not the freedom to do whatever one wants. For example, one cannot take off all your clothes and walk down the street. Freedom is an inner state of mind. There is only one place to be free and that is one's inner state of mind. You can feel enslaved in situations where you have actual freedom and feel free in the states of actual enslavement. A person can pray, "O Lord, please help me forget that, or to see it differently". One is asking for illumination instead of perception. Freedom vs. license means that you are free to be, but you are not free to do.

The lure of hedonism is irresistible in today's world, escalated by the media. This is a brainwashed generation we are in now, like never before. The media has subjected all of us to brainwashing. The realization that you have been brainwashed gives you skepticism about what you are holding in mind, so it is good to ask, "Is that my idea or was that imposed?" The brainwashing happens in the media faster than you can catch it. Next time you see that, you have to laugh at it. **Enslavement by the senses,** as the Buddha pointed out, is the attractions of pleasure via the senses. That takes some conscious effort to transcend the bondage to the senses and the attractions and aversions.

Ego/self-aggrandizement - the great "me" Bombast (180) and Hate websites: The next thing that is prevalent in our society is the great ego self, the aggrandizement of the great and wonderful 'me' and in political times, one sees bombast (180) live with all the elaborated language and fancy presentation. That is entrancing political rhetoric. If one turns down the volume a little bit so one does not hear the exact words you find that the energy, the tonality, is the same on both sides. Truth has no place in politics. Then we have the hate websites, which are shocking. When the president's wife, Mrs. Reagan was in the hospital, there were hate websites that gloated over that. It gives them great glee. This is incomprehensible that it was out there on the web, but the source of the edit is proud that they are the author of what is admittedly evil. Evil is legal, and not only that, it is profitable. "It is safe to pray for the various hatred websites and associated people" (calibrates true.) Jesus Christ says do not go to war with them because they do not play by the same rules as you do.

The next dilemma of our current society, especially by the media is what to do about what we consider adverse to life. The ideologists do not see the difference between one's idea about a thing and a thing itself. In international politics right now, should we step into the cage of Komodo dragon or not? It brings back what is necessary for **survival vs. "Accommodation".** Do we have the right to do what we need to do to survive? That which threatens life itself and takes delight in killing, should we accommodate that? The ideologists cannot differentiate politicized theory with an actually in reality. We do not have to believe these people, just as we do not believe in accommodating the Mafia and can take steps to eliminate them, just as we take steps to eliminate the Mafia.

FREEDOM: MORALITY & ETHICS (3)

Respect vs. joining

Megalomania of claims of God's authorization

Victimology: politicized specialness & exploitation

Worship of "freedom" & its narcissistic appeal:

"Do what you want"

Slide 151

SLIDE 151: FREEDOM: MORALITY & ETHICS (3)

This slide was introduced at the November 2008 lecture, DVD disc 2 at 003215.

The proper attitude towards those who you do not approve of because they would like to blow you up soon, is you **respect them, but you do not have to join them**. Ah, you can **respect them without joining them**. Political correctness draws a fuzzy line, thinking to respect means you have to join them. You do not have to line up with your enemies. You can respect their viewpoint. One can respect that if you grew up in a culture that teaches certain things, that women and dogs and things like that are unclean, then you are going to have that viewpoint. So you can respect the fact they have that. If one is a woman, you would not want to move to that country, and one would not want to be their doggie, either. One can respect the fact that they consider dogs unclean and have a derogatory view towards women. It does not mean a person has to join them. What is the worst place in the world for a woman to be, what country, walking down the street with her doggie? Those countries have 'decency police' so she would be instantly arrested by the decency police and incarcerated. The decency police are there to make sure that these prejudices are respected and the violators are put in prison. In some cultures, like Pakistan, when a rape occurs, the woman is imprisoned. The woman, once she is raped is put in prison in Pakistan, not the man, but the woman. Is that bizarre or what? So you can respect the fact they see and think that way, but you do not have to join it.

There is the **megalomania** in the same culture, **of claims of God's authorization**. They are claiming God's authorization for all kinds of manner of extremism, blowing up women and children and various things. One can see the megalomania in that, the megalomania of claims of God's authorization. The megalomaniac says that, if I kill all these people or a busload of children that will please God. These are distortions of morality and ethics, the direct opposite of our viewpoint.

Victimology is very current and we are looking at the prevailing ideologies in today's society. There is a race for victimology creating **specialness,** an entitlement. To prove that you are a victim becomes dear and if you try to 'un-victimize' the people, they go into a rage because the payoff of being a victim is so enormous. In political circles, one automatically comes into specialness, an entitlement. The race for being the victim gives you moral superiority and therefore you can figure out anything you can be a victim of; one is a victim of so many things one cannot even recall them all anymore. Each one of us is a victim of being a human being born here, a victim of gender, race, age group, etc. Everybody is somehow a victim of something and this is a specialty in today's political world. Politicize the **specialness and the exploitation** of it. Of course, the real payoff is you get money in the end as a special committee awards huge grants to explore "your victimization and how it all came about." Of course, how it came about is in your own head. Here we have the opposite of **the worship of freedom** and **its narcissistic appeal** of **"do what you want."** Does freedom mean license?

FREEDOM: MORALITY & ETHICS (4)

Cultural narcissism

Free speech in the Bill of Rights (cal. 350)

Free speech in current society (cal. 180)

Palin hanging in effigy

Struggle for "Moral Authority"

Chocolate vs. Vanilla

Choice vs. vilification

Slide 152

SLIDE 152: FREEDOM: MORALITY & ETHICS (4)

This slide was introduced at the November 2008 lecture, DVD disc 2 at 003800.

Narcissism distorts by superimposing self-interest and selfishness on truth. Almost all political statements in the media are distortions and the media impact on society is enormous. Narcissism feeds on itself, with a sense of grandiosity and people want to propagate their beliefs. **Cultural Narcissism** refers to whole cultures where you have to admire them, and make excuses and extend special privileges. **Free Speech in the Bill of Rights** calibrates at 350 and that is conservative centrism. **Free speech in current society** calibrates at 180, despite all demonstrators, parades extolling free speech in current society and pushing license to do anything you want, including the freedom of the flashers. Politics gives us endless examples of this.

Hanging Sarah Palin in effigy calibrates about 90, so one cannot get too excited about free speech when they express it at a consciousness level that calibrates at 90 which is "wickedness". Hiding under the sheep's clothing of freedom is actual evil in the form of wickedness. We cannot pretend it does not exist. We can say we refuse to join it. The failure to detect and diagnose wickedness makes one prone to it. The failure to discern that which is truly wicked and evil, means one then becomes vulnerable to it because one does not know what it is one is embracing. The hangers of effigy of **Sarah Palin** immediately came on television and hid behind freedom of speech, freedom of expression, and tried to justify what they were doing. They said, "It was just fun, just fun", and they were lying (tested true.) "They were merely gleefully acting out evil" tests true. Evil takes great glee in its own demonstrations and expressions. The core of evil is severe narcissism.

Freud postulated two primary energies in the unconscious: Life and death, Eros vs. Thanatos. Deep in the unconscious, there are two main drives, one is for life, pro-life, Eros is love, life; and Thanatos is death. That which is evil, then, has an attraction in the unconscious of humanity and that is one's enemy. The enemy is not out there, it is within man, the enemy that one gives validity and power to, because one projects one's own death wish, one's own worship of evil and death onto the world. "Freud's Eros was correct" (tests true), and "Freud's Thanatos was correct" (tests true). It reminds one of the joy and fun of killing and destroying and attacking the Pieta, because that which is beautiful summons up hatred from that which is evil. That which is evil hates innocence and beauty.

The **Struggle for moral authority** is very fierce and in fact, it is almost the basis for war. To prove who has the moral superiority and we see that in our dealings with the Middle East. Who has the morally superior position, beyond blame, and who is to blame? It is all about who has the moral high ground. It is not about how many people are going to die, but who has the moral high ground because that gives one the authority to attack and kill.

Chocolate vs. Vanilla: choice vs. vilification: We do not have to have a war between chocolate and vanilla because one can choose one without becoming the enemy of the other. Just because you choose chocolate, does not mean you have to hate vanilla, and you can choose vanilla and you do not have to hate chocolate or strawberry. You have choice. It is not necessary to vilify its opposite.

FREEDOM: MORALITY & ETHICS (5)

Confusion of ideology with reality

Constraint by mirroring

Biological foundation of ethical concern for others

Macaque monkey experiment

Oxytocin and inborn morality

Freud: Id, superego, and ego

Eros vs. Thanatos

Slide 153

SLIDE 153: FREEDOM: MORALITY & ETHICS (5)

This slide was introduced at the November 2008 lecture, DVD disc 2 at 004830.

The difficulty with the "far left" is their confusion of **ideology with the actual reality** in the world. One is an abstract concept, the other is a literal reality and it is not helpful to neglect the truth of the actual reality as expressed in the world. **Constraint by mirroring is a biological phenomenon.** There are mirroring neurons within the brain, so that when one watches something happen, the mind is also mirroring that and the neurons are registering it with a differentiation. There is a differentiation in the neuron whether the thing actually happened or one just witnessed it. If you want to learn how to do something, you do not have to actually go out and practice it. You can just witness it and if you have watched it enough times you can go step right on the dance floor and go dancing, because you watched it and have practiced it mentally in watching. In mirroring, one may be witnessing many things, but one's mind will direct one to do the most familiar thing. So mirroring means that one's neurons are becoming familiar with everything witnessed, which is equivalent to rehearsing. Mirroring therefore results also in constraint, because that which one mirrors may not be on the positive beneficial human side.

All of this points to the significance of a **biologic foundation of ethical concern for others,** which is a relatively recent discovery in the last 25 years or so. If one is merely ethical, other people learn by witnessing ethical behavior. So ethical concern for others is not just religion or taught morality, but it is imitative in which learning by example has a biologic basis. One picks up what is integrous and what is loyalty to one's brothers in the military service without even thinking about it because it has a biologic foundation.

Macaque monkey experiments show that morality and ethics are just not intellectual or religious phenomena but are like mirroring, embedded in the mammalian species. You have two cages. In one, if the monkey pushes this button, he gets a small amount of food. If he pushes the other button, he gets a large amount of food. The macaque monkey quickly learns which button gives the larger amount of food. Left to his own devices, the macaque monkey will always push the big, more food button. Now you put another monkey in second cage right next to the first and every time this macaque monkey pushes the big win lever and gets the large amount of food, by example, the monkey in the next cage gets a painful electric shock. Very quickly, the macaque in its cage will stop pushing the big button even though it gives him more food that he likes better, and he will satisfy himself with the lesser one so that the other monkey does not get shocked. A macaque monkey will actually take less to prevent the other monkey to be shocked, so we certainly have hope for humankind. That is also interesting because of the discovery of **oxytocin** and the part that it plays with the endorphins released in the brain by spiritual energy consequent to spiritual evolution.

There is a certain **inborn morality**, a biologic morality, so one can't get away with the excuse of not knowing any better. **Freud**'s concepts about the structure of the human psyche include the **Id** which are the animal instincts; the **superego** being one's conscience, and the **ego** as the part dealing with reality. Freudian psychoanalysis postulates two types of instincts in the unconscious: **Eros** (life giving) and **Thanatos** (death wish.) People are very entranced by death, e.g. after the French Revolution when thousands were guillotined, millions watched it, just fascinated watching somebody die. Death fascinates people in all of its manifestations and that is the attraction of death, both conscious and unconscious.

FREEDOM: MORALITY & ETHICS (6)

The herd instinct

Roar of the crowd

Arena

Pursuit of "make wrong"

Injustice Collectors (cal. 165)

High road vs. low road - enough rope to hang self

Win at all costs - karmic cost

No solutions to false equations

Slide 154

SLIDE 154: FREEDOM: MORALITY & ETHICS (6)

This slide was introduced at the November 2008 lecture, DVD disc 2 at 010300.

"The herd instinct, the roar of the crowd, arena": The way the old Roman emperors kept the people happy was by putting on grand displays in the Colosseum, gladiator fights to the death, having criminals torn to pieces by lions, etc. Life has not changed that much. As demonstrated by the burning of her effigy, we can hang Sarah Palin by her neck, and have people out there cheering. The cheer of the crowd is still the same. We are not far away from the Roman Colosseum, and electrocutions would be public and everybody would sign up in advance, if that were legal. The roar of the crowd can drive people on to do great deeds also and can have a positive influence when used judiciously.

The pursuit of "make wrong": One way to victory in today's world, especially the media world is the "make wrong" and therefore there is a lot of competition for making the other person wrong. They make them wrong because of what they wear or what their mother-in-law did or because of a "distant cousin having been arrested in adolescence". Spiritually evolved people become more sophisticated and wake up to the fact that they are being manipulated, controlled by all of it, being made a fool by all of it. Making others wrong calibrates close to **injustice collectors**. Injustice collecting is also rivalrous, to see who has been done the most injustice for the longest time, even if you have to go back centuries. Well, everybody's ancestors were made wrong as they were once slaves; it is just a matter of how many generations one goes back to check that fact. In Athens and Rome, the number of free citizens was only one-tenth. The free person who owned his own self was only one out of ten. That just casts a different light on it, to see phenomena as part of the evolution of human consciousness. The freedom of the individual citizen is really a very relatively recent development in human society.

High road vs. low road - enough rope to hang self: Once you see the opera Dr. Faustus, it somehow by its theatrical impact, gets across to you the difference between integrity, honesty and dishonesty, the narcissistic endeavor for power over others, money and influence, and the willingness to sell your soul in order to win. Although people hypothetically know there is a cost to this, they do not actually really know it, as it ends up as **karmic propensities**. With a certain kind of karma, our propensity is to make the other person wrong. With a different kind of karma, our propensity is to find an excuse for the other person. We as spiritually committed people by our own spiritual dedication tend to uplift the world and we uplift the world, not by what we say, not by what we do, but by what we have become. We turn down all the payoffs: to feel better than others, to make other people wrong and we reinforce our awareness of the inner innocence of all that lives. All that live are innocent, even within wickedness there is the core of innocence.

In everyday politics, the participants present that which is completely fraudulent and their conscience does not even twitch because in their game, **winning at all cost is all that matters**, the narcissistic gain and winning for the glamour, disclaiming any restriction due to truth. **No solutions to false equations**: An equation is a statement of equality between two expressions. The "hypothetical is not the Real" means people cannot be other than they are. The 'unintended result' arises out of denial due to a positionality that ignores context.

WHAT IS THE WORLD? (1)

1. **Being born a human is rare, fortunate, and the consequence of good karma - 455**

2. **The world is a trap of illusion; therefore, salvation depends on nonattachment to its linear and emotional qualities - 230**

3. **The perceived world is the result of the projection of human consciousness, and therefore akin to a Rorschach card - 450**

Slide 155

SLIDE 155: WHAT IS THE WORLD? (1)

This slide was introduced at the February 2009 lecture, DVD disc 1 at 005920.

One projects out into the world one's view of the world, depending on what one's level of consciousness is. When one stops projecting out, one sees the world as it is. **Being born a human is rare, fortunate, and the consequence of good karma (455).** That is what the Buddha teaches: on the one hand, it is a good thing to be born a human because there are karmic improvements you can make in yourself, and on the other hand, a human life entails old age, suffering, and death. So avoid it if you can, but if you are here, be glad that you are here because of good karma. This world is a world of maximum spiritual opportunity, where one can gain good karma and undo negative karma. Instead of cursing your human existence, saying "Oh, why was I born?" and all that kind of stuff, you say, "Well, this is a world of great opportunity because I can choose to condemn or I can choose to forgive." The fact that we have freedom of choice means we can undo the negative and gain positive karma. Therefore, the best spiritual advice is to be kind and loving to all of life in all of its expressions. So if you are going to be beheaded you say to the headsman, "Thank you so much for doing a very good job". Bless him for his work.

The world is a trap of illusion; therefore, salvation depends on nonattachment to its linear and emotional qualities (230). The world is not a trap; that one is 'trapped' is merely a negative belief to be undone, as one is completely free and does not have to follow the trap of illusions. **The perceived world is the result of the projection of human consciousness, and therefore akin to a Rorschach card (450).** One projects out into the world what one thinks the world is, because of what one is and not because of what the world is. People will come back from New York City and say New Yorkers are all cold and unfriendly. Another person will come back and say every person was friendly there. People there are very friendly, that is because you are very friendly and benign. However, if you are below 200, they will say, "Listen, I do not know you" and walk away. What you see is not what you think is out there but a projection of your own self. One person would see everyone as hateful while another would see everyone as trustable. People seem to project onto the world their own inner state of mind. So how can you transcend entrapment of your own illusions? How do you know you are perceiving reality at all?

The chimpanzee, the white tiger, and the friendly lion look friendly and trustable, and each one of them ended up savaging or killing their respective trainer. So how can you find out what the truth of it is? Without calibrating it, you cannot. Below level 200, people also respond to a group consciousness, so it is only a matter of time before people living in a violent community become violent. It is only a matter of time before they do dog fighting and things like that, as the 'group consciousness' begins to dominate. All of us have an individual consciousness, and are under the influence of a 'group cultural consciousness'. As one spiritually evolves, one's consciousness becomes progressively immune to negativity. So people will say "Let's go to town and shoot them all up" and you say, "I do not feel like it today." It does not appeal to you anymore. It is not a matter of being a 'goody goody' but it just no longer has any kind of reality for you.

WHAT IS THE WORLD? (2)

4. **The true reality of the world is unknowable due to the limitations of human intelligence - 450**
5. **The world is a comedy, a tragedy, a political game board, and more - 240**
6. **This is a purgatorial world of hardship & suffering; therefore, seek heaven - 350**
7. **The world is a rare opportunity for maximum spiritual growth and evolution by the undoing of bad karma and the earning of spiritual merit - 510**

Slide 156

SLIDE 156: WHAT IS THE WORLD? (2)

This slide was introduced at the February 2009 lecture, DVD disc 2 at 000500.

The true reality of the world is unknowable due to the limitations of human intelligence (450). The world is unknowable only to the ego, but to the spirit, it is quite knowable. A person's ego can make gross miscalculations and say, "Here kitty, kitty, kitty", to the lion, or play with the chimpanzee or tame a white tiger, miscalculating with wild animals, because a wild animal does not respond as a person. The wild animal phenomenon happens with chimpanzees, white tigers and lions; the trained wild animal in the end kills the trainer. These trained animals suddenly go berserk and kill you, and you cannot trust them because animals have a group consciousness; animals have a perceived memory, an individual memory, but their consciousness is a group consciousness. If one watches a flock of birds, one sees that the birds are following each other, as the skies are filled black with birds. How can they stay in formation like that? Each bird stays in formation, similar to a bunch of flying airplanes. Actually, each bird in that flock is not following the other birds at all. What is happening is there is a pattern in their mind, and each bird is following not the other bird at all, but an energy pattern in their minds. Each bird, like a radio, is tuned to the same radio frequency and is following an inner imprint or inner pattern. Each bird is therefore individual and yet, follows a group consciousness.

So all animals follow a group consciousness, therefore an ape that seems tame now, his memory track is that this is a safe place to be, but his group consciousness is that of the animal and at any moment he can turn dangerous. Because he is responding to the group consciousness, therefore any wild animal cannot be trusted at the level of absolute trust. It is only a matter of time before his group consciousness will take over. The lion eats the trainer, while the white tiger rips out the neck of the trainer, and the chimp tears at his trainer's face. So the animal is only very partially who you think it is, it is more the 95% instinctual animal. Therefore, you can never safely turn your back on a wild animal. The fact that one gets away with it many times, does not mean it is safe to do so. This applies to spiritual students in their dealings with humans under 200 as well.

The world is a comedy, a tragedy, a political game board, and more (240). This is a positive statement about the world but lacks trust in divinity to reach the level of equanimity or neutral. **This is a purgatorial world of hardship and suffering; therefore, seek heaven (350).** This statement reflects the level of acceptance as it does not deny the fact of the purgatorial nature of the human world and yet there is owning of responsibility for one's own mental and spiritual evolution.

The world is a rare opportunity for maximum spiritual growth and evolution by the undoing of bad karma and the earning of spiritual merit (510). The best thing to do is be thankful to the Lord for this lifetime, because in this lifetime one can undo the negative and gain positive karma by serving God, Self and all of humanity. The world is a rare opportunity for maximum spiritual growth. Undo the bad, and the earning of the new, that calibrates at 510. That is a very trustable teaching.

WHAT IS THE WORLD? (3)

8. **The world is a meaningless kaleidoscope of sensations. Any meaning is purely a projection - 250**
9. **The world is the theatrical stage for the comedy of the absurd - 220**
10. **The world and human life are the consequence of the fall of Adam and Eve due to disobedience and succumbing to the temptation of curiosity. Life is therefore penitential for original sin - 190**

Slide 157

SLIDE 157: WHAT IS THE WORLD? (3)

This slide was introduced at the February 2009 lecture, DVD disc 2 at 000650.

In one of the last books Dr. Hawkins wrote, "Reality, Spirituality and Modern Man" (2008), Chapter 16: Transcending the World, pp. 304-308, he gave about 40 different ways of seeing the world, but he did not calibrate any of them. He thought that it would be interesting to go back and pick a number of them that tend to be prevailing and calibrate them, and that is the topic of discussion in the series of slides entitled "What is the World?", including this slide.

The world is a meaningless kaleidoscope of sensations. Any meaning is purely a projection (250). To say the world is a meaningless kaleidoscope of sensations and that all meaning is purely a projection calibrates only at 250. In other words, it is true to a certain extent, that there are kaleidoscopic sensations. In and of itself they lack any intrinsic meaning for the average mind. All meaning is something one imposes on the world. To the more advanced mind, the meaning of the world is the presence of Divinity as the perfection of all that is. **The world is the theatrical stage for the comedy of the absurd (220).** This is a common presumption. Often it is part of humor. Absurdity is part of humor.

The world and human life are the consequence of the fall of Adam and Eve due to disobedience and succumbing to the temptation of curiosity. Life is therefore penitential for original sin (190). This is a certain interpretation of the Bible. The view that "Eve fell for the temptation of the serpent and pulled Adam down with her" disregards the nature of human consciousness itself. Within everyone's consciousness is really the consciousness of the child. The reason you believe anything is that basic to everyone there is within oneself the innate, pure consciousness of the child. An alternative interpretation of the Biblical story is that the serpent was aware that the consciousness of the child still resided in Eve and so he appealed not to her disobedience but to her curiosity: "Trust me, I won't hurt you, you can trust me, you can trust me." Eve was the victim of her own inner innocence. Because of her innocence, she did not suspect anything other than innocence prevailing anywhere. Eve was sinless, with lack of sophistication, lack of being aware. The innermost layer of the mind, as childhood innocence, prevails in everyone, and 'evil' can manipulate that.

We know that the super-billionaire 'ripoff-er' Bernie Madoff made off with hundreds of billions of dollars stealing peoples' money. How did he get away with it? Because in each one of us is the trusting child, that wants to believe in the goodness of the world. The child within us is trusting. We have to be careful. It is not just the evil of the world, but the innocent trustingness within our own inner child that gets one into trouble a good deal of the time. First, the inner child is curious. Secondly, it does not know anything about evil, as it has not lived long enough and does not think to be on guard. It would not even guess that a good friend would rip them off for millions of dollars and would not even suspect it. Some of us have a hard time getting over that intrinsic innocence of the child and we have the tendency to be overly trusting and trust others who are not quite trustworthy.

WHAT IS THE WORLD? (4)

11. **The world & humanity were created by God and are therefore divinely inspired and intrinsically holy - 545**
12. **The world is merely a physical product of the physical universe - 190**
13. **Life and therefore humanity are purely accidental products of Darwinian biological evolution (mechanistic reductionism) - 190**
14. **Survival is due to natural selection by survival of the fittest - 440**

Slide 158

SLIDE 158: WHAT IS THE WORLD? (4)

This slide was introduced at the February 2009 lecture, DVD disc 2 at 000915.

The world and humanity were created by God and are therefore divinely inspired and intrinsically holy (545). When the ego subsides, the intrinsic beauty, perfection and holiness of all that exists shines forth as a radiance from the world itself. The world is illuminated and the energy of luminosity shines out of everything that exists. When one first perceives it, one has to pull the car over to the side, stop everything and one is not able to function for some time. The intrinsic beauty and perfection of 'all that exists' shines forth because all that exists is God, nothing that exists is not God. The Divinity of His essence does not shine forth for the common person because they tend to project onto it their perceptions and belief systems about the world.

The world is merely a physical product of the physical universe (190). This is the pedestrian scientific viewpoint. There are professional atheists, some of them are humorous, too, and they 'pooh-pooh' any other depiction of the universe, stating that the world is merely a physical product of the physical universe and God is an illusion. God is an illusion and the professional atheist feels sorry for spiritual aspirants and mystics. Bill Maher is funny. He likes to ridicule anything that is not just strictly the most pedestrian physical view of the world. "The view of the world that Bill Maher presents which is that it is just a physical phenomenon and that God is just an illusion calibrates at 190" (tests true). There is quite a big difference between seeing the world at 545 and seeing the world of pedestrian materialism at 190.

Life and humanity are purely accidental products of Darwinian biological evolution (mechanistic reductionism, cal. 190). This is the idea that the universe is physical and it is nothing but a product of physicality, an expression of physicality. In the schools, we have now a conflict between the different explanations of evolution between creationism and Darwinian biologic evolution. Then we have a more sophisticated view:

Survival is due to natural selection by survival of the fittest (440). Intellectually that is true. "Natural selection" is the concept that a species will adapt to its environment and pass down those adaptations to their offspring over time. Those that do not adapt will die before breeding and therefore those unfavorable traits will not survive.

WHAT IS THE WORLD? (5)

15. **The world & the universe are merely passing illusions created by the ego to keep itself separate from God - 220**
16. **Human life is an expression of God's Will by which the Godhead fulfills the actualization of infinite potentiality - 560**
17. **Man descended from the stars and fell from the heavens - 160**
18. **Man descended from monkeys - 160**

Slide 159

SLIDE 159: WHAT IS THE WORLD? (5)

This slide was introduced at the February 2009 lecture, DVD disc 2 at 001845.

The world and the universe are merely passing illusions created by the ego to keep itself separate from God (220). The calibration of 220 tells us that it is true, but not really or overwhelmingly true. This is sort of a spinoff from some spiritual teachings that say that the world and the universe are merely passing illusions. What it should say is, how you see them are really passing illusions created by the ego to keep itself separate from God. However, the ego does not do these things merely to keep itself separate from God. The ego does these things because that is the biologic nature of the ego. It does not know anything about God. How could it do what it does in order to keep itself separate from God when it does not even know anything about God? It is a part of *A Course in Miracles,* too and one does not have to agree with it. The ego would have to know the answer to the whole conundrum in order to have created the conundrum; you would have to know about God to keep yourself separate from God, and if you knew about God then you would not be just a secularist. It is a self-defeating conundrum. It is a fact that the ego does maintain its separation from God, but not because that is its purpose but because that is the consequence of a fallacy. Its purpose is not the fallacy.

Human life is an expression of God's Will by which the Godhead fulfills the actualization of infinite potentiality (560). All that is, is not only created by God, all that is, is God. How the world is perceived then would be a positionality and not the Reality of the world. When the ego collapses, the radiance of Divinity shines as the essence of all that is, like a blinding light. Suddenly the awareness opens up to you and you have to pull your car over to the side of the road. Even a box of Kleenex is an example of divine perfection. What strikes you at first when this phenomenon begins to unveil itself is the stunning realization that it 'is', that anything 'IS'. It is the stunning realization of existence as God. To exist as 'this', or to exist as 'that' does not really make that much difference. What is stunning is that they exist at all. That anything has existence is the first stunning thing. After a certain degree of the development of inner awareness, you go past a certain stage and can begin to function again. These states of consciousness tend to come and then they recede because if they continue it is almost impossible to function. In a state of divine illumination, it is almost impossible to function in the world. In fact, it is hard even to stay in the world, because at that level you have permission to leave. You see you are not a physical body, so you are not going to die anyway. It is just that you depart from the physicality. The infinite potentiality of Divinity is to be anything and everything. It could be a flower or it could be a thing that you wave in the air.

This one is funny: **Man descended from the stars and fell from the heavens (160).** Then we have the next one, Darwinian biologic certitude that **man descended from the monkeys (160).** Ah, poor monkeys, they always get blamed for it. It is so interesting how one life form energizes another life form just by virtue of their existence, just by virtue of the fact that we are. You say, "What good am I, what good can I serve the world? Of what worth am I?" The first worth you have is that you are. One has already fulfilled one's function just by being here.

WHAT IS THE WORLD? (6)

19. The world and earthly life are the optimum venue for the evolution of consciousness in human form from its animal origins to its spiritual enlightenment and salvation - Man is therefore the crossover from the animal to the angelic - 255

20. The world and its human life are only one dimension of existence among many dimensions - 450

Slide 160

SLIDE 160: WHAT IS THE WORLD? (6)

This slide was introduced at the February 2009 lecture, DVD disc 2 at 003020.

The world and earthly life are the optimum venue for the evolution of consciousness in human form from its animal origins to its spiritual enlightenment and salvation. Man is therefore the cross-over from the animal to the angelic. Although this viewpoint is true, it is not the highest truth. It is only 255.

The world and its human life are only one dimension of existence among many dimensions (450). So one can see that there is a degree of election, each one of us has elected to be in this dimension. "Each one of us has elected to choose this human existence", (tests true). Each one of us of our own free will has chosen to be here. Goodbye, alibis. Each one of us may not remember it. We do not remember that moment in spiritual evolution that we agreed and chose to reincarnate. Is that okay with everybody? Whatever happens on this planet, there are always some protestors. God bless the protestors, as they add certain aliveness to everything. If you have a carnival for goodness and giving away free money, there would be protestors. That is why one need not go to peace meetings because the protestors are so violent one is afraid to go to them.

WHAT IS THE WORLD? (7)

21. **The world represents the fusion of the linear and the nonlinear and actually exists outside the domain of time and causality - 485**

22. **The world offers the gift of life itself via beingness & existence, whereby consciousness is made experiential & thus reified as the Ultimate Reality out of which arises a capacity for existence/awareness - 520**

Slide 161

SLIDE 161: WHAT IS THE WORLD? (7)

This slide was introduced at the February 2009 lecture, DVD disc 2 at 003230.

The world represents the fusion of the linear and the nonlinear and actually exists outside the domain of time and causality (485). Causality is a projection from the human mind. Everything is happening of its own, autonomously and spontaneously. Nothing is being caused by anything else. What is happening is that potentiality manifests as actuality. So, the potentiality of everyone reading this is to become enlightened, no excuses. Everyone has chosen to be here. The next time you feel down and discouraged and everything is going wrong, you ask yourself, "Now why did I choose to be here then? If things are so screwed up and I am so hopeless and the world is so screwed up, why am I here, why am I here?" To ask that question periodically is the basis of wisdom: What is the meaning of my existence? What is the truth of my existence to the degree that I can know it? Then one day comes an understanding, which is nonverbal. It is just an awareness of how that which could have been is. At the same time, from that 'which is' originates that 'which could be'. It is not a one-way street. It goes in both directions simultaneously.

The world offers the gift of life itself via beingness and existence, whereby consciousness is made experiential and thus reified as the Ultimate Reality out of which arises a capacity for existence/awareness (520). The 'I' of the Self is the Eye of God witnessing the unfolding of Creation as Now. Belief systems are so powerful that they are like the television set. They interpret and process everything. You see nothing as it is on television because the angle has been preselected, the lighting has been selected, the sound has been selected, the verbal subscription has been selected, the politicalization has been selected, the grammar has been selected, etc. Thousands of selections have occurred before you even get a chance to view it on television. So when you say you saw something, you did not really see it. What you saw was a processed interpretation of it, with multiple slants; you need to know why they choose a particular scene to put up, the selection of the scene, etc. This is important. It contains a hidden message of visual imaging in the soundtrack.

So what we see is an edited world. Within everyone is the processor, which is pretty much like a TV production studio. It selects what it considers important, how to interpret it, how to feel about it, etc. The Reality comes to you in a meditated state, not necessarily formal meditation. It happens very often when you walk in the woods, not thinking about anything in particular. Then all of a sudden, time seems to stop. The whole woods become silent. You can hear every leaf fall. It is magical. Suddenly the world is mystically beautiful.

WHAT IS THE WORLD? (8)

23. The spiritual evolution occasioned by human life allows for the eventual discovery and human awareness of Divinity as its Source - Thus, the relinquishment of the ego/self reveals the spiritual Reality of the Self by which the Reality of God becomes manifest and subjectively experienced as the Self (God Immanent) - 570

All contextualizations of the world are conjectural mentations as life is lived solely by subjective experience - 225

Slide 162

SLIDE 162: WHAT IS THE WORLD? (8)

This slide was introduced at the February 2009 lecture, DVD disc 2 at 003445.

The spiritual evolution occasioned by human life allows for the eventual discovery and human awareness of Divinity as its Source. Thus, the relinquishment of the ego/self reveals the spiritual Reality of the Self by which the Reality of God becomes manifest and subjectively experienced as the Self (God Immanent). This statement calibrates at **570**. It means we are here to discover the spiritual reality behind our sense of existence and discover that it is the reality of God that has become manifest, and that is experienced as the Self. We have the "self", that is the one we beat ourselves up about. Then we have the "Self". The Infinite Self ("S") is the source of consciousness itself. Consciousness does not identify in and of itself, it does not identify itself as separate or individual in the first place. It is the introduction of the "humanness" that makes the mind assume that that which "is" is called "me". There is a story of the cat where the cat asks, "Who am I?" You tell him "You're a cat". You can read the cat 4 or 5 pages about cats from the encyclopedia. The cat listens respectfully, then says, "But that's not who I am". You ask the cat, "Who are you?" The cat replies, "I'm just me". This story crystallizes all of this into sort of a comical story. What each one of us really experiences is our own experience of experiencing. The only thing that you are experiencing is that you are experiencing. What your experience is of is irrelevant. Whether you experience if your hand is here or there or this is a Kleenex box, etc. is irrelevant. What is of interest and significant in value is that you are experiencing, period. You are experiencing, so therefore, by reductionism, you can get back to the point that which I am is not different from experiencing, therefore that which I am, in reality is always experiencing experiencing. You experienced it that way when you were a kid, in a different way when you are rich, in a still different way when you are poor, when you are sick, when you are well, etc. That which you are is experiencing your own existence. You experience your own existence.

Eventually we say, "How do I experience what I experience? How can I know that I know?" The spiritual reality of the Self is due to the reality of God, experienced as the Self, God Immanent. It is because of the "Self" that the "self" presumes that it is "me". It is because of the presence of God within. Were it not for the presence of God within, you would not have consciousness and without consciousness you would not know that you "are". Everyone presumes that their consciousness is innate to their existence. Everyone presumes that everyone knows that one "is". Many things "are" but do not know that they "are" (calibrates true). There are humans who "are", but are not conscious that they "are" (Calibrates as true). That one always befuddles people, they say, "How can that be? How can you 'be' and not know that you 'are'?". It is because they "are" without being aware of their own existence as existence. That is a lower level of consciousness below 200. They "are" but they are not aware that they "are". If you look at it and reflect on it, you can understand it eventually. **All contextualizations of the world are conjectural mentations as life is lived solely by subjective experience.** That is true to a certain extent (calibrates at 225) and means this viewpoint is true but not overwhelmingly true, not spiritually true.

WHAT IS THE WORLD? (9)

24. **Man is just a highly evolved hominid and therefore merely a biological species and genus, and spirituality is a product of imagination - 160**
25. **Man is an environmental disaster, and the sooner he self-destructs and returns the world to Nature, the better - 120**
26. **Mankind is on a learning curve of biological/social evolution - 450**

Slide 163

SLIDE 163: WHAT IS THE WORLD? (9)

This slide was introduced at the February 2009 lecture, DVD disc 2 at 004010.

Man is just a highly evolved hominid and therefore merely a biological species and genus, and spiritually is a product of imagination (160) is a current political positionality. There is a skeptic's dictionary that calibrates at about 160 and that is where this viewpoint comes from. Merely a biologic species and spirituality is a product of imagination: it is an interesting book because everything that is spiritual gets ridiculed in it. Because from that particular book, only pedestrian physicality is real and anything beyond the most mundane consciousness level of 170 or so is unreal. **Man is an environmental disaster, and the sooner he self-destructs and returns the world to nature, the better (120).** This is sort of the crazy environmentalist who worries that the sheep in New Zealand are belching and passing intestinal gas and emitting methane into the environment. The environmentalist says we should all become vegetarians, because to eat animals you have to have animals and animals pass gas and contaminate the environment with methane. These people think the environment is God, and God is vulnerable. The extremes to which people can go are really quite interesting.

There are some people in India (a sect of "Jain" monks) that put a cloth over their face so they do not accidently inhale bacteria and therefore kill the bacteria. They do not want to harm the bacteria, so these people have not accepted something within themselves that is profoundly human. They have demonized it. In psychiatry, this is called a reaction formation, which is a defense mechanism in which emotions and impulses, which are perceived to be unacceptable, are mastered by exaggeration of the directly opposing tendency. The fact that you are so far over on this side, means that you are really over on the other side.

Mankind is on a learning curve of biological/social evolution (450). That would explain many of the phenomena, e.g. if you calibrate different regions of the world and the different countries in the world, you will see extreme differences. There are huge sections of the world that live at consciousness level 160-170. They live by death and terrorism by beheading people and torture, belittling of women, children and animals, etc. Then there are people that live close to the highest levels of consciousness and they wish no harm to any living being and are benign in their viewpoint.

WHAT IS THE WORLD? (10)

27. 'Meaning' is a semantic/linguistic construction with no inherent reality; therefore, any and all statements are equally valid - 150

28. 'I have invented the world I see' - 350

29. There is no point in trying to save the world, for the world you see does not even exist - 370

30. The world is an opportune place for redemption and salvation - 575

Slide 164

SLIDE 164: WHAT IS THE WORLD? (10)

This slide was introduced at February 2009 lecture, DVD disc 2 at 004500.

'Meaning' is a semantic/linguistic construction with no inherent reality; therefore, any and all statements are equally valid (150). This is part of the current political collapse of the intellectual basis of the country. Meaning is more than just semantics; on a superficial level, something can be superimposed on the meaning. When you can see the difference between appearance and essence, meaning shines forth from the essence. It differentiates perception, being what you think a thing is, from essence. So all the consciousness research constantly approaches the same question: What is the difference between the essence of this and its appearance? Consciousness calibration cuts through appearance, and what is calibrated is essence. Because we all cannot discern the wolf in sheep's clothing, therefore consciousness calibration is incredibly unique. It is the first time actually in man's history, other than by divine revelation, that man has had the capacity to discern truth. It is as if you accidently fell into something of profound significance and application, which the world does not even know about. The majority of the people in the world would not even begin to understand, even if you explained it to them. "You mean to tell me that without even going to that place in Cuba, without even going there, one can look at the name or a picture of somebody, one can ask specific questions, where he was, what he did, what he decided, what he said, what he suggested we serve and what his intentions are when he leaves?" One can know it with certitude. All you have to do is calibrate him. You could do the same with an animal in the zoo. To be able to discern truth from falsehood is extremely sophisticated, and extremely rare.

I have invented the world I see (350). There is no point in trying to save the world, for the world you see does not even exist (370). The world is actually an opportune place for redemption and salvation (575). So what the world really is calibrates close to 600. What you see in the prior two statements is only in the 300's. If you calibrate lower, you will see the world as intrinsically evil. There are two confusing things in the Bible. One is, Jesus says evil is in the eye of the beholder, condemn not, do not stone the woman because what you see is in the eye of the beholder. The seeming contradiction is in the Lord's Prayer, where it says, "But deliver us from evil". If evil is only projection, you would not need protection from it. The implication is that we should not try to defeat evil, but avoid it. So even with evil, the choice is left to our own consciousness and our own level of spiritual evolution. How should we hold it? "It is safe to pray for evil-doers, the sources of hate and pray they see things differently" (calibrates true.)

WHAT IS THE WORLD? (11)

31. **One's perception of the world is consequent to the observer's level of consciousness - 485**
32. **The human world is a spiritual hospital & rehabilitation unit - 265**
33. **Karma is God's own bail-out plan and rescue package - 350**
34. **The world is getting hotter due to human causes - 105**
35. **The world won't end on 12/21/2012 - True**

Slide 165

SLIDE 165: WHAT IS THE WORLD? (11)

This slide was introduced at the February 2009 lecture, DVD disc 2 at 005600.

One's perception of the world is consequent to the observer's level of consciousness (485). At a certain point, one sees the beauty and divinity of everything that exists. At lower levels, everything looks ugly, seen in a utilitarian way for its functional value. Then at a different level, the only thing in one's mind is money. "How much is this worth? How much could I get to do this?" How much is your soul worth? Jesus said that your soul is worth more than the rest of the world put together. He asked, "What will it profit a man if he gains the whole world, and loses his own soul?" Ramana Maharishi said, "There is no point worrying about the world you see because the world you see does not even exist." What he means by that is you do not see the reality, you only see what you project out there. At a certain level, you look out there and see that everyone has all the resources needed to survive at whatever their level of consciousness is. Then at certain other level of consciousness, it takes very little to survive because your needs are very minimal. **The human world is a spiritual hospital & rehabilitation unit (265).** That is an easy one to accept, that everybody is here for rehab.

Karma is God's own bail-out plan and rescue package (350). One sees that as a joke but it does calibrate around 350. Divine intention is we have the chance to undo the negative karma and create positive karma. The majority of the people here have had a previous human existence. Most people have been here a number of times, but they do not remember those lifetimes. However, in an altered state of consciousness you can remember them, via past life recall. There are specific techniques for past life recall. Monroe Institute teaches one and there are people in many cities that do past life regression. In a relaxed state, self-hypnosis is very simple: You just picture yourself going down the stairs, count yourself going down and a previous specific lifetime somehow just resumes. In any case, just be aware that this is not your first and only time here on Earth. Of course, that is helpful to know because if you screw up this lifetime, you can come back again. Many people spend their lifetime addicted to alcohol, drugs, gambling, sex, food, etc. They do these things to an excessive degree and need to come back to rehabilitate themselves, undo negative karma and earn positive karmic merit. Thus, the viewpoint that "**this is a spiritual hospital & rehabilitation unit**" has a certain reality for some people. Of course, that is similar to what the Buddha teaches also, as the law of karma is a basic Buddhist belief. Christianity does not teach that. Christianity comes from a different direction and does not get into the whole subject of karma. It just has no opinion about it, does not say yes or no.

The world is getting hotter due to human causes (105). The world is not getting hotter due to human causes. The Earth's temperature change is due to the sunspot/magnetic storm activity on the surface of the Sun. Currently that activity has decreased, implying that we are actually going into a cooler period over the next few decades. That is how the human world is a **spiritual hospital & rehabilitation unit** as one learns many new lessons, e.g. how to discern truth from falsehood. What Dr. Hawkins discovered in consciousness research is one of the reasons he came back here with this timeless message: "It is possible to discern truth from falsehood. You have within yourself that capacity." **The world won't end on 12/21/2012 (true).** People worried about it because of the Mayan calendar. Dr. Hawkins said jokingly, "If you are a Mayan, worry about it. That only applies to Mayans. If you are not a Mayan, forget about it."

WHAT IS THE WORLD? (12)

36. With the removal of perception, the Radiance of Divinity shines forth as the exquisite beauty and perfection of the world - 645

Slide 166

SLIDE 166: WHAT IS THE WORLD? (12)

This slide was introduced at the February 2009 lecture, DVD disc 2 at 010300.

With the removal of perception, the Radiance of Divinity shines forth as the exquisite beauty and perfection of the world (645). With the removal of perception, in other words, when you stop projecting out, and you see the world as it is, the radiance of Divinity shines forth as exquisite beauty and perfection of the world. Dr. Hawkins described the first time he saw that. He had surrendered everything to God and was in a higher rarefied space, hardly anyone had been there. He saw a few who had been there, the great Sages. Then it dawned on him that he had surrendered everything to God, but he had not surrendered life to God. He had surrendered all that he had, all that he had been, all he believed, and everything he could say about himself. Then he said, "This, too, I surrender to Thee, O Lord" and he laid down his life to God. There were a few moments of very intense agony as he felt himself dying. That which Dr. Hawkins had been, died. Suddenly, the door opened, and the exquisite perfection and radiance of Divinity shone forth like a blinding light. The beauty, the radiance of Divinity, the perfection of all that exists was so stunning that it knocked him off his feet. In ordinary life, we blind ourselves to it because for one thing, one cannot really function in the world in that state and he could not function for several years. By revelation, one sees the true Reality of life, the exquisite perfection of all that exists. Everything you see is an expression of Divinity, Divinity as this table, Divinity as this paper, Divinity as this soda bottle, Divinity as this pointer, coffee, person... You see the perfection. You become aware of the perfection of all that exists. This is because you have let go of judgmentalism. You do not process anything. Ordinarily, mind instantly processes the input from the senses. That processing happens in 1/10,000th of second. It is very hard to get ahead of it. In a highly meditative state, you can suddenly cross that barrier of 1/10,000th of a second and see things as they are, before the processor gets to it. The processor comes in 1/10,000th of a second and edits everything. Therefore, in ordinary life, what you are constantly witnessing is what you constantly have processed; you are not seeing "What Is" but what has been processed, interpreted, given a name, judged right or wrong, pro and con, anti... In one instant, one can catch it, however.

Dr. Hawkins recalled the time he discovered it when a rabbit ran in front of the car. Just as the rabbit ran in front of the car, his foot pushed down the brake and stopped the car, and he caught that he did it before he thought of doing it. He caught the ego trying to take the credit for saving the rabbit's life. No, the foot stepped down, and slowed and saved the rabbit's life and the ego jumped in 1/10,000th of a second and claimed credit. In higher meditative states, what happens is that you eventually cross over the processor. Time comes to a stop. Judgmentalism stops. Mentalization stops. So that is the divine state and it occurs at the level of 600 and up, where the internal processor stops processing information and just experiences the world as it is with no intervention, with no editing. When you have those experiences, you see the world the way it is. If you can remove yourself from the world,because you do not have to go anywhere or do anything, you have no responsibilities, no television set and nothing to read, you can stay in this Divine state for long periods. In such periods, one can forget that one has a body or a connection to it. Dr. Hawkins describes that in such a state when he passed the mirror and saw somebody in the mirror and it scared him. He did not know who was in the house. Another time, he tried walking through a wall. The physical body smacked right against the wall because he no longer identified himself as the physical body. These are the expanded states of consciousness facilitated via meditation, contemplation, prayer, fasting, religious/spiritual techniques, etc., but once attained they require getting used to.

101 WAYS TO HAPPINESS (1)

1. **Source is within, not without**
2. **Want what you have instead of have what you want**
3. **Happiness is an inner decision**
4. **Give up "poor me"**
5. **Choose instead of crave, want, desire, or get**

Slide 167

SLIDE 167: 101 WAYS TO HAPPINESS (1)

This slide was introduced at the April 2009 lecture, DVD disc 1 at 003940.

The world is very intrigued with happiness, and the media is preoccupied with it to sell products,

e.g. buy this car, or have whiter teeth, prettier hair or swirlier skirts, etc. The promise is that whatever you buy is going to bring you greater happiness, make you happy. The illusion is always that the source of happiness is out there. The first thing to realize is that there is no source of happiness out there. **The source is within, not without.** "That" does not have the capacity to make you happy; you project onto "that" the capacity to make you happy. Desirability, the world thinks, is something that is "out there." There is a famous book in Alice Bailey's series of books, "Glamour: A World Problem", in which she describes the energy of glamour as what we project onto a thing that makes that thing desirable. The source of happiness is within your Self but projection makes perception, which is the illusion that makes one look for things outside for happiness.

The secret is to **want what you have, instead of have what you want**. Look over everything you have and decide that even if it is frumpy, a little beat up and worn, it is still yours and it is adorable. If you want what you have, then look around and say, "Whatever it is, it is mine and I love it." Cheap chrome furniture, so what? It is better than no furniture. You look at whatever you have and see that it is desirable. You look in the mirror and you just say, "that which I am seeing in there is desirable." Yes. One thing you have is your own existence. What you have to settle for, then, is the fact that you exist and have life and all that it should take to make you happy is that you are. Be satisfied with the fact that you are. If you start from that state, you are happy all the time: "I am happy that I am. I am happy that currently I am in a physical body and I get to experience this plane of existence. I am happy that eventually I will get out of the body and not be restricted to this protoplasmic world. I will be in another dimension where other exciting adventures are waiting to be explored." Want what you have instead of craving what you do not have. You clearly see that **happiness is an inner decision**. Once you decide to be happy, nobody can do anything about it. The main source of happiness is just satisfaction that you are.

There are certain things you have to give up, and that is why people just do not like being happy too much. You have to **give up "poor me"**, as that is not being grateful to the Creator. By acceptance of everything as it is we eliminate the negatives. We choose it to be that way. You **choose, instead of craving, desiring, wanting, or grasping** for happiness. You see that happiness is completely within yourself. Stop projecting the source of happiness outside yourself. Because then you are not going to be happy unless you have something. That is the miserable state of someone like Eeyore, the famous character in the Winnie-the-Pooh books, as he says, "Oh, well, it won't do any good anyway. What good is happiness?"

101 WAYS TO HAPPINESS (2)

6. **Surrender all cravings to God**
7. ***Joie de vivre* is independent of events**
8. **Is it the child, adult, or parent that wants?**
9. **Differentiate actual from symbolic win or gain**

Slide 168

SLIDE 168: 101 WAYS TO HAPPINESS (2)

This slide was introduced at the April 2009 lecture, DVD disc 1 at 005350.

One has to **surrender all cravings to God**. This is for a more spiritually evolved person in whom the love of God becomes the priority. Would I rather crave this thing and be unhappy or be thankful for my existence? The happiness is in the willingness. If you were asked, "Could you surrender this to God?" you would respond by saying, "Yes, I could." That is the beginning of happiness right there. Then, the next step is merely "would." So realize that it is not that you cannot, it is just you will not. You can let go of anything that you want to.

There is a hard-to-describe ***joie de vivre* independent of events**. *Joie de vivre* is a certain attitude, a style of happiness in which if you lost all your money today, and someone asks, "Why are you happy?" You respond, "I am happy because I lost all my money today." *Joie de vivre* is the realization that happiness is a superior style. *Joie de vivre* is part of a decision to have a certain attitude towards life, an existential position of being happy and grateful and enjoying in whatever expression your life is expressing right now. Being a human, you never know what is going to happen next. Any moment suddenly one can get a heart attack and fall over. You could suddenly win the lottery. The joy of life is independent of what actually happens, as you play the game for the sake of the game, not for the necessity of winning the game, because that is not in your hands in any case. The way to experience *joie de vivre* is to be good-natured, humorous, light-hearted and helpful to others and because you are that way to others, that is what you become.

Within our self, we have unconsciously, the child, the adult and the parent. So who is it that is happy or unhappy? Sometimes, if you become the child, the parent in you will get angry and become guilty. So, **is it the child, the adult, or the parent in you that wants**? The parent is your conscience, the adult is your performance and your inner child is the one that is curious and "wants". Part of *joie de vivre* is that the inner child is still there. Why are you happy and skipping? Part of happiness is that your child is still active, your adult is well integrated and you have a loving parent; that your conscience is not brutal and negative; that you have total inner acceptance of yourself.

We also have to **differentiate the actual from symbolic win or gain**. People kill each other and do terrible things over things that intrinsically have no reality, but are merely symbolic. For symbolic reasons they bomb each other. Our life is not only actual, emotional, with the child, the adult and the parent inside, but it is appealing to the archetypes of all these things within us on a symbolic level. Having a lot of money in some parts of the world is useless. They do not have anything to sell you with it. In other parts of the world, without money, you are nothing. The meaning of money then, is symbolic. The joy of the game of life comes from playing the game, not from winning or losing, because in human life, there is no way to win or lose. Winning and losing is all a fantasy you project onto events.

101 WAYS TO HAPPINESS (3)

10. Differentiate narcissistic ("rich and famous") from mature goals

11. Be pleased with the direction/alignment instead of just completion

12. Practical reality vs. fantasy and glamour of "success"

13. Choose decision instead of just hope

Slide 169

SLIDE 169: 101 WAYS TO HAPPINESS (3)

This slide was introduced at the April 2009 lecture, DVD disc 2 at 000040.

We are talking about the roads to happiness. If you stop and examine yourself, you begin to wonder what your goals are, and if you do not know what your goals are, it is fun to just sit down and write them down. What are my goals in this life? Being rich and famous seems to be an obsession with the television industry. Rich and famous is what they feed on. So how does one **differentiate the narcissistic goal, such as being rich and famous, from mature goals**? How many people have written their goals down, just to make them more conscious? You actually write them down, "My goals in this life are ____." Then you can prioritize them. Of course, one good goal is to be happy no matter what happens. Then if you win, you say, "Hooray, I won" and if you lose, you say, "Thank God I lost." Sometimes it is much better to lose than win.

Be pleased with the direction/alignment instead of completion. Instead of saying, "I won't be happy until I reach there, or I won't be happy until I have $84000 saved up", just be happy that you are in the direction of trying to be thrifty and think about your older age and provide for it. Be happy that you are in a certain direction / alignment. Of course, in spiritual work that is very much so, because there is no way you can actually really tell where you are at in your spiritual evolution. To be happy with the fact that your direction is to achieve enlightenment or salvation, to bring about happiness to others in itself is gratifying. So be happy with the things you have assigned a value to, to be friendly and cheerful, to be uplifting to others, etc.

We are talking about **practical reality versus fantasy and glamour of "success"**, as in Hollywood success and TV star success, which is symbolic and has to do with our projecting value onto it. It is not that a person has stardom or money etc., it is that you have projected desirability onto that. In and of itself it has no attraction. Nothing in this world has any attraction unless you project attractiveness onto it. It is "that attribute that you have projected onto it", that makes it desirable. The main thing is to pursue a thing because that is what you are. If you are studious, then being a studious person is what you are. The thing is to enjoy the process, enjoy the process of life, and enjoy the various stages of life. It is fun to be a kid, it is exciting to be an adolescent, and it is great to be a young adult. Middle age has many wonderful things about it. Older age is self-rewarding as you are too old to give a rap about anything anymore.

Where you want to go now, you **choose decision instead of just hope.** Do not do something just because others ask you to do it. That way you do not end up blaming it on other people because no matter which way you go, there are risks involved. Even if you decide to stay at home and not go anywhere, you could become decrepit. One's decision can bring you back to being rich with what matters to God.

101 WAYS TO HAPPINESS (4)

14. Flexible vs. rigid

15. Cancel "...and then I'll be happy"

16. Let go of clutching and grasping

17. Clarify goals and ideals

18. Realize all value is arbitrary

19. Happiness is a nap on a train or a plane

Slide 170

SLIDE 170: 101 WAYS TO HAPPINESS (4)

This slide was introduced at the April 2009 lecture, DVD disc 2 at 000820.

Choose to **be flexible versus rigid**. The weed that bends with the current is flexible and survives, while the one that is stiff and inflexible perishes in the current. There is an old Taoist teaching, which asks to be flexible and to bend with the wind, bend with the current rather than break, to be able to change, to switch roles easily as needed. You can also see your life as a sequence of roles; you are not only what you are, but you are also fulfilling certain social roles to the best of your ability and understanding. The parent, the adult, the child, etc. those are all roles.

Then we learn not to make our happiness dependent on anything, like "I will be happy if I get an "A" on this thing." So you have to **cancel, "...and then I'll be happy."** That way, your happiness is not provisional about anything except the direction that you are going. You say, "I am going in this direction, I am choosing spiritual evolution as a lifestyle, and it gives my life meaning and significance, and serving God in every way that I can." One way you serve God is by being happy. God's will for you is happiness, and therefore to be happy is pleasing to God. God's demand is that you be happy (calibrates true.) So being happy is fulfilling your human potential and we are created in that style by Almighty God.

Make the happiness independent of phenomena, therefore you do not have to clutch and grasp at things. **Let go of clutching and grasping** at things as that is a good way to lose them.

Clarify **your goals and ideals**. Many spiritual people have actually sat down, listed what their goals are and prioritized them, and of course, in actual life, we are doing that all the time, but it is unconscious. We are choosing one goal over another constantly, but to make them conscious and intellectually aware is of great value.

Realize that all value that you contribute to anything is arbitrary; because you value it does not mean that it is so. It just means that you value it. The only value that is independent of personal opinion is the scale of consciousness, indicating a precise mathematical level. Valued and looked at from Consciousness itself, many would disregard that also as having any value, so even that which is of confirmatory value would not be valuable in another person's eyes. In our culture, honesty and integrity are virtues; there are other cultures in which honesty and integrity is idiotic and stupid. On the other side of the world, if the price of an object is $6.00 and you sell it for $6.00, they say you are an idiot. Now how do you accommodate yourself to a culture that thinks that truth, honesty, etc. is a defect? It is a little hard to figure how you are going to accommodate something that is diametrically opposed to your own set of values. Clarify goals and ideals, realize all value is arbitrary, and realize there are huge cultures in which honesty is not valued but actually regarded as stupidity.

Happiness is a nap on a train or a plane. Relax wherever you are! You relax your body and have a quick nap, and you can be happy no matter where you are, feeling refreshed.

101 WAYS TO HAPPINESS (5)

20. **Live one day at a time**
21. **Happiness is a cat's purr or a dog's wagging tail**
22. **Faith vs. skepticism**
23. **Gratitude for what one has & is**
24. **Detached vs. crave**
25. **Glass half full or half empty – optimist or pessimist**
26. **Spiritual vs. material goals**

Slide 171

SLIDE 171: 101 WAYS TO HAPPINESS (5)

This slide was introduced at the April 2009 lecture, DVD disc 2 at 001405.

Live one day at a time. This is one of the greatest sources of happiness and is an axiom of the 12-Step program. People who practice the 12-step program are happy. Is "to live one day at a time" rational? Well, yesterday is gone forever and so it has no reality. Tomorrow is not here yet, so it has no reality. The only thing that is actually real is what is right now. **Happiness is a cat's purr or a dog's wagging tail**. They both calibrate at 500. It is hard to be angry, upset and in self-pity when a kitty is purring in your arms. You got this kitty and she is going "purr, purr, purr..." There is nothing nicer than hearing a kitty's purring and watching a dog's tail wagging. Another source of happiness is the resolution of **faith versus skepticism**. Skepticism is a narcissistic position. Faith is a much higher position. The skeptic thinks skepticism will lead him to truth and happiness and that is why he is a skeptic. It is his faith in his skepticism that gives him that feeling, something paradoxically funny. Now if he were skeptical about his skepticism, he would be making progress.

We learn to be **grateful for what we have and what we have become**. We have traveled for a long time through life to become what we are at this moment. We are the product of the past and attracted by the future; so here we are in no-man's land between the past, which is over, and the future, which is not here yet. Therefore, we live in a complete vacuum. The past is over, and the future is not here yet, so the only place one can exist is in this present moment. The only thing you have to worry about is this present moment.

Detached versus crave means if it happens it is terrific and if it does not, it is okay. The capacity to become detached is a learned technique. Everybody should practice becoming detached from something you think you just have to have to be happy. Pick something arbitrarily and start becoming detached from it. You say, well, if I become detached from it, then I will not get it. That is wanting to become detached and still be attached; a sneaky trick of the ego that will not succeed. Detached means if it happens, great, and if it does not happen, that is fine too. One way or the other, it is all the same because that which I am in reality is not going to be affected one way or the other. If I have not learned how to derive happiness from my own existence, then nothing could possibly make me happier. If I cannot be happy when my net worth is this much, how will I be happier if I am worth twice as much? This leads to **gratitude for what one has and is**. To seek truth for its own sake and to go wherever one has to go to learn truth is therefore a great goal. Be grateful that you are even interested in integrity and truth. You realize that about 98% of the world is not interested in truth.

The whole attitude of life is summed up in, **"Is the glass half-full or is it half empty?"** How your perception of life is, how you contextualize it, and are you **optimistic or pessimistic**? The optimist thinks that increasing one's consciousness level will increase one's happiness. That is optimistic, and is fulfillable by choosing **spiritual versus material goals**. Because spiritual goals cannot be lost, spiritual goals are valuable beyond all time and beyond the physical. Material goals come and go. Yesterday all these famous people were multi-millionaires and today they have lost much of their money due to stock market fluctuations. Anyway, that should not affect their happiness because the capacity to make more money is there. It is the capacity then, and not the thing itself that is valuable.

101 WAYS TO HAPPINESS (6)

27. Surrender to God's will

28. Capacity to let go

29. Be pleased with progress

30. Avoid self-judgment

31. "Good" and "bad" are circumstantial

32. "Win" is provisional

33. Simplicity vs. complexity

Slide 172

SLIDE 172: 101 WAYS TO HAPPINESS (6)

This slide was introduced at the April 2009 lecture, DVD disc 2 at 002925.

'Surrender to God's will' is a sophisticated understanding that really evolves as your own level of consciousness evolves. When you are a kid you think God's will is that you go to church, do not use certain bad words, etc. so your understanding of what is God's will evolves over the decades and you can't really explain it. It is more a contextualized knowingness that in this instant in evolution, 'this is the way' to go rather than 'that way'. 'Knowingness' evolves and we call this wisdom, certain spiritual wisdom. To **'surrender to God's will'** then brings about an evolution of one's wisdom. Is it God's will that I take up arms to fight, or is it God's will that I surrender? Do I take up arms against the slings and arrows of outrageous fortune, or battle them? This is really a conundrum, which is permanent in all the evolutionary phases of life.

What does it mean to surrender to God's will at that point? For some people to surrender to God's will means to obey the command and shoot the enemy, while for others, to surrender to God's will means they cannot kill another human under any circumstance. This is where spiritual evolution leads to progressive sophistication. What is God's will for you at this moment, in these circumstances, what is the highest thing you can do? **The capacity to let go** is freedom. The capacity to **'surrender to God's will'** increases **the capacity to let go**. To let go becomes progressively easier and easier. Eventually you reach the point where you can let go of anything. Surrendering to God's will is the capacity to let go and we surrender ourselves to God out of love for God and therefore the capacity to let go is almost infinite.

Be pleased with your own progress, that some capacity to let go is there. It is a matter of the human will. The minute you hear yourself say that you cannot let go of something, tell yourself what the truth is, that you will not let go of it. That puts it in a different domain, because something you cannot let go of today you may be able to a week from now, a year from now or a decade from now. Being a movie star is hard to let go of as an adolescent fantasy, but by 80, you have gotten over it. Be pleased with your progress, you do not have to want to be Clark Gable at 80 to be happy. You **avoid the self-judgment** that is in the internalized parent; there is the child in you, there is the adult, and then judgmentalism is the inner parent or the super ego that is constantly judging everything you do. So if you want to enjoy life the child has to stay alive, but the adult has to watch one's child as the child can be obstructive. Having your inner kid alive and well is part of happiness so that you as the mature adult can let the kid play periodically, preventing the punitive parent from showing up also in the process.

"Good" and "bad" are circumstantial. Many times, we see people that think that something is good and we see it as bad, or vice versa, so what is good is how you define it. Whether something is a win or a loss is dependent on circumstances, therefore a **"win" is provisional** and it depends on what you mean by win. **Simplicity vs. complexity**: that which is super complex is harder to achieve than that which is simple. One way to make life better is to take something that is staggeringly complex and boil it down to its inner principles. If something is too complex, it just cannot be handled and gets discarded, like college algebra. Algebra has outlived its usefulness as any computer can solve the same problem in one thousandth of a second. What takes you all evening the computer can do in no time at all. Life moves on from complexity to simplicity. That which was undoable from complexity is now doable through simplicity. It is best to try to simplify life's problems.

101 WAYS TO HAPPINESS (7)

34. Realistic expectations

35. Value is in the eye of the beholder

36. Give up skepticism

37. Sense of humor

38. Accept karmic propensity

39. See essence rather than perception

40. Jocular instead of morose

Slide 173

SLIDE 173: 101 WAYS TO HAPPINESS (7)

This slide was introduced at the April 2009 lecture, DVD disc 2 at 004320.

What can one **realistically expect** of life and of others and of events? Consciousness levels below 250 tend to take on rigid positions, an impediment in a world that is complex and multi-factorial rather than black and white. Taking such positions creates polarization, which in turn creates division. Rising above oppositions that dissipate one's energies, the neutral condition allows for flexibility and nonjudgmentalism and a realistic appraisal of problems. To be Neutral means not getting your way is no longer experienced as defeating, frightening, or frustrating, e.g. "Well, if I don't get this job, then I'll get another." The expectation that life will be okay if one can roll with the punches is a typical 250-level attitude. This attitude is nonjudgmental and does not lead to any need to control other people's behaviors. Correspondingly, because Neutral people value freedom, they are hard to control. If you are going to be interested in politics, for example, you have to modify your expectations. If you expect honesty, integrity and all of that in politics, forget it. Just get realistic as politics is in a different world with different values. You cannot judge the world of politics by the standards of your world. Their world is not your world. In their world, making it happen takes a few bucks here and a few bucks there, lying here and testifying falsely there. That is what their game is. You cannot use your rules and put them in their domain because in their domain you would be an idiot. So values are contextual, it depends on who you are and where you are in life, therefore we cannot judge others.

Value is in the eye of the beholder. What you think is valuable is what is valuable to you, but may not be equally valuable to others. You have to **give up your skepticism** and learn to live by faith, accompanied by surrender to and acceptance of a Higher Will. You can be skeptical about anything except your skepticism. A **sense of humor** serves you in all of the ways to be happy, enhancing every one of them.

Accept karmic propensity: Many things are karmic or coming out of the unconscious; this means a propensity, a tendency based on your previous actions and intentions. It is not cause and effect but a probability. When we investigate it with consciousness research, we find that there is a high likelihood that if you have a lot of negative karma, you will happen to be in an earthquake or similar disaster, so it is a propensity, not a causality. It is not just 'one's negative karma' that is the cause of the earthquakes or other mass disasters around where one lives. Karma does not cause anything, but the likelihood of certain things happening is increased.

See **essence, rather than perception**, the wolf hiding in sheep's clothing. Appearance is not essence, and the cover is not the book. Illusions look real, error is often convincing, which is an unpleasant fact to consider and accept. Everyone secretly believes that one's own personal view of the world is 'real', so one has to be forgiving continuously.

Be **jocular instead of morose.** Everyone loves laughter and life. Be the one who has the biggest smile, the loudest laughter, and is the most approachable. Fill the room where you are with your infectious goodwill and do not treat anyone as a stranger.

101 WAYS TO HAPPINESS (8)

41. **Good will regarding all of life**
42. **Easy-going vs. rigid**
43. **Reduce expectations**
44. **Generous instead of stingy**
45. **Modify the "inner voice"**
46. **Be gracious to self and others**
47. **Surrender the need to control**
48. **Let go of desire for applause**

Slide 174

SLIDE 174: 101 WAYS TO HAPPINESS (8)

This slide was introduced in April 2009 Lecture, DVD disc 2 004610.

Good will regarding all of life pays off the most and makes all the rest of the path easier. All you need is that one, and a hundred other ways to be happy come about. In that state, if somebody ate your hamburger when you went to the men's room, you will say, "Well, I guess he was hungry and didn't have any money." Goodwill towards all of life builds up your positive karma bank account recorded forever by the universe.

You can be uplifting, **easy-going vs. rigid,** by reducing expectations of others. If you do not expect anything of them at all, you are never disappointed. If somebody is integrous, honest, and educated, one falls over with joy. Easy-going means being flexible, as things are not always going to go the way you want them to go, so be willing to change. **Reduce your expectations of others**. If you have good will towards all of life, you will see what an effect you will have on people. When you are in a store and they ring you up on the cash register, you thank them very much. You say, "thank you a lot for ringing that all up" and they will go, "huh?" They do this hundreds of times before somebody says, "Thank you for ringing that up."

Be generous instead of stingy. Be generous with yourself, not generous with one thing or another. Generosity is an attitude towards life, a "givingness", a nurturance. You walk through the woods and the trees in the woods know that you love them. "The trees in the woods know that one is glad and loves them" (calibrates true.) All of life bows down before that which reflects God's love. All of life, then, responds to not what you have, not what you do, not what you say, but what you have become. People say, "What can I do to save the world?" The best advice is, "Stay home, stay out of traffic. Keep away from parades and demonstrations." All of us affect the consciousness level of the world. What can you do to bring about world peace? The best advice is, "Avoid peace marches." Instead, become as generous and loving as you can towards all of life in all its expressions. As you step over the little bug instead of stomping it, you have now done more for the world than parading around with banners. Generosity is an attitude; it is not monetary, although it can take a monetary expression.

Modify the inner voice so that it reflects your spiritual attitudes. You go inside to your inner thoughts and talk to your inner thoughts until you have gotten your inner voice to be reflective of your spiritual commitment and intention. **Be gracious to yourself and others**. That is part of generosity. We often remember to be gracious to others, but you can be gracious to yourself also by having a more easy-going conscience that understands your humanness. If you were perfect, you would not be here, so part of perfecting is correcting an overly strict superego. One way to have a more forgiving inner conscience is to be aware that it is not the act, but the intention behind the act that matters. An act can go wrong even though your intention is good, so you develop a more flexible, easy-going, loving and forgiving attitude.

Surrender the need to control others. It is not necessary to control everything that happens in the world because there is positive karma that will correct many a thing. All you need to do is hold what you desire and value in mind and it tends to manifest within your life. **Let go of the desire for applause**. One does not have to have applause for what one does in life. You do not have to have recognition. Doing good things unexpectedly for other people is so pleasing that you do not need applause.

101 WAYS TO HAPPINESS (9)

49. Be glad instead of mad

50. Acceptance instead of resistance

51. Generous instead of stingy

52. Candid with self and others

53. Silence the mind

54. Give up thinkingness

55. Forgiving vs. vindictive

Slide 175

SLIDE 175: 101 WAYS TO HAPPINESS (9)

This slide was introduced at the April 2009 lecture, DVD disc 2 at 010530.

Be glad instead of mad. Some people are glad that they are mad. Some people are mad that they are glad. Be glad that you are glad. You want to have **acceptance of the phenomena of life instead of resisting** it. Like a reed in the wind, be flexible and yield to life on life's terms, let go and allow the natural course of events to flow; like a ship on the ocean, let the wind do all the work, taking you to wondrous new shores.

Be generous instead of stingy. Generosity is its own reward. It is a comfortable place to be. All the ways to happiness recommended are subjectively and experientially very comfortable. Each thing is its own reward. That you have been generous is pleasing and it leaves you with a higher self-esteem. **Be candid with yourself and others**. If you don't like them diced, and you like them sliced, say, "I'd really like them sliced better than diced."

In the meantime, you **silence the thinking mind**. That can take some decades of spiritual work generally, before the mind stops talking. First, you withdraw interest from it. Do not care what the mind thinks. Stop calling it "my mind." That is grandiose; it is not *your* mind. It is *the* mind, and everybody shares in it. The current thing in the media is that everybody has to speak their mind. They think that is a great step forward in the evolution of consciousness, "This is a right, a Constitutional right." Those people who live in a certain political domain think that their duty to society is to express their mind. That is only a very rudimentary understanding. Anybody can babble away and talk and they go and listen to the "man on the street". Spiritual students need not care what the "man on the street" thinks, knowing that less than one in ten million of the population is interested in truth and enlightenment. He is going to think whatever TV told him to think. Whatever he says, he heard it on television today or yesterday. Everybody feels he has to express himself and he does not realize that it is just narcissistic egotism. Why should the world give a rap what you or I think? Because the mind has nothing to do with truth and it jumbles along and blabbers all day long. The mind is an idiot. Knowingness comes about nonverbally, in a nonlinear dimension. Knowingness is knowingness without thinking about it. The way to silence the mind is to stop giving it narcissistic egocentric energy, "Oh, wonderful mind, I wonder what you think about this?"

Give up thinkingness. Thinkingness is the narcissistic egocentric idea that what you think is important, that you have to have a voice in everything. Know that the world can get along fine without your thinkingness or advice. Thinkingness is a narcissistic and naïve investment that can be given up.

Forgiving is gracious and feels wholesome rather than being **vindictive**, which brings on discomfort and disease. One does not have to get even, because karma is automatic. That which is evil will bring about its own downfall by virtue of its own evility. You do not have to make yourself an energy field out there to go out and correct the world.

101 WAYS TO HAPPINESS (10)

56. Work on inner traits instead of external ones

57. It only takes a bone to make a dog happy – small things of life

58. Sing "Don't worry, be happy" in your mind

59. Choose spiritual values and goals

Slide 176

SLIDE 176: 101 WAYS TO HAPPINESS (10)

This slide was introduced at the April 2009 lecture, DVD disc 2 at 011220.

Work on your inner traits instead of external ones. The inner traits include a person's feelings, motivations, alignment and intention. The external traits include a person's appearance, physical features, what a person is good at, where a person lives and with whom, who a person is in life, i.e. their jobs and social roles. People work on their outer traits; it is developing the inner traits that saves you all the work. You automatically say "thank you" when somebody serves you with something, because you feel gratitude. Therefore, you can see the simple small things of life make the difference. We think that we are not really accomplishing anything unless it is a major project, unless you save the unwed mothers, or save the poverty- stricken in India or do something big. No, it is the **small things of life** that accumulate into a positive karma field, and it is true that **it only takes a bone to make a dog happy**. Ask yourself, "What does it take to make me happy?" Dr. Hawkins said for himself the answer is, "All it takes is a sip of soda." A sip of soda is all it took to make him happy.

There is a nice song, **"Don't Worry, Be Happy" and you sing that little song in your mind**. That actually was a recorded song many years ago, by Bobby McFerrin and is available in the form of a singing prop, "Big Mouth Billy Bass". If you have had a feeling of good will towards all of life, including people encountered in the phenomena of your life, and you feel gratitude, say something like, "Here I am in a nice house, I have got doggies and kitties, I have got TV in the other room, and I have got my sweetheart here. What more could I want? Nothing, being completely 100% satisfied."

Prioritize your goals. **Choose spiritual values and goals,** the energy that they put out, what they stand for; it is their lovingness, their lovableness, their presence that makes all the difference. To love and appreciate that you are, and that it is what you are that contributes to the world. It is what the doggie is that makes you feel happy. You see the wagging tail of a dog; the dog is not really doing anything for you, he just is. The kitty purrs and what is it doing? It just is. What is it? It is a kitty purring and you feel an inner gladness about the goodness of life. So, with spiritual evolution you become more and more aware of the goodness of life. You get the intention of the people you are with, the people who designed the place where you are, the gifts of nature, the beautiful flowers and all the things you could possibly want that are here for you. What more could you ask? What is the purpose of the world? It is here for you. Why is this book here? It is here for you. Everything is here for your comfort. Now, you have to see beyond the egocentric, as to what it means, "The world is here for you." Out of Divine intention, that which is here is here for you, because the divinity of all that exists shines forth. The essence of all that exists is Divinity Itself. All you are seeing is Divinity in its various expressions all around you: Divinity in its expression as the flowers, Divinity as a soda pop, Divinity as a wonderful friend, Divinity as a Kleenex, etc. You have a Kleenex available because God wants you to have a Kleenex available. If God did not want you to have a Kleenex, there would not be any Kleenexes. Happiness is therefore a goal within easy reach of a grateful heart.

101 WAYS TO HAPPINESS (11)

60. Choose spiritual friends and groups

61. Go from complete to complete

62. Identify with Self rather than self

63. Accept limitations of humanness

Slide 177

SLIDE 177: 101 WAYS TO HAPPINESS (11)

This slide was introduced at the April 2009 lecture, DVD disc 2 at 011930.

Choose Spiritual friends and groups. The alignment with spiritual friends and groups itself has a positive karmic effect. The effect of a spiritual group is very powerful, well known in certain circles such as Alcoholics Anonymous. A person does very well in the energy field of AA, which of course is at 540 and over. They do very well and so they say, "I don't need AA anymore and will just go out on my own." Next thing, they are back in the bar, saying "poor me, poor me". The field of energy of the group supports you. A group with a powerful collective intention is overwhelming and literally affects the consciousness level of all of humanity.

One influences all of humanity by becoming the most spiritually evolved and aware creature that one can be.

One serves God and all of humanity by being as spiritually advanced as one is capable of being. Do not see yourself as wanting, lacking or incomplete. That which you are now is complete. You do not go from incomplete to complete, you **go from complete to complete**, "I am completely all that I am right now. I am completely all that I am right now. I am -- So I move from complete to complete to complete. If I could be sweeter, more loving, more generous, more adoring than I am right now, I would be so." You go from complete to complete because you are and you have all that you could possibly want. You are completely all that you can be right now. Then maybe next year you will be completely all that you can be next year with a new car. That is just what completion is. That is not what it is here and that is not where it will be ten years from now. Part of being complete is having what you need, what you like, etc. Go from complete to complete. Do not go from lack to fulfillment, you go from fulfillment to fulfillment, "If I could be taller, handsomer and richer, I would be. I am good where I am, now, okay."

So, in doing this you end up **identifying with the large Self**. The large Self is infinite and perfect and beyond all time. It is beyond imperfection and you identify with that. **The "small self"** is only our temporary expression in this domain. The Self is complete and needs nothing. It is beyond time, Self-fulfilling, the presence of God as Love Itself, with no beginning and no end. Without the presence of God within you, you would not exist. Therefore, the small self owes its existence to the large Self and humility is when this self begins to acknowledge that this Self is its source: "an Infinite Presence of Infinite Love, with no beginning and no end, not different from that which I am. That which I am always existed, and will always exist. It has no beginning and no end." That comes as a revelation all of its own, without a single thought. Also in that state, you have permission to leave the world. There is no reason further to continue in a physical existence, as the purpose of one's human lifetime is complete, allowing the spirit for its next great adventure in a different domain. You have permission to leave the world and the knowingness of the reality of that which you are is the presence of God within you. One is happy to be here when you realize that you could actually leave if you wanted to.

Accept the limitations of humanness, protoplasm. You have chosen to learn what can be learned only in the world of protoplasm. Humanness has the karma of protoplasm. Therefore, humanness is a temporary condition, a protoplasmic awareness, and we must accept the limitations of humanness, it is okay to be a human.

101 WAYS TO HAPPINESS (12)

64. Happiness is a destination and direction

65. Reflective vs. impulsive

66. Thoughtful rather than critical

67. Be content instead of complaining

68. Realize life is a learning curve

Slide 178

SLIDE 178: 101 WAYS TO HAPPINESS (12)

This slide was introduced at the April 2009 lecture, DVD disc 2 at 012715.

Happiness is a destination and direction, as you move progressively higher up the scale of consciousness. It is an intention that you wish to be happy and not make it dependent on anything external. "I will be happy if I get that car, I'll be happy if I get that promotion, I'll be happy if I get a fried egg sandwich" may be where one starts the spiritual journey but that attitude keeps happiness away. Happiness is an overall intention, a destination and direction.

One way to get there is **reflection versus impulsivity**. Meditation is a wonderful spiritual technique, but it is limited in time and space, e.g. you cannot drive your car and also be in a meditative state. **Being reflective versus impulsive,** as you move through the world and make decisions, you become increasingly reflective of all the nuances and the implications and the overall spiritual context. **Impulsiveness** results from the lack of incorporation of social values and respect for authority. The 'Id' aspect of the ego expects to be self-indulgent with no consequences or accountability and sees social structure as a frustrating its impulsiveness. This brings up the superego, the punitive inner parent within us and the task of the inner adult is to acknowledge impulsiveness without triggering guilt attacks of self-hatred, anger, or resentment of self or others and through **reflection**/contemplation, become spiritually aware. The Self is experienced as compassion for all of life in all its expressions, including its evolution as one's personal self. Consequently, forgiveness replaces condemnation, which is a sign that it is now safe to proceed deeper into serious inner inventory without undue stress.

Thoughtful rather than critical: Thoughtfulness is caring, a form of unconditional love, but one can always find something to criticize like criticizing the weather, e.g. this place is too windy and blowing my hat off or it is too hot, too cold, etc. One can enjoy the downside of being a human and then realize that it is not really a downside. Any human should complain about the wind blowing your hat off all the time. Stand up for being a human. Complaining can be brave, courageous and honest: I am here to complain about the weather, I am here to complain about taxes.

Be contented instead of complaining but also one can be content with complaining. Why should we not be complaining? We can be content "with" complaining, i.e. with a call for action where required within or without. Any human worth his salt is going to complain. Somebody who does not complain is not worth the bother. If you care about life, you will complain about it. One reason for complaining is that because you care about life, you can register a suggestion for improvement. If you did not care about life, you would not complain. You would not complain about the neighborhood if you do not live there. To be content instead of complaining is a goal and **realize that life is a learning curve**. You are some place on the curve. You are not perfect, nor are you completely an idiot. So be willing to accept that you are where you are. Happiness is a destination and a direction and all these ways are helpful to keep in view: Reflective versus impulsive, thoughtful rather than critical, be content instead of complaining, and realize life is a learning curve.

101 WAYS TO HAPPINESS (13)

69. **Pray**
70. **Contemplate**
71. **Affirm God is my Source and solution**
72. **Sing an inner song**
73. **When feeling down, say to yourself, "Yours is the saddest story I've ever heard!"**

Slide 179

SLIDE 179: 101 WAYS TO HAPPINESS (13)

This slide was introduced at the April 2009 lecture, DVD disc 2 at 013200.

We **pray** for help. You ask yourself, "does praying do any good? Am I just talking to myself?" Praying helps but there can be a doubt that it is just imaginary, like grade school kindergarten stuff. "Praying is beneficial", "Benefits yourself", "Benefits loved ones", "Benefits the world", "Benefits all of humanity" (all these calibrate true.) So praying is not just a grade school exercise that you do, but praying actually is an expression of what you have become. You have become gracious. Thank the Lord for all the gifts of this day, both seen and unseen. You ask for God's direction in your life and dedicate all your actions towards Divinity in all of its expressions. One of its expressions is creation and part of creation is humankind. **So pray, contemplate, and affirm that God is my Source, inspiration and solution.** These are some of the most helpful spiritual techniques to put to good use at various times.

One can **sing an inner song**, "Don't Worry, Be Happy" Sing an inner song. You hear a child sitting there happily in his highchair, he has mush all over his face, mush all over his lap and he is just going 'hum, hum, hum...' Now inside of you is still the inner child. So one way to be happy is to speak to your inner child and parent it. You go, 'hum, hum, hum…' and continue humming, looking around and walking around until you can get good at it. You can teach your inner child to hum all the time. Then of course, the inner mother says, "don't be humming like that in church and the grocery store" and so you learn how to hum quietly, softly. Finally, your mother says, "stop that, people are going to think you're mental or something" and so you learn to hum to yourself without making any noise, hum to yourself even when talking, in the back of your mind. Confirm God as your Source and solution, and sing an inner song.

If you are feeling down, you can put this on your mirror wherever you put yourself together in the morning. It says, **"Yours is the saddest story I've ever heard!"** People love self-pity. Instead of criticizing yourself for self-pity, enjoy it. As Dr. Hawkins shared, "Yours is the saddest story, you have gone and lost your thumb. I am not even ready to leave this world and the thumb has gone ahead of me. I go to heaven, and there is the thumb waiting for me, saying, 'Where have you been, for God's sake, I've been waiting here for 45 years for you to get here.' That is sad. Poor old thumb. Oh, aw, darn it. So, I can have a temper tantrum.

Temper tantrum and self-pity are good to acknowledge and be aware of, (Ha, Ha.)"

101 WAYS TO HAPPINESS (14)

74. Insist on being miserable and gloomy

75. Make faces at yourself in the mirror

76. Be grateful for the gift of life

77. Live one day at a time

78. Be your own best friend

Slide 180

SLIDE 180: 101 WAYS TO HAPPINESS (14)

This slide was introduced at the April 2009 lecture, DVD disc 2 at 013910.

When you are down and out, what is wrong is to fight it. When you are down and out and you are fighting being miserable and gloomy, **insist on being miserable and gloomy**. Acknowledge to yourself all your problems such as your socks do not match, you have a hole in one of them, all your shirts are dirty and wrinkled, the bedding fell on the floor during the night and the cat slept on it, etc. Insist on being miserable and gloomy. Happiness is not going to do any good anyway. What good is happiness? You can be happy and someone can run over you the next day, ha-ha! You can be happy and you do not pay your income tax, and they put you away. You can be happy and go over the speed limit, and they give you a ticket. What is there to be happy about? It is better to be miserable and gloomy and feel the feelings. At least nobody interferes with you then, and the feelings eventually run out.

Make faces at yourself in the mirror. That is a great technique and you cannot beat it, making faces at yourself in the mirror. You look at yourself and you go, (made all kinds of faces). It is hard to stay depressed and miserable when you make faces at yourself in the mirror. When you do that, tell yourself "Yours is the saddest story I have ever heard." Ha-ha. You have a sad, sad story. Every year you are a year older. One more year creeping, all day it is just creeping on you. Say, "I heard you are creeping", and make faces at yourself in the mirror. That is a very good one. You stop taking yourself so seriously. You see all of the options opening up to you. It is a wonderful spiritual practice. It is a spiritual technique, the holy churches of the giggles, the way to God through giggles.

Be grateful for the gift of life. When everything else settles down, you say, "Well, this is wrong, that is wrong, these bad things have happened to me, but I've had the gift of life. By living the gift of life in a certain way, I have great hope of and look forward to the afterlife." Be grateful for the gift of life: If you do all these exercises, you will be grateful for the gift of life, because you really enjoy life. It is easy to be grateful if you enjoy life. If you let your inner kid loose, you are fearless and spontaneous and you love everything that you encounter throughout the day. You end up feeling grateful for the gift of life. How else would one express one's love for everyone present except by being present? Sometimes, it is only by being here and now, jabbering away and enjoying everyone's presence that one can have a wonderful time. So be all that you can be to everyone all the time, either physically present or not necessarily physically present. To be all that you can be to life, and if nothing else, you reflect back to life its beauty so that life knows that you are recognizing its beauty. When you walk through the woods, the trees realize the divinity of your essence. Trees actually know it. The trees are actually aware in a nonverbal contextual knowingness (tests true).

Live one day at a time and do the best you can. Yesterday is gone forever and tomorrow never gets here. Tomorrow is going to be tomorrow's tomorrow. So live only today, being present to what is present. And try to **be your own best friend**. That is the way to recognize and be aware that your life counts. Be kind, be a good neighbor to yourself.

101 WAYS TO HAPPINESS (15)

79. Expansion vs. diminution of problems

80. Clarify confusion of Self with social role

81. Play the role of martyr? Injustice Collector?

82. Play the role of hero?

83. Play the role of victim?

84. Play the role of morally superior?

Slide 181

SLIDE 181: 101 WAYS TO HAPPINESS (15)

This slide was introduced at the April 2009 lecture, DVD disc 2 at 014455.

Expansion vs. diminution of problems: Diminish problems. They are all nothing, an artifact of perception, an illusion. You have to choose whether you are going to expand on a problem or diminish it. Are you going to be a diminisher or an expander? Are you the one to say, "OH MY GOD, we are out of eggs!" and expand the problem, or are you the one who very calmly says, "We are out of eggs, so we'll have cereal for a change." Both options are available and your day is either ruined, as we are all out of eggs or you can be happy with acceptance that, oh great, we will have cereal for a change.

Clarify the confusion of your Self with your social role. The Self is one thing; your social role is quite another. You can learn to be in the higher Self and fulfill any social role without changing identification. Am I **playing the role of martyr or injustice collector**? Oh, the world loves injustice collectors, "Look how they did me wrong." Claim the moral high ground, "Look how the world is mistreating me because of everything, my age, my sex, my color, my religion, my country I live in. Look how the world is treating me unjustly." You have the option of **playing the role of the victim or the hero.**

Play the role of morally superior, gooder than you, yep. The competition for moral superiority in this world is intense. You think it is money. No, it is moral superiority, to make somebody wrong. For example, if someone believes in heterosexual marriage, they can hate and curse those that are not in a heterosexual marriage, "Who do you think you are?" "If it were not for heterosexual marriage, you would not be here, idiot." We defend and make excuses for our thoughts and are jealous of our beliefs. We prize them and alternately despise and punish ourselves with guilt and self-hatred. The self-image is the stage upon which the drama of our life unfolds, and all along, we have been in love with it. To let go of it brings up fear of loss. To the self, all love objects external to it are a source of happiness. The self thrives on injustice, martyrdom, failure, and guilt and secretly 'loves' the position of victimhood, extracting a distorted pleasure from pain and suffering. The 'loser' is an almost romanticized figure in music and folklore e.g., the 'bag lady', the rejected lover, etc.

We think that the loss of a love object brings grief, but actually, the grief is about the loss of the attachment itself, which is due to the illusion that one has lost a source of happiness, and that the source of happiness is 'out there'. If one looks at the sensation of happiness, it becomes clear that it is actually located within, and felt under favorable circumstances when the mind experiences a desired outcome. The external event with the desired outcome merely triggers an inner innate capacity. With the discovery that the source of happiness is actually within one's inner self and therefore cannot be lost, there is a reduction of fear. Viewed from Reality, thoughts are actually an 'out there' and can be dispensed with altogether because they interfere with the achievement of true happiness.

101 WAYS TO HAPPINESS (16)

85. Let go of being injustice collector

86. Let go of being provocative

87. Stop pushing one's luck

88. Avoid catastrophe

89. Do not buy a house in the flood plain or on the edge of a mud cliff

90. Do not win the lottery

Slide 182

SLIDE 182: 101 WAYS TO HAPPINESS (16)

This slide was introduced at the April 2009 lecture, DVD disc 2 at 014550.

Let go of being an injustice collector, nursing grievances and, by paranoid extension, collecting grievances to justify hostility. We watch that all day on television, "Oh, how unjust it is!" There is a competition for injustice collectors in the media, as if looking out for the reward of being the most martyred. It is a basic dictum that perception finds what it seeks. In Reality, there is no such thing as a 'justified resentment'.

Let go of being provocative to others. The spiritually advanced person no longer needs to look outside themselves for happiness. Every time you see yourself getting provoked, you say, "Well, I may have triggered that." So see yourself, your unconscious intention as the trigger and source of events. If you see an event happen in your life that you are not happy about, ask, "How could I have been the trigger of that?" instead of blaming it on the other person. The other person is impatient, so you get mad at them for being impatient, and then you recall that you kept them waiting for ten minutes while you stood there and brushed your teeth.

Stop pushing one's luck. People like to say they are not responsible for what happens in one's life. Let us say you had a doctor's appointment at nine in the morning and the weather news said there was going to be a tornado in your area around that time and to stay off the route to your doctor's office. Instead of pushing your luck and then blaming it on the weather, you can just cancel the doctor's appointment. Simple enough, but you can see how many people would push it, keep the doctor's appointment, go off the road, get rescued by a tow truck and have a long sad story. So do not keep pushing your luck. **Avoid catastrophes**, but when caught unawares in one, pray in earnest, surrendering at great depth to God. "Man's catastrophe is God's opportunity", as almost all survivors of major disasters spontaneously recount that they prayed in earnest, and some even went into a state of profound peace subsequent to prayer and surrendering to God. They report being in a state of profound stillness and peace that was outside of time, and they were almost sad when the disaster such as a tornado ended and they returned to a normal mental state. It is important to note that the discovery of the Presence of God is not due to fear but to the surrender precipitated by the fear.

Do not buy a house on the flood plain or on the edge of a mud cliff. Every so often, there is a sad story that someone built a house on the edge of a mud cliff and the mud cliff slid down along with the house. Ask yourself, "Who in the world would build a house on the edge of a mud cliff?" People seem to do it all the time. You can drive down certain places on the California coast and sure enough, you see the phenomenon of "mud cliff house". The house is just edging itself closer and closer to the edge. The cliffs keep falling down and they keep buying houses right on the edge of the cliff. Soon enough, the cliffs start falling down. Do not buy one there.

Do not win the lottery. Have you ever seen the story of what happens to people's lives when they win the lottery? The divorce rate is close to 100%, murder and suicide rates go up dramatically, and surprisingly, half of them become bankrupt. How can you win the lottery and go bankrupt? They figured out how to do it.

101 WAYS TO HAPPINESS (17)

91. **Do not ski in an avalanche area**

92. **Give up the self-importance of being the protester**

93. **Obey the law - be polite to police**

94. **Stop demonstrating**

95. **Give up saving the world**

96. **Mind your own business**

Slide 183

SLIDE 183: 101 WAYS TO HAPPINESS (17)

This slide was introduced at the April 2009 lecture, DVD disc 2 at 014705.

Do not ski in an avalanche area. This is one of the things difficult to digest when watching the news. Someone goes up in the avalanche area and of course, he almost dies, his skis turn over and they have to send an ambulance and a plane to get him. Anybody who wants to climb, it would be good to make them post a several hundred, or $1000 bond with the state. It will act as a deterrent, motivating prudence if everyone did so before attempting to climb mountain peaks, etc. The people who did not make it have cost the taxpayers a fortune. It makes sense that if someone is going to climb a high mountain like Mount Everest you have to post a prohibitively expensive bond with the parks department.

Give up the self-importance of being the protester. Protesters calibrate in the levels of Pride (~180), indicating defective reasoning, narcissism, and progressive inability to differentiate *res interna* from *res externa*. In contrast, persons above 200 rely on reason, fact, and the balance that results from inclusion of context, replacing emotions and partiality of levels below 200.

Obey the law - be polite to the police. All these things seem so simple, yet every day on the news, one sees people mouth off to the police. A cop is the last person one would want to offend. Unrestrained by society, the narcissistic ego is like an engine without a flywheel, and with maturity one begins to understand that the police and laws ensure one's true freedom by denying the ego's illusory substitute of unaccountability and irresponsibility.

Stop demonstrating. Every day one sees demonstrators out there. They have these big signs because they are going to demonstrate. Always ask, "Who cares what you think?" They are pro- this or anti-that. Why would anybody care what you think about anything? Anyway, they take it very seriously. Stop demonstrating, and focus on self-transformation instead, thereby best serving yourself and others.

It is a good idea to **give up saving the world.** Strive for spiritual purification instead, realizing that the world is within you, a gift from God. The spiritual aspirant has to give up the vanities of opinionation and the duties of saving the world. One's inner spiritual evolution is of greater value to society than any form of doingness, however noble it may seem.

It is a great idea to **mind your own business.** The ego does not want to hear, "mind your own business." It says instead, "It is my responsibility as a citizen to get out there and demonstrate." The core error is that the ego's dualistic, distorted perception sees everything in terms of the perpetrator/victim model. This releases hatred and the production of the "straw man", who is then subject to vilification and attack. Until now, it has actually escaped man's discernment that truth brings peace, whereas falsehood brings fear. By that sign, it is possible to tell the difference.

101 WAYS TO HAPPINESS (18)

97. Give up being important

98. Improve oneself instead of others

99. Pay your income taxes

100. Smile and the world smiles with you

101. Dedicate all actions to God

Slide 184

SLIDE 184: 101 WAYS TO HAPPINESS (18)

This slide was introduced at the April 2009 lecture, DVD disc 2 at 014745.

Give up being important. What goes on with demonstrators, protesters, and marchers is that they get a feeling of being important. The narcissistic core of the ego is concerned only with an inflated self-importance. When it dawns on the ego that the universe is indifferent to its wants, it goes into a rage that transposes into patterns of interpersonal conflict. The best defense against this is to see others as equals, lessen expectations, and via humility, surrender the fulfillment of one's wants to God.

Improve yourself instead of others. The ego focuses externally and takes great pride in finding flaws in others. The beginning step in spirituality is to shift the focus from others to one's own inner self. Trying to improve others instead of yourself is a fool's game that keeps you stuck in thinkingness and imagination. This becomes an insurmountable bar to the nonlinear domains that start at level 500. The steps to self-realization take one from the materialistic plane through self-improvement, to the plane of morality and virtues that lead eventually to the realization of the nonlinear levels of love, from where advancement to the nondual levels becomes a possibility.

Another idea is to **pay your income taxes**. This never seems to dawn on the leaders of our country. There is not a big name leader out there who is not behind in his or her income taxes or else involved in some kind of a financial issue. That is the funniest thing. No matter who they are, the President's cabinet often consists of people who do not pay their income taxes. The news leaks every so often that even the head of the tax department has not paid his taxes.

Smile and the world smiles with you, cry and you cry alone. Everything we see is the result of our thoughts. There are no "idle thoughts" and our meaningless thoughts give rise to the perception of an illusionary world. Every thought we have brings either love or fear; either a smile or a cry. A neutral result is impossible because a neutral thought is impossible and we influence everything and everyone around us with our thoughts. We as humans communicate our state of awareness to others all the time but are mostly not aware of this fact. Becoming conscious of this "secret", no sane human will want to see others sad and will take every opportunity to make life more joyful for all by transforming into a smiling, joyous person. What the people in the world actually want is the recognition of who they really are on the highest level, and to see that the same Self radiates forth within everyone heals their feeling of separation, and brings about a feeling of peace.

Dedicate all actions to God: If you dedicate all your actions to God, they automatically become changed and purified. If you dedicate this demonstration to God, you have to fool yourself into thinking that your ego is Divinity, because nobody is going to be pleased about you demonstrating except your ego. All of these ways to happiness bring about an inner humility and it is the inner humility that stops listening to the voice of the ego and in its place chooses the silence of God. That God is 'All That Is' becomes readily apparent without a single thought. The Divinity of all that exists shines forth. All that exists is Divinity. Without Divinity there is no sky, there is no earth, there is no table, and there is no audience. The only thing that exists is Divinity, period. All is God in the infinite number of expressions as people, as stage, as sore knee, as cane, as a cup of coffee (calibrates true.) The capacity to exist is solely that of Divinity. That makes life simple.

101 WAYS TO PEACE (1)

1. **Let go of trying to change and control others**
2. **Let go of wanting to 'get even'**
3. **Let go of wanting to be 'right' and making others 'wrong'**
4. **Practice discernment rather than judgmentalism**

Slide 185

SLIDE 185: 101 WAYS TO PEACE (1)

This slide was introduced at the August 2009 lecture, DVD disc 1 at 005415.

Peacefulness has to be a decision that one makes and can exist right in the middle of war, devastation and catastrophe. To develop a peaceful nature, the first thing to do is to **let go of trying to change and control others**. Do not tell them how to vote. Give up questionable advertising. The ego always wants other people to be different than they are, thinking, "Why can't they be more like me? If I cannot change them, if I'm stuck with them, well, then at least I can control them." Just noticing and becoming aware of how often your mind would like to change people and make them different than they are will help you overcome this defect.

The next important thing to have peace of mind is to **let go of wanting to 'get even'**. You can let go of wanting to get even if you understand divine justice; it saves you the bother of getting even because everything is taken care of by the Divine presence of God. All things then, karmically, have their own karmic payoff and you do not have to do anything. It is not necessary to bring down your enemies because they will bring themselves down by their own hand and in that process, you are not stuck with any new karma. The minute you get even with them or conquer them, etc., you now have the karma of that. If somebody falls over, it is better that it happens of its own rather than you putting a bullet in them. The mind thinks and the spirit knows.

Let go of wanting to be right. This is extremely difficult in the human condition. In our society, getting even and being right is acceptable behavior, so most people do that. The other thing that goes on is **making other people wrong**. If you are right, then the other people must be wrong. The struggle for moral superiority, of being right is intense. Data that is in conflict with personal beliefs are best handled by viewing such information as a 'possible alternative' rather than as a 'make wrong', which automatically summons up the ego's indignation. Although the human mind likes to believe that it is 'of course' dedicated to truth, in reality, what it really seeks is confirmation of what it already believes. The ego is innately prideful and does not welcome the revelation that much of its beliefs are merely perceptual illusions.

We learn to **practice discernment rather than judgmentalism**. All things are in the process of evolution. Perception arbitrarily selects a cross-section of Reality, and puts it up on the screen, showing how reality looks, taking it out of the timeless context of karmic evolution, like a camera that records an instantaneous point in time and place. The reason you cannot judge anyone based on perception is that all you have is an appearance, a snapshot. What a thing looks like based on perceptual limitations is not what it is. Discernment is interested in finding out the essence of something, differentiating truth from falsehood. So when you ask the Holy Spirit for a miracle, you are asking for a recontextualization of the illusion of sequence/appearance. The Holy Spirit dissolves the illusion, as sequential observation is not Reality and that is not how things are happening. All judgments - good or bad - are rooted in perceptual illusion, as being human we are not aware of the evolutionary context of time at that point. When we admit that we are gullible and easily seduced by the senses and deluded by glamour, we have the beginning of discernment, which can be the simple process of avoiding everything that makes one go weak with the muscle test.

101 WAYS TO PEACE (2)

5. **Be modest with opinions**
6. **Perfect diplomacy skills and gentility**
7. **Be gracious and considerate**
8. **Keep serenity as a goal**
9. **It is okay to be 'wrong' or undecided**
10. **Calibrate options; be flexible**

Slide 186

SLIDE 186: 101 WAYS TO PEACE (2)

This slide was introduced at the August 2009 lecture, DVD disc 1 at 005905.

The way to have peace in your own life is to silence opinionation. In fact, it is not necessary to have an opinion about anything. One can completely accept the way things are going at this time and if God wanted them to be different, they would be. We learn to **be modest with our opinions,** and can give them up completely at a later stage. You say, "It seems to me at this time, that this is the way it appears to be." That is flexible. "It seems to me a certain way." That leaves room for you to move out of the way.

We learn to **perfect diplomacy skills and gentility**. In the upper classes of society, everybody has money, but it does not mean anything. Everybody has a title also but the most important thing is the capacity for diplomacy and gentility, the art of dealing with people in a sensitive, thoughtful and effective way. Every one of them is gracious and polite with a quietly appealing manner. That means considerate of others, having sensitivity to the needs of others. If someone has been standing a long time, the gracious ones ask, "Wouldn't you like a chair to sit? Could I get you something to drink, maybe water or a cup of coffee?" The top people in the world are extremely gracious, and solicitous of your comfort. This means not just physical comfort but psychological comfort, and spiritual comfort as well. Disagreements are fine because you want the other person to be honest with what they are.

You **become gracious and considerate** of others. People say, "What has all this got to do with God?" God is gracious and considerate. When you get to heaven, He says, "Would you like to float on this cloud here? Would you like to float over the sea?" God comes disguised to us in many different ways, as 'God is in everyone' is an experiential reality at spiritually advanced levels. So, when you hear, "Can I get you a cup of coffee, would you like to sit down? You look like you've had a long trip", what is talking to you is not a person, what is talking to you is Divinity. Because Divinity is that quality of consciousness; it is not a personhood, it has no gender, no age. Gentility, consideration for others are aspects of unconditional love. Unconditional lovingness is concern for the welfare of others, putting them first, that they have the most comfortable seats.

Keep inner serenity as a goal. What is the point of winning the argument and then not being able to sleep all night? "I guess I told him off! Boy, did I ever tell him off" are afterthoughts you do not want to have. You keep a sense of humor. Everything is comical when you look at it a certain way, from a high space. Here people are struggling to achieve all these things.

It is okay to be 'wrong' or undecided. People say, "What do you think about that?" You can say, "I don't know, I just haven't thought about it, I really can't tell you." People say, "Well, that's being wishy-washy." You can love being "wishy-washy". Another thing you can do when you are undecided, is to **calibrate the options and be flexible**. You do not have to have an opinion on everything or on anything. People say, "What do you think about so and so?" You can say, "Well, I don't know, I just haven't given it much thought yet. I am going to think about it after dinner tonight."

101 WAYS TO PEACE (3)

11. It is not necessary to have an opinion on everything

12. Avoid peace demonstrations

13. Remember that Socrates was short and ugly

14. Value wisdom over being 'right'

15. Seek wise counsel

Slide 187

SLIDE 187: 101 WAYS TO PEACE (3)

This slide was introduced at the August 2009 lecture, DVD disc 1 at 010815.

It is not necessary to have an opinion on everything. All opinion is merely provisional, tentative, and transitory. The ego's structuring of mental processes misidentifies opinion as truth and actual reality (e.g., solipsism). If you want to live a peaceful life and be peaceful, one of the first rules is **avoid peace demonstrations**. Peace demonstrations invariably are violent, and have dogs, water cannons, police all over the place, and thugs. Usually what goes on at a peace demonstration is thuggery. One can start a riot anywhere in a few minutes for a few dollars. The communists learned how to do that, and perfected the art of it. You go to the nearest low-class bar. You say, "I got fifty bucks here. Now what I want you to do, there are some guys out there that stole my car and my girlfriend and I want you to give them a good poke in the nose and teach them a lesson." Ten dollars apiece, one can get five persons to leave any bar anytime and you have two shots at a beer when you get back. The next thing you know there is a riot on the street and then they call the police. All spontaneous demonstrations are staged; if it was not staged, why would they all be on a street corner? How do you get fifty people on a street corner? You get it by "barroom organizing". Nearest barroom will get you demonstrators in two minutes and demonstrators love demonstrating, so they will pull in more demonstrators. Next thing you know the knuckles are going and the police are there, it is wonderful excitement, everybody's adrenalin goes up, and they are having a good time. So, if you want to be peaceful, avoid peace demonstrations because they are too violent.

All of you who pine to be beautiful and rich and all, **remember that Socrates was short and ugly**. It is okay to be short and ugly. Socrates became world-famous for centuries. He was neither tall nor handsome, nor rich. **Value wisdom over being right**. It is not necessary to be right unless you feel that you have to fight for your image, the image that you have to be right. It is of greater value to be understanding.

One thing that people ignore in our current society is to **seek wise counsel**. You do not have to solve everything all by yourself without discussing it with anybody. Everybody should have somebody, a mentor that one looks up to, that one respects. It can be just a very good friend. Instead of keeping everything to yourself and sweating it out, you can talk to people that you respect because you get feedback. There is a reason for it other than just the practicality. It is so that you do not get so egotistical about whatever your conclusion is: you did not conclude to do that all by yourself, you discussed it with a friend and the two of you decided that. Well, if two of you decided that, then you will not say, "Well, I am the one that picked the winning ticket, you know what I mean, l picked the winning ticket." If you discuss the best ticket to buy with somebody else, then it is a shared, joint decision and that protects you from egotistical inflation. We are looking for ways to transcend the ego and allow the spirit to take over and this is one of the ways. You get feedback from other people as they have other ways of looking at it and so, sometimes they will say, "That sounds good, but you could look at it this way too", and you had not thought of that. So it is good to have a confessor, a counselor, a therapist, everybody should have a psychotherapist, everybody. People who think they do not need a therapist are the most gone of all. Have a good spouse, have somebody you can confide in, share, share in reaching decisions, and it serves your highest good.

101 WAYS TO PEACE (4)

16. **Realize you influence others by what you *are* vs. do**
17. **Avoid activism and pedantry**
18. **Be grateful for your assets**
19. **Mankind has survived millions of years without your help**
20. **Be your own best friend**
21. **Be wary of 'do-gooders'**

Slide 188

SLIDE 188: 101 WAYS TO PEACE (4)

This slide was introduced at the August 2009 lecture, DVD disc 2 at 000800.

Realize that you influence others by what you are, not just by what you do. We subtly are constantly influencing actually all of mankind by what we are. What you are is more important than what you do because what you are radiates out an energy that influences everyone. What you are, what you have become is more powerful. People say, "What can I do to help mankind?" Well, become the most loving, evolved person that you can. Love all of life in all of its expressions. Be respectful of nature and beauty. Esteem beauty and nature. Realize that you influence others by what you are, not by what you do. You radiate out loving energy into the field of consciousness, which influences everyone. The best thing that you can do for the world is to sit down and shut up. The kind thoughts that you have towards others, the kindly thoughts, the kindly intention that you have towards others tends to influence all of mankind, the whole field of consciousness of mankind. Realize that you are influencing others right now, not by what you say, but by what you are.

That is why it is best to **avoid activism and pedantry**. People say, "Well, isn't that the American way?" It is the American way of certain people in America at certain times, but it is not a way of being in the world. Once you choose spirituality as a lifestyle, you can give up the activist signs and the parades, most of which is egoistic display. Most activism is egocentricity, "Look at me, how important I am. And listen to me because what I have to say is so important." It is not important to anybody except you. Activists get on TV and they have a thing around their neck saying they are a blogger-activist. They actually get on TV and someone asks, "What have you blogged lately?" Their answer is, "Screw you" or something like that.

Be grateful for your assets. Be glad if you are smart or good-looking, or if you are tolerant, or your biggest asset is that you have become interested in spiritual evolution and spirituality, and serving God and your fellow man. It is helpful to your ego to remind yourself that **mankind has survived millions of years without your help**. The ego thinks, "I don't know how mankind got along without me all these years." Intrinsic to spiritual evolution is humility. Therefore, "Yours is the saddest story I have ever heard" is a good one. And one can also add to it another sentence, "Mankind has survived without you so far." That way you do not take yourself so seriously. By doing all these things, you become your own best friend. Putting a little thing on your mirror that says, "Yours is the saddest story I have ever heard" and "Mankind has survived millions of years without you," you are already **being your own best friend**. You are putting a leash on your ego, reminding yourself of the reality that you are of benefit to humankind to the degree that you radiate God's unconditional love to the world. **You are your own best friend** and you are doing everything you can for the world.

Be wary of do-gooders. The world is full of do-gooders. The history of do-gooders is rather catastrophic. There are always do-gooders in politics. They like to control other people. They are after one thing or another: candy, peanut butter, booze, chewing tobacco, etc. There is always a do-gooder going to do something good for you, meaning control you. What they mean is they want to control you in a certain way, "It is for your own health." One can counter, "Let me worry about my health. The longer I live, the more it costs the taxpayer."

101 WAYS TO PEACE (5)

22. Read *Do-Gooders* by Mona Charen

23. Let others win

24. Beware of unintended consequences

25. The innocent child is present in everyone

26. Pray to see things differently - reframe/recontextualize

Slide 189

SLIDE 189: 101 WAYS TO PEACE (5)

This slide was introduced at the August 2009 lecture, DVD disc 2 at 001520.

Read "Do-Gooders: How Liberals Hurt Those They Claim to Help (and the Rest of Us) (2005)", an interesting book by **Mona Charen**. Dr. Hawkins experienced some of it in detail. At one time, he had the largest psychiatric practice in the United States for many years in addition to a hospital practice. He was also in charge of many state hospitals where there were up to 9000 patients. The do-gooders came along and said, "Well, there is no such thing as mental illness, that's just a myth." It was a stupid thing to say, not well-thought out at all but the authorities fell for it, opened the doors of the state hospitals and let these poor "victims" out. Victimology pictured these poor souls as being the victims of the system and that the hospital was unjustifiably incarcerating them. The reality was these people were not capable of taking care of themselves on the outside. The authorities closed the doors to these hospitals, all these patients went out into the street and they became today's street people. The street people you see in any big city years back were in a hospital. In the mental hospital they received three meals a day, balanced by dietitians, free medical treatment and legal protection, they got all kinds of protection. Anyway, Mona Charen details that do-gooders always have something wonderful they think will be good for you.

Another way to peace is to **let others win**. Letting others win is very gratifying and it makes them very happy. So, letting other people win arguments, you say, "you're right, honey, you're right, dear, yep." Your spouse may say, "We'll do as you say, we'll do as you say, yeah." That puts her on top. Now you have to think of a way to counter that, to be on top of that one. **Beware of unintended consequences**. This is a relatively well-known phenomenon in society: you intend for a thing to go in a certain direction and there are other factors involved that you are not aware of which result in unforeseen results.

Realize that in trying to develop compassion for people and their propensity to make grave errors, there is **the innocent child that is present in everyone**. The innocent child in all of us says, "Let us go save the mentally ill, they are being imprisoned against their will, mental illness is just a myth anyway." Who believes that? The innocent child is present in everyone. You can also call it the idiot child. The reason you believe what you believe is that the innocent child in you believes it. Within us is the child, the adult and the parent and so the child within you tends to believe the adult and especially the parent. The parent within you says, "Well, I read it in the paper or I saw it on television or I read a good book on it." That is enough to impress the child. All the political discussions that you hear so heatedly on TV and other places are appealing to the innocent child in other people: "This one must know what they are talking about, because he has this title, the czar of something, they must know what they are discussing." The innocent child believes that. The government believes it. The voters believe it. Who would even suspect that none of them know what they are doing?

Pray to see things differently, **reframe and recontextualize**. To lower levels of consciousness, prayer is an attempt to 'get' something for self or others, such as a new car, a job, recovery from an illness, etc. With progress, the act of supplication becomes a dedication instead of a request. Prayer becomes surrender rather than supplication.

101 WAYS TO PEACE (6)

27. **Accept that the majority of people calibrate below 200**
28. **"Judge not lest ye be judged"**
29. **All viewpoints are arbitrary**
30. **Renew thankfulness, gratitude**
31. **The mind is an 'it', not a 'you'**
32. **Critics are a dime a dozen**

Slide 190

SLIDE 190: 101 WAYS TO PEACE (6)

This slide was introduced at the August 2009 lecture, DVD disc 2 at 002230.

Accept that the majority of people calibrate below 200, and reduce your expectations so you will not be disappointed. The fact that they are surviving and they still have a job and are taking care of the kids is good enough. Humanity is not anywhere as evolved as you think it is. A lot of the criticism that we have of others, politics, or anything else in our society, is the expectation of a higher level of consciousness than people are at, as the majority of people cannot tell truth from falsehood. The human mind, humanity, people, whole nations, whole civilizations are unable to tell truth from falsehood. We tailor our expectations of the world and become more forgiving.

"**Judge not lest ye be judged**." It does not mean to go to sleep and be unaware of reality and the essence of things. What it means is to realize that people cannot help being themselves because of their own inner limitation. Therefore, everyone is intrinsically innocent. To say they could be better is a hypothetical egotism. To recognize that somebody is a crook who is on the take is merely a recognition of the truth. That is different from judgmentalism. Judgmentalism says he should not be that way. Well, if he could be different than he is, he would be.

All viewpoints are arbitrary, because they all represent positionality, and are the result of framing. Looked at from this viewpoint, it looks like "this"; looked at from a different viewpoint it looks like "that". All viewpoints are arbitrary and therefore, you judge not. Realize that any judgment that you can make represents a viewpoint and that viewpoint itself is arbitrary. That saves us the problem of getting into fixed positionalities of rigidity. A spiritually evolved person avoids rigidity. It does not mean they lose the certainty of reality as they have known it, but it is no longer an arbitrary position. There are people who do not believe in God and one can understand them completely. They rant and rave about the evil of religion and Godness and all that. Suffering of humanity is due to the lack of spiritual evolution and the ignorance that accompanies being deaf, dumb and blind to the presence of Divinity. Therefore, we **renew thankfulness and gratitude**. Every day and every night we pray, "Our Father, who art in heaven, etc." If you watch TV shows like the *Ice Road Truckers*, this person as he is driving this truck, he is saying "The Lord's Prayer" out aloud, 30 below zero in this huge giant truck. He is about half a minute from death, if the ice breaks through he is a dead goner. And he is saying "The Lord's Prayer" out loud. "Our Father, who art in Heaven," he says, as he drives his truck up near Alaska. Very impressive is his utter simplicity.

In the enlightened state, you realize you are not the body, you are not the mind, you are something that goes beyond and encompasses both of them. **The mind is an "it," it is not a "you."** The mind is what talks all the time. The spirit does not talk. When you listen to the mind, you can refer to it as "it." That is what "it" is thinking, not "you." The real "I," the Self with a capital "S" is the presence of Divinity within, the radiance of consciousness itself, without which you would not even know you exist. The source of all awareness is the Self with a capital "S," which is not different from Consciousness itself. Consciousness, then, is the radiance of Divinity as all that exists. Out of Consciousness arises the universe and all that exists. **Critics are a dime a dozen**. People will say, well, "That is the American way", to get up and speak your piece. It is wonderful that people do that, and then, they should sit down. Hold your sign up, "I have heard what you have to say, thank you."

101 WAYS TO PEACE (7)

33. **Review *Extraordinary Popular Delusions and The Madness of Crowds* by C. MacKay**

34. **Keep a sense of humor: Cattle gas vs. gas of 70 million bison as the cause of earth warming**

35. **Everyone assumes they are right and others are wrong**

Slide 191

SLIDE 191: 101 WAYS TO PEACE (7)

This slide was introduced at the August 2009 lecture, DVD disc 2 at 003450.

Accepting that the majority of people are below 200 is a little difficult. To help you with this, review ***Extraordinary Popular Delusions and the Madness of Crowds*** **(C. Mackay).** Refer to this book very often because the majority of humankind can be seriously wrong and an opinion held generally by the populace makes it seem true. The fact that everybody believes a thing is interesting should be taken into account, but it should not be persuasive.

Keep a sense of humor. The government is going to tax people for cattle. Every cow is going to cost you a $15.00 federal tax. The reason given is that cattle emit methane, which is a cause of earth warming, so **cattle gas is what is causing the earth to warm**. Just think what went on when there were **70,000,000 bison** running across the face of the United States. 70,000,000 bison, all doing 'you-know-what', must have made quite a noise. The earth would have gone into a fiery ball with seventy million bison emitting methane at the same time. Oh, so earth warming is today's major delusion and madness of the crowd and it is highly politicized. Everybody gets out there about earth warming. It becomes very fervent, very fervent. Certain politicians are not going to allow something or other because that is going to save the earth. Oh, you are going to save the earth, yeah, okay.

Everyone assumes they are right and others are wrong. When you are having an argument with someone, put yourself in the other person's place and say, "to their hearing, what I am saying is wrong." So maybe discuss an alternate view to what is causing earth warming. I am aware that the other person has been thoroughly brainwashed and does not believe what I say at all. I do not even know why I am talking to them except that you have to be polite and make conversation. So one can say, "Well, an alternate view is that earth warming has to do with the magnetic activity on the surface of the sun and sunspots, as ice core drillings back through ten million years have demonstrated. That is just an alternate view." So one does not care if they believe it or not. One does not have a positionality, and is not harmed or hurt if they want to tax the cows.

101 WAYS TO PEACE (8)

36. Seek to understand others rather than change them

37. Serve God rather than the narcissistic ego

38. Seek to participate rather than dominate

39. It's okay to have faults

Slide 192

SLIDE 192: 101 WAYS TO PEACE (8)

This slide was introduced at the August 2009 lecture, DVD disc 2 at 003830.

Seek to understand others rather than change them. It is not necessary to change people to see things your way. The only world one can change is one's own and by becoming all that one can be, one influences others automatically. **Serve God rather than the narcissistic ego**. To serve God means to be spiritual and send forth love and good will towards people. Spiritual advancement comes by Grace, which results in the humility that acknowledges the state yet does not take credit for the condition. That would result in ego inflation. You can send forth good will towards all of life in all of its expressions. The recommended rule of life is to serve all of life and have reverence for all of life in all its expressions. It is an error to claim personal credit or specialness.

Therefore, all you have to do is to **participate rather than dominate**. You do not have to win every argument. You can share a teaching or put a thought in the other person's mind and say, "so I have heard," like the Buddha, who is alleged to have said that all the time before his enlightenment. So one can say, "I have heard", and give others an alternate view. **It is okay to have faults**. All human beings have faults. As someone said, "I have faults, but being wrong is not one of them." That is a humorous way of juxtaposing the Reality and the human condition.

101 WAYS TO PEACE (9)

40. Avoid struggle for the moral high ground

41. Support others to find good about themselves

42. Concede to ‘what is’ versus ‘what ought to be’

43. It’s okay to just ‘be’ rather than ‘do’ or ‘have’

Slide 193

SLIDE 193: 101 WAYS TO PEACE (9)

This slide was introduced at the August 2009 lecture, DVD disc 2 at 004000.

Avoid struggle for the moral high ground. Everyone naively presumes that their own perception, opinions, and comprehension of life and its events are 'real, true and factual', and therefore 'right'. Hence, if other people have a different viewpoint, they are 'wrong, misinformed, prejudiced, politically incorrect, or ignorant'. Thus, being 'right' is associated with pride and self- esteem which then has to be defended as per the constant national and international contentious political struggle for the moral high ground. America gives away the moral high ground to its avowed enemies via much publicized violence, sexually provocative celebrities, school shootings, and politically supported decline of ethics or honesty. America's enemies view these phenomena in a poor light, resulting in an image of America as decadent and therefore deserving of destruction.

Support others to find good things about themselves. Even though they are a psychotic, raving idiot, they are kind to their mother. "You are very kind to your mother." Yep. Find something good. "You can really cook and fry bacon really well." **Concede to "what is" versus what you think things "ought to be."** You have to watch out when your mind starts telling you things ought to be such and such a way. Be very suspicious of "ought," the things that "ought" to be different. People "ought" to be smarter. People "ought" to agree with you. No. People ought to pay their taxes honestly. What do you mean, "ought to", and who is wise enough to say what "ought to be?" Concede to what people actually are. People will take advantage of loopholes if they are available. Instead of making them wrong about it, you can blame it on human nature. It is human nature to chisel a little bit if you can get away with it. The majority of people calibrate below 200, therefore, the majority of people would cheat on their income tax if they could get away with it (tests true.) What do you know about that? This is creative tax reporting exemplified by naming your cat as a dependent, deducting your veterinarian bills as medical treatment, etc. Concede to "what is" so there is no point in making people wrong about that. Everybody is into survival and therefore they do what they think will bring about an increase in the likelihood and value of their survival. We can just presume that people will do what they consider best for their survival.

It is okay to just "be" rather than "do" or "have." The lowest levels of consciousness are concerned with what you have; cars, private planes, houses, whatever. The next higher levels are the levels where what you do is what makes you important: your title, what you do for a living, etc. And in the end, it is what you have become that really matters. It is what you are that is the most important factor in your happiness.

101 WAYS TO PEACE (10)

44. Surrender your will to God

45. Let bygones be bygones

46. 'If you don't have anything good to say about a person, then say nothing at all'

47. Realize mankind has been at war 93% of recorded history – 'whirled peas' is unlikely

Slide 194

SLIDE 194: 101 WAYS TO PEACE (10)

This slide was introduced at the August 2009 lecture, DVD disc 2 at 004330.

Surrender your will to God and therefore you can **let bygones be bygones**. Love is the opportunity to surrender the personal will to God and to reassess the overall purpose of the gift of human life. While the surrender of one's will to God is a well-known premise of all true spiritual traditions and teachings, its application outside the fields of religion or spirituality has only recently been recognized in our society as crucial to the resolution of other individual or collective human problems. Life itself depends on becoming conscious via major self- confrontation with something that the higher Self has picked that will force one to grow because there is no turning back. The only options are to surrender one's will to God or go insane and die. Once one is into the addictive alcoholic or other process, there is no turning back. There is only confrontation with owning the truth about one's self. Recovery depends on accepting that process, moving joyfully into it, and being grateful, living one day at a time and letting all prior resentments go, letting bygones be bygones.

"**If you don't have anything good to say about a person, then don't say anything at all.**" Well, the mind really likes to say things that are not too complimentary about people. That is what gossip is all about. So, look at gossip as a source of amusement. The pervasiveness of non-integrity in today's society is also a product of the impact of the media. With the progressive decrease in acceptable standards of decency in the name of total freedom, the media output constantly pushes the limits of credibility and tolerance. Thus, positive commentary about the country or its leaders is actually unwelcome. Naïvely, people believe that the First Amendment means no restrictions, consequences or accountability. It just states that "government" cannot interfere, but others, such as employers, etc., can. Employee "bloggers" discovered this when they lost their jobs due to intemperate commentary.

It is important to realize that **mankind has been at war 93% of recorded history: 'whirled peas' is unlikely.** World peace is unlikely any time soon at the current level of humanity, as it is not a heavenly domain but a purgatorial one, ideal for the advancement of consciousness. During Dr. Hawkins' lifetime, he lived through 7 wars, one after another, not including the small wars in Africa and various places. The only time humanity was not at war was when it was probably too sick with the plague or too impoverished

101 WAYS TO PEACE (11)

48. Acceptance – "So there you are"

49. Fatalism - "What will be will be": Karmic influences

50. Develop a peaceful nature - Be aware of the power of Nature

51. See the beauty of all that exists

Slide 195

SLIDE 195: 101 WAYS TO PEACE (11)

This slide was introduced at the August 2009 lecture, DVD disc 2 at 004645.

Humankind has been at war almost all the time. **One can accept** this as the human condition and say, **"So there you are."** The news in the morning is that something or other happened, and one can say, "So there you are". In a way, that is being **fatalistic**. "So there you are" means that is the way the world runs, and that is the way things are in the world. That infuriates the do-gooders who feel that the world should not be that way. One can **accept** the fact that there will be people in the world who will say, "It should not be that way." Another way to explain it is **"what will be, will be."** What will be, will be is not just chance. It has to do with the power of **karmic influences**. It is as if we are all little pieces of iron filings with a magnetic north pole and a south pole, and the infinite field of consciousness, which is the Mind of God, is an infinite magnetic field. Now, what you have become determines where you are within that field. You have to picture yourself as an iron filing, with a north pole and a south pole. Here is this big powerful electromagnetic field, the Mind of God called consciousness. Now where you are within the field depends on the decisions that you make. As you say, "Well, I forgive that person," you move up higher in the field. If you say, "I am going to get even with that bad person," you move down in the field. It is clear that one cannot blame anything on God.

What historical religions do is that they blame one's fate or misfortune on God. This creates many atheists in the world. No, what happens to you is solely up to you alone depending on your choice: "I forgive him" or "I hate him"; "Oh, I'll overlook it" or "No, I'll get even." You can see how your "spirit", which is like a little electromagnetic iron filing, moves in the infinite magnetic field of the infinite power of consciousness itself. The power of consciousness is beyond man's imagination. Modern Science says that the power of the potential energy of one cubic centimeter of the infinite field of consciousness is greater than the power of the total mass of the entire universe. The power of the entire mass of the universe is less than the power of a tiny bit of consciousness. Why? Because consciousness is the field of God's will and the power of God's will is infinite. Consciousness has no beginning, has no end and is infinite. **"So there you are"** meaning, that is how it is.

Develop a peaceful nature. Be aware of the power of nature. Love all of nature and develop a peaceful nature. The power of Nature starts at the bottom with *Tama*s (calibration levels below 200), as the energy of resistance that is overcome by rajas (calibration levels 200–499), the energy of constructive activity and effort; *Raja*s is the response to motivation and dedication to actually reach *Sattva*, the state of tranquility calibrating at levels 500-599. Moksha is peace and enlightenment and calibrates at 600 and over. **See the beauty of all that exists**. As the level of consciousness advances, the innate perfection and stunning beauty of 'All That Exists' shines forth like a luminous radiance. All of life becomes more beautiful as innate illumination reveals the Divinity of Creation.

101 WAYS TO PEACE (12)

52. Value quietude

53. Let go of willfulness; silence the inner child

54. Practice the virtues

55. Recall "Peace on Earth, good will toward men."

56. Strive to be angelic vs. Luciferic

Slide 196

SLIDE 196: 101 WAYS TO PEACE (12)

This slide was introduced at the August 2009 lecture, DVD disc 2 at 005120.

Value quietude. You do not have to turn the radio on the instant you walk into the house. All languaging is a paradox because nothing can actually be as it is languaged to be. Revelation is a revealed knowingness, understood without words or concepts. The mind is accustomed to obtaining, getting, deriving, or discovering meaning or information. In the state of enlightenment, all is self-revealing of its essence as its existence. Ultimately, everything is knowable only by virtue of the identity of 'being it'. All languaging is paradox, a substitute for God. The enemy is really the inner child, the innocence of the inner child and the inner child's willfulness. **Let go of willfulness; silence the inner child** by being aware of its patterns. Willfulness is the ego itself. The surrender of willfulness/positionality brings peace in all circumstances. Within most people is a child who is merely imitating being an adult. As people grow up, they take on various identifications and copy what they conceive of as adult behaviors and styles; however, it is not the adult who is doing this but the child. Therefore, what we see in daily life are people acting out the programs and scenarios that they identify with as a child. The young child, as well as most animals, already exhibits curiosity, self-pity, jealousy, envy, competitiveness, temper tantrums, emotional outbursts, resentments, hatreds, rivalries, competition, seeking the limelight and admiration, willfulness, petulance, blaming others, disclaiming responsibility, making others wrong, looking for favor, collecting 'things', showing off, and more. These are all attributes of the child. The inner child is naïve and impressionable, easily programmed, and easily seduced and manipulated. Despite one's best efforts, willfulness and desire for gain or control continue to erupt repetitiously. These were learned accretions to the ego during its evolutionary development over eons of time and therefore, it is not necessary to feel guilty. These patterns are part of one's inheritance as a human, but that is not what one is.

As spiritual beings, we **practice the virtues**. We do not claim perfection, only progress. We try our best to forgive people even though they seem to be evil or wrong. We practice the virtues but may not be able to master them, as we are admitting that we are evolutionary, that the degree of our fulfillment of our human potential is in constantly growing.

Recall "Peace on Earth, good will towards men." This is a very good one because very often the power of this arises in childhood when you hear that the angels announced the coming of Christ on Christmas Eve. The origin of this quote is taken from the bible where countless angelic beings were sent forth by Almighty God to proclaim the Savior's birth. It was in the birth of this child that Almighty God would bring forth the propitiation for redemption for all of humanity and the demise of Lucifer. **Strive to be angelic, rather than Luciferic**: The Luciferic error proclaims that the ego is God. The basis for the error is the unwillingness to surrender sovereignty from the 'I' of the ego to the Allness of God. To acknowledge the absolute divinity of the Infinite Supreme is unacceptable to entities that are deluded into claiming godship. Luciferic is an entity that has declined truth for pride and control over others (levels below 200.) Angelic are entities at or above the calibrated levels of 500 and are selfless, loving and beneficent to all of Creation.

101 WAYS TO PEACE (13)

57. Practice 'no attractions, no aversions' (Buddha)

58. Accept the social roles of others

59. Study to understand others

60. The 'Near-Death Experience' is one of total peace

Slide 197

SLIDE 197: 101 WAYS TO PEACE (13)

This slide was introduced at the August 2009 lecture, DVD disc 2 at 005235.

Practice "no attractions and no aversions" (Buddha): That requires some discipline. You can do it by asking yourself, "Could I let go of wanting to be attracted to that?" You begin to see that the attraction is something you project onto things. A thing is not attractive in itself at all. Its attraction is due to an energy that you project onto it. Now, that is quite a surprise for most people who think the attraction is in the thing. The attraction is in you. You are very attracted to a doughnut if you are hungry and you like doughnuts. If you do not like doughnuts, if you hate them, you do not think doughnuts are attractive, you think they are ugly. The practice of no attractions and no aversions results in peace. How to be peaceful, how to be 'one-up' in a conversation and keep your cool, here is an inner secret if you are going to have an argument with somebody. They are a debater, and as the debater gets up with you, you say, "You have something on your chin. Is that mayonnaise?" In an innocuous, harmless situation, just say, "Is that something on your chin? Is that ketchup? No, is that lettuce? Is that mayonnaise on your chin?" That completely throws the other person off their mindset and then you swoop in, waiting for them like a hawk on the edge of the field. "Is that mayonnaise on your chin?" They have lost the game; you threw them off their cool with the feint, a French term indicating maneuvers designed to distract or mislead, done by aiming at one place or point merely as a distraction from the real place or point of the maneuver.

Accept the social roles of others. In other words, people are fulfilling what they see as their social role. It is not really actually who they are. They are acting out a social role and their definition of the understanding of how they are supposed to be, what they are supposed to be, how they are supposed to look and how they are supposed to talk. So everybody has a whole set of programs of what their behavior and appearance and everything should be like. That is the **value of studying to understand others**. To understand what runs them, and out of that comes compassion. Out of that arises compassion. Understanding others brings compassion.

The near-death experience is one of total peace, which is hard to explain. The peace of God that goes beyond understanding is a peace of great profundity. Transforms the appearance of the world and takes you out of all possible suffering. People are afraid of death. Actually, the near-death experience is one of absolute and total peace. Although people fear death, the actual experience is one of infinite peace.

101 WAYS TO PEACE (14)

61. Only the ego is vulnerable; the real Self is eternal

62. Live in each instant, which is innately peaceful

63. Detach from control; be the 'Witness/Observer'

64. Practice meditation and contemplation

Slide 198

SLIDE 198: 101 WAYS TO PEACE (14)

This slide was introduced at the August 2009 lecture, DVD disc 2 at 005845.

Only the ego is vulnerable; the Real Self is eternal. The real Self is invisible to other people. Therefore, if your feelings are hurt, or you feel you have to have something or win something, or you are lamenting losing something, remind yourself it is only the ego creating this experience. It is because of your relationship to the object that you mourn it when it is lost. Again, it is always going back to the ego to understand the ego and therefore not be its victim. Be its master instead of being its victim.

Live in each instant, which is innately peaceful. This comes about through spiritual work also. To live not one day at a time, not one hour at a time, but one instant at a time. As Dr. Hawkins shared after coming back to the lecture, late from the lunch break, "We were either going to make it back here in time, or we were not. What could I do? Susan was at the wheel, the traffic and other local conditions were there, helping or not helping." If you live in each instant, you are always in peace because non-acceptance of "What is", is suffering. "I lost poor so and so, and he got run over by a so and so, and then my cat drowned and then the next thing you know I had a flat tire, and then I got a ticket." You have a whole, long story and need to learn to live in each instant, which is innately peaceful.

Detach from control; be the "Witness/Observer." This is a little more sophisticated. It means that if you constantly let go of wanting to control things, change them, or being on top of them, what happens is the chatter of the ego stops. You then become merely the observer, the witness. This is a high spiritual state, in which you relinquish the personal self to the field of consciousness itself. In witnessing and observing, you think that there is a "you" doing "that". There is no '*you*' witnessing or observing. There is not any person there at all. The idea that there is a person there comes in after you have observed and witnessed. Observing and witnessing goes on autonomously, without any intervention on anybody's part. It does not need a personal self. Consciousness is aware. You do not have to interject yourself and say, "I'm aware." The witness/observer is a higher state that, without making conclusions, judgments, or trying to control anything, merely wants to witness. When you go out of body, there is only the witness/observer there, which does not have any particular intention about anything. It is just aware of what is going on, like people who leave the body in surgery and go up to the ceiling and witness the surgery. The witness/observer does not want to do anything, but witnesses everything, it just watches. "Say, what did you do when you were up near the ceiling?" "Didn't do anything, but I was aware of what was going on." Be the witness/observer, the state you can achieve by constant surrender and by contemplation. The contemplative state puts you in the witness/observer.

Practice meditation and contemplation. As you do that, the witness/observer becomes predominant and becomes more or less one's normal state. The only trouble with that is you are asking people questions all the time, "What day is it?"

101 WAYS TO PEACE (15)

65. Differentiate wants from needs

66. "Wear the world like a light garment."

67. Differentiate appearance from essence

68. Be kind to all of life

69. Have pets and a garden spot

Slide 199

SLIDE 199: 101 WAYS TO PEACE (15)

This slide was introduced at the August 2009 lecture, DVD disc 2 at 010350.

Differentiate wants from needs. What you want is one thing and what you need is another. People convince themselves that their wants are their needs. For example, they always have to have a raise in pay and everybody has to have more money. That is universal. No matter how much you make, you need more money. If you ask any multibillionaire about his main problem, he says, "Well, I just need more capital. I could buy the whole United States, instead of just the Eastern Seaboard, you know." Jesus Christ said, "**Wear the world like a light garment**." In other words, participate, see that it is there, but it is not central. The ego is not central. Wear the world like a light garment. So you are the witness/observer, you observe the world and **differentiate appearance from essence**. That is what we do when we use the arm to calibrate something. The appearance of a thing is one thing, the essence is another. The ego cannot tell essence from appearance. It just sees the sheep in wolf's clothing or vice-versa, the wolf in sheep's clothing. Differentiate appearance from essence.

Be kind to all of life for its own sake, because of your own reverence for life. You try to be kind to all of life in all of its expressions, no matter whether it is a toad, a bunny, a squirrel; whether it is another human being or whether it is a tree. You see some people take a hand ax and as they are going by a tree, they slam the ax into the tree, pull it out and walk on. What do you think, the tree doesn't know you just hit it with an ax? If you ask the tree, how was that, the tree would go "Owww!" All of life is aware of the nature of other life. In an advanced state of consciousness, you see that even a tree is aware of the divinity of your Self, the Self with a capital "S." As you walk by a tree, its consciousness is aware of the divinity of that which is walking by (tested true.) That is true, even a tree is aware of the divinity, the Godness within you. The tree is aware that an emissary of God is walking by. All of nature knows when that which is of divine origin is walking by. All the more reason to be kind to it. If consciousness expressed as life is aware of the divinity of your essence and bows to it out of respect for that life, you return the favor.

Therefore, you love the trees, love the kitties, love the doggies, and love all the living things because their essence is also that of divinity. This is God appearing as a kitty cat, this is God appearing as a mole, this is God appearing as a toad. See the little toad. Do you not see that the toad loves life? He loves being a toad. To take a hammer and hit the toad, one can see the extreme ungodliness of that act. Because that is denying the divinity of all that exists. All that exists is worthy of reverence. As we grow, we begin to revere all of life in all of its expressions, even the mad dog, which cannot help but be a mad dog, and even the raving maniac who cannot help but be a raving maniac. They cannot help themselves. Out of benevolence you send unconditional love to all of life and wish it well. It is very beneficial to **have pets and a garden spot**. The pet could be anything. The pet could be a dog, a cat, a bird or even cockroaches in a little box.

101 WAYS TO PEACE (16)

70. Decrease expectations of others

71. Mind your own business

72. Make a list of worries

73. Chocolate vs. vanilla is simply a choice

74. Differentiate emotional from spiritual viewpoints

Slide 200

SLIDE 200: 101 WAYS TO PEACE (16)

This slide was introduced at the August 2009 lecture, DVD disc 2 at 010940.

Decrease your expectations of others. Nobody is going to be at the level that you think he is at, so it is best to decrease your expectations of others. You see that our society programs everyone. Very few are the people who escape the programming of our human world. It is very good for your peace of mind to **mind your own business**. From level 200 on up, responsible social relationship is possible. While the lower emotional levels lead to involvement with others, at 200, the intention now shifts to alignment with others and the rewarding principle of mutuality rather than egocentricity. Without the constant interference of discord, there is the emergence of harmony as an operating principle that enables getting along with others and coordinating activities. The consequence is an increase in social approval and acceptance.

Make a list of your worries. If you cannot get rid of your worries, then it is important to make a list of them. One way to get on top of your worries is to make a list of them and prioritize them. Because when you identify them, you can deal with them. Otherwise, they are just sort of a vague thing: worrying about money, worrying about old age, worrying about your business collapsing, whatever it is. If you sit down and make a list of worries, they lose a good deal of power over you because you are defining them, and in defining them, you see how small they actually are. I mean, if you go flat broke you go on the county. So what is wrong with being on the county? If you are broke, have no money, and have no place to go, what better place to be?

Chocolate versus vanilla is simply a choice. What the world does is that it says the people on this side are chocolate and the people on this side are vanilla. And, they don't have to be seen as adversaries. You can see that you can choose chocolate and that does not mean you have to hate vanilla. You can choose vanilla, and that does not mean you have to hate chocolate. If you watch the political news, you would think the only way you can be vanilla is you have to hate chocolate or vice versa. Actually, you are just picking one of two choices.

Differentiate your emotional from your spiritual viewpoints. People will use an excuse like "Well, I feel this way." They use the emotional outlet. Why did you do that? "Well, I felt like it." That is the big excuse. That was your emotional viewpoint. What was your spiritual viewpoint? "Well, my spiritual viewpoint is somewhat different." You do not want to be the slave of the ego and its emotions. Do not forget that the ego, the basis of the mind, is the child. When you are talking about emotions, you are often talking about the inner child and not the inner adult.

101 WAYS TO PEACE (17)

75. Utilize logic instead of emotion

76. Ask for a miracle

77. Today is tomorrow's yesterday

78. Talk it over with friends

79. Accept "worst-possible scenario"

80. "Think about it tomorrow"

Slide 201

SLIDE 201: 101 WAYS TO PEACE (17)

This slide was introduced at August 2009 lecture, DVD disc 2 at 011310.

In fighting your way out of some emotional corner, **use logic instead of emotion**. A lot of people try emotion instead of just logic. If you use logic you can see, there is nothing to fear. When life is over, they bury you and that is the end of the problem, so what is the problem? When it is over, it is over, no more suffering. **Ask for a miracle**. Those of you who have done *A Course in Miracles* know that this in itself is a miracle. That asking for a miracle very often produces the miracle. You cannot find a thing, you have no idea where it is, your mind is completely blank and you ask the Holy Spirit, "Where is so and so?" Then you forget it and you walk in the other room and then out of nowhere, not out of logic, out of nowhere it comes to your mind, "You left it in the bathroom on the shelf." Everything you ever lose is in the bathroom on the shelf or on the kitchen shelf. Ask for a miracle. People feel they are not entitled to miracles or that they don't believe in them. People don't know what a miracle is. Very often, a miracle is merely the reframing, especially in time, e.g. healing is of the spirit and may, or may not show up in physicality due to karmic factors and local conditions.

Today is tomorrow's yesterday. It is yesterday already and here you are, worrying about it. You were worrying about getting back here on time and tomorrow is going to be yesterday. It is learning to live in the present moment and continuously accepting 'What Is'. Today is going to be yesterday soon and you will say, "We were worried about getting back on time yesterday." Aside from having a mentor, **talking things over with friends** is very important. The isolated person ends up pretty crazy. The Unabomber lived by himself in a small shed and terrified all industry and everyone. He did not have any friends to talk with. If he had talked it over with friends, they could have dissuaded him to take the action he was contemplating. No, he wanted to be all by himself in a small space and he is now all by himself in a ten by twelve space. He probably feels he is rattling around in that big cell. As you can see, a person with schizophrenia and delusions is unable to help himself. So, even though he was the Unabomber, you can't hate him, you can't want to get even with him. How can you see the Unabomber, except as a person who is spiritually lost? He was spiritually lost and completely egocentric.

Another way to drown your fears and worries is to **accept the worst possible scenario**. Picture it in your mind, "Well, the worst thing that can happen is I get a flat tire on the parkway and it's raining and I forgot my driver's license." That is the worst possible scenario. Then you say, "What if all that happened?" "Well, I'd catch hell from the cop and I'd have to pay the fine." If that is the worst possible scenario, you do not have to be frightened. As Scarlett O'Hara would say in the movie *Gone with the Wind*, "I'll **think about it tomorrow.**" In the modern world that would be criticized. Think about it tomorrow, this, that and the other. There is a certain wisdom to that because if you think about it tomorrow it does not look the same. For one thing, you have started a process going in your unconscious mind. You may be saying, "I can't think of how I am going to make any money, I haven't got any assets, and I've got no income and I've been cut off now." Then you say, "Well, I'll think about it tomorrow." In the morning, you get up and all of a sudden you remember, "I could take this to a hock shop and probably get a couple of hundred bucks." Yesterday you did not think of that. Today it is obvious.

101 WAYS TO PEACE (18)

81. Peace exists in the midst of war

82. 'Things could be worse'

83. Life is transitory

84. You were created by God

85. Go on a worry diet

86. Give up trying to be happy

87. Give up being rich and famous

Slide 202

SLIDE 202: 101 WAYS TO PEACE (18)

This slide was introduced at the August 2009 lecture, DVD disc 2 at 012120.

Peace is existent all the time, even in the midst of war. Once the experience of peace has occurred, we are no longer a victim of the world, for we have had a glimpse of the truth about it and of what we really are. The inner Self prevails resulting in an imperturbable peace, as the personal self with all of its feelings, beliefs, identities, and conflicts disappears. Dr. Hawkins describes his experience of peace in the middle of World War II when he served on a minesweeper. He and a colleague stood watch for four hours at night, each wearing a gun belt with a loaded 45, ready to shoot anything that moved. Once they were faced with a mine that was about to go off, and his colleague said, "Well, we might get killed," and then he says, "then what happens if it goes off?" Dr. Hawkins said to him, "Well, then we die." The colleague said, "You're right," and his fear went away and, there was peace that they were doing exactly what their duty was.

T**hings could be worse. Life is transitory.** The ego thinks that it is eternal, that its life is going to be forever. Once you accept the fact that life is transitory at best, and we are all going to go without physicality to the other side; the acceptance of that decreases a great deal of fear. In the infinite dimensions of time, we are all living together. The knowledge that "**you were created by God"** gives a certain solemnity, certain profundity. "We were all created by God" (calibrates true). Not the ego, but the Self is the essence of who you are. And when you leave the body, those of you who have had this experience of leaving the body, the witness/observer witnesses and observes the body, but feels no attraction to it at all. It seems meaningless, boring, not even attractive. You think you would try to get back in that body and reactivate it, but strangely enough it just lays there and it has no attraction.

You **go on a worry diet**. Make a list of your worries, if you do not have one already. You begin to take things off your worry diet that you are willing to let go of. "I will stop worrying about money." Worst that can happen to you if you do not have any money is you are poor. When you are poor, there are many things you cannot have. Can't have a new Cadillac. So you go on a diet and you start letting things go. "Could I be happy without a new Cadillac? Yep. Could I be happy if I didn't have a new pair of shoes? Yes." You have an ongoing acceptance. This acceptance is not the human will. This acceptance is being the witness/observer, a contemplative position. You can let go of your worries one by one by total acceptance. **Give up trying to be happy**. Do not try to be happy; just be happy. That is simpler than trying to be happy. You can see that trying to be happy is like a mouse chasing its tail. Why should you be happy? You should be happy because you *are*, coming from nothingness to the miracle of somethingness. **Give up being rich and famous**. Rich and famous people constantly succumb to failed marriages, addiction, alcoholism, suicide, or untimely death, e.g. the movie stars (Judy Garland, Marilyn Monroe, James Dean); the pop stars (Elvis Presley, Janis Joplin, Jimi Hendrix); the writers (Edgar Allan Poe, Jack London, Ernest Hemingway, F. Scott Fitzgerald), etc. In addition to such notorious examples of the price of celebrity are the uncounted thousands of less famous "successful" lives ruined by drug problems, or the twisting of personality whereby formerly decent folk become vain, cruel, self-centered, and inordinately self-indulgent. What people think is heroic is nothing but vainglory.

101 WAYS TO PEACE (19)

88. Walk the labyrinth

89. Do the Rosary

90. Spin the prayer wheel

91. Write a Will

92. Take out life insurance

93. Watch TV's Animal Channel

94. Bury the hatchet

Slide 203

SLIDE 203: 101 WAYS TO PEACE (19)

This slide was introduced at the August 2009 lecture, DVD disc 2 at 013010.

Walk the labyrinth. One can get the effect of walking the labyrinth by tracing a diagram of it with a pencil. If you have a diagram of the labyrinth and you take a pencil point, you start from the starting point and you follow the labyrinth where it goes with the pencil point. The effect on your consciousness is the same as if you walked it. "That is a mystical truth", (tests true). "Nobody knows the reason for it" (calibrates true). It is just a fact. If you are worried and cannot get off it, you find some place that has a labyrinth and walk it, or you get a copy of the labyrinth and you trace it slowly with the tip of a pencil and you follow it. There is something mysterious about the pattern; it brings a profound sense of peace by merely following a diagram of it with the eye, or tracing the same with a pencil. That is something similar to **doing the rosary** and **spinning the prayer wheel**. "Doing the rosary brings about greater inner peace", (tests true). "Spinning the prayer wheel brings about greater inner peace" (calibrates true). Whether you are a Christian, Buddhist or whatever, it does not say you have to be a Christian or a believer to do these things, it just says, "To do them." It does not say only Christians benefit from the labyrinth, or only Buddhists benefit from the prayer wheel, it says *anybody, anybody.* There is something mysterious, beyond beliefs. There is some other power and patterning in the universe, which nobody has discovered so far. In the perusal of the world's spiritual literature over the decades, one has never come across any explanation why such a geometric pattern should have such a profound effect. There is some recent research on the torus shape, which perhaps could be a plausible partial explanation of the phenomenon. Do the rosary, walk the labyrinth and spin the prayer wheel.

Another thing that will calm your nerves is to **write your will** and **take out life insurance**. The fact is we need to accept our mortality, therefore not to have a legal 'Will' or life insurance means a loss of a sense of reality. Somebody might as well benefit, you are going to croak anyway. Pick out a friend, a relative, or leave it to the Humane Society, if you do not have any friends or relatives. The importance of these things is that there is a certain generosity that your death will serve some positive benefit to life in its various forms. The Humane Society could use the insurance money so it can find more homes for more homeless pets, etc.

Watch Television's Animal Channel, it has very interesting things on it. The ego within us is primarily a self-interested animal that we inherited as part of being human. Like a pet, the inner animal can be comical and entertaining, and we can enjoy it without guilt and look forward to getting it trained, properly housebroken and civilized. **Bury the hatchet** means to make peace with others. We think we are punishing the other person by holding resentment against him or her, but we are actually suppressing love. In the beginning, we may not consciously feel this specifically about the other person, but we will begin to notice that we do have this aspect to our personality. As we keep surrendering our resistance to love, we will notice that within ourselves there is a desire to make a friendly gesture; we want to heal the separation, to repair the wound, to make good the wrong, letting the past go and burying the hatchet.

101 WAYS TO PEACE (20)

95. Give up being an adrenaline junkie

96. Quit when you are ahead

97. Let go of greed

98. Invoke your Buddha-Nature

99. Live in the space beneath thoughts

Slide 204

SLIDE 204: 101 WAYS TO PEACE (20)

This slide was introduced at the August 2009 lecture, DVD disc 2 at 013720.

Give up being an adrenaline junkie. That is a hard one. The term 'Adrenaline Junkie' was popularized by the 1991 movie *Point Break* in referencing people who favor dangerous activities for the adrenaline rush that accompanies them, e.g. bank robbers, psychopaths, skydivers, etc. Adrenaline junkies come in much more subtle forms also, creating drama, crises, higher stress levels and feelings of overwhelm in their lives, consciously or unconsciously. Below consciousness level 200, there is a predominance of adrenaline and animal-instinct survival responses. In contrast, consciousness levels over 200 are termed 'welfare emotions', which are benign and signify the emergence, and eventually the dominance, of spiritual energies.

One thing of importance is to **quit when you are ahead**. People push the greed button to the point that a hundred thousand dollars a year is not enough; they have to push to a hundred and five, push to a hundred and ten, etc. Of course, then they get fired so it is best to quit when you are ahead. **Let go of greed**. One has to be able to handle money without any thought of greed.

When you reach the full understanding of things, there is no reason to avoid them. Do not get caught by them. Detachment is different from nonattachment.

Invoke your Buddha-Nature. God/Buddha Nature 'is' and as such is complete. Therefore, it does not 'do' anything or 'go' anywhere, nor is there a time track of 'duration'. 'Now' and 'forever' are identical. "From the moment of birth on, the 'when' of when you leave this world is already preset" (tests true.) Why are we worrying about dying because it is already certified, signed, sealed, delivered and stamped? Some people say, "If the time of your leaving is preset, why bother with caution, why bother with safety, if it's all set?" That is fatalism, something different. The time has been pre-set since the beginning of time, because each one of us is part of God's creation. In the beginning of all time, the beginning of creation, there is not a "then" and a "now." In the infinite world of consciousness all places are here, all time is now. Every place is equally the center. When dealing with infinity, all the usual logic of thought is not applicable.

Thoroughly **live in the space beneath thoughts**. People say, how can I get the mind to stop? You do not have to get the mind to stop, just pay no attention to it. You will notice that thoughts are like the surface of the sea and beneath the surface of the sea is the stillness of the deep. Beneath thoughts, there is absolute silence. With spiritual advancement, you become aware that everything is happening autonomously of its own. One does not have to talk, the talkingness is happening of its own, there is no 'you' that is talking; you just witness that talkingness is happening of its own. Most of the things we worry about, take blame for and feel guilty over are autonomous; they happen of their own nature. For example, a seed opens up and sprouts of its own nature when it is time for it to do so, which is karmically determined. There is no point in hovering over it, trying to hurry it up or trying to slow it down.

101 WAYS TO PEACE (21)

100. Speak sanely to yourself in the mirror

101. Talk it over with your therapist or psychologist

Slide 205

SLIDE 205: 101 WAYS TO PEACE (21)

This slide was introduced at the August 2009 lecture, DVD disc 2 at 014245.

When you get crazy and everybody gets crazy some time, learn to **speak sanely to yourself in the mirror**. Look at yourself in the mirror and speak sanely to yourself. Give yourself a lecture and be kind to yourself and realize that you are crazier than a loon and stupider than you imagine: "The truth, buddy, is that you are a nut job and you're not too bright and how God tolerates your existence in the universe is simply the consequence of the fact that He created you." Then you realize that God cannot throw you out of the window because you are his handiwork. Right, about face, Oh, in the winning circle, there you are in the winning circle, talking to yourself in the mirror. Speaking to yourself in the mirror is not about bragging and vanity, but about starting to believe in yourself, and your possibilities. Our subconscious is susceptible to the things we say, and this talk will have a positive effect as we make positive statements while looking at ourselves confidently in the eyes. There is a difference between talking to yourself (in your head) rather than loudly in the first ("I") versus second ("you") person. The second-person self-talk has a beneficial effect because it brings up memories of receiving support and encouragement from others, especially in childhood.

Talk it over with your therapist or psychologist. Always have a counselor, a confidante, a therapist, a psychologist, a best friend, people that you can rely on, including a great spouse. They can serve as an advisor or sponsor in the healing process, to provide guidance and serve as an example to identify with, love, and respect. In formal therapy, there is dependence on therapists and their training and techniques, a reliance on a psychological theory to which the therapist and the patient both subscribe. Scientific research reveals that the results of therapy are not dependent on these factors; instead, the results depend on the interaction between them and the degree of the patient's desire to improve, as well as the patient's faith and confidence in the therapist. Therefore, psychic factors are operating of which psychotherapy is unaware.

Spiritual apathy is quite common as an expression of avoidance and reluctance to face inner conflicts that thereby become a deterrent to progress and growth. Having active spiritual advisors and sponsors can be very helpful. Motivation is aided and augmented in almost any human endeavor by having a mentor, confidant, or trusted friend. Apathy is often the result of isolation and cured by involvement in and the activity of positive relationships that provide a source of caringness. Apathy is indicative of the absence of love, which is its most powerful antidote.

101 WAYS TO SUCCESS (1)

1. **Internal vs. external**
2. **Personal, spiritual vs. worldly**
3. **Read Gingrich's book, *5 Principles for a Successful Life* and George Foreman's *Knockout Entrepreneur***
4. **Success as winning**
5. **Success as goal achievement**

Slide 206

SLIDE 206: 101 WAYS TO SUCCESS (1)

This slide was introduced at the October 2009 lecture, DVD disc 1 at 010000.

Peace and happiness eventually bring you to success. People think that peace and happiness are opposed to success. In fact, peace and happiness are an essential part of success. True success means you are pleased with how it is all going, etc. There is **internal success** -I am very pleased with something -and then there is **external success** as the world views it. So when you say, "I'm working on success," you mean within yourself, you can be very pleased with how you sawed a piece of wood or how you planted your garden, but the world wouldn't consider that success, so you have to decide, do you mean external or internal? Which are you aiming at? Are you aiming at being pleased with your own self? The hardest critic you have to deal with is yourself and he is the only one you have to please. If it does not turn out right, the one committed to success will try again. Success requires persistence: try, try again if at first you do not succeed. Go back to your desk and work on it some more. Success, then, is within you, a resolution of a project you have set up for yourself. Then there is external success as the world views it and that is a different animal than internal success. By success, do you mean **personal, spiritual or worldly**?

Interestingly enough, there are a couple of new books out on success: Gingrich's, ***5 Principles for a Successful Life*** and George Foreman's ***Knockout Entrepreneur***. George Foreman was a heavyweight champion of the world but he lost it at age 45. They ran out of money and his wife said, "You better go out and make some more money." George went back into the ring at age 45 and re-won the world's heavyweight title. Then he went on to create the Foreman Grill, which sold well and he became a multimillionaire in selling it. For George Foreman to re-win the title at age 45, which in boxing is middle age, is impressive and then to become a millionaire, we are looking at **success as winning**. He also won back his wife's respect. He was not a failure and he has won the world's respect. Everybody likes George Foreman, so likable and lovable, being very humanly human. To be successful, we do not have to be artificially perfect. Very often, the world loves us for our humanness and for our foibles and our nuttiness. This shows **success as goal achievement**.

Similarly, to do the Lecture called "101 Ways to Success" Dr. Hawkins had to come up 101 Ways to Success, so he did not achieve the goal until he got to 101 ways. Along the way, he describes that he found a couple of dozen that he thought about and decided that he did not like them too well, and he threw them away. Success, like happiness, is thus a direction, and a destination.

101 WAYS TO SUCCESS (2)

6. **Success as prominence, media attraction, celebrity status**
7. **Success as happiness**
8. **Imagine desired outcome**
9. **Build good karma balance**
10. **Harness desire and ambition**
11. **Workable plan**
12. **Self-confidence**
13. **Dedication**

Slide 207

SLIDE 207: 101 WAYS TO SUCCESS (2)

This slide was introduced at the October 2009 lecture, DVD disc 1 at 010500.

Success in the world's view is to be prominent, to be a media attraction and to reach celebrity status. There is a downward side to media attention. It sucks you in without your realizing it. People say, "Oh, it hasn't affected me." Oh, yes, it does. Being the big star on a TV show does affect you and there is a peculiarity to it, which unless you have been the guest on some big-name show, you do not appreciate it. You get why all the rock stars and all of them get into drugs because at the end of the program you cannot get off that high. You want to keep the high going, so one can have greater sympathy for people in the media who get into drugs because one can see they love that adrenaline rush, the cortisone shooting out, the endorphins shooting out, and suddenly they pull the plug on you. Suddenly you are nobody, you got nothing and all your hormones collapse and you are a nothing, a nobody. Typically, in that particular culture after the program is over, you meet over at somebody's house and everybody is high, you stay high until four in the morning. So one can get off being moralistic about it and just understand it. One thing about the decision to be loving towards all of life in all of its expressions is you achieve a greater understanding, you find that you are not prone to make right and wrong and you are no longer subject to criticizing people or putting them down. What you are interested in is understanding them. When they come out of the prisons and they continue the crime the same as before they went in, instead of condemning them, you begin to understand them. For them there is no other life except going back to mugging, drugs, pedophilia and whatever put them there in the first place, because that is their life, the only life they know. **Success as happiness**: If you are happy, what more can you ask than being happy? "Success is being happy. I'm happy, my dog's happy, my kitty's happy, my wife's happy, my neighbors are happy, what more can you want?"

You build a good karma balance: One way to achieve success, one attribute is to build a good karma balance. It means you have a deposit in a savings account. Everybody has a karma savings account (calibrates true). The little bug that you did not step on adds to your positive karma savings account and the next time a pot falls off the top of a building, it will miss you instead of hitting you on the top of the head. It does not take great achievements; you do not have to save the life of thousands of people by inventing penicillin. Good will towards all of life in all of its expressions builds up a positive karma balance and when you need it, it is there. It is like a savings account. Everyone has had a number of occurrences in life that seem miraculous, not explained by any kind of logic. That is positive karma balance. In other words, the goodness that you have radiated towards all of life to the best of your ability is now like a savings account and when you need it, it is there to draw on. You never know when you are going to need it. Lightning strikes without warning. So when your life is hanging in the balance or something about your life is hanging in the balance, if you have a positive karma balance, it swings the result in a favorable direction. On the other hand, if you have a negative karma balance, it swings the pendulum in a negative direction. It is a great idea to try to maintain a positive karma balance. The plus of random acts of kindness is really the operation out of which it works. By constantly building a positive karma bank account, you do not know when you are going to need it. You may not need it until the last five seconds of life. Other ways to success is you can **imagine the desired outcome**; you begin to image it. You can also **harness your desire and ambition into a workable plan through self-confidence anddedication.**

101 WAYS TO SUCCESS (3)

14. Satisfaction with progress

15. Override obstacles

16. Supportive relationships

17. Flexible vs. rigid

18. Enthusiasm

19. Self-rewarding

20. Dedication to the Highest Good

21. Pray for awareness of God's Will

22. Retain modesty - avoid hubris

Slide 208

SLIDE 208: 101 WAYS TO SUCCESS (3)

This slide was introduced at the October 2009 lecture, DVD disc 1 at 011625.

Satisfaction with your progress: How is it going? **You develop a certain momentum to override obstacles.** You need **supportive relationships** and if you do not have any, build some. It is really a very, very enjoyable part of life, having good friends. How can you live without good friends and people that you love? You do not tell them that you love them because that would make them nervous. You just love them, but you do not say anything about it. You say, "I'm so glad to see you," when you meet someone you have not seen in months. You are just happy as heck to see that person, a good friend that you love. So you become **flexible instead of rigid**.

You will notice that success is very common in the level of the 300s. The consciousness level of the 300s is not divine love, or not an intellectualism, but **enthusiasm**. Someone just keeps running around buying one casino after another. Why does he do it? Because he likes doing it. Does he need more millions? He does not need any more millions. Why does he keep doing that? He just loves doing it. Why does a person go out and play baseball once a week? Because of their enthusiasm, obviously they must love it. Everyone loves these enthusiastic people just because they love doing what they do and that is why they do what they do. Success is **self-rewarding**. A more advanced person **dedicates their life to the highest good** and **prays for awareness of God's Will. Retain modesty - avoid hubris**: Whichever way it turns out, we **retain modesty** about it instead of claiming personal credit.

101 WAYS TO SUCCESS (4)

23. Thankful rather than prideful

24. Incremental goals

25. Result of basic attitudes

26. Determination

27. Will power, 'grit'

28. Visualize goals

29. Chip away: incremental progress

30. Preparation

Slide 209

SLIDE 209: 101 WAYS TO SUCCESS (4)

This slide was introduced at the October 2009 lecture, DVD disc 1 at 012405.

We tend to be **thankful rather than prideful**. "Thank You, O Lord, Amen. All glory be to Thee, O Lord." So we dedicate our lives to God and ask for God's guidance in all of our decision- making and our way of being in the world. We tend to be thankful rather than prideful. We are pleased therefore with **incremental goals**. You do not have to become the star of the show tomorrow. The fact that you are making progress is sufficient. Success is a way of being in the world, a way in which you are. The way in which you are tends to radiate a certain energy and that certain energy tends to influence things that are around you. So, spiritually advanced people experience the world differently than people who are not. Everyone would light up as you came to one's attention. They just became lit up. Not because of who you are personally, so it has got nothing to do with you as a person. Something about that energy uplifts everyone. You tend to uplift all that come into contact with you. Success is not what you do but what you have become. What you are, then, transmits that energy to other people, of feeling friendly and confident, and more entitled to give you the truth than a falsehood, to be loving towards you rather than unloving. So what you are is already a guarantee of success. Your function will follow from what you are. What you are will determine what your judgments and your decisions are and the answers you get about certain things. And so, if in doubt, you can find somebody with whom you can do the simple test of truth versus falsehood. "Thank You, God, for all the gifts of this life." Very successful people have all been very modest people, worth enormous amounts of money but very modest as a person.

You do not have to become a worldly success overnight. It is a result of **basic attitudes**. There is also a certain **determination** to achieve certain standards. The thing to be happy about is that you have become an asset to the world. You have become that which is a gift to your children, to your parents, to your society, to your neighborhood. "The fact that you live where you live accounts for the fact of a reduction of the crime rate where you live" (calibrates true). Where you live the crime rate is already reduced because of the radiance that you emit from your aura. So that gives you great respect for the aura. Let us all say, "That which I am radiates peace and success to the world." It is not what you do, as there are all kinds of do-gooders. They are lurking around every corner saying, "Eat this, do not eat that, and do not smoke a cigarette." Well, humor is one of the best teachers there is. With humor, you do not take yourself too seriously. You say to yourself, "it seemed like a good idea at the time." You are thankful rather than prideful. We are satisfied with progress, incremental goals. Progress rather than perfection and this progress is a result of basic attitudes that we have accumulated by good positive merit.

One thing is determination, determination to do a good job. Another thing we call is **will power or "grit."** We **visualize our goals** and **chip away incrementally**. Almost everybody is guaranteed success with anything if you really want it. You say, "Well, I haven't been successful at this or that." Well, you don't really want it then, do you? "Did you sleep last night?" "Yes." If you really wanted it, you would have been working on it. When one is working one's way through medical school, one does not go to bed at eight o'clock at night. If you get to bed by three in the morning, it is good. It takes grit. Where do you get the grit? You get the grit from the willingness. The willingness to commit to something gives you the grit. And we can **visualize goals**, so picture yourself in the goal in which you want. You want to be a famous movie star? Picture yourself then in Hollywood. You **chip away incrementally and you prepare yourself in advance**.

101 Ways to Success (5)

31. **Fortitude**
32. **Picture result**
33. **Develop work rhythm**
34. **Create routine schedules**
35. **Inspiration**
36. **Harness the muse "Carpe Diem"**
37. **Special place and setting**
38. **Expert advice/consultation**
39. **Patience, persistence**

Slide 210

SLIDE 210: 101 WAYS TO SUCCESS (5)

This slide was introduced at the October 2009 lecture, DVD disc 2 at 000125. .

The next characteristics you need to emphasize in yourself are things already within you, so all we are asking you to do is to increase the voltage of things that are already within you. Everybody has **fortitude**. As Dr. Hawkins shared, "Everybody dragged themselves out to get here to this lecture, and got tickets and stood in line and found a seat and put up with the speaker and everything. That takes fortitude." Another trick, and we are talking about the tricks of worldly success, is to **picture the result**. Have an image in your mind. So if you are destined for some place, get an image of it. Get an image of what you want to accomplish. Get an image of your factory spinning out piles and piles of whatever it is you are manufacturing. Picture the books lining up that you have written or the poetry that you have had published. So picture the result, and picture yourself as successful. Then you **develop a certain rhythm to your work,** a certain work rhythm. These are all the habits of successful people. Fortitude, picturing the result and you develop a certain work rhythm. You **develop certain routine schedules**. **Inspiration**, then, is the fire underneath your feet that keeps you going.

Harness the muse "carpe diem." "Carpe diem" is "seize the day", for today is the day when you will get an interesting idea that will seize you. "Carpe diem" is success, not because of what you do, but because of what you have become. Success is a result of what you have become and not what you do. All kinds of people try for success and they seem to be futile, they just never make it. Harness the muse "Carpe diem", seize the day, means to capitalize on opportunities as they arise.

Many people have found that having **a special place or setting** is very useful to their creating work. If you are into literary work like writing books, etc., a special place and setting tends to facilitate it, where you have all your reference books and everything all around and if necessary, and so inclined, your cat is walking back and forth across the desk to give you company. Then there are times when you need **expert advice and consultation**. You need advice and consultation, and one form of that is the way we use the arm for muscle testing. Then with **patience and persistence**, success becomes closer and closer.

101 Ways to Success (6)

40. Hang out with successful people

41. Avoid naysayers and energy drainers

42. Practice the virtues - integrity

43. Look for helpful feedback

44. Imaginative enterprise

45. Be friendly and upbeat

46. Express appreciation

47. Teamwork

Slide 211

SLIDE 211: 101 WAYS TO SUCCESS (6)

This slide was introduced at the October 2009 lecture, DVD disc 2 at 000950.

Hang out with successful people, because you pick up from their aura a way of being in the world. Success is really a way of being cordial towards all of life in all its expressions. If you step over the insect, it is an aspect of your cordiality. You are cordial towards all of life whether it is a hungry kitty or it is a bug on the carpet, or it is a person in need or in pain or it is suffering, or somebody needs a ride on the road. It means that you have an abundance of the life energy, more than what you need for just your own survival and enough energy to radiate out to influence everything around you. The way to be successful, then, is by cordiality and caringness for the happiness of others. If you are constantly caring for the happiness of others, you do not have to worry about your own; it is automatic because you create a field and the field is what uplifts you to a state of happiness. **Avoid naysayers and energy drainers**. Those are the negative people. **Practice the virtues,** taking one's stand in **integrity**. **Look for helpful feedback** as fulfillment of potential has a positive feedback, helping reinforce commitment and intention. Engage in **imaginative enterprise** in which you pretend either in imagination or in daily life to enjoy certain activities and people and then surprisingly discover that the capacity for enjoyment and pleasure stems from within (i.e., *joie de vivre*). Experiment with other attitudes and personality styles resulting in surprising inner discoveries.

Always **be friendly and upbeat. Express appreciation** by thanking everybody for their efforts on your behalf. You say to the clerk in the grocery store who rings you up, "Gee, thanks a lot" and it is just a little bright flick of sunshine in her day. She feels better, she does not know why. It is not because of anything but by virtue of that which you have become. You radiate out thankfulness, acknowledgment and a positive energy field to everything and everyone. As you grow in awareness, you realize that life recognizes you. As you walk through the woods, the trees are aware of what you are. Do you know that all of nature knows that which you are? So as you plant the little plant, the little plant is now being blessed because never in all of its life has it been touched by the radiance of Divinity that comes down through the human kingdom. Here is this little nothing, nowhere plant and Divinity Itself is touching this little plant. As you walk through the fields then, the fields know that that which is Divine is in their presence. As you walk down the street, you are radiating that same energy to everyone on the street. Everyone in your neighborhood is safer because you live where you live, by virtue of the radiance of that which you emanate. If you picture yourself as radiating out an energy field that brings peace, happiness, success and safety to all within your aura, you own your own reality and you are affirming the Divinity of your own creation because it is the Presence of God within, which is the Source of it. We do not take anything for granted. We acknowledge everyone's presence. You are, in addition to being polite also intensifying that person's joy of their own existence.

To express appreciation is to uplift all of life and to bring Divinity closer to the experience of others as an inner experience. They do not recognize the source. All they know is that they feel happier and that they are more inclined to go into **teamwork**. Instead of "me, me, me", it now becomes "us, us, us". A whole team of people all together and it would not be the same without every one of them as an individual. It is nice to be somebody that people look forward to your coming, instead of hiding the china and locking up the children. "I put the dog away because so and so is coming." We influence everything around us. That is the important thing, because if you think you are just doing it for yourself, it will seem shallow. No, you become the best you can be in every way possible for the goodness of the world, for the benefit of the world and it is not being grandiose to realize that. Naturally, things are better because you are part of the world in which we all live.

101 Ways to Success (7)

48. **Group support**
49. **Dress the part**
50. **Find a coach**
51. **"When in Rome, do as the Romans do"**
52. **Identify, evaluate the successful**
53. **Watch for subtleties**
54. **Cut giant-size projects into bite-size portions**

Slide 212

SLIDE 212: 101 WAYS TO SUCCESS (7)

This slide was introduced at the October 2009 lecture, DVD disc 2 at 002245.

Traditionally, dedicated spiritual seekers have formed their own groups and styles of study and meditation. "**Group support**" of spiritual groups such as the 12 Step groups depends on the sponsor's power, derived from successful experience and, therefore, mastery of the presenting problem. Such spiritual groups radiate an energy field that then benefits the newcomer by individual and group alignment maintained by self-honesty.

Dress the part because a part of life is unconsciously role-playing. Of course, you can do that with hypnosis. You can tell people that they are something or not something and they will immediately begin to act and behave that way. "You're afraid of everybody and you don't have much confidence", and the person will instantly become hesitant and self-deprecating, etc. Life is an endless theater, so you **dress the part** that you are playing in the theater. The lack of a tie is an expression of male freedom. People you can trust do not wear a tie. You can change your whole mood and ambience by the way you dress. Of course, that is why there are dress codes in certain areas of life, because if you dress like a slob, you act like a slob, and if you dress neatly, then you have to act neatly.

Everybody needs a life coach. Everybody needs feedback, and it is helpful to share what you do with others. The people you are friendly with, you share it with them because you get feedback. People in any kind of business need a life coach, a person with twenty more years of experience than you have. You try out your ideas on them. That will save you all kinds of disasters and mistakes. So **finding a coach** can be helpful to everybody. Many times traditionally, people have used a priest, a rabbi, a neighbor's psychologist, a great-aunt, a great-grandmother, somebody who can give you some kind of a feedback on what you are saying. When Dr. Hawkins was in psychiatry and psychoanalysis, he had an analyst and even though he had finished his analysis years and years ago, he would go back and see his analyst periodically to share his experience and any areas for improvement. You want some kind of objective feedback from others, so you are not just "me, me, me" in the mirror all the time. We all need somebody who can give us trustable feedback. We trust them because we know what their intention is, our welfare.

"When in Rome, do as the Romans do" is something many people seem to fail to learn. It is due to narcissism, they insist on doing it their way when they are in a different culture. It is respectful to respect their culture and try to blend in. **Identify and evaluate the successful**. Become like them. Adopt what positive aspects they have. **Watch for subtleties**. A slight delay in a gesture of a split second has a completely different meaning. As you move forward into the world of success, you will find that subtleties have greater meaning than that which is overt. Nuances have to do with style and a way of being, and the way of being has to do with the degree of self-confidence as well as the training and the background of people. Some people are automatically polite when it is not even required. You are automatically polite and considerate of others all the time because that is what you have become. **Cut giant-size projects into bite-size portions** because giant-size projects are too dismaying. Dr. Hawkins described how he dug a ditch on both sides of the road for a quarter of a mile by just doing six feet a day at first, and when that became easy, he found he could do twelve, and the next day he could do eighteen, so we benefit from the confidence of that which we have accomplished.

101 Ways to Success (8)

55. **Activate the 'Ego Ideal' (Freud)**

56. **Capitalize on energy and inspirational surges**

57. **Have note pad next to the bed**

58. **Ask what does the world value, want, or need and supply it**

59. **Capitalize on frenetic energy surges**

60. **Plod along between bursts**

Slide 213

SLIDE 213: 101 WAYS TO SUCCESS (8)

This slide was introduced at the October 2009 lecture, DVD disc 2 at 004200.

Activate the Freudian "Ego Ideal", which is the internalization of admired qualities, achievements, or heroic figures that are inspirational and represent possibilities for growth and development. The admired figures are in accord with the individual's prevailing level of consciousness so that each level characteristically tends to have its commensurate inspirational leaders. Lack of such an internalized figure can stem from poor or absent parenting, or lack of self-esteem or sense of personal worth that leads to expectations of failure, pessimism, and the 'a motivational syndrome', characterized by the losing of interest in social endeavors and participation in activities. You will get **energy and inspiration in surges so you learn to capitalize on them**, instead of dismissing them by saying, "Well, I'll do that later today at four o'clock." When the urge comes on you at eight in the morning to complete a certain project, it saves a lot of expenditure of time, thought and energy to sit down and do it. It is not what you do, but it is what you are that provides the inspirational urge. You do not think it; you just become aware.

The next trick: **always have a notepad next to your bed**. With all the wonderful insights and wonderful phrases and thoughts you have had, just before you go to bed, you say, "I'll remember that in the morning." In the morning, you forgot what it was. Always have a note next to the bed as that is a sign of your enthusiasm. To be rational you a**sk what does the world value, want or need and then try to supply it**. Does your idea fit it or supply it? Those are the ways to guarantee success.

Capitalize on frenetic energy surges. Once every so often, you will get just a frenetic surge of energy. The thing to do is capitalize on it. Do not put it aside and say, "I will do it later when I have time at three o'clock", because at three o'clock the energy surge is not there. Many times Dr. Hawkins would jump out of bed at three in the morning, go into his study, write down a few significant words and then go back to bed. One learns from experience to write the ideas down when they are a hot topic in your mind. In this connection, Dr. Hawkins gave the example of Donald Trump's enthusiasm. People wonder what makes him run, he already has more millions than he could ever spend or utilize. The next thing you know he is going to take over sixteen more casinos in South America. Taking over all the gambling and building new casinos across the world has become a game he enjoys. Why does he do it? He does it because he likes to do it, for the fun of it as he just loves doing what he does. That is what makes him run. Not greed, he has enough money already, he could not possibly spend it all. It is the fun of the game, so capitalize on these frenetic energy surges.

In between bursts of energy, just plod along. There are times when you are just bursting with all kinds of brilliant energy and genius, strokes of genius, and you write these all down on the notepad next to your bed. Until that happens again, you plod along. As an example, in coming up with "101 ways to Success", Dr. Hawkins shared that 55 of them were inspirational, 10 of them were goofy ideas and the rest of them are from 'just plodding along'.

101 Ways to Success (9)

61. **Expect success**
62. **Nail down a specialty**
63. **Write about your project**
64. **Do a sales pitch on video**
65. **Promise yourself periodic rewards**
66. **Make photos of yourself in a successful role**
67. **Reward yourself for productivity**

Slide 214

SLIDE 214: 101 WAYS TO SUCCESS (9)

This slide was introduced at the October 2009 lecture, DVD disc 2 at 004815.

People who have an inner integrity begin to **expect success**. You know that if you put your mind to a project that it is going to turn out all right. If you are going to make a jug of iced tea for this afternoon, you know that it is going to be good iced tea. You can learn to depend on yourself. **Nail down a specialty** means that it is nice to get a little niche in the world that is all yours. Donald Trump has that niche in gambling casinos and so you do not have to do anything much in gambling casinos, figuring that belongs to Donald. **Write about your project**. It is a way of organizing yourself and it will bring in thoughts that you did not have until you actually wrote them down. These are practice steps. **Do a sales pitch on video**. That activates a whole lot of energies that you were not aware of before. Because we are visual, auditory, and cerebral, using these different modalities can be helpful. When you do a sales pitch, you are doing it in movement, you are doing it in speech, you are doing it as a style of presentation and as you do a video on some project, the understanding of the project will be different at the end of the video than it was at the start of the video. If you have a thing that can make videos at home, you give yourself a sales pitch on video for the project you are working on, whether it is designing a new dress or how you are going to fix up your car.

You want to **promise yourself periodic rewards**, that at a certain time you are going to acknowledge your own creativity and take pleasure in it and share it with your family or share it with your wife and then both of you can comment on it. That starts a further development of the thought process. Aside from doing videos, you can **make photos of yourself in a successful role**. If you take some photographs of yourself, you begin to notice that you look like a slob, with everything unbuttoned and hair is a mess, etc. You begin to be aware that that which you are also expresses itself nonverbally. Not only in style, language and gesture, but also the way you dress and your manner and the manner in which you carry yourself. Making photos of yourself in a successful role is a way of affirming that aspect of your life that you are trying to grow into. For example, take a picture of yourself and put it on your desk with the label, "President." You have a company going, a company you are working for, so you just put the sign that says "President" and take the picture of yourself as president. You have never really thought about being president of this company before, but the minute you do that you begin to see, yes, you could be, actually. All of a sudden, you see the pathway to becoming president. You begin to become that which you think you are. You become your role. Audio-visual is quite powerful. Much of what is happening in today's world is not the cause of the nightly news but a consequence of it. It is the nightly news that is causing tomorrow's news. You are creating today's news by what attention and energy you give to which subjects. The attention and energy that you give to certain subjects then creates the reality out of the audio-visual image of it. The TV news is quite powerful. One reason to track it is it tells you exactly what is happening in various areas of the world, which may or may not have surfaced yet, but you know that they are going to, soon.

Reward yourself for productivity, which begins at the level of Courage where you put back into the world as much energy as you take. At lower levels, individuals drain energy from society without reciprocating. Because accomplishments result in positive feedback, self-reward and esteem become progressively self-reinforcing.

101 Ways to Success (10)

68. **Give yourself a dollar for each great idea**
69. **"To thine own self be true"**
70. **Put together an inspirational collage**
71. **Be 'on the road' of enterprise**
72. **You don't have to be a genius to build a better mousetrap**
73. **Clarity of goals**

Slide 215

SLIDE 215: 101 WAYS TO SUCCESS (10)

This slide was introduced at the October 2009 lecture, DVD disc 2 at 005450.

Give yourself a dollar for each great idea. Then as time goes on you will see they pile up. Dr. Hawkins described the time when he was in Peru, near Machu Picchu, all by himself, in the middle of nowhere and there was this little girl standing there holding this llama. He had a camera, so he said to her, "Do you mind if I take your picture?" She said, "That'll be a dollar." And that is where Dr. Hawkins got the phrase "That'll be a dollar" from. People used to ask Dr. Hawkins questions after lectures, and many times he would say, "That'll be a dollar." And pretty soon he had collected a lot of dollars (which were donated to charity.) Anyway, this practice came spontaneously from this beautiful little girl, high up in the Andes.

"**To thine own self be true**", be true to yourself, to your own standards. That is to the integrity, the reality of that which you really are, to be true to that. If your innate nature is to be kind towards others and forgiving, then be true to that image. When the crowd is roaring for the guillotine, you are not in the crowd because that is not your way of seeing the world. The way you see the world, people make mistakes and you do not believe in beheading them for it. In the days of the guillotine, one can guess that there was quite a mob. During the French Revolution, there were 15,000 people guillotined to death. Some people were in the crowd and enjoyed watching the guillotine come down. Other people avoided it, so "to thine own self be true," be true to your own standards.

You **put together an inspirational collage**, a way of showing a collection of things that image what you are holding in mind. Collage is a technique where an artwork is made from an assembly of different forms including magazine clippings, artwork, texts, photographs, etc. glued to a piece of paper or canvas, thus creating a new whole. If you keep putting pictures of jet planes up on your bulletin board, somewhere out of the blue, one might emerge. You are trying to bring about a phenomenon in the world using a variety of techniques you can see. Unconscious suggestion, imaging, role-playing, pictorial, a collage of all the things you would have if you were that. If you want to be successful and have a Cadillac, you get pictures of Cadillacs and you put them up. **Be 'on the road' of enterprise**. That means you should be traveling in the direction that you have in mind for yourself, cultivating the relationships that will be supportive, cultivating the intellectual input, the learning, the courses you could be taking. **You don't have to be a genius to build a better mousetrap**. It means that this is a consequence of awareness. You see what the world needs and you just automatically try to invent something that will handle it. Over the years, one can invent a number of things just for one's own sake. Of course, any of them could become a product that you could then advertise, and sell and manufacture. **Clarity of your goals** is the first requirement for success. By success what are the exact goals, what do you mean by success? Clarify the goals means to nail down in a concrete fashion exactly what you mean by a success.

101 Ways to Success (11)

74. 'Do' instead of crave

75. Put heart instead of ego into the project

76. Which aspects are ego and which ones are soul?

77. Is success a feeling or a reality?

78. Self-rewarding vs. public adulation?

79. Success as adequate to lifestyle

Slide 216

SLIDE 216: 101 WAYS TO SUCCESS (11)

This slide was introduced at the October 2009 lecture, DVD disc 2 at 010045.

'Do' instead of crave. The only thing you can actually 'do' is to 'be' your potential to the fullest. That 'one is responsible for the effort but not the result' is a 12 step program basic dictum that curbs the ego. So, any of you that are interested in success, it is important to get a page and write down exactly what you mean by a success in all the details. You may like a little cozy place off in the woods some place and nobody knows you are there except the birds and the animals. Other people like the sound of city traffic and when traffic comes to a halt, they feel depressed. You have to decide what you are: a city person or a country person?

Put your heart instead of your ego into the project. Heart is passion. You put your passion into the project instead of just the ego's idea of gain. The ego sees success in terms of gain, titles, money, positions, etc. The heart sees it as fulfillment. If you put your heart into the project instead of your ego, you will find that it takes less energy. To fulfill it for the ego's ends takes energy, it takes energy away from you. If you are doing it out of the passion, out of the love for the project that does not take any energy out of you. In fact, by the time you finish the project, you will feel more energetic than you did before you started it. Many people in sport understand this very well. The love of the sport is what puts them out on the practice ground and they will do for the love of the sport that which they would never do for money. **Which aspects of your projects are ego, and which ones are from the perspective of the soul?** The ego is looking for gain and not only just gain, but the glamour of the gain. Which aspects of your project are ego driven, and which ones derive from the essence of that which you are?

Is success just a feeling or is it a reality? Is success something real or is it something you just project onto it? You say, getting to a certain level, in your eyes, makes you a success. Is that just a feeling or is that a reality? Would other people agree with you and would it make any difference? There are times when it does not make any difference whether other people consider you a success or not, so it is a feeling rather than a reality.

Self-rewarding versus public adulation means is success for you self-rewarding, or are you looking for the 'hurrah' of the crowd? What are you looking for? If it is self-rewarding, then you are independent of the public's reaction. So long as you want public adulation or public applause, you are now the victim of the media and everything out there. Self-rewarding implies that you want to be the best you can be, because you have taken a vow to do that. Self-rewarding means that you have fulfilled your understanding, rather than pleasing the public. If I am going to be a good congressman, I have to satisfy my own conscience, not necessarily please the public. So you are answerable, a person of integrity is answerable to themselves. A person of less integrity is only interested in the adulation of the crowd, the cheer of the crowd. If you are aware that that is your purpose, and that is acceptable to you, there is nothing wrong with it, but at least you are not fooling yourself.

Success as adequate to your lifestyle means success has to be appropriate to that which you are. Some people pretend greater success than they have. Other people are chronically poor-looking even though their mattress is stuffed with money.

101 Ways to Success (12)

80. Light-hearted vs. grim

81. Success as adequacy rather than Olympic star

82. Success as good partnership

83. Success as dependability and reliability

84. Success as responsible, reliable

85. Stop giving energy to self-doubt

Slide 217

SLIDE 217: 101 WAYS TO SUCCESS (12)

This slide was introduced at the October 2009 lecture, DVD disc 2 at 011030.

To be **light-hearted versus being grim**, that the pathway to success should be pleasant and easygoing instead of white-knuckled. You see many people trying for success and it is pathetic, your heart goes out for them, you say, good God! To such extremes they go for that which should be automatic, because **success is being adequate rather than being some kind of an Olympic star**. To be adequate means to utilize the faculties that you have just normally, but use them with a goal, a goal in mind.

One way to success is merely being friendly, pleasant and **good partnership**. If you think of somebody you want to accompany you on the road to success, you do not want somebody who is white-knuckled, boring and grim. Success is a more general kind of attitude of being **dependable and reliable**, being pleasant, agreeable, and friendly. Success is being **responsible as well as reliable**. It means you are willing to be accountable for your efforts.

Therefore, it is important to **stop giving energy to self-doubt**. Why give energy to that which is negative? The desire is to produce the best possible performance, whether you are on a job, or on a trip, or you are doing a minor repair on the car, whatever it is. There is a pleasure in knowing that you have done the best possible job you could at the time. You cannot compare it to the hypothetical, i.e. if you had had a hundred dollars' worth of equipment, you could have done a better job. If the car breaks down, you get it going again, the normal person is pleased, so there is just a normalcy to success. You watch the whole animal kingdom and they are happy when they have achieved something. A dog is as happy as a clam when she finds something she has lost and picks it up. There is just a normal mammalian kind of a pleasure in being alive and functioning in a successful, self- rewarding way.

101 Ways to Success (13)

86. Give up the excuse of 'trying' – just *do* it

87. Write down all the 'negatives' and bury them in the back yard

88. Identify helpful contacts

89. Do "Brain Gym" exercises of the road to be traveled

90. Energize each step

91. Avoid ethically dubious schemes

Slide 218

SLIDE 218: 101 WAYS TO SUCCESS (13)

This slide was introduced at the October 2009 lecture, DVD disc 2 at 011330.

Give up the excuse of 'trying' and make a decision to *do* a thing. You were not supposed to *try* to make things with your tinker toys; you were supposed to *make* them. Not *try* to make a locomotive with it, but *make* a locomotive out of that. You have to do it, not fake it. Do not try to do a thing, just do it because trying to do it puts it in the future and doing it puts it in the present.

Another trick is **write down all the 'negatives' and bury them in the backyard**. As a child in camp, many of us would dig a big hole in the back, we would all sit around the campfire and then we would all have to write our resentments against some other kids and put them in this hole. When we finished putting our resentments in this hole, we covered it up with dirt. It is not silly because you are actualizing something that would otherwise be in the abstract, non- specific. Acting out symbolically brings it to a different level.

Identify helpful contacts. Now we are back again to the practical, the value of having feedback from consultants and experts. Identify helpful contacts, those who would be helpful to you in developing your idea and moving it forward. You know, "if I were you I'd make it blue instead of green, it'll show up better." "Oh, you're right."

Do the "Brain Gym" exercises of the 'road to be traveled', i.e. the activities necessary in accomplishing a goal. Brain Gym is where you put your neurons through the whole exercise in connection with your project. For example, you picture yourself sitting down. Then you picture yourself picking up the pen. After that, you picture yourself writing a book. You picture yourself proofreading it, you picture yourself getting it typed, now you are going to read the typed copy, then you are going to correct the typed copy, then you picture yourself dictating the corrections, then communicating the corrections and finally, you picture yourself correcting the corrected copy. The Brain Gym goes through all the things that you have to do and somehow the neurons and the dendrites connect with each other.

You **energize each step**, not just the overall pattern but also each step of the way. That which you energize develops a certain momentum of itself. Highly successful people learn how to take advantage of momentum, how to energize, how to move those dendrites to be connected correctly, how to get yourself enthused. With yourself and your Brain Gym, there is a game of working towards fulfilling an end. You have a book in mind that you want to write, all kinds of little short things that you have noticed in life that you cannot make a whole book out of, but they are significant and things people do not recognize. Things you have noticed, especially in the media. When you are old enough, you can just publish your essays and commentaries and if people do not like them, it is OK. At least you have had your say. Everybody should have their say before they go. If you have not written a book of essays yet, you should start it now. These are your commentaries on life and the book reflects your values and many observations that other people do not make.

Avoid ethically dubious schemes. If there is anything that makes you uncomfortable about a thing, it is best to avoid it. One reason is that to the person you are now at this age it may be a little okay. As you get older, the ethical responsibilities seem to be more demanding and a morally dubious scheme that you pulled off at twenty-five, at forty-five it is going to bother you, at sixty-five it is really a burden and by eighty-five, you know you are going to meet God soon and it may be difficult to forgive yourself.

101 Ways to Success (14)

92. **Have supportive relationships: friends, family, cohorts**

93. **'Fake it till you make it' rehearsal**

94. **Select role model**

95. **Decide to be happy no matter what the result**

96. **Great success is often fortuitous - 'expect the unexpected'**

Slide 219

SLIDE 219: 101 WAYS TO SUCCESS (14)

This slide was introduced at the October 2009 lecture, DVD disc 2 at 012945.

Have supportive relationships: friends, family, cohorts. To illustrate this, Dr. Hawkins related a story from his childhood. When Dr. Hawkins was a kid, he was very shy. As a kindergartner he was in this play where he was supposed to be behind a big cardboard Christmas tree, and on the key word he was supposed to say, "Robin, hop, hop, hop", and he was supposed to hop, hop, hop in front of this tree and then back around behind the tree again. On the day of the play, the teacher said, "Robin, hop, hop, hop," but Dr. Hawkins 'the kid' would not come out, as he felt too shy. He stayed behind the tree. "Robin, hop, hop, hop," she would say louder and louder. No matter what, the kid would not come out from behind the tree.

Success is a style, a way of being in the world. This way of being guarantees that all outcomes will be all right, that all of them will be acceptable, and it is okay to be a shy robin and not come out from behind the tree. People say, "Why didn't you come out from behind the tree?" Dr.

Hawkins responds, "Because I was shy and that is okay. End of story. I was too shy to be a robin in kindergarten. If I have to be re-born, I would not go to kindergarten. They are always trying to get you into some rotten kindergarten play. That is all to pull out the parents and the aunts and the grandparents to go and see little Joey be a robin in the play. I feel sorry for the parents, the grandparents, the aunts and the uncles who have to go and see the little kid be a robin in the kindergarten play. It is a tough one and difficult to survive. Well, because you love little tots and they are all cute, you go and it is sort of a fun exercise." It is necessary to have **supportive relationships about you** and there should be coaches on that exercise helping you to **'fake it till you make it' rehearsal**.

Select a role model. It is educational to select a successful role model and pattern oneself in accord with those traits, such as determination, commitment, skill, and integrity. One does not become a success by envying and vilifying others, but by imitating them. The image you have of the perfect life is to be that which lights up the world wherever you go. "That which is lit up by the love of God and acknowledges God as creator, when they walk through the woods, the whole woods know it" (tested true). The decision to be happy, no matter what the result, means that the source of your happiness does not depend on the world, or your performance.

Decide to be happy no matter what the result, so that would be through the effort, by your commitment to express the best of that which you are capable, to be helpful to all of society in all of its ways. To be a happy person means that you live according to certain rules, guidelines and qualifications. Therefore, you do not have to have a result; you just have to be that way. The fact that you are as friendly as you can be and as helpful as you can be, does not mean that you have to be popular. If you are just doing that to be popular, that is quite different from doing that because that is what you are as a person.

Great success is often fortuitous-expect the unexpected. When Alexander Fleming noticed the Petri dish where growth of mold was able to kill bacteria, it was the basic discovery that led eventually to the discovery of penicillin and changed the history of World War II. People who used to die from infections now got a shot of penicillin and one million units of penicillin would cure just about anything. That was a fortuitous observation. The person, the witness, became enhanced by the observation. The fact that truth makes you go strong and falsehood makes you go weak is fortuitous. It is so automatic and infallible that one can incorporate it into one's lifestyle without ever thinking about it. It is fortuitous, but extremely useful. It does not create any product in the world, much less profit, but it does teach people to pay attention to the facts of life. If you happen to make an observation that leads to great discoveries what happens is, you are thankful, you are not prideful. Dr. Hawkins was very thankful that he discovered how to discern truth from falsehood in about an instant, at no cost. He was very thankful to Almighty God for such a wondrous gift.

101 Ways to Success (15)

97. **Avoid the 'winning the lottery' calamity**
98. **Keep a watchful eye on the ego**
99. **Realize the world has gotten along without you thus far**
100. **Success is whatever you say it is – win the hula hoop contest, eat more hot dogs in 10 minutes**
101. **Fame is only fame**

Slide 220

SLIDE 220: 101 WAYS TO SUCCESS (15)

This slide was introduced at the October 2009 lecture, DVD disc 2 at 013735.

Avoid the 'winning the lottery' calamity. You may have seen on television what happens to people who win thirteen million dollars or something like that. What happens to the life of the people who win the lottery is 100% calamitous. Divorce rate is 100%, suicide rate is extremely high, drugs and accident rates are much higher than normal. The most calamitous thing that can happen to you is to win the lottery. It is because it has both conscious and unconscious consequences. Of course, the media make it even worse. You can imagine how many friends you will have if they broadcast on evening television that you just won the lottery. Your mailbox is jammed and everyone wants something from you, "I'm a poor widow with five children and I have tuberculosis and four of my children have polio and we're all living in a Hogan in South America, surrounded by demons and a small donation would mean life or death to us." If that does not joggle some money out of you, one does not know what will. Avoid winning the lottery and do not buy a lottery ticket because you might win it. *Idiots* buy the tickets. It is a sucker's game. They get the money out of them. "Winning the lottery is probably the worst thing that can happen to you in our society-resist" (tested true). It is not just money, but also the energy all that pulls in, not to mention the media attraction. So, pray to God, "Dear God, please don't let me win the lottery tonight, Amen."

Keep a watchful eye on the ego, the grandiose "I am." When you are successful, the ego tends to jump in and say, "Boy, aren't I wonderful? I'm terrific and I must be really the best in the world." Keep a watchful eye on the ego, the narcissistic egocentricity, which is always hungry. The ego keeps itself alive by feeding on the energies and therefore it is always hopeful of taking over. Its enemy is spiritual alignment. The enemy of the ego is spirituality. Without spirituality to balance it, the ego runs everything, runs the person's life and runs him eventually into hopelessness. Keep a watchful eye on the ego. Realize that the ego, the egocentricity, is prideful and always looking to win.

Realize the world has gotten along without you thus far. That is one that brings one back to reality, to realize the world has gotten along without you thus far- aw, geez!

Success is whatever you say it is- win the 'hula hoop' contest, eat more hot dogs in ten minutes, etc., whatever people will do for publicity. Mark David Chapman shot John Lennon dead because he wanted to be famous. Talk about egocentricity. That is probably the all-time, world winner. Yet, there are more crimes reported recently of the same ilk. Can you imagine shooting somebody dead in order to be famous? Success is whatever you say it is. Shoot John Lennon, win the 'hula hoop' contest, look at all these people who see how many hotdogs they can eat in ten minutes.

In the end, after all the 101 ways, of course you are going to be successful. Then you realize that **fame is only fame**. It is not the magic chariot to Heaven and it is not going to fill your life with beautiful women clamoring to jump in bed with you. Today's fame is tomorrow's disgrace and it is the day after that is re-run. No matter how spectacular your life is, folks, someday you are all going to be a rerun. God has a big TV set, and He pushes a button and there goes a rerun on your life for review. Do you ever keep that in mind while acting, speaking or thinking? You run your life forward and you run it backward for fun and sometimes it is best just to push the "Erase" button. That particular incident we will just hit "Erase." As life goes on, you want to avoid the things you have to erase later on. That is one reason to be integrous.

HANDLING SPIRITUAL CHALLENGES (1)

Stress

EARLY LIFE

Birth: Sensory overwhelm, hunger, cold, noise, lights, separation, emotion, fear

Midwifery – warm-water, imprinting

Attitude – half-full or half-empty

Secure – safe vs. danger

Slide 221

SLIDE 221: HANDLING SPIRITUAL CHALLENGES (1)

EARLY LIFE

This slide was introduced at April 2010 lecture, DVD disc 1 at 005945.

It is instructive to go through the entire human lifetime from beginning to end, looking at the spiritual challenges of human life and see how best to handle the various stresses to which humans are automatically subject, from the very moment of birth. The stress starts in early life as **birth itself is a sensory overwhelm**. There are the powerful contractions coming down over the body, and then emerging out of warm darkness, safety and security into **lights so bright it is blinding, cold and overwhelmingly loud voices**. The environment is cold and no longer safe, warm and secure to the baby. So one starts out life behind the eight ball, in a negative sensory overwhelm and of course, you have not eaten yet, so you are **hungry**. You go through **separation anxiety, the emotion of fear**. The delivery can be assisted by midwifery. Nowadays, the **midwife can help birth the infant child into a warm tub of water**.

One of the first phenomena as soon as you are born is **the phenomenon of imprinting,** whereby **whatever you are surrounded by, you imprint, and that becomes your mother**. This has a profound effect on the rest of your life. What you have imprinted on is there relatively permanently and you will always associate that with safety and security. On the other hand, if the midwifery was bad, and you were not put in warm water, and made to feel secure you are going to be afraid of every new situation. What we imprint on, we tend to hold that as a mother. That is a very interesting thing to know. Whatever you are strangely attracted to, you can ask yourself, "What could I have imprinted on in childbirth?" Usually the first person you see is your mom, nobody else. The mother has traditionally been that which creates and sustains life and so the mother deserves reverence and really reigns supreme. The father is necessary for a few seconds and you can get rid of him. Everything relies on the mother. The mother in our culture, on a certain level, is almost divine. To speak against her, to turn against your mother is not thinkable. Midwifery tries to overcome the negative impacts of childbirth.

Out of this, you arise with an **attitude, either an optimist or a pessimist. Life is either half-empty or half-full** and that determines whether you are going to be an optimist or a pessimist, whether you are going to be **secure and feel safe or you are going to feel that life is dangerous**. One can see that right from birth itself, from the first few hours of life, it already sets your attitude: This is a safe world, life is safe, or it is a dangerous world.

CHILDHOOD (2)

Affection

Trust

Siblings, rivalry

Discipline

Confidence

Good/Bad

Birth order

Schooling

Religion, soul

Reverence - spirituality

Heaven vs. Hell

Sin, guilt

Parenting skills

Physical health

Heredity

Slide 222

SLIDE 222: HANDLING SPIRITUAL CHALLENGES (2)

CHILDHOOD

This slide was introduced at the April 2010 lecture, DVD disc 1 at 010800.

After the birth phenomena comes childhood itself. What has been your experience of **affection**? What has been your experience of **trust**? What has been your experience of **siblings** and **rivalry**? To be an only child is much different from being one of two children, which is much different from being one of three, which is much different from being one of five, etc. The next thing that sets our attitudes is the kind of **discipline** involved. Some people use positive discipline, other people use negative. Our sense of **confidence** arises out of our childhood. If you got strokes for being good and productive, or whether you were just ignored. This whole idea of **good versus bad**, whether you are a good person, whether life is good or you are a bad person, life is bad. Having bad circumstances at birth very often leads to the chronic criminals.

Life has been bad from the very beginning, bad mothering, bad environment, bad companions, and bad energy.

The next thing that really influences us considerably is **birth order**- were you the oldest of all, the youngest of all, the middle child? Traditionally, certain phenomena happen if you are the oldest child or the youngest one, what the birth order is.

In addition, what sets up our attitudes is our experiences, our experiences in **schooling**, our experiences in **religion**, our knowledge and awareness of having a **soul**, the capacity for **reverence** and for **spirituality**, and the preoccupation with **heaven vs. hell**. Are you really energized by the desire to move to Heaven, or is it merely a fear of hell? **Sin and guilt**, then, bring up all the fears of hell, and **parenting skills**, then, in bringing these across to the child.

The **physical health** and **heredity** are profound factors in influencing our attitudes throughout all of life. The reason we are looking at these things is that they set our life attitudes. Everybody reading this material right now has been interested in all these things in their life to some extent. Any self-aware person looks at all these various phenomena in their life and comes to a certain understanding about why they are the way they are. Does everybody here know why they are the way they are? If you do not know why you are the way you are, you need to research where you grew up. Well, you may need a psychiatrist. That is where the psychiatrist comes in, to help us to adjust to the phenomena that we do not seem able to grasp in ordinary life.

ADOLESCENCE (3)

World events

Emotional climate

Financial adequacy

Social acceptance

Education

Friends, comrades

Sexuality, hormones

Heredity

Slide 223

SLIDE 223: HANDLING SPIRITUAL CHALLENGES (3)

ADOLESCENCE

This slide was introduced at the April 2010 lecture, DVD disc 1 at 011130.

What follows after childhood is adolescence. If we can successfully come out of childhood, then we come into adolescence, where again we are in a world of **world events**. It is either a dangerous world or a safe world. It is an **emotional climate**. The **financial adequacy** of the family and yourself is very significant in how you adjust. The amount of **social acceptance, the education** that you receive, your **friends and comrades**, the emergence of **sexuality and hormones** and your preparation for it are all crucial factors in how you adjust to life. Here, of course, we are profoundly involved in **heredity**. The attitudes that we grow up with, then, are as you can see, the result of a complex interaction of biologic, social, family, and cultural relationships.

ADULTHOOD (4)

(Adverse Events)

Vocation	**Aging**
Courtship	**Political**
Marriage	**Intellectual**
Success	**Philosophical**
Family	**Introvert/Extrovert**
World conditions	**Physical appearance**
Health	**Financial**

Slide 224

SLIDE 224: HANDLING SPIRITUAL CHALLENGES (4)

ADULTHOOD
(Adverse Events)

This slide was introduced at the April 2010 lecture, DVD disc 1, at 011230.

After you have been through that battering ram of whammies of childhood and adolescence, you now become an adult. Now the problems really start. **Vocation**: What am I going to do, what am I going to be in this world? Am I going to get married, be single, am I going to be heterosexual or homosexual, am I going to be part of a group, am I going to be isolated. **Courtship** can profoundly affect your physicality, finances, mental make-up, and social status. **Marriage and family** become extremely important and again, adverse effects can happen to you in searching for success. **World conditions** affect us without our being aware of them. You can keep an eye on the news and periodically throughout the day catch up with world events, because world conditions affect your own emotional attitudes and expectations without you being aware of it. You say, "Well, that is all happening out there." In fact, "out there" is where you live; do not forget the human consciousness is collective. "Everyone is connected to the collective consciousness of mankind" (tests true). "Therefore, everyone is influenced by world events whether they know it or not-resist" (tests true). That is a good thing to know. You say, "Well, that has got nothing to do with me, that is those nut-jobs on the other side of the world." It does affect you. It affects your sense of inner security, your trust of your fellow human beings and your overall worldview, whether it is pessimistic or optimistic.

Of course, your **health** profoundly affects you and your **financial** situation. World conditions affect our wealth, our health, our financial comfort zone. Comfort zone is simple, just spend less than what you make. **Aging** has its own profound effects on attitudes and your **political** and **intellectual** capacity and interests. The eighties certainly are not the sixties, and certainly not the forties and definitely not the thirties, so someone in his eighties may say things because how long he has lived that he sees it that way. It is not political, it is not intellectual, it is just that he belongs to a different age group. His age group has lived through certain things that people in other age groups did not live through. Because they did not live through it, their understanding of it is different.

If your interests are in the 400s, if you are intellectually interested in the *Great Books of the Western World*, you will end up more **philosophic** and sophisticated. We have **the introvert versus the extrovert.** Have we found our comfort zone to be within ourselves, or only when we are with other people? To be an ambivert would be perfect, because then it is okay if you are alone, all by yourself and it is okay if you are surrounded by people. Of course, **physical appearance** profoundly affects all of us. Some people are good-looking and have to fight off the opposite sex. Some of us have to adjust to the fact that we are not looking like Hollywood. Happiness does not depend on that, no. We have known some ugly people, they are hard to look at and yet they were extremely happy, while some beautiful people are extremely miserable. You see handsome young men and lovely women who should be out there, successful in every area, but have a negative self-image which hinders them. These are some of the things we have to surmount, and by our spiritual evolution, we transcend them, which to other people are limitations.

ADULTHOOD (5)

(Adverse Events)

Social role

Catastrophic events

Doubt/Faith

War

Lonely

Moral failure

Seven Deadly Sins

Temptations

Old age, sickness,

poverty & death (Buddha)

Slide 225

SLIDE 225: HANDLING SPIRITUAL CHALLENGES (5)

ADULTHOOD (Adverse Events)

This slide was introduced at the April 2010 lecture, DVD disc 2 at 011230 but was not specifically reviewed.

Social role: With or without one's consent, society forces everyone into various social roles,

e.g. son, wife, one's occupation, etc. They all have the potential downside and often lead to stress and fear. Fear continues throughout life and ends with the fear of death itself, along with fear of the unknown. In normal life, a myriad of defense maneuvers and compensations make life tolerable, yet lurking in the shadows are inexplicable fears. **Catastrophic events** represent loss to the mind and a threat to survival. They indicate a major change and have in common the feeling of powerlessness due to their finality and permanency. The mind perceives that it cannot do anything about them. How to handle **catastrophic events** will depend on one's knowledge of the whole field of consciousness. **Doubt/faith:** A consequence of self-importance based on pride is its need to be constantly fed and propped up to offset the inner **doubt** and deficiency. Wholeness and completeness ensue from fulfilling the requirements of integrity based on **faith** in a Higher Power.

War has prevailed during most of human history. To be 'anti-war' is also an ego position that presumes omniscience. It is best to be 'pro' God's will and Divine providence for the world and humanity instead of being at the adverse effects of war. **Lonely:** The loss of hope and the will to live, along with the accompanying depression, frequently occur in **lonely** isolated persons. It is normal for ordinary people who have gone through the psychological depletion of severe stress, such as divorce, financial disaster, loss of loved ones, and the process of grieving itself to feel lonely. Suicide is a leading cause of death in adolescents.

Moral Failure can lead to a host of problems including repression of anger, aggression, inner hostility, general unpleasantness, undignified manners, and a spiritual setback. These conditions, if not worked through, will have deleterious consequences to health and overall progress. The **Seven Deadly Sins** are hubris, greed, lust, malicious envy, gluttony, inordinate anger, and sloth, and are abuse of one's natural instincts, e.g. gluttony abuses one's desire to eat. To throw off the Ten Commandments and simultaneously indulge in the **Seven Deadly Sins** has devastating consequences. **Temptations:** The spiritually wise reject the temptation of ego inflation of flattery, titles, worldly success, pomp, wealth, worldly power, and other temptations of illusion. True asceticism is a matter of economy of effort or projected value.

Old Age, Sickness, Poverty & Death (Buddha): If one thinks about their life, or looks at the world around them, they will see that life is full of suffering. It is only a matter of time before one experiences suffering of some kind, whether it is a cold, an injury or a sad event — and this suffering must be borne alone. The causes of suffering are desire, ill will, and ignorance which is the inability to see things as they really are. The more people free themselves from desire, ill will and ignorance, the greater their happiness is, no matter what is going on around them. The Buddha advocated the Middle Path in which avoiding the extremes of indulgence and denial leads to the end of suffering. The Buddhist path aims at developing good conduct (right speech, right action, and right livelihood), mind (right effort, right mindfulness, and right contemplation) and wisdom (right attitude, right view of life.)

Most Valuable Qualities for a Spiritual Seeker (1)
(Introduction)

- **Start with certainty and a feeling of security, instead of self-doubt or timidity**
- **Accept without reservation that you are worthy of the quest, and be resolved to totally surrender to the truth about God**

Slide 226

SLIDE 226: MOST VALUABLE QUALITIES FOR A SPIRITUAL SEEKER (1)

Introduction

This slide was introduced at the May 2011 lecture, DVD disc 1 at 005230.

Start with the certainty that if you are spiritually oriented, you will make progress. Start, therefore, with a feeling of **security**. **Instead of insecurity or self-doubt**, tell yourself that anyone who wants to evolve spiritually will receive the necessary assistance and his success is guaranteed by God, which is another name for his own Higher Power. Get rid of **self-doubt**, any idea that you are not worth it or you are not capable of it, or that it is not the right time in your life. It is always the right time in your life. **Accept without reservation that you are worthy of the quest**. Be resolved to **totally surrender to the truth about God** and that your spiritual evolution is aligned with His will for you.

Dr. Hawkins gave the example of Nisargadatta Maharaj, "He ran a 'bidi' shop, a local cigarette smoke shop. Politically incorrect in today's world, that is for sure. Anyway, he ran a smoke shop and he smoked endlessly himself. He would get excited and pound on the table and talk to his followers. He had a little attic up over his 'bidi' shop in Bombay. He was merely practicing the statement that his teacher had given him- 'I am', something simple. He really focused on it and of course, the real critical thing that works in spiritual work is the 'fixity of focus'. When you decide to go for it, it means you cannot deviate from the edge of the knife for even one split second. If you are going to surrender every sensation, impulse, thought to God as it arises into the focus of consciousness, it requires fixity of focus, which is like a laser beam. Enormous intention and you are not going to get off the edge of the knife for anything. Whoops and hollers on this side; sad, crying people on this side; wealth, happiness, seduction, nothing gets you off the edge of the knife. When you start that, you had better warn your friends because the end is near. This is devotion, dedication and the way of the heart. To live on the edge of the knife requires an enormous devotion. One can talk about the way of mind, which I tend to talk about in public. When you talk about the way of the heart, you very often cannot start it because the bliss state comes back, you cannot function in that state and that is the end of the lecture. People can come up and you can bless them, maybe, but that is all that you can do in that state."

Most Valuable Qualities for a Spiritual Seeker (2) (Intro-2)

- **The facts that are to be unreservedly accepted are simple and very powerful**

- **Surrendering to them brings enormous spiritual advancement**

Slide 227

SLIDE 227: MOST VALUABLE QUALITIES FOR A SPIRITUAL SEEKER (2)

Introduction (2)

This slide was introduced at the May 2011 lecture, DVD disc 1 at 005350.

The facts that are to be unreservedly accepted are simple and very powerful. Surrendering to them brings about enormous spiritual progress and advancement. Seemingly small steps in spiritual evolution often occur almost unnoticed, but it is the small shifts which occur out of sight below a mountain of snow that result in an avalanche. Sudden leaps in consciousness can occur with no warning. Therefore, it is best to be prepared for such a possible eventuality.

As Dr. Hawkins shared, "Ramana Maharishi was fifteen or sixteen, not particularly religious, just going about daily life. We checked him out by previously earned karmic inheritance he had. One day he falls to the ground and feels he has died. He felt himself dying. When somebody feels himself dying, you know that he has hit the end of the ego and that he is on the threshold of enlightenment, which is what he did. When he felt himself die, when I read he felt himself die, I knew this was the real thing because that is exactly what happens. Then he went into a bliss state and sat there for weeks. He did not eat and did not drink water and was dehydrated and eaten up by bugs and stuff. It is comical just the way it is. These bugs are eating him and he had not eaten anything, had not drunk anything and he could not care less. He was just in this incredible state.

Here in the US, we would have taken him to the hospital, given him a shock treatment and shot him full of Thorazine, but he was in India where some spiritually sophisticated people realized what had happened to him. They began to chase the bugs away, feed him, get him to drink water, etc. He did not speak for a few years. It is very funny, because in the meantime a fake guru, of which the world abounds, started taking credit for his blissed out state saying, 'this is my student, look at his blissed state,' so he started signing up students right and left. Ramana, being in a mute state, unable to speak or say anything, had nothing to do with it. Of course, he could not have cared less. I mean this person is making a living off him, so what is the difference? If you are a statue, let the birds use you how they will; it does not affect the fact that you are a statue. With coaxing and all, after a few years, Ramana began to learn how to speak. I do not know what he spoke of, but the condition is difficult to explain. So finding the levels of consciousness gave a bridge to try to make the nonlinear comprehensible to the linear."

Most Valuable Qualities for a Spiritual Seeker (3)

1. The living proof of God's love and will for you is the gift of your own existence

Slide 228

SLIDE 228: MOST VALUABLE QUALITIES FOR A SPIRITUAL SEEKER (3)

This slide was introduced in May 2011 Lecture, DVD disc 1 005420.

The living proof of God's love and will for you is the gift of your own existence. The fact that you *are* is the best evidence there is of God's love and will for you. Amen.

The true source of joy and happiness is the realization of one's existence in this very moment. The source of pleasure always comes from within, even though occasioned by some external event or acquisition. In any one instant of time, no such thing as a problem can exist. Unhappiness arises from going beyond the reality of the Now and creating a story out of the past or the future, which, because neither exists, has no reality.

There is a meditation we might call "What For?" When we note a desire, we can ask, "What for?" The answer is always," ...and then I'll be happier." Thus, the locus of happiness is always something that is outside oneself and in the future. This results in viewing oneself as the victim of outer circumstances. This is also a projection of one's power. The possible source of happiness is actually coming from within. There is neither time nor locus of happiness other than this instant now, which is permanent.

There is another meditation we could call "What if, and then what?" This exercise is based on the willingness to surrender the ego's illusions to the reality of God. We start with, "What if we let go of something we desire or value?" and ask, "And then what?" That brings up the next obstacle. We ask if we are willing to surrender it to God, which brings up the next obstacle.

Eventually, the willingness to surrender every illusion that happiness is 'out there' brings an awareness that one's existence from moment to moment is solely by the grace of God. One's life is sustained as a function of the presence of God, and the materiality that we thought sustained it is in itself an expression of God's will for us. One's own efforts to sustain life is a 'given' and not a personal invention. The ego thinks we survive in spite of God's will rather than because of it.

Most Valuable Qualities for a Spiritual Seeker (4)

2. **Do not compare yourself with others regarding 'holiness,' merit, goodness, deservingness, sinlessness, etc.**

   These are all human notions, and God is not limited by human emotions

Slide 229

SLIDE 229: MOST VALUABLE QUALITIES FOR A SPIRITUAL SEEKER (4)

This slide was introduced at the May 2011 lecture, DVD disc 1 at 005440.

Other valuable qualities for a spiritual seeker: **Do not compare yourself with others regarding 'holiness,' merit, goodness, deservingness, sinlessness, etc.** Realize **these are all human notions you have about being 'better' and God is not limited by human notions.** What others are or say is irrelevant. What is important is what you are. In reality, nothing thoughts say about one's self or others has any reality. All statements are fallacious and represent programming and positionalities. The true Self is invisible and has no describable qualities nor can it be the subject of any adjectives at all. The Self merely 'is' and is beyond verbs, adverbs, and adjectives. It does not even 'do' anything. The Scale of Consciousness does not denote 'better than', which is a program of the ego. The Scale merely denotes position or location that in turn denotes associated characteristics. A large tree is not 'better than' a small tree. Thus, the consciousness level denotes a locus on a learning curve and a stage of the evolution of consciousness. The joy of life comes from filling one potentiality at any given level. Each level has its rewards, and they actually feel the same to each person. Goal fulfillment is self-rewarding if the goal of the aspirant is one of devotion. Then a life dedicated to God is endlessly self-fulfilling, whereas, in contrast, a life devoted to gain is full of pitfalls and suffering.

On the Map of the Scale of Consciousness, one can identify the approximate level of any attitude or emotion since they are described rather verbatim. The purpose of the levels is to provide some direction and context for understanding the nature of consciousness. One can estimate one's own level of consciousness by identifying one's prevailing attitudes and positionalities. Thus, if one is always angry or seeing injustices, then anger/pride would be a fair level to identify with at this time and can be undone by a willingness to abandon judgmentalism and see that it is merely a positionality of the mind. How can you experience your own existence? We experience 'That Which I Am' as "I," the pronoun "I." It is very interesting that the pronoun "I" is capitalized just as the "G" is in God. You would think out of humility, man would have made himself a small "i" and God, the big "I," but he did not. Why is "I" the same as "God?" Is that grandiosity, megalomania, insanity, or what? No, it is because the truth is that the personal "I" is knowable only by virtue of the infinite "I" which underlies it. It is because of the universality and the Infinite knowingness of the "I" of the Self, the Presence of God within, which conveys to you the capacity to be aware of your own existence as the small "i" The small "i" knows that it *is* by virtue of the infinite "I", which is the source of its consciousness and awareness and existence. The ultimate statement, 'please define God,' then, is that God is the infinite "I" within, and without, the infinite "I" of all that exists. Beyond all dimensions, beyond all planes, beyond all universes, beyond all divisions. Therefore, you do not want to bring down the level of "I" by saying "Am"-ness because "I" as the Infinite Reality is at 1000. "I" as "Am"-ness is already a considerable condensation, because now you have put the condition of beingness and Is-ness upon it. Beingness and Is-ness means to come into manifestation, but the Infinite "I," that which you really are is the Unmanifest. To say "I Am" means that you are now manifest, limiting the realization of that which you are. At this moment, one may experience one's self as manifest, but that does not mean it is the Ultimate Reality, any more than you are your body or you are your mind.

Most Valuable Qualities for a Spiritual Seeker (5)

3. Accept that the concept of 'the fear of God' is ignorance

- **God is peace and love and nothing else**

Slide 230

SLIDE 230: MOST VALUABLE QUALITIES FOR A SPIRITUAL SEEKER (5)

This slide was introduced at the May 2011 lecture, DVD disc 1 at 005510.

Accept that the concept of 'the fear of God' is ignorance. God is peace and love and nothing else. Many people talk about the fear of God and use God as a threat. People sometimes think God is punishing them for some reason. That is not the case. It is their lack of alignment with Divinity that results is suffering. So, with spiritual evolution you become more and more aware of the goodness of life. You get the intention of the people you are with, the people who designed the place where you are, the gifts of nature, the beautiful flowers and all the things you could possibly want that are here for you. What more could you ask? What is the purpose of the world? It is here for you. Why is this message here? It is here for you.

Everything is here for your comfort. Now, you have to see beyond the egocentric, as to what it means, "the world is here for you." Out of Divine intention that which is here is here for you because the divinity of all that exists shines forth. The essence of all that exists is Divinity Itself. All you are seeing is Divinity in its various expressions all around you: Divinity in its expression as the flowers, Divinity as a soda pop, Divinity as a wonderful friend, Divinity as a Kleenex, etc. You have a Kleenex available because God wants you to have a Kleenex available. If God did not want you to have a Kleenex, there would not be any Kleenexes. Happiness is therefore a goal within easy reach of a grateful heart.

Most Valuable Qualities for a Spiritual Seeker (6)

4. **Realize that the depiction of God as a 'judge' is a delusion of the ego that arises as a projection of guilt from the punishment of childhood**

- **Realize that God is not a parent**

Slide 231

SLIDE 231: MOST VALUABLE QUALITIES FOR A SPIRITUAL SEEKER (6)

This slide was introduced at the May 2011 lecture, DVD disc 1 at 005550.

Realize that the depiction of God as a 'judge' is a delusion. It is an ego fixation, arising out of guilt. "Justice is inherent in the universe as a quality of its essence. Nothing escapes detection within the all-encompassing, timeless, infinite field of consciousness. Consequences are automatic, spontaneous, and guaranteed by the very structure of Creation. Everyone is at some point along the learning curve of the evolution of consciousness, and each level has its inherent characteristics. [...] The soul is the author of its own fate by the exercise of its own choice and selection. Each gravitates to its own concordant dimension. Spiritual paradoxes may appear in response to spiritual choice; for example, the spiritual seeker wants love and joy but that intention triggers the surfacing of all that obstructs it and prevents its appearance. Those who dedicate themselves to peace and love automatically pull up from the unconscious all that is cruel, unloving, and hateful to be healed. This may bring about consternation until judgmentalism about it is replaced with compassion, and forgiveness takes its place. These were, after all, what had obstructed the love and joy, so one can be thankful that these deterrents have been brought up to be resolved by the spiritual tools available." – "I: Reality and Subjectivity" (2003), Chapter 2: Spiritual Information and Practice, pp. 24-25

Realize that God is not a parent. What God becomes in most people's mind is a parent; rewards you and loves you if you are good and punishes you if you are bad. That is nothing but a parent, so realize that God is something much greater than a human 'parent'. In contrast to the ego's perceptions of God, the Absolute Reality of the Self is the manifestation of God as the very core of one's existence. "The concept and definition of God as 'Creator' rather than timeless Presence and ever-present, constant, ongoing Source results in conceptual limitations whereby God is defined in terms of time and causality and thus conceptually linked with the linear, observable daily world. Time itself is a cognitive and perceptual illusion and merely a projection of consciousness [...] God is considered to be not only a 'what' but also a 'who,' as well as a 'when', with personality characteristics that are primarily anthropomorphic (human- like), and particularly so as depicted by the Old Testament. [...] Out of these anthropomorphic projections arises an image of God about which the human is understandably somewhat ambivalent in that God is perceived as benevolent but, paradoxically, also capable of even throwing one's soul into Hell. Thus, God is perceived as being loving but also limited and likened unto one's human parent. [...] The seeming unfairness of human destiny is countered by more sophisticated religions such as Buddhism and Hindu, which teach the laws of karma." – "Reality, Spirituality, and Modern Man", Chapter 12: God as Hypothesis, pp. 226-227

Most Valuable Qualities for a Spiritual Seeker (7)

5a. Christ's teaching was essentially and simply to avoid the negativity (calibrated levels below 200), and the goal of his teaching was for his followers to reach Unconditional Love (calibration level 540)

Slide 232

SLIDE 232: MOST VALUABLE QUALITIES FOR A SPIRITUAL SEEKER (7)

This slide was introduced in May 2011 Lecture, DVD disc 1 005610.

Jesus Christ's teaching was essentially and simply to avoid negativity. His purpose for his followers (Christianity) was to reach the level of Unconditional Love. What Jesus Christ wanted us to reach was Unconditional Love, calibration level 540 and over. The following excerpt, paraphrased from the Question and Answer section of the December 2005 lecture "God, Religion, and Spirituality" is helpful in putting into perspective many of the statements on Lord Christ, Lord Buddha and Lord Krishna:

"Q: In the Bible, Jesus says something to the affect "I am the Way, the Truth, and the Light. No one comes to the Father except though me". How does that square with other religions in the world, like Buddhism that do not believe in Jesus Christ?

A: Jesus Christ is just a nominalization. You can remove the name Jesus Christ and it is still an energy field that you go through in evolution. The Christ Body is one of the highest etheric bodies, right before the Atmic. You do not get to the Atmic without going through the Christ Body. [...] When you let go of the selfish, the egotistical, the linear, you then become the expression of the Source of your own creation. You can label that anything, Buddhist or any other terms as the labels do not mean anything. Do not forget all labels are only historic designations. The great gurus of all time were already in existence in 10,000 BC. They calibrated at close to 1000 at 10,000 BC, but Jesus Christ came to speak to a certain group of people. He did not appear in India where the gurus already had dominion. He came to the people that were worshiping the golden calf. They needed the words of Jesus Christ. Whether you pursue Truth via one pathway or the other, it is irrelevant as there is so much karmic influence on that. So much karmic influence of what you have done, what you have tried, what you have failed at.

Each one typifies something you really want to learn about yourself. Jesus Christ taught forgiveness, so all that which is unforgivable comes up in someone destined for Christianity. Buddha, Socrates and Jesus Christ all taught the same thing. The Buddha said there is no point in attacking your enemies because they will bring themselves down by their own hand. Collectively when you become sufficiently advanced, they are all saying the same thing, different languaging."

Most Valuable Qualities for a Spiritual Seeker (8)

5b. Christ knew that once the level of Unconditional love was reached, the soul's destiny after death was certain and the soul was safe

- **This is essentially the same conclusion taught by the world's great religions, such as Lotus Land Buddhism**

Slide 233

SLIDE 233: MOST VALUABLE QUALITIES FOR A SPIRITUAL SEEKER (8)

This slide was introduced at the May 2011 lecture, DVD disc 1 at 005655.

Christ knew that that once the level of Unconditional Love was reached, the soul's destiny was certain and the soul was safe. This is essentially the same teaching as the world's other great religions, such as Lotus Land Buddhism. Sometimes spiritual seekers will become confused- are they following the right teacher, are they studying with the right teacher, are they reading the right books, are they going to the right church, do they belong to the right religion. What you do is you filter through the pathways and you see that the essence of all of them is almost identical. The essence, not the surface of it, but the essence is almost identical.

From "Transcending the Levels of Consciousness: The Stairway to Enlightenment" (2006), Chapter 5: Fear, pp. 111-112: "Even primitive belief systems of punitive, jealous, vengeful, and angry gods also provide resolutions by which redemption and salvation can be granted. Within rational and confrontable realms, these include absolution by confession, penance, and acceptance of a Savior, institution of a major change of behavior, prayer, entreaty, and basically surrendering one's will to God.

It is useful to realize that all life, from moment to moment, is based on faith by whatever name it may be called. Even the atheist clings to the belief system out of faith that the beliefs are authentic and valid. Research on the calibrated levels of consciousness verified the validity of the world's major religions and spiritual belief systems (*Truth vs. Falsehood*, 2005).

Peace can be the consequence of surrender to the inevitabilities of life. The religious/spiritual skeptic can look within and observe that the inner fundamental irreducible quality of life is the capacity of awareness, consciousness, and the substrate of subjectivity. Without consciousness, the individual would not 'know' or even 'know' if they 'know', so that consciousness is *a priori* awareness of existence, irrespective of the content of that existence. Thus, consciousness itself can be accepted as an obvious reality, without the elaboration of being Divine (as recommended by the Buddha). To 'be' is one thing; to *know* that one 'is' obviously requires a more transcendent quality."

Most Valuable Qualities for a Spiritual Seeker (9)

6. Realize that salvation and enlightenment are somewhat different goals

- **Salvation requires purification of the ego; enlightenment requires its total dissolution**
- **The goal of enlightenment is more demanding and radical**

Slide 234

SLIDE 234: MOST VALUABLE QUALITIES FOR A SPIRITUAL SEEKER (9)

This slide was introduced at the May 2011 lecture, DVD disc 1 at 005755.

Realize that salvation and enlightenment are somewhat different goals. Salvation is concerned with a 'yes' or 'no' answer to acceptance of a Savior. Enlightenment is concerned with becoming something beyond that which you have been. **Salvation requires purification of the ego; enlightenment is concerned with letting it go** and eliminating the ego. **The goal of enlightenment is somewhat more demanding than simply being a good person**. Enlightenment is something other than good personhood. It is advancing one's level of consciousness in the nonlinear realms.

From "Transcending the Levels of Consciousness: The Stairway to Enlightenment" (2006), Chapter 5: Fear, pp. 116-117: "The Judaic-Christian and Islamic religions provide resolutions of salvation and redemption, while Buddhism and Hinduism stress spiritual evolution from the limitations of the linear ego to higher nonlinear levels of spiritual identification. However contextualized, the consequences of sin/error/limitation/ ignorance are counterbalanced by Divine Mercy, Love, and Compassion.

From consciousness research, it becomes confirmably clear that the fate of one's soul is the consequence of one's own choices and decisions rather than by retribution of an angry deity. Thus, like a cork in the sea that rises to its own innate degree of buoyancy, or an iron filing that moves automatically within a universal electromagnetic field, each spirit determines its own evolutionary position within the nonlinear context of the overall infinite field of consciousness.

Divine Justice is innate and autonomous as a consequence of Creation itself. In addition, the overall omnipresence of Allness includes ever-present options for salvation. The Justice of God is thus perfect in that it also affords perfect freedom as well as the opportunity for the evolution of consciousness and spiritual awareness. (The above calibrates at 945; in contrast, anthropomorphic depictions of God calibrate at 75.)"

Most Valuable Qualities for a Spiritual Seeker (10)

10. Clarify that it is not a personal 'you' who is seeking enlightenment, but an impersonal quality of consciousness that is the motivator.

- **Spiritual inspiration and dedication carry forth the work.**

Slide 235

SLIDE 235: MOST VALUABLE QUALITIES FOR A SPIRITUAL SEEKER (10)

This slide was introduced at the May 2011 lecture, DVD disc 1 at 005850.

Clarify that it is not a personal 'you' who is seeking enlightenment, but rather a quality of consciousness itself that is the motivator. You like to think "I am this, or I am that," and actually, it is merely consciousness itself being what it is. **Spiritual inspiration and dedication carry forth the work,** your own spiritual momentum within yourself.

As Dr. Hawkins shared during the Lecture, "Handling Spiritual Challenges" in April 2010, "You are an unlimited being. You are subject only to what you hold in mind. If you think you are lovable, then you are lovable. If you think you are not lovable, then you are not lovable. We really become that which we hold in mind. The average person, then, has to surmount all these obstacles to fulfillment and go through these obstacles in order to reach enlightenment. We are interested primarily in reaching the levels of enlightenment and therefore, we want to transcend all these stresses of ordinary life. You work like a dog to reach enlightenment and then you realize there is nobody to become enlightened. You thought there was somebody here, an individual 'you' that is going to become enlightened and you find out that that is fiction. What a relief! Nobody here has to become enlightened. You do not have to buy into that goal in life. Say, "To heck with enlightenment. I just want to be stupid and ugly." To be happy if you are stupid and ugly means you are enlightened. [...]

We looked at all the factors that influence success. It is important to believe in yourself. No matter where you are in life, I want you to have a positive attitude towards that. Let us say you have done everything wrong, you are in jail and everybody has left you. You are a great success because you have now learned what does not work in this world. However, there are some people congenitally unable to learn what does not work in this world. You say, "Didn't they learn anything from experience?" The answer is "no." They apparently lack the capacity. Instead of condemning them, we should be compassionate, but also take proper protection. This person, as nice as they can be, and they can be quite amiable and pleasant, is unable to learn from experience, so all we can do is use precautions to prevent them from harming us."

Most Valuable Qualities for a Spiritual Seeker (11)

11. Comfort replaces insecurity when one realizes that the most important goal has already been accomplished

- **That goal is to be on the road to spiritual evolution**

Slide 236

SLIDE 236: MOST VALUABLE QUALITIES FOR A SPIRITUAL SEEKER (11)

This slide was introduced at the May 2011 lecture, DVD disc 1 at 010000.

Comfort replaces insecurity when one realizes that the most important goal has already been accomplished. The goal is to be on the road to spiritual evolution.

As Dr. Hawkins shared in 2005 Lecture 4, "Transcending Barriers": "I want you to live in such a way that your life is a prayer. I want you to live your life in such a way that you have no anxiety at all about meeting God. Are you willing to be answerable for who you are and what you have done with what you are? What more can anyone ask than that I live in such a way that frankly I am not scared of talking to God. I have done everything I can in every direction here. I have pushed myself to the limit to be the fulfillment of my potential. That relieves me of all guilt because now I can make a mistake. Yes, I make a mistake, but in the overall context, you see, I have sanctified that mistake by overall intention. By intention then our life becomes devotional. We become the prayer. By virtue of that, we invoke divinity and then through the heart, through the devotion, through the alignment with divinity, we empower all humankind and say, 'Gloria in Excelsis Deo! Glory be to God in the Highest!' And what more could be said?"

Most Valuable Qualities for a Spiritual Seeker (12)

12. Spiritual development is not an accomplishment, but a way of life

- **It is an orientation that brings its own rewards, and what is important is the direction of one's motives**

Slide 237

SLIDE 237: MOST VALUABLE QUALITIES FOR A SPIRITUAL SEEKER (12)

This slide was introduced at the May 2011 lecture, DVD disc 1 at 010215.

Spiritual development is not an accomplishment, but a way of life. It is an orientation that brings its own rewards, and what is important is the direction of one's own motives in life. There is no value in keeping a scorecard on yourself. A scorecard- how far have I come or how far do other people think I have come. The only one you have to answer to is yourself. The motivation to seek God is God. Nobody seeks God except under the influence of Divinity, because man, left to his own devices would never think of it. It is by virtue of the truth of the Reality of Divinity that the Reality of Divinity can be realized (apperceived and comprehended), which results in gratitude for the capacity for the recognition. Thus, devotion is not the same as piety, nor is it a mood, but instead it is a way of life and a way of being with oneself, God, and the world. The core of devotion is humility and the willingness to surrender all belief systems and illusions of 'I know'. The way is not by acquiring even more information or knowledge about God but instead by surrendering all suppositions.

Divinity emanates as consciousness/awareness, which sources Creation in its expression as the emergence of existence. The conditions implied by the terms 'beingness', 'existence', 'awareness', or 'consciousness' are without subject or object and devoid of causal qualities. The nonlinear is therefore a field of Infinite Power, by which manifestation emerges as the consequence of potentiality, which itself is an expression of Creation. Within that which is perceived is the unseen as the source of all that exists. Thus, spiritual evolution means to move from identification with content (linear 'mind') to context (nonlinear Mind). Spiritual evolution in itself brings forth the transformation in the non-form of Realization, which is beyond conceptualization or languaging and instead becomes apparent and dominant without the necessity of thought.

Most Valuable Qualities for a Spiritual Student (13)

13. Appreciate that every step forward benefits everyone

- **One's spiritual dedication and work is a gift to life and the love of mankind**

Slide 238

SLIDE 238: MOST VALUABLE QUALITIES FOR A SPIRITUAL SEEKER (13)

This slide was introduced at the May 2011 lecture, DVD disc 1 at 010310.

Appreciate that every step forward brings benefits to everyone. As you advance spiritually, it brings a value to everyone, to every human being. Because of the collective consciousness, every single person who improves helps elevate the level of consciousness of humanity. As that elevates, the incidence of war, suffering, ignorance, savaging and disease diminish. When you advance yourself, you are helping everybody. Appreciate that every step forward benefits everyone. In a holographic universe, the achievements of every individual contribute to the advancement and well-being of the whole. To become more conscious is the greatest gift anyone can give to the world; moreover, in a ripple effect, the gift comes back to its source. If we view time as the space that gives one the freedom to grow, to become more conscious, and to become aware, then time becomes our friend. It is over the passage of time that the illnesses of the body of middle and old age disappear. We have the time in which to explore and to become aware that there are options for how we limit ourselves by belief systems.

Apathy and depression are the prices we pay for having settled for and bought into our smallness. It is what we get for having played the victim and allowed ourselves to be programmed. It is the price we pay for having bought into negativity; it is what results from resisting the part of ourselves that is loving, courageous, and great. It results from allowing ourselves to be invalidated whether by ourselves or by others, the consequence of holding ourselves in a negative context. The way out is to become more conscious by looking for the truth for ourselves, instead of blindly allowing ourselves to be programmed, whether from without or by an inner voice within the mind, which seeks to diminish and invalidate, focusing on all that is weak and helpless. To get out of it, we have to accept the responsibility that we have bought into the negativity and have been willing to believe it. The way out of this, then, is to start questioning everything. The feeling state of apathy is associated with the belief, "I can't." The mind does not like to hear it, but in reality most "I can'ts" are "I won'ts." "I can't" is a cover-up for other feelings, which can be brought to awareness by posing the hypothetical question to oneself, "Is it true that I won't rather than that I can't? If I accept that 'I won't,' what situations will be brought up and how do I feel about them?" As an example, let's say we have a belief system that we can't dance. We say to ourselves, "Perhaps that's a cover-up. Maybe the truth is that I don't want to and I won't." The way we can find out what the feelings are is to envision ourselves as going through the process of learning to dance. As we do that, all of the associated feelings now start to come up: embarrassment, pride, awkwardness, the sheer effort of learning a new skill, and the reluctance about the time and energy involved. As all of the associated feelings are surrendered, it becomes very clear that the real reason is unwillingness—not incapacity.

One's spiritual dedication and work is a gift to life and the love of mankind. It is nice to know that what we think we are doing only for ourselves is actually benefitting everyone around us. To be kind to just one living being benefits everyone.

Most Valuable Qualities for a Spiritual Seeker (14)

14. There is no timetable or prescribed route to God

- **Although each person's route is unique, the terrain to be covered is relatively common to all**

Slide 239

SLIDE 239: MOST VALUABLE QUALITIES FOR A SPIRITUAL SEEKER (14)

This slide was introduced at the May 2011 lecture, DVD disc 1 at 010415.

There is no timetable or prescribed route to God. The approach to spiritual progress is not one of "getting somewhere," as there is no "where" to get. Instead, authentic spiritual teachings guide one to transcend one's ego and shed all illusions so that Truth stands revealed. The sun is always shining; one need only remove the clouds. Inasmuch as neither God nor Reality has any beginning or end and exists outside of time, no single act of God in time and space is tenable. Continuous creation by an ongoing and ever-present God does fit with what is apparent. There is no conflict between evolution and creation as one is merely an expression of the other in the visible domain. Evolution does not negate God but reflects God's presence as always present in everything that exists. Classically, elaborations of the above are the subject of ontology, the branch of philosophy concerned with the science of being. The biblical interpretation is expressed in the Gospel of John, Chapter 1, which states that in the beginning was God as the Word (Godhead), out of which emerged all of existence, including the Light of Life and human consciousness (calibrates at level 1,000). Thus, God is both Source and Creator. Because of creation, all that exists takes joy from its existence because of its innate Divinity, which is the consciousness of God.

That which is all knowing and always present registers everything. Consciousness detects and instantly registers every event, thought, feeling, and occurrence and thus knows everything completely forever. One can verify by simple muscle testing that every hair on every head is indeed counted, noticed, and filed away in the knowingness of Infinite Consciousness itself. This occurrence is impersonal and automatic and happens because of the innate qualities of consciousness. God has no personal stake in all this nor does he react. God does not get upset or offended or get his nose out of joint at any impertinence or lack of good taste. All actions, events, thoughts, ideas, concepts, and decisions are accompanied by an energy field that can be calibrated. Thus, by its own acts, the ego brings itself to its own level in the sea of consciousness. Like buoyancy, the impersonal quality of the sea of consciousness automatically determines the level to which one rises or sinks. This is merely the nature of the universe's being what it is. The explanation that the ego and perception use to describe the automatic outcome of actions is called 'judgment', which is an illusion, just as an explanation of events in the material world is ascribed to 'causality'. God is not limited by concepts, ideas, thoughts, or languages. Because of the quality of the omnipresence, the presence of God includes 'All That Is', including human thinking, but of itself does not partake of it. God does not talk to anybody. A voice booming out of the heavens is at best an interpretation of an inner experience that has been projected onto the physical world. Sound is a physical vibration. God is all present within the physical. That which is formless does not manipulate sound waves.

Although each person's route is unique, the terrain to be covered is relatively common to all. Whatever torments you go through in trying to perfect yourself, overcome self-centeredness and selfishness, etc., realize that this is common to all of humankind. People troop into church Sunday mornings, with everybody working on the same problem- how to be less selfish, how to be more giving, how to be more loving, etc.

Most Valuable Qualities for a Spiritual Seeker (15)

15. The work is to surmount and transcend the common human failings that are inherent in the structure of the human ego

- **One would like to think they are personal; however, the ego itself is not personal**

Slide 240

SLIDE 240: MOST VALUABLE QUALITIES FOR A SPIRITUAL SEEKER (15)

This slide was introduced at the May 2011 lecture, DVD disc 1 at 010505.

The work is to surmount and transcend the common human failings that are inherent in the structure of the human ego. Whatever defects you have are not just personal, they are not just yours, but in fact, they are the problem of the human ego itself. The problem is one of evolution in that humankind at this point has evolved to a certain point and that is as far as it has gotten as of today.

One would like to think they are personal; however, the ego itself is not personal. People would like to think, "Oh, me and my progress" or "me and my sins" or "me and my difficulties," and what you are talking about is not your personal self. The problem is the ego itself and so you stop taking the ego personally. There is a tendency to think one's problem is personal but it is really a collective problem one shares with all of humankind. That makes you feel a little less guilty. The problem is the human ego, which comes out of the structure of the brain itself, plus the human experience of life on this planet. We want to surmount and transcend the common human failings that are inherent in the structure of the human ego, not *your* ego, but the *human* ego. So one can say, "Well, that is characteristic of the human ego," just like one blames one's brain for having defective neurons. It is better to have poor neurons than to be wrong and bad, because it becomes the fault of nature then. You are always the pure witness of nature with all its upside as well as downside.

Most Valuable Qualities for a Spiritual Seeker (16)

16. The ego was inherited along with becoming a human being

- **Details differ based on past karma**

Slide 241

SLIDE 241: MOST VALUABLE QUALITIES FOR A SPIRITUAL SEEKER (16)

This slide was introduced at the May 2011 lecture, DVD disc 1 at 010855.

The ego was inherited along with becoming a human being. The ego is a product of the brain and the function of the brain and details differ based on past karma of how this expresses itself. So the ego is one thing, the brain function is another and then you add to it past karma. Now, karma is not that well understood in the western world, but once you grab on to karma you will find that it is a very handy tool. The entire unfolding and interaction in evolution of everything in the universe is totally karmic. Human life is no exception. Likewise, all possibilities are determined by the entire set of the universe and everything in it. A cat does not suddenly turn into a dog. It is 'karma' that results in the selection of the genes and chromosomes of one's birth, as well as the place, location, and conditions of it. A potential cat's energy field does not get attracted to enter the body of a dog. One can, with muscle testing, track the 'karma' of any entity. Within each entity, karma is a field of possible choices as well as consequences of past choices. Commonly, these prevailing sets of conditions are referred to as destiny, fate, or luck.

We can observe the association between actions and choices, both mental and physical, with consequences. In reality, these are not sequential but are actually concordant and seemingly separated by perception. From outside the duality of perception, an 'event' and its 'effects' are one and the same thing. Nothing actually moves except the point of perception itself. All religions, without exception, teach that decisions, choices, and actions are connected with consequences that appear and occur later in 'time'. If life is seen as a continuum from one realm to the next, then all religions are the same in that they teach that actions have consequences in another realm or condition of sequential life frame. All the religions teach that there will be a nonphysical life that supersedes the physical one. The confusion here arises from the misidentification of this life as physical and other lives as nonphysical, or recurrently physical. To begin with, this life is an inner, subjective experiencing that includes, but is independent of, the physical body. Thus, this current existence is not actually physical, either. This life is the subjective adventure of that mysterious entity called 'I'. This current experience of the 'I' may consider itself physical, but that in itself is an illusion. Whether successive life experiences include the illusion of physicality or not is really irrelevant to the inference and significance of the sequential progress of conditions. All 'lifetimes' are subjective, nonphysical, interrelated, and actually continuous. Each is conditioned and determined by choices, positionalities, and their consequences. All possibilities are included in the evolution of consciousness. Once consciousness stops identifying with form, it is then beyond karma.

Most Valuable Qualities for a Spiritual Seeker (17)

11. Intense prayer augments dedication and inspiration and facilitates progress

Slide 242

SLIDE 242: MOST VALUABLE QUALITIES FOR A SPIRITUAL SEEKER (17)

This slide was introduced at the May 2011 lecture, DVD disc 1 at 010950.

Intense prayer augments dedication and inspiration and facilitates progress. So we give loving service to all those who are around us. Intense dedication, prayer and appeal to God: "Dear God, please help me in this endeavor." You call upon all the good karma you can think of, all the people you have been nice to, all the money you put in the plate at church, all the old ladies you helped across the street, all the starving little doggies that you gave something to eat. Intense prayer and surrender to God can be consequent to crisis ('hitting bottom') and despair, but it can also be the result of integrous intention and dedication.

A Course in Miracles, which emerged in recent decades, provides an orderly progression of practices that lead to the ego's dissolution via insight and by means of following the recovery steps (the workbook calibrates at 600, the textbook at 550). The lives of many people have been transformed, and recovery from serious ailments has also occurred, thus attesting to the validity of the name of the year long course. Eventually, the seemingly 'extraordinary' becomes a new reality as though one now lives in a different dimension in which the ostensibly impossible manifests effortlessly as though orchestrated. The power of the field autonomously facilitates the emergence of karmic potentiality into a manifested actuality in a harmonious unfoldment. The dynamics are nonlinear and therefore incomprehensible to the intellect, which presumes the limitations of the linear Newtonian model of causality and is unable to conceptualize emergence, Divine Order, or Harmony.

Karmic research reveals that life patterns tend to be 'impersonal' in that certain energies have been set in motion that will express themselves in this lifetime through any available fortuitous channel. Such qualities as selfishness or cruelty to others in the past may rebound in this lifetime. Without karmic awareness, they might lead to denial and self-pity or indulgence in the role of martyr or victim. When these adverse life patterns are detected, they can be undone through intense prayer and forgiveness. If this is not done, the individual's psyche will energize the unconscious inner mechanisms of self-attack, guilt, self-blame, and depression.

Most Valuable Qualities for a Spiritual Seeker (18)

18. The Grace of God is available to all

Historically, the 'Grace of the Sage' is available to the committed spiritual seeker

Slide 243

SLIDE 243: MOST VALUABLE QUALITIES FOR A SPIRITUAL SEEKER (18)

This slide was introduced at the May 2011 lecture, DVD disc 1 at 011045.

The Grace of God is available to everyone. That is the most encouraging one of all. When you ask God for help, God's Grace is available to everyone. **Historically, the 'Grace of the Sage' is available to the committed spiritual seeker.** The consciousness of the spiritual teacher, especially the sage, radiates forth into the world. The grace of the sage is transmitted by the actual physical presence of the consciousness of the teacher. One wishes it would go via the written page, but the laws of consciousness are that the power of the teacher transmits into the consciousness of the student. Therefore, unfortunately, one does have to go to the actual physical presence of the teacher at some point in one's spiritual evolution. Happily, there is enough power available in the teachers that are available because it has accumulated over time. The spiritual power of the great teachers who once lived, but are no longer in a living physical body, is still available. It is transmitted down from one sage to the consciousness of the succeeding sages. There is a definite value to being in the physical presence of the consciousness of the teacher.

Dr. Hawkins states, "Within your aura is much that you have learned in this world, much of it is nonverbal, which you cannot share. You do not have enough time to sit down and describe to everybody everything you have ever known about life in a linear way. The total collectiveness of your entire life and all the wisdom and experience of it exists as an energy field. When you share that which you have become with others, they pick up the energy field of all that knowingness. That is how it is that the guru, the spiritual teacher, transmits enlightenment via an energy field. The aura of the teacher has within itself the collective wisdom throughout all of time. There is no amount of world time in which all of this can be 'laid out' in a linear lecture, intelligent class, kind of a format. You could extract some principles from it, but the principles are only basic principles. The way to enlightenment is instantaneous. From the energy field of the teacher, there radiates forth an energy field, whoosh! That field has within it the total knowingness of all that you need to become enlightened, which is not describable. It means becomingness of the Divinity within and becoming one with that Divinity in all of its expression. We transmit to others without any verbalization, without any formality, so when you ride the subway you are influencing all the people in that subway train. When you stand on the corner, you are influencing everything around you. Your own openness to awareness brings about the change. So, the way in which you hold all that you have learned in life, and hold it for others, you become not only what you are, but how that is held. How you hold who you are, how you frame who you are. If you frame yourself as a thankful gift of God to the world, then you are a gift of God to the world. If you frame yourself as a miserable worm, then you are a miserable worm, because you become what you say you will be. All of us need to own the infinite dimension of that which we are for the sake of the world, for the sake of ourselves. Each of us, let us hold out our hands to God and own the Divinity within us. That which is within us is the Source of the salvation of all of humankind, for which we thank Thee, O Lord, Amen."

Most Valuable Qualities for a Spiritual Seeker (19)

19. The strength of the ego can be formidable, and without the assistance of the power of higher spiritual beings, the ego cannot of itself transcend itself

Slide 244

SLIDE 244: MOST VALUABLE QUALITIES FOR A SPIRITUAL SEEKER (19)

This slide was introduced at the May 2011 lecture, DVD disc 1 at 011305.

The strength of the ego can be quite formidable, and without the assistance of the power of higher spiritual beings, the ego cannot of itself transcend itself. One indirect benefit one gets from being in the physical presence of the consciousness field of an enlightened teacher is that it diminishes the hold of the ego and increases your power to transcend it. This is because of your own intention. A person who does not wish this to happen, it will not happen.

You say, "I refuse to listen to this guy, I'm not going to pay any attention to these folks, bunk," then that is what will be with you and things will remain the same. Skepticism and doubt, therefore, is not of any great service. Due to the law of free will and the nature of consciousness being what it is, the great beings that are willing to help all of us are waiting for us to say "yes." When a person says, "If there is a God, I ask him to help me," then the great transformative experiences happen. The dualistic structure of the ego stems from the core factor of linear positionality. A centralizing image of a personal self emerges as the belief of an individual personal self as an agent, i.e., the 'thinker' of thoughts, the 'doer' of actions, and the repository of guilt and self-blame. Some qualities are suppressed and become buried in the unconscious, along with their emotions, which are the residuals of animal instincts. Only after evolution to consciousness level 200 does an etheric brain emerge that is functionally capable of spiritual awareness, intention, and karmic responsibility. Naively, personal consciousness identifies the self with body, mind, and emotions. Then, as a result of karmic 'merit', spiritual truth is heard and becomes inspirational, and, with further good fortune, a spiritual teacher is encountered. The high vibrational frequencies of the teacher's aura activate the nascent, etheric, higher spiritual bodies in the spiritual student. All the enlightened beings at the very top of the scale say that all is God and that a 'thing' is merely what it is (essence). They place no constriction or valuation of right or wrong on it. They see the sacredness of all of existence; therefore, there is no invalidation. If all is God, then to invalidate any part of it would be to invalidate God.

Instead, the great beings teach a principle that leads to understanding. The highest teachers say that if you follow a certain course, certain things will happen; they then leave the rest up to you. A very good example of such pure teaching in our society is that of Alcoholics Anonymous (AA). AA takes no position about whether you drink or not. It does not try to close up the liquor industry or try to convince you to stop drinking. However, it does say that for those who have a problem, this is what we do, and these are the results. If you continue to drink, these will be the results. There is no 'making wrong' or invalidation. No one is looking for any power nor do they wish to exploit anyone. AA has no possessions, no royalty, no government, no buildings, and no glamour. It is just pure spiritual principle that allows an individual to have the freedom to see the truth in it for oneself and to apply it in one's own life if desired. This is an example of a high teaching; AA calibrates at 540, which one would expect. An energy field that heals would have to be a teaching that is in a positive direction and calibrates at least at 540. AA stands, of course, as an example of healing based on the physical, mental, and spiritual aspects of man, as no healing from addiction can occur without

spiritual growth and development.

Most Valuable Qualities for a Spiritual Seeker (20)

20. Fortunately, the power of the consciousness of every great teacher or avatar, who has ever lived still remains and is available

To focus on a teacher or their teachings by meditation makes the power of that teacher available to the seeker

Slide 245

SLIDE 245: MOST VALUABLE QUALITIES FOR A SPIRITUAL SEEKER (20)

This slide was introduced at the May 2011 lecture, DVD disc 2 at 000050.

The qualities of a spiritual seeker, then, take advantage of the consciousness of the teacher. Apart from what is said and aside from what you think is going on, none of that is in fact happening. The power of the field of the teacher has come down through the centuries. As Dr. Hawkins said, "Whatever is speaking to you today is the accumulation of the influence of teachers going back to the Buddha. So, the energy field of the Buddha is here, now available- resist (calibrates true)." Every great teacher who ever lived leaves the power of that field within the collective consciousness of humankind. That is why humanity progresses. Otherwise, if every generation had to start from scratch, humanity would not be where it is today. **The power of the consciousness of every great teacher who has ever lived remains and is still available.**

To focus on a teacher or their teachings by meditation or visiting them or going to lectures or whatever, the power of that teacher is now available to the seeker. "So down through the centuries the power of the consciousness of the great beings is now here present-resist (calibrates true). Is now here available to every student" (True.) And is their karmic right" (true). It is your right, by virtue of your declaration, to benefit from the consciousness of all the great teachers who have ever lived."

Most Valuable Qualities for a Spiritual Seeker (21)

21. It is the will of every truly enlightened sage that every spiritual seeker succeed, and not just the members of some specific or exclusive group.

Slide 246

SLIDE 246: MOST VALUABLE QUALITIES FOR A SPIRITUAL SEEKER (21)

This slide was introduced at the May 2011 lecture, DVD disc 2 at 000405.

It is the will of every truly enlightened teacher that every student succeeds, and not just students of a particular group. You will hear that weakness and defect in various world religions and spiritual groups that they are selective therefore, they are only concerned with the enlightenment of members of their own special group and those who are not members of their group are infidels. So, beware of those who see everybody but themselves as infidels. "Those who think heaven and salvation is only for them are in error-resist" (calibrates true). They are in error, yes. Salvation and enlightenment is for all of humankind, because it is the will of God. It is the will of every truly enlightened sage that *every* seeker succeeds, not just members of your congregation.

Most Valuable Qualities for a Spiritual Seeker (22)

22. Just as the individual seeker of spiritual advancement benefits all mankind, thus also does the enlightenment of the Teachers benefit the seeker

Slide 247

SLIDE 247: MOST VALUABLE QUALITIES FOR A SPIRITUAL SEEKER (22)

This slide was introduced at the May 2011 lecture, DVD disc 2 at 000530.

Just as the individual seeker benefits all of humankind, thus also does the enlightenment of the Teachers benefits the seeker. The Teacher benefits from the student and the student benefits from the Teacher. That is good to know. Every loving or compassionate thought outweighs many thousands of negative thoughts held by others. We change the world not by what we say or do but as a consequence of what we have become. Thus, every spiritual aspirant serves the world. That to which seekers trust their very souls should be verifiably trustworthy and integrous. The basic essentials of researched and documented spiritual integrity, teachers, teachings, and organizations are provided in "Truth vs. Falsehood: How to Tell the Difference" (2005), Chapter 17: Spiritual Truth, pp. 379-382. In addition there is detailed information on Teachers in "Discovery of the Presence of God: Devotional Nonduality" (2006), Chapter 11: Teachers and Teaching, starting on p. 171, from which the following is excerpted:

"The evolved Teacher historically has been the primary source of Truth and spiritual information. The function has been to inspire, inform, and convey information that is not obtainable via ordinary mind. The Teacher has been unique in that the Source of the Knowledge has been intrinsic rather than external. That the Source of the Knowingness is Self-effulgent and not the result of linear processing resulted in the use of the descriptive term 'mystic' to denote that the Source of the information is the Self, not the self or ordinary mind, education, or intelligence.

The Illumined State is also accompanied and distinguished by a concomitant radiance of a specific spiritual energy via the aura, which is often pictorially represented by the symbol of the halo to denote that the energy field is innately radiant. That energy field is a permanent marker which persists beyond time or location. [...] Enlightenment is a very definite state or condition that is self-revealing when the obstructions to its realization have been removed, just like the sun shines forth with the evaporation or disappearance of clouds. The sun is likened to the Self in that it is self-effulgent and radiates the energy that is termed 'Illumination'.

The statistical infrequency of such a phenomenon in the human population tends to attract attention to the condition by virtue of not only its rarity but also its intrinsic value of uniqueness. The Teachings that ensue are a consequence of the condition itself and not of any personality. Because the process is not mental, emotional, or physical, it has been perceived as 'mystical', meaning mysterious or not within the province of the mind or intellect to comprehend via ordinary perception or conceptualization (i.e., nonlinear). [...] The linear manifest world (Creation) is itself an emergence from the nonlinear, which is depicted as the Unmanifest (the Godhead). The enlightened Teacher is therefore the example or confirmation within the visible, linear human domain of the Source, out of which Enlightenment and life itself manifest. An Enlightened Teacher is therefore the exemplification of the human potential as a demonstration within the visible world."

Most Valuable Qualities for a Spiritual Seeker (23)

23. That power and energy are available to call upon

- **There are no requirements or obligations**

Slide 248

SLIDE 248: MOST VALUABLE QUALITIES FOR A SPIRITUAL SEEKER (23)

This slide was introduced at the May 2011 lecture, DVD disc 2 at 000600.

The spiritual power and energy of every great teacher who has ever lived is currently available to call upon through the consciousness of one's current teacher. From the May 2011 Lecture: "So, therefore the consciousness that speaks to this audience now is empowered by all the great teachers that have ever lived-resist" (calibrates true). What a responsibility. Out of thanksgiving, you hold your own spiritual advancement, intention and enlightenment for the benefit of everyone, not just for the benefit of you. What you are doing for yourself, you do for everyone. So, be conscious of that fact, that your prayers, your enlightenment, and the progression of your level of consciousness benefits all of mankind and it is your gift to mankind that you share it. Therefore, you being here today is a gift to all of mankind. The presence of all now present is a gift to all of mankind-resist (calibrates true). Humanity thanks you."

There are no requirements or obligations. You do not have to sign up for anything. You do not have to agree to anything. You do not have to go into a contractual agreement. It may be helpful to reference "Truth vs. Falsehood: How to Tell the Difference" (2005), Chapter 17: Spiritual Truth, pp. 379-382 from which the following is excerpted: "Truth is true at all times and places, independent of culture, personalities, or circumstances. It is open to all; nonexclusive. There are no secrets to be revealed, hidden, or sold, and no magical formulas or 'mysteries'. Spiritual purity has no interest in the personal lives of aspirants, or in clothing, dress, style, sex lives, economics, family patterns, lifestyles, or dietary habits. There is no brainwashing, adulation of leaders, training rituals, indoctrinations, or intrusions into private life. Participants are free to come and go without persuasion, coercion, intimidation, or consequences. Truth is not 'anti' anything. Falsehood and ignorance are not its enemies but merely represent its absence. Truth does not intervene or have an agenda to propose, inflict, or promulgate. The effect of higher energies is innate and not dependent on propagation or effort. God does not need help anymore than gravity needs the 'help' of an apple's falling off the tree. Because Reality is nonlinear, it cannot be localized or encoded in restriction of form, such as secret messages, codes, numbers, and inscriptions, or hidden in runes, stones, the dimensions of the pyramid, the DNA, or the nostril hairs of the camel. Truth has no secrets. The Reality of God is omnipresent and beyond codification or exclusivity. Codes are indicative of man's imagination and not the capriciousness of Divinity. Emotionality is based on perception. Compassion results from the discernment of truth.

The Nature of God (1)

1. **God is both manifest as the Totality and Allness of Creation and simultaneously unmanifest as the Godhead, the Infinite Potentiality and source or 'voidness' prior to form**

2. **God is infinite beyond time or depictions of space or locality, without beginning or end**

Slide 249

SLIDE 249: THE NATURE OF GOD (1)

This slide was introduced at the May 2011 lecture, DVD disc 2 at 000835.

God is manifest as the Totality and Allness of Creation. At the same time, God is unmanifest as the Godhead, the Source of All That Is, prior to form. God is Infinite beyond time or depiction of space or locality without beginning or ending. People thought God lived down the street in a church, but no, God does not just live in church. Generally, people are very careful when they are near or in a church. They walk around and are careful not to have any sinful thoughts or anything like that because this is where God lives.

That is cute in a way, to think of the church or a temple or a similar place as God's house. That is a good explanation for children, but we are not children anymore and now we know that God is all the time everywhere. "God is in the grocery store. God is in the supermarket. God is everywhere, in every place, including supermarkets, bathrooms, parking garages, sidewalk cafés" (calibrates true). If God is going to have His way with us, He will. God is both manifest and unmanifest. God is Infinite beyond time or depiction of space or locality and has no beginning and no end. That which is Divinity has no beginning and no end.

The Nature of God (2)

3. God is omnipresent, omnipotent, and omniscient.

4. God is the source and substrate of consciousness, awareness, knowingness and sentience.

5. God is the sole source of the energy of life.

Slide 250

SLIDE 250: THE NATURE OF GOD (2)

This slide was introduced at the May 2011 lecture, DVD disc 2 at 001120.

God is omnipresent, omnipotent, and omniscient; God is the capacity to be everything, to be All That Is, to know all that is knowable. **God is the source and substance of consciousness, awareness, knowingness and sentience.** From the May 2011 Lecture: "The only reason anybody would be here today is because God is present in your consciousness. If it were not for God as the presence in your consciousness, you would not be at a lecture of this kind. So God makes sure that you get here. The only reason you are here is God said you should be here. Get busy with what you are supposed to do." God is the source and substance of consciousness, awareness, knowingness and sentience.

God is the sole source of the energy of life. Does this mean a turtle has God's consciousness in it, a turtle? "God is in the salamander. God is in the cougar. A turtle has God's consciousness. A turtle is an expression of God-resist" (calibrates true). Let us be kinder to the next turtle we meet. Anyway, God is the Source of 'All That Is'.

The Nature of God (3)

6. **God is the source of evolution and Creation, which are one and the same**

7. **God is the source and presence of peace, love, stillness, and beauty**

8. **God is beyond all universes and materiality, yet is the source of 'All That Is'**

Slide 251

SLIDE 251: THE NATURE OF GOD (3)

This slide was introduced at the May 2011 lecture, DVD disc 2 at 001410.

God is the source of evolution and Creation, which are one and the same. The simple and rather obvious truth is that evolution is Creation. Therefore, Creation is continuous, ongoing, and witnessed sequentially as evolution. Its source is the infinite power of the unmanifest becoming manifest as potentiality, with its inherent invisible patterning emerging in the visible physical domain as existence. Throughout the ages, this ultimate source has been universally intuited as well as subjectively experienced as Divinity, which alone has the power to transform the potential into the actual, the Unmanifest (i.e., the Godhead) into the Manifest, and nonexistence into existence (e.g., Bohm's enfolded and unfolded universes).

God is the source of all that is; **God is the source and presence of all peace, love, stillness and beauty.** As you are walking through the woods, you are not thinking about God or anything like that and all of a sudden, the sudden stillness of the woods is overwhelming, and one is suddenly in the presence of Divinity without being aware that it is Divinity. The stillness and beauty of the woods is the expression of God.

God is beyond all universes or materiality, and yet is the source of all that is; without God, nothing would be. That is scary that, if it were not for God, nothing would exist. Therefore, God is the source of all existence. God is the source of All That Is, without exception. "God is the source of All That Is, without exception. Even you and me" (tests true). That is sweet. You look at your spouse, your mother, your father, your sister, your brother, and then remind yourself that every one of them is created by the same Power that created you. That changes the way you see them and behave towards them. Even a toad takes on a different significance when you realize that even the toad is a creation of God.

The Nature of God (4)

9. **God is the sole source of existence and the potentiality of beingness**

10. **God is the ultimate context of which the universe and all existence is the content**

11. **God is the a priori formless source of existence within all form**

Slide 252

SLIDE 252: THE NATURE OF GOD (4)

This slide was introduced at the May 2011 lecture, DVD disc 2 at 001615.

God is the sole source of existence and the potentiality of beingness. God is the ultimate context of which the universe and all existence is the content. God is the *a priori* formless source of existence within all form. Divinity is the source of everything that exists without exception. Meditating on that can have quite a profound effect. To look about you and realize that all that exists is God, yes.

The Nature of God (5)

12. God is not within the province of the provable or the intellect

13. God is the source and essence of the subjective state of 'I-ness' called Enlightenment

14. God is the radical subjectivity of Self-realization

Slide 253

SLIDE 253: THE NATURE OF GOD (5)

This slide was introduced at the May 2011 lecture, DVD disc 2 at 001720.

God is not within the province of the provable or the intellect. As Dr. Hawkins shared, "Well, that is where I ran into trouble when I was an atheist. As a kid, I was very profoundly religious and one time I was walking along, not thinking about anything in particular and suddenly, I became aware of the totality of the pain and suffering of humankind. Although I had been a devout believer as a child and as I grew up, when I saw the complete suffering, the totality of the suffering of humankind, I became an atheist. I became just as devout an atheist as I had been a theist. It took me some decades to transcend that transition." God is not within the province of the provable or the intellect. Therefore, atheism and theism are both foolish play with the intellect. You can neither prove God nor disprove God.

God is the source and essence of the subjective state of 'I-ness' called Enlightenment. The sense of 'I-ness' is autonomous. There is no 'person' that experiences one's existence. One's existence is all that is. There is no duality between an "I," and consciousness in the state of enlightenment. The realization that 'that which you are' is all there is, that you are "it," that whatever there "is" is what you are.

God is the radical subjectivity of Self-realization. That is the realization of the Divinity of the essence of your own existence, that nothing exists other than God, that there is nothing that exists outside of Divinity. All that exists is Divinity in its various forms, including atheism. Anything that is capable of atheism is God. To be an atheist, you have to have consciousness; to have consciousness you have to have the presence of Divinity. Without God you cannot be an atheist, so, "thank God I'm an atheist," you can say to yourself. "Thank you, God, but I'm an atheist. I do not have to go to church and go to confession etc. I can eat meat on Fridays and use bad language, yep." God says, "Yep, whatever you want to be, it is you. However, do not forget the little details about karma." Although the concept of karma is not commonplace in the Western world, it is a confirmable reality calibrating at 999. Karma is a shorthand term for the totality of all factors present at birth, both physical and spiritual (i.e., the calibrated level of consciousness itself). This inheritance is both individual as well as collective, and therefore, every earthling shares in the collective karma of humankind itself and its worldly expressions. Karma includes the spiritual problems that are inherent to being a human being, including the fact that humankind has very limited spiritual understanding ('ignorance'). Thus, the purpose of human life is to overcome and transcend these inherited limitations via spiritual truth as revealed by the great religious and spiritual teachers. Everybody has some good karma somewhere in their spirit, no matter how seemingly depraved they may be. Everything happens of its own. You become an energy field, and pull down to yourself that which is the consequence of the field. Establishing favorable conditions is what we can do to aid spiritual growth. Karma of the spirit (the little iron filing), where it is in the field, is a consequence. It is helpful to ask yourself, "Does this serve my obligation to humankind? Am I willing to face God for my behaviors?

The Nature of God (6)

15. **God is descriptively immanent and transcendent**

16. **The human experience of the Presence of God is the same in all ages, all cultures, and all localities**

Slide 254

SLIDE 254: THE NATURE OF GOD (6)

This slide was introduced at the May 2011 lecture, DVD disc 2 at 002050.

God is All That Is and is all that is not (the linear and the nonlinear). **God is descriptively immanent as well as transcendent.** Religions, especially Christianity, Islam, and Judaism, emphasize Divinity as Transcendent. The mystics of the world's great traditions, especially those coming out of the East, such as the various Hindu and Buddhist schools of nonduality, focus instead on the Realization of Divinity as Immanent. Whether God is conceived of as transcendental, immanent, or both, is a province of *res interna*, and the realization that God is both immanent and transcendent (*res externa, extensa*) is a consequence of the Realization of the Self and Enlightenment. While the primary prerequisite for adherence to religion is faith, the essential required qualities needed for following the pathway of nonduality are humility, surrender, and devotional dedication to the pathway. It is readily observable that followers of religions presume 'I know' via scriptural authority, ecclesiastical doctrine, historical precedent, etc. In contrast, the spiritual devotee of nonduality starts from the basic, more truthful position, "I, of myself, *don't know*." In Christianity, Jesus Christ *is* The Way, and without His help (Grace), the ego (sin) cannot be transcended. Although "heaven is within you," its reality is not realizable without a Savior because of the sheer tenacity of the ego. Thus, Jesus taught the way to salvation. In contrast, the Buddha taught the pathway to Enlightenment, which, however, was not possible to realize without the Grace of the Enlightened Teacher. The traditional spiritual devotee usually combines the approaches of both faith and self-inquiry.

The human experience of the Presence of God is the same in all ages and cultures, and all localities. The expression of the awareness of the Presence of God is part of all cultures throughout all of time, and universally man intuits it. Even if you live on a deserted island in the middle of nowhere, people have a belief in a holy spirit or animal spirit, or in the clouds or the sun or the sky. Every culture includes Divinity in one or another description or form. The human experience of the Presence of God is the same in all cultures, all ages, and all localities. If you study anthropology and all the history of all the cultures of the world, you find that Divinity exists in various forms in every culture. Every culture has a name for Divinity, and they also have a name for that person who does not believe in it and those persons become "outcasts"

The Nature of God (7)

17. The effect on human consciousness of the experience of the Presence of God is subjectively transformative and identical throughout human history

It leaves a timeless mark that is verifiable as a calibration of a recorded level of consciousness

Slide 255

SLIDE 255: THE NATURE OF GOD (7)

This slide was introduced at the May 2011 lecture, DVD disc 2 at 002305.

The effect on human consciousness of the experience of the Presence of God is subjectively transformative and identical throughout all of human history. Just sitting on the edge of a cliff, you look out and suddenly there is a transformation of the entire world. The overwhelming stunning beauty of all of existence hits one like a huge thunder of beauty and light. It is as if you see what you have always seen, but at much greater depth. What you see is not only what exists, but also the Divinity of all that exists.

It leaves a timeless mark that is available as a calibration of a recorded level of consciousness. Suddenly the world lights up and you become aware of the stunning beauty, the incredible beauty. Everything is three dimensional. We thank God for that gift. That is why we call enlightenment a gift. It is not something that you have earned and acquired or paid for, etc. It is like a gift from Divinity. Suddenly as you are walking along, everything lights up and you see the miraculous.

The Nature of God (8)

18. The essence of God does not include human frailties, such as partiality, the desire to control, favoritism, duality, judgmentalism, wrath, righteous anger, resentment, limitation, arbitrariness, vanity, revenge, jealousy, retaliation, vulnerability, or locality.

Slide 256

SLIDE 256: THE NATURE OF GOD (8)

This slide was introduced at the May 2011 lecture, DVD disc 2 at 002605.

The essence of God does not include human frailties, such as partiality. It is beyond the desire to control, beyond favoritism, beyond duality, beyond judgmentalism, beyond wrath, righteousness, righteous anger, it is beyond resentment, limitation, it is beyond vanity, it is beyond revenge, it is beyond jealousy, it is beyond retaliation, it is beyond locality. So you become aware that what you are is consciousness itself, not the content of consciousness, but consciousness itself. It is not this body, but the capacity to comprehend the existence of this body. "So you can exist in different realms without a body. That is true-resist" (calibrates true). You can exist without a body. The older you get the less you need a body.

What good is it? Well, you know, it loves to eat dinner and loves ice cream. It seems we hang around for a few reasons. Anyway, that is impersonal, having to do with realizing the value of all that exists and allowing the enjoyment and recognition of it all. We thank God for ice cream, "Dear God, thank you for this wonderful ice cream." In response, a voice says, "Good deal, then tomorrow you shall have some more." As you can see, the variations and the understanding, comprehension and description of Divinity are widespread, depending on culture, time, and age.

Every culture has its own holy spirit, sometimes considered to be nature spirits, but still of a spiritual nature. When we need rain, one can remind the nature spirits that it has not rained for a month now, just in case God and the nature spirits had not noticed. The nature spirits nudge God and sure enough, within a week or two it always rains, "Thank you, nature spirits." As Dr. Hawkins shared, "In the non-linear states, there isn't any 'you' to have a say. There is no 'this' causing a 'that.' There is no center point of the ego/mind that is making decisions about what to say. In ordinary consciousness, you think there is a 'me' that is making a decision to say a 'that.' On top of that, you get purpose and intention and it becomes very elaborate. In the non-linear states, what happens is because of the nature, the quality of the Self within with a capital "S", the Purusha, that core of the Self out of which the expression comes forth, happens of its own. The question arises from the audience. That affects the Self, which then speaks back through this person here, this animal here. All right, so this condition is what we usually call a 'sage', with Ramana Maharshi, and Nisargadatta Maharaj as examples from recent history.

The Nature of God (9)

19. The variabilities of the depictions of Divinity reflect the variabilities of human perception and the projections of the impediments of the ego and its positionalities.

Slide 257

SLIDE 257: THE NATURE OF GOD (9)

This slide was introduced at the May 2011 lecture, DVD disc 2 at 002945.

The variations of the depictions of Divinity reflect the variability of human perception and the projections of the impediments of the ego and its positionalities. The negative views showing "God as an arbitrary punisher" is the God of insanity. How insane can you be not to know the top of the box from the bottom of the box? Is God at the top, the Source of the light, or is it as some religions say at the bottom, the great punisher waiting for you with whips and chains, and tortures so you have to get away from Him? Dr. Hawkins has described his experiential investigation of hells and said that no God would send anybody there. In fact, anybody who is evil would not even send anybody there. It is beyond evil, it is beyond any possibility of knowingness of what it could be. Never curse somebody to go to hell, as it is a truly bad deal because that which you condemn others to becomes your fate. You cannot condemn somebody to hell without automatically precipitating some hellish conditions and experiences later in life. Okay, so one can transcend all these limitations.

One can say that the Godhead is the Unmanifest out of which Divinity arises and the nature of Divinity is Creation and henceforth, everything that evolves out of Creation itself has the capacity for Creation. So all is in the process of being created as well as being Creator, one might say. Things are not arising in the world out of causality but out of creation. Everything, every what we call 'thing,' every what the world-mind calls 'event' is not sequential; it is only sequential from the viewpoint of the observer. Because you perceive things sequentially, you think that one thing is causing another. So, if we have these balls: A, B, C, D, the world assumes that you hit A with a cue stick and that hits B and that causes C, that causes D. That is the Newtonian paradigm of causality. Actually, the way it comes about is 'that' which causes A is simultaneously the cause of B, is exactly and simultaneously the same as the cause of C and is simultaneously the cause of D. Otherwise, God would have merely set the billiard ball rolling, disappear off into heaven which is up there, while you are down here.

That is God as transcendent, the trouble with religion. That is where the mystic gets himself burned at the stake. He says, 'No, God is Immanent.' That which is the source of life itself within one's Self, the source of existence and reality, the source of the awareness of your existence is the Presence of God as within, as Self, as the Ultimate Reality. That is the Truth of the enlightened sage, who says that God is not only transcendent, but also immanent; he does not just say that, the sage knows that they are not opposites. They are only two different ways of looking at it. When the Presence of God is realized as Immanent, we say the person is enlightened or a sage, or whatever you want to call it.

The Nature of God (10)

20. The purity of the Presence of God is traditionally the essence of the ineffable quality of holiness and is the basis for the depictive term 'sacred'

- **That which is devoid of content is the equivalent of innocence**

Slide 258

SLIDE 258: THE NATURE OF GOD (10)

This slide was introduced at the May 2011 lecture, DVD disc 2 at 003005.

The purity of the Presence of God is traditionally the essence of the ineffable quality called holiness and is the basis for the depiction of the 'sacred,' that which is sacred. **That which is devoid of content is the equivalent of innocence.** In an elevated state of consciousness you see the beauty, worth and inspiration of all that exists. As you are walking down the sidewalk, there is this little bug walking along. The enlightened person carefully steps over the little bug and blesses it by his concern. We bless the little bug because we realize that it represents the evolution of consciousness as life itself. We value life in all of its expressions. We appreciate all of life. To be appreciative of your own existence and the existence of all that is, is in itself a short course on enlightenment. "I am grateful to Thee, O Lord for this stage, for this audience, for this wonderful cane, I am thankful for the beautiful flowers, I'm thankful for a box of Kleenex." Just think, primitive man did not have Kleenex. He just blew his nose on his sleeve. There is an interesting anecdote about where buttons come from in the military uniforms. It is because in cold weather the soldiers' noses would be running and they would wipe them on their sleeve. The commander could not stand it so he had buttons put on their sleeves. Thank God for buttons on our sleeves, or we would all be a mess to look at. God is the source of all good things orchestrated in innumerable different ways.

The Nature of God (11)

21. When the obstacles of human mentation, emotionality, and the ego's structures from which they are derived are transcended, the Self as God Immanent shines forth of its own accord, just as the sun shines forth when the clouds are removed.

Slide 259

SLIDE 259: THE NATURE OF GOD (11)

This slide was introduced at the May 2011 lecture, DVD disc 2 at 003300.

When the obstacles of human mentation, emotionality, and the ego's structures from which they are derived are transcended, the Self as God Immanent shines forth of its own accord, just as the sun shines forth when the clouds disappear. You thought, "Enlightenment is a goal that I will pursue." Instead, you see that it is what happens when you remove its barriers. You do not have to do anything to become enlightened, except stop being unenlightened. How is that? I am 'What Is'? Something has to be there to question, "Who am I," "How did I get to be where I am?" and "How do I get enlightened?" Stop being unenlightened, it is simple. You are All That Is, you are All That There Can Be, and you are All That There Ever Was. One does not have to do anything, go anywhere, read anything, sit in yoga postures and do weird breathing. Enlightenment is an instantaneous realization, apperception. Why seek "what is", which already is, so there is no point in chasing your tail. Everybody should relax, be totally complete, satisfied and happy with just what you are this instant. Self-awareness shines forth of its own accord when the obstacles blocking it disappear. To know all that is knowable, all that has ever been known, and all that could be known, realize that in between a peanut butter sandwich and a root beer is the whole universe. When you eat that peanut butter sandwich and you wash it down with root beer, you have just experienced "All That Can Be Experienced" of the wondrousness and goodness of Enlightenment. That makes it easy. That what you want to happen has already happened and your only problem is that you have not recognized that it already is. It is not possible to exist and be conscious without being enlightened. You are all there is, there is nothing else. The fact that you are just a little piece of it may bother what remains of your ego, but you cannot be the entire Empire State Building at one time. You can only be one floor at a time. The wonderment of your own awareness, of your own presence, of your own existence is your Empire State Building. You are so used to looking at the Empire State Building that you are, that you do not realize that it is one of the great wonders of the world. That you exist is the ultimate miracle because you can see the opposite would be nonexistence. You have your choice between existence and nonexistence. Only the Presence of Divinity within you accords you the capacity to realize that you exist.

Other entities "are," but do not know that they "are". It has taken multitudes of millions of years to move from "being" to *know* that you "are." To "be" is one thing; to *know* that you "are" takes millennia. We are the product of eons, millennia, to move from that which "is" to that which *knows* that it "is." Mostly that which exists does so and does not realize it exists. To exist and know that you exist makes you enlightened. Everyone knows that "one is." The fact that you are here means you know that you "are." The difference between the unenlightened and enlightened is the knowingness that the unenlightened does not know that they are enlightened already and therefore, they are unenlightened. The enlightened knows they are enlightened already and therefore is enlightened. Consciousness is the capacity to recognize the essence of the reality of one's own existence, the capacity to stand apart and yet be that which is perceived. You are both "What Is" and that which realizes "What Is." The unenlightened person does not have that recognition. Other than being the totality of knowingness, nothing else is possible.

The Nature of God (12)

22. **God is the context and source of the karmic unity of all Creation, beyond all perceptual descriptions or limitations, such as time or space**

23. **Truth is verifiable only by identity with it and not by knowing about it**

Slide 260

SLIDE 260: THE NATURE OF GOD (12)

This slide was introduced at the May 2011 Lecture, DVD disc 2 (not shown in the Lectures).

God is the context and source of the karmic unity of all Creation, beyond all perceptual descriptions or limitations, such as time or space. From "I: Reality and Subjectivity" (2003), Chapter 10: The Nature of God, p. 165, "If the totality of the content of human consciousness is illuminated, then the consequences and derivations of the levels of consciousness become apparent, much like a map allows the fate of certain pathways to become clearer. Thus, the sage or avatar merely points out the consequences of going in various directions based on the revelation of the certainty of the absolute karmic unity and divinity of Creation that, in predictability, are comparable to the physical laws, such as those of gravity. The sage then confirms that the karmic laws of Creation supersede all the illusions and errors of the ego. The message to be conveyed by spiritual teachings is that just as the physical body is subject to the laws of Newtonian linear physics, the spiritual body is subject to the laws of the nonlinear spiritual truth, which are quite different. Because of the rudimentary level of the evolution of man's consciousness, the avatar, mystic, or sage has been illuminated in order to teach the difference between the two domains.

Human life seems to represent a staging process or dimension by which life as consciousness evolves from the simplest life energy, such as the cells of the body through elaboration as form, and progresses up through the animal kingdom, and up through the complexity of the primate and the evolution of an intelligence to enable comprehension. As intelligence develops, it becomes capable of investigation and comprehension of meaning and abstract derivation of essence apart from form, that is, content vis-à-vis context. Out of context arises the inference of and search for Source in the capacity for spiritual awareness. The spiritual sage emerges as a consequence of that level of consciousness which discovers its source and proclaims the discovery for the information of all. The spiritual information then illuminates the possibilities of the soul's destiny at the cessation of human physicality."

Truth is verifiable only by identity with it and not by knowing about it. The Presence of Self constitutes the classic *Purusha*, or Radiance of Self as Source. Self 'knows' by virtue of identity with Divinity itself. It thereby is its own Awareness, and by its Presence, it thereby makes itself 'known' as the 'Knower'. Thus, it does not know 'about' but is the Completion of its own Essence. By analogy, the only true authority on being a cat is that of the cat itself, by virtue of its being a cat. Thus, identity is authority by virtue of nondualistic Reality. The Teacher thus bypasses duality by virtue of identity with the Oneness of the Self, which is the true Teacher within the Teacher.

Calibrated Scale of Consciousness: The Enlightened and Divine States (1)

Sainthood	**Very close to Enlightenment**	**575**
Bliss	**"Sat-chit-ananda"**	**575+**
Enlightenment	**Bliss replaced by peace, stillness & silence**	**600**
"I Am"	**Awareness of the "I" as beingness or isness**	**650**
Self	**As Existence**	**680**
Self	**As Beyond Existence or Nonexistence**	**840**

Slide 261

SLIDE 261: CALIBRATED SCALE OF CONSCIOUSNESS: THE ENLIGHTENED AND DIVINE STATES (1)

The explanation for this slide is based on the transcript for Slide 2, first introduced at the March 2002 Lecture DVD, Disc 2, starting at 011100.

In the high 500s, one goes from Love to Unconditional Love. At **575**, we say those people are **saintly**. This is what the naïve spiritual seeker in the beginning thinks they are going to find. They are going to find someone who is saintly walking around in sandals, with long hair and a staff and a robe, who smiles sweetly at you. At that point, one may hear the sound of gongs, with "Om" in the background, and incense arising in the air. **Sainthood** may take different forms, but when it first hits you, this is how it hits you, so you're not going to really keep your job at XYZ Corporation very long, sitting there blissed out in front of the computer and you have accomplished nothing since this morning at 8, nor have you moved or gone for lunch. At that point, most people leave the world, especially a complex world like New York City and come to a smaller place very often, where other people are spiritually oriented and your condition is permissible. Which means you didn't have to change your clothes, you didn't have to eat, you could get skinny, you never bother getting a haircut, your beard got longer and longer, and you are just blissed out and it was okay. It was fine. "Hey, don't you think you ought to eat something," your friends would say to you. That was a safe community and therefore you so often see a shift to community. People will leave a complex, demanding world because it is so much in form and what happens with **Enlightenment at 600** is that the world of form is very, very difficult. It is very difficult to think in form, it takes energy, like understanding; comprehending what people are talking about. You have to keep saying, "What?" The meaningfulness of it comes to you from a different domain. There is a translation of form into non-form. The nonverbal communication becomes progressively important. That is why the communication with animals becomes very easy. You and the animal know exactly where they are at with each other without saying anything. The snake will coil up and start to strike and then this profound stillness and peace prevails and it dominates the snake. The snake cannot strike out of that field because it's a field of perfect peace and safety and it is more powerful than the snake and the snake is just entranced with you and sits there and looks at you for minutes and finally, he goes away by himself, and says goodbye, rattling his tail. All is safe in peace, because that is the domain prevailing.

The sense **"I Am" comes out at 650**. **That Which I Am as Existence (680),** anybody can reach through meditation. The letting go of identification with the physicality or the body as self, then letting go of the content of mind, becoming the witness of the content of mind, and then becoming the awareness. Behind the experiencer of the witness of the content of the mind, layer by layer you withdraw your identification from the particular, from the finite, from the definable, from the material. That Which I Am is the witness of all that is and the witness does not change depending on content.

As Dr. Hawkins describes his experience at age 3, "There was this body in a little wooden wagon and it was spring and the warm sunlight going on. Of course, this three-year old does not know how to talk, does not know words or anything and is stunned with the shocking fact of **existence, and instantly arose the fear of nonexistence**. That calibrates at **840.** In the nonverbal state, there was only the fear of nonexistence, because, if I exist, then it could have happened that I would have not come into existence. There was the fear, the polarity of existence versus nonexistence, which set the karmic spiritual conundrum for this lifetime. Somebody asked something about karma. You cannot come in at that level without having done a lot of prior spiritual work.

Calibrated Scale of Consciousness: The Enlightened and Divine States (2)

Sage	**700**
Sage: Self as God Manifest	**740**
"I": is complete and total, as the Ultimate Reality, the Supreme	**740**
"I": Self-Divinity as Allness (Beatific Vision)	**750**
Teacher of Enlightenment	**800**
God (Self) As Logos	**850**
Avatar	**985**

Slide 262

SLIDE 262: CALIBRATED SCALE OF CONSCIOUSNESS: THE ENLIGHTENED AND DIVINE STATES (2)

The explanation for this slide is based on the transcript for Slide 2, first introduced at the March 2002 Lecture DVD, Disc 2, starting at 011100.

The **"Sage"** is at 700. The sage seldom goes anywhere, and usually stays home and people come and visit him. The sage rarely moves beyond the level where he finds himself. **Self as God Manifest" is at 740**, the same level as **"I"**. Dr. Hawkins states, "The word "I" is sufficient. "I" is complete and total, because the **Ultimate Reality** of God is the Source out of which Consciousness and Awareness arises." In the same neighborhood is **"I" as Self- Divinity/Allness (Beatific, Vision) at 750**. The well-known teachers of recent years like Nisargadatta Maharaj, Ramana Maharshi, various ones like that calibrate at 700, 750, in that range. When Ramana Maharshi hit 700, he fell down at age fifteen, felt he was dying, which is correct. When the ego goes, it is death. The only death that you can experience is the death of the ego. You cannot experience death of the body because you are out of body already and observe the body lying nearby, not even interesting. Death of the ego, the self, takes all the energy you have to go through it. The transition from 750 to **800, Teacher of Enlightenment (Arhat)**, is as described in the words of Dr. Hawkins, "What happens is thirty years of silence. Because the transformation is so stunning that you are struck dumb for thirty years. The mind does not think. To think in the presence of the Infinite Presence would be the ultimate absurdity; it is not even a possibility. So out of that silence then arose some kind of an awareness of this bridge between the non-linear and the linear. The understanding of the calibrated levels of consciousness as a way of making the nonlinear comprehensible to the linear came of its own. The human mind is used to scales, calibrations, temperatures, and therefore, the calibrated levels of consciousness seemed to make sense and we stumbled on kinesiology as the ultimate tool and that the field of consciousness is infallible because it is based on That Which Is, that which has Reality and therefore it cannot be fooled. Level 800 would then be the capacity to teach this. These are not great teachers, you can be the greatest piano virtuoso in the world, but that does not make you a good teacher of the piano. You can be Heifetz, but be a very bad violin teacher. To be the virtuoso is one thing, but to be able to convey it to others and share it, teach it to others is something else, so it is a separate karmic commitment."

That which is Unmanifest and manifests at **level 850 as Logos** radiates forth as the Light within which one knows the content of Consciousness as form and mind and meaning and significance and all that it becomes within the linear domain as best expressed by Sir Isaac Newton. It takes the totality of God to account for the existence of everything at any moment anywhere in time. The consciousness of the **Avatar at 985** has the capacity to send forth and radiate into the world an energy field, which tends to recontextualize the reality of all humankind for centuries. What happened 2000 years ago defines right through the next 2000 years, and 2000 years and 2000 years our definitions of right and wrong, values, the 10 Commandments, the courts, the judiciary. Its influence on architecture, values, and mores: the impact on human behavior is profound, even without being stated. It is the power of that energy field which contextualizes the consciousness of all of humankind. So the value is not specifically the specifics of a teaching, but the fact that an energy field at 985 appeared within the consciousness of mankind, thereby transforming it, because power is a reflection of context.

Calibrated Scale of Consciousness: The Enlightened and Divine States (3)

Buddhahood	**At-oneness with God Manifest and Un-manifest**	**1,000**
Krishna/Christ Consciousness	**At-oneness with God Manifest and Un-manifest**	**1,000**
"I"	**As the Ultimate Reality beyond this dimension, transcending dimensions**	**1,100**

Slide 263

SLIDE 263: CALIBRATED SCALE OF CONSCIOUSNESS: THE ENLIGHTENED AND DIVINE STATES (3)

The explanation for this slide is based on the transcript for Slide 2, first introduced at the March 2002 Lecture DVD, Disc 2, starting at 011100.

Buddhahood At-oneness with God Manifest and Unmanifest calibrates at 1,000. Krishna/Christ At-oneness with Consciousness God Manifest and Unmanifest also calibrates at 1,000. These are the greatest enlightened beings of all time. They had not only the capacity of the Knowingness, but also the capacity to express it in society in a way that was sufficiently meaningful that it recontextualized all society for thousands of years. A context at 1000 has sufficient power to influence all of humankind throughout all of time. That power and that consciousness is still present. Although the entity that came and left and reflected it to us has come and gone, the energy remains, the energy remains. What is the difference between the levels 985 and 1000? The statement, "There is no 'cause' of anything," calibrates at 999. The Buddha's Law of Dependent Origination or Interdependent Co-creation calibrates at 965. Buddha's Law pertains to the evolution of form or existence, that is, the Manifest. However, the Buddha stated that the Ultimate (the Void) was beyond form and there was nothing that was permanent (i.e., the Law of Impermanence, or *anatta*). To see a cause, you would have to have something that is caused, and to see something that is caused is already within the world of form. To see that everything is coming out of the spontaneity of Creation, out of the Essence of That Which It Is calibrates at 1000. The law of infinite causation, dependent causation calibrates at 985.

The soul is the nonphysical residual of the ego, and as the ego dissolves, even the personal soul with its karmic propensities dissolves into the Unmanifest Oneness of the Ultimate Reality. As separate 'things' do not exist in the Nonlinear Reality, no explanation such as 'causality' is necessary. By analogy, once a drop of water falls into the ocean, it becomes one with the ocean.

"I" As the Ultimate Reality beyond this dimension, transcending dimensions calibrates at 1,100. There are stages or levels of enlightenment that are progressive. We can calibrate them so as to calibrate the different terms that have been used over the ages. These are not levels of Reality but levels of the degree of awareness of Reality. The levels do not denote 'better than' lower levels but only the position of perspective, much as one might describe the appearance of the world from different levels of the stratosphere, or the characteristics of the oceans at different depths below sea level.

Calibrated Scale of Consciousness: The Enlightened and Divine States (4)

"I" as Essence of Creation	**1,200**
Archangel	**50,000+**
The Supreme Godhead - God Unmanifest	**Infinite**
God Manifest as Divinity/Creator	**Infinite**
Divinity	**Infinite**

Slide 264

SLIDE 264: CALIBRATED SCALE OF CONSCIOUSNESS: THE ENLIGHTENED AND DIVINE STATES (4)

The explanation for this slide is based on the transcript for Slide 2, first introduced at the March 2002 Lecture DVD, Disc 2, starting at 011100.

The Essence of Creation as "I", the Self as God of all Universes, of which there are an infinite number, is **1200**. In the words of Dr. Hawkins, "To go from around 700 or so, which does not happen very often, on upwards is not a pleasant experience. It is not like the high 500s. It is not exquisite kundalini energy coming up through you and pouring out through yourself in an exquisite way. What happens now is that the nervous system is over-taxed, and goes into exquisite pain. It is like a burning sensation of hot barbed wire. It is a horrible sensation and it is throughout your whole aura, so you cannot escape it, no matter what. This means that there is some awareness out, that there is something holding up the progression. That only happens if you are karmically destined to progress, and then consciousness keeps going and it is not satisfied with 700. It should be-it is absolutely, totally, infinite bliss, the knowingness of the oneness with the Divine Presence, but something out of some place can force it to grow and it goes beyond that. Then there are these horrible experiences which go on for years. You can be driving along perfectly fine and suddenly a thought goes through the air somewhere and the extreme discomfort starts. You find out what the error is, and you correct the error, usually in the form of a prayer and then it disappears. This goes on for quite a painful period. It seemed like a moment when the mind disappeared, obliterated by an Infinite Presence of crystal clarity, exquisite beauty, exquisite gentleness and profound power. In the pits of hell, the atheist says, beyond any hope, 'If there is a God I ask him to help me.' Infinite silence, then suddenly this Infinite Presence, absolute silence, as though you grabbed onto a 50,000 volt live wire, the power was so infinite. So the response to the prayer was a thought by that archangel, like an archangel was cruising by and he hears this screech from the pits of hell and he gives it a thought instantly. That which you were was obliterated for all time and the Radiance shines forth and there you are, barely able to see in the light.

All is an evolution of consciousness and we call that evolution 'karmic.' The word 'karma' here does not mean reincarnation. Karma means that consciousness evolves and each thing becomes an expression of its essence and we call that 'karma.' You cannot be a human being here sitting in a body without already the karmic inheritance that allows you to do so. There is no point to worry about karma because that which you are *is* your karma. The ego is your karma. There is no necessity to look for where it arose from, any more than it is not too interesting how you broke an ankle. The problem is how to fix it. As a physician, I do not care how you broke it-fell down stairs or you had a battle with your wife- that is all immaterial. You want to fix what the condition is *now* because the condition *now* is the inheritance of the past. It was the walking down the steps, the slipping on the banana peel, the argument with the spouse, the not paying attention. So, however it arose karmically-as spiritual students our presentation is that, how we experience ourselves in the present moment, as compared to how we would like to become in due time."

The **Archangel** is 50,000 and up. And the supreme and ultimate Realization is **God as Unmanifest** as well as **Manifest** because that which is Manifest is both, is both Manifest and beyond both. The Ultimate Reality is beyond either Manifest or Unmanifest, all of which are definitions of mind and when mind stops, they are meaningless.

Basic Ego Positionalities (1)

1. **Phenomena are either good or bad, right or wrong, just or unjust, fair or unfair**
2. **The 'bad' deserve to be punished and the 'good' rewarded**
3. **Things happen by accident or else they are the fault of somebody else**

Slide 265

SLIDE 265: BASIC EGO POSITIONALITIES (1)

The four slides from 272 to 275 discuss fundamental ego positionalities that are helpful in understanding the ego. These are also explained in "I: Reality and Subjectivity" (2003), Chapter 3: Spiritual Purification, pp. 44-50. "Spiritual realizations arise spontaneously and not as a consequence of thought processes. They arise in awareness as though coming out of intuition. [...] In experience, it just becomes apparent—it 'dawns on you'. Truth arises out of subjectivity and is obvious and self-revealing. This very often occurs when one is occupied with something totally unrelated. It 'comes out of nowhere' as a gift, a given. It is like the answer to an unspoken question. It is satisfying, solves an underlying puzzle, and is freeing in its effect on the psyche."

– "I: Reality and Subjectivity" (2003), Chapter 3: Spiritual Purification, p. 43

1. **Phenomena are either good or bad, right or wrong, just or unjust, fair or unfair.** To an enlightened being, all phenomena are of equal value. If it is sunny, then it is a nice sunny day and if it is raining, it is equally fine as a great rainy day. "Perception is edited observation in contrast to the terms 'vision', 'realization', and 'awareness', which refer to meaning and comprehension and therefore to a greater expanse of observation that includes not only the field but also the context. Context is inclusive rather than exclusive, and 'proximate field' places the observed presumed event or linear designation within a time frame. [...] Eventually, supposed 'events' or 'things' are seen as transitory, evolutionary epiphenomena of observation without any independent existence." – "Truth vs. Falsehood: How to Tell the Difference" (2005), Chapter 5: The Essential Structure of Truth, p. 48

2. **The 'bad' deserve to be punished and the 'good' rewarded.** "This world can be viewed as a spiritual workshop wherein the consequences of past mistakes can be reworked so that, hopefully, one will 'choose differently this time'. The consequences of past actions are not due to some judgment or mechanism of 'punishment' on the part of the spiritual universe; instead, they are merely innate to its intrinsic design. They are neither good nor bad. One does not get punished by some arbitrary God for past errors; instead, one merely follows them through to their consequences and learns that what is depicted as 'sin' is essentially error based on ignorance." – "I: Reality and Subjectivity" (2003), Chapter 5: Spiritual Reality, p. 97

3. **Things happen by accident or else they are the fault of somebody else.** "So-called accidents are an illusion of perception in the domain of form, which is based on a linear expectation. With muscle testing, the hidden elements are revealed and the illusion of 'accident' disappears. The only hypothetical possibility for a true accident to occur would require that it 'happen' outside the Allness of Creation, which is an impossibility. For a so-called accident to be observable, by definition it would have to have occurred within the discernible universe. Everything represents the consequence of the effect of the entire universe throughout all time. Nothing is outside the karmic, balanced harmony of the universe." – "I: Reality and Subjectivity" (2003), Chapter 5: Spiritual Reality, p. 85

Basic Ego Positionalities (2)

4. **The mind is capable of comprehending and recognizing truth from falsehood**

5. **The world causes and determines one's experiences**

6. **Life is unfair because the innocent suffer while the wicked go unpunished**

Slide 266

SLIDE 266: BASIC EGO POSITIONALITIES (2)

4. The mind is capable of comprehending and recognizing truth from falsehood. "One thing is obvious—the mind is totally unreliable. It cannot really be depended upon at all. It is not able to be consistent, and its performance is sporadic as well as erratic. It will forget to take the keys to the office, forget telephone numbers and addresses, and be the source of frustration or annoyance. The mind is contaminated by emotions, feelings, prejudices, blind spots, denials, projections, paranoias, phobias, fears, regrets, guilts, worries, anxiety, and the fearsome specters of poverty, old age, sickness, death, failure, rejection, loss, and disaster. In addition to all the foregoing, the mind has also been innocently and erroneously programmed by endless propaganda, political slogans, religious and social dogmas, and continual distortions of facts, not to mention falsifications, errors, misjudgments, and misinformation. [...] Above all else, the primary defect of the mind is not only its content, usually irrelevant or in error, but it has no means of telling truth from falsehood." – "The Eye of the I: From Which Nothing Is Hidden" (2002), Chapter 7: The Mind, pp. 97-98

5. The world causes and determines one's experiences. "Spiritual progress is based on acceptance as a matter of free will and choice, and thus everyone experiences only the world of their own choosing. The universe is totally free of victims, and all eventualities are the unfolding of inner choice and decision. [...] To the higher self, human life is composed of games and charades because, unconsciously, everyone knows that death is not an actual possibility. Why else would anybody risk their 'life' for political gain or money? [...] The ego engages in performances that are utterly convincing to the players and onlookers. On a certain level, each player is providing a spiritual service to others by acting out the lessons that need to be learned for the benefit of all. Acts of courage awaken the soul to its own innate power, which it will need to reach the ultimate awareness." – From "The Eye of the I: From Which Nothing Is Hidden" (2002), Chapter 4: The Basics, pp. 61-62

6. Life is unfair because the innocent suffer while the wicked go unpunished. "It is well to keep in mind at all times that the ego/mind does not experience the world but only its own perceptions of it. The media exploit emotionality and sensationalism in images and languaging to elicit sentimentality, indignation, or outrage, or to satisfy prurient curiosity. When seen for what they are, these invitations to reactivity can be declined. [...] The oneness of life appears to perception as multitudinous. What makes the appearances of the world seem real is a projection of the Radiance of the Self. The movie itself has no intrinsic reality as perceived. The actual locus of the sense of realness lies totally within consciousness as subjectivity." – "I: Reality and Subjectivity" (2003), Chapter 11: Transcending the World, pp. 179-180.

Basic Ego Positionalities (3)

7. **People can be different than they are**

8. **It is critical and necessary to be right**

9. **It is critical and necessary to win**

Slide 267

SLIDE 267: BASIC EGO POSITIONALITIES (3)

People can be different than they are. "From the hypothetical, moralistic viewpoint, one is not supposed to give in to 'weakness', and who is to be blamed for the fact that the evolution of consciousness has not brought one to saintly resolve, a healthy brain, and beneficial genes? We could blame the rhinencephalon, that old animal brain that is rapacious in order to survive. We could blame parents or society. We could blame the Pavlovian conditioning of the media. [...] In this kaleidoscope of interacting factors, whom should we blame? Who should wear the sackcloth and ashes and beat their breast? When any single act is disassembled, it will be found to have no single determinative cause, and the 'who' that ostensibly performed the act no longer even exists. [...] We can see from the inherent complexity of even a simple act that only the omniscience of God would be capable of judging; thus arises the spiritual dictum, "Judge not." It is vanity that leads the ego to think it is capable of judging others or itself." – "I: Reality and Subjectivity" (2003), Chapter 12: The Emotions, pp. 194-195

It is critical and necessary to be right. "The ego's investments take the form of pride and identification with belief systems; therefore, these also have to be defended. This results in a hyper alertness to danger, like that of the animal in the wild. All that is valued has to be defended; therefore, danger lurks everywhere. The ego is ever watchful of every slight, slur, or encroachment on its turf. [...] Because of the ego's investments, innumerable positionalities, and false identifications, its fears are endless and continuously propagate. They subside only when the identification of 'me' with the positionalities is withdrawn, and the fears relating to physical survival and being separate diminish as a result of total surrender of one's life and survival to God." – "I: Reality and Subjectivity" (2003), Chapter 12: The Emotions, p. 199

"To be offended signifies that one is defended, which, in itself, signifies the clinging to untruth. Truth needs no defense and therefore is not defensive; truth has nothing to prove and is not vulnerable to being questioned for an answer." – "I: Reality and Subjectivity" (2003), Chapter 18: "No Mind", p. 323

It is critical and necessary to win. "Because emotional appeal and personal charisma are deemed as necessary to win, they frequently tend to override rationality and truth or spiritual principles. These factors bring down the overall calibrated levels of political parties from the lofty 500s of love or the 400s of reason to the practical 'get it done' attitude of the high 200s and 300s, which is characterized by willingness, service, and productivity. Although politics may cite moral or even religious issues, it sometimes does so primarily for secular reasons, e.g., to win votes." – "Truth vs. Falsehood: How to Tell the Difference" (2005), Chapter 10: America, p. 149.

Basic Ego Positionalities (4)

10. Wrongs must be righted

11. Righteousness must prevail

12. Perceptions represent reality

Slide 268

SLIDE 268: BASIC EGO POSITIONALITIES (4)

Wrongs must be righted. "Guilt is the consequence of the memory of regretted past actions as they are recalled. These can be transcended only by recontextualization. Mistakes are the natural, impersonal consequence of learning and development and therefore unavoidable. [...] The present self 'is', and the former self 'was', and, in truth, that which 'was' is not identical with that which 'is'. Regret and guilt result from equating the present self that 'is' with the former self that 'was' but actually is no more; they are not the same. [...] The past cannot be rewritten, but it can be recontextualized so as to be a source of constructive learning. Regret over past events or decisions can be ameliorated by realizing that they 'seemed like a good idea at the time'. [...] Past errors are due to limitation and belong to a certain point in the timeline of evolution, not only personally but also collectively. What was acceptable in the past is no longer acceptable. Ignorance is due to fallacy of perception or interpretation." – "Transcending the Levels of Consciousness: The Stairway to Enlightenment" (2006), Chapter 2: Guilt and Vindictive Hate, p. 49

Righteousness must prevail. "Negativity originates from the mind of man who manufactures the endless array of false gods, all of whom demand worship and sacrifice. The God of Reality has no 'needs' and is not subject to being pleased or displeased, much less appeased. [...] One of the main levers that tilted the world in a negative direction was the self- defeating conceptual weapon called 'righteousness', which calibrates as Pride at 190. It has been the primary destructive force and Achilles' heel for the last several thousand years of man's history. It was the great, highest excuse for every form of imaginable savagery and barbarism." – From "The Eye of the I: From Which Nothing Is Hidden" (2002), Chapter 4: The Basics, pp. 55-56

Perceptions represent reality. "The entire perceptual illusion that the ego claims to be reality is completely and totally the product of positionality. This is very important to unravel and understand in one's own experiential awareness. If you observe carefully, you will note that at the time the mind is taking a position, that position stems from choice, training, desire, emotion, or political or religious viewpoint. From the arbitrary positionalities of moralizing, all actions and events can be categorized as right or wrong. From that positionality stem all the pointless sacrifice and sufferings of the world. [...]The Buddha said there is nothing to judge because perception can only see illusion. Perception is always partial and limited by an arbitrary context. In truth, no judgment is possible." – "The Eye of the I: From Which Nothing Is Hidden" (2002), Chapter 12: The Search for Truth, pp. 180-181.

Examples of Limiting Postulates (1)

1. **There is a right side and a wrong side to every conflict**
2. **There is a cause for everything**
3. **Someone is responsible for everything**
4. **Someone is to blame for unfortunate events and accidents**

Slide 269

SLIDE 269: EXAMPLES OF LIMITING POSTULATES (1)

The four slides from 276 to 279 discuss fundamental ego postulates that are helpful in understanding the ego. These are also explained in "I: Reality and Subjectivity" (2003), Chapter 13: Mind, pp. 216-220. "What have been naïvely believed to be personal opinions can then be seen to be simply products of a field. It can also be observed that many basic postulates have such wide acceptance that they are automatically uncritically subscribed to. We can call this phenomenon "being at the effect of the postulates," which, in the unaware person, occurs primarily outside awareness. To the spiritual student, this awareness is of critical importance because each postulate establishes a context that is a constraint and limitation, with its resultant dualities of perception and belief." – "I: Reality and Subjectivity" (2003), Chapter 13: Mind, p. 217

There is a right side and a wrong side to every conflict. "By taking responsibility for the consequences of their own perceptions, observers can transcend the role of victim to an understanding that "nothing out there has power over you." [...] We may observe how throughout history, society has tried to "treat" social problems by legislative action, warfare, market manipulation, laws, and prohibitions-all manifestations of force-only to see these problems persist or recur despite the treatment. Although governments (or individuals) proceeding from positions of force are myopic, to the sensitive observer it eventually becomes obvious that conditions of social conflict will not disappear until the underlying etiology has been exposed and "healed."" – "Power vs. Force: The Hidden Determinants of Human Behavior" (2012 edition), Chapter 3: Test Results and Interpretation, pp. 94-95

There is a cause for everything. "Contemplation of the Map of Consciousness© can, for instance, transform one's understanding of causality. As perception itself evolves with one's level of consciousness, it becomes apparent that what the world calls the domain of causes is in fact the domain of effects." – "Power vs. Force: The Hidden Determinants of Human Behavior" (2012 edition), Chapter 3: Test Results and Interpretation, p. 94

Someone is responsible for everything. That is faulty perception as in Reality, nothing is happening. "In Reality, nothing changes; no events occur. There are no real names for anything nor is there any seeming sequence or separation of so-called occurrences." – "I: Reality and Subjectivity" (2003), Chapter 8: The Mystic, p. 144

Someone is to blame for unfortunate events and accidents. "As we have observed repeatedly, in a universe where everything is connected with everything else, there is no such thing as an "accident;' and nothing is outside of the universe. Because the power of the actual elements is unseen and only the manifestation of effects is observable, there is an illusion of "accidental" events." – "Power vs. Force: The Hidden Determinants of Human Behavior", Chapter 18: Wellness and the Disease Process, p. 242 (2012 edition).

Examples of Limiting Postulates (2)

5. **There is an answer to every question**
6. **Everything has an opposite**
7. **Everything has a meaning**
8. **Everyone is capable of reason**
9. **Everyone's reality is really basically the same**

Slide 270

SLIDE 270: EXAMPLES OF LIMITING POSTULATES (2)

There is an answer to every question.

"Q: Many questions that arise, therefore, are not really answerable.

A: That is true. That is because they are often just tautologies. They merely mean what they are defined to mean but have no corollary in existence. The mind presumes that a mentation that seems logical and intellectually reasonable must have a concordant reality. This is a major source of fallacy in human life." – "I: Reality and Subjectivity" (2003), Chapter 7: The Radical Reality of the Self, pp. 126-127

Everything has an opposite. God has no opposite. "Evil is not the opposite of God but simply the denial of God, just as falsity is not the opposite of truth but its refusal. The deification of the self does not lead to God-ness but to the grandiose delusions of egomania and religious psychosis." – "I: Reality and Subjectivity" (2003), Chapter 20: Perspectives, p. 364

Everything has a meaning. "Neither God nor Truth can be found within the limitation of content only for, by simple observation, content is only definition or description whereas context supplies meaning, significance, and concordance with the reality of existence itself. This is important to comprehend not only in spiritual work but also in everyday social and political policies. [...] To ignore context is the greatest source of catastrophe for every generation of man, and it continues on in the present time with the same catastrophic consequences." – "I: Reality and Subjectivity" (2003), Chapter 13: "Mind", p. 220

Everyone is capable of reason. "The basic fallacy is the presumption that 'other people' are ruled by ethics, logic and reason, which is a grave error. That is why this country is always 'surprised' by the response of other countries or segments of society that have very different agendas. [...] Such societies are ruled by expediency, hatred, greed, selfishness, emotionality, etc. Thus, 'food for the poor' sent to other countries is customarily commandeered by the rich who feel no obligation to the 'undeserving' lower class." – "I: Reality and Subjectivity" (2003), Chapter 7: The Radical Reality of the Self, p. 127

Everyone's reality is really basically the same. "As is obvious, each level of human consciousness therefore has its own innate 'reality', and conflict is inevitable between people and cultures that are diametrically opposed to each other. What brings praise in one subgroup would result in ridicule in another. For example, [...] Are honesty and morality reality-based bulwarks of stability in society or merely 'politically repressive semantic constructs'? Is truth an absolute (essence), or is it arbitrary and merely a relative reflection of transitory public opinion (appearance, perception) that solely reflects social bias? – "Reality, Spirituality, and Modern Man" (2008), Chapter 1: Overview, p. 37.

Examples of Limiting Postulates (3)

10. Some things are better than others

11. Time marches on

12. Some things are more valuable than others

13. Reason is a reliable tool

14. Logic is proof

Slide 271

SLIDE 271: EXAMPLES OF LIMITING POSTULATES (3)

Some things are better than others. "Each entity has its work to do in its contribution to the whole. One brick is not better than another because it is bigger or higher up in the building. 'Greater' or 'lesser' or 'better' are judgmental terms arising from positionality. Each entity that lives takes equal joy from the awareness of existence. The Divine Presence in All That Is imbues that quality as a consequence of Creation. The animal, the plant, or the human are equal in their joy of existence." – "The Eye of the I: From Which Nothing Is Hidden" (2002), Chapter 11: Along the Pathway, p. 173

Time marches on. "Everything exists outside of time and not within it; therefore, nothing exists in time nor is subject to it. Time is merely a style of perception. [...] 'Now' is also a concept. There is only foreverness; that which is the Self is felt/known as a quality of always and is not experienced as a current instant that would be analogous to a place or episode in linear time. In the nonlinear Reality, there is no time track upon which to position a moment or an instant denotable as 'now.'" – "I: Reality and Subjectivity" (2003), Chapter 11: Transcending the World, pp. 181-182

Some things are more valuable than others. "With the elimination of preference, all form is seen to be equal in value; in fact, its common value is only that it has form. The weed is the same as the diamond—each may differ in appearance but not in intrinsic value. Their beauty is equal because it is innate in all form. Everything is equal by virtue of having existence." – "I: Reality and Subjectivity" (2003), Chapter 11: Transcending the World, pp. 180-181

Reason is a reliable tool. "The shortcomings of this energy level (400: Reason) are the failure to clearly distinguish the difference between symbols and what they represent, and confusion between the objective and subjective worlds that limits the understanding of causality. At this level, it is easy to lose sight of the forest for the trees, to become infatuated with concepts and theories, ending up in intellectualism and missing the essential point. [...] Although Reason is highly effective in a technical world where the methodologies of logic dominate, Reason itself, paradoxically, is the major block to reaching higher levels of consciousness." – "Power vs. Force: The Hidden Determinants of Human Behavior" (2012 edition), Chapter 4: Levels of Human Consciousness, pp. 110-111

Logic is proof. "Spiritual reality is verifiable but not provable. The term 'proof' is limited in application to the Newtonian paradigm of reality, which is based on form, and an implied process called causality. Proof is limited to content and form." – "I: Reality and Subjectivity" (2003), Chapter 5: Spiritual Reality, p. 105.

Examples of Limiting Postulates (4)

15. **There is a self-existent, discoverable, objective reality 'out there'**
16. **Man is superior to animals because he can think**
17. **Everyone knows right from wrong**
18. **The guilty deserve punishment and the good deserve rewards**

Slide 272

SLIDE 272: EXAMPLES OF LIMITING POSTULATES (4)

There is a self-existent, discoverable, objective reality 'out there'. "By analysis, it will be discovered that the common term "relationship" is itself an illusion that originates solely within the mind of the observer. It is an arbitrary viewpoint set up by selection of what is to be compared to what (i.e., a mentalization). To select two points for mental focus and attention does not magically change what is 'out there' that now have a 'relationship', just as selecting stars to look at does not cause a 'constellation' to be a reality in the sky. Connecting the dots is imaginative but all 'constellations' are within the observer's imagination. They are not facts about astronomy nor do they have reality as *res externa*, i.e., nature." – "Truth vs. Falsehood: How to Tell the Difference" (2005), Chapter 12: Problematic Issues, p. 215

Man is superior to animals because he can think. Man and animal are both part of Creation and one part of Creation is not superior to another. On the other hand, man's karmic inheritance includes potentiality of realizing his immortality whereas the animal does not have that potentiality. "Mankind lives in the realm of tension between emotional instincts and the counterbalancing power of spiritual awakening (i.e., the animal/angel conflict)." – "I: Reality and Subjectivity" (2003), Chapter 6: Realization, p. 112

Everyone knows right from wrong. "The lowest levels of human consciousness are those of criminality, as represented by the inability to delay or control animal impulses, pleasure at defiance, and the lack of capacity to learn from experience. The defect is represented in the inherent and often genetic incapacity to discern right from wrong. [...]Uncontrollable willfulness and defiance are seen during the infant state of the 'terrible two's' in which the omnipotence of the infantile ego is pitted against parental control. Parents may lack the energy or volition to respond appropriately, so the child fails to learn impulse control and is unable to discern the basic survival lesson of right from wrong. This is concordant with very low consciousness levels, especially those below 90, as represented by criminality." – "Reality, Spirituality and Modern Man" (2008), Chapter 13: Doubt, Skepticism and Disbelief, pp. 262-263

The guilty deserve punishment and the good deserve rewards. The Scale of Consciousness does not denote 'better than', which is a program of the ego. Each level of energy has its rewards, and they actually feel the same to each person. "Force is the universal substitute for truth. The gun and the nightstick are evidence of weakness; the need to control others stems from lack of power, just as vanity stems from lack of self-esteem. Punishment is a form of violence, an ineffectual substitute for power. When, as in our society, the punishment rarely fits the crime, it can hardly be effectual; punishment is based on revenge at the weak energy level of 150." – "Power vs. Force: The Hidden Determinants of Human Behavior" (2012 edition), Chapter 11: Power in the Marketplace, p. 189.

Authentic vs. Pathologic State (1)

Authentic	**Pathologic**
Samadhi	**Catatonic**
Religious Ecstasy	**Mania (bipolar Hyper-religiosity)**
Illumination	**Grandiosity Enlightenment**
Religious delusion	
Piety	**Scrupulosity – (obsessive/compulsive)**
Inspiration	**Imagination**

Slide 273

SLIDE 273: AUTHENTIC VS. PATHOLOGIC STATE (1)

Samadhi vs. Catatonic: Catatonic refers to someone who is apparently awake but immobile or unresponsive to external stimuli, with an inability to move normally and can be associated with schizophrenia and other mental illnesses. "In traditional spiritual literature, there are descriptions and classifications of various advanced levels of consciousness described as states of *Samadhi*. Often these are descriptively associated with states of meditation consequent to transcending the limitations of the ego." - "Transcending the Levels of Consciousness: The Stairway to Enlightenment" (2006), Chapter 17: Self-Realization, p. 288

Religious Ecstasy vs. Mania (bipolar hyper-religiosity): Religious ecstasy is the experience of a beatific vision characterized by greatly reduced external awareness and expanded interior mental and spiritual awareness, accompanied by euphoria. Most self-proclaimed messiahs, on the other hand, are suffering from the manic phase of a bipolar (manic-depressive) mental disorder. "Religion is the means, not the end; it is the map, not the territory; it is the cover, not the book. [...] The great teachers taught the Truth about Divinity, not religion, which came centuries later. While the veneration of religion and scriptures is understandable, it is their truth and God that are meant to be worshipped and sought." – "Truth vs. Falsehood: How to Tell the Difference" (2005), Chapter 16: Religion and Truth, pp. 331-332

Illumination vs. Grandiosity: The authentic enlightened state of Illumination emerges at consciousness level 600, which is that of Infinite Peace and Bliss illuminated by the Light of the Radiant Self. "This grandiosity represents succumbing to the temptation of what might be called 'godification', into which many world-famous leaders have fallen via greedy financial and sexual exploitation, control, and manipulation of followers for personal gain ..." – "Reality, Spirituality, and Modern Man" (2008), Chapter 11: Belief, Trust and Credibility, p. 210

Enlightenment vs. Religious Delusion: A religious delusion is experienced as an assumption rather than a belief and is quite unlike a subjective religious experience. "Illumination, Self- Realization, and Enlightenment denote the Divine states that have historically demonstrated the highest levels of consciousness. These conditions represent the transcendence of the limitations of the constraints of the linearity of the ego and the emergence of the Radiance of the Infinite Reality and source of Existence." – "Transcending the Levels of Consciousness: The Stairway to Enlightenment" (2006), Section Four – Overview, p. 271

Piety vs. Scrupulosity – (obsessive/compulsive): Piety is the quality of being religious, with reverence for God and devout fulfillment of religious obligations. However, hyper-religiosity itself, which appears as piety, can and does become an error as exhibited by scrupulosity or obsessive-compulsive disorder in which the person lives in fear of guilt over even minor trivia, such as making just a normal mistake.

Inspiration vs. Imagination: Motivation for spiritual growth is the consequence of inspiration instead of the desire for imaginary (perceptual) gain. The individual is free to ignore inspiration or to follow its dictates and interpretations of reality vis-à-vis imagination, fantasy, or emotional options.

Authentic vs. Pathologic State (2)

Authentic	Pathologic
Visions	Hallucinations
Authentic Spiritual Teacher	False guru, imposter, spiritual con-artist
Experiential	Intellectual
Devotion	Zealotry, hyper-religiosity

Slide 274

SLIDE 274: AUTHENTIC VS. PATHOLOGIC STATE (2)

Visions vs. Hallucinations: Spiritual discernment is a rare gift and, historically speaking, it does not occur until the 'third eye' opens with spiritual vision. Until that happens, any spiritual seeker, no matter how earnest, can be easily fooled. The differentiation between a Divine messenger and a religious-content hallucination can be made by the technique of consciousness calibration.

Authentic Spiritual Teacher vs. False Guru, Imposter or Spiritual Con Artist: The spiritual teacher who has reached spiritual maturity remembers that the devotee is frequently enthusiastic but naïve, easily deceived by false teachers or teachings that are attractively packaged. Guidance is an inestimable value of the guru who steers the student away from enticing pitfalls of spiritual seduction and glamour. The teacher's function is to inspire, to instruct, and to confirm by personal testimony the truth of teachings and to encourage students who are struggling with the path. "Zealous enthusiasm is no substitute for truth, nor is the belief in the faith of thousands or even millions of followers. [...] If spiritual imposters were not impressive, charismatic, believable, and convincing, they would have no followers. It actually takes an expert or a person of very advanced consciousness to tell the difference. The reason for this spiritual error is that the error of the false guru is one of context, and the context is beyond the limited perception of the initiate. Erudition is also not a guarantee of truth. There are teachers of great brilliance, but when one does research, one finds that the heart chakra is out of balance. In contrast, very loving teachers who are 'all heart', but in whom the third eye or crown chakra is 'out', lead followers down an errant path to possibly the most painful of all human experiences in which spiritual disillusionment leads to depression and even to suicide." – "The Eye of the I: From Which Nothing Is Hidden" (2002), Chapter 5: Circumventing the Ego, p. 72

Experiential vs. Intellectual: When it pertains to the spiritual, the mind with its **intellect** is not reliable as it has no experiential evidence to follow at all, and, therefore, it usually blindly follows social, ethnic, or family precedent. Most people's spiritual and religious beliefs are determined by the 'accident' of birth and cultural identification. The ego adopts the belief systems as 'mine', and then proceeds to defend them. Whether the beliefs have any validity cannot be ascertained by the mind and therefore have to be overly defended, and often to a fanatical degree, primarily because they are vulnerable to attack. Truth that is **experiential** does not have to be defended. It is merely a matter of fact. Therefore, 'believers' are the most vociferous and militant in expressing their views. The true seeker of truth is forewarned to avoid the influence of believers, aggressive proselytizers, and religious fanatics of all persuasions.

Devotion vs. Zealotry, Hyper-religiosity: "The defect of the far-right position of any religion is the activation of spiritual **zealotry**. True spiritual integrity comes from courage in the promotion of truth. Therefore, that is reflected in the energy of the heart as **devotion** to one's spiritual beliefs. Spiritual hatred, however, comes out of the spleen, which then triggers the release of animal-type behaviors." – "Truth vs. Falsehood: How to Tell the Difference" (2005), Chapter 16: Religion and Truth, p. 344

Authentic vs. Pathologic State (3)

Authentic	Pathologic
Committed	**Obsessed, brain-washed by cult**
Dark night of the soul	**Pathologic depression**
Detachment	**Withdrawal, indifference**
Nonattachment, acceptance	**Passivity**

Slide 275

SLIDE 275: AUTHENTIC VS. PATHOLOGIC STATE (3)

Committed vs. Obsessed, Brain- washed by Cult, Victimized: It is important to know that it is actually extremely rare for a human to be **committed** to spiritual truth to the degree of seriously seeking Enlightenment, and those who do make the commitment do so because they are actually *destined* for Enlightenment. "Frequently, serious spiritual students become waylaid by attractive, deviant pathways, schools, and teachings and thereby devote time and energy in fruitless pursuit of spiritual illusions. This may take up years, decades, or even whole lifetimes that sometimes end up in regret or even bitter disappointment. With the current availability of the techniques of calibrating levels of truth, such errors can be circumvented. There are even professional 'deprogrammers' to assist in recovery from **cult indoctrination and brainwashing** that can result in severe loss of reality testing and rationality, even to the degree of cult group suicide or bombing the innocent, allegedly 'for God.'" – "Discovery of the Presence of God: Devotional Nonduality" (2006), Chapter 12: The Devotee, pp. 203-204.

Dark Night of the Soul vs. Pathologic Depression: The dark night of the soul is often a sign of significant spiritual progress for it is not really the soul (higher Self) but the ego that is in the dark. Some comfort can be obtained by recalling the spiritual dictum that one can only go as high as they have been low, or that Jesus Christ sweat blood in Gethsemane, or that the Buddha reported that he felt as though his bones were being broken and he was being attacked by demons. **Pathological depression** is different. From "Transcending the Levels of Consciousness: The Stairway to Enlightenment" (2006), Chapter 3: Apathy, p. 84: "Intrapsychic repression of unacceptable drives and conflicts depletes psychic energy that is unavailable for normal adaptational operations. This results in apathy expressed as exhaustion, feeling tired and below par, and the lack of pleasure in living (anhedonia). Lack of pleasure through normal means may be artificially compensated through various addictions. When escapism is blocked or unobtainable, **the inner depression** returns, which may result in acting out and desperate measures of avoidance. Many actually choose to die rather than face the inner conflicts and own the responsibility for either the conflict itself or for seeking help and resolution."

Detachment vs. Withdrawal, Indifference: "One participates but is not involved in or attached to it (the world). One can observe without being judgmental. **Detachment** would require **withdrawal** from the world, whereas **nonattachment** allows participation as there is no stake in outcomes. The game is entertaining but which side 'wins' is of no importance." – "I: Reality and Subjectivity" (2003), Chapter 8: The Mystic, p. 146.

Nonattachment, Acceptance vs. Passivity: "At this level of awareness (350: **Acceptance**), a major transformation takes place, with the understanding that one is oneself the source and creator of the experience of one's life. [...] Acceptance is not to be confused with **passivity**, which is a symptom of apathy. This form of Acceptance allows engagement in life on life's own terms, without trying to make it conform to an agenda." – "Power vs. Force: The Hidden Determinants of Human Behavior" (2012 edition), Chapter 4: Levels of Human Consciousness, p. 109.

Authentic vs. Pathologic State (4)

Authentic	Pathologic
Transcendent state	Mutism
Trusting	Naïve
Advanced state	Psychosis, egomania
Beatific	Euphoria
Humility	Low self-esteem
Spiritual sharing	Proselytizing
Commitment	Religiosity
Inspired	Messianic

Slide 276

SLIDE 276: AUTHENTIC VS. PATHOLOGIC STATE (4)

Mutism is a neuropsychological disorder related to impairment of speech. "In the **transcendent state**, all is continuous, and nominalization or denotation is of appearance only, as nothing is actually separate. All is self-evident and self-effulgent, which cannot be adequately described in language." – "I: Reality and Subjectivity" (2003), Chapter 2: Spiritual Information and Practice, p. 35. "The spiritual seeker goes through developmental stages. There is the **naïve** initiate who is gullible, overly **trusting**, and vulnerable to persuasion and proselytizing by spiritual politicians and power seekers. In this stage, that which is nonintegrous is not detected, and everyone is seen as trustworthy and lovable. [...] As spiritual progress continues, the **naïveté** of the aspirant is replaced by greater wisdom and discernment." – "I: Reality and Subjectivity" (2003), Chapter 19: The Way of the Heart, p. 338. "There are different levels of Samadhi, classically described with Sanskrit designations. [...] The more **advanced state** is a permanent awareness that persists continuously so that returned functioning in the world is possible, as determined by karma or prior decision, choice, or agreement." – "The Eye of the I: From Which Nothing Is Hidden" (2002), Chapter 12: Explanations, p. 199.

"Evil is not the opposite of God but simply the denial of God, just as falsity is not the opposite of truth but its refusal. The deification of the self does not lead to God-ness but to the grandiose delusions of **egomania** and religious **psychosis**." – "I: Reality and Subjectivity" (2003), Chapter 20: Perspectives, p. 364. **Beatific** bestows bliss, blessings, happiness, or peace**.** Many stimuli can induce **Euphoria**, including psychoactive drugs, exercise, social activities, etc. "The comfort of drugs may also provide escape from the inner barrenness. When the temporary drug-induced **euphoria** subsides, the return of the downside becomes intolerable, so the drug dependence is not just an addiction but also a lifestyle. [...] Self-condemnation is projected onto God and society which are therefore blamed for the condition." – "Transcending the Levels of Consciousness: The Stairway to Enlightenment" (2006), Chapter 3: Apathy, p. 77-78.

Social craving is often compensatory to self-doubt, **low self-esteem,** and the need for external sources of pleasure. "When we have adequate self-esteem, we are motivated by **inner humility** and gratitude and, therefore, we have no need for the constant eliciting of strokes and pats from others (or God). When we stop wanting to be liked, we find that we are." – "Letting Go: The Pathway of Surrender" (2012), Chapter 18: Relationships, pp. 265-266. Authentic **spiritual sharing** is the exact opposite of **proselytizing**. From "The Eye of the I: From Which Nothing Is Hidden" (2002), Chapter 5: Circumventing the Ego, p. 68: "**Proselytizing** is best done by example rather than by coercion and lapel grabbing. We influence others by what we are rather than by what we say or have. [...] Each person has their own karma or destiny to fulfill, and it is best not to confuse these missions."

Spiritual progress requires intense motivation and devotion that then becomes a total **commitment** to a task and its relentless pursuit. This acquired faculty can then be used in both the practice of formal meditation as well as in daily life. This capacity is volitional and the result of a decision and is therefore quite different from **Religiosity**. A sage is **inspired** to the perfection of being a perfect mirror to reflect God's grace to be shared by all whereas most self-proclaimed messiahs are suffering from the manic phase of a bipolar (manic-depressive) mental disorder. Political leaders are the best known **messianic** personalities, and they can be mesmerizing with their grandiose egomania.

Authentic vs. Pathologic State (5)

Authentic	Pathologic
God Shock	Schizophrenic
Spiritual Ecstasy	Disorganization, manic state, High on drugs
Genuine spiritual leader	Spiritual politician, cult leader
Free	Psychopathic
Teaching	Controlling

Slide 277

SLIDE 277: AUTHENTIC VS. PATHOLOGIC STATE (5)

The prominent characteristics of **Schizophrenic Disorganization** are disorganized speech and behavior, which may impair one's ability to carry out daily activities such as showering or eating. **God shock**: "Physical incarnation may or may not continue because intrinsic to very advanced states of consciousness and spiritual development is the awareness of an invitational permission to leave physicality (level 600). [...] The circumscribed personal identity disappears, and the self is replaced by the Allness of the Self. There may be a period of initial '**God shock**' in which the mind is silenced and functioning is autonomous, without volitional intention or the prior customary pursuit of goals. [...] Hunger seems to disappear, and one can go for days without eating. One may be surprised to see a body reflected in a mirror." – "Reality, Spirituality and Modern Man" (2008), Chapter 19: Practicum, pp. 357-358. The **spiritual ecstasy** of the very high 500s is an authentic state, recorded (e.g., Ramakrishna or the great Christian saints) and thereby given credence and acceptance as a possible reality for those who are exceptionally motivated or gifted.

The **manic state, high on drugs** is quite different: "We will use the example of somebody who bases survival on something outside himself, such as an **addict**. When we threaten to take away his bottle or supply or flush his **drugs** down the toilet, he goes into a rage. Now it is very clear to us what the source of the anger is, is it not? The source of the anger is exactly the same fantasy as the source of happiness being something outside of him and which has been placed on some external object—a person, place, or thing. To place the source of our happiness on something outside ourselves creates a negative energy field because it is basically a lie." - "Healing and Recovery" (2009), Chapter 12: Depression, pp. 374-375.

Characteristics of a **genuine spiritual leader** are detailed in slides 39-42, "Identification and Characteristics of Spiritual Truth, Integrous Teachers, and Teachings". From "I: Reality and Subjectivity" (2003), Chapter 1: Teachers and Students, pp. 9-11: "Even when the pretenses of a charismatic leader are exposed, many duped followers merely resort to denial in the face of the obvious. Such examples are now commonly documented on the Internet by research groups. (For example, **a cult leader** recommends risky investments; another 'channels' a teacher/guide 'from the other side' who, for a hefty fee, gives a spurious reading about a person who does not even exist, etc.) [...] Devotees are exploited and controlled by abuse of their naïve trust and misplaced faith. "By their fruits one can know them."

In contrast, that which is of God brings beauty, love, joy, forgiveness, compassion, peace, and freedom." One is **free** to subscribe to a quality or position. All positionalities are voluntary. "When we realize that some people are unable to change of their own volition, we begin to see that they are ill or perhaps lack essential critical brain function. Historically, this was called 'moral imbecility'. Currently, it is referred to as '**psychopathic** personality'. This defect shows up as early as ages two or three through the inability to control impulses or delay gratifications. There is some intrinsic defect in the ability to learn from experience and an intrinsic inability to fear consequences." – "I: Reality and Subjectivity" (2003), Chapter 18: "No Mind", p. 323. **Authentic teaching is non-controlling**: Spiritual purity has no interest in the personal lives of aspirants, or in clothing, dress, style, sex lives, economics, family patterns, lifestyles, or dietary habits.

Newtonian vs. Quantum Mechanics (1)

Newtonian	Quantum
Orderly	Disorderly
Logical	Illogical
Predictable	Unpredictable
Deterministic	Free
Literal	Creative
Pedestrian	Imaginative
Reductionist	Progressive
Separate	Intermingled, interconnected
Discrete	Diffuse
Cause	Potentiate

Slide 278

SLIDE 278: NEWTONIAN VS. QUANTUM MECHANICS (1)

This slide is a subset of slide 19 and was not actually shown in any lecture. Additional information has been provided below to help in making the transition from the Newtonian linear (force) to the nonlinear (Power) domain. To facilitate understanding of the transition from the macroscopic, 'objective', ordinary world of form and logic to the subjective, 'microscopic', nonlinear reality of subjectivity, it may be useful to summarize the differences between the old linear Euclidian/Newtonian paradigm of reality and the more advanced understanding of nonlinear dynamics and the science of Quantum Mechanics and sub-atomic advanced theoretical physics.

These are explained in "I: Reality and Subjectivity" (2003), Appendix D: Quantum Mechanics, starting on p. 431. No statement of objectivity has any validity except as a subjective reality; therefore, the absolute infinite reality is subjectivity. Quantum is the infinite potentiality of the Context out of which what we call 'reality' (manifest world of form) arises. The field of infinite potentiality of quantum mechanics is Consciousness itself. It shows ignorance for anyone to take the position that quantum is unreal and Newtonian is real. It is only out of Subjectivity (what some call unreal) that the objective world appears. The Absolute infinite reality is Subjectivity, which is not out there, elsewhere, at some other time, for other people. A good part of the world refutes the reality of the nonlinear domain and spirituality because it cannot comprehend it, and does not want to be answerable to a spiritual reality. It wants to be free of that threat, so it can do what it wants to do. What is important for the spiritual student to grasp is that the various substratum of what we assume to be reality are profoundly affected and are alterable by the mere act of human observation. Aside from the advanced mathematics, a student of quantum theory may conclude that what one discovers is a product of intention in that, what one discovers depends on what one is looking for. It is difficult for a mind used to the world of the Newtonian measurable finite world to make the jump to the nonlinear domain.

The scale of consciousness tries to establish a way of comprehending going from the known to the unknown, and making it more comprehensible in the style of understanding the mind is accustomed to. The calibrated levels represent a perspective, an arbitrary point of observation, which is significant only in relationship to the whole. Each selected level is therefore the viewpoint from an arbitrary perspective. It does not denote a different reality but instead shows how such a reality is experienced or perceived. Thus, it is not that reality 'is' that way, but that it 'feels' or 'looks' that way. "The nonlinear domain is invisible, without form, and beyond time, dimension, or measurement. It includes qualities and meanings, and power emanates from its intrinsic essence. The source of power and creation is in the invisible, nonlinear domain and by the exercise of will can result in form. The visible world is therefore the world of effects and the interaction of forces. It is out of inspiration and volition that action arises by assent of the will, which has the capacity to activate possibilities or options... (The linear and the non-linear) are not separate but mutually inclusive, and ... the linear is contained within the nonlinear, just as all form is included within the formless. These are, therefore, not two different realms but are the same viewed from two different points. In common parlance, we speak of digital versus analog, left brain versus right brain, holistic versus specific, or limited versus unlimited to imply that there are two different, contrasting approaches to reality." – "The Eye of the I: From which Nothing is Hidden" (2002), Chapter 20: Duality versus Nonduality, Science versus Spirit, pp. 297-298.

Newtonian vs. Quantum Mechanics (2)

Newtonian	Quantum Mechanics
Atomistic	Nonlocal coherence
Forced	Reactive
Caused	Responsive
Provable	Comprehensible, Measurable, Observable
Sequential	Simultaneous
Settled	Potential
Temporal	Time dependent/independent
Computational	Stochastic/chaotic

Slide 279

SLIDE 279: NEWTONIAN VS. QUANTUM MECHANICS (2)

This slide is a subset of slide 19 and was not actually shown in any lecture. Additional information has been provided below to help in making the transition from the Newtonian linear (force) to the nonlinear (Power) domain. The characteristics of linear as compared to nonlinear are listed in "The Eye of the I: From which Nothing is Hidden" (2002), Chapter 20: Duality versus Nonduality, Science versus Spirit, pp. 297-298.

"The material reductionist sees history as merely a 'biological evolution with survival as its primary goal'. This mechanistic, 'hardcore' scientific view believes that life spontaneously arose in some unknown manner as a fortuitous convergence of matter and energy. The linear Newtonian paradigm is based on the notion that intrinsic to evolution, there is a mysterious intention or cause. It is also teleological in that it presupposes that evolutionary events accrued 'in order' to bring about a specific end or purpose, such as survival. How a nonthinking organism could have a purpose, intention, or desired end is not explained. [...] Essential to an in-depth understanding of the evolution of life is the subtle but critical comprehension that is axiomatic to higher awareness: The manifest world of form is intrinsically devoid of power. It is not capable of cause; it is an outpicturing, a consequence, an effect, a result, a product, a display in manifestation of the effects of power that originate and reside within the nonlinear domain. Life originates only from preexistent life. Life is the unfoldment of the potentiality of the unmanifest infinite power of God. Evolution is the progressive unfoldment of Creation as it manifests its potentiality as form (i.e., material physical existence). [...] The light of the consciousness of Divinity irradiated materiality and thus spawned life. Note that 'life' has a completely different essence, quality, capacity, and characteristic from inert material. It is not even in the same logic class or category as materiality. The energy of life has an innate, critically essential quality that is totally absent from inert matter. It has intelligence, the capacity to learn, adapt, assimilate, accumulate, and utilize information. It is of a domain altogether different from matter. It has a unique essence and potentiality that are not shared by matter. Matter is analogous to a copper wire that is inert and has no actual function until an electric current courses through it, at which time it becomes a 'live wire'." – "I: Reality and Subjectivity" (2003), Chapter 23: Homo Spiritus, pp. 401-403

"The infinite field of Consciousness includes all that has ever been, is or could be. Everything leaves a trackable track within the infinite field of Consciousness, which itself is timeless and nonlocal.

Within the field of Consciousness, all time is now and everywhere is right here. In my fingertip anything and everything anywhere in the universe can be calibrated. Why is that? Because (the substrate of) the tip of my finger is everywhere There is no beginning and no end and what people have difficulty with is that Consciousness is nonlinear. It does not traverse time. It does not go from 'here' to 'there'. It does not 'start' here and end 'there'. It is everywhere present now. What Cleopatra thought, did, what she calibrated at is knowable now as it was at the time of Cleopatra because between then and now there is no time in the nonlinear universe. Beyond time and dimension, all places are here and all time is now. Everywhere is right here and all time is right now. Otherwise, having time and distance will be linear. Consciousness is nonlinear. Consciousness is the infinite Context. That is simple." – Paraphrased from the opening several minutes of the March 2008 lecture, "The Clear Pathway to Enlightenment.

Newtonian vs. Quantum Mechanics (3)

Newtonian	Quantum Mechanics
Limited	Unlimited
Actuality	Possibility
Permanent	Altered by observation
Constricted	Expansive
Content	Context
Objective	Subjective
Force	Power
Certain	Uncertain
Finished	Poised

Slide 280

SLIDE 280: NEWTONIAN VS. QUANTUM MECHANICS (3)

This slide is a subset of slide 19 and was not actually shown in any lecture. Additional information has been provided below to help in making the transition from the Newtonian linear (force) to the nonlinear (Power) domain.

"Focusing on form is de-energizing, exhausting. Let us get to the essence. Truth is very, very brief. The Absolute Truth is absolutely wordless. What is interesting about quantum mechanics is that as you get to smaller and smaller submicroscopic, sub-particles, subatomic, sub-electrons, sub-photonic reality, that consciousness has an observable effect. The basic experiment that gives the whole thing away is as follows. When an atom of matter and one of anti-matter meet, they extinguish each other, and when they do, there's a discharge of two photons. The photons head off in different directions in the universe. They have no spin to them. However, if a human being looks at one photon, it instantly begins to spin. At the same time, on the opposite side of the universe, with no connection between the two whatsoever, the other photon begins to spin in exactly the opposite direction at exactly the same instant. The mere act of observation, witnessing, changes reality. So, that's the space in which prayers are effective, the space in which that which you hold in mind tends to manifest, energy follows thought.

The Presence of God within expresses itself as the infinite potentiality out of which arises subjective awareness as consciousness. The Presence is radically subjective. It's not 'out there,' elsewhere, some other time, for other people. The average religious concept of God is that God arose somewhere back there in time, rolled the dice, now he's disappeared, up there with his feet up, in an easy chair, waiting for time to end, at which time we're going to have Judgment Day-Oh! So, God's waiting elsewhere, in time and space-heaven- heaven is up there someplace. Astronauts have been up there, they haven't found any heaven up there. Where is heaven? God is elsewhere in time and place. How can you experience a God which isn't even here? The God of Judgment Day: "Was" and "will be," but is not "now," huh? So, God disappears, rolls the dice, takes off, and now how does the world keep going? It goes like billiard balls, supposedly causality, so the explanation, then, of what the world considers reality is over here (Newtonian side). Actually, the explanation is over here (Quantum side). So, any concept of objectivity, then, is a subjective judgment. There is no such thing as objectivity. There is only subjectivity. The subtle feelings of "is-ness," existence, the subtleties and inferences, are not on the level of the gross. They don't even exist in time or space. They're comprehensible. They're not local to any place. That's the whole basis of the Heisenberg principle. There are not measurables in Reality. In quantum reality, there are only observables. You can witness certain things, but you can't measure them, because the minute you try to measure it, it already changes. You can't measure the same thing twice in quantum mechanics. One observation totally changes it. When you go back, it isn't there anymore.

The above shows that spiritual work is very, very powerful, because it is the subjective reality out of which observables, supposed reality, appearances arise in the first place. People say, "How can I get from 150 to 200?" Well, you just follow, 'be kind to your neighbor.' So, here we have infinite, infinite power (Quantum side). How much power is available in the quantum potentiality is infinite, without beginning, without end, without limitation, without design or form. Consequently, power is infinitely powerful." - Paraphrased from June 2002 Lecture, "Realizing the Root of Consciousness: Meditative and Contemplative Techniques", DVD disc 1 at 013600- 014900.

Spiritual Teachers – 500s: Historical Examples

Brother Lawrence	**575**
Father Pio	**585**
Confucius	**590**
Rumi	**550**
Socrates	**540**
Dilgo Khyentse Rinpoche	**575**
Swami Prabhavananda	**550**

Slide 281

SLIDE 281: SPIRITUAL TEACHERS – 500S: HISTORICAL EXAMPLES

This slide was introduced at the September 2011 lecture, DVD disc 1 at 003050.

These are historical examples of Spiritual Teachers in the 500s, the energy field of Love: **Brother Lawrence** (575): The most powerful tool that is in the province of the 'will' is devotion. It is not just spiritual truth but the degree of one's devotion to it, which empowers it to become transformative. A great classic that demonstrates the efficacy of simplicity and devotion is that of Brother Lawrence's "The Practice of the Presence of God" (1692), which emphasizes the importance of constancy. Many have found this simple "Practice of the Presence of God" to be quite beneficial. **Father Pio** (585), also known as Padre Pio was a priest, and mystic, and is a saint of the Catholic Church. He was born in 1887 and died in 1968. Padre Pio became famous for exhibiting stigmata for most of his life, thereby generating much interest and controversy. He was both beatified (1999) and canonized (2002) by Pope John Paul II. **Confucius** (590) was a Chinese teacher, politician, and philosopher, traditionally credited with having authored or edited many of the Chinese classic texts, including The "I Ching" (or *Book of Changes*). Confucius was born in 551 BC and died in 479 BC, and his principles emphasized common Chinese tradition and belief including personal and governmental morality, correctness of social relationships, justice and sincerity. **Rumi** (550), also known as Jalaluddin Rumi was a 13th-century Persian poet, jurist, Islamic scholar, theologian, and Sufi mystic. Rumi was born in 1207 and died in 1273 and his influence transcends national borders and ethnic divisions with his books being very popular in much of the East as well as the West.

Socrates (540) was born around 470 BC in Athens, Greece and died in 399 BC in Athens and is credited as one of the founders of Western philosophy. Although Socrates himself wrote nothing, he appears to be a man of great insight, integrity, and self-mastery in "Plato's Dialogues". Socrates taught that all human error or wrongdoing is involuntary, for man can only choose what he believes at the time to be a good that will bring happiness. His only error is that he cannot discern the real good from the illusory good and thus mistakenly chooses externals (illusions) instead of Truth. Instead of vilifying the ego and indulging in guilt, shame, and self-hatred, it is far more productive to accept it for what it is, appreciate its historic value, and adopt it as one would a naïve pet. By heeding Socrates' time-proven dictum that "Man chooses always only what he believes to be the good," hatred is replaced by compassion and forgiveness. Socrates was committed to truth with such sincerity that he followed the order to drink hemlock and accept death rather than violate the tenets of truth. He had the choice to save himself by compliance with the prevailing authorities, but to do so would be violating his own teachings. Thus, he chose to follow the dictum "To thine own self be true."

Dilgo Khyentse Rinpoche (575), was a Buddhist Vajrayana master, scholar, poet, teacher, and head of the Nyingma school of Tibetan Buddhism from 1987 until his death in 1991. The current Dalai Lama regarded Dilgo Khyentse Rinpoche as his principal teacher in the Nyingma tradition and of Dzogchen. **Swami Prabhavananda** (550) was an Indian philosopher, monk of the Ramakrishna Order, and religious teacher. He founded the Vedanta Society of Southern California, the largest Vedanta Society in the West. He was born in India in 1893 and died in 1976 in California.

L O V E (1)

- **Love is the Ultimate Law of the Universe (calibrates at 750)**
- **Love God with all thy heart, soul, & mind**
- **Love thy neighbor as thyself**
- **"Love makes the world go round"**
- **"Love is a many splendored thing"**
- **Love is a way of being in the world**
- **Love is a way to God**
- **Love facilitates healing**
- **Duck story**

Slide 282

SLIDE 282: LOVE (1)

This slide was introduced at the September 2011 lecture, DVD disc 1 at 003140.

Love is the Ultimate Law of the Universe: This statement calibrates at 750. **Love God with all thy heart, all thy soul and all thy mind.** You become that love and then everything happens appropriately, automatically due to what you are. **Love thy neighbor as thyself.** It is like, 'how may I be of help to you, how may I comfort you, may I loan you some money when you are broke, may I help you find a job, how may I console you when you have suffered a major loss in your family.' Lovingness is a way of being in the world, and that way you light up the world.

"Love makes the world go round." As Dr. Hawkins shared, "I was glad during World War II I didn't have to kill anybody. I had to maintain this ship. I was a bosun's mate and I brought the ship through all kinds of terrible storms. One time the ship went over ninety degrees. I was standing on the bulkhead, with one foot on the bulkhead and the other at the wheel. I stayed at the wheel for some twenty hours nonstop because everybody else was sick, everybody was terribly seasick and laying on the floor, throwing up, and so I just stayed at the wheel. Love empowers us, and allows you to steer a ship for close to a whole day without food or drink or anything. Forgiveness and love is transformative. We have to forgive ourselves for our trespasses. I forgive myself for the errors I have made, O Lord, when I was less evolved, Amen."

"**Love is a many splendored thing**," as the popular song goes. Experientially, this statement is true. When we have surrendered all of the resistances to love and let go of the negative feelings that block love, then the world is radiant with the splendor of love. **Love is a way of being in the world.** As you become loving, it is your way of being, so lovingness is a way of being. It is not an emotion but a way of being in the world. Once you become loving, there are certain things you can never do again. You can also perform the miraculous, without labeling it miraculous. You can do things other people cannot do and people do things for you that they would not do for others. It is best not to tell people that you love them because they will get scared. They will think you have designs on them. Lovingness is a way of being, and it transforms everything around you because of the radiation of that energy. People that are hateful, in your presence will suddenly become willing to forgive others. They would find an excuse to defend the person instead of attack them. We become defenders of love and life and we stop being attackers.

Love is a way to God. Because you become loving, you radiate the energy of God wherever you go. Some people are a blessing to be in the world and other people are like a curse. Lovingness is a way of being that transforms everything around you because of the radiation of that energy. It happens of its own. We do not have to "do" anything, and we do not have to call it anything. Love is the energy that silently transfigures every situation. **Love facilitates healing.** If physicians would say a prayer for their patients to get better, then that would help them recuperate most of the time.

Duck story: A duck hunter shot a duck and the duck fell to the ground, badly injured. After the duck fell to the ground, its female mate flew down on top of him and put her wings over him to shelter him. The hunter was utterly amazed and had a transformation within his own heart and he gave up hunting as a sport. After that, he never hunted or killed another duck again. Love has a transformative power.

L O V E (2)

- **Love - calibrates 500 and over**
- **Heart chakra – calibrates 505**
- **Energy of the heart – (ex. Bagpipes)**
- **Love of pets**
- **Love of freedom**
- **Romantic love**
- **Loveless = flat**
- **Love of purpose**
- **Golden Rule ("Do unto others...")**

Slide 283

SLIDE 283: LOVE (2)

This slide was introduced at the September 2011 lecture, DVD disc 1 at 004240.

Love calibrates at the level of 500 on the Map of Consciousness® and goes up to just below 540. **The heart chakra calibrates at 505. Bagpipes,** as an example of the energy of the heart at 505, signify valor rather than just courage and therefore instill consternation in a would-be enemy. There is sound but it is enshrouded in stillness and timelessness. Music of high calibration presents an energy field directly that bypasses the intellect and negative mentation. **Love of pets:** Love for God or nature or even one's pets, opens the door to spiritual inspiration. The desire to make others happy overrides selfishness. Some people are so limited that they experience this phenomenon of contributing to the welfare and happiness of others only with their favored pets, but at least that is a start. Because of social conditioning in our society, people even suppress and repress their positive feelings. Our repressed and suppressed emotions on the psychic level influence life events. Suppressed love re-emerges as excessive adoration of pets and various forms of idolatry. The basic rule of the psychic universe is that "like attracts like", so that the person who has let go of a lot of inner negativity is surrounded by loving thoughts, loving events, loving people, and loving pets. **Love of freedom:** Freedom is availability of alternate options rather than the suppression of other viewpoints and presupposes mutual respect and forbearance. The United States Constitution and the Bill of Rights establish freedom from imposition of religion by government (theocracy), yet simultaneously, freedom of religious expression (e.g., Christmas trees, Santa Claus, the Menorah.) 'Free speech' means the freedom of ideas and expression of viewpoints, not excess of emotionality and infantile actions.

Romantic love: It is only a very recent development that personal romantic love has evolved in importance and expression. At first, the male-female relationship was primarily rooted in lust, desire, and possession, which led to craving and control. Eventually, the male was required to defend and support the family, and pair-bonding, affection, mutual support, and love emerged as progressively important.

Loveless = flat: Major segments of society operate on the level of loveless-ness, e.g. dourly functioning of giant corporations and government agencies. Gratitude does not appear nor considered socially appropriate. Love is 'belittled' as 'touchy-feely' and socially restricted to romance, mothers and their children, or one's dog. Expressed elsewhere, it becomes an embarrassment. To 'care for' is a wide-open avenue for the expression and expansion of love that is socially acceptable and leads one out of the 'flat' experience of life.

Love of purpose: The goal as well as appeal of a purpose driven life is to give meaning, spiritual value, and significance to life, and thus, like science, to make a major contribution to society and the value of human life. People looking for meaning, direction, and improved relationships look toward integrity, purposeful self-fulfillment, and spiritual significance.

The energy of Willingness is the level of the **Golden Rule: "Do unto others as you would have others do unto you."** In successful relationships, this results in a mutuality of partners as helpmates and companions. This mutuality is the result of alignment with each other's welfare rather than just the more animal-driven emotional involvement that often has a fractious downside. Willingness is supportive rather than competitive for gain or dominance, and relationships involve service to each other's growth and goals rather than to just one's own.

L O V E (3)

- **Love of attributes**
- **Love increases perceived value**
- **Love increases happiness**
- **Love as "Agape" (570) - Universal Love**
- **Love as virtue**
- **Love as enthusiasm: *"I love doing this!"***
- **Love as forgiveness**
- **Love as acceptance**

Slide 284

SLIDE 284: LOVE (3)

This slide was introduced in September 2011 Lecture, DVD disc 1 004315.

Each level of consciousness represents an energy field that has innate attributes. Jealousy, retaliation, vengeance, partiality, etc., are all attributes of the egoic levels and not of God. The qualities that must be inherent for Divinity to be Divinity, and to be the Infinity called God are as follows: beyond form; beyond duality; beyond human attributes; without parts, actions, or motives; complete and total; beyond time and space, without beginning or end; and lacking in nothing. Out of this Supreme arise infinite compassion, stillness, silence, and peace. **Love of these Divine attributes** leads towards the Divine.

Love increases perceived value: As Dr. Hawkins shared, "You can encourage your fellows to make life better for everybody around you. That's because of your presence, things go better, or the eggs get fried better, or the duckies got saved, or the kitty got fed this morning. To share your love with everything around you, to all forms of life, kitties and doggies and other people, and even villains, yes. A captured villain, it is up to you to make his life tolerable and say, 'I'm sorry that I have to hold a gun to your head, but that's my job. Don't make me pull the trigger, thank you.'"

Love increases happiness: The rate of happiness is directly dependent on the level of consciousness and is close to 100% in the levels of 500 and above. **Love as "Agape," which is Universal Love, calibrates 570.** Agape is a word derived from ancient Greek and means the highest form of love, charity; the love of God for man and of man for God embracing a universal, unconditional love that transcends, that serves regardless of circumstances.

Love as virtue: Love is the highest of all virtues. As a learning device, it is often surprisingly effective to 'pretend' to be the quality that is desired, and then, much to one's surprise, discover that it has been a non-activated and latent aspect of one's own potentiality. Many people make self-improvement the number one priority in their lives and identify with admired figures instead of envying them. It is important to discover that we are making a difference in the world and that our life is significant.

Love as enthusiasm reevaluates the worth of our life and recontextualizes it, viewing it differently in order to give it a different value in our own eyes, thereby raising our own energy pattern consequent to a more positive way of looking at life. We can be very active and vigorous into old age, we can have a very significant and valuable life that is highly enjoyable when **we love doing what we are doing**, and our physical health can continue right to the very end.

Love as forgiveness: Forgiveness is an aspect of love that allows us to see life events from the viewpoint ofgrace. We forgive ourselves for the errors we made when we were less evolved. We transcend the smaller aspects of ourselves by accepting and loving them. **Love as acceptance:** There is a total acceptance of our own humanness and that of the other. If we are really in tune with others, we forgive them when we see a passing jealousy or reactivity. We realize it is only natural and we know that they, in return, are aware of our passing resentment. Yet, they are overlooking it; they accept our humanness, and they understand the situation. They know us so well that they recognize the likelihood of a passing resentment in certain situations, but they know, also, that we are going to let it go. The people with whom we share a relationship of loving acceptance are okay with our humanness and their own. No matter the surface emotions, we remain aware of the shared alignment to love, acceptance, and harmony with each other and the world.

L O V E (4)

- **Love as motivator**
- **Love of Creation - Life - Existence**
- **Love as appreciation**
- **Love as kindness**
- **Love as essence of relationship**
- **Love as group energy, i.e. Alcoholics Anonymous (540)**

Slide 285

SLIDE 285: LOVE (4)

This slide was introduced at the September 2011 lecture, DVD disc 1 at 004545.

"There are many types of love other than the personal or romantic love, and they infuse our everyday experience: love of pets, love of family and friends, love of freedom, love of purpose, love of country, love of attributes, love of creation, love as virtue, love as enthusiasm, love as forgiveness, love as acceptance, love as motivator, love as appreciation, love as kindness, love as essence of relationship, love as group energy (for example: Alcoholics Anonymous), love as admiration, love as respect, love as valor, love as fraternal bonds of unity (buddies, classmates, shipmates, teammates), love as friendship, love as loyalty, love as affection, love as cherishing, love as self-sacrificing maternal love, love as devotion.

"Love is a many splendored thing," as the popular song goes. Experientially, this statement is true. When we have surrendered all of the resistances to love and have let go of the negative feelings that block love, then the world is radiant with the splendor of love. On the level of love, this radiance is no longer hidden from us." – "Letting Go: The Pathway of Surrender" (2012), Chapter 12: Love, p. 17.

L O V E (5)

- **Love as admiration**
- **Love as respect (love of country & countrymen, military)**
- **Love as valor**
- **Love of shipmates**
- **Bonds of Unity**
- **Fraternal Love (buddies, classmates, teammates)**
- **Love as friendship, loyalty**

Slide 286

SLIDE 286: LOVE (5)

This slide was introduced at the September 2011 lecture, DVD disc 1 at 004945.

"Love is ordinarily conceptualized as having to do with relationship and the vicissitudes of compatibility and interaction as well as expectations, and thus, emotionality. Relationships bring up desires for control and possession, resulting in conflict that surfaces as anger or even hatred. Thus, unsatisfactory experiences of purported 'love' are not the result of love but of emotional attachment and 'involvement'.

More evolved patterns of relationship that are free of negativity are consequent to basing a relationship on mutual alignment rather than on possessive emotional involvement. This is of critical importance and redefines the essence of true relationship. It could be pictured as being mutually parallel and vertical rather than horizontal (e.g., control), which acts as a tether between people via their 'solar plexus' instead of alignment via the heart.

Spiritual love is neither erotic nor possessive and is seen in mature love mates and in the platonic love of the strong bonds that are formed by shipmates, for example, or military units, or teams. Love of country and one's countrymen eventually extends to all of humanity, and then eventually to the Creator as the Source of Life. Love is gracious and expansive and eventuates as love of all life and all Creation. Thus emerges the Buddhist prayer for the enlightenment and salvation of all sentient beings so they may transcend the bondage that underlies suffering itself. The ideal of unconditional compassion and mercy to all life in all its expressions requires transcendence of dualistic perception and its illusions.

Devotion to Truth and life is transformative and results in transcending linear perception to awareness of nonlinear essence as the Ultimate Reality. This becomes self-revealing as the self dissolves into the Self and reveals the perfection of Divinity of all existence that shines forth as the Essence and Glory of Creation." – "Reality, Spirituality and Modern Man" (2008), Chapter 14: Spiritual Pathways, pp. 288-289

L O V E (6)

- **Love is letting go of fear (Jampolsky)**
- **Love as affection ("Honey")**
- **Love as cherishing**
- **Maternal Love – self-sacrificing**
- **Lovingness as an existential style**
- **This lecture is the result of Love and the "miraculous"!**

Slide 287

SLIDE 287: LOVE (6)

This slide was introduced at the September 2011 lecture, DVD disc 1 at 005025.

"This love is the mechanism of reassurance, and very often we can quiet another person's fears by our mere physical presence, and by the loving energy that we project to them and with which we surround them. It is not what we say, but the very fact of our presence that has the healing effect.

We can learn another one of the laws of consciousness: **Fear is healed by love. This is the central theme of the series of books by psychiatrist Jerry Jampolsky** (e.g., **Love is Letting Go of Fear**). This was also the basis of the healing that went on at the Attitudinal Healing Center in Manhasset, Long Island, of which I was co-founder and medical advisor.

Attitudinal healing has to do with group interaction with patients who have fatal and catastrophic illnesses, and the whole process of healing has to do with the letting go of fear and replacing it with love.

This is the same mechanism of healing demonstrated by the great saints and illumined healers, whose very presence has the power to heal because of the intense vibration of love which they radiate. This healing power—the basis of spiritual healing—is also transmitted by loving thoughts. The multitudes of people down through recorded history who have healed by just this kind of love are legendary. In recent history, for instance, Mother Teresa is credited with healing great numbers of people by these very mechanisms of unconditional love and illumined presence." – "Letting Go: The Pathway of Surrender" (2012), Chapter 6: Fear, p. 93

Love as affection ("Honey," "Sweetheart"): As Doc said to Susan, "Every morning I give thanks for your love. Every night I thank God for it."

Love as cherishing; Maternal love- self-sacrificing: As Susan Hawkins shared during the September 2011 Lecture on Love, "I was speaking to some ladies who were up front here before the lecture started. We were talking about what it is for us to be wives and mothers, and how important it is for each one of us to hold that spiritual torch in our family. How it's up to us to keep that spirituality strong as women of the world should be, so I just wanted to pass that along to everybody that we as women, as wives and mothers need to inspire our children and mates to take up that torch and follow God.

L O V E (7)

How Animals Affect Your Life

• **Song Bird's Song**	**500**
• **Kitty's purr**	**500**
• **Dog's wagging tail**	**500**
• **Family Cat**	**245**
• **Family Dog**	**250**

- **Having a dog increases lifespan by 10 years!**

Slide 288

SLIDE 288: LOVE (7)

This slide was introduced at the September 2011 lecture, DVD disc 1 at 005225.

"When you think of all the idiotic exercises, crazy diets and stuff that people go through, why don't they just buy a dog and get to live ten more years? Save yourself all those horrible low- cholesterol diets and crap. You get to die of cholesterol poisoning when you are 90." Doc said these words during the September 2011 Lecture, and also that without a dog he would have been dead already. He and Susan loved and adored their dog, Kelsey. Continuing the narrative by Doc, "All the other dogs jumped around, and Kelsey just lay in the corner like this. (Doc poses with his chin resting on his hands like front paws, looking out over them.) Kelsey got me through the heart. The fact that owning a dog adds ten years to your life, I mean, that is just a major issue, is it not, ten years is quite a while. Okay. Kelsey asked me to bring that up, so I said, 'I'll bring it up, Kelsey.' That was my promise to her."

"**A songbird's song** we can add to the 500s. We go into rapture and the poet has done so throughout time about the song and the nightingale. The sound of a singing bird at 500, the same as a **kitty's purr** and a **dog's wagging tail**. So, somehow mankind gets back the goodness and love that we give to the animal kingdom. Somehow comes back to us, because these are close to us. And Alex, the trained African Grey parrot, the subject of a thirty year experiment (1977-2007) by an animal psychologist, calibrates at 401. Alex can think. Four hundred is the beginning of intellect. So, Alex can actually think. When she says, "take two greens and one orange and make three," he does that, he actually can think. Cats as a genus, as a species calibrate at 240. **The family cat**: Once you have a cat and it gets adopted by a family, it jumps five points to 245 just because of the presence of humans. It has the capacity to respond to the presence of humans by jumping five points. So, the family cat is 245, about the same as a racehorse, the same as dogs. A dog is 245, but if a family adopts it, its consciousness jumps to 250. The cat's purr calibrates at 500. The dog's wagging tail calibrates at 500." - Paraphrased from the November 2003 Lecture, "Realization of the Self and the 'I'", DVD disc 1~ 015500-015800.

"The more we love, the more we can love. Love is limitless. Love begets love. This is why psychiatrists recommend having a pet. A dog, for example, brings love and expands love in the heart of the owner. Love prolongs life. In fact, research documents that having a dog extends the owner's life by ten years! Just think of all the bizarre exercises, diets, and other regimens that people go through to add relatively small amounts of time on to their life, when they can simply get a dog and add ten years! Love has a powerful anabolic effect. Love increases endorphins, which are life-enhancing hormones. You live ten years longer with a dog in your life because a pet dog catalyzes the energy of love, and that energy of love heals and prolongs life." – "Letting Go: The Pathway of Surrender" (2012), Chapter 12: Love, p. 177

Solar Plexus vs. L O V E

- ***Love is from the heart!***
- **Attachment and ambitious craving are from the solar plexus**
- **"LOVE" OF:**

Wealth	**Fame**
Power	**Being "Right"**
Glamour	**Publicity**
Stardom	**Public Attention**

Slide 289

SLIDE 289: SOLAR PLEXUS VS. LOVE

This slide was introduced at the September 2011 lecture, DVD disc 1 at 005640.

"We can simplify the levels of consciousness into three major states: inert, energetic, and peaceful. These three states are related to the decision-making process. The first state— inertia—is reflective of the emotional levels of apathy, grief, and fear. The nature of these feelings is to interfere with our concentration on the situation at hand and engage us instead in concentration on our own thoughts, most of which are in the realm of "I don't know," "I'm not sure," and "I don't think I can." [...] The second state, which is higher than inertia, is that of being "energetic." The emotions underlying this state are those of desire, anger, and pride. The nature of these feelings is to interfere less with concentration than the previous lower state because some positive thoughts are allowed to flow through and mix with the negative feelings. This is the state of the "go-getter." Although things are accomplished, there is unevenness of performance because of the mixture of positive and negative thoughts and ideas. Negative feelings such as ambition, desire, or "proving oneself" tend to drive the "go-getter," and at times the decision-making is compulsive or impulsive.

Characteristic of this level of consciousness is **personal self-gain** as the primary motivating factor. Therefore, many of the decisions are unsustainable because they are based on a win-lose situation rather than on a win-win situation. A win-win decision would have occurred had the feelings and welfare of the other persons involved in the situation been taken into account.

Using language relating to the body's energy centers, we say that people on this level are motivated by their **"solar plexus"** (third chakra). This means that they seek to attain success and to master the world. But they are **self-centered** and driven by **personal motives, with little concern for the welfare of others or of the world** in general. Because their decisions benefit primarily themselves, their success is limited to personal gain. Any benefit to the world is purely secondary and the results, therefore, fall far short of greatness.

The third and highest level is the peaceful state, based upon the feelings of courage, acceptance, and love. Because these feelings are purely positive and non-disturbing by their very nature, they allow us to concentrate completely on the situation and observe all of the relevant details. Because of an inner state of peace, inspiration brings forth ideas that solve the problem. In this state, the mind is free of worry, and its ability to communicate and concentrate is unimpeded. From this state come solutions to problems that are placed in a win-win context; because everyone benefits, everyone lends their energy to the project and success is shared by all." – "Letting Go: The Pathway of Surrender" (2012), Chapter 19: Achievement of Vocational Goals, pp. 287-289.

L O V E - 500 Level (1)

- **Love is a progressively unconditional energy field.**
- **Lovingness is a way of being in the world.**
- **Love is forgiving, nurturing and supportive.**
- **Love emanates from the heart.**

Slide 290

SLIDE 290: LOVE - 500 LEVEL (1)

This slide was introduced at the September 2011 lecture, DVD disc 1 at 005810.

Love is a progressively unconditional energy field. The more you love, the more you can love. That is one reason to have a dog. You live ten years longer because it brings up the energy of Love and the energy of Love heals and prolongs life. When you are thankful for your life, you are thankful to God because of your life and you say, 'I thank Thee, O Lord, for my life and I thank Thee, O Lord for all the miracles of this life.'

Love is a way of being in the world. You just become that; in everything you do and say, every movement then is energized by the lovingness which you own within yourself. Everything you say as you talk you feel like an energy running out. You want to share what you hold in your heart as a knowingness experientially and hold it in your heart for everyone, that they should all be feeling it. You pray for the inner experience of Divine Love for everyone present. God bless all in the name of the Lord, the Father, and the Holy Ghost.

Love is forgiving, nurturing and supportive. In our society we look to the woman as the representative of maternal love as the ideal. **Love emanates from the heart.** Our love for God and for all of Creation, everyone is seeing and picking up out there, that vibration. Because of our presence, everyone around us feels good. Love encompasses us all and the kitties' love and the doggie's love and the love of all our friends are all forms of God's love for us.

From "Letting Go: The Pathway of Surrender" (2012), Chapter 12: Love, pp. 176- 177: "Eventually, we just become love. Everything we do and say, every movement we make is energized by the lovingness that we have owned within ourselves. Whether speaking to a large audience or petting the dog, the energy of love is felt to be pouring out. We want to share what we hold in the heart as an experiential knowingness, and we hold it in the heart for everyone and everything, that they would be feeling it, too. We pray for that inner experience of infinite love for everyone around us, including the animals. Our life is a blessing to everything around us. We acknowledge to others and to our animals the gift that they are to us. [...] In the state of love, we wake up every morning and give thanks for another day of life, and we seek to make life better for everyone around us. Because of the presence of love, things go better; the eggs get fried better; the ducky gets saved; the kitty gets fed; and the doggie is adopted from the pound and brought home. We share our love with everything around us, all forms of life: kitties, doggies, other people, and all living things. Yes, even the villains. If it is our job to watch over the captured villain, we seek to make his life tolerable. We say, "I'm sorry that I have to hold a gun to your head, but that's my job." We try to be as gracious and generous as we can be, without exception.

L O V E - 500 Level (2)

- **Reason deals with particulars, whereas love deals with wholes and essence.**
- **Love accomplishes great feats because of its purity of motive.**
- **Love takes no position and is inclusive.**
- **Love augments the positive.**
- **Love focuses on life's goodness in all of its expressions.**

Slide 291

SLIDE 291: LOVE - 500 LEVEL (2)

This slide was introduced at the September 2011 lecture, DVD disc 2 at 000235.

Reason deals with particulars, whereas love deals with wholes and essence. Love accomplishes great feats because of its purity of motive. It may be instructive to listen to a dialog on the stage between Susan and Doc that illustrates this point. Doc, to Susan: "I'm going to sing something funny, and then I want you to say, 'get lost, bum.' All I got is love, all I got is love, then you say, 'get lost, bum.'" To Susan: "Well, Baby, all I got is love, all I got is love." Susan: "Get lost, bum." Doc laughs, then says, "I ain't got nothing but love, honey." Susan says, "Get lost, bum!" Doc: "We thought we'd have fun with that one." Susan: "I know." Both sing: "I can't give you anything but love, Baby." Doc to Susan: "Get lost, bum." Susan: "Oh, get lost, bum." Susan sings: "I can't give you anything but love." Doc: "Love is all I can afford. Get lost." Doc laughs and Susan says, "I won't quit my day job." Doc: "I think that's funny." Susan concluded by saying, "Dave and I would hope that you carry on our work. And that what we have brought to you, that you remember and teach others."

Love takes no position and is inclusive. When love is a primary in one's personal experience, the conditions are irrelevant. If you have decided to love a certain situation, then it is unconditional. Even if they hoot and say, 'you are terrible,' you still love them. Well, a mother's love is unconditional. Dr. Hawkins related this story from his childhood in this connection, "I remember as a kindergartner or first-grader, we wore long stockings in the wintertime when I was a kid. I went to school and that day I had diarrhea and was one unholy mess, with long socks and diarrhea. Somebody had to clean me up when I got home. That is love because I remember being told, 'don't feel bad about it, you couldn't help it,' so it was not only the cleaning me up, but the relief of my guilt that I had done such a terrible thing. We bless others by our forgiveness. I realize that, in a certain way, nobody can help being other than what they are. Considering the world situation at the time, Adolph Hitler did what he thought was the most necessary thing to do. Nine attempts to kill him all failed, and so, even with Adolph Hitler I say, he was dedicated, he thought he was being of service by what he did. I did the same thing in World War II, I thought that kamikaze pilots are doing what they think they should do for their country. Even though they are trying to kill us and bomb us, I did not hate them. I respected kamikaze pilots, willing to give up their life for their country. So I respected them, and I still do."

Love augments the positive. Love focuses on life's goodness in all of its expressions. "Out of humility, all opinions about others are surrendered. In a certain way, nobody can help being other than what they are. Love knows this truth and takes no position. Love augments the positive about others rather than their defects. It focuses on life's goodness in all of its expressions. Unconditional love is a love that doesn't expect anything from others. When we have become loving, we have no limitations or demands on others that they should be a certain way in order to be loved. We love them no matter how they are. Even if they are obnoxious! We feel sorry for the criminals that they saw a life of crime as their best option." – "Letting Go: The Pathway of Surrender" (2012), Chapter 12: Love, pp.179-180.

L O V E - 500 Level (3)

- **By level 500, approx. 90% experience happiness as a basic quality of life.**
- **With spiritual intention, Love becomes a way of life.**
- **The capacity for Love is limitless.**
- **The more one loves, the more one can love.**

Slide 292

SLIDE 292: LOVE - 500 LEVEL (3)

This slide was introduced at the September 2011 lecture, DVD disc 2 at 000940.

By level 500, approximately 90% of people experience happiness as a basic quality of life. With spiritual intention, Love becomes a way of life. The capacity for Love is limitless. The more you love, the more you can love because it is a nonphysical thing and because it is nonphysical, the Infinite Love of Almighty God is the ultimate expression. As you go up the scale of consciousness, you see you are going from that which is definable, measurable, and scientifically verifiable, to that which is becoming progressively ineffable. As you cross over at 500, you left the world of science. Science cannot measure that, cannot put it in a box, cannot take its temperature, cannot get its atomic weight, and cannot get its vibration on a spectrometer. It has left the world of science, the Newtonian paradigm of reality; and so, at 500, Love is the real emergence of the nonlinear, the spiritual reality of the nonlinear, which is the Presence of God as Love. People say, 'Where do you find God?' God is Love, God is everything; loving within yourself is already the Presence of God. Anybody who is interested in spiritual work and spiritual development has already within them the Presence of God that is pulling them like a magnet. It is not that you are pursuing God, but it is like the magnetism of the Self, that which you are. The Truth of That Which You Are is drawing you inevitably, like a moth to the flame it cannot be resisted.

From "Healing and Recovery" (2009), Chapter 1: A Map of Consciousness, pp. 39-40: "The way to heal the small self is to reject taking a polarized, right/wrong position, which makes it our enemy, and instead view life with loving compassion and see the intrinsic innocence of the child. We first see the innocence of the child's consciousness and then the programming that is superimposed. It is because of the child's lovingness and trustingness that it is so programmable, and we begin to see the innocence even within those who seem most hateful. Out of compassion to see into the hearts of things, one finds the intrinsic innocence within the ego that then gets healed through that compassion and love. We can love our humanness and that of others, and instead of condemning it, we now say, "I see the seeming validity of that at that time."

For example, instead of being ashamed of anger and hatred, we say to ourselves, "Well, being angry was inevitable at that time," because a person who has never hated will not move up to Love since they have never cared that much about life. If one does not care enough about life to have gotten angry and actually hated, then they would be down at the level of Apathy.

When we look at our humanness from the viewpoint of forgiveness and compassion, we can then love it and hold it within our greatness. We look at our smallness like we look at the child and begin to heal it through understanding and compassion. When we do this, we are putting forth a very powerful energy field that is healing. When we look at ourselves from compassion and lovingness, we begin to heal. We also now know that what we forgive in others is forgiven within ourselves and disappears from our perception of the world.

L O V E - 500 Level (4)

- **It is discovered that to be loving is also to be lovable.**
- **Love also appears in the animal kingdom - bird's song, dog's wagging tail, kitty's purr.**
- **Love heals. Love uplifts others.**
- **Love is present everywhere - its presence only needs to be realized.**

Slide 293

SLIDE 293: LOVE - 500 LEVEL (4)

This slide was introduced at the September 2011 lecture, DVD disc 2 at 001050.

It is discovered that to be loving is also to be lovable. Love appears in the animal kingdom-the bird's song, the dog's wagging tail, the kitty's purr. Love heals. Love uplifts others. Love is present everywhere-its presence only needs to be realized. This leap of consciousness is possible consequent to willingness and inspiration. Love approaches Unconditional Love at level 540, which is the level of Healing. It requires the willingness to choose appreciation of the body instead of the 'make wrong' of the body, the lovingness of our life instead of the 'make wrong' of our life, the lovingness of the being that we are instead of the criticism of it. Superimposed around the physical body is an energy body whose form is very much like that of the physical body and whose patterns actually control the physical body. This control is at the level of thought or intention. The more energy we give it, the more power it has to manifest itself physically. Love prevails at level 500 but does not become unconditional until level 540. This means that some form persists from 500 to 540, so that Love is conditional. The full flowering of Love emerges only when it becomes unselective. It is characterized by lovingness, which is unconditional, because it is what one has become. This leap is accomplished by the 'letting go of the polarity of the opposites', which is an intrinsic error of mentation. After this happens, there are no longer 'good trees' or 'bad trees'. Instead, all trees are seen as perfect and beautiful just as they are. Each living thing is a perfect sculpture in its expression of its essence.

The act of a human sharing love with an animal like a dog, cat, horse, or bird raises the consciousness level of both at least 5 points. Just naming your dog Spot raises its consciousness 5 points; a family dog is 250 while dogs generally are at 245. Most people's consciousness only rises 5 points in a lifetime. Ads on TV calibrate higher if there is a dog in them wagging its tail. Some animals that calibrate in the 200s as a species can respond to love, which is in the 500s (Cat's purr, dog's tail wagging, songbird's song) for reasons that have not been researched. Koko, the gorilla, at 405 calibrates higher than almost 95% of the world population. Over 200, the value of others becomes important. Animals above 200 become herbivores. People below 200 do not know they exist, so for them it is really nothing to kill others; they have no sense of taking life. They do not understand existence as "I am". Above 200, one has the beginning of morality, ethics, and concern for others.

"As we move beyond the level of acceptance, which we do by owning back our own power to know, we move into a loving state that is forgiving and understanding, with the beginning of revelations and the experience of all life as loving. We begin to see that love is present everywhere. Therefore, we move on up to a God who is merciful and represents unconditional love. The realization that lovingness is a basic reality leads to an inner state of joy. Out of that comes compassion, the transfiguration of consciousness that reveals the perfection of all creation." – "Healing and Recovery" (2009), Chapter 15: Death and Dying, p. 455.

Unconditional LOVE (1)

- **The teaching of Jesus Christ was essentially to avoid negativity - levels below 200.**
- **The goal of his teaching was for his followers to reach Unconditional Love (level 540)**

Slide 294

SLIDE 294: UNCONDITIONAL LOVE (1)

This slide was introduced at the September 2011 lecture, DVD disc 2 at 001125.

The teaching of Jesus Christ was essentially to avoid negativity-the levels below 200. The goal of his teaching was for his followers to reach the level of Unconditional Love, which calibrates at 540. Unconditional Love is love that does not expect anything when given. When you have become loving then you have no limitations or demands on people out there that they should 'be this way' so they can be loved. You love them no matter how they are, even though they are obnoxious. You feel sorry for the criminal that they did not know any other lifestyle, and that their life was so pathetic that this is all they had left, e.g. to run down the street and grab someone's purse. Unconditional Love has no hidden agenda and no attachments or requirements, no strings attached, and nothing to expect back when given. The more loving we are, the more lovable we are. At 540, you love everybody and everything, even Adolph Hitler. You look at him as a person who was taken over by negative energies and you are willing to even forgive Adolph Hitler, who could not help what happened to him, that he was overcome by evil. So instead of hating evil, you feel sorry that some people have become overwhelmed by evil. Adolph did what he thought he was required to do by honor and its contextualization at the time; he was captured by certain ideals, captured by the thinkingness of the time. You could see that everybody who violates the law of love is really a victim of some other societal belief system or the pressures of the time.

During World War II, Dr, Hawkins did not hate the Japanese, even after Pearl Harbor; he did not hate Hitler or anybody else. He still had to conduct himself, but without hate. He did it out of a sense of duty and loyalty to his fellow man. Some ninety ships went down in the Okinawa typhoon during the War while he was at the helm the whole time, as all his shipmates were extremely seasick. He was just thankful that he could sustain his life in order to save the lives of his shipmates. Everyone was lying on the deck, throwing up for days, and so steering the ship was up to Dr. Hawkins. We serve our fellow man out of a commitment and understanding our human nature as God would have us understand it.

"Interestingly enough, there is a scientific basis for Jesus Christ's admonition to bless and love our enemies. On the level of energy, the lower feelings have a lower vibration frequency and lower power. When we are in lower energy state such as anger, hate, violence, guilt, jealousy or any other negative feelings, we are psychically vulnerable to the other person. In contrast, forgiveness, gratitude, and loving-kindness have a much higher energy vibration and much greater power. When we shift out of a lower to a higher energy pattern, we create a protective shield on the energetic level, as it were, and we can no longer be psychically vulnerable to that other person. When we are in a state of anger, for instance, we are vulnerable to the energy depletion brought about by the other person's counter-anger. Paradoxically, if we really want to affect other people, then we ought to really love them. Then, their anger at us will boomerang back upon them with no effect upon us!" – "Letting Go: The Pathway of Surrender" (2012), Chapter 18: Relationships, pp. 260-261.

Unconditional L O V E (2)

- **Jesus Christ knew that at the level of Unconditional Love (540), the soul's destiny was certain.**
- **This is taught by the world's great religions, such as Lotus Land Buddhism.**

Slide 295

SLIDE 295: UNCONDITIONAL LOVE (2)

This slide was introduced at the September 2011 lecture, DVD disc 2 at 001530.

Jesus Christ knew that at the level of Unconditional Love, which calibrates at 540, the soul's destiny was certain. This is also taught by the world's other great religions, such as Lotus Land Buddhism. Jesus said, "Resist not evil." The way to handle evil is to ignore it, to walk away from it, to look away from it. Instead of fighting the negative, you embrace the positive; so the way you handle the negative in the world is not by opposing the negative, because then you get locked into a positionality with it, and you can't get beyond the negative. Instead, you just emphasize the positive. That is what Christ taught, and that is what the churches are doing now. They are emphasizing the positive-love and compassion, forgiveness, mercy, being helpful to others, and loving service towards mankind, and they have stopped emphasizing fighting evil. "Sin" literally means "error," not evil. The Buddha also said there is only one "sin," and that is ignorance.

When Jesus Christ talks about hell, he is talking about that which you create for yourself. He is not talking about something arbitrary, like a cosmic jail you get thrown into. He is saying that if you follow certain kinds of behavior, you will bring enormous suffering upon yourself that is self-created. There is no punitive God hanging out there waiting for you to trip over things so He can kick you and throw you into jail, a cosmic torture chamber. Most people picture God as some kind of monster who waits for you to trip over the defects of your own humanness, and now you are guilty of humanness; and because you are guilty of humanness, we are going to throw you into this endless torture pit. This horrible God, the God of the Old Testament, the God of punishment and fear sits there waiting for you to screw up. One creates inner hell for oneself; there is no arbitrary, punitive God hanging out, waiting for you. The negative gods are self-created so one is always living in the prison created by one's own ego. The more purified one becomes spiritually, the less any such negative god could have any reality because it does not exist within you any more to project out into the world to fear. Because your hatred of other people and fears now diminish practically to zero, only a benevolent god would have any reality to you; so everyone lives with the very god they create. Therefore, we can stop feeling sorry for people because they are recreating for themselves everything that they experience every second. Jesus said your chances of reaching enlightenment are so slim in this lifetime that what you best do is purify yourself, become as loving as you can, and when you leave the physical body, you will go to heaven; and in heaven, there are higher spiritual teachers. There is not all that negativity. From heaven, then, you can progress farther. Pure land Buddhism says the same thing: "You believe in Buddha, and then He is your savior. When you die, you go to the pure land, which is like a heaven."

Diagnostic Differential: Infatuation vs. Love (1)

QUALITY	PASSION/ATTRACTION (Level 145)	LOVE (Level 500+)
Locus	self/ego	Self/spirit
Origin	Animal instinct	Spiritual state
Mental Function	Impaired	Uplifted
Intention	Mate, get	Bond, enjoy
Duration	Transitory	Permanent
Emotions	Excess/imbalance	Calm/balance

Slide 296

SLIDE 296: DIAGNOSTIC DIFFERENTIAL: INFATUATION VS. LOVE (1)

This slide was introduced at the September 2011 lecture, DVD disc 2 at 001555.

When you are horizontally aligned with people, you 'have to have' them, therefore, you have to control them, so controlling your relationship is crucial, whether it's a job or a business. If your happiness comes from 'out there' it is always at risk. We wanted to differentiate between infatuation, which can become severe to the point of murder and suicide; and love, which is alignment. They have two different qualities. First of all, you can calibrate the difference. You say, "so and so is involved with so and so, are they really in love?" Well, passionate attraction and ego involvement calibrates at 145. Then Love, actually is 500 and up, so they have completely different qualities and people very often confuse them.

What is the **locus** of an aligned relationship? In involvement, it's the ego/self and in alignment it's the Self with a capital "S." It's the **spiritual Self**. There is the dim awareness that you are answerable over long periods of time for your integrity and therefore, very often you turn down what could be a win and say, 'the heck with it.' Because the way we phrase it in our mind, in the long term, it is not going to make any difference. The long term is, 'you win the battle, but you lost the war.' So, in love, you are willing to turn down temporary gain for long term gain.

The **origin** of infatuation is, then, in frantic mating- the **animal instinct**, and in alignment, it is a **spiritual state** where the welfare and happiness of the other person becomes equal to your own. In fact, you are willing to sacrifice your life for them. If there is only room for one in the lifeboat, the person you love gets the seat.

What happens **to mental function**? We know that the person who is madly in love has **impaired** reality testing. People that are aligned are **uplifted**, uplifted by the relationship. Your life is better, more enjoyable, you are more grateful for it and therefore, you are grateful for the relationship. The **intention** in infatuation is a quick acquisition, to **mate, or get** that person, while in alignment it is to **bond** with them and **enjoy** with them and live through life side by side, side by side.

The **duration** of infatuation is **transitory**. You hear it said, "Love is supposed to be close to hate." That is a bizarre thought, isn't it? If you love something, why would you hate it? That which ends up as hate or jealousy was not love, it was the ego's infatuation in 'having to have,' and 'if you leave me, I'll kill you, bitch.' 'Catch you with another woman, you're a dead man.' So, infatuation is transitory. Alignment is a **permanent** arrangement, calm and steady. The relationship that has been going on for some time develops calmness to it. You know that it is steady because you know you can count on the relationship, you can count on that person. As far as loss, what happens with loss? In this relationship of involvement/ infatuation, you go into depression, rage, hate, blame, murder and suicide. Here in alignment, you merely go into regret, grief and sadness at loss, which is different than suicide, depression, rage, hate or murder. There is gratitude and satisfaction even if it should come to an end. You went 'this far' with someone and now you must part, for reasons of which neither one has any control. The change of the nature of life itself or you get conscripted into the army, or whatever. Therefore, you're grateful for whatever you do have with that person or did have with that person. You don't have to have them forever. It allows flexibility.

Diagnostic Differential: Infatuation vs. Love (2)

QUALITY	PASSION / ATTRACTION (Level 145)	LOVE (Level 500+)
Brain physiology	Left brain-physical	Right brain-etheric
Emotional	Frustration, frantic, fearful, tormented	Gratitude, peaceful, self-fulfilling
Stability	Desperate	Enhanced
Bodily functions	Impaired; loss of appetite & sleep	Improved

Slide 297

SLIDE 297: DIAGNOSTIC DIFFERENTIAL: INFATUATION VS. LOVE (2)

This slide was introduced in September 2011 Lecture, DVD disc 2 001700.

The infatuation/attachment kind of relationship releases adrenalin and excitement. It pours out sex hormones. A spiritually aligned relationship produces endorphins. Endorphins are what accompany joy and happiness. Adrenalin has to do with conquest, etc. Infatuation is **"left-brain physicality"** whereas alignment is **right-brained**, and the etheric body and **etheric brain** play a large part in the relationship.

The emotions in infatuation are excess and imbalance, and emotional quality, then, is frantic. Here in Love, they are calm and balanced and the emotional quality is self-fulfilling. You feel sort of settled in life, and, of course, the brain physiology is completely different.

How about **stability**? Frantic relationships become **desperate** whereas, an aligned relationship is **enhanced**. The desperation comes from 'must have' that person, 'must control' that person, 'must have' that job, 'must have' that car, 'must have' that money, 'must have' that title, all the frantic 'having to have.' Frantic 'having to have' gives it a frantic nature. It's okay for it to be frantic if you realize that, in evolution its franticness is based on reality. When it didn't get what it thought it needed, it died. So, the ego's experience throughout great eons of time is that, if its desires and wants were not satisfied, it died. That is why it is so frantic. That is why it is so frantic and it reacts with such volatility to frustration. They 'must' win the election. The extent to which some of these crazy politicians go to, to try and win an election is unbelievable. How much does this job pay, anyway? Even the governor of the state, in big money terms, is peanuts. What does he get paid, $140,000 a year? Any guy, in any kind of thriving business, who knocks his brains out seven days a week, will end up at the same place. It is control and power and prestige, those are the things they are willing to die for. And lie and put their hand on a Bible and swear on a Bible, that makes one shudder. The same as the atheist, not the honest atheist who says, 'in and of myself, with my intellect, I can't prove the existence of God,' he's just being honest. But the one who gets out there and vilifies Divinity, writes an editorial for the "New York Times." As death approaches, what will be going through their mind? Even if one does not like the Pope, why would you want it to go on record?

Bodily functions: When you are frantically addicted in a relationship, you are **impaired**, you quit eating, and there is **loss of appetite and sleep**. On the other hand, in a good relationship, your body **improves**.

Diagnostic Differential: Infatuation vs. Love (3)

QUALITY	PASSION / ATTRACTION (Level 145)	LOVE (Level 500+)
Description	Craving	Contentment
Pathology	Suicide, despair, stalking	Well-being
Judgment	Impaired	Improved
Perception	Exaggerated	Illuminated
Intention	Possess, own, control, capture	Be with

Slide 298

SLIDE 298: DIAGNOSTIC DIFFERENTIAL: INFATUATION VS. LOVE (3)

This slide was introduced at the September 2011 lecture, DVD disc 2 at 001750.

Infatuation/involvement is coming from addiction and **craving**, from lack; whereas, in an aligned relationship it's fulfilling and you feel **content**. You feel fulfilled that that person adds something additional to your life and therefore, you are very grateful. In an aligned relationship, there is **gratitude**, e.g. for fellow workers on the job, people who work for you one can have tremendous gratitude all the time. Everybody being aligned makes for harmony. The **pathology** in infatuation, everybody knows too well-murder and **suicide**, **stalking**, **despair**, depression, throwing yourself off a bridge. A thousand people throw themselves off the Golden Gate Bridge in San Francisco. Infatuation/involvement throws people off the bridge. "No point to live if I can't have what I want," so you throw yourself off. Fulfillment of an aligned relationship gives you a state of **well-being**.

Here in involvement, **judgment is impaired**, and here in alignment your judgment is **improved**, because you try to work out mutuality. That requires working things through in your mind. Somebody wants this, you want that, so you try to think through how that can work, how can we work that so we get to go to the picnic and the zoo on the same day, for example. You have improved rationality because you think of ways that you wouldn't have thought before, so judgment is improved.

Perception here in infatuation, becomes glamorized and **exaggerated**. There seems to be willingness to sacrifice your soul for temporary gain, like in the story of Faustus. One must realize that every time one sells out, one is building up a karmic accountability, answerability. So, because of the awareness of the answerability, it curtails extremism. Everyone is answerable for everything to the universe. No escaping it. The only way you'd escape it is to get outside the universe, which is not possible. Within the infinite field of consciousness, everyone is answerable, answerable.

Glamorization makes a thing seem more tempting. This is part of addiction to the ego's payoff. You begin to anticipate, then you begin to exaggerate, then you get hooked on the image of it. Soon you begin to crave it. You begin to want it. You've allowed it to build up. The minute the thought of a drink goes through your mind, stop it then. The minute the image of a martini hits your head, stop it, right there! Because it will get more and more attractive, it will attract more and more energy. Soon, it will be a want; then it'll be a 'must;' pretty soon, it'll become a 'just one;' then it'll be a lie and then you'll be back hooked again. The way to stop any craving or desire is the minute it hits your mind. At that point it's vulnerable. Once it attracts to it more and more energy from the ego, it becomes more and more difficult. It takes greater and greater sacrifice and self-control. The perception in alignment is **illuminated** because you realize the intrinsic value of the other human being and their commitment to you and your relationship. You feel constant gratitude. You watch how people will go to any length to get you what you like- you want a certain kind of crumpet and she goes all the way across town to get you it because it's your favorite. You are grateful for that kind of life.

Diagnostic Differential: Infatuation vs. Love (4)

QUALITY	PASSION/ATTRACTION (Level 145)	LOVE (Level 500+)
Productivity	Disrupted	Enhanced
Self-Image	Inflated	Positive
Balance	Erratic	Steady
Hormone/ endocrine	Adrenaline/ sex hormones	Endorphins/ oxytocin

Slide 299

SLIDE 299: DIAGNOSTIC DIFFERENTIAL: INFATUATION VS. LOVE (4)

This slide was introduced at the September 2011 lecture, DVD disc 2 at 001845.

Productivity in involvement/infatuation is disrupted. The worst employee is somebody who is "madly in love" as they are mentally deranged most of the time. Here in alignment you have a positive and enhanced state. The self-image in involvement is inflated. If you get what you want, this now results in ego inflation. Spiritually you are in worse shape than when you didn't get it. Now you think you know who you are. The inflation of the narcissist is also self-feeding, so narcissism, which is that society should cater to your wants, etc., has become the law of the land. Now the law of the land is inflated narcissistic egotism, in which you can imagine yourself as slighted by anything that happens. In alignment, however, it's a positive effect on the self-image. The positive is the fulfillment of the potentiality of happiness and this is part of the fulfillment of that potential. The self-image in alignment is not inflated whereas in infatuation it is more vulnerable than it was. The social image of the person who is 'madly in love', of course is that they're impaired and we call it 'madness,' 'madly in love.' Here the image is one of balance and equanimity, therefore it's **enhanced**.

The balance of the relationship in a possessive relationship is **erratic**; it is over stimulated and over emotionalized. In alignment, it is calm and steady. So, the relationship that has been going on for some time develops calmness to it. You know that it's steady because you know you can count on the relationship, you can count on that person. Glamour, what a powerful energy it is. And how the famous, "Hundred Most Influential People in the World," play with glamour. It isn't just power, it's the glamour of power. It isn't just wealth, it's the glamour associated with it. It's just not being the winner, it's the glamour of being the winner. So, you are hooked on the pleasure of glamour. Everything you get hooked on, you have somehow glamorized it. To be in control, how wonderful that is. Glamorization, then, is the other thing. The ego juice payoff then becomes glamorized, which means it's magnified, overwhelmingly important. In the long run, you won't even remember it. What you'll kill yourself for at 23, by 35, you don't even remember it anymore. And by 80, you don't even recognize it was in your lifetime.

The intention is what sets the calibrated level of consciousness. Not the glamorization, not the wantingness, but the intention. What is the intention? That is why spiritual alignment is so powerful. It invokes the spiritual will which is capable up to level 850. The human will is only as effective as your calibrated level of consciousness. A person who calibrates at 205 decides by reason that they will overcome a certain defect and that decision has the power of 205. But it takes 850 to beat it. It's only by spiritual intention. In an addictive relationship, the intention is to possess, capture, control, and own the other person. Whereas in mature relationships it is just the joy of being with them and that you are sharing life with them. You become aligned with your friends, not just your ultra-exclusive relationship, but your friends and the people who work with you, people that you hang out with in the social groups and the spiritual groups are all aligned, and therefore, compatible, because of the intention. Here there is no desire.

Diagnostic Differential: Infatuation vs. Love (5)

QUALITY	PASSION / ATTRACTION (Level 145)	LOVE (Level 500+)
Social Image	**Inflated**	**Enhanced**
Intellectual function	**Romanticize, lower Mind**	**Realistic, higher Mind**
Level of consciousness	**Lowers**	**Raises**
Style	**Involvement (horizontal)**	**Alignment (vertical)**

Slide 300

SLIDE 300: DIAGNOSTIC DIFFERENTIAL: INFATUATION VS. LOVE (5)

This slide was introduced at the September 2011 lecture, DVD disc 2 at 001920.

When you are involved with someone that does not mean you are aligned with that person. You might even kill them, 'I was so attached to her that I had to kill her when I saw her flirting with somebody else.' Alignment means that your purposes are aligned, so that is why a spiritual overall field in a relationship ensures its longevity and the positive effect it has on others, so that you become an example. The more you love, the more you can love. Sometimes love is misconceived as an attachment. Attachment is one thing and love is another. You can love something and either be attached or not be attached. In infatuation/involvement the intellectual functions are romanticized by lower mind (cal. 155); and in alignment they are realistic, as to higher mind (cal. 275). In intellectual function, what happens when you're infatuated with a goal, its reason now becomes distorted to subserve and rationalize reaching that goal. It involves all kinds of violations of truth. Because, to win means to win at any cost, even if it means chopping your head off. The effect on consciousness level here is quite deleterious. The person who is 'madly in love' calibrates at 145 like Romeo and Juliet. They both commit suicide. To be madly, crazily, infatuated in love is what Hollywood feeds us constantly and as a romanticized relationship calibrates quite low. A mature relationship, coming out of alignment, coming out of side-by-sideness instead of horizontalness, calibrates at 500 plus.

"The persona interacts with everything. It will say something because that is the conversational interaction of the moment. There is no great intrinsic reality to it. Because of the alignment and the lovingness between the two, everything becomes recontextualized. No matter what the person says, it does not have any effect on the alignment whatsoever. The person could be angry at you one second and it does not really mean anything because in the next second the anger is gone. If something was really going to threaten the relationship, it would have a different impact. Because you are both aligned and committed to reach God, that makes you 'parallels' or vertically aligned and not horizontally at the solar plexus level. A little static on the radio is not exactly a major transmission. You could say something back and forth out of your animals. Do not forget you are an animal, so the cause for disparity is really your animal. Let us say now my animal goes to the refrigerator and says, "Where in the world is the pickled herring?" The partner's animal will come up and say, "Right here, in front of your eyes!" I say, "All right, all right!" as I do not want to mix it up. It is never physical; it is just a nuisance, the annoyance of the animal being annoyed. The animal thinks there is a bone over there and he goes over there and in the end the bone falls down the steps and the animal is annoyed. It is just the annoyance of the animal that is coming up and not the real you. The real you has not changed any position, so annoyance between partners is more the animal coming up. So if you say that is my animal, it is not really who I am, you end up kidding each other a good deal." – Paraphrased from June 2007 Lecture, 'What is real?"

Diagnostic Differential: Infatuation vs. Love (6)

QUALITY	PASSION / ATTRACTION (Level 145)	LOVE (Level 500+)
Relatedness	**Demanding**	**Harmonious**
Goal	**Satisfy, own**	**Fulfill**
Pattern	**Individualism**	**Concordance**
Loss	**Depression, rage, hate, blame**	**Grief, regret**

Slide 301

SLIDE 301: DIAGNOSTIC DIFFERENTIAL: INFATUATION VS. LOVE (6)

This slide was introduced at the September 2011 lecture, DVD disc 2 at 002125.

"Love is ordinarily conceptualized as having to do with relationship and the vicissitudes of compatibility and interaction as well as expectations, and thus, emotionality. Relationships bring up desires for control and possession, resulting in conflict that surface as anger or even hatred. Thus, unsatisfactory experiences of purported 'love' are not the result of love but of emotional attachment and 'involvement'. More evolved patterns of relationship that are free of negativity are consequent to basing a relationship on mutual alignment rather than on possessive emotional involvement. This is of critical importance and redefines the essence of true relationship. It could be pictured as being mutually parallel and vertical rather than horizontal (e.g., control), which acts as a tether between people via their 'solar plexus' instead of alignment via the heart. Spiritual love is neither erotic nor possessive and is seen in mature lovemates and in the platonic love of the strong bonds that are formed by shipmates, for example, or military units, or teams. Love of country and one's countrymen eventually extends to all of humanity, and then eventually to the Creator as the Source of Life. Love is gracious and expansive and eventuates as love of all life and all Creation. Thus emerges the Buddhist prayer for the enlightenment and salvation of all sentient beings so they may transcend the bondage that underlies suffering itself. The ideal of unconditional compassion and mercy to all life in all its expressions requires transcendence of dualistic perception and its illusions." – Excerpted from "Reality, Spirituality and Modern Man" (2008), Chapter 14: Spiritual Pathways, pp. 288-289

From "Transcending the Levels of Consciousness: The Stairway to Enlightenment" (2006), Chapter 14: Love, pp. 247-248: "At lower levels of consciousness, what is perceived as love is conditional and identified with possession, passion, romance, and desire, which are projected onto people or objects to give them an exciting specialness and glamour that tend to fade after the prized object or relationship is obtained. As the excitement of acquisition fades, so does the allure of the exaggerated desirability. Infatuations tend to be frantic with a fear of loss that leads to despair. Interference with the possession can result in very severe emotional reactions such as rage, jealousy, or even murder and suicide. Thus, there is a drivenness, possessiveness, or jealousy that can be imbalanced and excessive, leading to obsession due to the projected, exaggerated, and inflated emotional image. Society tends to look upon such excesses as a temporary madness ('madly in love'), with its transitory but intense loss of reality testing, along with immunity to rational intervention or caution. [...] As becomes evident, the contrast is between ego involvement (the self) versus consensual alignment of Self that indicates mutuality of the higher intention of serving the relationship rather than just the personal ego's wantingness or cravings."

Because the conditions of Love and passionate desire are frequently confused, the chart on p. 249 of "Transcending the Levels of Consciousness: The Stairway to Enlightenment" (2006), Chapter 14: Love can be helpful in the differential diagnosis, which is often puzzling to the participants and observers.

Ego Dynamics of L O V E

- **The capacity for Love increases as positionalities are surrendered**
- **Love is a quality of Divinity and emerges in accord with spiritual practices**
- **Example: Be kind to everything and everyone, including oneself, at all times with no exception**
- **Love illuminates the Essence and therefore the lovability of others**

Slide 302

SLIDE 302: EGO DYNAMICS OF LOVE

This slide was introduced at the September 2011 lecture, DVD disc 2 at 002210.

The capacity for Love increases as positionalities are surrendered. Yes, because it opens the heart. Instead of perception, the heart knows. The mind thinks, argues and carries on like that, but the heart just continues. **Love is a quality of Divinity and emerges in accord with spiritual practices. For example: Be kind to everything and everyone, including oneself, at all times with no exception. Love illuminates the Essence and therefore the lovability of others.** Even when others are very, very bad, we can still love them. The mind could be critical and disagree, but the heart loves no matter what. The heart does not put any conditions on what's out there. Only the mind does. From "Transcending the Levels of Consciousness: The Stairway to Enlightenment" (2006), Chapter 14: Love, pp. 250-251: "The capacity for Love increases as the limitations of the narcissistic ego's perceptual positionalities are surrendered.

This is accompanied and supported by an increase in spiritual energy that emanates from the Self, in contrast to desire, which emanates from the self. Love emerges as a consequence of spiritual alignment and accord with spiritual principles and practices and is accompanied by the increased spiritual energy. Perception is replaced with vision that allows for the awareness of the intrinsic value of all that exists. [...] From calibration levels 500 to 539, the love is still subject to conditions and partialities based on considerations and qualitative values, as well as the influence of belief systems.

The limitations may be frustrating to spiritual aspirants who try to 'see past the behaviors and love the person', which is easier said than done. Limitations may be consequent to unpleasant past experiences as well as karmic influences and also affected by social programming and belief systems, some of which may be outside of awareness and operate unconsciously.

The relinquishing of judgmentalism greatly increases the capacity of Love, as does surrendering the wanting of anything from others. Thus, people are not perceived according to what they have or do but by appreciation for what they are and have become.

Love is self-fulfilling and thus does not seek gain or to compensate for lack. Because it does not need to 'get', it is therefore free to peacefully 'be with' and appreciate. To Love, the world is more benign and its people appear more friendly and available. There is an increased feeling of safety and identification with mankind in general and concern for the welfare and happiness of others. The energy field is accompanied by a radiant aura that intrinsically has an effect on others who themselves then tend to become more benign as do their perceptions. This energy field has an influence on all life, which intuits the safety of Love through the field effect. Characteristic of this level are an unmistakable 'sweetness' of personality, speech, attitudes, and lifestyle that is inwardly nurturing."

Transcending Level 500 (1)

- **A key to making Love unconditional is the willingness to forgive**
- **With forgiveness, events and people are re-contextualized as simply "limited", not "bad" or "unlovable"**
- **Forgiveness ensues from the willingness of humility to surrender the world and its events to Divinity**

Slide 303

SLIDE 303: TRANSCENDING LEVEL 500 (1)

This slide was introduced at the September 2011 lecture, DVD disc 2 at 002410.

From "Transcending the Levels of Consciousness: The Stairway to Enlightenment" (2006), Chapter 14: Love, p. 252: "The limitations of Love have to do with perceived qualities and differences. By inner self-honesty and examination, these areas of limitation are revealed, usually as residual judgments or as the impact from prior experience. **A key to making Love unconditional is the willingness of forgiveness** to undo past reservations, experiences, and viewing people as unlovable. **By the willingness to forgive and surrender one's perceptions, they may be re-contextualized and now seen simply as limited or influenced by programming as spiritually underprivileged and reflective of the ego's proclivity to be blind to falsity.** By intention, awareness may be changed from the perceptual duality of good/bad to witnessing 'desirable' versus 'less desirable', or even just preferable or less preferable.

Forgiveness ensues from the willingness of humility to surrender the world and its events to God. The change in appearance that is the consequence of deep surrender is a focus of the well-known *A Course in Miracles*, where the miracle is the consequence of the re-contextualization of the limitation by which the inner innocence and innate holiness of others and life are revealed. This is a subjective transformation that is not under volitional control. A transformative mechanism is the relinquishment of faith in the validity of one's ideas and thinkingness itself and seeing that they are only images from the past, with no current validity or reality."

From "2002 Lecture Series: The Way to God", September: 'Devotion: The Way to God through the Heart', (Paraphrased): "All the pathways of love talk about forgiveness. But, forgiveness truly is not possible if you continue to see somebody as bad, evil, wicked, or at fault. It's only when you can remove your own projections, and your own perceptions, and not label them as anything, that you realize that basically, they are innocent—that they don't know any better. In that way, you can stop hating them. ...Forgiveness is not really possible until, to a certain degree, you transcend dualistic perception, which labels everything as good and bad, deserving and undeserving, etc. The doorway to unconditional lovingness is the dawning on you that everything is innocent. Some are conscious, some are not conscious—that's the difference."

Transcending Level 500 (2)

- **Pray to the Holy Spirit for a miracle to see the Truth about the situation or person**
- **Surrender all perceptual positionalities and their egoistic gain to the revelation of Truth**

Slide 304

SLIDE 304: TRANSCENDING LEVEL 500 (2)

This slide was introduced at the September 2011 lecture, DVD disc 2 at 002440.

Pray to the Holy Spirit for a miracle to see the Truth about the situation or the person. When we ask for a miracle, we are surrendering our perception of how we see a situation or a person. Through "A Course in Miracles", for instance, the miraculous occurs when we surrender our perception of the situation or person to the Holy Spirit. Then it is transformed and when it is transformed, we see that the person or the situation is still is lovable. We see that somebody we are angry at cannot help but be that way. So, instead of being angry or hateful, we feel sorry for them and say, 'It's too bad that they cannot see it the way we are seeing it,' because you know their life is painful the way they are seeing the world and when they see it our way, the world stops being painful. Whenever there is any conflict within us because of our perception of a person or a situation, we are not to accept the situation or the person but instead to go within and forgive the situation or the person by surrendering our perception to the Holy Spirit and asking for a miracle. That resolves the conflict within us. **And Surrender all perceptual positionalities and their egoistic gain to the revelation of Truth.** From "Transcending the Levels of Consciousness: The Stairway to Enlightenment" (2006), Chapter 14: Love, pp. 252-253: "**By surrender, the request to the Holy Spirit for a miracle is thereby the willingness to surrender one's perceptual positionalities and their egoistic gain to the revelation of Truth.** The phenomenon is often accompanied by a re-contextualization of time, place, and intention, and it is a literal, experiential phenomenon that is transformative in itself."

"Reluctance to forgive is a consequence not only of unwillingness to let go of the ego juice of perceived injustice but also the illusion that others do not 'deserve' it. In reality, it is the forgiver and not the forgiven who benefits the most. [...] In actuality, and psychologically, it really could not be done by the ego/mind at all because it lacks the necessary power when it is caught up in the energy field of hate, which calibrates at only 30. Therefore, the transformative source of power cannot originate from the mind or the personality called the personal 'I'. The necessary power resides in the nonlinear quality of consciousness termed the 'Will', which alone can open the gates to the power necessary to dissolve the ego's positionality.

By invitation, the Holy Spirit transforms comprehension by virtue of the presence of the healing power of Grace. What the ego cannot lift with all its might is like a feather to the Grace of God. As a consequence of the process of transformation, not only are the views of others transformed from hateful to benign, but the view of self is also transformed." – "Transcending the Levels of Consciousness: The Stairway to Enlightenment" (2006), Chapter 2: Guilt and Vindictive Hate, pp. 55-56.

Transcending Level 500 (3)

- **Remember: This domain is one of MAXIMUM SPIRITUAL OPPORTUNITY, with a multitude of options, which aids the evolution of consciousness**
- **One can be grateful instead of resentful about the past**
- **The Buddha: "Rare is it to be born a human being, rarer still to have heard of Enlightenment, and even rarer still to pursue it"**

Slide 305

SLIDE 305: TRANSCENDING LEVEL 500 (3)

This slide was introduced at the September 2011 lecture, DVD disc 2 at 002635.

From "Transcending the Levels of Consciousness: The Stairway to Enlightenment" (2006), Chapter 14: Love, p. 253: "The difficulties of this world appear to be the consequence of all different levels of evolutionary development being thrown together simultaneously, which results in social turbulence. Simultaneously, however, the availability of such a wide spectrum allows for the greatest opportunity for growth and the undoing of 'bad karma' and, by choice, accumulating the merit of 'good karma'. Thus, **this domain is one of maximum spiritual opportunity with a great multitude of options and choices that provide maximum potential for the evolution of consciousness about which one can be grateful instead of resentful. As the Buddha taught, 'Rare is it to be born a human being, rarer still to have heard of Enlightenment, and even rarer still to pursue it'.**"

"Inner peace is the consequence of humility and acceptance of one's karmic inheritance, with its intrinsic gifts as well as limitations. It is very helpful to know that even one's human existence is the consequence of assent by the will. Like any limiting ego position, it is not the position itself that requires relinquishment but the emotional pay-off or energy that holding onto that position provides to the ego. To realize that Pride is a limitation is already a great step in itself.

Notable is that Pride is intrinsically a statement of lack, and it is therefore constantly needy and seeking to be fed and propped up to compensate for its insufficiency. Also notable is that the more it is fed, the more voracious its appetite, which eventually becomes insatiable.

Frustration of pride easily leads to rage; thus arose the wise adage to be cautious with the prideful for they can become spiteful or vengeful.

The spiritually wise reject the temptation of ego inflation of flattery, titles, worldly success, pomp, wealth, worldly power, and other temptations of illusion. Lastly, there is the paradoxical, concealed temptation of pride in one's humility, i.e., the so-called spiritual ego, where even piety or humility can be a display.

Assumed poverty can also be a form of ostentation and can be worn as a badge out of spiritual pride. True asceticism is a matter of economy of effort or projected value. It is not the possessions themselves but the importance attached to them. Thus, one can be wealthy but unattached to the wealth itself, which is a matter of indifference, e.g., "to wear the world like a loose garment," as suggested by St. Francis of Assisi." – "Transcending the Levels of Consciousness: The Stairway to Enlightenment" (2006), Chapter 8: Pride, pp. 157-158.

Unconditional Love, Joy and Ecstasy (1)

- **As Love becomes unconditional, it begins to be experienced as inner Joy**
- **Joy arises from within each moment of existence, not from any outer source**
- **The hallmark of this state is compassion. At this level, people have a notable effect on others**

Slide 306

SLIDE 306: UNCONDITIONAL LOVE, JOY AND ECSTASY (1)

This slide was introduced at the September 2011 lecture, DVD disc 2 at 002820.

As Love becomes unconditional, it begins to be experienced as inner Joy. Joy is where you think the dog is run over and probably killed but when you get there, you realize that it was only hurt a little bit and is still alive and its tail wags and your heart just jumps with joy. The doggie's okay, not really badly hurt. So you jump with joy. You jump with joy when you get up every morning, you are glad to see yourself in the mirror every day. 'Hi, how are you today?' **Joy arises from within each moment of existence, and not from any other source.** Yes, it is from within. It is not dependent on anything out there. Whether the audience laughs or not does not matter. Whether they are enjoying what you are saying is irrelevant. That is their problem. One is self-sufficient because the experience of Love as the Radiance of Divinity is everywhere present. It is like the sun just shining everywhere on the desert no matter where you go.

The hallmark of this state is compassion. At this level, people have a notable effect on others. Acceptance of human limitation, both individually and collectively, allows for forbearance, forgiveness, and compassion rather than condemnation. Compassion and forgiveness do not mean approval. Those who live in the energy fields below 200 are subject to relentless torment. In the Christian tradition, one is taught to pray for sinners. At the same time, one is advised to also avoid and dissociate from non-integrity and negativity ('evil') rather than confront it. The 'sinful' can be seen as unfortunates whose spiritual growth is still rudimentary. The average person's psyche is overwhelmed by layers of programmed belief systems of which they are not even aware. Out of naïveté and the belief in the principle of causality, the supposed causes and their solutions are sought 'out there' externally. With maturity and the wisdom of spirituality, the search becomes directed inwardly where the source and resolution are finally discovered. Owning one's own inner flaws allows for nonjudgmental respect for others and opens the door to compassion for all humanity. When we look within, we can really see that anything we have ever done in our lifetime was done out of innocence, and when our main intention is to understand that, it becomes healed out of compassion. We provide a safe space and context about our spiritual work by being centered in the Heart — not the physical heart, but from the ultimate compassion, the owning of ourselves from this level, the joy of the spiritual work, and the saying "thank you" to all the things that come up out of gratitude.

Unconditional Love, Joy and Ecstasy (2)

- **Everything happens effortlessly by synchronicity**
- **One sees the world and everything in it to be an expression of Love and Divinity**
- **The state is impersonal, not personal and represents the power of the energy field, not of the individual**
- **There is the capacity to love many people simultaneously - Love has no limits**

Slide 307

SLIDE 307: UNCONDITIONAL LOVE, JOY AND ECSTASY (2)

This slide was introduced at the September 2011 lecture, DVD disc 2 at 003050.

The more you love, the more you can love. From "Power vs. Force: The Hidden Determinants of Human Behavior" (2012 edition), Chapter 4: Levels of Human Consciousness, pp. 113-114: "From level 540 and up is the domain of saints, spiritual healers, and advanced spiritual students. Characteristic of this energy field is the capacity for enormous patience and the persistence of a positive attitude in the face of prolonged adversity. The hallmark of this state is compassion. People who have attained this level have a notable effect on others. They are capable of a prolonged, open visual gaze, which induces a state of love and peace.

At the high 500s, the world one sees is illuminated by the exquisite beauty and perfection of creation. **Everything happens effortlessly, by synchronicity, and the world and everything in it is seen to be an expression of love and Divinity.** Individual will merges into Divine will. A Presence is felt whose power facilitates phenomena outside conventional expectations of reality, termed miraculous by the ordinary observer. **These phenomena represent the power of the energy field, not that of the individual.**

One's sense of responsibility for others at this level is of a different quality from that shown at the lower levels. There is a desire to use one's state of consciousness for the benefit of life itself rather than for particular individuals. **This capacity to love many people simultaneously** is accompanied by the discovery that **the more one loves, the more one can love**.

Near-death experiences, characteristically transformative in their effect, have frequently allowed people to experience the energy level between 540 and 600."

Unconditional Love, Joy and Ecstasy (3)

- **Unconditional Love is the goal of the majority of spiritually committed people**
- **Unconditional Love (540) is a practical and reachable goal**
- **The goal of Unconditional Love is reachable by very simple means**
- **Example: "To live with care and kindness" on a daily basis - without exception**

Slide 308

SLIDE 308: UNCONDITIONAL LOVE, JOY AND ECSTASY (3)

This slide was introduced at the September 2011 lecture, DVD disc 2 at 003140.

"The truth of one's real self can be discovered through the pathway of everyday life. To live with care and kindness is all that is necessary. The rest reveals itself in due time. The commonplace and God are not distinct." – "I: Reality and Subjectivity" (2003), Introduction, p. xxv

Question: "A lot of us would like to live that example of 'living with care and kindness on a daily basis,' but when we try to apply it, it just doesn't work. So, can you give us some tips as to how we can achieve that?"

Doc: "Well, it's because of how we are viewing the world. In other words, when we place expectations on the world then we set ourselves up for disruption. I have no expectation that there will be coffee in the morning in the kitchen or not. One can have great hopes. It may or may not be there. We can have great hopes when we get home today the doggie will not have had an accident in the living room, but if doggie had an accident, you are prepared to forgive her. Unconditionally loving means no conditions. Because it is the way that we are, and not the way the world has to be. The doggie does not have to be the way you want her to be. You would prefer it, but she is only a doggie and if she has to go wa-wa, she is going to go wa-wa. Hopefully not before we get home..."

From "Healing and Recovery" (2009), Chapter 2: Assisting Healing, pp. 52-53: "If we look at the basic physics of the energies involved, we can see why fear at calibration level 100 is overpowered by Love at 500 because these are exponential powers. Therefore, the power of Love is represented by 10500, whereas Fear is only 10100, a very big difference.

To put oneself in an energy field of 540 is to automatically heal oneself. A loving thought then heals, and a negative thought creates illness. Choosing to become a loving person results in the release of endorphins by the brain, which has a profound effect on the body's health and happiness... Happiness arises from the willingness to let go of that which is negative and to allow love to replace it in consciousness because the essential nature of consciousness, unless it has been impaired, is lovingness. We see this in the young child who is only innocence, and lovingness is the expression of the essence of human nature. It is as if the child has not yet been programmed to go into fear, doubt, or limitation. It is essential to capture that essential expression of lovingness in order to help any illness within us, as well as to let go of the negativity of the belief system."

Unconditional Love, Joy and Ecstasy (4)

- **There is a silent, nonverbal benefit of being in the actual presence of such a teacher**
- **Silent transmission of the high-frequency energy of the teacher's aura:**
  - **The 'Silent Teaching'**
  - **'Transmission of No-Mind'**
  - **'Grace of the Teacher'**
  - **'Benediction of the Teacher'**
- **It happens of its own and is not personal**

Slide 309

SLIDE 309: UNCONDITIONAL LOVE, JOY AND ECSTASY (4)

This slide was introduced at the September 2011 lecture, DVD disc 2 at 003345.

There is a silent, nonverbal benefit of being in the actual presence of such a teacher. The Buddha transmitted it in giving his disciple a flower, symbolic of the transmission of the energy. To have been in the presence of a great teacher, you will never be the same. The most beneficial thing that can happen to you is to have been in the presence of a great teacher, because you pick up the vibration, which cannot be taught via words or lectures, but actually only from the field. You pick up the energy field of a teacher by the physical presence within the aura. But then it lasts for more than a lifetime, because you become that and then you yourself also become the source of it for others. So your kindness and lovingness becomes a pattern for someone else and is transmitted out. It is because the vibration is transmitted out that humankind is still alive. It would have destroyed itself a long time ago. So, it is worthwhile to go a long distance to see a teacher that would have that. All they need to do is pick up the energy field of the teacher. Then, when they go home, they bring it back to where they came from. People came from all different countries around the world and Dr. Hawkins felt greatly honored by that, and also to be requested to go to certain places in the world because they wanted his energy there. Doc: "It was a great privilege to go to South Korea and be able to be of service, yes. We prevented a war from happening there by virtue of our having been there, um hum, yes. That was a great privilege."

The silent transmission of the high- frequency energy of the teacher's aura is referred to as: The 'Silent Teaching', The 'Transmission of No-Mind', The 'Grace of the Teacher', The 'Benediction of the Teacher', etc. It happens of its own and is not personal. That is the transmission of Grace by virtue of the energy field of the teacher, which radiates forth unconditionally. Doc: "It is the ocean that's uplifting the ship. That is your universal lovingness. Being unconditionally loving as a way of existing, as a way of being in the world uplifts everyone, no matter who. I can remember walking down the street with a complete stranger walking towards me and I felt the aura of that person coming towards me. As that person walked by, they got this profound whack of love and they experienced the miraculous. The miraculous occurred without the person's awareness and without my having to acknowledge it. I looked him in the eyes and he looked at me in the eyes and it was profound, we both became different. One moment is all it took to transform, in the heart of the city of New York City."

Ego Dynamics of Unconditional Love (1)

- **To align with Love as a primary goal invites spiritual energy that emanates from the Self**
- **This energy facilitates and supports the evolution of consciousness**
- **One relinquishes seeing the personal self as a causal agent**
- **Joy stems from the inner subjective experience of one's own existence**

Slide 310

SLIDE 310: EGO DYNAMICS OF UNCONDITIONAL LOVE (1)

This slide was introduced at the September 2011 lecture, however not actually shown.

Question: "So we are uplifting the world by being unconditionally loving towards everything? We are actually helping mankind?"

Doc: "That is so. I can remember meeting the doorman at a very high-class apartment building and as I came to see him, I saw him transform. As I came to speak to him, I saw him go from bored and disappointed to happy. Because I could feel the energy just pour out. I just adored this person, just loved him. He was transformed and we were both transformed in the instant, by the presence of Divine Love. It was Divine Love that brought about the transformation. The world did not look the same."

Question: "So is that what all of us are supposed to do, to go forth from this lecture and project this type of love towards mankind? Is that what you're saying?"

Doc gets up from his chair: "Is everyone here willing to be unconditionally loving towards all of life in all of its expressions?" Audience says, "Yes." Doc claps his hands and says, "See, because from you it is transmitted to others, so you only look like a thousand people but you are going to be influencing millions as a consequence during your lifetime-resist" (Tested true). "Okay, not because of what you do, but because of what you have become. What you have become transforms the world. What a great blessing, O Lord. Amen."

From "I: Reality and Subjectivity" (2003), Chapter 7: The Radical Reality of the Self, pp. 131-132: "In Reality, nothing requires an explanation. Nothing is caused by anything else. Existence requires no explanation nor does it have any dependence on any other state or quality. This understanding is clarified by the realization that nothing in and of itself has any 'meaning'. Therefore, neither does it have a 'purpose'. Everything is already complete and merely self- existent as its own self-identity.

As an example, 'space' just 'is'; it just 'stands there' doing nothing at all. It cannot be measured because measurement is solely an arbitrary mentation. No reason is necessary. It would be lapsing into pointless mentation to ask, "Why is space," or "What is its purpose?" There is no 'why' to any reality. Nothing in the universe requires a 'why', nor does any truth reveal itself by even asking the question."

Ego Dynamics of Unconditional Love (2)

- **The innate perfection and stunning beauty of all that exists shines forth like a luminous radiance**
- **All of life becomes more beautiful as its illumination reveals the Divinity of the Creator**
- **The energy also uplifts the state of others who are enveloped by the field ("Grace of the Teacher")**

Slide 311

SLIDE 311: EGO DYNAMICS OF UNCONDITIONAL LOVE (2)

This slide was introduced at the September 2011 lecture, however it was not actually shown.

From "Transcending the Levels of Consciousness: The Stairway to Enlightenment" (2006), Chapter 15: Unconditional Love, Joy, and Ecstasy, pp. 258-259: "By alignment with Love as a primary goal, along with spiritual dedication, the evolution of consciousness is supported and facilitated by an infusion of the powerful spiritual energy that emanates from the Self. The influx of this unique energy starts at calibration level 200 and progressively increases. Its observable effect is the change in brain physiology (as per the Brain Function chart) from dominance of the animalistic left brain to the benign, spiritually-oriented right brain.

Acceleration of spiritual energy is facilitated by the relinquishment of narcissistic, egoistic self-interests, such as the seeking of personal gain. The energy is facilitated by the intention and alignment of humility, mercy, compassion, and dedication to the relief of suffering of others in the forms of benevolence, mercy, and kindness.

The spiritual energy catalyzes the transformation of linear positional perception to the greater context of the nonlinear inclusiveness that transcends the limitations of time, space, sequence, or the limitation of the perception and belief in the operant principle of cause and effect. Thus, the revelations that ensue are aptly described as 'miraculous' and transformational.

The source of joy stems from the inner subjective experience of the innate source of one's existence itself, unimpeded by the limitation of presuming the personal self to be a causal or primary agent. By humility and surrender, the imaginary control is relinquished to God and Divine Will. This frequently results in what the world denotes as saintly (cal. 555) and selfless attitudes and behaviors.

As consciousness continues to advance, **the innate perfection and stunning beauty** of all that exists shines forth like a luminous radiance. **All of life becomes more beautiful as innate illumination reveals the Divinity of the Creator**. The subjective experience of the flow of the spiritual energy is felt as an exquisite sweetness. It feels as though it flows up the back and into the brain itself, as well as flowing out through the heart region, where it may spontaneously flow externally and even for some distance to influence external events. **The energy also influences the subjective state of others who are enveloped by the field, which has an uplifting effect** (**the traditional Grace of the Teacher**)."

Ego Dynamics of Unconditional Love (3)

- **Spiritual energy ('kundalini') facilitates transformation:**
  - **-- from perception to vision**
  - **-- from linear to nonlinear**
  - **-- from limited to unlimited**
- **Its power is subjective, and thus the energy of motor performance is inexhaustible**
- **Example: Dancing in the chapel all night**

Slide 312

SLIDE 312: EGO DYNAMICS OF UNCONDITIONAL LOVE (3)

This slide was introduced at the September 2011 lecture, however it was not actually shown.

Do not be glamorized by miracles, and do not try to force the Kundalini energy. It will rise through the chakras as a consequence of that which you have become. In the high 500's, the Kundalini energy runs up your spine, and is an exquisite sensation as it runs up your back, up the spine and into the brain. If you think of the left side of the brain, it runs to the left side; you can run it on one side of the brain or the other. It goes on for a varying period of time, like a couple years. Then it comes down and would come out of the heart and the heart region and it is exquisitely pleasurable, indefinably exquisite. On occasion, it would flow outside to somewhere, this energy would of its own. That is the time of the miraculous also, and many of the "Siddhis", certain occult powers. They come about as a result of the energy field, which exists on its own so that the miraculous happens within the field as a result of the field. It has nothing to do with you as a person. It is the energy doing that; the energy has the capacity to do that. There is no decision on anybody's part.

From "Transcending the Levels of Consciousness: The Stairway to Enlightenment" (2006), Chapter 15: Unconditional Love, Joy, and Ecstasy, pp. 259-260: "Spiritual energy ('kundalini') potentiates the transformation from **perception to vision**, and from **the limited linear to the unlimited nonlinear** nature of existence. This is an expression of the basic reality that all comes into existence by virtue of potentiality's becoming actuality when conditions (including karma) are favorable. This confirmation is also facilitated by intention and spiritual alignment. Thus, no 'person' performs miracles; they are the impersonal consequence of the spiritual energy field itself that acts like a catalyst, as does the energy radiating from the auras of advanced teachers that catalyzes the spiritual intentions of the spiritual student. [...] Unlike the calm tranquility that returns again at level 600, subjectively, the state of Ecstasy is one of very high energy and **tireless capacity**. The beauty of Creation is radiantly exquisite, and the innate Divinity and perfection of all Creation shine forth with a brilliant and overwhelming intensity. Its **power is subjectively experienced, and thus the energy and strength of motor performance becomes inexhaustible**. No tiredness occurs, nor does one have to stop to eat or even perform basic physiological functions. Instead, for instance, **one can dance nonstop for endless hours without food, rest, or respite**. Without consciousness calibration, the world would not know whether the state is pathological or one of 'Divine Intoxication'. [...] Although the state of ecstasy is recognized in spiritually-advanced communities and the subjective experience has been described by well-known mystics such as Ramakrishna, it is unknown to the world at large to which it is really incomprehensible."

Ego Dynamics of Unconditional Love (4)

- **Beauty of Creation is radiantly exquisite**
- **Innate Divinity and perfection of all Creation shine forth with brilliant and overwhelming intensity**
- **While functioning in the world is still possible, the high 500s may require leaving the ordinary world of commerce, and abandoning one's prior social world and occupation**

Slide 313

SLIDE 313: EGO DYNAMICS OF UNCONDITIONAL LOVE (4)

This slide was introduced at the September 2011 lecture, however it was not actually shown.

The **beauty of Creation is radiantly exquisite. Innate Divinity and perfection of all Creation shine forth – with brilliant and overwhelming intensity.** "All credit is due to God whose Radiance shines forth as Creation and who, by the Holy Spirit, inspires and illuminates all understanding and realization of Divine Truth. Amen." – "I: Reality and Subjectivity" (2003), Acknowledgements, p. xv

"The Buddha is said to have avoided using the term 'God' because of the prevalence of misconceptions surrounding it. He wanted to avoid all the limitations that that conceptualization confounds. The Self as Awareness is often referred to in literature as Light. As recounted in Genesis, the Unmanifest became Manifest first as Light, which was the radiance of the energy of God that took form as the universe.

The term 'Self' also overcomes the dualistic notion that one is separated from God. Historically, the picture that there is a sinner down here on Earth and there is a God up there somewhere in heaven is the viewpoint of the ego. Thus, to most people, the term 'God' implies 'otherness'. However, there is no separation in the Allness of Creation, so it is impossible for the created to be separate from the Creator. Enlightenment is therefore the revelation of the Self when the illusion of the reality of a separate self is removed.

The constant awareness of one's existence as 'I' is the ever present expression of the innate divinity of the Self. This is a universal, constant experience that is purely subjective and of which no proof is possible or necessary. The 'I' of the Self is the expression of Divinity as Awareness, which is therefore beyond time and form. The truth of this identity is obscured by the duality created by perception and disappears when all positionalities are relinquished." – "I: Reality and Subjectivity" (2003), Chapter 7: The Radical Reality of the Self, pp. 128-129

While functioning in the world is still possible, the high 500s may require leaving the ordinary world of commerce, and abandoning one's prior social world and occupation. From "Transcending the Levels of Consciousness: The Stairway to Enlightenment" (2006), Chapter 15: Unconditional Love, Joy, and Ecstasy, p. 260: "While functioning in the world efficiently is still possible, the high 500s may require leaving the ordinary world of endeavor and commerce and abandoning one's social world and prior occupation. By persistent spiritual alignment and practice, the spiritual energy may continue to flow and increase to the level of Ecstasy (cal. 575), which becomes incapacitating to ordinary worldly function and thereby requires retreat from the customary world of endeavor. It is best to be prepared for the fact that the world has little or no understanding of such a state or the actual necessity for such a transition that others may even resent or find unsettling."

Spiritual Phenomena: The *Siddhis*

- **From level 540 to the high 500s**
- **"Miraculous," "supranatural" phenomena**
- **No "person" performs miracles - they occur spontaneously when conditions are appropriate**
- **Not explicable by reason, logic, or cause and effect**

Slide 314

SLIDE 314: SPIRITUAL PHENOMENA: THE SIDDHIS

This slide was introduced at the September 2011 lecture, however it was not actually shown.

From "Transcending the Levels of Consciousness: The Stairway to Enlightenment" (2006), Chapter 15: Unconditional Love, Joy, and Ecstasy, pp. 262-263: "**From consciousness level 540 and up into the higher 500s, phenomena occur spontaneously** that are **inexplicable by reason, the customary conceptualization of logic, or cause and effect**. They are an accompaniment to the progressive dominance of the spiritual energy (kundalini) and **occur as a consequence of the contextual field rather than by volition**. They are witnessed and seen to **occur autonomously**. These have been classically termed *siddhis* (Sanskrit) and denote **'supranatural' or 'miraculous/mystical powers'**, as they are not explicable by logic.

In the early stages of their appearance they may be sporadic, but as consciousness advances, they become frequent and sometimes continuous. They are unintended and arise of their own accord. These include faculties such as distant viewing, precognition, clairvoyance, clairaudience, extrasensory perception, psychometry, bilocation, and the occurrence of the miraculous, including spontaneous healings and transformations. There are also unique facilitations that are beyond expectation or possible explanation.

The capacities or phenomena are **not within personal control**; they are **not the consequence of 'cause and effect'**. Therefore, students are forewarned not to claim them as personal as they occur independently of the person's 'I', or self. Thus, as said previously, no 'person' performs miracles for they are solely a consequence of the Spirit. Inflation of the spiritual ego is precluded by honesty and humility, which results in temptation of exploitation for gain.

The phenomena tend to emerge and become strong for variable durations of years. Some seem to fade away and become less predominant, and others continue permanently.

The kundalini energy flow is itself extraordinary in that subjectively, the sensation can only be described as exquisite as it flows up the back and into the brain, emerges as though through the heart chakra, and then goes on out into the world where its presence facilitates the unfoldment of the truly wondrous. The occurrences are witnessed as happening without intention. It is as though Divine qualities are brought into manifestation via higher realms that transcend the mundane physical world.

Eventually, the apparent 'extraordinary' becomes a new reality as though one now lives in a different dimension in which the seemingly impossible manifests effortlessly as though orchestrated. The power of the field autonomously facilitates the emergence of karmic potentiality into a manifested actuality in a harmonious unfoldment. The dynamics are nonlinear and therefore incomprehensible to the intellect, which presumes the limitations of the linear Newtonian model of causality and is unable to conceptualize emergence, Divine Order, or Harmony."

Transcending Joy and Ecstasy (1)

- **The reluctant devotee holds back and clings to doubt and to "the familiar"**
- **Surrender all doubt to Divine Providence**
- **Surrender all belief systems, all perceptions, all positions, all attachments**
- **Surrender attachment even to the exquisite state of Ecstasy, which is beyond description**

Slide 315

SLIDE 315: TRANSCENDING JOY AND ECSTASY (1)

This slide was introduced at the September 2011 lecture, however was not actually shown.

From "Transcending the Levels of Consciousness: The Stairway to Enlightenment" (2006), Chapter 15: Unconditional Love, Joy, and Ecstasy, pp. 263-267: "Transcendence requires the relinquishment of all attachments, even those characterized by self and society as 'responsibilities'. Thus, relationships, positions, titles, and social roles are eventually abandoned to the commitment to realize the Self or reach the state of Enlightenment. **The reluctant devotee who holds back clings to doubt and asks naively, But what about? The solution is to surrender all the 'but what about's' to God and Divine Providence.**

A major transition also necessitates responsibility to others by making necessary and realistic adjustments and helping others to accept the required changes. This transition may therefore take considerable courage and patience as well as conviction, for it brings up residual doubts, attachments, guilt, and the like.

The eventuality of a major leap in consciousness is seldom taken into consideration as a serious possibility, much less a likelihood, among most aspirants who, unless forewarned, may not have made anticipatory plans. Therefore, serious students should be informed and also have spiritual alliances or relationships that are capable of recognizing advanced states of consciousness. [...]

The transcendence of spiritual ecstasy and joy **depends on the willingness to surrender all to God, no matter what, including even the exquisite state of ecstasy**, which is of a dimension beyond description. The state itself is now a temptation and can delay the evolution to the state of Enlightenment. At first, there is a reluctance and dismay to surrendering such a glorious condition to God, and yet, there arises a knowingness that even this wonderment, too, must be released. The anguish and hesitancy of having to take the step reveals that an attachment to the condition and its wonderment has already unwittingly taken place. Then, because of commitment and intention, there is conviction that yes, this, too, must be surrendered "to Thee, O Lord," and with its surrender, an infinite Peace prevails that is beyond all understanding or description at level 600. The condition reveals itself to be the actuality of the Peace of God."

Transcending Joy and Ecstasy (2)

- **Devotion (555) and surrender allow for the inflow of spiritual energy, which dissolves resistance**
- **The self-revelation becomes progressively recognized as Divinity**
- **The inner state is progressively dominant as self diminishes by the eclipse of the Self**

Slide 316

SLIDE 316: TRANSCENDING JOY AND ECSTASY (2)

This slide was introduced at the September 2011 lecture, however was not actually shown.

Devotion (555) and surrender allow for the inflow of spiritual energy, which dissolves resistance. The self-revelation becomes progressively recognized as Divinity. The inner state is progressively dominant as self diminishes by the eclipse of the Self. From "Transcending the Levels of Consciousness: The Stairway to Enlightenment" (2006), Chapter 15: Unconditional Love, Joy, and Ecstasy, pp. 263-267: "The surrendering of all limiting beliefs, positionalities, doubts, and attachments allows for the inflow of spiritual energy, which is the concomitance of devotion (cal. 555). Persistent devotion to spiritual truth and love allows for the dissolution of resistances. [...] The inner state is progressively dominant as self diminishes by the eclipse of the Self. The consequent changes, both inner and outer, turn out to be more major than anticipated."

From "I: Reality and Subjectivity: (2003), Chapter 17: The Inner Path, pp. 291-292: The straightest way to enlightenment is through devoted introspection, meditation, and contemplation of the inner workings of the ego so as to understand consciousness. The process is energized by intention, dedication, and devotion, and the total effort is supported by spiritual inspiration. The dedication is focused on the process itself as a surrender to God. The focus needs to be intense, and it is energized by fixity and deliberateness of intention. The process is one of discovery and becomes **progressively self-revealing**.

Every period of focus and practice is equally valuable. Eventually, the tool of 'one- pointedness of mind' becomes perfected, which in itself is quite an accomplishment that requires devotion to the task. The devotion becomes self-fulfilling and rewarding.

The actual focus, as explained elsewhere, can be either context or content, that is, central (like focusing on the eye of a fly) or peripheral. Context is all inclusive of the totality of the person and the process—the mind, the body, the style of the practice, the person, the setting, the room, the building, the city, the county, the state, the continent, the world, the sky, the planets, the galaxy, the universe, and the mind of God. With practice, either style becomes familiar. In fact, one could try both to see which is the more natural. It is also possible to become equally adept at either focus (central or peripheral).

Under ordinary life circumstances, the automatic functioning of the ego/mind is taken for granted and not subject to scrutiny. The very process of studying the mind already begins to diminish the ego's grip. The sense of self begins to shift locus, and the feeling of one's inner 'I' begins to progress through the layers of consciousness.

This simple drill/process/praxis will reveal evermore rarified levels as the ego's 'gravity field' of fascination with mental content, thoughts, feelings, and dialog is transcended. The layers or fields move from the literal, concrete 'thingness' and form of the linear domain and begin to shift from specifics to context."

Transcending Joy and Ecstasy (3)

- **At level 600, the distinction between "subject" and "object" disappears – total Oneness, no separation**
- **The consequent changes, both inner and outer, turn out to be more major than anticipated - ("God shock")**
- **Serious aspirants are forewarned that sudden leaps in consciousness are possible - It is advisable to make anticipatory plans**

Slide 317

SLIDE 317: TRANSCENDING JOY AND ECSTASY (3)

This slide was introduced at the September 2011 lecture, however was not actually shown.

From "Transcending the Levels of Consciousness: The Stairway to Enlightenment" (2006), Chapter 15: Unconditional Love, Joy, and Ecstasy, pp. 264-266: "The eventuality of a major leap in consciousness is seldom taken into consideration as a serious possibility, much less a likelihood, among most aspirants who, unless forewarned, may not have made anticipatory plans. Therefore, serious students should be informed and also have spiritual alliances or relationships that are capable of recognizing advanced states of consciousness. [...] The emergence of progressively higher levels of consciousness requires periods of adjustment, such as that required by a new pair of glasses, and thus, worldly function may be impaired periodically due to shifts of orientation. In this reorientation, phenomena are discovered to be happening spontaneously of their own rather than via the usual presumed premise and perception of cause and effect. Pleasure is no longer something one acquires but is innate consequent to the power of the field rather than via some agency or personal decision. It is also progressively discovered that there is actually no 'doer' of actions, and one witnesses the autonomous unfoldment of karmic potentiality from a new paradigm of reality that is beyond the presumptive dualistic principle of causation. Thus, life becomes an endless series of revelations of intrinsic charm and delight that initially seem amazing. Then comes the realization that what appears to be miraculous is merely the constant unfolding of the potentiality of the evolution of Creation by which the subjective experience of time dissolves and is replaced by the knowingness of all Is-ness. Likewise, the perception of 'change' is replaced by the progressive emergence of the on-goingness of Creation as becoming the fulfillment of potentiality's actualizing into manifestation.

With neither past nor future, likewise, there is no 'now', and it is comprehended that the past, present, or future are all illusory contextualizations consequent to the limitation of a paradigm. With the surrendering of all belief systems and positionalities, the unfoldment of Creation is self-revealing. The unfolding process may bring up presentations, uncertainties, or transitory doubt that have to be surrendered to faith and devotion as there is very rarely a really advanced spiritual teacher available for consultation. At these points, the Knowingness inherent as a vibratory frequency within the field of consciousness itself unfolds and reveals the reality of the emerging paradigm. By virtue of the Radiance of the Self, the revealing effulgences are silent. The world then becomes a revelation of Essence rather than an appearance.

The self-revelation becomes progressively recognized and identified by Knowingness as Divinity. The major shift of paradigm cannot be anticipated or even really imagined, and its onset is sometimes described cryptically as **'God shock'**. The consequence is profound awe by which the mind goes silent in the presence of Divinity and disappears at level 600. Henceforth, all is merely as it is as a continuous unfoldment that reveals itself as neither beginnings nor endings nor divisions such as 'then', 'now', or the 'future'. Realization no longer occurs as a consequence of mentalization, thought, or by the agents of a personal self because it no longer exists."

CONCLUDING MESSAGE: TRUTH AND RADICAL HONESTY

"There are only a few things you really need to know. To merely hear them already begins the process. Just before the world disappears altogether, you notice that everything is happening spontaneously. The most important thing to know is that everything is happening in and of its own. Nothing is being caused by anything. All phenomena are the automatic consequence of the field. The field is one of infinite, invisible, omnipotent power, all encompassing, like a giant electromagnetic field. No beginning; no ending, either spatially or in time. Forever and always present.

This field is infinitely powerful. The human mind cannot conceive of the Infinite except as a concept. Its presence is exquisitely gentle and exquisitely powerful. The field is so powerful that potentiality is activated by the field, to become an actuality. All things happen by virtue of the infinite power of the field. What the world considers evolution is the witnessing of Creation, which is continuous. The unmanifest, beyond the linear, becomes manifest by Divine Providence as the totality of Creation and this happens effortlessly. Within the field, potentiality is actualized by intention. Therefore, each thing comes forth, manifesting its karmic inheritance, you might say its innate potential, and when the conditions are appropriate, then the potentiality becomes an actuality in and of itself; in and of itself, as a consequence of the infinite power of the field. The field is so powerful that if you continuously hold a thought it will become a happening. Otherwise, no one would become enlightened. Therefore, one's intention is all- powerful.

The ego is very clever. As a potentiality begins to manifest, it takes credit for it. What happens is that the mind, in 1/10000 of a second, claims credit for the manifestation. If you are strictly, radically honest - beyond the capacity of most people to be honest, much less radically honest... To be radically honest means to somehow beat that 1/10000th of a second... to completely surrender to the fact that all things happen by Divine Providence, the Will of God and for no other reason. The only opponent to this understanding is the ego. And the ego's job is to claim to be God and it does that job well. The ego is a liar. To understand the workings of the ego frees you from its coils. One thing we do is try to understand the ego in ways that have not really been discovered or described before.

The infinite field of Power registers in the person's consciousness and travels down through the acupuncture system and the basic premise of the infinite field is that it instantly recognizes truth. The infinite field of Consciousness registers all that ever happens in time. Every thought, every feeling, every movement, every action is recorded forever. There is no such thing as privacy; you never did have any. Everything radiates an energy which can be read thousands of years later. You have access to all the information that exists now or ever within one second." - Paraphrased from the opening ~ 6 minutes of DVD disc 1 of 3 of the October 2004 Lecture, "Witnessing and Observing".

ABOUT DR. HAWKINS

Biographical Note

Dr. David R. Hawkins (1927-2012) was renowned as a physician, author, lecturer, and researcher of consciousness. After serving in the United States Navy during World War II, he graduated from the Medical College of Wisconsin in 1953. For the next 25 years, he lived in New York, where his pioneering work as a psychiatrist brought major clinical breakthroughs, especially in the treatment of schizophrenia and alcoholism. His research findings were published widely in medical, scientific, and psychoanalytic journals. As Medical Director of the North Nassau Mental Health Center (1956-1980) and Director of Research at Brunswick Hospital (1968-1979) on Long Island, he had the largest practice in New York.

In 1973, Dr. Hawkins co-authored Orthomolecular Psychiatry with Nobel Laureate chemist Linus Pauling, initiating a new field within psychiatry and leading to appearances on numerous talk shows. He spoke at the Oxford Forum and Westminster Abbey, as well as Harvard University, University of Argentina, University of Notre Dame, University of California, Fordham University, and the Institute for Noetic Sciences. He also served as a psychiatric advisor to Catholic, Protestant, and Buddhist monasteries.

Dr. Hawkins received numerous recognitions for his scientific and humanitarian contributions, including: the Huxley Award for the "Inestimable Contribution to the Alleviation of Human Suffering"; Physicians Recognition Award by the American Medical Association; 50-Year Distinguished Life Fellow by the American Psychiatric Association; the Orthomolecular Medicine Hall of Fame; Who's Who in the World; and a nomination for the prestigious Templeton Prize, which honors progress in science and religion.

In 1983, Dr. Hawkins established the Institute for Spiritual Research, a nonprofit organization dedicated to consciousness research. During the 1980s, his lectures at such events as the First National Conference on Addictions and Consciousness (1985) and Whole Life Expo (1986), both held in California, recontextualized addiction by illuminating the underlying spiritual drive for inner peace and how to cultivate it apart from substances. During the 1990s, he served as the Chief of Staff at Mingus Mountain Estate Residential Treatment Center for adolescent girls in Prescott Valley and was the consulting psychiatrist for several recovery houses in Arizona.

Dr. Hawkins spent the last three decades of his life in Arizona, working to correlate the seemingly disparate domains of science and spirituality. In 1995, at the age of 68, he received a Ph.D. in health and human services. That same year saw the publication of his book "Power vs. Force", which was ultimately translated into 25 languages with over a million copies sold, and evoking praise from such notables as Mother Teresa and Sam Walton. "Power vs. Force" presented his trademarked and copyrighted "Map of Consciousness," now used by health professionals, university professors, government officials, and business executives worldwide. Many other books followed.

In recognition of Dr. Hawkins's contributions to humanity, he was knighted in 1996 by the Sovereign Order of the Hospitaliers of St. John of Jerusalem by authority of the Priory of King Valdemar the Great. From 1998 to 2011, Dr. Hawkins traveled widely as a lecturer throughout the United States and overseas, speaking to sold-out audiences about the science of consciousness and the reality of advanced spiritual states. In 2000, he was bestowed the title "Tae Ryoung Sun Kak Tosa" (Teacher of Enlightenment) in Seoul, Korea. His final lecture, entitled, "Love," occurred in September 2011 and was attended by 1,700 people from around the world. Dr.

Hawkins was active to the very end. Just before his passing in September 2012, he completed a video-recorded dialogue series and finished his 12th book.

Throughout Dr. Hawkins's life, he participated in a wide range of civic and professional endeavors, often in leadership roles. As a physician, he co-founded or served as medical advisor for many organizations, including the Schizophrenia Foundations of New York and Long Island, the Attitudinal Healing Center of Long Island, the New York Association of Holistic Health Centers, and the Academy of Orthomolecular Psychiatry. He was co-director of the Masters Gallery of Fine Arts.

Born with an exceptionally high IQ, he became a member of Mensa International in 1963. As a young doctor, he was attracted to Buddhism and joined the first Zen Institute in the United States. At the time of his death, he had been a member of St. Andrew's Episcopal Church for many years. He was the first president of the Country and Western Dance Club of Sedona, a member of the Veterans of Foreign Wars, American Legion, and the Sedona Elks Lodge. He was an archer, carpenter, blacksmith, musician (bagpiper, violinist, pianist), designer of prize- winning 16th-century French Norman architecture, and lover of animals.

Internationally, Dr. Hawkins was the founder of Devotional Nonduality (2003), a spiritual pathway that applies the core truths of the world's great traditions: kindness and compassion for all of life (including oneself), unconditional love, humility, inquiry into the nature of existence, surrender, and self-realization. Since 2002, "Hawkins Study Groups" have autonomously sprung up in many cities around the world, from Los Angeles to Seoul, from Cape Town to Melbourne; the groups study and practice the principles of his books, such as: "We change the world not by what we say or do but as a consequence of what we have become." His life exemplified that principle.

AUTOBIOGRAPHIC NOTE

At age three, there occurred a sudden full consciousness of existence, a nonverbal but complete understanding of the meaning of "I Am," followed immediately by the frightening realization that "I" might not have come into existence at all. This was an instant awakening from oblivion into a conscious awareness, and in that moment, the personal self was born and the duality of "Is" and "Is Not" entered my subjective awareness.

Throughout childhood and early adolescence, the paradox of existence and the question of the reality of the self-remained a repeated concern. The personal self would sometimes begin slipping back into a greater impersonal Self, and the initial fear of non-existence—the fundamental fear of nothingness—would recur.

In 1939, as a paperboy with a seventeen-mile bicycle route in rural Wisconsin, on a dark winter's night I was caught miles from home in a twenty-below-zero blizzard. The bicycle fell over on the ice and the fierce wind ripped the newspapers out of the handlebar basket, blowing them across the ice-covered, snowy field. There were tears of frustration and exhaustion and my clothes were frozen stiff. To get out of the wind, I broke through the icy crust of a high snow bank, dug out a space, and crawled into it. Soon the shivering stopped and there was a delicious warmth, and then a state of peace beyond all description. This was accompanied by a suffusion of light and a presence of infinite love that had no beginning and no end and was undifferentiated from my own essence. The physical body and surroundings faded as my awareness was fused with this all-present, illuminated state. The mind grew silent; all thought stopped. An infinite Presence was all that was or could be, beyond all time or description.

After that timelessness, there was suddenly an awareness of someone shaking my knee; then my father's anxious face appeared. There was great reluctance to return to the body and all that that entailed, but because of my father's love and anguish, the Spirit nurtured and reactivated the body. There was compassion for his fear of death, although, at the same time, the concept of death seemed absurd.

This subjective experience was not discussed with anyone since there was no context available from which to describe it. It was not common to hear of spiritual experiences other than those reported in the lives of the saints. But after this experience, the accepted reality of the world began to seem only provisional; traditional religious teachings lost significance and, paradoxically, I became an agnostic. Compared to the light of Divinity that had illuminated all existence, the god of traditional religion shone dully indeed; thus spirituality replaced religion.

During World War II, hazardous duty on a minesweeper often brought close brushes with death, but there was no fear of it. It was as though death had lost its authenticity. After the war, fascinated by the complexities of the mind and wanting to study psychiatry, I worked my way through medical school. My training psychoanalyst, a professor at Columbia University, was also an agnostic; we both took a dim view of religion. The analysis went well, as did my career, and success followed.

I did not, however, settle quietly into professional life. I fell ill with a progressive, fatal illness that did not respond to any treatments available. By age 38, I was in extremis and knew I was about to die. I didn't care about the body, but my spirit was in a state of extreme anguish and despair. As the final moment approached, the thought flashed through my mind, "What if there is a God?" So I called out in prayer, "If there is a God, I ask him to help me now." I surrendered to whatever God there might be and went into oblivion. When I awoke, a transformation of such enormity had taken place that I was struck dumb with awe.

The person I had been no longer existed. There was no personal self or ego, only an Infinite Presence of such unlimited power that it was all that was. This Presence had replaced what had been "me," and the body and its actions were controlled solely by the Infinite Will of the Presence. The world was illuminated by the clarity of an Infinite Oneness that expressed itself as all things revealed in their infinite beauty and perfection.

As life went on, this stillness persisted. There was no personal will; the physical body went about its business under the direction of the infinitely powerful but exquisitely gentle Will of the Presence. In that state, there was no need to think about anything. All truth was self-evident and no conceptualization was necessary or even possible. At the same time, the physical nervous system felt extremely overtaxed, as though it were carrying far more energy than its circuits had been designed for.

It was not possible to function effectively in the world. All ordinary motivations had disappeared, along with all fear and anxiety. There was nothing to seek, as all was perfect. Fame, success, and money were meaningless. Friends urged the pragmatic return to clinical practice, but there was no ordinary motivation to do so.

There was now the ability to perceive the reality that underlay personalities: the origin of emotional sickness lay in people's belief that they were their personalities. And so, as though of its own, a clinical practice resumed and eventually became huge. People came from all over the United States. The practice had two thousand outpatients, which required more than fifty therapists and other employees, a suite of twenty-five offices, and research and electroencephalic laboratories. There were a thousand new patients a year. In addition, there were appearances on radio and network television shows, as previously mentioned. In 1973, the clinical research was documented in a traditional format in the book, Orthomolecular Psychiatry. This work was ten years ahead of its time and created something of a stir.

The overall condition of the nervous system improved slowly, and then another phenomenon commenced. There was a sweet, delicious band of energy continuously flowing up the spine and into the brain where it created an intense sensation of continuous pleasure. Everything in life happened by synchronicity, evolving in perfect harmony; the miraculous was commonplace. The origin of what the world would call miracles was the Presence, not the personal self. What remained of the personal "me" was only a witness to these phenomena. The greater "I," deeper than my former self or thoughts, determined all that happened.

The states that were present had been reported by others throughout history and led to the investigation of spiritual teachings, including those of the Buddha, enlightened sages, Huang Po, and more recent teachers such as Ramana Maharshi and Nisargadatta Maharaj. It was thus confirmed that these experiences were not unique. The Bhagavad-Gita now made complete sense. At times, the same spiritual ecstasy reported by Sri Ramakrishna and the Christian saints occurred.

Everything and everyone in the world was luminous and exquisitely beautiful. All living beings became Radiant and expressed this Radiance in stillness and splendor. It was apparent that all mankind is actually motivated by inner love but has simply become unaware; most lives are lived as though by sleepers unawakened to the awareness of who they really are. People around me looked as though they were asleep and were incredibly beautiful. It was like being in love with everyone.

It was necessary to stop the habitual practice of meditating for an hour in the morning and then again before dinner because it would intensify the bliss to such an extent that it was not possible to function. An experience similar to the one that had occurred in the snow bank as a boy would recur, and it became increasingly difficult to leave that state and return to the world. The incredible beauty of all things shone forth in all their perfection, and where the world saw ugliness, there was only timeless beauty. This spiritual love suffused all perception, and all boundaries between here and there, or then and now, or separation disappeared.

During the years spent in inner silence, the strength of the Presence grew. Life was no longer personal; a personal will no longer existed. The personal "I" had become an instrument of the Infinite Presence and went about and did as it was willed. People felt an extraordinary peace in the aura of that Presence.

Seekers sought answers but as there was no longer any such individual as David, they were actually finessing answers from their own Self, which was not different from mine. From each person the same Self shone forth from their eyes.

The miraculous happened, beyond ordinary comprehension. Many chronic maladies from which the body had suffered for years disappeared; eyesight spontaneously normalized, and there was no longer a need for the lifetime bifocals.

Occasionally, an exquisitely blissful energy, an Infinite Love, would suddenly begin to radiate from the heart toward the scene of some calamity. Once, while driving on a highway, this exquisite energy began to beam out of the chest. As the car rounded a bend, there was an auto accident; the wheels of the overturned car were still spinning. The energy passed with great intensity into the occupants of the car and then stopped of its own accord. Another time, while I was walking on the streets of a strange city, the energy started to flow down the block ahead and arrived at the scene of an incipient gang fight. The combatants fell back and began to laugh, and again, the energy stopped.

Profound changes of perception came without warning in improbable circumstances. While dining alone at Rothmans's on Long Island, the Presence suddenly intensified until everything and every person, which had appeared as separate in ordinary perception, melted into a timeless universality and oneness. In the motionless Silence, it became obvious that there are no "events" or "things" and that nothing actually "happens" because past, present, and future are merely artifacts of perception, as is the illusion of a separate "I" being subject to birth and death. As the limited, false self dissolved into the universal Self of its true origin, there was an ineffable sense of having returned home to a state of absolute peace and relief from all suffering. It is only the illusion of individuality that is the origin of all suffering. When one realizes that one is the universe, complete and at one with All That Is, forever without end, then no further suffering is possible.

Patients came from every country in the world, and some were the most hopeless of the hopeless. Grotesque, writhing, wrapped in wet sheets for transport from far-away hospitals they came, hoping for treatment for advanced psychoses and grave, incurable mental disorders. Some were catatonic; many had been mute for years. But in each patient, beneath the crippled appearance, there was the shining essence of love and beauty, perhaps so obscured to ordinary vision that he or she had become totally unloved in this world.

One day a mute catatonic was brought into the hospital in a straitjacket. She had a severe neurological disorder and was unable to stand. Squirming on the floor, she went into spasms and her eyes rolled back in her head. Her hair was matted; she had torn all her clothes and uttered guttural sounds. Her family was fairly wealthy; as a result, over the years she had been seen by innumerable physicians and famous specialists from all over the world. Every treatment had been tried on her and she had been given up as hopeless by the medical profession.

A short, nonverbal question arose: "What do you want done with her, God?" Then came the realization that she just needed to be loved, that was all. Her inner self shone through her eyes and the Self connected with that loving essence. In that second, she was healed by her own recognition of who she really was; what happened to her mind or body did not matter to her any longer.

This, in essence, occurred with countless patients. Some recovered in the eyes of the world and some did not, but whether a clinical recovery ensued did not matter any longer to the patients. Their inner agony was over. As they felt loved and at peace within, their pain stopped. This phenomenon can only be explained by saying that the Compassion of the Presence recontextualized each patient's reality so that he or she experienced healing on a level that transcended the world and its appearances. The inner peace of the Self encompassed us beyond time and identity.

It was clear that all pain and suffering arises solely from the ego and not from God. This truth was silently communicated to the minds of the patients. This was the mental block in another mute catatonic who had not spoken in many years. The Self said to him through mind, "You're blaming God for what your ego has done to you." He jumped off the floor and began to speak, much to the shock of the nurse who witnessed the incident.

The work became increasingly taxing and eventually overwhelming. Patients were backed up, waiting for beds to open, although the hospital had built an extra ward to house them. There was an enormous frustration in that the human suffering could be countered in only one patient at a time. It was like bailing out the sea. It seemed that there must be some other way to address the causes of the common malaise, the endless stream of spiritual distress and human suffering.

This led to the study of the physiological response (muscle testing) to various stimuli, which revealed an amazing discovery. It was the "wormhole" between two universes—the physical world and the world of the mind and spirit—an interface between dimensions. In a world full of sleepers lost from their source, here was a tool to recover, and demonstrate for all to see, that lost connection with the higher reality. This led to the testing of every substance, thought, and concept that could be brought to mind. The endeavor was aided by my students and research assistants. Then a major discovery was made: whereas all subjects went weak from negative stimuli, such as fluorescent lights, pesticides, and artificial sweeteners, students of spiritual disciplines who had advanced their levels of awareness did not go weak as did ordinary people. Something important and decisive had shifted in their consciousness. It apparently occurred as they realized they were not at the mercy of the world but rather affected only by what their minds believed. Perhaps the very process of progress toward enlightenment could be shown to increase man's ability to resist the vicissitudes of existence, including illness.

The Self had the capacity to change things in the world by merely envisioning them; Love changed the world each time it replaced non-love. The entire scheme of civilization could be profoundly altered by focusing this power of love at a very specific point. Whenever this happened, history bifurcated down new roads.

It now appeared that these crucial insights could not only be communicated with the world but also visibly and irrefutably demonstrated. It seemed that the great tragedy of human life had always been that the psyche is so easily deceived; discord and strife have been the inevitable consequence of mankind's inability to distinguish the false from the true. But here was an answer to this fundamental dilemma, a way to recontextualize the nature of consciousness itself and make explicable that which otherwise could only be inferred.

It was time to leave life in New York, with its city apartment and home on Long Island, for something more important. It was necessary to perfect myself as an instrument. This necessitated leaving that world and everything in it, replacing it with a reclusive life in a small town where the next seven years were spent in meditation and study.

Overpowering states of bliss returned unsought, and eventually, there was the need to learn how to be in the Divine Presence and still function in the world. The mind had lost track of what was happening in the world at large. In order to do research and writing, it was necessary to stop all spiritual practice and focus on the world of form. Reading the newspaper and watching television helped to catch up on the story of who was who, the major events, and the nature of the current social dialogue.

Exceptional subjective experiences of truth, which are the province of the mystic who affects all mankind by sending forth spiritual energy into the collective consciousness, are not understandable by the majority of mankind and are therefore of limited meaning except to other spiritual seekers. This led to an effort to be ordinary, because just being ordinary in itself is an expression of Divinity; the truth of one's real self can be discovered through the pathway of everyday life. To live with care and kindness is all that is necessary. The rest reveals itself in due time. The commonplace and God are not distinct.

And so, after a long circular journey of the spirit, there was a return to the most important work, which was to try to bring the Presence at least a little closer to the grasp of as many fellow beings as possible.

The Presence is silent and conveys a state of peace that is the space in which and by which all is and has its existence and experience. It is infinitely gentle and yet like a rock. With it, all fear disappears. Spiritual joy occurs on a quiet level of inexplicable ecstasy. Because the experience of time stops, there is no apprehension or regret, no pain or anticipation; the source of joy is unending and ever-present. With no beginning or ending, there is no loss or grief or desire. Nothing needs to be done; everything is already perfect and complete.

When time stops, all problems disappear; they are merely artifacts of a point of perception. As the Presence prevails, there is no further identification with the body or the mind. When the mind grows silent, the thought "I Am" also disappears, and Pure Awareness shines forth to illuminate what one is, was, and always will be, beyond all worlds and all universes, beyond time, and therefore without beginning or end.

People wonder, "How does one reach this state of awareness," but few follow the steps because they are so simple. First, the desire to reach that state was intense. Then began the discipline to act with constant and universal forgiveness and gentleness, without exception. One has to be compassionate towards everything, including one's own self and thoughts. Next came a willingness to hold desires in abeyance and surrender personal will at every moment. As each thought, feeling, desire, or deed was surrendered to God, the mind became progressively silent. At first, it released whole stories and paragraphs, then ideas and concepts. As one lets go of wanting to own these thoughts, they no longer reach such elaboration and begin to fragment while only half formed. Finally, it was possible to turn over the energy behind thought itself before it even became thought.

The task of constant and unrelenting fixity of focus, allowing not even a moment of distraction from meditation, continued while doing ordinary activities. At first, this seemed very difficult, but as time went on, it became habitual, automatic, requiring less and less effort, and finally, it was effortless. The process is like a rocket leaving the earth. At first, it requires enormous power, then less and less as it leaves the earth's gravitational field, and finally, it moves through space under its own momentum.

Suddenly, without warning, a shift in awareness occurred and the Presence was there, unmistakable and all encompassing. There were a few moments of apprehension as the self died, and then the absoluteness of the Presence inspired a flash of awe. This breakthrough was spectacular, more intense than anything before. It has no counterpart in ordinary experience. The profound shock was cushioned by the love that is with the Presence. Without the support and protection of that love, one would be annihilated.

There followed a moment of terror as the ego clung to its existence, fearing it would become nothingness. Instead, as it died, it was replaced by the Self as Everythingness, the All in which everything is known and obvious in its perfect expression of its own essence. With nonlocality came the awareness that one is all that ever was or can be. One is total and complete, beyond all identities, beyond all gender, beyond even humanness itself. One need never again fear suffering and death. What happens to the body from this point is immaterial. At certain levels of spiritual awareness, ailments of the body heal or spontaneously disappear. But in the absolute state, such considerations are irrelevant. The body will run its predicted course and then return from whence it came. It is a matter of no importance; one is unaffected. The body appears as an "it" rather than as a "me," as another object, like the furniture in a room. It may seem comical that people still address the body as though it were the individual "you," but there is no way to explain this state of awareness to the unaware. It is best to just go on about one's business and allow Providence to handle the social adjustments. However, as one reaches bliss, it is very difficult to conceal that state of intense ecstasy. The world may be dazzled, and people may come from far and wide to be in the accompanying aura. Spiritual seekers and the spiritually curious may be attracted, as may be the very ill who are seeking miracles. One may become a magnet and a source of joy to them. Commonly, there is a desire at this point to share this state with others and to use it for the benefit of all.

The ecstasy that accompanies this condition is not initially absolutely stable; there are also moments of great agony. The most intense occur when the state fluctuates and suddenly ceases for no apparent reason. These times bring on periods of intense despair and a fear that one has been forsaken by the Presence. These falls make the path arduous, and to surmount these reversals requires great will. It finally becomes obvious that one must transcend this level or constantly suffer excruciating "descents from grace." The glory of ecstasy, then, has to be relinquished as one enters upon the arduous task of transcending duality until one is beyond all opposites and their conflicting pulls. But while it is one thing to happily give up the iron chains of the ego, it is quite another to abandon the golden chains of ecstatic joy. It feels as though one is giving up God, and a new level of fear arises, never before anticipated. This is the final terror of absolute aloneness.

To the ego, the fear of nonexistence was formidable, and it drew back from it repeatedly as it seemed to approach. The purpose of the agonies and the dark nights of the soul then became apparent. They are so intolerable that their exquisite pain spurs one on to the extreme effort required to surmount them. When vacillation between heaven and hell becomes unendurable, the desire for existence itself has to be surrendered. Only once this is done may one finally move beyond the duality of Allness versus nothingness, beyond existence versus nonexistence. This culmination of the inner work is the most difficult phase, the ultimate watershed, where one is starkly aware that the illusion of existence one transcends is irrevocable. There is no returning from this step, and this specter of irreversibility makes this last barrier appear to be the most formidable choice of all.

But, in fact, in this final apocalypse of the self, the dissolution of the sole remaining duality of existence versus nonexistence—identity itself—dissolves in Universal Divinity, and no individual consciousness is left to choose. The last step, then, is taken by God.

—David R. Hawkins

For a list of available audio and video recordings
and other publications on consciousness
and spirituality by Dr. Hawkins,
please contact:

Veritas Publishing
PO Box 3516
Sedona, AZ 86340
U.S.A.
Phone (928) 282-8722
Fax (928) 282-4789
www.veritaspub.com
info@veritaspub.com